GLOBAL HEALTH LAW

GLOBAL HEALTH LAW

Lawrence O. Gostin

 Harvard University Press

Harvard University Press
Cambridge, Massachusetts
London, England
2014

Printed in the United States of America

Library of Congress Cataloging-in-Publication Data

Gostin, Lawrence O. (Lawrence Ogalthorpe), author.
Global health law / Lawrence O. Gostin.
pages cm
Includes bibliographical references and index.
ISBN 978-0-674-72884-4 (hardcover : alk. paper)
1. Public health laws. 2. Public health laws, International. 3. Public health—International cooperation. I. Title.
K3570.G67 2014
344.04—dc23 2013030764

For my wife, Jean;
sons, Bryn and Kieran;
and their loving partners, Jen and Isley

Contents

Preface

This is a unique moment to offer a systematic account of global health law. The promise of potential solutions to improve life prospects for the world's population has captured the imagination of a new generation of philanthropists, scientists, celebrities, entrepreneurs, students, and citizens eager to make a difference in our interconnected planet. International development assistance for health—a crucial aspect of foreign policy—has quadrupled over the past two decades, from $5.6 billion in 1990 to $26.9 billion in 2010, with the private and voluntary sectors taking on an ever-increasing share of the total. Given the rapid and expanding globalization that is a defining feature of today's world, the need for a robust system of global health law has never been greater.

Throughout this volume, I stress the important diplomatic, political, social, and economic factors that give scope, substance, and structure to global health law. The policy objectives that make global health law so vital and vibrant range from the imperative of safeguarding the population's health to national security, economic prosperity, and sustainable development, through to normative commitments to human rights and social justice.

My goals in writing this book are to (1) define the field of global health law within the broader currents of global governance for health; (2) systematically describe and analyze the major sources of law, together with their institutional frameworks; and (3) develop critical themes that ought to guide global health in the twenty-first century.

Definitions

The definition of global health law developed in Chapter 3 captures the field's mission, sources of law, key participants, and ethical foundations. Global health law encompasses both "hard" (e.g., treaties that bind states) and "soft" (e.g., codes of practice negotiated by states) international instruments that shape norms, processes, and institutions to achieve the highest attainable standard of physical and mental health for the world's population. To achieve this goal requires creative methods to mobilize resources, set priorities, coordinate activities, monitor progress, and ensure accountability among diverse global health actors. The value of social justice should infuse the field, ensuring equitable conditions of health for the world's most disadvantaged people.

International law, however, has inherent limitations, as sovereign states are often reluctant to surrender their autonomy or act against self-interest. International legal norms are frequently vague and hard to enforce, with states often unwilling or unable to robustly implement them domestically. Consequently, global health scholars have turned to a new language of governance, which includes not only law, but also multiple levers to effect change. "Governance"—the method by which organized society directs, influences, and coordinates public and private activities to achieve collective goods—recognizes the complexity of the global health architecture and the many ways that norms and institutions can guide health-promoting activities.

Although many scholars talk about global health governance, I prefer the broader concept of global governance for health (GGH). The former principally describes the norms and institutions within the health sector, while the latter is more encompassing, extending beyond the health sector. As is true of global health law, GGH encompasses diverse fields, such as agriculture, trade, development, human rights, and the environment. Undoubtedly, effective GGH is a complex undertaking, navigating the cross-currents of politics, power, and vested interests.

Institutions

Global health law and broader governance rely on institutions charged with advancing their missions—whether that mission is health or a different aim that nonetheless affects the socioeconomic determinants of health. Primary among these institutions is the World Health Organization as the "directing and coordinating authority on international health work," but there are also multiple international agencies that affect health directly or indirectly, such as UNAIDS, the World Bank, the Global Fund, the GAVI Alliance, and the World Trade Organization. In this volume I consider how effectively these and many other institutions operate—their goals, methods, and governance strategies, particularly how open they are to scrutiny, accountability, and civil society engagement.

Themes

Several themes permeate the pages of this work, reflecting my understanding of the innovative reforms needed to achieve the book's aim of global health with justice:

Health equity By global health with justice, I mean achieving the highest attainable standard of physical and mental health, fairly distributed. Many, perhaps most, global health endeavors measure their success by overall public health improvements, such as rates of infant and maternal mortality, injury or disease burden, or longevity. Although these metrics are certainly necessary, they can often mask stubbornly persistent inequalities within and between countries—rich/poor, urban/rural, or North/South. If health gains, for example, are concentrated among the middle and upper classes while leaving the lower and working classes stagnant, we may have advanced global health, but not with justice.

Global solidarity My career spanned mental health, AIDS, and public health before turning to global health. (I describe this personal journey in "From a Civil Libertarian to a Sanitarian," *Journal of Law and Society* 34, no. 4 (2007): 594–616.) What strikes me about my development as a thinker and advocate is that I initially believed—as many do—that global health was primarily concerned with foreign assistance: poorer states lacked the capacity to deliver health services, while richer states lacked the political will. That was overly simplistic. Genuine health improvement requires global solidarity, with all states and stakeholders taking mutual responsibility for health. I outline the government's primary duty to safeguard its inhabitants' health, together with the international community's obligation to develop capacity. The former requires governments to take ownership of, and amply fund, health programs, while the latter requires a new theory of international assistance. "Health aid" presumes a charitable relationship of a generous donor and a needy recipient, but health should be an equally shared obligation. Global solidarity demands equal partnerships where all actors—domestic and international—do their fair share to assure the conditions for people everywhere to be healthy and safe.

Health in all policies (HiAP) Sticking with the theme of government responsibilities, it is clear that solutions have to go beyond the health sector. So much of what government does has profound effects on the public's health—for good or bad. A broad range of policies—agriculture, urban planning, transportation, energy, and the environment—affect people and their habitats. That is why an "all-of-government" approach to health is so essential, and beyond that an "all-of-society" approach. Even government with all of its resources cannot fully create the conditions for people to be healthy. All of society—businesses, media, academia, and philanthropy—affects human well-being. Just think about the role of the food, alcohol, and tobacco industries to get a sense of the influence of the private sector—and imagine the changes that could result if strategic assessments of the health impacts of policies and practices became the norm rather than the exception.

Multiple regimes The international analogue of HiAP is the influence of multiple regimes on public health. In an era of rapid globalization, migration, and urbanization, health threats span the globe. Even if the health and development sectors did everything right, a gaping hole in global governance for health would remain. To name just a few of the multiple regimes that affect health, consider *trade,* which brings prosperity, but also the transmission of disease and lifestyle risks beyond borders; *intellectual property,* which incentivizes innovation, but also makes essential medicines less affordable; and the *environment,* which provides a habitat for humans and animals, but also exacerbates health hazards through flooding, heat waves, and widening geographic zones for disease vectors.

Good governance Governments, international organizations, and other global health actors can operate effectively only if they are governed well, adhering to universal values enshrined in international human rights law. Well-governed entities are *honest* (avoiding corruption), *transparent* (open to public scrutiny), *deliberative* (with stakeholder and community engagement), *efficient* (managed well), and *accountable* (assuming responsibility for successes or failures). Well-governed entities set clear targets, monitor progress, and change course when needed. Absent sound governance, global health leaders cannot achieve the aim of health with justice, as scarce resources will be wasted and implementation mismanaged.

Health-promoting priorities In the final chapter I pose a thought experiment to demonstrate the importance of setting the right priorities. Imagine a Rawlsian world where—not knowing the position you will occupy in life (rich or poor, healthy or sick, living in the global North or South)—you have to choose between two stark visions: population-based public health or personal health care. Would you want to live in a world where you had nutritious food, potable water, sanitation, safe roads, and freedom from noxious vectors? Or would you prefer full access to medical care in the event of injury or illness? To me the answer is self-evident. I would unhesitatingly choose to inhabit an environment with healthy living conditions (a preventive, public health strategy) than to gain access to medical care after becoming ill. There are good reasons for preferring a healthy community from both a historical and an empirical perspective. And yet most of global health is organized around the medical, individualized model. Global health with justice will only come once the existing architecture incorporates the vision of a collective, population-based approach to health for all.

The right to health I return often to the imperative of health as a fundamental entitlement. This may appear odd to scholars who see the obvious flaws inherent in socioeconomic rights, as I do. Certainly, the right-to-health framework suffers from imprecise standards, many of which are only progressively realizable and often unenforceable. Truthfully, it will be hard to overcome these deficiencies. But human rights law is the only universally applicable international regime designed to safeguard public health. Virtually all states have consented to the right to health as a legally binding norm through treaty adoption and/or national constitutions. Rather than abandoning the framework, I chose to adopt it, while recognizing the need to clarify the standards, monitor progress, and ensure accountability for results. Reflecting the thought experiment above, to achieve global health with justice requires viewing the right to health as more a collective than an individual right, which assures that healthy and safe conditions are equally available to all people, everywhere.

Readership

I have in mind diverse audiences for this book. Most importantly, it is designed for scholars, practitioners, and passionate advocates in global health—whether the reader's primary interest is in law, governance, human rights, foreign policy, or health. It is intended to be useful for policy makers, global health leaders, civil society organizations, and the informed public that cares about global health with justice.

The book should also provide a valuable reference tool for scholars, practitioners, and activists who want to understand the international legal regimes affecting health and innovative ideas for global governance for health. My aim has been to make the book accessible to a nonlegal audience while also making it engaging and informative for more in-depth study.

This book is designed for teachers and students of global health law and governance. I have sought to define the field and offer a useful and systematic method of instruction for courses in schools of law, public health, medicine, health administration, international affairs, and other fields. I would very much like to see global health law, and broader governance, as part of global health curricula across disciplines. I am on the executive board of the Consortium of Universities for Global Health (CUGH), which encompasses academic institutions devoted to teaching global health and serving health needs around the world. CUGH demonstrates the vibrancy of global health as both an undergraduate concentration and a graduate-level course of study. This text should serve a broad range of faculty and students who are passionate about global health.

GLOBAL HEALTH LAW

Global Health Narratives: Listening to the Voices of the Young

I BEGIN THIS BOOK with the voices of young people living in poverty—the daily lives of girls and boys, young women and men, who inhabit filthy, congested cities or remote rural villages. These global health narratives are told by the young people themselves, or by passionate community activists living alongside them. The stories of Alois, Shefali, Ti Charles, Eneles, Namubiru Rashida, Johnny, and Molly speak for themselves.

Alois's Story: A Young Man, Age Sixteen, Living in Rural Zimbabwe

I am the oldest in my family. My father works at Indigo Mine and my mother died of AIDS a couple of months ago. I have two brothers and two young sisters who follow after me. We live in a three-roomed house with electricity, running tap water, and flush toilets. Indigo Mine social welfare workers maintain the households' sewage system for our community in extreme cases of blockages. In the event of electricity power cuts, we use wood to make fires for cooking.

Currently I am unemployed. I was unfortunate not to proceed with my education, because my father could not afford to send all of my brothers, sisters, and me to school at once. The money he earns is not quite adequate for the family's basic welfare in terms of clothing and food. Often the food is not adequate to last for a month. Local shops sell foodstuffs at unaffordable prices, and to get cheaper basic commodities I have to travel to the big city, located thirty-four kilometers away.

However, at our local school there is a child-feeding program serving porridge, beans, and groundnuts to prevent malnutrition.

Our local health clinic is located five kilometers away. The clinic provides services for common diseases and injuries, emergencies, maternity care, HIV testing, and referrals to a public hospital in town. I remember that when my mother was ill, she had to collect her medication from the town because the local clinic did not provide antiretroviral medication. The major barriers to accessing health services are distance, unavailability of drugs, and lack of money. Some people resort to faith-based and traditional healers.

What worries me is the state of my father's health. He drinks beer and smokes tobacco while being exposed to dust and pollution from where he works. After our mother's death, everything changed; he got married to another woman who treats my sisters in a cruel way. They have no time to play after school—all is work. Sometimes when my father is drunk, he beats my stepmother, and we end up being confused and feeling insecure. I just wish my mother was alive. If she got tested early, she could have survived and seen her children grow.

Shefali's Story: A Young Woman, Age Sixteen, Living in Dhaka, Bangladesh

This story is told by Atiya Rahman and Sameera Hussain, BRAC University, Dhaka:

Home to over three million slum dwellers, Dhaka, the capital of Bangladesh, is one of the most densely populated cities in the world. Living on land that they do not legally occupy, slum dwellers have limited access to electricity, water, and sanitation.

Already married for two years, Shefali is pregnant and has recently come to live with her husband, Mujib, in Korail, the largest urban slum in Bangladesh. Her family cohabits with her mother's family as a joint family. Shefali's mother has lived in the slum for ten years doing part-time domestic work, and Mujib earns a living as a rickshaw driver.

Shefali grew up in a village in Kurigram, the poorest district in Bangladesh. Due to financial constraints at home, her mother migrated to Dhaka seeking a livelihood. Shefali continued to live with her father and siblings on her mother's remittance, until her family decided she should get married—despite the minimum legal age of eighteen for marriage for girls in Bangladesh.

Shefali is well aware of the reasons she "had to get married": she was old enough to ease the financial burden of her family. Education for a girl of her age would cease to be free for her in the village, and marriage was the natural next step.

Petite and slight, Shefali is physically weak and, at six months into her pregnancy, is not visibly pregnant. Because she has a very basic education, she is aware of the need for antenatal care and seeks health information for pregnant women in the slum. She says she urgently needs to find free care so that she does not cause further financial hardship for her family: "I heard that they have free deliveries here. I wanted to find out whether this is true."

There are no hospitals in Korail, only some health centers run by nongovernmental organizations, where women who are expecting no complications can give birth. Shefali feels reassured that there are birthing centers in the slum that provide services at little or no cost. Getting to a hospital entails walking through narrow alleyways and roads unfit for vehicles; then, upon reaching the main road, patients would have to make their way through two hours of traffic.

Ti Charles's Story: A Young Man, Age Twenty, Living in Coastal Artibonite, Haiti

This story is told by Jean Jacques Solon and Franciscka Lucien, Partners In Health, Haiti:

Lack of access to health services can push families into economic despair and instability in a small coastal town in Haiti's lower Artibonite region, where Ti Charles and his family live. Ti Charles's experience speaks to the fate of many young people from communities like his throughout Haiti.

His story begins on a normal day two years ago, uneventful by his own account, that ended in a life-changing injury by nightfall. As the day came to an end, then-eighteen-year-old Ti Charles sat outside with a friend, passing the time in the neighborhood *[lakou]*. With the sun now set and no electricity available in the community, the friends headed back to their homes. The *lakou* was quiet, with many of their neighbors attending a *pwogram* (an event within the community), when a passenger riding by on a *moto*, a small motorbike that is common in the rural communities and urban streets, sent into the air the bullet that would ricochet before piercing Ti Charles's leg.

Without the means to access health services, Ti Charles remained home for more than a month as his leg worsened from the bullet wound. His mother had passed away because the family lacked access to health services until it was too late. Faced with not only the challenge of insufficient money but also little knowledge of the nearby facilities serving the community, Ti Charles's injury continued to worsen, forcing him to drop out of school. He passed the days in the one-room home that slept him and four family members, with little food, clean water, or sanitation.

Had his story ended there, Ti Charles believes he probably would have become a statistic within a sea of people who lack health care: "I would have died. The bullet was right near my vein, and my leg was so bad I couldn't even walk." One month later, at the recommendation of a neighbor, Ti Charles visited the Partners In Health/Zanmi Lasante Hôpital Bon Sauveur in Cange. Ti Charles believes that making the two-hour trek to the hospital, which is located in a rural community in Haiti's Central Plateau, changed his life: "I'm now part of the network of Zanmi Lasante patients."

Having since returned to school, he imagines a future in which he will complete his education and fulfill his dream of becoming an auto mechanic.

Eneles's Story: A Young Girl, Age Fourteen, Living in Neno District, Malawi

This story is told by Victoria Smith, Partners In Health, Malawi:

If you ask Eneles how she spends her time, she'll give you an answer that might sound similar to that of a fourteen-year-old girl living anywhere in the world: "I go to school, I go to church, I play with my friends." Eneles, a small-framed girl with a thoughtful face and short-cropped hair, lives with her mother and five brothers and sisters in a tiny village nestled in the mountainous terrain of southwestern Malawi.

Malawi, a landlocked country in sub-Saharan Africa, is one of the poorest nations in the world. And Neno District, which Eneles calls home, is one of its most remote districts. Running water and electricity are rare, and the roads are not paved, making travel particularly treacherous during the five-month rainy season that runs from December to April. Nearly one-quarter of the 125,000 people living in Neno face a walk of more than five miles to reach the nearest health facility.

The seven members of Eneles's family share a two-bedroom structure with an earthen floor, thatched roof, and outdoor pit latrine. They sleep on mats on the floor, sharing three blankets and mosquito nets between all seven people. As one of the older children, Eneles helps her family with chores—she sweeps and cleans the house and makes the daily trip to a nearby borehole to collect water for cooking, drinking, and washing. She helps her mother cook their meals over an open fire. They can cook outside during the dry season, but when it is raining they often move the cooking indoors, which makes the home very smoky.

The rainy season is hard for Eneles and her family. "When it rains, the grass from the roof falls into the house and the roof leaks," Eneles explains. "I get wet from the rain when sleeping." The rain also makes Eneles's daily trip to school very difficult—she lives more than an hour's walk from her rural school, and when it rains the road turns into a muddy pit. "It is good to have flip-flops," she says, pointing at her thin plastic shoes.

Her mother has been the primary caretaker and provider for the family since Eneles's father's death from tuberculosis in 2005. Her mother does piecework—washing clothes and gardening—to feed her family. She also maintains a small garden of maize, beans, and cassava to provide additional food. Eneles's mother stretches her small resources as far as possible, but she often does not have enough to make ends meet. Eneles understands her mother's sacrifices, but feels that sometimes it is not enough: "I never go without food and we always have three meals a day, but I usually still feel hungry after we eat, because we didn't get enough food."

When asked about the health of her family, Eneles hesitates. "Well, some are healthy and some are not," she says. Her father passed away when she was very young; Eneles barely remembers him. Her mother and youngest brother, Blessings, have both tested positive for HIV and are receiving antiretroviral treatment. Blessings also suffered from malnutrition, which improved once he began therapy. More than one in ten people are HIV-infected across the district.

Eneles has suffered with her own chronic health problems. "I have had asthma for as long as I can remember," she explains. She visits a chronic care clinic at the hospital once a month, walking three hours each way with her mother. "The medicine helps, but sometimes they run out at the hospital. I walk all the way to the hospital, and then I have to turn around and go home without any medicine."

But Eneles is optimistic about her future. She is in her final year of primary school and hopes to move to secondary school next year. Eneles feels passionate about education: "I must go to school so that I can have a place in this world." She dreams of studying nursing at the university.

Namubiru Rashida's Story: A Young Woman, Age Eighteen, Living in Gaba, a Suburb of Kampala, Uganda

I am a university student in my first year of study. I am firstborn out of a family of seven children. Each child has his or her own mother but was born to the same father. My mother has two children, a boy and a girl, each with their own father. I stay in a very rowdy place with no clean water and no good toilets or bathrooms; the toilets are shared by all university students who stay around this place. I have to move a long distance every day looking for clean water in order to bathe and cook.

At night, the conditions worsen; there is hardly electricity. The mosquito noise fills up the place. Cockroaches move around me and this makes me sick. Even when I fall sick, I hardly go to the hospital. My mother, who would have helped me out with medication fees, lives in the village, far away. She is living with HIV/AIDS; because of this, the relatives advised her to go back to the village to farm, because she needs fresh fruits and vegetables that she cannot access in Kampala because she has no job. It is out of the crops that she grows that she saves money to pay school fees for my younger brother, who is also at university now and doesn't know the whereabouts of his father.

Life is too hard and complicated for me. I have to cook food for my brother and myself. My father gives my stepmother money to send to me, but I rarely get this. Even when I request him to send it directly to me, he does not. This forces me to cook one meal a day because I lack money to access all the food I would need to get healthy.

A lot of violence happens to the university students, especially the girls; they are always raped and their property is stolen. I fell prey to a thief who robbed my handbag as I was moving from the university library one night. My handbag had the money I was left with for upkeep for the next two months and my valuable property, including my cell phone. I was not raped; I was saved by a group of boys who were also moving from the library. From then on, I learned to move with friends in a group.

I intend to leave home after I finish school. I do not want to go back into my father's home to stay with my stepmother, and neither can I go to the village to stay with my mother. I will rent out a small place to stay. I am thinking of getting a job, however small the salary will be after school, to begin a new life and look after my mother and sibling.

The following two global health narratives come from the Blackfeet Tribal Reservation in the U.S. state of Montana. These stories are told by Anna Bullshoe, a courageous American Indian woman who is fighting the scourge of alcohol and drugs on her reservation—a public health crisis that is utterly destroying the social fabric. In 2012, half of all infants born on the Blackfeet Reservation came into the world with an alcohol or drug dependency acquired from their mothers—a problem that is threatening an entire generation. These American Indian narratives from the wealthiest country in the world show that health injustice exists not only "over there" but also right at home.

Johnny's Story: A Young Man, Age Twenty, Living on the Blackfeet Reservation

I start my days with a cup of joe; then I corral, ride, and break horses, and smoke a bowl of weed—about six or seven times a day, if I have it. Otherwise, I smoke whenever it shows up. It's a stress reliever. My father used drugs, snorting coke in front of me, taking my birthday money. He even did a line of coke with me. And he used alcohol since before I was born. Not my mother, though. She drank once that I can remember. I have never seen her drink again.

My dad was abusive to all of us. He was verbally abusive, and I watched my father beat my sister with a belt. It was not a spanking—he beat her. And I was backhanded by him. In my marriage, I have also been abused physically, mentally, and emotionally. My partner ran me over with a car. I, in turn, assaulted her family members. It was in self-defense. I have since moved on and am now single.

It makes me mad when people in the community do the heavier drugs. What I mean is: what little kids get to eat, did they get the shoes or clothes they needed, it depends on whether adults do drugs. I know that it can't be stopped, but it's unfair that the grown-ups get what they want and the children do without.

I live with my mom and my sisters, but keep pretty much to myself. Drugs have made me a hermit. I try to stay away from Browning [a nearby small town in Montana], because I am trying to stay sober. Whenever I come to town, I just want to drink, and my friends are trying to talk me into getting high on whatever.

I have friends who smoke bad drugs in front of their kids, meaning meth. Then they try to care for their kids. They touch them and hold them, and I wonder if the smoke and everything affects their kids. I have walked into a house and there were many people smoking meth, and it's like, "Hey, don't let your kids be here."

If I could, I would turn our reservation into a dry reservation. As for drugs, I would find out what houses are dealing and gather solid information, then prosecute them for what they are doing. Check the houses. Check the people. Watch the houses. Watch the people. You can tell who is doing drugs and who is not.

Molly's Story: A Young Woman, Age Twenty-Four, Living on the Blackfeet Reservation

On a typical day, I get up early on weekdays to drop off my mother at work and my younger sister at school. Then I try to find some kind of employment, run errands, or just wait for my mother and sister. When I get home, I relax by reading or watching TV.

For the last two years, I've lived with my mother, brother, and sister, and off and on with my older brother and his family. I hardly see my father. I know he abuses alcohol. I must have been around two, I remember him coming home drunk. I think he did more coke than anything. It was kind of a shock to me when he rushed me into his house before my twenty-first birthday because his dealer had shown up. I saw the exchange and the dealer was male. I think the drugs may have been prescription pills, but they could have been hard drugs.

I don't drink. The smell of alcohol makes me sick. I don't do other drugs because I have seen how it tears families apart, and I want no part of it. Every once in a while I will smoke weed. Honestly, it makes me realize how close I came to being right there—seeing friends and family doing drugs and knowing what a fool I was to put myself in those situations.

I remember before my parents split, I was about four or five and my mom and dad were arguing. My dad pushed my mom down. She got up and said she was done and took us kids. We all went to my grandmother's.

My siblings have abused me physically, but mostly mentally. Like they thought my parents were favoring me when in reality I was a go-between from my father to my mother. It made me feel worthless. I was told that I was just wasting space and I didn't deserve to be here. It took me some time to deal with this. When your family is broken due to drugs and alcohol, everyone is hurt. In my own relationships, I've launched emotional attacks, trying to get back at them for hurting me, but it *always* backfired.

Several of my cousins smoke weed. Actually, one of my cousins did pills with her last two children. I know she miscarried but I do not know if the pills were the cause.

If I could make a change, I would want all narcotics and meth away from here, because it is causing family abuse and suffering. I would be out there helping to do something. Some parents are very good people, but they forget about their kids when it comes to drugs. It even causes death to some children.

How would I do it? Right now, do raids. You can go down the street and six out of every ten houses would be selling drugs. People come up and ask if you want to buy drugs—even in schools. They don't try to even hide it anymore.

And watch the children. We have to make sure they're safe.

After conducting these interviews with young American Indians, Anna Bullshoe organized a tribal Women's Health Council—a group of women in their seventies and eighties, "ready to take on the world to save our children." The Women's Council went on a media blitz to take on the infant addiction crisis on the Blackfeet Reservation, appearing on tribal radio every week "to let the public know that we are pushing for no tolerance on drugs and alcohol. We are also letting the people know just how far we have come in letting drugs into our society and what it is doing to the children." Anna organized a women's task force to find solutions. But the women tribal elders are poor and lack power on the reservation. The radio station is demanding money, which the women cannot afford. Meanwhile, the tribe's political leaders—virtually all men—seem to turn a deaf ear, often more concerned with casino revenue than with the health of Indian children. Anna is desperately looking for funding to sustain her grassroots campaign.

When I met Anna on the Blackfeet Reservation, I saw tribal workers dumping raw sewage into a lagoon adjacent to the village health clinic. No one even noticed—a testament to how accustomed the tribal community was to enduring unimaginable health hazards. But the real sign of complacency and neglect was the sight of children playing in rough fields, being approached by drug dealers, and teetering on the edge of another lagoon that reeked of untreated sewage, with windswept garbage seemingly everywhere. In the Indian-run casino, young people spent the day with their eyes fixated on slot machines, smoking cigarettes, and drinking hard liquor. It was a school day.

PART I

Failures in Global Health and Their Consequences

Health Inequities in Today's Globalized World

THIS FIRST PART OF THE BOOK lays the foundation for themes that will permeate throughout—particularly global health with justice, in which all people live and work in conditions that allow them to lead healthy, productive lives. Chapter 1 considers four fundamental issues, which are among the most pressing in global health today: (1) the services universally guaranteed under the right to health, (2) states' duties to safeguard the health of their own populations, (3) international responsibilities to contribute to improved health in lower-income countries, and (4) the governance needed to ensure that all states live up to their mutual responsibilities.

Chapter 2 examines the forces of globalization, looking for explanations of why health hazards change form and migrate everywhere on the earth. The global movement of goods, services, and ideas enables the rapid dissemination of pathogens and unhealthy lifestyles—behavioral risk factors, such as diet, tobacco use, and physical activity—across the world. Globalization demonstrates the interconnectedness among all countries, and all people, so that no state can insulate itself from transnational health threats. This chapter will deepen readers' understanding of the urgent need for collective global action to safeguard the population's health.

Collective action, however, will remain out of reach without the norms, processes, and institutions formed through international law in the broader currents of global governance for health. As explained in Chapter 3, the boundaries between law and governance are indistinct, with elements of law bleeding into governance, and vice versa. This chapter categorizes and explains three major sources of global health law: international health law (principally WHO normative instruments, discussed in Chapters 6 and 7), the human right to health (Chapter 8), and interconnecting legal regimes that have an impact on health. Part I concludes with six "grand challenges" in global health: (1) global leadership, (2) international collaboration, (3) harnessing creativity, (4) sustainable financing, (5) setting priorities, and (6) influencing multiple sectors.

CHAPTER 1

Global Health Justice

Toward a Transformative Agenda for Health Equity

CONSIDER TWO CHILDREN—one born in sub-Saharan Africa and the other in Europe, North America, or another developed region. The African child is almost eighteen times more likely to die in her first five years of life. If she lives to childbearing age, she is nearly 100 times more likely to die in labor. Overall, she can expect to die twenty-four years earlier than the child born into a wealthy part of the world.[1] Collectively, such vast inequalities between richer and poorer countries translate into nearly 20 million deaths every year—about one in every three global deaths—and have done so for at least the past two decades.[2] Put simply, the health gap between the rich and the poor is pervasive and unjust, with few signs of improvement.

The basic human needs of the world's poorest people continue to go unmet. In 2010, 780 million people lacked access to clean water and 2.5 billion people were without proper sanitation facilities, while approximately 870 million people faced chronic hunger.[3] Deteriorating infrastructure (e.g., electricity and roads) and worsening environmental conditions have compounded these threats to health in impoverished areas of the world. The health challenges that are the focus of the Millennium Development Goals (MDGs)—child and maternal mortality, HIV/AIDS, and malaria—persist as major health threats, as do neglected tropical diseases. Emerging infectious diseases (EIDs) continue to threaten the world's population, while the tremendous burden of noncommunicable diseases (NCDs) and the devastation of severe injuries continue to grow.

Yet these vast health disparities are not even fully captured by contrasting rich countries with poor ones: profound inequalities are found *within* countries, as marginalized populations trail far behind national averages. In Nairobi, Kenya, for example, the child death rate in impoverished slums is many times the rate in the wealthiest neighborhoods. These deprivations arise amid splendor for a lucky few, with one-third of the world's largest fortunes held by people in low- and middle-income countries. Even within wealthy states, dramatic health differences are tied to social disadvantage, with the poorest people often having life expectancies similar to those inhabiting the least developed countries. A black, unemployed youth in Baltimore, for example, can expect to live thirty-two years less than a white professional in the same city.[4] With the happenstance of one's birth still the greatest determinant of health, the current state of world health is one of deep injustice.

Although the global health gap remains unacceptably large, the international community has taken major steps to improve health and advance development. The United Nations adopted the MDGs to lift disadvantaged people out of poverty and disease (see Box 1.1). The Paris Declaration on Aid Effectiveness and the Accra Agenda for Action call for clearer targets and indicators of success, harmonization among partners, alignment with country strategies, and mutual accountability for results. The Global Fund to Fight AIDS, Tuberculosis and Malaria has emerged as a major international financier, pooling billions of dollars for health programs in more than 150 developing countries.[5]

Meanwhile, both domestic and international health investments have increased. For example, from 2000 to 2010 governments in sub-Saharan Africa more than doubled their per capita health spending, from an average of fifteen dollars to forty-three dollars (in nominal dollars and including on-budget external assistance).[6] International health assistance increased from less than $6 billion annually in the early 1990s to $10.5 billion in 2001, and then climbed to $26.9 billion in 2010.[7]

But despite unprecedented engagement, the international community has not fundamentally changed the reality for the world's least advantaged people. Will progress be achieved for poor and marginalized populations? Or will they come to form a permanent global health underclass? The fight against the most endemic and intractable diseases, such as AIDS and tuberculosis (TB), is at risk of slowing, or even reversing. Health inequities within many countries are growing. New global health challenges are arriving in force, particularly the rapid growth of NCDs and the impact of climate change, especially on water and food supplies (see Chapter 2, Box 2.3). Will countries mitigate these new, complex health threats, or will inequities be further compounded? Now is a pivotal time for global health—a moment of both promise and peril.

BOX 1.1 The Millennium Development Goals and Beyond: Toward a Post-2015 Sustainable Development Agenda

Recognizing the failure to meet the needs of the world's poor, the UN General Assembly, on September 8, 2000, unanimously adopted the Millennium Declaration.[1] The Millennium Development Goals (MDGs), which followed the Declaration, are the world's most broadly supported and comprehensive development targets, creating numerical benchmarks for tackling poverty and hunger, ill health, gender inequality, lack of education, lack of access to clean water, and environmental degradation by 2015.[2]

Child health MDG 4 calls for a two-thirds reduction in the mortality rate of children younger than five years old between 1990 and 2015. Globally, child mortality has fallen from twelve million deaths in 1990 to 6.9 million deaths in 2011. There are, however, gaping inequalities: 33.9 percent of child mortality occurs in South Asia and 48.7 percent occurs in sub-Saharan Africa, whereas 1.4 percent occurs in high-income countries.[3] Health inequalities among children are actually growing.[4]

Maternal health MDG 5 calls for a three-quarters reduction in the maternal mortality ratio between 1990 and 2015, together with universal access to reproductive health services. Maternal mortality is dropping, from 543,000 deaths in 1990 to 287,000 in 2010. The improvements, which mask extreme variations, are largely attributable to better care during pregnancy and skilled childbirth attendants.[5] To mobilize action, the 2010 MDG Summit launched the Global Strategy for Women's and Children's Health.[6]

HIV/AIDS, malaria, and other diseases MDG 6 aims to halt and reverse the spread of HIV and the incidence of malaria and other diseases. Even with historic global engagement to prevent AIDS-related deaths and nearly 10 million people on treatment by the end of 2012, under 2013 WHO treatment guidelines a further 16 million people in resource-poor settings will require treatment.[7] Malaria remains a major killer. Despite significant progress in some countries over the past decade, malaria deaths climbed from about one million in 1990 to nearly 1.2 million in 2010. Climate change and growing resistance to antimalarial medications pose major threats. In 2010, roughly 1.2 million people died of tuberculosis, with 85 percent of new cases occurring in Asia and Africa. Multidrug-resistant (MDR) and extensively drug-resistant (XDR) TB pose deep challenges.[8]

Food, water, and sanitation MDG 1 aims to halve extreme poverty and hunger by 2015, compared with 1990. The environmental sustainability goal, MDG 7, calls for halving the proportion of people who lack basic sanitation and safe drinking water by 2015, relative to 1990. The world has already met the water target, but this still leaves 11 percent of people without this necessity. The sanitation target is severely off track. At the current pace, 33 percent of the population—2.4 billion people—still will not have access to basic sanitation by 2015.[9] The hunger target is off-track as well, though in 2013 the United Nations reported that it was within reach with accelerated progress. Yet even achieving the target could leave more than 11 percent of the world's population without enough to eat, and far more people still suffering nutritional deficiencies.[10]

Most MDG targets have not been met, partially as a result of four global crises: finance, food, energy, and climate change.[11] In 2008 WHO Director-General Margaret Chan observed that even though "the health sector had no say when the policies responsible for these crises were made…health bears the brunt."[12]

In 2012 the UN launched a process to formulate post-2015 sustainable development goals, including a focus on health systems. As of 2013 the UN was considering the following health-related sustainable development goals: universal health coverage, healthy life expectancy, and enhancing MDGs 4–6 while reducing the burden of noncommunicable diseases (NCDs). The UN High-Level Panel of Eminent Persons on the Post-2015 Development Agenda offered "ensure healthy lives" as an illustrative health sector goal, with targets focused on women and children, along with reducing the burden of infectious diseases and NCDs. Separate High-Level Panel illustrative goals addressed food security and universal access to water and sanitation.[13]

NOTES

1. United Nations General Assembly (UNGA), Resolution 55/2, "Millennium Declaration," September 18, 2000.
2. United Nations (UN), *The Millennium Development Goals Report 2005* (New York: UN, 2005), 3.
3. United Nations Children's Fund (UNICEF) et al., *Levels and Trends in Child Mortality Report 2012* (New York: UNICEF, 2012), 9–10.
4. Save the Children Fund, *Born Equal: How Reducing Inequality Could Give Our Children a Better Future* (London: Save the Children Fund, 2012), 15. Across thirty-two surveyed countries, the gap between the richest and poorest children has grown by 35 percent since the 1990s.
5. World Health Organization (WHO) et al., *Trends in Maternal Mortality: 1990–2010* (Geneva: WHO, 2012), 26–29.
6. Ban Ki-moon, *Global Strategy for Women's and Children's Health* (New York: UN, 2010).

7. Joint United Nations Program on HIV/AIDS (UNAIDS), *UNAIDS World AIDS Day Report 2012* (Geneva: UNAIDS, 2012); "Realities in Global Treatment of H.I.V.," editorial *New York Times*, July 24, 2013, A26.
8. Rafael Lozano et al., "Global and Regional Mortality from 235 Causes of Death for 20 Age Groups in 1990 and 2010: A Systematic Analysis for the *Global Burden of Disease Study 2010*," *The Lancet* 380, no. 9859 (2012): 2095, 2105; WHO, *Global Tuberculosis Control 2011* (Geneva: WHO, 2011), iv, 9–10, 49. The number of malaria deaths cited is nearly double the levels WHO had estimated, in part due to evidence suggesting large numbers of deaths in individuals older than age five. WHO, *World Malaria Report 2011* (Geneva: WHO, 2011), 74.
9. UN, *The Millennium Development Goals Report 2013* (New York: UN, 2013), 47; UNICEF and WHO, *Progress on Drinking Water and Sanitation: 2012 Update* (New York: UNICEF, 2012), 15.
10. UN, *The Millennium Development Goals Report 2013* (New York: UN, 2013), 10.
11. UNGA, Resolution 65/1, "Keeping the Promise: United to Achieve the Millennium Development Goals," October 19, 2010.
12. Margaret Chan, "Globalization and Health," transcript of speech to UNGA, October 24, 2008.
13. UNGA, Resolution 67/81, "Global Health and Foreign Policy," December 12, 2012; "Health and the Post-2015 Development Agenda," editorial, *The Lancet* 381, no. 9868 (2012): 699; The World We Want 2015, *High Level Dialogue on Health in the Post-2015 Development Agenda, Gaborone, 4–6 March 2013: Meeting Report* (The World We Want 2015, 2013); High-Level Panel of Eminent Persons on the Post-2015 Development Agenda, *A New Global Partnership: Eradicate Poverty and Transform Economies Through Sustainable Development* (New York: UN, 2013).

The solutions to these global health challenges cannot lie in maintaining the status quo. Certainly, there is no simple solution to health threats that have endured for centuries. But transforming global health law—and more broadly, global governance for health—could dramatically improve health for all and reduce deep health inequalities. Global governance for health—i.e., the organization of norms, institutions, and processes that collectively shape the health of the world's population—goes beyond the health sector. It requires remediating the unfair and detrimental health influences of international regimes (e.g., trade, intellectual property, and finance policies), and developing stable, responsive, democratic political institutions that are focused on good governance and capable of implementing an all-of-government approach to health.

This chapter presents four defining questions for the future of global health—questions to which the answers would offer clear pathways toward lasting and innovative solutions:

1. What are the essential services and goods guaranteed under the right to health?
2. What duties do all states have to meet the health needs of their own inhabitants?
3. What duties do wealthier states have to improve the health of poor people outside their borders?
4. What governance strategies are needed to create effective institutions and structures for global health improvement?

Reviewing these four critical questions will make readily apparent how important law can be to the future of global health. Each global health problem is shaped by law's language of rights, duties, and rules of engagement, such as setting high standards, monitoring progress, and ensuring compliance. It is only through law that individuals and populations can claim entitlements to health services, and that corresponding state obligations can be established and enforced. And it is through law that norms can be set, fragmented activities coordinated, and good governance (e.g., transparency, stewardship, participation, accountability) ensured. The goal of this book is to show the potential of law, both national and global, to dramatically transform prospects for good health, particularly for the world's most disadvantaged people.

But before turning to those questions, let me first set out the moral and legal underpinning of my approach: the concept of health aid as charity must be jettisoned in favor of a justice-based commitment to mutual responsibility beyond state borders. The principles for which I argue in this chapter—those of shared national and global responsibilities, social justice, and the right to health—form the normative perspective that will run throughout this book's evaluation of global health law and governance.

Reconceptualizing "Health Aid"

"Global health" means different things to different people.[8] Often the term is used as shorthand for health assistance provided by affluent countries to poor countries, in a donor-recipient relationship, as a form of charity—a concept I will refer to as "health aid."

Framing the global health endeavor as health aid is fundamentally flawed, because it implies that the world is divided between donors and countries in need. This is too simplistic. Collaboration among countries, both as neighbors and across continents, is also about responding to health risks together and building capacity collaboratively—whether it is through South-South cooperation (see Box 1.2), ensuring the supply of essential vaccines and medicines, or demanding fair distribution of scarce lifesaving technologies. New social, economic, and political alignments are evident, for example, in the emerging health leadership of countries such as Brazil, India, Mexico, and Thailand.[9]

Likewise, the concept of "aid" both presupposes and imposes an inherently unequal relationship in which one side is a benefactor and the other a dependent. This leads affluent states and other donors to believe that they are giving "charity," which means that financial contributions and programs are largely at their discretion. It also means that donors decide the amount and objectives of global health initiatives. As a result, the level of financial assistance is not predictable, scalable to needs, or sustainable in the long term. These features of health aid could, in turn, mean that recipient countries do not accept full responsibility for their inhabitants' health because they can blame donors for shortcomings.

Conceptualizing international assistance as "aid" masks the deeper truth that human health is a globally shared responsibility, reflecting common risks and vulnerabilities—an obligation of health justice that demands a fair contribution from everyone (e.g., North and South, rich and poor). Global governance for health must be seen as a partnership, with financial and technical assistance understood as an integral component of

BOX 1.2 **South-South Cooperation**

Africa's first public antiretroviral plant in Mozambique, established in 2012 with Brazil's support, exemplifies the burgeoning role of South-South cooperation.[1] The growing economic and political strength of developing countries, especially the BRICS (Brazil, Russia, India, China, and South Africa), is driving innovations in global governance. The Group of Twenty (G20) major economies have become an important force in international relations. The Foreign Policy and Global Health Initiative draws its leadership largely from the South, consisting of five Southern countries (Brazil, Indonesia, Mexico, Senegal, and Thailand) and two Northern ones (France and Norway). South-South health cooperation is increasingly occurring through regional alliances, such as the twelve-nation South American Health Council, aimed at strengthening health systems and negotiating fair prices for essential medicines. Today's health cooperation emphasizes knowledge sharing and capacity building.

NOTE

1. PharmaAfrica, "New ARV Drugs Plant Launched in Mozambique," July 22, 2012, http://www.pharmaafrica.com/new-arv-drugs-plant-launched-in-mozambique/.

the common goal of improving global health and reducing health inequalities. As the African Union has observed, the world has moved to "a new era of shared responsibility and global solidarity."[10]

A Shared Obligation: The Right to Health and Reinforcing Frameworks

The right to the highest attainable standard of health, first enshrined in the WHO Constitution, is the most important health-related international legal obligation. What makes the right to health a compelling framework for holding states accountable is that it has wide international acceptance as binding law (see Chapter 8).

As described by the UN Committee on Economic, Social and Cultural Rights, the right to health, which covers public health, health care, and the underlying determinants of health, contains four "interrelated and essential elements," requiring that acceptable and good health goods, services, and facilities be available and accessible to everyone. States must respect, protect, and fulfill the right to health. That is, they must refrain from interfering with people's ability to realize this right (e.g., discrimination in access to health services), protect people from violations of this right by third parties, and actively ensure the full realization of this right.[11]

Although the right to health offers a critical framework for national and global responsibilities for health, it also suffers from obvious limitations:

1. The right to health contains broad aspirations, and fails to structure obligations with sufficient detail to render them susceptible to rigorous monitoring and enforcement.
2. The oversight body—the UN Committee on Economic, Social and Cultural Rights (CESCR)—possesses few enforcement powers beyond reviewing state reports on treaty implementation and making recommendations.
3. The International Covenant on Economic, Social and Cultural Rights (ICESCR) requires states to deliver on its promises "progressively," rather than immediately. This offers only a staggered and uncertain path toward full realization.
4. The legal duty falls primarily on the state, not the international community, to provide health services to its own people, even if the country has few resources and limited capacity.

These structural limitations in the right-to-health framework can be overcome. The CESCR and the special rapporteur can continue to develop clear, enforceable standards and to press states harder toward implementation. The duty to "progressively" realize the right to health could be interpreted to require states to meet precise indicators or benchmarks of tangible progress. The ICESCR's text requires states immediately "to take steps" to achieve "the full realization" of the right to health. The CESCR affirms that states must "move as expeditiously and effectively as possible towards that goal."[12] The all-important capacity problem can be overcome through the ICESCR's insistence that states use "the maximum of [their own] available resources," and that the international community provide "assistance and co-operation, especially economic and technical."[13]

The right to health—and related entitlements, such as the right to food, clean water, and adequate sanitation—continues to evolve and gain international acceptance.[14] Meanwhile, two other paradigms join the human rights framework in recognizing global health as a shared responsibility, a partnership, and a priority that requires international cooperation: human security and global public goods. Unlike the right to health, these two frameworks do not have the force of law, but they have gained international recognition (see Box 1.3).

BOX 1.3 Two Global Health Paradigms

Human security is emerging as a complementary paradigm for understanding global vulnerabilities, as it addresses shortcomings of the traditional national security paradigm in international affairs. Under this approach, people (not states) become the central focus, which allows international interventions to address atrocities, such as genocide.[1] The human security approach focuses on "political, social, environmental, economic, military, and cultural systems that together give people the building blocks of survival, livelihood, and dignity." The Commission on Human Security has stated that "good health is both essential and instrumental to achieving human security."[2] There is an interplay between health and human security: extreme health inequalities may foment conflicts, and conversely, military conflicts may threaten health and health systems in myriad ways.

Global public goods (GPGs) have two characteristics: (1) they are nonrivalrous (once supplied to one person, the good can be supplied to all others at no extra cost), and (2) they are nonexcludable (once the good is supplied to one person, it is impossible to exclude others from the benefits). States have a shared responsibility to provide public goods that the market cannot deliver, and that no country can provide on its own. Traditional GPGs, such as clean air, uncontaminated water, and infectious disease control, require collective action, because no state or private actor has sufficient incentives to provide the good in sufficient quantity. Health services would not seem to qualify as public goods. For example, there is an additional cost to supplying medicine to additional people (rivalry exists), and it is possible to provide medicine to one person but not another (people can be excluded). However, global health scholars often view health as a GPG because of its positive externalities. Whether or not health fits into the GPG framework, it has widely shared benefits—it enhances people's capacity to contribute to political and cultural life, enriches economies, and fosters social cohesion.[3]

NOTES

1. Keizo Takemi et al., "Human Security Approach for Global Health," *The Lancet* 372, no. 9632 (2008): 13–14.
2. Commission on Human Security, *Human Security Now* (New York: Commission on Human Security, 2003), 4, 96.
3. Richard Smith et al., eds., *Global Public Goods for Health: Health Economics and Public Health Perspectives* (Oxford: Oxford University Press, 2003), 10–17.

Four Defining Questions for the Future of the World's Health

Having explained the moral and legal underpinnings of my approach, I now want to sketch preliminary answers to the four questions raised earlier in this chapter. Taken together, these questions are critically important for the future of the world's health (see Figure 1.1).

1. What are the essential health services and goods guaranteed to every human being under the right to health?

The first foundational challenge is to specify the essential health services and goods that make up the core obligations of the right to health. This clarification would help define key health interventions and give greater substance to a state's fundamental duties to meet the health needs of its inhabitants. It would also provide a foundation for assessing affluent states' obligations to low- and middle-income countries. The right-to-health framework militates against a narrow definition of vital services. Rather, services should encompass three essential conditions that give everyone a fair opportunity for a healthy, safe, and productive life (see Chapter 14):

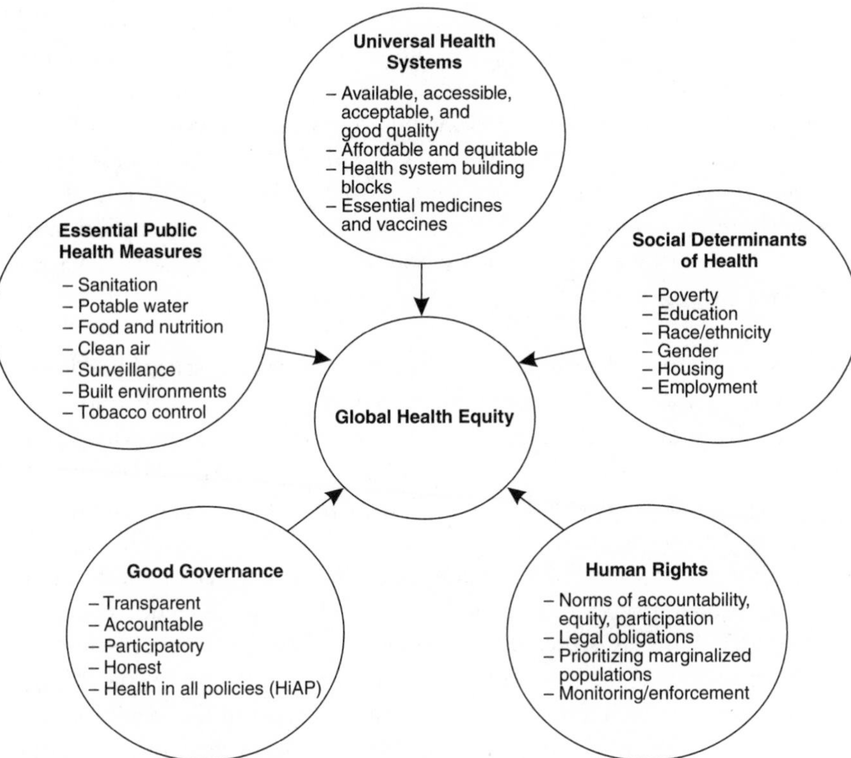

Figure 1.1 **Key determinants of global health equity**

1. Public health services The first essential condition for good health is population-based services that create an environment in which people and communities can lead healthier, safer lives. As critical as effective health care systems are, people who cannot access nutritious food, whose water contains harmful bacteria, and whose lungs are smothered by pollution and tobacco smoke hardly live in conditions that are conducive to living healthy lives. Public health services—which are essential to maintaining and restoring human capability and functioning—include sanitation, potable water, clean air, nutritious food, vector abatement, tobacco and alcohol control, injury prevention, and healthy built environments.

2. Universal health systems The second essential condition for good health is a well-functioning health care system to provide clinical prevention, treatment, and palliative care for all people who are ill, injured, or suffering. According to the WHO, the building blocks of such a system include health care services, a health workforce, health information, medical products and technologies, sustainable financing, leadership, and governance.[15] Health systems should ensure high-quality health care (e.g., primary care, emergency care, specialized care for acute and chronic diseases and injuries, pain relief), including essential vaccines and medicines for all inhabitants (see Chapter 4, Box 4.2). The WHO identified three dimensions of universal health coverage: the proportion of the population covered, the level of services covered, and the proportion of costs covered by prepaid, pooled funding—each of which can be informed by the right to health (see Chapter 8).

3. Socioeconomic determinants of health The third essential condition for good health is elimination of the underlying social and economic causes of injury, disease, and early death, such as inequities based on income and gender, and lack of (or poor-quality) education, employment, and housing. Even if she lives in a village with an effective health system, a woman who is abused by her husband, lacks the educational and economic wherewithal to leave him, or has no confidence in a justice system to protect her, will still be unhealthy and unsafe. Indeed, 35 percent of women globally suffer intimate partner violence or sexual violence from non-partners.[16] And in the famous Whitehall study in the 1960s, civil service clerks in the United Kingdom had most of the conditions required for good health—for example, living in one of the world's wealthiest countries and being covered by the National Health Service—yet they were four times more likely to die young than colleagues at the top of the civil service hierarchy.[17] Something necessary for good health was missing.

Socioeconomic determinants are mostly ensured outside the health sector, such as in ministries of education, transportation, and commerce. This reality, and the relative nature of many determinants (e.g., equality, stress), prevents them from being quantified within a set of health goods and services to which all people are guaranteed under the right to health—even as these determinants remain crucial for human flourishing.

Excluding the broader determinants of health, how much would health goods and services cost? The WHO, based on the work of the High-Level Taskforce on Innovative International Financing for Health Systems, estimated that health interventions to meet the health-related MDGs and treat chronic diseases would require states to spend, on average, a minimum of about sixty dollars per capita, which could achieve near-universal health care coverage.[18] This is only a fraction of the cost because it includes few of the population-based public health services needed for healthier and safer populations.

In considering costs, it is worth bearing in mind that most health investments would more than pay for themselves. Health services contribute to increased productivity and economic growth—including, over the longer term, children's education and healthy development—as well as maintaining a healthy workforce.

2. What are states' responsibilities for the health of their own populations?

States hold primary responsibility for upholding their inhabitants' right to health. This requires governments, within their capacity, to provide the funding for and delivery of all the essential goods and services guaranteed to every human being, and to progressively achieve the highest attainable standard of health. The elements of a state's duties to its inhabitants include at least the following:

Provide adequate health resources within the state's capacity Despite the considerable need for expanded health services, developing countries' health expenditures as a proportion of total government spending are significantly lower than the global average (less than 10 percent compared with more than 15 percent).[19] This low spending comes even as African heads of state pledged in the 2001 Abuja Declaration on HIV/AIDS, Tuberculosis and Other Related Infectious Diseases to commit at least 15 percent of their government budgets to the health sector[20]—a pledge reaffirmed at their 2010 summit.[21] At the present rate of increase (from 2000 to 2009), average health sector spending among African countries will not reach the 15 percent target until 2046—more than four decades after the Abuja Declaration.[22] Meeting in 2012, African health and finance ministers committed to "increase domestic resources for health through enhanced revenue collection and allocation, re-prioritization where relevant, and innovative financing."[23]

States' own health spending is influenced by foreign assistance, which accounts for 15 percent of total health expenditures in low-income countries, and can be as high as two-thirds of the total in some countries. Unfortunately, developing countries often reduce their domestic health spending in response to increasing international assistance—the so-called substitution effect.[24] Of course, the purpose for which domestic health spending is being diverted matters a great deal. For example, certain essential non-health sector expenditures, such as agriculture, education, or social security, can improve health. Yet some governments use these funds for purposes much less likely to improve health—such as the police or military—or waste precious resources through corruption and inefficiency.

It is unrealistic to expect that affluent states will carry out their responsibilities if lower-income states do not provide necessary resources within their own economic constraints. A firm commitment by lower-income countries to make a clearly defined effort, consistent with their human rights obligations, could convince wealthier countries to accept their mutual responsibilities. It would therefore be beneficial to reach a global agreement on the minimum domestic effort necessary to uphold the right to health. States that do not live up to that minimum will have a weaker platform from which to claim international assistance. Furthermore, they would bear greater responsibility for ill health in their countries, and for epidemics spilling over to other countries.

Govern well Money alone will not ensure good health. Governments must manage national economic and social resources effectively. Public officials who exercise authority have a duty of *stewardship*—a personal responsibility to act in the interests of those they serve (see Chapter 3). Sound governance is *honest,* in that it is avoids corruption, such as public officials seeking personal gain or diverting funds from their intended purposes. It is *transparent,* in that institutional processes and decision making are open and comprehensible. It is *deliberative,* in that stakeholders have an opportunity to provide genuine input into policy formation. Good governance is also *accountable,* in that leaders give reasons for decisions and assume responsibility for successes or failures, and the public has the opportunity to disagree with and change the direction of policies. Good governance enables states to formulate and implement sound policies, manage resources efficiently, and provide effective services.

Despite the importance of good governance, health sector corruption is a major problem. A World Bank survey of twenty-two developing countries found that health was among the most corrupt sectors. Health sector corruption includes fund leakage, drug diversion, informal payments to providers, accreditation and licensing bribes, and professional absenteeism.[25] Foreign assistance, in particular, is considered "ripe territory for corruption."[26] Public officials can profit from foreign assistance, which is often given with substantial discretion and little accountability. A vicious cycle of corruption can easily occur: corrupt countries perform poorly, and therefore they increasingly depend on aid.

Allocate scarce resources equitably and efficiently States should have the authority to set their own health priorities. But in doing so, they have a responsibility to allocate scarce resources ethically. A state should fairly and efficiently distribute health services for its entire population. This requires paying special attention to the needs of the most disadvantaged—such as poor people, minorities, women, and people with disabilities—and ensuring that health services are accessible and acceptable irrespective of socioeconomic status, language, culture, religion, or locality.

3. What responsibility does the international community have for improving the health of people in low- and middle-income countries?

States' duties are not limited to caring for their own people, but also extend to fostering a functioning, interdependent global community in which mutual survival is a matter of common concern. Increased globalization has compelled states to understand the broad need for collective action. But a more difficult question remains unanswered: to what extent are states, particularly wealthier ones, responsible for the health of inhabitants in other countries? This is a particularly vexing problem because enunciating sound principles demonstrating that State A has specific duties toward the people of State B is exceedingly difficult. Even if a cosmopolitan perspective did point toward transnational obligations, the issue of which states have duties to whom, and for what, would remain unclear.[27]

Notwithstanding the conceptual complexity, finding innovative ways to hold richer states accountable for international assistance is imperative. Unfortunately, a deep burden of avoidable morbidity and premature mortality rests on those states that have the least capacity. As stated above, the WHO estimates that a basic set of health services would cost a minimum of sixty dollars per person annually, plus additional investments to meet fundamental human needs. The politics of taxation cannot realistically allow for government revenue that is more than 20 percent of the gross national income (GNI) in low-income countries.[28] If these states allocated 15 percent of government revenue to the health sector, as African leaders promised in the Abuja Declaration, only states with a GNI of more than $2,000 per person per year would have the capacity to provide the essential package of health services.

The actual minimum GNI that would enable countries to have the capacity to provide the essential health package, using only internal resources, would need to be appreciably higher than $2,000 per capita—given that this figure is based on an incomplete set of essential health services (e.g., only a limited number of NCD services) and does not cover fundamental human needs. More than one-third of the world's people live in countries with per capita GNI of less than $2,000. External support will be needed to provide the essential health package to these people, who number in the billions.

In 2001 the WHO Commission on Macroeconomics and Health calculated that affluent states would need to devote approximately 0.1 percent of GNI to international development assistance for health.[29] Other data suggest a similar or slightly higher proportion of GNI may be necessary.[30] Yet in 2010 official development assistance (ODA) for health care from traditional donor countries—members of the Organization for Economic Cooperation and Development (OECD)—was less than 0.05 percent of GNI, or less than half of what is required by this measure.[31]

If low- and middle-income countries are to provide their inhabitants with a reasonable standard of health services, wealthier states will have to ensure financing that is predictable, sustainable, and scalable to needs. The High-Level Taskforce on Innovative International Financing for Health Systems reported in 2009 that health spending (from all sources) in 49 low-income countries needed to increase from $31 billion to $67–$76 billion annually to achieve the MDGs. And even this recommended funding level largely excludes fundamental human needs.[32] However, the world is not on track to meet these and other funding requirements, and in the aftermath of the 2008–2009 global financial downturn, prospects for future growth in international health assistance appear grim. It is even possible to see a retrenchment in the near term.

Although the volume of international financial responsibility is vital, the long-term reliability of funding is equally important. Financial assistance for health is typically provided in the form of grants with limited duration, generally three to five years. Domestic politics in wealthy countries contribute to the short-term nature of these grants. Elections that may lead to new governments with different priorities, along with annual appropriation cycles and changing geopolitical interests and national priorities, make it difficult for governments to make firm long-term commitments. Furthermore, the international community seems to believe that short-duration grants will encourage poorer states to take their fate in their own hands and mobilize additional domestic resources.

Regrettably, the actual effect might be quite the opposite. As long as donor commitments remain short-term and unreliable, governments are "understandably reluctant to take the risk of relying on increased aid to finance the necessary scaling up of public expenditure."[33] But that does not mean they will refuse the financial assistance that is available. It is more likely that they will limit their own domestic health spending. Health ministers understandably do not want to increase their budgets to a level that would be unsustainable should foreign assistance be reduced in the future.[34] Furthermore, the short-term nature of assistance makes states reluctant to invest in recurrent costs (such as health worker training), exacerbating severe human resource shortages (see Chapter 11).

Financial assistance that is not based on an understanding of mutual responsibility, and is unreliable in the long run, is therefore an inefficient expenditure of resources because it is limited in its ability to improve the public's health. This alone should be sufficient reason to consider a global agreement on norms that clarify national and global responsibilities for health, transforming ineffective short-term financial assistance into effective sustained funding.

International responsibility extends well beyond financing, however. Many regimes have a significant impact on public health. States often adopt policies that impede, rather than facilitate, health among the world's poor, such as intellectual property rules that reduce access to essential medicines; restrictive macroeconomic policies that limit government revenue or the ability to invest in health; agricultural policies, such as farm subsidies and biofuel production targets, that affect global food markets; and energy policies that exacerbate climate change, with its adverse effects on health. States should limit these conflicts between health and other policies by adopting a health-in-all-policies approach, conscientiously assessing the health impact of policies with the aim of ensuring that they promote health (see Chapter 14).

4. What kinds of global governance mechanisms are required to ensure that all states live up to their mutual responsibilities for improving health?

The preliminary answers to the first three questions should be sufficient to demonstrate the need for better global governance for health, based on genuine partnerships.

This paradigm shift to mutual responsibility for global health grounded in the right to health will require more than an agreed-on set of responsibilities and principles. It will also require constructing a more forceful, purposeful, efficient, and accountable set of institutions and arrangements. A global governance structure that can at last make health for all a reality will have to successfully address six "grand challenges" in global health,[35] which are explored in greater detail in Chapter 3:

1. *Foster global health leadership* to mobilize, coordinate, and focus a large and diverse set of actors around a clear mission, common objectives, effective approaches, sustained action, and mutual accountability.
2. *Improve collaboration and coordination* among multiple players to reduce fragmentation and duplication.
3. *Harness the creativity, energy, and resources for global health,* including civil society, the private sector, philanthropists, and public-private partnerships.
4. *Ensure predictable, sustainable, and scalable funding* by countries themselves and the international community.
5. *Prioritize essential health needs,* including clean water, nutrition, sanitation, tobacco control, vector abatement, and health systems.
6. *Influence multiple sectors to promote health* to minimize conflicts between health and other sectors and to maximize the extent to which all sectors contribute to health.

These broadly imagined innovations in global governance for health are ambitious, and they face powerful political and economic obstacles. There remains considerable distrust between the global North and South. Convincing wealthy states that they should bind themselves to sustainable levels of assistance, scalable to real needs, will be difficult. And it will be just as difficult to persuade poorer countries to fulfill their own responsibilities for health assurance and good governance.

Yet mutual responsibilities come with reciprocal benefits. Countries in the global South would benefit from increased respect for their strategies; greater and more predictable funding from more accountable development partners; reform of regimes that harm health, such as trade and agriculture policies; and improved health for their populations. The global North would benefit from greater confidence that development assistance is spent effectively; the prospect of reduced foreign assistance obligations over time, as host countries build sustainable health systems; and better protection from global public health threats for their own populations. All countries would benefit from the economic, educational, environmental, and security benefits that come from healthier populations. And all would experience a sense of shared satisfaction from participating in a historic venture to make unprecedented progress towards global health equity.

Above all, innovations in global governance for health are necessary to bring an end to stubbornly persistent health inequalities based on the happenstance of one's birth. My goal in this book is to reveal in vivid detail the yet untapped potential of global health law to redress the dire state of global health today. I offer a systematic account of the international law regimes that powerfully influence health—for good and bad—in the key realms of WHO treaties, human rights, and trade. Most importantly, I demonstrate the potential for law and global governance for health to make a dramatic difference in the lives of people throughout the world, with particular attention to the most disadvantaged.

Globalized Health Hazards

The Need for Collective Global Action

CHAPTER 1 EXPLAINED why solutions to profound global health challenges require a framework of mutual responsibility. No state, not even the most wealthy, can insulate itself from the forces of globalization that propel health hazards throughout the world. In Chapter 2, I aim to deepen understanding of globalization and demonstrate the urgent need for collective global action to tackle the world's most pressing health threats.

Globalization can be understood as a process characterized by changes in a range of social spheres, including the economic, political, technological, cultural, and environmental arenas. Globalization is restructuring human societies, ushering in new patterns of health and disease, and reshaping the determinants of health. Indeed, the globalization of trade and investment, travel and migration, information and communication, and culture and lifestyles is obscuring the traditional boundaries between national and international health.

The determinants of health (e.g., pathogens, air, food, water, lifestyle choices) do not originate solely within national borders. Health threats inexorably spread to neighboring countries, regions, and even continents. People's lives are profoundly affected by commerce, politics, science, and technology from all over the world. Global integration and interdependence occur "as capital, traded goods, persons, concepts, images, ideas, and values diffuse across state boundaries."[1] It is for this reason that law and policy must be transnational, extending beyond sovereign nations.[2] There is no other way to truly ensure the public's health than through cooperation and communal action.

This chapter searches for answers as to why health hazards change form and migrate everywhere on the earth. Exploring this issue requires an understanding of the global dimensions of injury and disease, as well as humankind's role in harming the planet. Human beings, and the societies they form, are deeply interconnected. The actions of individuals affect their neighbors near and far. Whether it is the act of polluting a waterway or the air, overusing scarce resources, or entering the stream of travel and commerce, people's actions have inescapable health consequences.

This chapter analyzes (1) the cross-border spread of infectious diseases; (2) the global profile of NCDs and the mechanisms by which they are spread; (3) the neglected subject of injuries, which children and adults in lower-income countries sustain at vastly disproportionate rates; and (4) the hazards posed by international commerce in food, drugs, and consumer goods. The three main health threats covered in the chapter (infectious diseases, NCDs, and international commerce) are inter-related, as discussed in Box 2.1.

BOX 2.1 The Interrelationships between the Three Main Global Health Hazards: Infectious Diseases, Noncommunicable Diseases, and Injuries

Although global health experts like to talk about them as distinct categories, the lines between the three major health hazards—infectious diseases, NCDs, and injuries—are becoming blurred.

Pathogens: The link to cancers Globally, more than 20 percent of malignancies have been causally linked to human pathogens, including hepatitis B and C virus (liver cancer), human papillomavirus [HPV] (cervical and anogenital cancers), and Helicobacter pylori [H. pylori] (stomach cancer).[1] Every year, for example, cervical cancer affects nearly half a million women and takes more than a quarter of a million lives, with 80 percent of cases occurring in developing countries. Many of these deaths are preventable by screening (e.g., mammograms and pap smears)[2] and by vaccinating girls and young women against HPV.[3] The routine administration of HPV vaccines, for example, has reduced both HPV infections and associated cervical cancers in the United States.[4]

Alcoholic beverages: The link to NCDs, infectious diseases, STDs, and injuries About 2.5 million people around the world die each year from the deleterious consumption of alcohol.[5] Alcohol contributes to most major chronic diseases, such as cardiovascular disease, cancer, and diabetes. By lowering behavioral inhibitions, it can lead to unprotected sex and HIV/AIDS transmission. Heavy alcohol use is also a risk factor for tuberculosis, as it impairs the immune system and increases a person's susceptibility to infection as well as to reactivation of latent disease.[6] In addition, alcohol can increase carelessness or violence, resulting in injuries both unintentional (e.g., car crashes, falls) and intentional (e.g., self-inflicted injuries or suicide, assaults, murders, and partner or child abuse). Injuries account for 50 percent of alcohol-attributable deaths. Alcohol consumption has resulted in increasingly high injury rates in low- and middle-income countries.

NOTES

1. H. Zur Hausen, "The Search for Infectious Causes of Human Cancers: Where and Why," *Virology* 392, no. 1 (2009): 1–10; Peter Boyle and Bernard Levin, eds., *World Cancer Report 2008* (Lyon: International Agency for Research on Cancer, 2008), 128.
2. Mark Schiffman and Sholom Waeholder, "From India to the World—A Better Way to Prevent Cervical Cancer," *New England Journal of Medicine* 360, no. 14 (2009): 1453–1455.
3. Lawrence O. Gostin and Catherine D. DeAngelis, "Mandatory HPV Vaccination: Public Health vs Private Wealth," *Journal of the American Medical Association* 297, no. 17 (2007): 1921–1923. HPC vaccination is also recommended for boys and young men to protect against genital warts and some anal cancers. See "Genital HPV Infection Fact Sheet," Centers for Disease Control and Prevention (CDC), http://www.cdc.gov/std/HPV/STDFact-HPV.htm.
4. Lauri E. Markowitz et al., "Reduction in Human Papillomavirus (HPV) Prevalence among Young Women following HPV Vaccine Introduction in the United States, National Health and Nutrition Examination Surveys, 2003–2010," *Journal of Infectious Diseases* 208, no. 3 (2013): 385–393.
5. World Health Organization (WHO), *Global Status Report on Alcohol and Health* (Geneva: WHO, 2011), 24–28.
6. Jürgen Rehm et al., "The Association between Alcohol Use, Alcohol Use Disorders and Tuberculosis (TB): A Systematic Review," *BMC Public Health* 9, no. 1 (2009): 450–462.

Globalization and the Spread of Infectious Diseases: Man-Made and Controllable

Despite remarkable advances in medical research, common infectious diseases remain among the leading causes of death, accounting for 16.7 percent of global mortality.[3] AIDS, tuberculosis, malaria, measles, pneumonia, and diarrheal diseases are associated with poverty, as are tropical diseases such as schistosomiasis, lymphatic filariasis, and dengue. It is important to stress, however, that infectious diseases transcend borders and affect both rich and poor countries, with far-reaching consequences for national health systems and human security.

More than 335 infectious diseases have emerged over the last half century. Emerging infectious diseases (EIDs) are caused by newly identified organisms, such as lyme borreliosis, severe acute respiratory syndrome (SARS)-associated coronavirus (SARS-CoV), and hepatitis C or E. Moreover, the incidence of EIDs is increasing, which suggests that their threat to global health is growing (see Box 2.2).[4] In addition to the continual discovery of new human pathogens, there has been a reemergence of old infectious diseases—such as dengue, mumps virus, streptococcus, and staphylococcus aureus—which are rapidly increasing in incidence and geographic range.[5] "Natural genetic variations, recombinations, and adaptations allow new strains of known pathogens to appear to which the immune system has not been previously exposed and is therefore not primed to recognize," such as novel influenzas.[6]

BOX 2.2 Novel Corona Virus Case Study: SARS and MERS-CoV

Severe acute respiratory syndrome (SARS) is a viral respiratory illness caused by SARS-associated coronavirus (SARS-CoV). SARS is spread primarily by close person-to-person contact, usually by respiratory droplets (droplet spread) produced when an infected person coughs or sneezes. First reported in Asia in February 2003, within months SARS affected twenty-nine countries, infecting 8,098 people and killing 774. After China, Hong Kong, and Taiwan, Canada was hit the hardest.[1] The global outbreak caused significant economic harm, especially in Asia and in Ontario, Canada. Public fears significantly curtailed international travel, tourism, and commerce in goods and animals.

SARS sent shock waves around the world, causing widespread fear and confusion regarding its cause, source, modes of spread, and appropriate interventions.[2] Quarantine and isolation were widely used in Asia and Canada to contain SARS transmission. In Toronto 13,000 people were quarantined.[3] Quarantine was used predominantly for asymptomatic contacts of infected persons, including health care workers who had been in hospitals in which SARS was transmitted. Although quarantine in Toronto was accomplished by a variety of means, home quarantine was the predominant venue. To prevent a shortage of essential health care staff, health care workers were subject to "work quarantines" that required them to travel directly from home to work. Less restrictive measures, including social distancing, were also widely used, such as school closures and cancellation of public events. At the other extreme, China used highly restrictive measures, including cordoning off neighborhoods.

While Canada generally adopted voluntary approaches, Mainland China, Hong Kong, and Singapore used more coercive measures, such as confining residents in a large housing complex. Surveillance cameras were placed in homes where people were quarantined; to avoid fraud, the inhabitants were required to take their temperature on camera. Electronic wristbands or ankle bands also were used as enforcement measures. Singaporeans faced fines of more than $5,000 for breaching home quarantine orders. Chinese citizens faced even harsher criminal penalties.

The effectiveness of quarantine remains in doubt. SARS was diagnosed in 0.22 percent of quarantined contacts in Taiwan, 2.7 percent in Hong Kong, and 3.8 percent in Beijing.[4] In Toronto only a small percentage of people who were quarantined had a suspected SARS diagnosis, and even a smaller percentage had a laboratory-confirmed diagnosis.[5] In hindsight, large-scale quarantine may have been unnecessary. The public feared SARS because of the disease's novelty, communicability, and rapid spread. Some of this trepidation proved to be rational. But in the end, the 9.6 percent case fatality rate was less than first feared, and the total number of deaths was a small fraction of seasonal influenza deaths.[6]

To understand the constantly evolving threat of pathogens, consider a recent emergence of a novel coronavirus (nCoV) – a beta coronavirus known as the Middle East Respiratory Syndrome Coronavirus (MERS or MERS-CoV). In September 2012 scientists reported this novel coronavirus in a Qatari man with a travel history to Saudi Arabia, and it has since infected others in Qatar, Saudi Arabia, Jordan, Tunisia, and the United Arab Emirates, as well as in France, Italy, and the United Kingdom.[7] Globally, from September 2012 to November 4, 2013, the WHO reported 150 laboratory-confirmed cases of infection with MERS-CoV, including 60 deaths.[8] MERS-CoV does not appear to be easily transmissible from humans to humans, and it probably has an animal origin (possibly bats or camels).[9] Health officials are remaining vigilant to the possibility that a future mutation could render the virus transmissible between humans. The WHO convened an Emergency Committee under the International Health Regulations to advise the director-general. However, the committee decided that MERS-CoV did not meet the conditions for a "Public Health Emergency of International Concern" (PHEIC) under the International Health Regulations.[10]

NOTES

1. Public Health Agency of Canada, *Learning from SARS—Renewal of Public Health in Canada: A Report of the National Advisory Committee on SARS and Public Health* (Ottawa: Health Canada, 2003), 1.

2. David P. Fidler, *SARS, Governance and the Globalization of Disease* (Houndmills, UK: Palgrave Macmillan, 2004), 71–105; David P. Fidler, "Developments Involving SARS, International Law, and Infectious Disease Control at the Fifty-Sixth Meeting of the World Health Assembly," *ASIL Insights* (June 2003).
3. Tomislav Svoboda et al., "Public Health Measures to Control the Spread of the Severe Acute Respiratory Syndrome during the Outbreak in Toronto," *New England Journal of Medicine* 350, no. 23 (2004): 2352–2361.
4. CDC, "Efficiency of Quarantine during an Epidemic of Severe Acute Respiratory Syndrome—Beijing, China, 2003," *Morbidity and Mortality Weekly Report* 52 (2003): 1037–1040.
5. Svoboda et al., "Public Health Measures to Control the Spread of the Severe Acute Respiratory Syndrome," 2352.
6. Lawrence O. Gostin, "Pandemic Influenza: Public Health Preparedness for the Next Global Health Emergency," *Journal of Law, Medicine and Ethics* 32, no. 4 (2004): 565–573.
7. "Middle East Respiratory Syndrome (MERS)," CDC, http://www.cdc.gov/coronavirus/mers/.
8. "Middle East Respiratory Syndrome Coronavirus (MERS-CoV)–Update," WHO, November 4, 2013, http://www.who.int/csr/don/2013_11_04/en/index.html.
9. Chantal B. E. M. Reusken et al., "Middle East Respiratory Syndrome Coronavirus Neutralizing Serum Antibodies in Dromedary Camels: A Comparative Serological Study," *The Lancet Infectious Diseases* (August 9, 2013).
10. WHO, "WHO Statement on the Second Meeting of the IHR Emergency Committee concerning MERS-CoV," July 17, 2013, http://www.who.int/mediacentre/news/statements/2013/mers_cov_20130717/en/.

Preexisting, well-recognized infections, such as tuberculosis, malaria, nosocomial infections, and foodborne diseases, are also resurgent, due to antimicrobial resistance. Known infections such as West Nile virus, monkeypox, and Chikungunya virus are similarly spreading to new geographic areas or populations.

Disease emergence is driven by anthropogenic and demographic changes, representing a hidden cost of intense economic development.[7] Disease amplifiers, therefore, are principally man-made and controllable.[8] Human beings congregate and travel, live in close proximity to animals, pollute the environment, and rely on overtaxed health systems. This constant cycle of congregation, consumption, and movement allows infectious diseases to mutate and spread across boundaries.

The global population is also vulnerable to deliberate manipulation and dispersal of pathogens. Individuals and groups—whether motivated by politics, religion, or ethnic animosity—seek to destabilize social

Mass congregation

- The world's population grew from 1.6 billion at the beginning of the twentieth century to 6.1 billion by the century's end. By 2050 the global population is expected to reach 9.1 billion.
- The number of people living in urban centers has increased from 2.26 billion to 3.01 billion between 1990 and 2003. The rate of urbanization is highest in developing countries.

Environmental degradation

- Water and air pollution increase respiratory and gastrointestinal diseases.
- Climate change results in extreme weather, which creates breeding grounds for disease.

Human-animal interchange

- Many infectious diseases, including HIV/AIDS, Ebola, SARS, and avian influenza originated in animals but crossed over to humans.
- Cattle diseases endanger human health and stifle international trade.

Overtaxed health systems

- Overtaxed health centers lack equipment and training for sterilization and infection control.
- Health care professionals improperly prescribe medicines, creating drug-resistant viruses and bacteria.

Spread of infectious diseases

- Seventy-five percent of all deaths from infectious diseases occur in Southeast Asia and sub-Saharan Africa.
- Lower respiratory diseases, HIV/AIDS, diarrheal illnesses, tuberculosis, and malaria account for more than 90 percent of deaths from infectious diseases.

Figure 2.1 **The interacting factors that influence the transnational spread of infectious diseases**

structures. Bioterrorists have incentives to move pathogens to places where they will have the most destructive impact—often densely populated urban areas.[9]

These human activities, and many more, have profound health consequences for people in all parts of the world, and no country can shield itself from the effects. The world's communities are interdependent and reliant on one another for health security (see Figure 2.1).

Transnational Spread of Infectious Diseases

Mass Congregation, Migration, and Travel

Infectious diseases spread among populations and geographic areas as human beings congregate, migrate, and travel. Mass movement of people occurs naturally as individuals travel from rural to urban settings in search of livelihoods and social attachments. (In 1900, only 13 percent of the world's population lived in urban areas; by 2008, half the population was living in urban settings; and by 2025, 70 percent of the population will be urban.)[10] Mass migrations are also fueled by famine, civil unrest, and natural disasters.[11] The unsanitary conditions in refugee camps and other mass settings are deeply troublesome from a humanitarian perspective. Population density—whether through voluntary or forced migrations—places a strain on drinking water, food supplies, and sewage systems. This provides a breeding ground for infectious diseases.

Modern travel—its volume, speed, and reach—is unprecedented. Today it is possible to travel anywhere in the world within twenty-four hours and come into contact with fellow passengers who may be harboring infectious diseases or transporting disease vectors. As Mary E. Wilson has stated: "When they travel, humans carry their genetic makeup, immunologic sequelae of past infections, cultural preferences, customs, and behavioral patterns. Microbes, animals, and other biologic life also accompany them. Today's massive movement of humans and materials sets the stage for mixing diverse genetic pools at rates and in combinations previously unknown."[12]

The swine influenza A (H1N1) pandemic offers a classic illustration of the rapid global spread of an infectious pathogen. By the time Mexico reported the first cases of novel influenza in April 2009, geographic containment was not feasible.[13] By June 11, barely two months after the first reports, the WHO raised the alert level to a full-blown pandemic; nine weeks after the first reported case, all WHO regions had patients with H1N1. Scientists are currently watching the emergence of a new avian influenza A (H7N9) outbreak first reported in China in March 2013 (see Chapter 12).[14] The virus was detected in humans and poultry, with the working assumption that human infections occurred after exposure to infected poultry or contaminated environments.

Human-Animal Interchange

People do not merely congregate together; they do so in close proximity to animals, through intensive farming, meat production (raising, slaughtering, and eating animals), and exotic animal markets.[15] These processes have transnational dimensions, with thriving markets in meat and livestock. Such interactions with animals entail serious risks as novel pathogens mutate and jump species.[16] For example, live bird markets, backyard flocks, traveling poultry workers, fighting cocks, and migratory birds are vectors for spreading avian influenza A (H5N1 and H7N9). Close contact with rodents imported to the United States caused outbreaks of monkeypox, and use of exotic civet cats for meat in China was the route by which the SARS coronavirus moved from animal to human hosts.

Zoonotic pathogens (those with nonhuman hosts) represent a threat to global economies and public health. Animal diseases have major economic consequences, as illustrated by outbreaks of bovine spongiform encephalopathy (BSE) and foot-and-mouth disease. More importantly, more than 65 percent of all EIDs are caused by zoonotic pathogens, with the vast majority having a wildlife origin.[17] Zoonotic disease outbreaks in the past decade (e.g., H5N1, SARS, H1N1, H7N9, and MERS) highlight the importance of understanding how humans interact with wildlife and domesticated animals in a globalized world.

Ecosystem Degradation

Human well-being is dependent on ecosystems, and ecosystems are sensitive to human activity. Ecosystem degradation in one geographic area affects other parts of the world; in this way, living systems (e.g., air, seas, forests, soil) are interconnected, as are people and places. Ecosystem degradation has multiple adverse effects. Air and water pollution increases susceptibility to respiratory diseases (e.g., asthma) and gastrointestinal diseases (e.g., cholera, E. coli), as well as cancers. The emission of heat-trapping gases (e.g., carbon dioxide, methane, nitrous oxide) contributes to climate change, which causes multiple health hazards (see Box 2.3). Finally, excessive and unsustainable uses of scarce resources (e.g., deforestation, strip mining, intensive farming or fishing) diminish natural assets needed for healthy living.

Health Systems

Trade in medical goods and services is increasingly globalized, as vaccines, pharmaceuticals, and medical equipment are developed, manufactured, and shipped internationally. The processes of globalization even affect human resources, as health workers migrate in search of better pay and working conditions (see Chapter 11).

The health care system plays an important role in the resurgence of infectious diseases. Clinicians often prescribe antibiotic and antiviral medications indiscriminately, causing microbial adaptation. (Farmers similarly overuse antibiotics in their herds and flocks.) These practices result in changes in the virulence of pathogens, as well as development of resistance to frontline medications. Researchers report a significant increase in drug-resistant microbes, particularly in developed countries.[18]

BOX 2.3 Climate Change, Globalization, and Human Health

There is a scientific consensus that climate change is anthropogenically forced, with impacts on ecological systems and human health already in evidence.[1] In August 2013, the Intergovernmental Panel on Climate Change reported with "near certainty" that human activity causes temperature increases, warning that sea levels could rise by three feet by the end of the century.[2] The grim toll already is estimated at 300,000 deaths annually, which is the result of growing malnutrition, diarrhea, and chronic and infectious diseases linked to environmental degradation, for example. Although climate change will affect the entire world, it will impose vastly disproportionate burdens on low- and middle-income countries.[3]

Systemic health threats linked to climate change include increasingly intense and more frequent natural disasters—such as tropical storms, floods, heat waves, droughts, and wildfires—that result in injury, disease, and mass dislocations to unsanitary shelters. Although the causal relationship between climate change and particular disasters is difficult to establish, the 2003 heat wave in Europe, the 2005 flooding in Mumbai, Hurricanes Katrina (2005) and Sandy (2012) in the United States, and the 2011 floods in Queensland, Australia, are indicative of the extreme events that are likely to occur with greater frequency in the future.

Climate change creates fertile conditions for, and alters the geographic range of, disease vectors such as mosquitoes, ticks, and rodents, bringing them into greater contact with human populations that are naïve to the diseases they carry. Malaria, for example, is expected to move to higher altitudes, and dengue to move farther north. Scientists also anticipate increases in foodborne and waterborne illnesses, both of which thrive in warmer conditions. Climate change also affects air quality, particularly in urban environments, as increased temperatures exacerbate air pollution—especially ground-level ozone and particulate matter. Rising temperatures and higher concentrations of carbon dioxide will also increase the concentration of allergenic aeropollens. The impact of climate change on air quality will add to the burden of respiratory and cardiovascular diseases, particularly among people with chronic illnesses such as asthma.

Climate change increases the scarcity of clean water for drinking, sanitation, and crop irrigation, resulting in diarrheal illnesses. Ecosystem changes and water scarcity will also impair crop, livestock, and fishery yields, leading to increased hunger and famines. Climate change will play a major role in putting Africa under severe water stress as early as 2020. These cataclysmic events may result in economic instability, mass migrations, civil unrest, and armed conflict in a time of competition for scarce resources.

The impact of climate change will be experienced in every region, but it will disproportionately burden the poor, exacerbating health disparities. Areas within Africa and South Asia (some of the world's poorest regions) face 30–50 percent reductions in staple food crops by 2020. The World Bank estimates that developing countries would bear 75–80 percent of the costs of climate change. Even 2°C warming above preindustrial temperatures—the minimum the world is likely to experience—could result in permanent 4–5 percent reductions in GDP for Africa and South Asia.[4]

Disadvantaged populations already live on the edge, struggling with scarcity of water and nutritious food, as well as high rates of infectious diseases. The world's poor also have the least capacity to ameliorate the devastation of climate change. Low-income countries have weak health systems, poor infrastructures, fewer technological capabilities, and the fewest resources for adapting to rapidly changing climatic conditions. Most of these states are in tropical and subtropical regions that are already subject to a highly variable climate. Climate change, therefore, challenges the international community to find solutions that will reduce this global injustice.

NOTES

1. Lindsay F. Wiley and Lawrence O. Gostin, "The International Response to Climate Change: An Agenda for Global Health," *Journal of the American Medical Association* 302, no. 11 (2009): 1218–1220.
2. Justin Gillis, "Climate Panel Cites Near Certainty on Warming," *New York Times*, August 20, 2013, A1.
3. Global Humanitarian Forum, *The Anatomy of a Silent Crisis* (Geneva: Global Humanitarian Forum, 2009), 1, 58.
4. Liliana Hisas, *The Food Gap: The Impacts of Climate Change on Food Production: A 2020 Perspective* (Alexandria: Universal Ecological Fund, 2011), 18–19; World Bank, *World Development Report 2010: Development and Climate Change* (Washington, DC: World Bank, 2010), 5.

This process has rendered some diseases (e.g., tuberculosis) hard to combat using standard medical countermeasures.

The public health system is responsible for monitoring health threats. However, poor countries often have weak infrastructures that can fail to rapidly detect and contain novel pathogens. This results in a mismatch in surveillance capacity: emerging disease hot spots are concentrated in lower-latitude countries, whereas the capacity for research and surveillance is overwhelmingly found in richer, developed countries. Global efforts for EID surveillance, therefore, are poorly allocated, requiring reallocation for "smart" surveillance.

Bioterrorism

Governments have devoted considerable attention to terrorism in the wake of the attacks on the World Trade Center in New York City on September 11, 2001, and the subsequent dispersal of anthrax through the United States Postal Service. In 2013 a U.S. federal grand jury indicted a Mississippi man for mailing letters contaminated with ricin (a lethal toxin) to the White House and Congress. Also in 2013 a woman was arrested and charged with mailing three ricin-laced letters to President Obama, New York City Mayor Michael Bloomberg, and a gun-control lobbyist in Washington, DC.[19] Although terrorism can entail any hazard (conventional, chemical, or nuclear), biological attacks have been high on the political agenda because pathogens can be easily disseminated, hard to detect, and politically destabilizing.

Bioterrorism is the deliberate release or dissemination of biological agents (bacteria, viruses, or toxins) to cause illness or death in people, animals, or plants. Biological agents (e.g., anthrax, botulism, plague, tularemia, viral hemorrhagic fevers) may be used in their natural state or in a human-modified form in which they are altered to increase their pathogenicity, make them resistant to medicines, or increase their transmissibility.

Social divisions and trepidation are greater when dangerous pathogens are released with the intention of harming the populace or destabilizing the political system. Biological weapons can be terrifying, and they evoke the most basic human instinct to protect self and society from external threats. Whereas political interest in naturally occurring infectious diseases may be low, bioterrorism captures the attention of the most senior officials. Bioterrorism, as a national security problem, is a matter of high politics.

The Epidemiological Transition from Infectious to Noncommunicable Diseases: A Double Burden in Low-Resource Countries

The spread of infectious diseases in a changing and interdependent world is to be expected, given human migration, travel, and trade. Less obvious is how and why NCDs have global dimensions. NCDs are chronic conditions that cause death, disability, or impairment in quality of life; they include heart disease, cancer, diabetes, respiratory disease, stroke, and mental illness. These diseases rob individuals of healthy years of life and devastate whole societies, undermining prospects for a stable future.

The world's disease profile is rapidly changing. Poorer countries that were once primarily concerned about infectious diseases now face a dual burden of both infectious and noncommunicable diseases. Whereas NCDs once were diseases of the well-to-do who ate calorie-dense foods and led sedentary professional lives, now people all over the world are prone to excess. Rising standards of living and harmonization of cultures are causing a remarkable epidemiological transition from infectious to chronic diseases.

Chapter 13 details the scope and impact of this transition to NCDs, which have become the leading cause of functional impairment and mortality, accounting for 65 percent of deaths worldwide. Some 80 percent of NCD deaths occur in low- and middle-income countries, where the toll rests disproportionately on people in the prime of their lives.[20] If the trend continues, by 2020 NCDs will account for 80 percent of the global burden of disease, causing seven out of every ten deaths in developing countries.[21] The drag on national economies from NCDs is palpable, as evidenced by lost productivity, rising health care costs, and family disintegration. And the gravity of the NCD pandemic is projected to worsen as populations age and dietary habits continue to evolve.

Despite the social and economic consequences, national and global health policies have failed to keep up with this "silent" pandemic. The international community appears to be stuck in the mind-set that global health is mostly about stemming infectious diseases. As a result, the MDGs do not even mention chronic diseases, the WHO's budget devotes few resources to them, and the Global Fund focuses only on three infectious diseases.

The world has only recently awoken to the sheer scale of suffering and early death caused by NCDs. It was not until September 2011 that the UN devoted a high-level summit to NCDs, and not until May 2012 that the World Health Assembly (WHA) adopted concrete targets. In May 2013, 194 WHO member states adopted the Global Action Plan for the Prevention and Control of Noncommunicable Diseases 2013–2020.[22] This document provides a comprehensive global monitoring framework for NCD prevention, including a set of measurable goals, indicators, and voluntary targets, as well policy options for states to implement in the prevention, monitoring, and treatment of NCDs (see Chapter 4, Box 4.4).[23] Nevertheless, the WHO and the UN are yet to amp up funding for NCD prevention, and the Framework Convention on Tobacco Control remains the only treaty to address a primary NCD risk factor. In addition, most high-level attention to NCDs has entirely excluded mental illness—a set of deeply consequential conditions that cause untold suffering, as well as social and economic disintegration.

The Harmonization of Culture and Behavior

What is causing this epidemiological transition, and why have risk behaviors moved from richer to poorer countries? High-risk lifestyles were once thought to be associated with abundance and excessive consumption. The affluent were more likely to consume high-energy diets and work in white-collar jobs that required less physical activity. Smoking cigarettes and drinking fine wine and spirits were glamorous pursuits. Movies, television, and magazines displayed images of well-heeled men and women, with successful careers and vibrant lifestyles, smoking and drinking. The poor seemed to have a different set of problems: malnutrition rather than overeating, lives filled with hard work rather than leisure, and lives cut short from injuries and infections rather than chronic diseases.

Yet just as infectious diseases move and change, so do NCDs.[24] The global rise in NCDs reflects transformations in diet, physical activity, and tobacco use worldwide. The process of industrialization, urbanization, economic development, and food market globalization leads to a harmonization of behaviors. What was once culturally attractive primarily in industrialized countries has gained popularity everywhere. Brand recognition, advertising, and the low cost and widespread availability of unhealthy products drives their consumption in all regions of the globe.

Visit any major city in the world and witness the effects of a blended culture, inspired by multinational corporations, media conglomerates, and the influence of tourists and immigrants as they travel globally. The high streets are filled with fast-food chains such as McDonald's, Burger King, KFC, and Dunkin' Donuts; the billboards display omnipresent images of Camel cigarettes, Hershey's chocolate, Coca-Cola, and Johnnie Walker whiskey; and movies and television run attractive images of alluring people smoking cigarettes and drinking alcoholic beverages. This is how risk behavior migrates from place to place and permeates all people and cultures. Perversely, as developing countries begin to grow and prosper, the emergence of behaviorally related chronic diseases stand out as "joint totems" of success.[25]

"It makes little sense to expect individuals to behave differently from their peers," wrote Geoffrey Rose in 1992.[26] The problem is that one's peers used to be neighbors, and so behavior varied across places according to cultural norms and local environmental influences. Today the drivers of behavior are broad and diffuse. In the age of the Internet, cable television, multinational corporations, and global markets, it is rarely possible to change behavior solely through domestic policies. States cannot meaningfully effect behavior change without global cooperation and solutions that are based on shared commitments to health. It is for this reason that law and governance must transcend frontiers.

A World of Hurt: Global Injuries

Injuries are often portrayed as accidents or random events that are unpredictable and therefore unpreventable, rather than as a public health threat. Thus, historically, injury prevention has been a neglected field of global public health.[27] Consider a story told by Mark Rosenberg about the social response to injuries: A driver killed a young female runner in Atlanta. In a flood of letters to the editor, half the writers blamed the runner, while half blamed the driver. "Not a single writer blamed the road." However, more often than not, vehicle or road design cause fatal crashes.[28]

Injuries are a leading cause of death and disability worldwide, resulting in more than five million deaths every year and representing 11 percent of the global burden of disease;[29] by 2020 that figure is projected to increase to 20 percent.[30] The injury epidemic has been compounded by rapid unplanned urbanization, increased motorization, and dramatic changes in the built environment in low- and middle-income countries.[31]

The WHO differentiates between unintentional injuries (those caused with no predetermined intent, such as road traffic incidents, poisonings, falls, burns, and drownings) and intentional injuries; the latter include injuries that are self-directed (e.g., suicide, self-mutilation), interpersonal (e.g., caused by domestic violence or murder), or collective (e.g., war-related injuries). I focus on unintentional injuries because they are more clearly related to globalization. But readers should realize that intentional injuries are an equally formidable public health threat, whether they are caused by civil unrest in North Africa or firearms in the United States. Indeed, in 2013 the UN adopted the Arms Trade Treaty, which restricts export of conventional weapons that could be used in violation of humanitarian or human rights law.[32]

The Unequal Distribution of Unintentional Injuries

Christine Grillo explains that in low-income countries, "children sustain injuries largely unfamiliar in high-income countries: They're burned while cooking on unsafe stoves, they drown by falling into uncovered wells, and they're poisoned by the kerosene used for lamp fuel. . . . The poorer you are, the more likely you are to get injured, and the care for your injury is worse."[33] The data reveal the marked inequalities in the global distribution of injuries, with more than 90 percent of all deaths and disability-adjusted life years (DALYs) occurring in low- and middle-income countries, mostly among young people.[34]

The economic burdens are staggering: road traffic crashes alone cost $65 billion (or 1–1.5 percent of GDP) annually.[35] Moreover, these figures underestimate the actual financial and societal loss. For every person killed, injured, or disabled, others are deeply affected. Many families are driven into poverty due to the expense of prolonged medical care, loss of a family breadwinner, or the burden of caring for persons with disabilities.[36] Unintentional injuries exemplify "the asymmetrical character of contemporary globalization and the unequal distribution within and across national borders of gains, losses and the ability to influence globalization's outcomes."[37]

Risk Factors: Gender, Age, and Poverty

Even within lower-income countries, marginalized populations are the most susceptible. Socioeconomic factors predispose individuals to injuries, with poverty being the biggest determinant. Simply put, people who live in the most impoverished areas and under the harshest conditions are the most likely to suffer from injuries, with age and gender also being key determinants.

The UN Convention on the Rights of the Child (CRC) guarantees all children the right to a safe environment and to protection from injury and violence.[38] Yet injuries are the single greatest cause of death and disability among children in lower-income countries. Drowning, for example, is a leading cause of disability and premature mortality in children younger than age five.[39] For older children, road traffic fatalities surpass drowning; traffic crashes are the top killer of children ages 15–19.[40] Increased mobility, crowded urban settings, and lack of adult supervision all contribute to unacceptably high rates of childhood injuries (see Box 2.4).

Males account for two-thirds of all injury deaths. Compared with women, men have higher injury rates in all categories except burns. This is due to the persistence of traditional gender roles. Men often suffer injuries in the course of labor, whereas women, as a result of their customary domestic role of cook and housekeeper, are more likely to suffer burns caused by kitchen fires, scalding water, or cooking on open fires. The home use of kerosene or paraffin lamps, which are easily knocked over and ignited, is also a significant cause of burn injuries.[41] Above all, gross poverty heavily influences injuries, irrespective of a person's age and gender.

BOX 2.4 Juan's Story

Fourteen-year-old Juan lives with his mother, father, four younger brothers, and two younger sisters in a small village outside Mérida, Mexico. Juan no longer goes to school because he has to help his father sell fruit at the roadside. Juan must help support his family because of a terrible injury sustained by his youngest sister, Martha. At age six, Martha fell into the water well in the backyard while trying to retrieve a dropped toy. Juan was the first one to find her, and he called his father. The two of them ran to the nearest clinic holding Martha, who was limp and not crying. The doctors resuscitated Martha, but she suffered devastating disabilities. Juan is heartbroken by his sister's injury. He feels responsible for Martha's fall, convinced it would not have happened if he had been there. But he is also proud of the wooden construction he built to put over the well to prevent a similar incident.[1]

NOTE

1. WHO and United Nations Children's Fund (UNICEF), *World Report on Child Injury Prevention* (Geneva: WHO, 2008), xviii.

Globalization's Impact on the Toll of Injuries

The processes of globalization dramatically affect injury rates among the world's poor. The rapid pace of industrialization, urbanization, and motorization in the developing world has not been accompanied by the same improvements in economic conditions, infrastructure, and safety regulations that have reduced injuries in the developed world. The uneven effects of globalization are particularly apparent in road traffic crashes and occupational injuries.

Globalization and Motorization

Travel to any crowded urban area in a poor or transitional country and witness the chaos of streets heaving with traffic; unsafe vehicles in a bad state of repair; and roads with no lane markings, barriers between traffic, or safety signage. A bewildering mixture of buses, light trucks, cars, motorcycles, bicycles, pedestrians, and even animals teems through the roads; drivers and passengers travel without safety equipment, such as seat belts, child safety seats, air bags, and helmets. Observe a young father weaving in and out of dense and frenzied traffic on a motorbike, with his wife and children hanging on—all without helmets.

This mix of pedestrians, bicycles, and motorized vehicles on unsafe roads that do not separate the different types of traffic is lethal. To further compound the problem, roadways are usually designed with the convenience of the drivers in mind and little thought for the safety of pedestrians. In Nairobi, for example, residents of Kibera, one of the largest urban slums in the world, suffer inordinate road traffic injuries as they run across dangerous roads to get to work, school, or shops. The peril of being on the roads in Kenya was vividly illustrated by a slew of fatal bush crashes—for example, on August 28, 2013 the sight of a wrenched and twisted wreck, killing more than forty people, shocked the nation. Perhaps the worst tragedy was how predictable the "accident" was—occurring on the same sharp bend in the road that killed countless others.[42]

It is no wonder that in cities as diverse as Bangkok, Beijing, Hanoi, and Mumbai, road traffic deaths are rapidly escalating, as more and more vehicles are added to roads that were not designed to hold them. Africa's global road fatality share is eight times higher than its motor vehicle share. The road fatality toll has grown by more than 25 percent in the last several years in large African countries such as South Africa and Zambia. Overall, low- and middle-income countries experience 80 percent of the world's total traffic fatalities, despite having only 52 percent of registered vehicles.[43]

Simply put, globalization is vastly increasing the number and variety of vehicles inhabiting crowded roads. At the same time, lower-income countries cannot afford—or fail to prioritize—safe vehicles, road design, and highway safety enforcement, all of which have dramatically reduced traffic fatalities in high-income countries.

Occupational Hazards

Work-related injuries are ubiquitous in low-resource countries, but no accurate data are kept. Most experts, however, predict that if these countries continue their current rate of industrial growth, the lack of attention to safety will ensure that occupational injuries double by 2025. Again, this situation is very different in the developed world, which has steadily decreased occupational injury rates over the years.

Most industrial work in low-resource countries, such as agriculture, manufacturing, and mining, is associated with high rates of injury from electrical, mechanical, and physical hazards. Now, the steady expansion of chemical and biotechnology industries has introduced new risks. Richer countries are shipping unwanted waste to poorer countries, a practice that exposes impoverished people to dangerous toxins and radiation. For example, the dumping of hazardous electronic waste, such as discarded computers, mobile phones, and video equipment, has serious consequences for workers and local communities.

Although some multinational corporations have policies prohibiting double standards in their safety regulations, so that local workers are not exposed to hazards disallowed in their home countries, these policies often are not rigorously implemented. Moreover, less-regulated small-scale factories and cottage industries expose workers to known hazards, such as asbestos, lead, and silica. The result is that these individuals increasingly suffer from poisonings and toxic exposures. Older children are also displaying symptoms from chronic exposure to lead, mercury, organophosphate, and pesticides.

Occupational health and safety laws cover only 10 percent of the population in low-resource countries. Without adequate regulations, businesses do not invest in quality equipment, or train workers to ensure safety. Companies often expect workers to take inordinate risks, because labor is cheap and plentiful. If developing countries do not soon implement effective safety standards, the health costs to workers in high-risk jobs will outweigh the financial benefits of industrial development.

The Neglected Injury Epidemic

The growing burden of injuries in lower-income countries is a burgeoning public health crisis fueled by urbanization and industrialization. The developed world has responded, steadily reducing injury rates. It is possible to prevent most injuries through technological innovation, safe design, and safety regulations. However, the same ingenuity and resources have not been applied in low-resource countries. The WHO devotes less than 1 percent of its budget to preventing injuries and violence. If the public health community wishes to close the injury gap between rich and poor, it must devise evidence-based solutions and demonstrate their effectiveness, engage the private sector, gain the cooperation of police and the courts, devote the necessary resources, and advocate for strong health and safety laws.

International Trade and Commerce: Safe Food, Drugs, and Consumer Products

Terror in Bangladesh: Global Routes of the Fashion Industry

On December 6, 2012 a fire at the Tazreen Fashions factory in Dhaka killed 112 workers. The *New York Times* described the horror that day:

> The fire alarm shattered the monotony of the Tazreen Fashions factory. Hundreds of seamstresses looked up from their machines, startled. Now

> they ran to a staircase. But two managers were blocking the way. Ignore the alarm, they ordered. Back to work. . . . Smoke was filtering up the staircases. Screams rose from below. There was nowhere to escape. . . . The factory was not a safe place to work. Yet, Tazreen Fashions operated at the beginning of the global supply chain that delivered clothes made in Bangladesh to stores in Europe and the United States—destined for some of the world's top fashion retailers.[44]

Five months after the heartbreak at Tazreen, an eight-story factory building in nearby Savar collapsed into a deadly heap. The Savar tragedy killed more than 1,100 workers—the worst manufacturing disaster since the Bhopal toxic chemical leak in 1984. Pointed questions were raised about why the factory building was not padlocked after terrified workers notified the police, government officials, and a powerful garment industry group about cracks in the walls.

The poignant words of a mother who lost two children at the factory are heartbreaking. Standing at the edge of the wreckage, she pressed her lips to photos of her two children, Asma and Sultan. For five days after the building collapsed, rescue teams retrieved bodies and survivors, but not her son and daughter. With tears on her cheeks, she began to shout, calling out their names and beckoning to them: "Today, I'm here! But you haven't come back!"[45] The breadth of human tragedy resulting from the Savar disaster revealed what years of abuse, inhumane conditions, and unthinkable dangers could not: workers in developing countries take enormous risks to eke out a living to cater to the fashion-conscious West.

Following the Savar building collapse, international labor organizations, NGOs, government officials, and European retailers created the Accord on Fire and Building Safety. Signed in May 2013, this legally binding agreement establishes a program of safety training, workplace inspection, and improvements to the employment conditions of thousands of Bangladeshi workers.[46] However, large U.S.-based retailers—including GAP Inc. and Walmart—refused to join the agreement, and created their own weaker program.[47]

Under pressure from the United States and the European Union, the Bangladeshi government amended the Bangladesh Labor Act 1996 to strengthen workers' unionization and collective bargaining rights and to provide for workplace inspection, personal protective equipment, injury compensation, and the creation of safety committees.[48] However, the amendments fall far short of international standards for protecting workers' rights, and enabling their participation in workplace safety decision making.[49] This is despite the fact that the Bangladeshi government earns

$18 billion in clothing exports annually, and the country has 3.5 million garment workers, most of whom are women.

The failure to secure improved working conditions and fair pay for Bangladeshi workers can be blamed on a range of parties, from factory owners, to the government, to global brands. But the culpability goes all the way down the supply chain—to us, the consumers who are willing to buy cut-price garments sewn under hazardous conditions.[50]

The global web of trade poses risks not only to workers but also to consumers. The dramatic growth in trade of goods has amplified the problem of unsafe consumer products as a source of deadly hazards. As the ever-expanding network of international commerce spreads, due to broadening consumer preferences and the easing of trade barriers, a dangerous array of contaminated, faulty, and counterfeit products are infiltrating national borders. Workers at the beginning of this global supply chain often suffer the brunt of injuries and death. However, the following subsection explores why product safety has become a ubiquitous challenge in both developed and developing countries.

The Expansive Demand for Consumer Goods

The sheer magnitude and exponential growth of the international trade in goods (e.g., food, drugs, and manufactured products) provides a lucrative source of income for trading partners. Global agricultural exports, for example, reached $1.7 trillion in 2011, with the top ten exporters reporting growth of more than 15 percent. The trade in pharmaceuticals has been equally impressive, reaching a value of $498 billion in global exports during 2011. Trade in manufactured goods increased 6.5 percent between 2010 and 2011, to $11.5 trillion.[51] Although the largest exporters are located in high-income countries, China has emerged as the second-largest merchandise trader after the United States. International trade brings benefits by sating consumer preferences, providing ready access to lower-cost or unseasonal products, and fueling economic development through export revenues. But it also brings with it major hazards for consumers.

Easing Trade Barriers

Aggressive political efforts to lower trade barriers can adversely affect product safety. World Trade Organization (WTO) agreements allow countries to set their own safety standards while abiding by international guidelines. But such treaties can also weaken national health protections, pressuring states to accept imports that do not meet domestic sanitary or safety requirements, on pain of trade sanctions. Free trade zones exacerbate product safety risks because they often have lax regulatory oversight.[52]

Trade Amplifies Product Hazards

Product hazards, such as contaminants and pathogens, can enter the stream of international commerce during production, processing, or transport. The increased global reach of goods creates opportunities for widespread and rapid disease outbreaks. For example, the longer time and distance required for the international movement of agricultural products allows pathogens to grow or food to spoil if improperly handled and stored. Trade also creates new entry points for contamination through transshipping (transferring goods between multiple vessels) and subcontracting. Three product categories pose serious health hazards if rigorous safety checks are not in place: agricultural and processed foods, pharmaceuticals and medical devices, and other manufactured goods, such as toys.

Agricultural and Processed Foods

Microbial pathogens, mycotoxins, parasites, prions, antibiotic residues, adulterants, and environmental pollutants can all cause foodborne infections. The global burden of foodborne disease is difficult to measure, due to underreporting and the difficulty of diagnosis;[53] however, the WHO estimates that diarrheal diseases arising from microbes and parasites cause 1.9 million child deaths annually. The problem is pervasive, with foodborne disease affecting up to 30 percent of the population in developed countries each year—though the true burden is borne by developing countries, where unsafe food production, handling, storage, and preparation conditions facilitate the spread of foodborne illness and make treatment difficult.[54]

Numerous disease outbreaks have spread globally through the trade of contaminated foods. For example, in 1996 a major outbreak of cyclosporiasis, resulting in more than 1,400 cases, occurred in the United States and Canada; it was traced to raspberries imported from Guatemala. In 2001 a salmonella outbreak originating from shelled peanuts produced in Asia hit three continents.

The intentional alteration of products can also spread foodborne diseases across borders. For example, in 2007 farmed seafood exported from China tested positive for unapproved, carcinogenic antibiotics and chemicals used to protect the stock from river pollution.[55] Variant Creutzfeldt-Jakob disease (vCJD)—a deadly neurodegenerative zoonotic disease linked to consumption of brain or spinal cord tissue of cows infected with BSE—has also spread internationally. The United Kingdom experienced a costly BSE outbreak during the mid-1980s that resulted in more than 200,000 infected cattle in 24 countries, as well as 153 human deaths from vCJD.

Pharmaceuticals: The Global Reach of Fake Medicines

Pharmaceuticals—prescription and over-the-counter, branded and generic—circle the globe in both legal and illicit commerce. Fake medicines fall into several overlapping categories:

1. *Falsified* medicines falsely represent the identity or source of the drug; the manufacturer of a falsified drug is usually unknown. Falsified drugs are packaged with untrue or misleading labels (e.g., contents, dose, expiration date).
2. *Substandard* medicines are lawfully produced but do not meet quality specifications set by national regulatory agencies; the manufacturer of a substandard drug is often legitimate and licensed. Substandard medicines may lack therapeutic value and often originate in states with low regulatory capacity.
3. *Unregistered* medicines are not granted market authorization in a country, and are therefore illegal. Unregistered drugs may be of good quality, but they are sold outside the controlled distribution chain and are therefore suspect.
4. *Counterfeit* medicines infringe on a registered trademark and are manufactured unlawfully. Article 41 of the Agreement on Trade-Related Aspects of Intellectual Property Rights (the TRIPS Agreement) obliges WTO members to legally protect registered trademarks. Civil society objects to the use of "counterfeit" as a generic term to describe any drug that is not what it claims to be because the problem of drug counterfeiting is seen as a deliberate conflation of public health and intellectual property concerns.[56]

Taken together, these inferior medicines can include products that lack the active pharmaceutical ingredient (API), have insufficient or too much API, contain toxic additives, or are sold in phony packaging. Fake medicines are hazardous because their contents may be poisonous or lack therapeutic value, resulting in drug resistance, treatment failure, or even death—such as the 2012–2013 deaths attributed to Massachusetts drug compounders that allowed deadly bacteria to contaminate products.

There is a thriving, highly lucrative black market in fake medicines, because they are inexpensive to make and have high profit margins. Furthermore, states often lack strict enforcement and criminal penalties. In scope and profit margins, the international market for illegitimate medicines rivals the illicit drug trade—often with the same cartels manufacturing or diverting medicines from the legitimate drug supply. Global sales of fake medicines amount to billions of dollars annually, with commerce expanding rapidly.[57] Globally, 15 percent of drugs are estimated to be illegitimate. Fake medicines are even more prevalent in low-resource countries: more than 30 percent of medicines in Africa, Asia, and Latin America are illegitimate.[58] Medicines sold over the Internet from illegal sites that conceal their physical address have been found to be fake in more than 50 percent of cases.[59]

Table 2.1 illustrates the real-life impact of fake medicines. Quoted in a 2013 *Washington Post* article, Rodgers Stephan (a Tanzanian who is HIV-infected) said, "People have stopped taking their drugs and they don't know what to do, who to trust or which place to go." This is a huge problem in Uganda, Tanzania, Nigeria, and the Democratic Republic of the Congo.[60]

Although two treaties have been drafted to regulate fake medicines, there is currently no international law or effective governance resulting from them. The Council of Europe's Convention on the Counterfeiting of Medical Products and Similar Crimes Involving Threats to Public Health (the MEDICRIME Convention) would criminalize the intentional manufacture, supply, or trade in counterfeit medicines, ingredients, or accessories. Twenty-two countries signed the Convention in 2011–2012, but only Spain and Ukraine have ratified it.[61] The Anti-Counterfeiting Trade Agreement (ACTA) sets standards for intellectual property protection, creating a regime outside the WTO and the World Intellectual Property Organization (WIPO). Eight countries signed the ACTA in October 2011, and the EU and twenty-two of its member states followed suit in January 2012 (but only Japan has formally ratified it).[62] Amid concerns that the ACTA may be overly broad and that its negotiation processes lacked transparency, many original supporters have now rejected the treaty. In December 2012 the EU withdrew from the ACTA, and asked the Court of Justice of the European Union to determine the treaty's compatibility with fundamental human rights and freedoms.[63] As of 2013, an insufficient number of states parties had ratified the MEDICRIME Convention or the ACTA, so the treaties have not been implemented. Beyond these fledging efforts, a group of experts recently proposed a treaty to cover all fake medicines of public health concern,[64] and the Institute of Medicine in the United States has proposed a Global Code of Practice.[65]

Table 2.1 **The Public Health Impact of Fake Medicines**

Fake medicine	Country/year	Report
Avastin (cancer)	United States, 2012	Affected 19 medical practices. Lacked active ingredient
Viagra and Cialis (erectile dysfunction)	United Kingdom, 2012	Smuggled into the U.K. Contained undeclared active ingredients with possible serious health risks
Truvada and Viread (HIV/AIDS)	United Kingdom, 2011	Seized before reaching patients. Was a diverted authentic product in falsified packaging
Zidolam-N (HIV/AIDS)	Kenya, 2011	3,000 patients treated with falsified antiretroviral therapy
Alli (weight loss)	United States, 2010	Smuggled into the U.S. Contained undeclared active ingredients with serious health risks
Antidiabetic traditional medicine (lower blood sugar)	China, 2009	Contained 6 times the normal dose of glibenclamide. Caused 2 deaths, 9 hospitalizations
Metakelfin (malaria)	United Republic of Tanzania, 2009	Discovered in 40 pharmacies. Lacked sufficient active ingredient
Heparin (anticoagulant)	Europe, New Zealand, and North America, 2008	Caused hundreds of allergic reactions and deaths. Was a contaminated drug originating in China

Source: "Medicines: Spurious/Falsely-Labelled/Falsified/Counterfeit (SFFC) Medicines, Fact Sheet No. 275," WHO, http://www.who.int./mediacentre/factsheets/fs275/en/, (accessed 11/17/13).

At the instigation of emerging states concerned with the excessive focus on intellectual property (e.g., Argentina, Brazil, and India), the WHA launched an initiative on fake medicines in May 2012.[66] Buenos Aires hosted the initial meeting in November 2012, which produced a report discussed at the 2013 Health Assembly.[67]

Other Manufactured Goods

Contaminants and defects in other manufactured goods have become an urgent concern. In 2007 an international recall was issued for tens of millions of children's toys after the discovery of hazards such as lead paint and small magnets that caused intestinal damage when swallowed. The vast majority of these hazardous products, including Barbie dolls, Hot Wheels and Thomas the Tank Engine toys, and baby bibs, were traced to manufacturing plants in China.[68] That same year, China exported a variety of other dangerous products, including formaldehyde-contaminated wool blankets, lipsticks contaminated with carcinogenic "Sudan red" dyes, and toothpaste contaminated with diethylene glycol (see Box 2.5).[69]

BOX 2.5 Melamine-Contaminated Exports from China

The rapid pace of globalization has allowed China to emerge as a major exporter of goods around the world. With a massive workforce and swift adoption of new technologies, China's ability to produce goods at a low price has made it an attractive supplier to foreign markets. Its economic potential, however, has been marred by international product safety concerns traced back to Chinese factories. Ninety-four percent of the 472 U.S. Food and Drug Administration (FDA) recalls of consumer products in 2007 involved Chinese imports.[1]

In 2008 some 300,000 infants in China became ill from consuming tainted formula. Infant poisonings from contaminated formula also sprang up across Asia. The poisonings were eventually linked to melamine, a synthetic chemical commonly used in plastics, glues, and cleansers.[2] Food dealers in China were adding melamine to boost the nitrogen content in infant formula in order to avoid government penalties for low protein content and to make the product appear milky. However, melamine dissolves poorly and can cause kidney stones in the urinary tract, which is why it is not approved by the Codex Alimentarius.

The melamine contamination was linked to twenty-two dairy companies in China, but the tainting scandal did not end there. The adulterant was also used in animal feeds, resulting in contaminated eggs. The melamine scare prompted many countries to ban or restrict Chinese dairy and soy-based products. These import restrictions took a significant economic toll, prompting China to take action to improve food safety.[3]

NOTES

1. Russell Gips, "From China with Lead: The Hasty Reform of the Consumer Product Safety Commission," *Houston Law Review* 46, no. 1 (2009): 545–583.
2. Julie R. Ingelfinger, "Melamine and the Global Implications of Food Contamination," *New England Journal of Medicine* 359, no. 26 (2008): 2745–2748.
3. Andrew Jacobs, "China Issues Broad Rules to Improve Dairy Safety," *New York Times*, October 20, 2008, http://www.nytimes.com/2008/11/20/world/asia/20iht-milk.1.17993757.html.

Product hazards associated with companies such as the Mattel toy corporation (which holds a reputation for "quality and testing"), are just the tip of the iceberg.[70] The constant pressure across industries to reduce costs leads suppliers to cut corners to remain competitive. As a result, governments must reevaluate safety standards, strengthen regulatory agencies, and seek international cooperation to protect their citizens.

States have a responsibility to protect their inhabitants from hazards posed by foreign, as well as domestic, goods. As supply chains become increasingly complex and domestic regulatory systems become more strained, international cooperation will become essential. Global governance is the only way to truly protect the welfare of consumers around the world.

The Benefits and Burdens of Globalization

Globalization brings enormous opportunities for prosperity, as well as serious risks to health and safety. Travel and migration, environmental pollution, international trade, and information dissemination can rapidly spread diseases—and even amplify them—from one end of the globe to the other. This is true whether the disease is caused by a pathogen, a behavior, the environment, or a dangerous activity. A country's level of development, moreover, can have a significant impact on its population's susceptibility to health hazards.

States have both individual and collective responsibilities. Governments have a duty to safeguard their own populations through domestic health and safety regulations. But states also must act together, as no single state has the necessary resources and knowledge to defend its population from international threats. Thus, Chapter 3 explores the role of global health law and governance in meeting the complex challenges of globalization and reducing the daunting burden of injury and disease worldwide.

CHAPTER 3

Global Health Law in the Broader Currents of Global Governance for Health

THIS CHAPTER DEFINES global health law and examines its salient features; it also discusses the importance of broader global governance in meeting the major challenges in today's global health landscape. The distinction drawn between law and governance, however, should not imply that these are entirely separate concepts. Instead, they are interrelated, with no clear boundaries: law is a major aspect of governance, and features of governance can take the form of law—such as the constitutions, bylaws, and processes of global health organizations.

At the same time, a wide variety of "soft" normative instruments could be classified either as law or governance. Although they are characteristically nonbinding, soft norms are negotiated between states and create expectations of conformance. The Pandemic Influenza Preparedness (PIP) Framework discussed in Chapter 12, for example, is a non-treaty-based agreement that could create binding contractual obligations between stakeholders to share the benefits of vaccines.

My definition of global health law is expansive, capturing the field's mission, sources of law, key participants, and ethical foundations:

Global health law is the study and practice of international law—both hard law (e.g., treaties that bind states) and soft instruments (e.g., codes of practice negotiated by states)—that shapes norms, processes, and institutions to attain the highest attainable standard of physical and mental health for the world's population. Normatively, the field seeks innovative ways to mobilize resources, set priorities, coordinate activities, monitor progress, create incentives, and ensure accountability among a proliferation of global health actors. The value of social justice infuses the field, striving for health equity for the world's most disadvantaged people.

To be effective, global health law must foster collective action, facilitating partnerships among state and nonstate actors and across public and private spheres.[1] Accordingly, my definition of global health law is prescriptive as well as descriptive: it sets out the international legal framework that is needed, but is not yet established, to empower the world community to advance global health, consistent with the values of social justice.

This chapter explains the major sources of global health law—both hard international law and soft (nonbinding) instruments that create international norms. If viewed narrowly, global health law is a sparse field; few international instruments have been explicitly adopted for, and dedicated to, the protection of public health—most of them fall within the framework of the WHO's normative standards. The WHO has negotiated only three treaties: the International Health Regulations, the Framework Convention on Tobacco Control, and the Nomenclature Regulations. The WHO has also negotiated multiple soft instruments to enhance health-promoting norms—e.g., resolutions, global strategies, and codes of practice (see Chapter 4).

My definition, however, is far more inclusive, viewing global health law as a dynamic and complex field. Seen from this broader perspective, global health law encompasses the concept of health as a fundamental human entitlement, as well as encompassing multiple legal regimes outside the health sector. The right to the highest attainable standard of physical and mental health—embedded within a large network of human rights norms, institutions, and processes—is a growing and expansive field that intersects with health.

At the same time, multiple international legal regimes that are not specifically designed to alter health outcomes nonetheless have profound effects on the public's health and safety. It will become clear in this and subsequent chapters that international regimes (e.g., trade, food, arms control, labor, and the environment) play a major role in promoting—or adversely affecting—health. If global health actors do not find ways to influence these regimes by placing health closer to the center of their mandates, it will be impossible to achieve the goal of health for all with justice for the most disadvantaged.

Whatever the form of global health law—hard or soft, existing within the WHO or outside it—it is vital to consider the infrastructure, human capital, and resource constraints needed for robust implementation. To achieve the goal of global health with justice, states and stakeholders must not only marshal the political will to adopt international norms, but must also have the capacity to put them into practice. Meeting basic obligations under emerging global health law and governance frameworks requires the hard work of building the capabilities—and political will—needed to realize rights on the ground.

The Role of International Law

Although the use of international law to improve the public's health has a long history, and has achieved significant advances in the last two decades, its potential has not been fully realized. In the past, societies handled most public health matters through domestic law—and even in this context, law was a neglected instrument for advancing population health and safety.[2]

Major economic and political changes, such as the end of the Cold War and the acceleration of globalization, have had a significant impact on public health around the world, forcing critical health concerns into the international spheres of policy, politics, and law. The rapid spread of EIDs, such as SARS and novel influenza strains, has solidified political recognition of health as a common concern that spans geographic boundaries. The need for collective action in an increasingly globalized world has intensified interest in international solutions to complex health threats.

With global health taking a more central place in foreign policy, embedded in concerns for security, trade, development, and humanitarian relief, it has risen in diplomatic negotiations at the highest levels. Today global health can be found on the agenda of major power structures, such as the G8, G20, and the UN. Major global health decisions were once the province of dominant powers in Europe and North America. But in a newly multipolar political climate, power blocs from the global South—led by states such as Brazil, China, India, and South Africa—provide a counterpoint to the traditional powers, which historically reserved their strongest global health efforts for issues that impacted their own security. For these rapidly emerging states, global health justice and economic development are more natural drivers of their political ambitions.

Global health law rests primarily within the domain of public international law. The subjects and sources of international law have traditionally been narrowly defined to give priority to state sovereignty. Public international law focuses mainly on the interactions of sovereign states and can broadly be characterized as the rules and processes that govern the conduct and relations among states, including their rights and obligations.

States remain the major subjects of international law; however, international organizations and—through the development of human rights law—individuals are also now considered subjects of international law.

Although there is a wide and complex array of legal sources, most international law today can be found in bilateral, regional, and multilateral treaties. This treaty-based system bears little similarity to domestic statutes and regulations. (Box 3.1 offers a simplified introduction for readers who have not studied the field.)

International law has serious limitations, owing to its state-centric orientation. Because international law primarily addresses the rights and duties of sovereign states, it cannot easily govern nonstate actors, ranging from individuals and civil society to foundations and private enterprises. Although international organizations and states increasingly interact with nonstate actors and incorporate them within global health forums, international law does not adequately capture their creativity and resources. Nor does it sufficiently coordinate their activities or foster their accountability.

BOX 3.1 **Sources of International Law**

Article 38 of the UN's Statute of the International Court of Justice (ICJ) offers the most authoritative statement of the sources of international law. It lists three primary sources: treaties, custom, and general principles.[1] Judicial decisions and scholarly publications are listed as secondary sources.[2]

Treaties are international agreements between states, governed by international rules.[3] Treaties are commonly analogized to contracts, because parties give their consent to be bound and those who do not consent are not legally bound. Even if states accede to treaties, they may express reservations—in the form of unilateral statements made at the time of signing or ratification, intended to exclude or modify their legal obligations. Treaties primarily govern the conduct of states, and they address national interests, such as security and commerce. However, treaties often also have significant impact on private parties, such as corporations (e.g., trade law) and individuals (e.g., human rights). Multinational treaties may have important regulatory effects that extend beyond the signatory parties, because they bring order to relationships between intergovernmental organizations, states, and individuals; provide some stability and predictability in international relations; and institutionalize norms of ethical global conduct in such vital areas as trade, human rights, health, and the environment.[4]

Customary international law (CIL) refers to legal norms that have been established by general and consistent state practice.[5] A rule of CIL forms when a practice is repeated and widely accepted as a legal obligation by a significant number of states. A rule of CIL is binding on all states, except those that persistently object. Customary international law can be fundamental, but also controversial. They are fundamental because of their universal character, often rising to a level of compelling international law *(jus cogens). Jus cogens* is a peremptory norm of international law, such as the prohibition against genocide or the slave trade, which applies to all states regardless of their objections.[6] CIL can be controversial because scholars cannot easily determine when conduct attains customary status. What exactly is "consistent," a "practice," or a sense of "legal obligation"? Despite the conceptual and pragmatic difficulties, CIL is an important aspect of international law, because it represents the norms of communities and nations.

General principles of law are an amorphous body of law that emphasizes broad principles of domestic or municipal law that are recognized in the legal systems of civilized nations.[7] Where treaties and custom do not exist or are vague, tribunals may fill the gap with general principles of law. To become a general principle, a rule must be recognized in most of the world's legal systems—i.e., common law, civil law, significant religious law (e.g., Sharia, or Islamic law) and ideological legal cultures (e.g., Socialist law). Given the proliferation of treaty law, modern tribunals rely less on general principles and consider them a secondary source of law.

NOTES

1. UN, "Charter of the United Nations," (1945), entered into force October 24, 1945, arts. 92–96; UN, "Statute of the International Court of Justice" (1945), entered into force October 24, 1945, art. 38. However, decisions of the ICJ have no binding force except between the parties to the case.
2. Ian Brownlie, *Principles of Public International Law,* 8th ed. (Oxford: Oxford University Press, 2008), 19–25.
3. UN, "Vienna Convention on the Law of Treaties between States and International Organizations or between International Organizations," (1969), entered into force January 2, 1980, art. 1(a).
4. John H. Jackson, *The World Trading System: Law and Policy of International Economic Relations,* 2nd ed. (Cambridge: The MIT Press, 1997), 24–34.
5. "Customary international law results from a general and consistent practice of states followed by them from a sense of legal obligation." Restatement (Third) of the Foreign Relations Law of the United States § 102 (1987).
6. UN, "Vienna Convention," art. 53.
7. Henry J. Steiner et al., *International Human Rights in Context: Law, Politics, Morals,* 3rd ed. (Oxford: Oxford University Press, 2008), 85–96.

The state-centric nature of international law poses other major global health problems. The overriding principle of sovereignty has driven the international system toward "law" that is essentially voluntary. In signing and ratifying treaties, which are the primary source of global health law, states establish international legal rules by consenting to them. There is often no supranational authority to monitor, adjudicate, and enforce international law against states. Furthermore, many international health instruments contain few incentives—or penalties—to encourage compliance.

Because states are loath to sacrifice their freedom of action through the codification of binding treaties, they often accede to only limited international obligations; or they may ratify more robust treaties but fall short in effectively implementing them. Moreover, the drive to establish universal consensus in contemporary treaty negotiations often results in weak norms that reflect the lowest common denominator. Although weak or vague norms and inadequate implementation are endemic in international law, the problem is particularly acute in the realm of social and welfare rights, including the right to health.

Overall, the limitations of international law—failure to capture non-state actors, lack of enforceability, and vague standards—permeate and deepen the challenges facing global health law. To become a more powerful catalyst for change, global health law must evolve to (1) set priorities, (2) coordinate activities, (3) create incentives, (4) monitor outcomes, (5) stimulate investments, (6) ensure accountability, and (7) facilitate dispute resolution among key actors, both public and private. Global health law, therefore, is an endeavor that involves both convergence and contestation over the most appropriate strategies for creating the conditions that will enable people to attain the highest possible level of physical and mental health.

International Health Law: The World Health Organization's Normative Standards

As discussed above, the scope of global health law is conventionally limited to a few WHO-negotiated health treaties—perhaps most aptly labeled "international health law." Although it is commonly stated that the Framework Convention on Tobacco Control (FCTC) is the only WHO-negotiated treaty, this is not the case. As explained in Chapter 4, the FCTC is the only agreement approved by the WHA under article 19 of the WHO Constitution (which grants the assembly the power to "adopt conventions or agreements" by a two-thirds vote).

The assembly, however, also possesses quasi-legislative powers under article 21 to adopt regulations on a broad range of health topics. Using this authority, the WHA has adopted two additional international instruments: the Nomenclature Regulations (to establish and revise international nomenclatures of diseases, causes of death, and public health practices, and to standardize diagnostic procedures) and the International Health Regulations (IHR) (to establish norms and processes for collective action on public health emergencies of international concern). Article 21 regulations are treaty-based instruments because they create binding obligations on member states to comply with health-promoting standards.

The WHO was founded as a normative organization with a broad mission and extensive legal powers. Yet scholars have criticized the WHO for failing to fully exercise its constitutional authority to negotiate treaties; these experts argue that international health law can have a significant role in global health, reforming norms and influencing states and stakeholders—much in the way that the FCTC has enhanced tobacco control strategies at the national and international levels.[3]

The focus on treaties, however, understates the WHO's normative role, which also includes the power to adopt a variety of soft, nonbinding instruments. The WHO's normative powers are discussed in more detail in Chapter 4. For now, it is sufficient to explain that article 23 of the WHO Constitution empowers the organization to make "recommendations" to members; these recommendations, although voluntary, do require states to report annually on compliance (article 62). The International Code of Marketing of Breast-Milk Substitutes (1981) and the Global Code of Practice on the International Recruitment of Health Personnel (2010) are the two most prominent sets of formal recommendations. Each code creates detailed normative standards, along with compliance-enhancing features such as progress monitoring and civil society engagement.

Beyond article 23 recommendations, the WHA has approved a wide range of global strategies, action plans, and guidelines—often with features that are reminiscent of treaties or formal recommendations. For example, the Global Strategy on Diet, Physical Activity and Health and the Global Strategy to Reduce the Harmful Use of Alcohol establish standards on health-promoting activities, with monitoring, reporting, and broad stakeholder engagement. Similarly, the WHA's Mental Health Action Plan 2013–2020 establishes benchmarks for mental illness prevention and treatment.[4]

Although the international community often strives (with limited success) to craft multilateral treaties—on issues ranging from intellectual property to arms control—the health field is populated principally by softer international instruments. Global health scholars often disagree about the relative benefits and disadvantages of hard versus soft law, but in reality there is no right answer. And in many cases, the actual impact—and even the form—of hard and soft law is difficult to distinguish.

From the perspective of politics and international relations, soft norms are far easier to negotiate than international treaties. States are more likely to accede to a norm if there is no formal obligation to comply. Assembly delegates can assent to a soft law instrument without the formal national constitutional processes entailed in signing and ratifying a treaty, which require agreement at the highest levels of government. Not only are soft norms easier politically and legally, they usually can be negotiated more quickly than international law, using fewer resources. And because these norms are nonbinding, states may be prepared to accept more far-reaching standards.

Even though soft norms lack binding rules and enforcement, they can build consensus over time. The consensus-building process begins with the negotiations themselves, in which states debate and then agree to principles, in partnership with key stakeholders. Civil society, in turn, can use agreed-on principles to pressure their governments for greater compliance. At the same time, the WHO is learning how important it is to build accountability mechanisms into codes, including timelines for compliance. Box 4.4 in Chapter 4 demonstrates the elaborate development of global strategies, which are designed to foster consensus and norm acceptance over time and among multiple stakeholders. Codes of practice, as well as global strategies, set clear national targets for achieving goals, while urging states to report to the WHO on tangible progress.

The WHO's voting body, the World Health Assembly, has 194 member countries—more than the UN itself. Resolutions adopted by the WHA are a significant expression of political will and the expectations of the international community. Assembly resolutions can lead to progressive development and deepening of international norms, and they are sometimes enacted into domestic law, referenced by treaty bodies in other sectors, or even incorporated into international law.

Given the political and pragmatic benefits of soft norms, it is not surprising that the WHA rarely negotiates binding treaties.[5] But it is precisely because soft norms seem to be flouted, and underresourced, that global health scholars and civil society often urge treaty making. In one empirical study, for example, 93 percent of respondents reported that the WHO

Global Code of Practice on the International Recruitment of Health Personnel has not had a meaningful impact on policies, practices, or regulations in their countries.[6] This highlights a gap between the existence of a soft norm and the behavior of actors.

There are also good reasons why international law, with its creation of binding obligations, is sometimes necessary in order to deal with difficult problems in global health. First, not only are states more likely to comply with treaties as a matter of international relations, but treaties also provide an important legal source that civil society can draw upon in seeking reforms in national courts—as they have done using human rights instruments (see Chapter 8). Civil society often points to the obligatory nature of international trade law as a model because the WTO system has a formal and binding dispute resolution process (see Chapter 9). Still, many of the most pressing challenges in global health are diffuse in nature, and therefore not easily susceptible to a legal framework modeled on the international trade regime.

Second, legal mandates may be better able to resolve collective action problems than voluntary codes. Health is often thought of as a global public good from which all states benefit (see Chapter 1, Box 1.3). Yet states face costs associated with doing the right thing, such as changing domestic policies or funding poor countries to build their capacity. In these circumstances, mutually agreed binding commitments by all states may be the best way to elicit cooperation. In many spheres, ranging from trade to climate change, states have recognized the need for international law to ensure that countries equitably share the burdens.

Third, there is a risk that soft health norms may be overridden by hard norms in other regimes, such as trade and intellectual property (see Chapter 9). The WHO, for example, has not adopted hard norms pertaining to food, alcohol, physical activity, injuries, pain medication, or mental health. If the WHO acts in these realms principally through voluntary consensus while other sectors develop hard law, this weakens and sidelines the organization. It is small wonder that the WHO appears to have little influence over vital sectors such as trade, human rights, and the environment.

Although the debate over the merits of hard and soft norms will continue, the truth is that there is a role for both. Soft norms are easier to achieve and can build consensus, but they cannot formally compel sovereign states to expend resources and comply with standards. Certainly, most WHO norm setting will continue to be soft, reflecting the agency's historical preferences and expertise. However, the WHO could do more to assert its authority and its mandate by serving as a platform for the negotiation of major treaties. Greater use of hard law would boost the legitimacy of the regulatory system, raising the moral, legal, and political stakes for compliance by national governments.

Health as a Fundamental Entitlement

International health law originating with the WHO is not the only body of law designed explicitly to promote human health. The human rights regime explicitly enshrines health as a fundamental entitlement. The International Covenant on Economic, Social and Cultural Rights (ICESCR) guarantees everyone "the enjoyment of the highest attainable standard of physical and mental health" (article 12). The ICESCR also captures underlying social determinants of health, including food, clothing, housing, social insurance, child protection, education, and shared scientific benefits.

Chapter 8 is devoted to the right to health and other health-related human rights. But it is important to stress here that human rights law is a vital aspect of the corpus of global health law. The WHO Constitution proclaims health as a "fundamental right." Interpretive instruments—such as General Comment 14 on the right to health and UN special rapporteur reports—must be read in conjunction with WHO normative standards. Human rights law, together with human rights institutions, contains detailed guidance on implementing the right to health.

Human rights law, therefore, is a health regime in its own right, but it also connects with multiple other regimes. Given that the WHO's constitution incorporates the right to health as central to its mission, the organization's normative standards should reference human rights instruments. Similarly, human rights law can help inform multiple non-health-related treaty regimes, such as WTO agreements. Although there is no clearly established hierarchy among health- and non-health-related treaties, states and international organizations should conform their activities to reflect the values of health and human rights wherever possible.

To get a sense of the interconnections between health, human rights, and non-health regimes, consider international tobacco disputes. These disputes arise under WTO and investment treaties, but they are deeply informed by the FCTC (see Chapter 7). Although it is true that dispute bodies must rely primarily on the law laid out in their own regimes, they should take account of potentially conflicting international obligations under WHO and human rights treaties.

A state, for example, might impede the free flow of trade, or diminish private economic investments, when enacting strict tobacco control laws, such as requiring the plain packaging of cigarettes. But it is equally important to recognize that these states have affirmative obligations under human rights law and WHO normative standards. How is it possible to conform to the right to health and to the FCTC without graphic cigarette warnings, tobacco taxes, and clean air laws? Given the major health impacts of multiple regimes, global health actors simply cannot be effective without actively engaging non-health-related sectors—a topic to which we now turn.

Interconnecting International Law Regimes

Beyond WHO treaties and the human right to health, numerous international legal regimes affect health and safety—either by enhancing health-related norms or detracting from them. Some of these regimes, such as international trade and intellectual property, are so fundamentally important to global health that I have devoted an entire chapter to their doctrines and practical impact (see Chapter 9). Free trade is vital to economic development, but it can also undermine national strategies that are designed to keep unsafe products from entering state territory. Intellectual property protections, such as patents, can create incentives for innovation, but they also can impede access to affordable medicines.

Interconnecting legal regimes can enhance or undercut health policies. As discussed in Chapter 2, Box 2.3, climate change creates health threats by expanding the geographic spread of disease vectors (e.g., malarial mosquitoes), raising sea levels (resulting in floods), exacerbating the frequency or strength of natural disasters (e.g., hurricanes, tsunamis, heat waves), and creating scarcity (e.g., of food, water, or land). The food and agricultural sectors confront hunger and food insecurity while navigating the politics of agricultural subsidies and food aid. Humanitarian law deals with the devastating consequences of armed conflict, such as the infliction of disability and death, or the destruction of food supplies, health facilities, and infrastructure (e.g., electricity, telecommunications). Finally, mass migration creates overcrowded and unhygienic conditions, breeding violence (e.g., rape), prostitution, malnutrition, and disease transmission.[7]

These above-mentioned international regimes that appear to be so clearly connected to health only begin to scratch the surface. Still other regimes include (to name just a few of the most obvious examples): the

WHO/ UN Food and Agriculture Organization (FAO) Codex Alimentarius Commission, which develops harmonized international food standards for consumer protection; the World Organization for Animal Health (OIE), which monitors and controls zoonotic diseases that can jump species, causing human disease outbreaks and even pandemics; and the International Labor Organization (ILO), which has adopted numerous agreements guaranteeing safe workplace conditions, along with social benefits. In addition, the international arms control regime contains multiple diverse agreements on weapons, ranging from land mines, nuclear weapons, and small arms to biological and chemical weapons—all of which can maim and kill.

Each of these regimes—and many more—affect the air we breathe, the water we drink, the land we inhabit, the goods we purchase, the rights we claim, and the conflicts we wage. It is easy to see how a large and diverse set of international legal regimes can either complement or grossly obstruct the attainment of public health and safety goals. This is why global health law—and broader global governance for health—must encompass multiple regimes. Unless global health leaders understand these regimes and influence their direction, it will be impossible to fulfill the mission of global health with justice.

Interrelationships between International and Domestic Law

Thus far, this chapter has characterized global health law within the contours of international relations—i.e., cooperation and mutual accountability between states and stakeholders to solve enduring collective-action problems. But a discussion of global health law would be incomplete without examining the interrelationships between international and domestic law. Even though national and international law take different forms, with very different legal effects, each sphere informs the other. To appreciate the impact of international legal regimes, it is important to see how their norms infuse domestic law and policy. Conversely, national health regulation (or its absence) can reinforce (or undermine) the aims of international law.

The adoption of global norms into the domestic sphere could help overcome the weak compliance and ineffectiveness inherent in international law. However, the incorporation of international law—whereby a sovereign state adopts an international agreement in domestic legislation—is a complex matter, dependent on the international regime and the domestic legal system.[8] Some national systems give legal effect to international norms without incorporation—e.g., a treaty has the effect of law once it is ratified. Other states require the explicit incorporation of a treaty before it can have legal force.

Most states have rules in between these two extremes. The Supremacy Clause in the U.S. Constitution, for example, mandates that "all Treaties . . . shall be the supreme Law of the land." However, before an agreement can be classified as a "treaty," it must be ratified by two-thirds of the Senate. And even then, a treaty has limited effect unless it is "self-executing"—i.e., judicially enforceable upon ratification.[9]

International norms can influence domestic law in other ways. Many states—particularly newer democracies—enshrine the rights to health and/or to life in their constitutions. Domestic courts, in turn, often use international norms—or decisions by regional or international tribunals—to interpret health-related constitutional or legislative entitlements. At the same time, international health-related rights undergird civil society campaigns for public health laws and policies—such as access to essential medicines, stricter tobacco control, or universal health coverage.

International law depends substantially on effective implementation at the domestic level. This requires governments to have the political will, and the capacity, to fully comply. Many health-related international instruments urge states parties to develop implementation capacities, while encouraging the international community to provide technical and financial assistance. The IHR, for example, relies on domestic pandemic preparedness and cooperative action. The treaty, however, has only vague capacity-building language, and an independent review found poor domestic implementation, with inadequate financial assistance from wealthier states.[10]

In all these ways, international law informs domestic law and remains heavily reliant on it for successful outcomes. The rights and obligations contained in international law cannot be fulfilled without robust domestic implementation through legal, policy, and economic reforms.

Global Governance for Health

Law has inherent limitations in its ability to solve the complex health challenges the world faces. Many—perhaps most—of the grand global health challenges discussed below are not readily susceptible to law's traditional approach of regulatory standards, dispute resolution, and enforcement. The perceived deficits in law have pushed the international community to a new language of global governance, in the health sector and beyond—one that recognizes the complexity of the global health architecture, the proliferation of actors, and the multiple ways that norm development can guide health-promoting activities. Governance can also avoid the arduous process of negotiating full-fledged treaties, as well as the problem of states' intransigence in assenting to obligatory arrangements.

To understand global governance, it is helpful to begin with a definition of governance: it is the method by which organized society directs, influences, and coordinates the activities of multiple private and public actors to achieve collective goods. It is important to note that governance is not synonymous with government.[11] The international health system lacks the defining characteristics of government, such as hierarchy, sovereign authority, and enforcement powers. This is why scholars invoke the looser concepts of governance or architecture.[12]

When global health scholars employ the term "governance," they conventionally frame it as global health governance (GHG).[13] In standard usage, GHG is limited to the norms and institutions that operate within the health sector—for example, norm development by international health organizations such as the WHO and the Joint United Nations Program on HIV/AIDS (UNAIDS). By contrast, my approach is more aptly termed *global governance for health* (GGH)—a more encompassing idea that extends beyond the health sector.[14]

I define global governance for health as the collection of rules, norms, institutions, and processes that shape the health of the world's population. Governance strategies aim to organize divergent stakeholders, and manage social, economic, and political affairs, to improve global health and narrow health inequalities.

As is true of global health law, GGH encompasses diverse fields, such as agriculture, trade, development, human rights, and the environment. The range of stakeholders is similarly diverse, including multilateral organizations, states, civil society, philanthropic organizations, and industry. Legal rules—including public international law, national legal systems, and institutional bylaws—play a major role in providing the core architecture of GGH.[15] However, although law can be an important tool in global health, it is only one among many aspects of governance.

Undoubtedly, achieving effective GGH is a complex undertaking. The challenge is to pursue a fundamental objective—optimal health, equitably distributed—while navigating various crosscurrents; these include politics (domestic and global), power dynamics (in the global North and South), vested interests (e.g., the corporate profit motive), economic power (e.g., wealthy states, foundations), security (national and human), and international relations.

How can the international community coordinate fragmented activities, design positive incentives, and create synergies in public and private spheres amid the complexity of global health?[16] Certainly, there is no one-size-fits-all answer that can apply across all countries and actors. Nor are top-down "command and control" rules likely to be effective. But governance does require guiding multiple actors toward common goals to better address the key determinants of health and ensure programmatic effectiveness. Orchestrating the mandate of GGH amid the complex dynamics of globalization is an enormous challenge, but the first essential reform would be to inculcate the universal values of good governance—values that are inherently important even beyond the health sphere.

Universal Values of Good Governance: The Responsibilities of Stewardship

Leaders who exercise power, expend resources, and make policy have a duty of stewardship—i.e., a personal responsibility to act on behalf of, and in the interests of, those whom they serve. Good governance has broad applicability, extending beyond governments to encompass non-state actors, such as international organizations, corporations, and foundations.[17] Entities that serve the public or discrete constituents should observe the universal values of good governance.

First, sound governance is *honest,* in the sense that it avoids corruption, such as public officials seeking personal gain or diverting funds from their intended purposes. It is *transparent,* in the sense that institutional processes and decision making are open and comprehensible to the people. It is *deliberative,* in the sense that officials consult with stakeholders and the public in a meaningful way, giving them the right to provide genuine input into policy formation, implementation, and evaluation. It is *efficient,* in the sense that it manages the public's affairs and resources wisely and effectively. Finally, good governance is *accountable,* in the sense that leaders monitor and report progress, assume responsibility for successes or failures, and allow the public the opportunity to disagree and change direction.

Honesty: Fighting Corruption

Leaders with integrity act on behalf of their constituents so that their decisions and actions are genuinely in the interests of those whom they serve. They should never act out of self-interest or to benefit selected or preferred groups (e.g., family or the elite). As honest stewards, leaders must direct funds to the most pressing public needs. Common failures in honest governance include misdirecting funds to curry favor with powerful sectors (e.g., the military), misusing public resources to win over political rivals (e.g., creating lucrative government posts), enhancing a leader's own prestige (e.g., building presidential residences), or advancing the interests of a favored ethnic group. In the most egregious cases, authoritarian leaders siphon money from the public purse, depositing huge sums in secret offshore accounts.

As an illustration, consider Equatorial Guinea, a nation that was enriched after the discovery of oil reserves in 1996 and now has a per capita GDP equivalent to Spain's. Yet the country's resources have been badly misused, with more than 70 percent of the population living on $2 a day, and poverty and infant mortality actually rising since the discovery of oil.[18] The country's economic gains have instead furnished lavish lifestyles for a small elite surrounding the government.

Corruption undermines social cohesion and fosters public distrust of government. Monopoly power, unchecked authority, unaccountability, and weak enforcement create opportunities for corruption.[19] The popular uprising in India in 2011, led by Anna Hazare, shows the depth of public outrage over corruption, as well as the difficulty in combating it. Despite much debate in the Indian Parliament and further protests, even by 2013 the full parliament had failed to adopt antigraft legislation.

Governments have a duty to fight corruption, including aggressive prosecution of dishonest officials. The World Bank estimates that countries that control corruption and assert the rule of law can expect, in the long run, a fourfold increase in per capita incomes.[20] International anticorruption treaties, such as the UN Convention against Corruption and the African Union (AU) Convention on Preventing and Combating Corruption, require states parties to develop independent agencies to prevent and prosecute corruption. In 2011 the South African Constitutional Court held that the country's constitution and international law impose a "pressing duty" to establish and maintain an independent body to fight corruption, stating that "corruption undermines the Bill of Rights and imperils our democracy."[21]

Health institutions have extensive public and private resources, and they are among the most corrupt sectors in many developing countries.[22] Health sector corruption not only erodes public trust, it also impedes access to health services and discourages international assistance, ultimately harming the public's health.

Transparency: Openness

Governments, like all institutions that serve the public interest, have an obligation to operate transparently, with open governance and free flows of information. Transparency is bound up with other obligations of good governance, such as civic participation and public accountability: individuals cannot participate in government if they lack accurate and timely information, and governments cannot meaningfully be held accountable if relevant information is not freely accessible.

The free flow of information and open forms of decision making are central characteristics of transparency. The public should understand the factors that go into making policy: (1) the facts and evidence, (2) the goals to be achieved, (3) steps taken to safeguard individual rights, (4) reasons for the decision, and (5) fair and open processes for stakeholders to voice concerns. Open governance can be accomplished in many ways, including public forums, open Internet access, publication of policy proposals, and the right to make verbal and written comments. Without transparency, the public cannot have confidence that officials are governing well and making efficient use of resources.

Deliberative Decision Making: Public Participation

Free flows of information are necessary to support public participation. Listening to citizens' concerns is an expression of a government's commitment to fairness and justice. Civic participation also gives communities a stake in their own health—it provides a feedback mechanism for informing policy and arriving at more considered judgments. Deliberative decision making requires genuine listening, as well as attention to the views of relevant constituencies—the public, stakeholders, and the disadvantaged, who might not be heard if their input is not actively sought.

Civil society plays an indispensable role in free and open governance. If a government harasses or imposes rigid rules on grassroots groups—for example, by imposing onerous registration requirements, requiring an "official" sponsor, creating bureaucratic hurdles, proscribing foreign funding, or monitoring grassroots activities—it will chill a vibrant civil society sector.

Effective Performance: Monitoring, Benchmarks, and Quality Improvement

Good governance requires effective performance, including sound policies, efficient management, and rational priority setting. This requires evidence-based policy making, setting defined benchmarks, and evaluating progress. The international community is urging governance reforms to accelerate the effective use of health resources. The Paris Declaration on Aid Effectiveness and the Accra Agenda for Action, for example, call for clearer targets and indicators of success, coordination among partners, and mutual accountability for results.[23] Rigorous performance measurement, against ambitious benchmarks, is a hallmark of sound governance.

Accountability: Taking Responsibility for Actions

Accountability is the most important principle of good governance, with leaders being held to account for their decisions and taking full responsibility for their actions. Fair democratic processes are important, but accountability goes well beyond free elections. It comes from adhering to the rule of law so that officials justify their decisions under national and international standards. Checks and balances among the branches of government prevent concentrations of power. For example, public officials must be subject to political and judicial oversight in the execution of their duties. Civil society should also be empowered to hold policy makers to account.

Sound governance—honesty, transparency, engagement, efficiency, and accountability—can be a powerful tool for human well-being. Adherence to these values—not only by governments but also international institutions, foundations, and industry—can help overcome the grand challenges identified in the next section.

The Six Grand Challenges of Global Governance for Health

Despite the proliferation of actors, initiatives, and funding in the global health space, the current architecture appears incapable of redressing unconscionable health inequalities. This inertia can be attributed to six fundamental challenges—the result of enduring political, legal, economic, and social obstacles to achieving health with justice.[24] Because these global health challenges are interconnected, a systemic approach is required (see Table 3.1). Governance challenges are not static; they involve

Table 3.1 **Grand Challenges in Global Governance for Health: A Typology**

Key governance challenge	Description	Importance to global health
Empower the World Health Organization to be an effective leader in global health	The WHO's core leadership functions include: setting, monitoring, and enforcing priorities, norms, and standards, and coordinating activities	Leadership creates visibility, political will, and resources for global health; it encourages stakeholders to achieve common goals
Harness the creativity of diverse stakeholders in philanthropy, business, and civil society	Effective GGH creates a climate and incentives for generous philanthropy, corporate social responsibility, and engaged civil society	Nonstate actors have the resources, know-how, and advocacy skills to find innovative solutions to complex problems
Facilitate collaboration, coordination, and partnership among multiple players	Proliferation of actors, programs, and initiatives leads to fragmentation, competition, and confusion on the ground	Coordination ensures that diverse actors know about ongoing programs and work cooperatively toward common goals
Set priorities to fulfill the conditions needed for public health, strengthen health systems, and address socioeconomic determinants of health	Human needs include sanitation, water, food, and pest control; health systems afford universal access; socioeconomic determinants include education, housing, and jobs	Resources should meet essential needs and avoid programmatic silos, such as disease-specific activities that fail to build health systems
Ensure predictable, sustainable, and scalable funding	Health resources (domestic and global) are below agreed targets, are unpredictable and have short-term horizons, and fail to meet ongoing needs	With ample, predictable, and sustainable funding, countries can plan for the long term and build enduring capacity
Ensure maximum effectiveness for global health assistance	Stakeholders fail to set detailed targets, monitor progress, and measure outcomes reliably	Aid effectiveness is vital in order to achieve key health indicators with rigorous methodologies and continuous improvement

Table 3.1 (continued)

Key governance challenge	Description	Importance to global health
Create systems for good governance that are honest, transparent, and accountable	Stakeholders may be corrupt, inefficient, and unaccountable	Good governance ensures more effective use of resources and maintains public trust
Enter genuine partnerships with host countries; empower them to set priorities, run programs, and develop core capacities and sustainable services	Donor influence over priorities and operations may create dependence and skew services to what donors want, rather than what countries need; donors may "go around" health ministries by funding northern NGOs	Genuine partnerships give host countries a stake in programmatic success, enable them to plan and develop domestic capacities, and show respect for their sovereignty
Reform existing institutions rather than creating new entities; facilitate provision of health assistance through multilateral organizations	New initiatives often overlook existing institutions such as the WHO, thereby weakening them and adding to a patchwork GGH system that lacks coherence	Reforming existing institutions enables them to exercise their authority, giving them ample funding and greater legitimacy
Overcome the problem of state-centricity in international law and governance	States defending their sovereignty eschew international norms, collective solutions, and shared obligations, while impeding inclusion of nonstate actors	A collective response to solving common problems holds the best chance for genuine improvement in global health

Source: This table consolidates key GGH challenges offered by the following scholars: Devi Sridhar, "Seven Challenges in International Development Assistance for Health, and Ways Forward," *Journal of Law, Medicine and Ethics* 38, no. 3 (2010): 459–469; Lawrence O. Gostin and Emily A. Mok, "Grand Challenges in Global Health Governance," *British Medical Bulletin* 90, no. 1 (2009): 7–18; Lawrence O. Gostin and Allyn A. Taylor, "Global Health Law: A Definition and Grand Challenges," *Public Health Ethics* 1, no. 1 (2008): 53–63.

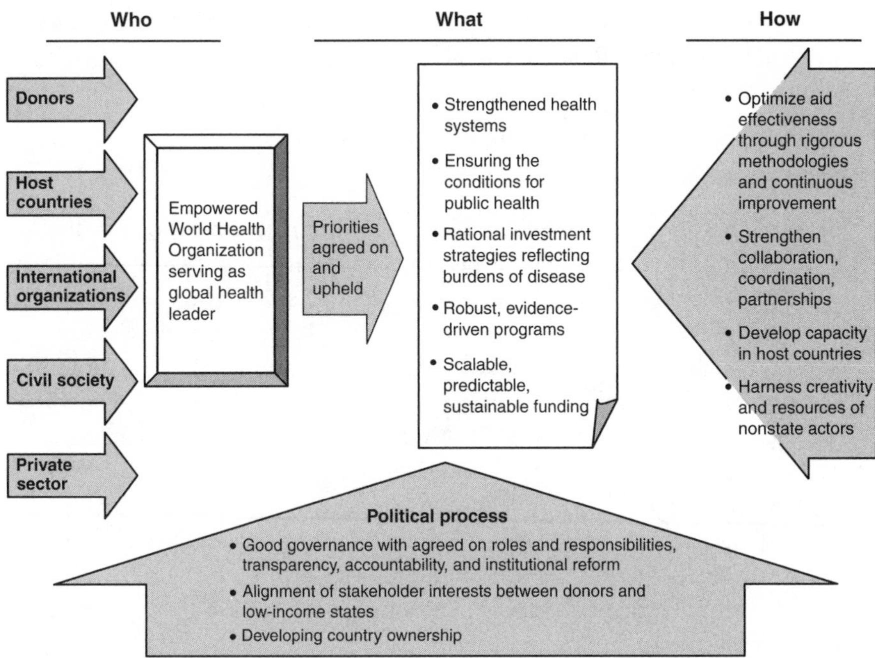

Figure 3.1 **A governance dynamic for addressing the grand challenges of global governance for health (GGH)**

a complex interplay of relationships. Figure 3.1 depicts a governance dynamic, showing *who* must act, *what* they must do, and *how* to accomplish global health goals.

1. Fostering global health leadership

Achieving any worthwhile objective requires leadership, and in the realm of global health, the WHO is the only agency with the legitimacy to provide that leadership. Chapter 4 is devoted entirely to this transformative, but underperforming, agency. For now, it is important to emphasize that unless the WHO can mobilize states and stakeholders around an inspired mission, guiding their activities toward collective goals, progress will be hard to achieve. Exercising global health leadership is a daunting task, given the proliferation of actors and the manifold health influences of multiple sectors. Powerful states, moreover, often refuse to cede authority. But these difficulties should not mask the imperative for strong leadership in a complex and splintered world. Although leadership need not entail top-down, rigid governance, the WHO could mobilize, coordinate, and focus a diverse set of actors around common aims, effective programs, sustainable action, and shared responsibilities.

2. Improving collaboration and coordination among multiple players

Multiple actors beyond the traditional state-centric governance system now occupy the field of global health. The deluge of actors and initiatives, often focusing on specific diseases, includes more than forty bilateral donors, twenty-six UN agencies, twenty global and regional funds, and ninety global health initiatives,[25] not to mention the proliferation of aid organizations, religious missions, and volunteers operating on the ground.[26] This crowded global health landscape results in fragmentation and duplication in the areas of funding, programs, and activities. Fragmentation can have crippling effects, with developing countries facing "a bewildering array of global agencies from which to elicit support."[27] Consequently, health ministries are overburdened with the task of "writing proposals and reports for donors whose interests, activities, and processes sometimes overlap, but often differ."[28]

Related to this fragmentation is the competition for funding and human resources between international actors and local service providers.[29] This encroachment on capable local entities hinders national ownership of health services. Well-funded foreign organizations that create AIDS clinics or other state-of-the-art facilities can offer more lucrative salaries and better working conditions than local providers, draining domestic capacity and making it more difficult for developing countries to provide sustainable services.

The GGH system should foster effective partnerships and coordinate initiatives to create synergies and avoid destructive competition. Developing countries must take ownership by setting their own priorities, developing national health plans, and managing programs. Donor countries must align behind these objectives, support local systems, and share information to avoid duplication.

3. Harnessing the creativity, energy, and resources of multiple stakeholders to innovate for global health

This proliferation of actors, of course, should be celebrated, as it brings sorely needed resources and creativity to global health. The goal is not to dampen the passion of stakeholders, but rather to harness their resources and creativity.

Foundations Private and charitable funding, once relatively insignificant, now accounts for nearly one-third of all development assistance for health.[30] Foundations, often founded by industrialists such as Henry Ford, John D. Rockefeller, and Bill Gates, provide valuable resources and technical expertise. Wealthy foundations are sometimes criticized, however, for exerting undue influence on the global health agenda, and for insufficient accountability. Although foundations should align with national strategies and global priorities, it is also vital to foster these organizations' ongoing commitment to global health because waning philanthropic interest would leave a gaping hole in research and services.

Businesses The private sector can deliver health-promoting goods, services, and technologies (e.g., medicines, healthy foods, safe products); lend expertise, infrastructure, and business acumen (e.g., research, marketing, distribution); follow health-promoting employment practices (e.g., safe workplaces, green spaces, reduced emissions); and contribute to health through corporate philanthropy, such as funding, training, and donations of drugs and vaccines (see Figure 3.2). The GGH system, however, must find better ways to engage the private sector, such as providing incentives to reduce market risks for public goods, regulating businesses to ensure health and safety for workers and consumers, and developing rigorous standards for avoiding conflicts of interest.

Civil society Civil society has repeatedly demonstrated the capacity to support members of its communities, and to advocate for social change. A fully engaged civil society can provide much-needed services because it understands local needs and customs, engendering the trust of marginalized communities. Civil society groups can also be effective advocates. Through their grassroots connections, they can garner public attention, lobby for policy reform, raise resources, and call attention to human rights violations. The GGH system often sidelines civil society groups when it should be embracing their unique voices, expertise, and passion.

International nongovernmental organizations (NGOs) offer valuable expertise and services to countries in need, whether in the face of a humanitarian crisis (e.g., Save the Children in war-torn Syria), endemic disease (e.g., Partners In Health fighting cholera in Haiti), or ongoing privation (e.g., Oxfam feeding the hungry). They also advocate for global health reform (e.g., Médecins Sans Frontières's Campaign for Access to Essential Medicines), often through coalitions (e.g., the International

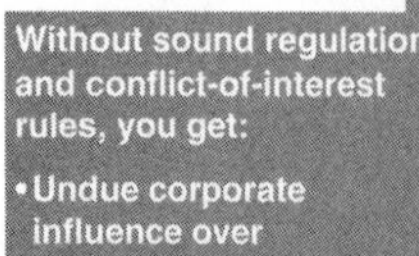

***Figure* 3.2 The role of business in global health: risks and benefits**
Global health is a $30 billion industry. For much of its history, it was the purview of governments, but now nonstate actors play a crucial role in solving complex health problems. The private sector powerfully affects global health, but how can businesses be incentivized to maximize health-producing activities and minimize harmful activities?
Adapted from Kate Taylor et al., "The Need for New Vaccines," *Vaccine* 27S, supplement no. 6 (2009): G3–G8, doi:10.1016/j.vaccine.2009.10.014.

Campaign to Ban Landmines). Yet these vital organizations face huge challenges, such as inadequate funding, violence against aid workers, and states that impede their efforts. The GGH system must support and facilitate the work of NGOs because they perform an indispensable service for the world's most neglected people.

Civil society, however, incorporates a vast array of entities, not all of which are dedicated to the public interest. NGOs, for example, are not always what they appear to be, and some have names and purported goals that are decidedly deceptive. Can you tell the difference between the Food Integrity Campaign and the Center for Food Integrity? The former is a legitimate advocacy group whereas the latter is an industry front group. It is just this sort of confusion that corporate interests count on.

4. Ensuring predictable, sustainable, and scalable funding

States need health funding that is predictable, sustainable, and scalable to needs; this requires adequate domestic resources, supplemented with international assistance. Sadly, many lower-income states do not sufficiently invest in public health, and international assistance is sporadic and discretionary.

Low- and middle-income country health expenditures as a proportion of total government spending are significantly lower than the global average (less than 10 percent, compared with more than 15 percent), and are well below promised levels. Despite repeated pledges to spend at least 15 percent of their budgets on the health sector, African states reached only 9.6 percent by 2010 (see Chapter 1).

At the same time, international health assistance is discretionary. From year to year, affluent states and foundations may increase or decrease funding, initiate new programs, discontinue existing programs, or place restrictive conditions on the use of resources. In this environment, ministries of health cannot plan for the long term—a situation that undercuts their ability to build infrastructure, hire health workers, and operate programs.

Affluent states also make promises but then fail to meet them. OECD countries do not come close to fulfilling their pledge, made in 1970, to spend 0.7 percent of GNI on official development assistance. More than forty years later, their real contribution has reached only 0.29 percent.[31]

Low-income countries account for over half the global disease burden, but less than 2 percent of global health spending.[32] Foreign assistance is a major part of low-income countries' health budgets, arguably displacing local initiatives and creativity. External resources account for 26 percent of the total health expenditures in low-income countries, rising to as high as 30–65 percent in more than two dozen countries.[33] Clearly, this mismatch between domestic and international resources is unsustainable in the long run.[34]

5. Setting priorities to ensure the conditions needed for the public's health

The GGH system must agree on key priorities to ameliorate the leading causes of illness, injury, and premature death. Although disease-specific programs and crisis interventions remain important, the international community should stress three essential conditions needed for the public's health and safety: public health services, universal health coverage, and socioeconomic determinants of health (see Chapter 14).

Building enduring health systems is critical to population health and safety. The international community is divided about the relative value of vertical (disease-specific) programs, horizontal programs (those that build health system capacity), and diagonal programs (a combination approach in which disease-specific programs also significantly invest in health systems). Vertical programs that focus on a single health condition have political appeal because they target major global concerns such as AIDS, malaria, tuberculosis, and maternal and child mortality. Furthermore, the results of vertical programs can be more easily measured and evaluated.

Yet vertical programs may neglect health systems that address a broad range of health needs. Horizontal programs aim to strengthen health systems holistically, preventing and treating the entire range of health conditions. Beyond addressing a spectrum of health conditions, strong health systems foster self-sufficiency, giving countries the tools to safeguard their own populations.

Although they address specific diseases, programs such as the Global Fund, the GAVI Alliance, and the President's Emergency Plan for AIDS Relief (PEPFAR) increasingly stress the value of health systems. These so-called diagonal programs retain their core mission of preventing and treating particular diseases, but they also recognize that health system capacity both supports their aims and improves the population's overall health.

6. Influencing multiple sectors to promote health

Global health actors can achieve only partial success through health sector reform. Multiple sectors—such as trade, intellectual property, migration, and the environment—have a powerful impact on the public's health; sometimes that impact is beneficial, but often it is harmful. Currently, the health community is self-contained and somewhat insular, concerned principally with health sector reforms.

A related problem is that international health law tends to have vague standards and weak enforcement. This puts health in a weaker position compared with regimes that have well-developed norms, adjudication, and compliance—such as the WTO. At the same time, there is no clear hierarchy of rules; therefore, if policies in diverse regimes conflict with each other, there are few means of resolution. For example, intellectual property rules may render drugs unaffordable, thus undermining the right to health. Trade and investment treaties may undermine state power to enact tobacco control laws required under the FCTC.

The GGH system must find ways to make health more of a priority in other regimes. This could require the exercise of greater political power, or the reform of international rules, to ensure that trade, finance, and investment regimes complement, rather than undermine, health objectives.

What seems certain is that a narrow focus on the health sector will not ensure global health with justice.

These grand challenges—leadership, coordination, stakeholder creativity, funding, priorities, and multisectoral impact—represent some of the most complex problems facing the GGH system. It is not simply the amount of money spent that is important, but also how resources are invested and used. Above all, there is an urgent need for strong and strategic leadership, a subject that I take up in Chapter 4 by examining the World Health Organization's powers, financing, achievements, and reform agenda.

PART II

Global Health Institutions

PART II CONTAINS A DISCUSSION of the institutional structures that undergird global governance for health. Governance requires institutions to do much of the work in global health, including setting health-promoting norms and priorities; mobilizing and expending resources to achieve health with justice; consulting with and guiding multiple actors to work more effectively and cooperatively; and setting targets, monitoring progress, and ensuring accountability for results.

This part of the book begins with the most important institution in the global health architecture: the World Health Organization. With its rich history, constitutional authority, and worldwide legitimacy, the WHO is in a unique position to provide international leadership. Yet the organization, as we will see in Chapter 4, is undergoing fiscal challenges and is currently in a phase of introspection and reform.

As vital as the WHO is to global governance for health, today the organization is situated among other quite powerful actors. Reflecting the complexity of the global health landscape, Chapter 5 analyzes the workings of key global health and development institutions—both "old" institutions, such as the World Bank, and "new" ones, such as the Global Fund to Fight AIDS, Tuberculosis and Malaria (the Global Fund); the GAVI Alliance; and the Bill & Melinda Gates Foundation.

The discussion of these, and other, institutions is both descriptive and normative. I explain their governance processes, but I also advance ideas for more effective institutional functioning—measuring their decision making and activities against the standards of good governance articulated in Chapter 3. Readers will also find more in-depth discussion of key institutions important to global health later in the book, including the WTO and UNAIDS (see Chapters 9–10).

CHAPTER 4

Fulfilling the Promise of the World Health Organization

THE WORLD HEALTH ORGANIZATION is the global health leader, endowed with a progressive constitution and international legitimacy. There is no substitute for the WHO, with its incomparable normative powers and influence. The WHO is a specialized United Nations agency with an expansive mandate and unequaled expertise. Virtually every country is a member of the agency, which provides the potential for democratic accountability and global impact. It is highly unlikely that the UN would grant the same expansive authority and global reach to an international organization created today.

Despite this rich heritage, the WHO faces a crisis of leadership.[1] Today the agency finds itself in a transformed political and economic landscape. Although it was once the only global health institution, it now operates in an arena filled with powerful actors, such as the Global Fund, the GAVI Alliance, PEPFAR, and the Bill & Melinda Gates Foundation. Where multilateral organizations and states once dominated the global health environment, there is now a proliferation of stakeholders, ranging from industry and trade associations to public-private partnerships, foundations, and civil society. Powerful health impacts arise from overlapping and sometimes competing legal regimes, such as agriculture, trade, security, and the environment.[2]

While remaining true to its bold vision of health for all, the WHO must adapt to a changing political climate, demonstrating leadership and delivering results. And it must do so as health challenges multiply, including humanitarian disasters, emerging infectious diseases, injuries, and NCDs. As the world's health needs are growing, public expectations are rising, fueled by advanced medical and informational technologies. Funding, however, has not kept up with mounting needs and expectations, as the WHO competes for scarce resources amid an ongoing global financial crisis. The WHO Director-General, Margaret Chan, announced a $300 million budget deficit for 2010–2011 as she launched the greatest structural reform in the organization's history.[3] To this day, despite promising budgetary reforms, the WHO has not fundamentally closed the gap between its resources and the demand for its leadership.

This chapter tells the story of the WHO—its origins, founding ideals, core functions, and governing structures. The WHO was born after the devastation of World War II as a normative agency endowed with unprecedented constitutional powers. But even as it has achieved stunning successes, such as the eradication of smallpox, it has failed to live up to the exalted expectations of the postwar health and human rights movements. The chapter concludes with an analysis of the WHO's ambitious reform agenda, together with proposals for fundamental change.

The Birth of the Premier Global Health Leader

Origins and Predecessor Organizations

The origins of the WHO, and the international health institutions that preceded it, can be traced to the first International Sanitary Conference. Held in Paris in 1851, the conference attempted unsuccessfully to establish an international covenant on infectious disease control. European states eventually adopted the first International Sanitary Convention in 1892, a predecessor to the WHO's International Health Regulations (IHR) (see Chapter 6).

States realized that an authoritative agency was needed to oversee implementation of the 1892 convention. The first international health bureau, however, was formed across the Atlantic. The International Sanitary Office of the American Republics—later the Pan American Sanitary Bureau (PASB), and now the Pan American Health Organization (PAHO)—emerged in 1902. Five years later, delegates of twelve predominantly European states signed the Rome Agreement, creating the Office International d'Hygiène Publique (OIHP), based in Paris. The Rome Agreement entrusted the OIHP with revising and administrating international sanitary agreements. The raison d'être of each of these early international health organizations was the implementation of infectious disease control treaties.

World War I became the next turning point, culminating in the League of Nations. The league's covenant obligated states "to take steps in matters of international concern for the prevention and control of disease," with the Geneva-based League of Nations Health Organization (LNHO) created in June 1921. The LNHO published periodic epidemiological reports on mortality rates and communicable diseases, along with standardized definitions of diseases and their causes—functions that the WHO still undertakes. In 1926 the OIHP and the LNHO signed a cooperative agreement for an Eastern Bureau for International Epidemiological Intelligence, based in Singapore.

In the aftermath of the Great War, a key question emerged as to how the LNHO and the OIHP could coexist. Although governments sought to form a new united health organization, "two autonomous international health organizations were to exist side by side—one in Paris and the other in Geneva—for thirty years."[4] It would take another war to unify their functions. With the outbreak of the Second World War, international public health work virtually ceased, with only the PASB continuing to operate.[5] During the war, the United Nations Relief and Rehabilitation Administration (UNRRA) took over some OIHP, LNHO, and Eastern Bureau functions, which were transferred to the WHO in the postwar era.[6]

International cooperation and action on health are rooted in this history. It is impossible to understand global health institutions and politics without seeing the connections to trade, war, and geostrategic interests. These relationships of power and politics continue to influence global health priorities and agendas today.

The Creation of the WHO

The United Nations was established in response to the horrors of World War II, and one of its primary functions was the protection of global health.[7] In 1945 the UN Conference on International Organization in San Francisco unanimously approved the creation of a specialized health agency. On February 15, 1946, the newly constituted UN Economic and Social Council called for an international conference to consider how to create such an agency. The sixty-one delegates of the International Health Conference convened on June 19, 1946, and signed the Constitution of the World Health Organization—the "Magna Carta for world health."[8] As the first specialized UN agency, the WHO's constitution entered into force on April 7, 1948, when the required twenty-six countries ratified it—a date now celebrated annually as World Health Day. The WHO Constitution expresses the universal aspiration[9] that health is "basic to the happiness, harmonious relations and security of all peoples."[10]

Regionalization was a matter of intense debate at the conference, with delegates concerned that regional arrangements should both "assure unity of action by the central Organization on health matters of worldwide import and allow for adequate flexibility in handling the special needs of regional areas."[11] Perhaps the most difficult issue was the WHO's relationship with the PASB. Ultimately, the PASB's status was preserved, retaining its identity, resources and name, but it would also act as the WHO regional office for the Americas.[12] To this day, the agency has a dual identity—as both an independent international organization (PAHO) and a WHO regional office (the Americas Regional Office [AMRO]).

The WHO convened its first World Health Assembly in June 1948, with delegates from fifty-three of the WHO's original fifty-five member states attending. The assembly declared malaria, tuberculosis, venereal disease, children's and women's health, nutrition, and environmental sanitation as the agency's priorities of the time.

The first assembly also took over two major legal responsibilities from precursor organizations. It adopted the WHO Regulations No. 1 Regarding Nomenclature with Respect to Diseases and Causes of Death—a uniform classification that dated back to the late nineteenth century as the International List of Causes of Death (see Box 4.6 later in this chapter). It also synthesized the two existing international sanitary conventions—one on maritime and land traffic and the other on air traffic. By 1951 the assembly had adopted the International Sanitary Regulations as the WHO Regulations No. 2—renamed in 1969 and now known as the International Health Regulations.

Governing Structure: Membership, Organs, and Division of Powers

The WHO is an intergovernmental organization comprised of 194 member states and two associate members (territories that lack full sovereignty). This inclusive state representation—together with the principle of one country, one vote—defines WHO governance.

The agency's governing structure includes the World Health Assembly (WHA), the Executive Board (EB), the Secretariat, and the regional offices. Broadly speaking, the WHA is the steering and policy-making organ of the agency; the EB is the executive arm, overseeing and implementing WHA policy; and the Secretariat—led by the director-general

(D-G)—is the technical and administrative arm, both advising and serving the WHA and the EB. Six regional committees focus on health matters within their geographical areas, supported by 147 country offices. Most country offices are located in developing countries where the WHO delivers programs.

The World Health Assembly

The WHA is the WHO's principal decision-making body, convening every May in Geneva, Switzerland, to set policy and approve the budget—and, every five years, to appoint the D-G. A majority of members of the EB can also convene a special session. In addition to determining the WHO's policies, and reviewing and approving reports and activities of the assembly, the WHA instructs the EB and D-G on actions and investigations (see Box 4.1).

BOX 4.1 **The World Health Assembly and Executive Board**

The World Health Assembly (WHA) is comprised of delegates, representatives, and observers. The assembly elects members of the Executive Board (EB).

WHA delegates Each member state is entitled to send three delegates to the assembly; in practice, delegates are often accompanied by alternates and advisors. Members must select delegates based on technical competence in health; in practice, they often come from ministries of health or foreign affairs (WHO Constitution, article 9).

WHA representatives Associate members of the WHA can appoint representatives based on technical competence (article 8). The EB also sends representatives (WHA Rule 44); while the board chairman is appointed ex officio, together with three other EB members. Additionally, the WHA can admit intergovernmental and nongovernmental organizations to participate in the assembly as nonvoting representatives.[1]

WHA observers Although the WHO Constitution does not mention observers, in practice the WHA invites potential members and "quasi-permanent observers" to participate in its activities. Currently there are seven observers: the Holy See (Vatican), the Order of Malta, the International Committee of the Red Cross (ICRC), the International Federation of Red Cross and Red Crescent Societies, the Palestinian Authority, the Inter-Parliamentary Union, and Chinese Taipei (Taiwan).

EB membership Members elected by the assembly are entitled to designate individuals to serve on the EB for a three-year term. The Constitution limits the board's size to thirty-four persons, to ensure efficient operation and realize "equitable geographic distribution" (article 24). Board members are expected to act in their personal capacities; in practice, however, governments often influence their delegates' decisions.

NOTE

1. World Health Organization (WHO), Resolutions WHA 8-26 and WHA 8-27, "Rules of Procedure of the World Health Assembly," (1955), Rule 19.

The WHA meetings are held in plenary and in two committees: Committee A deals predominantly with the program and budget, while Committee B deals predominantly with administration, finance, and law. Although the WHA decides important issues in plenary (e.g., admission of new members, the D-G's appointment, and EB elections), the two committees conduct most of the assembly's work. A Committee C has been proposed to increase transparency, coordination, and engagement, but the WHA has thus far declined to form such a committee (see "World Health Assembly 'Committee C'" later in this chapter).

In WHA plenary sessions, a simple majority is required for adoption of resolutions, but a two-thirds vote is required for consequential constitutional decisions (e.g., conventions or constitutional amendments), or decisions made under the Rules of Procedure (e.g., the suspension of member voting privileges). Each member has one vote, although by tradition most decisions are made by consensus.

The Executive Board

The board meets in public twice a year—a main meeting in January and a shorter meeting following the WHA in May—with the option to convene special sessions. The D-G sets the EB's agenda in consultation with the board chair.

The board's main function is to facilitate the assembly's work—i.e., to give effect to its decisions and policies, perform entrusted functions, provide advice, and submit for approval a general program of work. Under article 29 of the WHO Constitution, the assembly can also delegate any of its powers to the board. The board not only submits the assembly's provisional agenda but also proposes resolutions on technical matters.[13] Beyond executing the assembly's wishes, the board is empowered to take emergency measures to deal with events that require immediate action, such as combating emerging diseases, organizing humanitarian relief, and undertaking urgent research (article 28(i)).

The Secretariat

The Secretariat is comprised of the D-G and technical and administrative staff. The D-G is the WHO's chief technical and administrative officer (article 31), acting as the ex officio secretary of the assembly, the board, and all commissions, committees, and conferences. The assembly appoints the D-G for a five-year term (renewable once), following the board's nomination. Although rotational regional representation has been the subject of intense debate, the assembly has not supported the idea.

The D-G is responsible for appointing Secretariat staff, and for ensuring their efficiency, integrity, and internationally representative character. The D-G's responsibilities extend far beyond the technical and managerial, requiring political acumen. As the world's global health leader, the D-G must raise resources, influence and coordinate states and stakeholders, and secure the WHO's standing and prestige. The D-G must be a steward of the organization's human and financial capital; a diplomat, negotiating agreements or mediating disputes; the public face of global health; and a person of integrity, displaying high ethical standards and political neutrality.

The Secretariat serves the WHO and therefore cannot take instruction from any government or external organization, or have a conflict of interest, including improper remuneration (article 37). The Secretariat includes approximately 7,000 experts and support staff, all on fixed-term appointments, who work at headquarters, regional offices, and in-country. The Secretariat is responsible for the WHO's day-to-day management, as well as serving the assembly and board.

The Regional Offices

Chapter XI of the WHO Constitution (articles 44–54) empowers the WHA to create regional organizations to meet health needs within defined geographic areas. Each regional organization consists of a regional committee, comprised of member state representatives, and a regional office. The regional committees' functions include formulating health policy of an "exclusively regional character," supervising regional offices, and advising the D-G on international health matters. The regional offices are the administrative organs of the regional committees. There are six WHO regional offices, based in Washington, DC (Region of the Americas);

Copenhagen (European Region); Cairo (Eastern Mediterranean Region); Brazzaville (African Region); New Delhi (South-East Asia Region); and Manila (Western Pacific Region).

The Milestones: From Disease Eradication to Health Systems

In its early years, the WHO launched major campaigns against the great scourges of the time, including tuberculosis, malaria, and smallpox. The control of yaws, a tropical disease that affects the skin and bones, represents perhaps the WHO's earliest achievement. The Global Program for Malaria Eradication during the mid-1950s was a vast undertaking—justifiably so, given that the disease caused 1 million deaths annually, mostly among African children. But ultimately the campaign proved unsuccessful, due to high drug resistance rates; low effectiveness of insecticides; and problems with planning, logistics, and resources. Although the WHO abandoned its aspiration of global malaria eradication in 1969, this goal is now "back on the table."[14]

Perhaps the organization's most dramatic success was the eradication of smallpox. In 1958 the WHA directed the D-G to study the means to eradicate smallpox[15] and made worldwide eradication a "major objective" the following year.[16] The Global Smallpox Eradication Program (1959–1967) and the Intensified Smallpox Eradication Program (1967–1980) culminated on May 8, 1980, when the thirty-third assembly historically declared, "the world and all its peoples have won freedom from smallpox."[17] Today Russia and the United States have the last known repositories of smallpox virus, while the WHO debates the merits of destroying the repositories, amid speculation that the virus may have slipped into the hands of extremists.

In the late 1980s, the WHO targeted two other diseases for global eradication: dracunculiasis (guinea worm disease) in 1986 and poliomyelitis in 1988. Today both diseases are close to eradication, but the daunting challenge of achieving global disease eradication is evident from the ongoing pandemics of malaria, hookworm, and yaws.[18] The most recent vaccine-preventable disease the WHO is considering for global eradication is measles, although no target date has been set.[19]

Notwithstanding these successes, by the late 1960s, the WHO had expressed dissatisfaction with vertical, disease-specific programs, which the organization saw as "static" and "fragmented."[20] This led to a new emphasis on health systems and health education. Most famously, the 1978 Alma-Ata Declaration on Primary Health Care called for "health for all" by the turn of the millennium so that everyone could "lead a socially and economically productive life."[21]

Thirty years later, the WHO renewed its drive to improve primary health care (PHC), calling for "health system strengthening" marked by universal coverage and health equity. Out-of-pocket health care fees often pose an insurmountable barrier to PHC, with many poor people having to choose between "impoverishing" high fees and going without vital care, thus falling into a downward spiral of sickness and poverty (see Box 4.2).

BOX 4.2 The Declaration of Alma-Ata: "Health for All" by 2000

The landmark 1978 Alma-Ata Declaration on Primary Health Care called for universal primary health care (PHC), setting the target of attaining for "all peoples of the world by the year 2000 . . . a level of health that will permit them to lead a socially and economically productive life." The declaration specified that affordable and accessible PHC must be scientifically sound, socially acceptable, aimed toward maintaining physical and mental health at every stage of development, and available as close as possible to where people live and work.[1]

Due to limited health budgets and human resources, the global community largely fell short of this vision. Structural adjustment programs and user fees during the 1980s and 1990s erected barriers to access and eroded health systems. Health budget constraints led to "selective" primary health care that provided only a restricted package of inexpensive health goods and services. This narrow, technocratic approach to PHC was far from the comprehensive, participatory approach envisioned at Alma-Ata. Most low-income countries, especially in Africa, saw little progress, even as services improved in many middle-income countries, such as Brazil, Chile, and Thailand.

On the thirtieth anniversary of Alma-Ata, the WHO's 2008 World Health Report called for a renewal of the global community's commitment to PHC. The WHO advocated four reforms: (1) universal coverage to improve health equity, (2) reorganization of service delivery to create people-centered health systems, (3) public policy to integrate public health with PHC and implement health-in-all policies, and (4) leadership to foster citizen participation. A 2009 WHA resolution recommended strengthening health systems, with better planning, financing, and coordination.[2] WHO Director-General Margaret Chan explained that PHC must be fair as well as efficient, with solutions that are created, owned, and sustained by local communities.[3]

Two years later, the 2010 World Health Report declared the dual goals of expanding access to PHC and reducing the "impoverishing" impact of health costs, noting that health spending drives 100 million people below the poverty line every year. To avoid these deleterious effects, the WHO estimates that direct out-of-pocket payments should be no more than 15–20 percent of total health spending, and that prepaid pooled funding, through taxes and other revenue, is required.[4] The following year, the sixty-fourth WHA adopted a universal health coverage resolution, asking the director-general to seek a UN General Assembly discussion on this issue.[5] In December 2012, the UN General Assembly responded, passing a resolution supporting universal health coverage, while also recognizing its importance in the post-2015 development agenda.[6]

NOTES

1. WHO, *Declaration of Alma-Ata*, (1978).
2. WHO, Resolution WHA62.12, "Primary Health Care, Including Health System Strengthening," May 22, 2009.
3. Margaret Chan, "Return to Alma-Ata," *The Lancet* 372, no. 9642 (2008): 865–866.
4. WHO, *World Health Report: Health Systems Financing: The Path to Universal Coverage* (Geneva: WHO, 2010), 53, 79.
5. WHO, Resolution WHA64.9, "Sustainable Health Financing Structures and Universal Coverage," May 24, 2011.
6. UN General Assembly (UNGA), Resolution 67/81, "Global Health and Foreign Policy," December 12, 2012.

Halfdan Mahler, the legendary WHO D-G from 1973 to 1988, framed the Alma-Ata Declaration as "a holistic concept calling for efforts in agriculture, industry, education, housing, and communications."[22] The Alma-Ata Declaration, and its health-for-all campaign, was an early precursor to the WHO's Commission on Social Determinants of Health report in 2008, which found that the conditions in which people are born, grow up, live, work, and age powerfully affect their well-being.[23]

Despite its embrace of health systems, the WHO never lost its ambition to fight endemic diseases. In 1988 the WHA launched the Global Polio Eradication Initiative (GPEI)—with Rotary International, the CDC, and UNICEF. The 2008 assembly intensified its eradication efforts, as wild poliovirus transmission stubbornly persisted. The WHA's Strategic Plan for 2010–2012 targeted key geographic areas, such as Afghanistan, India, Nigeria, and Pakistan. The GPEI has faced a unique challenge compared to past eradication initiatives, with local mistrust of vaccination efforts due largely to the geo-political environment of the last remaining bastions of poliovirus and the use of a fake vaccination campaign by the U.S. government's Central Intelligence Agency (CIA) in Pakistan, as part of its attempts to find Osama bin Laden.[24] Not only has this affected the GPEI's vaccination uptake rates, but medical staff administering the vaccinations in Nigeria, Pakistan, and Afghanistan (the last three polio-endemic countries) have been targeted and killed because of their work. Despite these challenges, as well as an outbreak of wild poliovirus type 1 in the Horn of Africa and war-torn Syria in 2013, the GPEI launched the Polio Eradication and Endgame Strategic Plan 2013–2018, to "end all polio disease."[25]

The AIDS pandemic represents the WHO's greatest challenge in combating a single disease. The Global Program on AIDS, launched in 1986, grew into the largest program in the WHO's history. Although the organization's presence in AIDS response remains strong, the WHO ceded leadership to the Joint United Nations Program on HIV/AIDS (UNAIDS) on January 1, 1996 (see Chapter 10).

This did not deter the WHO from launching its landmark "3 by 5" Initiative with UNAIDS on World AIDS Day 2003, with the goal of ensuring access to antiretroviral therapy (ART) for 3 million people in the developing world by the end of 2005. The Global Fund and PEPFAR—which were founded around the same time—injected badly needed resources. The initiative achieved half its goal, with access to ART in low- and middle-income settings increasing from 400,000 people to 1.3 million. Even though the target was not reached, "there is little doubt that, without the initiative, the numbers of people on treatment would not have tripled or increased eight-fold in Africa."[26] Ultimately, the WHO initiative "made the idea of a Universal Access goal possible."[27]

If the WHO's early history was marked by eradication campaigns against ancient scourges, and if AIDS became a defining challenge later in the twentieth century, then the early twenty-first century could be exemplified by the organization's battle against newly emerging diseases, notably SARS, pandemic influenzas, and the novel coronavirus MERS. The WHO identified SARS as a global health threat in 2003, raising the agency's profile with highly visible updates and travel advisories and instigating the launch of the new framework for global cooperation for pandemic disease threats, the IHR (discussed in "WHO Regulations No. 2: The International Health Regulations" later in this chapter and in Chapter 6).

Before the emergence of SARS, the WHO was tracking avian influenza A (H5N1), with the first human case reported in Hong Kong in 1997.

H5N1 was of particular concern not only because of its impact on commerce, with the culling of large bird flocks and restricted trade, but due to the fact that 60 percent of known infected human patients died. Inefficient human-to-human transmission has contained the epidemic, but 380 people had died by October 8, 2013, and new cases continue to be reported.[28]

In late 2006, Indonesia refused to share H5N1 virus specimens with the WHO, claiming that sharing was unfair unless the country could be ensured equitable access to vaccines. The WHO feared that Indonesia's refusal to share the virus would impede surveillance and response—a fear exacerbated by the 2009 H1N1 "Swine Flu" pandemic. The WHO began contentious negotiations in May 2007, which culminated in the Pandemic Influenza Preparedness (PIP) Framework for the Sharing of Influenza Viruses and Access to Vaccines and Other Benefits in May 2011.[29] Although the PIP Framework represented a diplomatic triumph, it also demonstrated the challenges the WHO faces in bridging the North-South divide (see Chapter 12). Box 4.3 shows how MERS—in the aftermath of SARS, H5N1, and H1N1—is testing the WHO's normative leadership.

BOX 4.3 Connecting the Dots: WHO Leadership in Responding to MERS

While the WHO has triumphed diplomatically with the successful negotiation of the PIP Framework and the revised IHR, its leadership in the operation of these norms has been put to the test by the Middle East Respiratory Syndrome (MERS)—a novel coronavirus called MERS-CoV, first reported in Saudi Arabia in 2012. MERS has not demonstrated sustained human-to-human transmission, but has a high fatality rate among laboratory confirmed cases. As of November 4, 2013, there were 64 deaths among 150 reported cases, all linked to countries on or near the Arabian Peninsula.[1]

The emergence of MERS has challenged the WHO to revisit bitterly contested legal terrain over ownership and sharing of highly pathogenic viruses—raising crucial questions of international law and public health: is there a responsibility to share viral samples with the international community? Is it lawful and ethical to claim intellectual property rights over biological materials?

Origins of the Controversy

As described by David Fidler, the controversy arose in June 2012 when a patient suffering from pneumonia and kidney failure died in Jeddah, Saudi Arabia.[2] With no identified cause of the illness, Dr. Ali Zaki, a consulting physician, sent blood and sputum samples to the Erasmus Medical Center in the Netherlands, which successfully identified the novel coronavirus. Erasmus shared samples of the coronavirus with other laboratories under a material transfer agreement (MTA), a contract commonly used to share pathogens. Erasmus filed for a patent in the Netherlands for the gene sequence of the MERS coronavirus with the aim of developing diagnostic tools, vaccines, and antiviral drugs for MERS. Saudi Arabia immediately voiced disapproval, stating that Dr. Zaki violated national procedures for sending MERS samples abroad, which resulted in the Erasmus Medical Center incorrectly asserting intellectual property rights over future scientific advancements arising from the coronavirus sample.[3] In January 2013 the WHO convened an urgent meeting in Cairo, Egypt to address MERS but failed to consider the emerging legal issues arising out of Saudi Arabia's concerns.

Duty to Share Viral Samples under the IHR

Under the IHR, WHO members must notify and share information with the WHO concerning events that may constitute a public health emergency of international concern (PHEIC) (see Chapter 6). This novel coronavirus is clearly reportable under the IHR. In July 2013, however, the IHR Emergency Committee concerning MERS-CoV concluded that "the conditions for a PHEIC have not at present been met"—a decision reaffirmed at the committee's third meeting in September 2013.[4] The WHO has not accused Saudi Arabia of neglecting its responsibilities under the IHR, but has pressed the government to provide more information in a timely fashion. These concerns are reminiscent of China's perceived failure to promptly report SARS, which provided an impetus for the revision of the IHR. Global communication and transparency during disease events are fundamental principles of the IHR.

Viral Sovereignty: Who Owns MERS?

In 2007 Indonesia claimed sovereignty over Influenza A (H5N1) samples under international law. Its claim was based on the Convention on Biological Diversity (CBD), which recognizes that countries have sovereign control of biological resources found within their territories.[5] While Saudi Arabia has not formally claimed sovereignty over MERS samples, it has insisted on its legal right to control sharing of the virus. The Pandemic influenza Preparedness (PIP) Framework, adopted by the sixty-forth WHA on May 24, 2011, represented a hard-fought, WHO-brokered resolution of the Indonesia H5N1 dispute, with norms and procedures for sharing the benefits and burdens of viral samples and the resulting therapeutic advancements (see Chapter 12). MERS, however, reveals the limitations of the PIP Framework, which is confined to influenza. Thus, even though SARS was also caused by a coronavirus, no international virus-sharing agreement currently covers biological samples other than novel influenzas. This represents a major gap in global health governance.

Intellectual Property Rights over Biological Materials

The patent application by Erasmus, and its restrictive MTA agreements, raise the ethical problem of whether intellectual property (IP) claims will thwart international research relating to MERS. Put simply, do the IP claims by Erasmus discourage international scientific research and cooperation? (See Chapter 9 for a broader examination of IP and global health.) At the WHA in May 2013, Margaret Chan stated categorically, "No intellectual property should stand in the way of you, the countries of the world, protecting your people."[6] She also argued that virus sharing should not occur bilaterally between laboratories, but rather through WHO Collaborating Centers.

The controversy over MERS demonstrates the WHO's vital ongoing global health governance functions, especially its mandate to create norms and foster international cooperation. MERS has highlighted the gaps in international rules for sharing biological materials and the fair allocation of benefits resulting from scientific advancements. The revised IHR and the PIP Framework are a beginning, but they merely scratch the surface of normative rules needed to achieve more harmonious and robust international cooperation.

NOTES

1. WHO, "Middle East Respiratory Syndrome Coronavirus (MERS-CoV)–update," November 4, 2013, http://www.who.int/csr/don/2013_11_04/en/index.html.
2. David Fidler, "Who Owns MERS?" *Foreign Affairs*, June 7, 2013, http://www.foreignaffairs.com/articles/136638/david-p-fidler/who-owns-mers.
3. Declan Butler, "Tensions Linger over Discovery of Coronavirus," *Nature*, January 14, 2013, http://www.nature.com/news/tensions-linger-over-discovery-of-coronavirus-1.12108.
4. WHO, "Statement on the Second Meeting of the IHR Emergency Committee concerning MERS-CoV," July 17, 2013, http://www.who.int/mediacentre/news/statements/2013/mers_cov_20130717/en/; WHO, "Statement on the Third Meeting of the IHR Emergency Committee concerning MERS-CoV," September 25, 2013, http://www.who.int/mediacentre/news/statements/2013/mers_cov_20130925/en/.
5. David P. Fidler, "Influenza Virus Samples, International Law, and Global Health Diplomacy," *Emerging Infectious Diseases* 14, no. 1 (2008): 90.
6. Thomas J. Bollyky, "The Battle for Affordable Drugs," *CNN*, June 3, 2013, http://globalpublicsquare.blogs.cnn.com/2013/06/03/the-battle-for-affordable-drugs/.

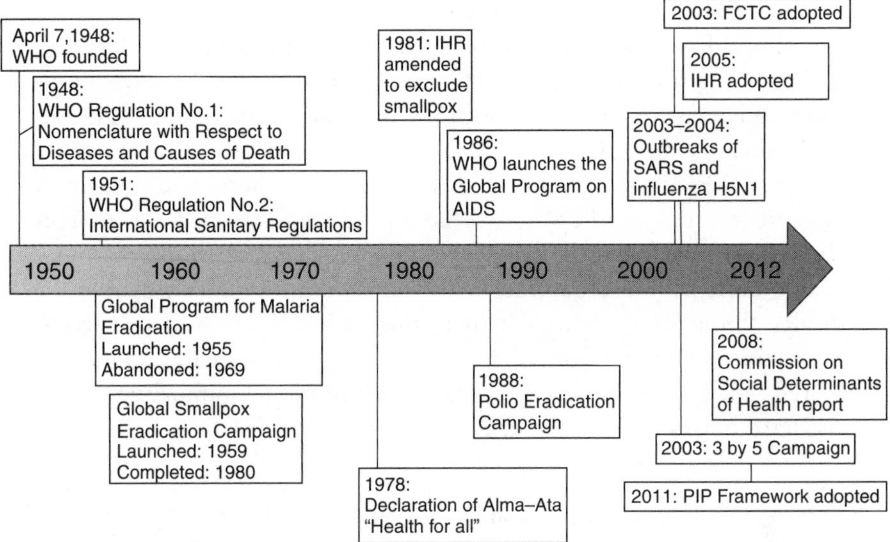

Figure 4.1 **Timeline of major milestones in the history of the World Health Organization**

Most of these milestones in the WHO's history involved scientific and technical expertise. But, as we will see next, the WHO Constitution designed the agency to also be a normative institution, developing international law in the realm of global health. Many of the WHO's modern achievements have involved normative development—mostly soft norms, but also two landmark treaties (see Figure 4.1).

The WHO Constitution: A Progressive Vision of a Normative Institution

Mission and Core Functions

The WHO Constitution created a normative institution with extraordinary powers. The constitution's first article enunciates a bold mission: "the attainment by all peoples of the highest possible level of health." The preamble defines health as "a state of complete physical, mental and social well-being and not merely the absence of disease or infirmity." Moreover, the preamble places human rights as a central theme, affirming that "the enjoyment of the highest attainable standard of health is one of the fundamental rights of every human being without distinction of race, religion, political belief, economic or social condition."

The constitution unmistakably establishes the WHO as the premier global health leader, stating that the agency should "act as the directing and coordinating authority on international health work"—working in close collaboration with UN agencies, national health ministries, and professional organizations (article 2).

Article 2 grants the WHO extensive normative powers to carry out its mission, authorizing the WHA to adopt "conventions, agreements and regulations, and make recommendations with respect to international health matters." The organization principally exercises its normative authority through soft power—either constitutionally authorized recommendations or more informal action by the assembly, board, and/or the Secretariat. The WHO rarely exerts its constitutional authority to exercise hard power by negotiating binding international law.

Recommendations: Soft Global Health Norms

The WHO's most salient normative activity has been to create soft standards that are underpinned by science, ethics, and human rights. Although not binding, soft norms are influential—particularly at the national level, where they can be incorporated into legislation, regulation, or guidelines.

Article 23 of the WHO Constitution grants the WHA the authority "to make recommendations to Members," and article 62 requires states to report annually on the action taken to comply with recommendations. The assembly's two most prominent recommendations—the International Code of Marketing of Breast-Milk Substitutes (1981) and the Global Code of Practice on the International Recruitment of Health Personnel (2010)—are described in Box 4.4.

Apart from these notable exceptions, the assembly rarely explicitly invokes article 23. In practice, however, failing to invoke article 23 seems to be inconsequential. States are not obliged to comply with the recommendations. Moreover, the WHO has not enforced article 62's reporting requirements, rendering the difference between constitutional recommendations and other soft norms less significant.

The WHO uses a variety of legal and policy tools to set norms, with varying levels of institutional support. First, the WHA can pass a resolution, which expresses the will of member states, representing the highest level of commitment. Second, the Secretariat can set a standard on a grant of authority from the assembly or the board, but without the governing authority's formal approval. Finally, the Secretariat can convene expert committees and disseminate their findings without formal endorsement.

BOX 4.4 World Health Assembly Recommendations under Article 23

The International Code of Marketing of Breast-Milk Substitutes

The International Code of Marketing of Breast-Milk Substitutes was the first WHA recommendation explicitly authorized under article 23 of the WHO Constitution.[1] During the 1970s, a decline in breast-feeding rates prompted the WHO to produce the code in cooperation with UNICEF. Its goal was to promote the healthy growth and development of infants through breast-feeding. The WHO mediated a politically charged agreement between stakeholders, including the infant formula industry. The WHA adopted the code in 1981, with the United States as the sole dissenter.[2]

The code states that industry should not promote breast-milk substitutes to the public; health care facilities and professionals should not promote breast-milk substitutes; and industry should not provide free samples of breast-milk substitutes to pregnant women, new mothers, or families. The WHA called for all governments to adopt the code into national legislation and report biannually on implementation. As of 2012, eighty-four countries had enacted legislation implementing all or part of the code and subsequent WHA resolutions.[3] The code creates a monitoring role for civil society—for example, it is used by the International Baby Food Action Network as a mandate to act as a "watchdog" on corporate practices that undermine breast-feeding.[4]

The Global Code of Practice on the International Recruitment of Health Personnel

The WHA adopted a Global Code of Practice on the International Recruitment of Health Personnel in May 2010. This code provides a multilateral framework for tackling the global health workforce shortage and the impact of health worker migration, particularly in lower-income countries. Implementation of the code has proved difficult, compounded by the fact that only fifty-one states—most of them European—reported on implementation by 2013.[5] The norms and impact of the code are discussed in detail in Chapter 11.

NOTES

1. Sami Shubber, *The International Code of Marketing of Breast-Milk Substitutes: An International Measure to Protect and Promote Breast-Feeding* (The Hague: Kluwer Law International, 1998).
2. UNICEF, "National Implementation of the International Code of Marketing of Breastmilk Substitutes," April 2011.
3. WHO, *Country Implementation of the International Code of Marketing of Breast-Milk Substitutes: Status Report 2011* (Geneva: WHO, 2013), 5–6, citing UNICEF, "National

Implementation of the International Code of Marketing of Breastmilk Substitutes" (April 2011).

4. "Code Watch Reports," International Baby Food Action Network, http://ibfan.org/code-watch-reports (accessed 10/10/13).
5. WHA/WHA Doc. A66/25, "The Health Workforce: Advances in Responding to Shortages and Migration, and in Preparing for Emerging Needs," April 12, 2013.

The more directly the assembly approves the normative content, the more likely member states will be to support and implement the standard. To build political support for the WHO's most important initiatives, the assembly often adopts a request-development-endorsement process. For example, the WHA charged the Secretariat with developing both the Breast-Milk Substitutes and Health Personnel Recruitment codes, followed by formal endorsement. Beyond article 23 recommendations, the assembly has placed its full weight behind major global strategies, such as the Global Strategy on Diet, Physical Activity, and Health; the Global Strategy to Reduce the Harmful Use of Alcohol; the Global Strategy for the Prevention and Control of Noncommunicable Diseases; and the Comprehensive Mental Health Action Plan (see Box 4.5).

Most norms are less formal than full-fledged regulatory texts, such as codes of practice, or even broad policy frameworks, such as the global strategies discussed in Box 4.5. Given the diverse and complex technical fields within the WHO's purview, the organization has developed a variety of mechanisms for gathering and disseminating expert advice. The Secretariat convenes expert advisory panels and committees to provide technical guidance.[30] The Expert Committee on Drug Dependence, for example, guides the agency in the discharge of functions assigned under the Single Convention on Narcotic Drugs (1961). The Expert Committee on the Selection and Use of Essential Medicines helps revise WHO's Model List of Essential Medicines, drugs that "satisfy the health care needs of the majority of the population . . . [and] should therefore be available at all times in adequate amounts and in the appropriate dosage forms, and at a price that individuals and the community can afford."[31] Expert committee reports are advisory but can exert influence on scientific development, while the Model List of Essential Medicines serves as a model for national drug registries and procurement strategies.

BOX 4.5 World Health Organization Global Strategies

WHO global strategies offer comprehensive recommendations on health promotion and disease prevention to multiple sectors. Here, I describe three of the most visible global strategies on behavioral risk factors, as well as one action plan that cuts across these strategies. The WHO has adopted multiple other strategies, such as Stop TB, the Global Strategy for Containment of Antimicrobial Resistance, and VISION 2020, a global initiative that aims to eliminate avoidable blindness by 2020.

Global Strategy on Diet, Physical Activity and Health

The WHA mandated the formulation of the Global Strategy on Diet, Physical Activity and Health in May 2002 to reduce the major NCD risk factors that cause cardiovascular disease, cancer, and diabetes.[1] The strategy was developed through an elaborate process that included a joint WHO/FAO expert consultation report, broad stakeholder consultations, and Executive Board approval, culminating in WHA adoption—thereby giving the strategy institutional legitimacy.[2]

This global strategy has four main objectives: (1) facilitate public health action to reduce chronic disease risk factors; (2) increase public awareness and understanding of the role of diet and physical activity in causing, preventing, and managing NCDs; (3) engage all sectors to develop and implement action plans for sustainable behavioral changes; and (4) promote science and research. Subsequently, the WHA adopted an Action Plan for NCD Prevention and Control (2008–2013)[3] and recommendations for marketing of foods and non-alcoholic beverages to children (2010)[4] (accompanied by an implementation plan).[5] In 2011 the UN held a High-Level Summit on NCDs, adopting a major political declaration on the prevention and control of these diseases.[6]

Global Strategy to Reduce the Harmful Use of Alcohol

Harmful drinking is socially destructive, causing violence, suicide, and vehicle crashes as well as contributing to cardiovascular disease and cancer. The Global Strategy to Reduce the Harmful Use of Alcohol was initiated by the WHA in 2008 and adopted in May 2010.[7] The multiphase process encompassed stakeholder consultations; draft strategy development by states, regions, and the EB; and finally, WHA endorsement. The strategy identifies ten target areas, including health services, community action, pricing, and reducing the illicit sale of alcohol. Given the magnitude and complexity of this global health threat, the strategy urges broad stakeholder engagement, with key roles for the WHO, civil society, academia, and industry.

Global Strategy for the Prevention and Control of Noncommunicable Diseases

Noncommunicable diseases (cardiovascular diseases, cancer, diabetes, and chronic respiratory diseases) are the leading causes of death globally, with lower-income countries bearing the disproportionate burden (see Chapter 13). Reducing behavioral risks (e.g., smoking, harmful alcohol use, poor diet, and physical inactivity) can significantly lower the burden of NCDs. At the turn of the twentieth century, the WHA adopted the Global Strategy for the Prevention and Control of Noncommunicable Diseases.[8] The strategy aimed to map NCDs and their social/economic/behavioral/political determinants, address modifiable risk factors, and advance health care for NCD prevention and treatment. In 2008 the WHA strengthened implementation of the global strategy,[9] but the impetus for urgent action did not come until the UN High Level Summit on NCDs in 2011.[10] In 2013 the WHA adopted the Global NCD Action Plan 2013–2020, establishing nine voluntary targets, including a 25 percent reduction in premature mortality from NCDs by 2025.[11]

Comprehensive Mental Health Action Plan 2013–2020

While not a global strategy, the Comprehensive Mental Health Action Plan 2013–2020 warrants attention due to its importance and its connection with all three of the above global strategies. As set out in the WHO Constitution, health is not simply a state of physical wellness, but also one of mental and social wellbeing. Suicide is the second most common cause of death among young people worldwide; 10 percent of the total global burden of disease is attributable to mental, neurological, and substance-abuse disorders.[12] In 2013 the WHA adopted the Comprehensive Mental Health Action Plan 2013–2020,[13] recognizing that socioeconomic and behavioral factors can impact mental health. The major objectives of the action plan call for enhanced leadership, governance, information systems, and research into mental health, as well as the implementation of strategies for the prevention and treatment of mental disorders. In order to monitor the progress, the action plan sets measurable global targets, including an increase in service coverage of at least 20 percent for severe mental disorders, and a reduction of the suicide rate in countries of at least 10 percent.[14]

NOTES

1. WHA, Resolution WHA55.23, "Global Strategy on Diet, Physical Activity and Health," May 18, 2002.
2. WHA, Resolution WHA57.17, "Global Strategy on Diet, Physical Activity and Health," May 22, 2004.

3. WHO, *2008–2013 Action Plan for the Global Strategy for the Prevention and Control of Noncommunicable Diseases* (Geneva: WHO, 2009).
4. WHA, Resolution WHA63.14, "Marketing of Foods and Non-alcoholic Beverages to Children," May 21, 2010.
5. WHO, *A Framework for Implementing the Set of Recommendations on the Marketing of Foods and Non-alcoholic Beverages to Children* (Geneva: WHO, 2012).
6. UNGA, Resolution A/66/L.1, "Political Declaration of the High-Level Meeting of the General Assembly on the Prevention and Control of Non-communicable Diseases," September 19, 2011.
7. WHA, Resolution WHA63.13, "Global Strategy to Reduce the Harmful Use of Alcohol," May 21, 2010.
8. WHA, Resolution WHA53.14, "Global Strategy for the Prevention and Control of Noncommunicable Diseases," 2000.
9. WHA, Resolution WHA 61.14, "Prevention and Control of Noncommunicable Diseases: Implementation of the Global Strategy," May 24, 2008, implementing WHO, *2008–2013 Action Plan for the Global Strategy for the Prevention and Control of Noncommunicable Diseases.*
10. UNGA, Resolution A/RES/66/2, "Political Declaration of the High-Level Meeting of the General Assembly on the Prevention and Control of Non-communicable Diseases," January 24, 2012.
11. WHA, Resolution WHA 66.10, "Follow-Up to the Political Declaration of the High-Level Meeting of the General Assembly on the Prevention and Control of Non-communicable Diseases," May 27, 2013.
12. WHA, Resolution WHA66.8, "Comprehensive Mental Health Action Plan 2013–2020," May 27, 2013, 4; Christopher J. L. Murray et al., "Disability-Adjusted Life Years (DALYs) for 291 Diseases and Injuries in Twenty-One Regions, 1990–2010: A Systematic Analysis for the Global Burden of Disease Study 2010," *The Lancet* 380, no. 9859 (2012): 2204, 2207.
13. WHA, Resolution WHA66.8, "Comprehensive Mental Health Action Plan 2013–2020."
14. Shekhar Saxena, Michelle Funk, and Dan Chisholm, "World Health Assembly Adopts Comprehensive Mental Health Plan 2013–2020," *The Lancet* 381, no. 9882 (2013): 1970.

The WHO has established a network of collaborating centers, linked to research institutes and universities, to support agency functions ranging from nursing, nutrition, and mental health to human rights. The Global Outbreak Alert and Response Network (GOARN) offers another salient example. GOARN is a technical collaboration of institutions that pool human and technical resources for the rapid identification, confirmation, and response to disease outbreaks of international importance.

The Negotiation of Treaties: Hard Law

As discussed above, the WHO Constitution envisages a normative institution that uses law and exercises power to proactively promote the attainment of the highest possible level of health. The WHO Constitution sets out separate processes for the negotiation of "agreements" or "conventions" on the one hand, and "regulations" on the other. Yet despite the WHO's impressive normative powers, modern international health law is remarkably thin. The WHA has adopted only three treaties in its sixty-five-year history, two of which predate the agency—the Nomenclature Regulations and the International Health Regulations. The processes for adoption of each of these different instruments are set out here:

Conventions or agreements Article 19 grants the WHA the power to "adopt conventions or agreements" by a two-thirds vote. A convention or agreement—which is a binding international treaty—enters into force for each member when the country's government accepts it in accordance with national constitutional processes.

This is consistent with standard treaty-making processes, with states having unfettered choice about entering into an international convention or agreement. However, article 20 is exceptional because it directs members to "take action" by accepting or rejecting the convention or agreement within eighteen months of adoption by the WHA, presumably even in cases where the member state's WHA delegation voted against the treaty's adoption. Each member must notify the D-G of the action it has taken, such as submission of the treaty for ratification. If a member does not accede to the treaty within the allotted time, it must furnish a statement of reasons. This is a powerful mechanism that is highly unusual in international law, which is predicated on the sovereignty of states. The requirement that states furnish reasons for failing to "take action" is also unusual in international law, because it obliges states to seriously consider the treaty in accordance with national constitutional processes.

Articles 20 and 62 give the D-G monitoring authority consistent with the obligation on members that accede to a treaty to report annually on its implementation. More generally, Chapter XIV of the constitution requires members to report annually on "action taken" and "progress" in improving health, as well as to transmit health information at the request of the EB.

The WHO did not negotiate a health convention until 2003, when the assembly adopted the Framework Convention on Tobacco Control.[32] Although a laudable achievement, the FCTC is almost sui generis because it regulates the only lawful product that is uniformly harmful. The FCTC was politically feasible because the tobacco industry was vilified for obfuscating and denying scientific realities; engineering tobacco to create nicotine dependence; engaging in deceptive advertising; and targeting youth, women, and minorities. Chapter 7 is devoted to the global response to tobacco.

Regulations The WHA's quasi-legislative powers under article 21 empower the WHO to adopt regulations on a broad range of health topics: (a) sanitation, quarantine, and other interventions to prevent the international spread of disease; (b) nomenclatures of diseases, causes of death, and public health practice; (c) standards for diagnostic procedures for international use; and (d) standards for the safety, purity, and potency of biological and pharmaceutical products moving in international commerce, as well as the advertising and labeling of such products.

The WHO's authority to adopt regulations is even more remarkable than it is for agreements or conventions. Under article 22, regulations enter into force for all members after due notice is given of WHA adoption, except for members that notify the D-G of rejection or reservations within a specified time. Consequently, states must proactively opt out or they are automatically bound. Perhaps standing alone in international law, the WHO Constitution permits the imposition of binding obligations without a state's express assent.

Indeed, the regulations may even enter into force for states that notify the D-G of a reservation to the treaty. International law has evolved since the adoption of the WHO Constitution. Under the Vienna Convention and current state practice, a state that has made a reservation to a treaty may still be recognized as a party, provided that the reservation is compatible with the treaty's overall purpose.

WHO Regulations No. 1: The Nomenclature Regulations Article 2 specifically empowers WHO to establish and revise international nomenclatures of diseases, causes of death, and public health practices, and to standardize diagnostic procedures. The first World Health Assembly, held in 1948, adopted WHO Regulations No. 1 Regarding Nomenclature with Respect to Diseases and Causes of Death, which formalized a longstanding international process for disease classification. By providing standardized nomenclature, the regulations facilitate the international comparison of morbidity and mortality data. The Nomenclature Regulations require states to use the current version of the International Classification of Diseases (ICD), which is now in its tenth edition (see Box 4.6).

BOX 4.6 The International Classification of Diseases

The International Classification of Diseases (ICD) is the international standard diagnostic classification for epidemiological, health management, and clinical purposes. It uses uniform data to characterize and monitor the population's health, and to assess resource allocation and quality of health services. The ICD classifies diseases on vital records, such as death certificates, offering a standardized form for compiling national morbidity and mortality statistics.

The ICD's origins date back to the First International Statistical Congress (ISC), held in Brussels in 1853. The ISC asked William Farr and Marc d'Espine to prepare an internationally applicable, uniform classification of causes of death. Farr, a statistician of the General Register Office of England and Wales, dedicated his life to improving these classifications. The International Statistical Institute (the successor to the ISC) adopted the International List of Causes of Death in 1893.

The WHO assumed responsibility for the ICD at its creation, with its constitution charging the organization "to establish and revise as necessary international nomenclatures of diseases, of causes of death and of public health practices; and to standardize diagnostic procedures as necessary" (article 2(s)(t)).[1] In 1948, the first World Health Assembly adopted WHO Regulations No. 1 Regarding Nomenclature with Respect to Diseases and Causes of Death.[2] The assembly amended the Nomenclature Regulations in 1956[3] and completely revised them in 1967, stipulating that states must use the current revision of the ICD for morbidity and mortality statistics.[4] The WHA endorsed the tenth edition (ICD-10) in 1990—the most recent version, which came into use in 1994. With medical knowledge fast evolving, the WHO plans to publish the ICD's eleventh edition by 2015.

NOTES

1. WHO, "Constitution of the World Health Organization" (1946), entered into force April 7, 1948, art. 2(s)(t).
2. WHO, "World Health Organization Regulations No. 1 regarding Nomenclature (Including the Compilation and Publication of Statistics) with Respect to Diseases and Causes of Death," July 24, 1948.
3. WHA, Resolution WHA9.29, "Amendment of Nomenclature Regulations," May 21, 1956.
4. WHO, "Regulations regarding Nomenclature (Including the Compilation and Publication of Statistics) with Respect to Diseases and Causes of Death 1967," May 22, 1967.

WHO Regulations No. 2: The International Health Regulations As highlighted earlier in the history and development of the WHO, the IHR date back to a series of European sanitary conferences held in the nineteenth century to deal with infectious-disease control. The WHA adopted the International Sanitary Regulations (ISR) in 1951 as WHO Regulations No. 2, covering six quarantinable diseases: cholera, plague, epidemic louse-borne typhus, relapsing fever, smallpox, and yellow fever. The twenty-second assembly (1969) revised and consolidated the ISR and renamed them to the IHR. Minor revisions to the IHR followed, with the twenty-sixth assembly (1973) amending cholera requirements, and in 1981, the thirty-fourth assembly excluding smallpox as a result of its global eradication the previous year. By the time the forty-eighth assembly (1995) called for its fundamental revision, the IHR applied only to cholera, plague, and yellow fever—the same three diseases discussed at the first Sanitary Conference in 1851. Following the outbreak of SARS and avian influenza threats in the early 2000s, the assembly completely revised the IHR in 2005, and the new version mostly entered into force in 2007 (see Chapter 6).

Hard versus Soft Norms

For the most part, the WHO has eschewed norm setting, preferring scientific and technical solutions to the deep-seated problems of global health. And even when it has acted normatively, it has mostly chosen soft law, in the form of guidelines, codes, or recommendations, rather than hard, binding international law. Prominent scholars have chastised the WHO for its reluctance to create binding norms,[33] although this is beginning to change with international instruments such as the FCTC and the IHR. However, there may be good reason for opting for soft instruments, which former U.S. Secretary of State Hillary Clinton called "smart" power in her January 2009 confirmation hearing.[34] (Chapter 3 discusses the benefits and disadvantages of soft versus hard norm setting.)

National Health Legislation

The WHO Constitution underscores the vital interaction between national and international law, with both required for effective promotion of population health. Article 63 directs member states to "communicate promptly to the Organization important laws, regulations, official reports, and statistics pertaining to health." Formerly, the OIHP published excerpts of national public health legislation, a function that the WHO took over at its inception.[35]

The WHO's International Digest of Health Legislation (IDHL) publishes extracts from and translations of public health laws and regulations among member states. The organization, however, has decreased support for this vital constitutional function, both by reducing IDHL staff and discontinuing print publication in 1999. Today the IDHL is available electronically, although it provides only a fragmented account of domestic health legislation. However, efforts to revive or renew the service are ongoing.

The WHO Reform Agenda: Proposals to Assure the Future of WHO Leadership

On March 10, 2011, the day before convening the D-G's Ad Hoc Advisory Committee on Reforming the WHO, Margaret Chan called together all staff at headquarters, with regional staff joining by satellite. She announced an alarming budget deficit and staff layoffs, calling for fundamental reform. That May, the WHA endorsed the reform agenda, while the EB launched "a transparent member state–driven and inclusive consultative process on WHO reform."[36]

In 2012 the WHA and the EB defined three reform objectives: (1) *improved health outcomes,* with the WHO setting priorities agreed by member states and partners; (2) *greater coherence in global health,* with the WHO playing a leading role in enabling multiple actors to become more effective; and (3) *pursing excellence* that is effective, efficient, responsive, objective, transparent, and accountable.[37]

The reform agenda reveals keen self-awareness of the challenges the WHO faces, but why has the agency not been able to fully succeed in meeting them? Why are so many allies concerned about the organization's future? Why has it been so hard for the agency to change and adapt? I conclude this chapter with eight proposals for ensuring that the WHO can reclaim its rightful place as the world's premier health organization.[38]

1. Encourage members to become shareholders

During the meeting of the Ad Hoc Advisory Committee on Reforming the WHO, the D-G said something that was telling—and brave. She observed that member states do not behave as "shareholders" with a genuine stake in the organization's success. That critique has a ring of truth. States, of course, want the agency to succeed, but they often act in ways that thwart effective action. Members want the WHO to be adequately funded, with control over its finances. Nevertheless, they resist higher mandatory assessments, push unfunded mandates, and sometimes fall into arrears in paying their dues.

Members want the WHO to exert leadership, harmonize disparate activities, and set priorities. Yet they resist intrusions into their sovereignty and they want to exert control. In other words, "everyone desires coordination, but no one wants to be coordinated." States often ardently defend their geostrategic interests. As the Indonesian virus-sharing episode discussed earlier in this chapter illustrates, the WHO is pulled between power blocs, with North America and Europe (the primary funders) on one side and emerging economies, such as Brazil, China, and India, on the other. An inherent tension exists between richer "net contributor" states and poorer "net recipient" states, with the former seeking smaller WHO budgets and the latter seeking larger budgets.

Overall, national politics drive self-interest, with states resisting externally imposed obligations for funding and action. Some political leaders express antipathy to, and even distrust of, UN institutions, viewing them as bureaucratic and inefficient. In this political environment, it is not surprising that WHO members fail to act as shareholders.

The WHO cannot succeed unless members do indeed act as shareholders, foregoing a measure of sovereignty for the global common good. It is in all states' interests to have a strong global health leader that can safeguard health security, build health systems, and reduce health inequalities. But that will not happen unless members fund the organization generously, grant it authority and flexibility, and hold it accountable.

2. Transform the WHO's internal culture from technical excellence to global leadership

The WHO reform agenda aptly stresses the value of human capital, which is at the heart of the organization's strength and credibility. The reform promises better recruitment and retention of experienced staff. Human resources are indispensable, but the reform fails to adequately address two critical problems.

First, the organization's financial crisis prompted a downsizing of personnel, and it is unclear how current staff levels can meet burgeoning health challenges. Without adequate resources, the Secretariat can neither expand nor even retain professional staff.

Second, the reform fails to consider the *kinds* of human resources that are needed in a globalized world. The WHO is comprised primarily of scientists, epidemiologists, physicians, and nurses. As vital as these functions are, leadership requires expertise in norm development, with the ability to influence key sectors. The WHO needs lawyers, diplomats, mediators, and economists, as well as experts in agriculture, trade, intellectual property, and human rights.

The WHO's aversion to norm development may well be due to the fact that the agency lacks funding and expertise, and does not see its comparative advantage over other UN institutions. Yet a stronger focus on norm setting is a design choice that the WHO should consider in setting its agenda, allocating its resources, and developing its workforce. Norm development is an integral aspect of the WHO's constitutional mandate.

3. Give voice to stakeholders and harness the creativity of nonstate actors

As a UN agency, the WHO is comprised solely of member states, which govern through the WHA and the EB. This governing structure affords the WHO legitimacy and influence, enabling the organization to stand alone as the voice of the community of nations in global health. Yet this state-centric focus often sidelines valuable stakeholders—public, private, and philanthropic.

If nonstate actors are not given a voice in the WHO, they will redirect their energies elsewhere. This process has been gradually hollowing out the WHO, as resources and influence move to bilateral programs (e.g., PEPFAR), innovative partnerships (e.g., the Global Fund and the GAVI Alliance), and foundations (e.g., the Gates Foundation).

Beyond major competing institutions lies a world with numerous stakeholders. Many of these actors have become disillusioned with the WHO because they feel that the organization has not heard their voices or reflected their interests. As a coalition of NGOs lamented: "we urgently need a larger role for 'little heard voices' as many of us have had difficulties making our voices heard at [the] WHO, which in comparison with other UN institutions is not accommodating to public interest organizations."[39] A major function of leadership is to harness the resources and energy of key stakeholders. The distant and sometimes distrustful relationship between the WHO and nonstate actors could be changed to enlist these stakeholders in a strategic alliance.

Nonstate actors play no formal role in WHO governing structures. The assembly and board do not fully recognize stakeholders beyond states. This contrasts with other international organizations that have mechanisms for incorporating third parties into their governance and decision-making processes. For example, UNAIDS includes representatives of civil society on its governing board, although with nonvoting status. More recent partnerships, like the Global Fund and the GAVI Alliance, seat civil society organizations, businesses, and foundations as voting board members (see Chapter 5).

Multistakeholder engagement Currently there is no single platform for global health dialogue between international organizations, states, partnerships, foundations, businesses, and civil society. The WHO would become more effective by giving voice and representation to these multiple stakeholders. To achieve this goal, the D-G proposed a World Health Forum in 2011—multistakeholder meetings under WHO auspices to increase effectiveness, coherence, accountability, and reporting to formal governing structures.[40] States, however, rejected the forum, while civil society feared it would advance corporate interests. In its stead, the D-G proposed a combination of stakeholder forums targeted to key policies, separate consultations with different constituencies, and web-based and in-person meetings.

To be effective, these proposals must influence the WHO's agenda, priorities, and governing structures. For example, the agency could create a meaningful platform for developing an innovative "Framework for Global Health" that could be adopted by the board and the assembly, monitored by civil society, and accompanied by genuine accountability mechanisms (see Chapter 14).[41]

Whatever the ultimate forms of engagement, they must be fair and inclusive, ensuring a voice for marginalized communities as well as the resources to enable civil society participation.[42] This requires transparent and representative selection processes, with agreed-on action agendas. It also requires proactive outreach to disadvantaged communities that are least likely to be aware of such programs, or have the means to participate. If the WHO does not make a stronger commitment to inclusion, civil society may be marginalized, with the private sector dominating the global health conversation.

Official NGO status The WHO makes it very difficult for nongovernmental organizations to gain "official relations" status, which is prerequisite for nonvoting participation in WHO meetings. NGOs with this status may attend EB and WHA sessions and make prepared (but not extemporaneous) statements.

With limited exceptions, to enter into official relations an NGO must (1) be international, representing "a substantial proportion of the persons globally organized" in the field; (2) have a constitution, governing body, and administrative structure, with a voting membership; and (3) have major activities that are relevant to WHO's health-for-all strategy. Even then, most NGOs must have two years of informal relations prior to applying for admission into official relations.[43] This burdensome process often excludes NGOs that are domestic, poorly funded, small, or have a specific mission—even if they are influential. Currently, most NGOs in official relations are Northern-based.[44]

The EB and the WHA should lower the bar for NGO participation, and should be more welcoming to civil society. For example, the WHO could offer scholarships that would enable NGOs in developing countries to participate. It could also expand opportunities for civil society input, such as allowing extemporaneous statements, facilitating NGO side sessions, and conducting open hearings. In 2004 the WHA postponed for "further study" a proposal to simplify the process for nonstate participation.[45] The proposal is still pending, with little prospect of success.

World Health Assembly "Committee C" As explained earlier in this chapter, scholars and diplomats have proposed the formation of a third WHA committee (Committee C) that would be comprised of major stakeholders, such as international organizations, foundations, multinational health initiatives, and civil society organizations.[46] The objectives would be to increase transparency, coordination, and engagement of stakeholders. The two extant WHA committees are comprised solely of states, and their business is concerned mostly with governance and financing of the agency. Yet the assembly's mandate extends beyond the WHO, granting it authority to "direct and coordinate" global health activities while also collaborating with specialized agencies, governments, professional groups, and other actors (article 2).

The constitution grants the assembly power to establish additional committees, and to invite nonvoting representatives (article 18). A Committee C could debate health initiatives, give stakeholders a venue for presenting their activities and plans, and discuss harmonization of activities.

Conflicts of interest Conflict of interest is a vital ethical concern for WHO governance as perceptions of probity underpin the confidence others bestow on the organization. The WHO must be careful to ensure that cooperating entities are genuinely devoted to the public interest, without pecuniary or other competing interests.[47] Although this is true for all groups, it is especially pertinent when engaging the private sector, such as the food, alcoholic beverage, pharmaceutical, and biotechnology industries (the WHO already has strict rules to exclude tobacco companies or entities that are funded by them). The WHO has a duty to set and oversee health and safety standards for businesses, which is another reason not to grant businesses privileged access. For example, it would be inappropriate for the food or marketing industries to fund nutrition guidelines. Contributors finance areas of their own interest, and companies may profit by influencing WHO decision making. The EB should design a clear, transparent process for managing conflicts, including monitoring and enforcement.

Although foundations do not have the same potential for conflicts as the private sector, they can still exercise considerable influence. Wealthy philanthropists such as Bill Gates and Michael Bloomberg donate vast resources, but they can also skew the world health agenda. For example, the Gates Foundation and other undisclosed sources helped fund the WHO blueprint for reform, raising the question of whether there is sufficient separation between the interests of the WHO and wealthy donors, which are not fully transparent or accountable.

4. Improve WHO governance through transparency, performance, and accountability

The WHO reform agenda aptly stresses both the organization's governance and broader global health governance. Chapter 3 describes the idea of good governance that demands transparency, honesty, results-based performance, and accountability. Without good governance, the WHO's legitimacy will erode as stakeholders shift their support to other, better-functioning institutions.

As a member-owned intergovernmental agency, the WHO must be open to scrutiny, with its evidence, reasons, and dealings with outside parties plainly disclosed. Most importantly, good governance requires tangible results, with clear targets and plans for achieving them. The D-G's 2013 proposal for a "results chain"—standard indicators to measure outputs and impact—is an important step. The WHO's proposed 2014–2015 budget includes numerical indicators for each program area and deliverables at country, regional, and headquarters levels.[48]

Stakeholders demand clarity about how their resources will achieve improved health outcomes. Yet an independent evaluation graded the WHO as "weak" on key parameters, such as cost-consciousness, financial management, public disclosure, and achievement of development objectives.[49] The importance of objective, third-party assessments in addressing these concerns is reflected in the reform agenda, which promises to establish independent evaluation of the WHO's work.[50]

5. Exert the WHO's constitutional authority as a normative organization

This chapter has emphasized the WHO's mission as a normative institution, charged with directing and coordinating global health activities. The justification for norm creation is not simply that it is mandated by the WHO Constitution but also that it will drive change far better than scientific and technical support alone. Norm development can set the global health agenda, guide priorities, harmonize activities, and influence the behavior of key state and nonstate actors.

If the WHO is to reassert its constitutional authority as a normative institution, then what principles should it adopt? What is the most effective combination of hard and soft norms? And how can it facilitate implementation of, and compliance with, health norms?

Human rights and global justice The WHO's history and constitutional design point to human rights as a primary source for norm development. What is striking about the postwar consensus is that the United Nations envisaged health and human rights as two great, intertwined social movements, with the UN Charter, the Universal Declaration of Human Rights, and the WHO Constitution as the defining instruments. The first two sentences of the constitution's preamble define health expansively and proclaim "the highest attainable standard of health" as a fundamental human right, with the WHO intended as the vanguard of the right to health.

Yet despite some notable achievements, the organization has been reticent to venture into norm development, and it rarely invokes the right to health. Certainly it has not been a leader in the health and human rights movement, leaving that role to civil society and the UN special rapporteur. In sixty-five years, the WHA has not passed a single resolution on the right to health. Exemplifying states' reluctance to develop right to health norms, in 2008 the United States strenuously objected to an innocuous WHO-OHCHR fact sheet on the right to health, emphasizing "the seriousness of our concerns" and reiterating "our request that it be rescinded."[51]

Soft and hard norms As discussed earlier in the chapter, the WHO has rarely exercised its law-making powers, negotiating only two major treaties. This represents a missed opportunity because law can be a powerful public health tool. Just as tobacco and health security transcend borders, justifying the FCTC and the IHR, so too do a range of major health hazards, such as NCDs, mental illness, and injuries.

Soft norms complement international law—a fact that the WHO increasingly realizes with codes of practice, global strategies, and action plans. States are more likely to buy into expansive standards if they are not legally bound to them, providing the WHO with an opportunity to issue bold guidance on highly consequential issues, such as health systems, access to essential medicines, and the socioeconomic determinants of health. The organization could go beyond declarations, reports, and commissions by negotiating normative standards for adoption by state and nonstate actors. Soft instruments, moreover, can become the building blocks for subsequent treaties, with greater potential for enforcement and accountability.

Implementation and compliance If norms are to have "bite," they must include effective mechanisms for accountability. Although the WHO's comparative advantage is not in policing, the agency is well constituted for convening, monitoring, and reporting. The convening process itself could lay the groundwork for gaining stakeholder buy-in. Once the normative instrument is adopted, ongoing monitoring could provide a feedback loop, with actors reporting on progress. The lack of capacity in developing countries remains a key challenge, requiring innovative financing and technical assistance.

Traditionally, international instruments have been directed primarily at states, leaving out many stakeholders. Extending normative influence to businesses, foundations, the media, and civil society could help ensure compliance. Advocates could exert political influence and rally public opinion. For example, NGOs could issue "shadow reports," holding stakeholders to account for failing to live up to their promises.

The "all-of-society" approach The *all-of-government* or *health-in-all policies* (HiAP) approach recognizes that ministries of health cannot accomplish major reforms on their own. HiAP urges all government departments to take health into account in their policies and practices. Beyond governments, an *all-of-society* approach seeks to include all social sectors—such as corporations, charitable foundations, the media, and academia—to achieve meaningful results.

6. Increase coherence within the WHO worldwide to ensure a unified voice and policy across headquarters, regions, and countries

Within the WHO's worldwide organizational structure, the headquarters, regions, and state offices all have vital roles. Ideally, headquarters sets the agenda and priorities while offering normative standards, technical expertise, and country support. Regions provide input for global decision making, implement global plans, and have greater control over matters of a predominantly regional nature. Country offices act at the national and local level, building capacity and helping to translate norms to fit country circumstances.

The question of whether the WHO should be more centralized or less centralized in its structure and governance is the subject of ongoing debates. There are clear advantages to allocating power and resources at each level. Centralization facilitates greater coherence and efficiencies of scale, whereas decentralization promotes innovation and responsiveness to local conditions and cultures.

Although the relative merits of centralization are debatable, the WHO needs to operate more cohesively. It is harmful and confusing when different entities purport to speak on behalf of the organization, expressing contradictory strategies and policies, or when activities at the various levels appear to be in tension, undermining overall impact. Furthermore, an international institution cannot exert leadership when control over its resources and workforce are dispersed and its regional and national actors have too much independence. The D-G must have greater control over the WHO's worldwide resources, workforce, and norm development.

Better alignment of the various levels of the organization is consistent with its constitutional design. Regions are supposed to be "an integral part of the Organization" (article 45). And according to article 50(a), regional governance must relate to "matters of an exclusively regional character." The constitution does not afford regions control over global challenges, but rather limits their role to providing "advice, through the Director-General . . . on international health matters" (article 50(e)). Moreover, regional offices are "subject to the general authority of the Director-General" (article 51).

Despite this, the WHO's culture has evolved to give regions considerable authority over policy and resources, resulting in fragmentation. The WHO regional offices are uniquely independent within the UN system, having authority over regional personnel, including country representatives. States within the region elect regional directors; therefore, the D-G has limited power to hold regions accountable. The D-G must also devote fixed proportions of the WHO's budget to regions. The regional committees meet annually to formulate policies, review budgets, and assess progress. The WHA and the EB formally approve decisions but do not provide tight fiscal and policy oversight.

Furthermore, states within the regions often have little in common and do not act in harmony, making coherence difficult. For example, high-income states—such as Australia and New Zealand in the Western Pacific region, and Canada and the United States in the Region of the Americas—may have decidedly different interests than developing countries within their respective regions. Israel is in the European region, while its Arab neighbors are in the Eastern Mediterranean region; North Korea is in the South-East Asia region, while South Korea is in the Western Pacific region.

The WHO must therefore align its global, regional, and national resources to better serve health needs at all levels. The organization's leadership depends on greater harmonization and control through the governing structures of the board, assembly, and D-G. The WHO headquarters should exercise more oversight over regional personnel and decision making. At a minimum, the agency should fully disclose the funds held within each regional office, and how regions meet objectives. Even if decentralized decision making remains the norm, the WHO should apply the same yardstick across regions to assess efficiency. A coherent worldwide structure would enable the WHO to more effectively steer global health activities.

7. Ensure funding that is predictable, sustainable, and scalable to needs

By its own admission, the WHO is "over-extended and overcommitted," with insufficient resources to meet expanding needs, and resources that are not fully within its control.[52] The Global Fund, PEPFAR, and the Gates Foundation have financial resources that overshadow the $3.98 billion budget the D-G proposed for 2014–2015. The CDC has more than three times the budget of the entire WHO.[53]

As discussed earlier in the chapter, the WHO had a budget deficit of at least $300 million in 2010–2011. To close the deficit, members set the WHO's 2012–2013 budget at $3.96 billion—nearly $1 billion less than the D-G sought, with 300 headquarters staff members (more than 10 percent of personnel) losing their jobs. Despite a quadrupling of global health funding for the decade ending in 2010, and a doubling of the WHO's budget, the agency finds itself in crisis. A combination of unfunded mandates from its members, growing health challenges, a long-term rise in the value of the Swiss franc, and poor fiscal control have all contributed to the current predicament. The global economic downturn placed greater pressure on WHO funding levels, with the 2014–2015 budget figure replicating the $3.96 billion in 2012–2013, which, when inflation is taken into account, represents a slight decrease in the overall budget, consistent with worldwide flatlining in global health expenditure.

While the budget has frozen, this has allowed the WHO to reshuffle its priorities, with infectious diseases taking a $72 million cut, but NCDs receiving a $54 million increase.[54] In light of the MERS and H7N9 Influenza outbreaks in the Middle East and East Asia respectively, the WHO intends to approach members for emergency funding in times of crisis or outbreak.[55] These changes demonstrate the importance of budget, and budget reform, in attaining both the WHO's global health and organizational priorities.

While budget allocation is central to the reform process, the success of the WHO is also dependent on how the WHO obtains its funding. The WHO's financing structure derives from two main streams. The first is assessed contributions to cover part of its budget, the costs of which are apportioned among members according to each country's wealth and population. The assessed contribution levels appear to be more a function of political will than a careful assessment of actual global need. The second stream, extrabudgetary funding, is sourced from voluntary contributions by member states and private funders, and it is often earmarked for specific diseases, sectors, or countries.

The agency's dire financial position is not due solely to insufficient funds, but also to its lack of flexibility in spending resources. From 1998 to 1999 about half (48.8 percent) of its budget was from discretionary sources—voluntary funds—whereas today that figure has grown to nearly 80 percent.[56] This eighty/twenty split undermines the organization's effectiveness and flexibility to meet rapidly changing health threats.

Having voluntary funding represent such a disproportionate amount of the agency's total budget is untenable. Extrabudgetary funding has transformed the WHO into a donor-driven organization, restricting its ability to direct and coordinate the global health agenda. The rationale for the shift towards extrabudgetary funding is clear: by tying funding to specific programs, donors ensure that their resources influence the activities and direction of the organization. Donor preferences often change from year to year, impeding longer-term strategic planning and capacity building.

Extrabudgetary funding, moreover, skews global health priorities. Compared with extrabudgetary funding, assessed contributions are more aligned with the actual global burden of disease. For example, in 2010–2011, the WHO's extrabudgetary funding was primarily for infectious diseases (65 percent), with negligible allocations for NCDs and injuries.

Yet NCDs account for 65 percent of all deaths worldwide, and injuries account for 11 percent of the global burden of disease.[57]

The WHO reform agenda proposes broadening the funding base by attracting donations from foundations, emerging economies, and the private sector. Although these stakeholders are worthwhile, they are unlikely to behave differently than traditional donors and will prefer to control their funds through earmarks. Furthermore, reliance on philanthropic and corporate funding opens the agency to the charge that it is not fully independent.

To increase the WHO's control over its budget and better align financing with organizational priorities, the 2013 WHA said it would approve the budget in its entirety, rather than only the portion funded by assessed contributions. The assembly aims to increase predictability and alignment of WHO financing with the organization's program of work to better reflect institutional priorities and the global burden of disease. More realistic budget financing dialogues with states and other major WHO contributors, and increased budget flexibility could help reduce the impact of drastic fluctuations in voluntary allocations, while curtailing the ability of wealthy donors to sway the WHO's agenda through earmarked contributions.[58]

But beyond these reforms, the ideal solution to the problem of donor-driven priorities would be for the WHA to set higher member contribution levels. The assembly should commit to increasing assessed contributions so that mandatory dues would comprise at least 50 percent of the overall budget within five years. Members could also give untied voluntary contributions above their assessed dues, and provide longer-term commitments. Member states must become genuine shareholders in the WHO's future, act collectively, and refrain from exerting narrow political interests. Failing decisive WHA action, the WHO could consider charging overheads of 20–30 percent for voluntary contributions to supplement its core budget. Although overheads are a familiar model in academia, the WHO would have to guard against the risk that charges might drive donors toward other multilateral organizations. Whatever the formula, there is little doubt that the WHO will never reach its potential unless members ensure that financing is predictable, sustainable, and scalable to global health needs.

8. Exercise leadership in global governance for health by exerting influence within and beyond the health sector

Harmonizing global health WHO leadership requires not only effective governance of its own affairs but also global governance—i.e., exerting influence within and beyond the health sector. The proliferation of global health actors is well known. The global health landscape suffers from poor coordination, unstable funding, and a lack of clear priorities. Rich contributors often tie resources to specific programs or diseases, and charities choose their particular causes. Global health, in effect, is bundled into silos without a coherent overall strategy. Ministers of health cannot guide—and may not even be aware of—all the foreign initiatives on their own soil. All of this undermines countries' ownership and effectiveness of health services, which are supposed to be overriding objectives.

The more rational course is to align international resources behind global priorities and national health plans. This would leverage the WHO's comparative advantage of identifying maximally effective strategies, such as health systems, development, and socioeconomic status determinants. It would also empower lower-income countries to implement national plans that meet their population's needs.

Influence beyond the health sector Harmonizing global health initiatives and aligning them with national health plans is necessary but not sufficient. The WHO must also exert influence in other regimes that affect health. Intellectual property rights affect access to essential medicines; trade in services affects health worker migration; and climate change affects food, disease vectors, and natural disasters. Human rights law covers social determinants, and humanitarian law protects civilians in times of armed conflict. The WHO needs to be at the table in major forums, advocating for health with a powerful voice. The agency should demonstrate why health is important, and how complementary sectors could adapt to protect human well-being. This will require the Secretariat to develop the core expertise in international relations, diplomacy, and law that is needed to carry real weight. It will also require the assembly to provide a mandate and resources for GGH.

The WHO's reform process, with its focus on core business, should not scale back on global governance. Through strategic engagement, forceful assembly resolutions, political courage, and adroit diplomacy, the WHO holds real potential to increase its impact beyond the health sector. For example, the WHO could urge governments to use health indicators that are attentive to human rights, such as equality, participation, and accountability. Similarly, the WHO could deepen its involvement in climate change negotiations to prioritize health in the development of adaptation strategies.[59] Finally, the WHO could enhance its intersectorial influence by spearheading a new health-focused consortium comprised of senior leaders of global institutions, such as the WTO, the IMF, the

World Bank, and the FAO. The consortium's objective would be to ensure a sustained, high-level focus of multiple regimes on health.

The WHO is the only institution with the legitimacy to rationalize global health funding and activities, and to advocate for health in the trade, intellectual property, and environmental sectors. Yet fundamentally reforming global governance will be difficult because powerful states and corporations are intent on pursuing their vested interests and maintaining the status quo. Global Health Watch, for example, reported that rich states use their funding leverage to pressure the WHO "to steer clear of macroeconomics and trade . . . and to avoid such terminology as the right to health."[60]

Political support from member states will be essential for reform. Whereas the G8 previously dominated the world agenda, today the G20 could become transformative, reducing the WHO's reliance on a narrow band of states. Powerful G20 states have interests in health, development, and access to medicines that diverge from the neoliberal model. Today a different set of powerful actors could place health and development at the center of global governance.

Concluding Reflections: Systemic Tensions within the WHO

With its progressive constitution and unmatched expertise, the WHO is well positioned to lead in world health. But the organization faces critical institutional tensions that it must overcome if it is to have a healthy future:[61]

- *A servant to member states.* Member states tightly control the organization, demanding faithfulness to their often-conflicting demands. Members govern the organization, electing the D-G, charting the work plan, approving the budget, and steering the agency's overall direction. When the governing bodies exert such close control, it can chill the Secretariat from acting as the moral leader for world health and advocating passionately on behalf of the disadvantaged.
- *A short-term horizon.* The WHO's efforts are often directed toward short-term emergencies at the expense of enduring health needs. Health security crises—ranging from SARS, influenza, and bioterrorism to humanitarian disasters—take disproportionate resources, leaving too little room for addressing intractable health threats, such as NCDs and injuries.
- *A paucity of resources.* The WHO's level of resources is entirely incommensurate with the scope and scale of global health needs.

Despite the agency's vast responsibilities, its budget pales in comparison with national and even local health budgets. This paucity of funding cripples the organization's effectiveness, spreading its resources too thin to make a genuine impact.

- *Earmarked funding.* The flow of funds to the agency is not only insufficient, but also highly restricted. This conflicts with the WHO's core mission of achieving health for all, with fair allocation of resources. The WHO must have greater authority to direct its resources to areas where needs are greatest and its comparative advantages are clearer.
- *Insufficient capacity for global implementation.* The WHO lacks global implementation capacity, due to its decentralized structure. The regions have wide autonomy. Each regional office is constituted by, and answers to, member states of that region. The regional directors report to regional members rather than to the D-G. Regionalization hampers the organization's ability to speak with a single voice and implement global strategies.

Despite progress, serious questions remain about whether the WHO reform process will make a meaningful difference. The WHO has established measurable programmatic targets and taken steps to align its funding with priorities; however, assessed contributions in the 2014–2015 budget were unchanged from the previous budget. Rather than adopting far-reaching proposals to better engage civil society, the organization planned to explore options for a framework to guide interaction among all stakeholders—an exploration with a target date of 2015.[62]

Yet if the WHO is to hold its rightful place as the global health leader, it must undergo fundamental reform. Member states hold the future of the WHO in their hands. If they invest in and support the organization, this would pay dividends in health security and human well-being. The WHO's current malaise can be overcome, if the political will is there. Members would guarantee the WHO's future by acting as shareholders; the Secretariat would govern itself well while exercising normative influence within and beyond the health sector; the governing bodies would actively engage stakeholders; and the assembly would ensure the resources and flexibility needed to meet evolving health challenges.

CHAPTER 5

Old and New Institutions

From the World Bank to the Global Fund, the GAVI Alliance, and the Gates Foundation

THE GLOBAL HEALTH LANDSCAPE is evolving at a dizzying pace: whereas the World Health Organization stood unrivaled in the aftermath of World War II, today there are nearly 200 international health agencies and initiatives.[1] This does not even include the myriad international NGOs and foundations that play vital roles in global health. These new institutions bring a host of benefits—more funding, an enhanced voice for civil society, and innovative ideas—but also a mismatch between health needs and available funds, a fractured approach to health planning and financing, and inadequate leadership and accountability. Scholars and advocates, recognizing these deficits, have called for fundamental restructuring of the global health architecture.[2]

This chapter tells the story of the evolution of global health institutions, in search of insights for reform. Institutional reform must respond to the major health needs facing developing countries while retaining the flexibility to respond to emerging health threats still on the horizon, such as emerging infectious diseases (EIDs).

A reimagined institutional architecture will need to return to the founding values of the WHO—namely, the right to health and a comprehensive vision of health for all—while responding to new realities. Globalization has accelerated, marked by the rapid dissemination of information, people, goods, and services—fanning the spread of infectious diseases. The diffusion of cultural norms and behavioral habits also brings with it a rising tide of NCDs.

The world's geopolitical power structure has also undergone vast changes since the WHO's formation. Emerging economies such as the BRICS countries now have substantial economic and political clout, but they also have high burdens of disease and poverty. Calamitous threats such as climate change have emerged, which compete with health needs for political attention while deepening the challenges facing global health institutions. Multiple regimes (for example, trade and intellectual property)—both compatible with health and competing with it—further test global health institutions.

In the midst of these sizable changes, international institutions and governments have agreed to key reform principles, such as harmonization among partners, alignment with national strategies, and country ownership of health systems.[3] In the past, success was measured in dollars, such as the amount of financial assistance devoted to a particular health threat. But success should now be gauged by measurable improvements in health outcomes—ideally, not just incremental changes, but deep and lasting improvement in health and longevity.

In this chapter, I identify three phases in the evolution of the global health architecture and point to a future "reforming" phase. The first phase is marked by a dominant WHO that sets the global health agenda. Although Chapter 4 systematically examined this still singularly important institution, here I return briefly to the WHO, reminding readers of its founding values, as well as the factors that contributed to its decline. The WHO's decline—in part of its own making and in part due to the rise of the Washington Consensus on neoliberal economic policies—led to the second phase, in which the World Bank Group became a dominating force in global health. The World Bank brought notable strengths in terms of expertise and resources, but also counterproductive policies that would undermine health systems in many countries.

This chapter's main focus will be on the complex third phase in which we now find ourselves. Having arisen from the failings of previous arrangements and from such new dynamics as the Millennium Development Goals and the response to the AIDS pandemic, phase three is marked by the formidable quantity and diversity of health actors. Some of the main global health institutions have tightly focused priorities, such as the Global Fund (AIDS, tuberculosis, and malaria), UNAIDS, and the GAVI Alliance (vaccines). Government initiatives such as PEPFAR also reflect the fundamental changes wrought by the AIDS pandemic. This new phase is also characterized by the entry of wealthy philanthropists such as Bill and Melinda Gates—who bring not only creativity and a huge influx of resources but also outsized influence.

The chapter closes by drawing on the lessons learned and posing major questions that have emerged from the first three phases of global health architecture to point toward a fourth phase, marked by the need for major reform. The reform movement should, I argue, advance the timeless founding values of the WHO—the right to health guided by strong leadership—within the changing sociopolitical realities that mark today's global health landscape.

Phase One: A Preeminent World Health Organization

In its first decades, the WHO functioned as the singular global health authority that its constitution envisioned, with countries relying on its technical advice and normative leadership. It operated in a sparsely occupied landscape where governments were the chief actors in global health—including governing the WHO. Few other global health institutions existed at the time. UNICEF collaborated with the WHO on childhood immunizations and the World Bank made its initial forays into health, while bilateral agencies provided assistance to select developing countries. The United States Agency for International Development (USAID), the largest bilateral agency, focused on supporting economic growth from its inception in 1961, but in the 1970s its mandate expanded to encompass health, with a focus on food, nutrition, and family planning. Global health actors beyond governments were few, although philanthropies such as the Rockefeller Foundation actively supported disease control in the developing world.

A Powerful WHO

In the late 1970s and early 1980s, the WHO reached the peak of its power under the dynamic leadership of Director-General Halfdan Mahler. Perhaps the WHO's boldest initiative at that time was mobilizing countries behind a new approach to health—primary health care—in which successes were beginning to be realized by the "barefoot doctors" of China and community-based health programs in Latin America, Bangladesh, and the Philippines.

Culminating in the Alma-Ata Declaration (1978), the new focus on primary health care held out the promise of transforming health systems. Previous approaches combined an emphasis on tertiary care (inherited from colonial powers) and disease-specific programs, which failed to meet most population health needs. Alma-Ata established principles for comprehensive health systems, with the promise of "health for all." Its vision matched the expansive definition of health in the WHO Constitution and would heavily influence the right to health for decades to come.[4]

Meanwhile, over the protest of industry, in 1977 the WHO published its first list of essential drugs. Later, in 1981, the World Health Assembly approved the International Code of Marketing of Breast-Milk Substitutes, again in the face of industry resistance.

Marking the pinnacle of the WHO's leadership, in 1979 scientists confirmed that the organization's smallpox eradication campaign had achieved its lofty goal. This was a time when the organization effectively set the global health agenda, spearheaded bold initiatives, and espoused a vision of health with justice.

The WHO's Declining Influence

Ironically, the WHO's successes contributed to its declining influence by creating opposition to its progressive policies and causing divisions within the global health community. The United States, protective of commercial interests, opposed the essential drugs list, viewing it as a threat to the pharmaceutical industry. The United States also saw the breast-milk substitutes code as harmful to the interests of baby formula manufacturers. In declining to ratify the International Covenant on Economic, Social and Cultural Rights, the United States resisted global health leadership anchored on the right to health.

More significantly, the tide turned against the WHO's primary health care initiative. Seen by international agencies as too expensive and overly broad, the comprehensive vision of the Alma-Ata Declaration gave way to "selective primary health care," a limited package of cost-effective health interventions. UNICEF adopted this limited approach and supported what became known as GOBI—growth monitoring, oral rehydration, breast-feeding, and immunizations—as the basic interventions of primary care. Initially proposed as a step toward comprehensive primary care, selective primary health care became an end in itself. Donors supported this approach, which was inexpensive and amenable to short-term, easily monitored results.[5]

Support for selective primary care was a reflection of the neoliberal ideology—dubbed the Washington Consensus—that was taking root. It was an era marked by expanding debts in developing countries, often a result of loans for large national development projects. A global recession in the late 1970s and early 1980s, along with falling commodity prices, left many of these states unable to repay the loans. Seen as evidence of government inefficiency, and limiting the money that states had available to invest, the debts contributed to the rise of an ideology that favored tight government budgets, privatization, and trade liberalization.

It was bound to be a difficult time for an organization such as the WHO, which worked through governments and had just set forth the ambitious agenda of health for all. And the WHO did not help its own cause. In 1988 Hiroshi Nakajima replaced the popular Halfdan Mahler as director-general. Accused of cronyism and corruption, an autocratic management style, and financial mismanagement, Dr. Nakajima proved unpopular with staff and with the WHO's main funders. Despite U.S. and other opposition, he was elected to a second term in 1993, leading to an investigation into whether Japan, his home country, used aid and trade to court votes.

The loss of confidence in the WHO resulted in its major funders demanding more control over how the organization used their money, as they supplanted the WHO's core funding with so-called extrabudgetary support. By gutting the organization's core budget, member states instigated the unsustainable funding patterns that continue to this day. By severely weakening the WHO's control over its own budget, this shift further undermined the organization's leadership and effectiveness. Extrabudgetary funding raised the profile of single-disease control programs at the expense of broader primary health care. Moreover, major member states such as those of the former Soviet Union and the United States were in arrears in paying their mandatory assessments, creating deficits for the WHO in the early 1990s.

By then, the WHO was no longer at the pinnacle of the global health institutional structure. Instead, that position belonged to the World Bank, with its rising political and economic power. The decline of the once predominant global health institution would also force the WHO to transform itself to revive its relevance and authority, leading to a new role at the center of the global health partnerships that began to proliferate in the late 1990s.[6] With its evolving position in a widening global health landscape, the WHO began to lose its identity and uniqueness. Whereas it once controlled the global health agenda, the WHO found itself as coequal with other actors—often becoming a rival for resources and influence.

Lessons Learned

Several lessons can be gleaned from the WHO's decline that can inform the next stage in the evolution of global health institutions. One is the importance of an effective, trusted leader at the helm and of a transparent selection process that meets the highest standards of integrity.

Dr. Nakajima, along with the questions over his reelection, cast a long shadow. Although successive directors-general have brought legitimacy back to the organization, elections continue to be conducted without full transparency. In the latest D-G election in 2012, the incumbent, Margaret Chan, ran unopposed.

Yet even the most dynamic leadership may not be enough. With its movement away from comprehensive primary care and its constitutional underpinning of the right to health, the WHO lost some of its legitimacy. At the same time, the organization never capitalized on a growing civil society movement that revolutionized global AIDS policy and has forcefully advocated on behalf of the public's health. Instead of harnessing the energy of NGOs, the WHO marginalized them. Rather than asserting moral leadership when dealing with powerful international actors such as the World Bank, the IMF, and the WTO, it tended to defer to them.

The turn away from the Alma-Ata Declaration also highlights the inescapable connection between leadership and the power of the purse. The WHO relied on other institutions to fund comprehensive primary health care, reflecting its own fragile financial position. Yet UNICEF, the World Bank, and many bilateral donors favored selective primary health care. Had the WHO been able to combine its normative authority with the economic capacity to execute its priorities, it could have more effectively set the global health agenda.

Phase Two: The Rise of the World Bank

The WHO's primacy in the post–World War II decades matched the times—from the idealism that infused the founding of the UN system (the UN Charter, the Universal Declaration of Human Rights, and the WHO Constitution) to the belief that states could improve people's lives (from the welfare states of Europe to the newly independent states of Africa). The political climate of the 1980s and 1990s, in contrast, was a time of neoliberal economic policies and skepticism toward the state. It is fitting, then, that these decades saw the rise of a bank as the most influential global health institution.

The World Bank's foray into global health began when Robert McNamara assumed its presidency in 1968, several decades after its establishment (see Box 5.1). McNamara's belief in the World Bank as a development agency—not merely a financial institution—coincided with a changing perception of development as a means to address human needs, not just economic growth.

BOX 5.1 **World Bank History, Governance, and Funding Arrangements**

History The World Bank and the International Monetary Fund (IMF) were established at the Bretton Woods Conference in 1944. The bank began operations in 1946, with an initial focus on financing post–World War II reconstruction in Europe. Its ambit soon became global, as it made large-scale capital and infrastructure investments to spur economic growth through the 1960s. In the 1970s it began to invest directly in meeting people's basic needs. The bank defines its mission today succinctly: "Working for a world free of poverty."[1]

Structure The World Bank Group consists of five institutions, three of which provide health funding. The International Development Association (IDA) provides grants and interest-free and low-interest long-term loans to low-income countries, with countries in or at risk of "debt distress" receiving all or much of their financing through grants. The International Bank for Reconstruction and Development (IBRD), the first World Bank institution, provides market-rate loans to low- and middle-income countries. The International Finance Corporation (IFC) is the World Bank Group's private sector arm, providing loans, equity, and technical assistance to spur private investment in developing countries.

Governance A Board of Governors, which includes all member states, and a smaller Board of Executive Directors govern four of the World Bank Group's institutions, including the IDA, IBRD, and IFC. The Board of Governors' powers include admitting and suspending members and reviewing budgets. The executive directors make policy, including approving loans and appointing the bank's president.

The five countries with the greatest ownership stake in the IBRD each appoint an executive director, while the Board of Directors elects the remaining Executive Board members. These elected members, presently twenty in number, represent country groups and several individual countries.

Voting power on the IBRD Boards of Governors and Boards of Directors is based on the number of IBRD shares each country holds, linked to economic clout. Thus, unlike the WHO's one state, one vote model, wealthier countries have disproportionate power in governing the bank, even as reforms have modestly increased the shares of developing countries.[2]

Funding arrangements The IBRD raises money to issue loans from bond sales and interest from loan repayments. By contrast, to support its grants and low- and no-interest loans, the IDA receives contributions, mostly from traditional donors and a handful of developing countries. IDA replenishment occurs every three years. Donors provided $31.7 billion at the sixteenth replenishment, the majority of the IDA's $49.3 billion funding package for July 2011 through June 2014. The seventeenth replenishment was on track to be at a similar level of financing.[3]

NOTES

1. Jennifer Prah Ruger, "The Changing Role of the World Bank in Global Health," *American Journal of Public Health* 95, no. 1 (2005): 60–70; "The World Bank: Working for a World Free of Poverty," World Bank, http://www.worldbank.org/ (accessed 11/18/13).
2. World Bank Group, "Spring Meetings Update: Voice Reform and Capital Increase," presentation to the United Nations Economic and Social Council, May 21, 2010.
3. UK House of Commons, International Development Committee, *International Development Committee—Fourth Report: The World Bank* (London: House of Commons, 2011); World Bank, *IDA Replenishment—Second Meeting, July 1–4, 2013, Chairperson's Summary* (2013).

The bank's first loan for family planning went to Jamaica in 1970; for nutrition, to Brazil in 1976; and for basic health services, to Tunisia in 1981. In 1974, in an early public-private partnership, the bank joined the WHO, the United Nations Development Program, and the FAO, along with private entities and NGOs, in initiating the largely successful Onchocerciasis Control Program, which was designed to eliminate river blindness in eleven West African nations. At the end of the 1970s, the bank established its Population, Health, and Nutrition Department—the forerunner to today's Health, Nutrition, and Population (HNP) program, one of the pillars of the bank's Human Development Network.[7] This shift was justified under the bank's development mandate, with internal studies linking population health to economic productivity.[8]

The WHO's decline in the late 1980s created space for the World Bank. The global economic downturn and the neoliberal ideology that was becoming popular in the halls of power also contributed to powerful actors—including the United States—favoring the bank's policies, such as selective primary health care. The bank's influence gained from its financial resources, and its connection to ministries of finance further enabled it to become, for a brief period, a dominant global health institution.

The World Bank developed considerable analytical capacity, building its in-house expertise in health economics and reducing its reliance on the WHO. The bank also brought multisector engagement to its health work, linking sectors such as water, sanitation, and agriculture.

Financing Health

The debt and fiscal crises of the late 1970s and early 1980s led the World Bank to focus on loans to help stabilize countries' economies. Notably, these loans began the practice of conditioning social sector loans on broader macroeconomic reforms—a practice that became deeply problematic.

The bank's health lending began in earnest in the mid-1980s. Leading campaigns included the Safe Motherhood Initiative in 1987, which grew in the 1990s to account for nearly one-third of the bank's HNP lending. From less than 1 percent of the bank's loan portfolio in 1987, HNP activities grew to 11 percent a decade later, peaking at more than $2 billion in 1996. In the late 1990s, the bank prioritized its HIV/AIDS response (see Box 5.2) and initiatives to improve health system performance and

BOX 5.2 The World Bank's Multi-Country HIV/AIDS Program for Africa (MAP)

The MAP program established the World Bank as a major international HIV/AIDS funder, although PEPFAR and the Global Fund would soon eclipse the bank's resources. Launched in 2000, the bank envisioned a fifteen-year, three-stage program emphasizing vulnerable populations, scaling up to cover countries where the disease was spreading. By 2011 cumulative MAP funding had reached $2 billion across thirty-five African states. MAP supported 50,000 civil society organizations, 1.8 million orphans and vulnerable children, and treatment for opportunistic infections for 288,000 people. MAP focused on capacity building and technical support rather than on treatment, which became the primary missions of PEPFAR and the Global Fund.[1]

The bank credits MAP's first phase with spurring political commitment around AIDS, particularly the rise in multisector national programs. The *Lancet* opined that MAP's strongest contribution was in promoting a multisectoral response, although others saw the bank's methods as undermining health ministries and devaluing other pressing needs and gender equality.

Beyond these questions lie doubts as to the program's overall effectiveness. Eight years into MAP, the *Lancet* observed that its "impact on HIV/AIDS is unclear." The bank's 2009 internal review found that a mere 29 percent of AIDS programs performed satisfactorily.[2]

NOTES

1. "Multi-Country HIV/AIDS Program (MAP)," World Bank, http://go.worldbank.org/I3A0B15ZN0 (accessed 10/10/13).
2. "The World Bank and HIV/AIDS in Africa," editorial, *The Lancet* 371, no. 9626 (2008): 1724.

financing reform. Nutrition and population programs declined, with funding for family planning and programs to reduce high fertility decreasing from 11 percent to 2 percent of the HNP lending portfolio from 1997 to 2006.

Before the dramatic increase in global health funding in the first decade of the new millennium, the World Bank had become the world's largest health funder. Yet despite the bank's precipitous rise in spending, health outcomes often failed to improve. A 2009 internal review conceded that there was "a lack of evidence that the Bank's HNP support is really delivering results to the poor." Performance was especially low in Africa, where only 24 percent of projects were rated as satisfactory, including the bank's vaunted AIDS programs. The poor performance resulted from the complexity of multisector grants and a lack of institutional capacity. Similarly, a lack of openness to learning, both from self-scrutiny and external scrutiny, may have enabled challenges to go unresolved or even unnoticed.[9]

The 2009 review of the bank's water and sanitation projects holds an important lesson that demonstrates the necessity of adopting a HiAP approach: the need to deliberately aim to improve health. Few of these projects had the express goal of improving health outcomes, and even fewer monitored improvements. The bank's projects rarely addressed hygiene despite its centrality to health. Ironically, World Bank loans to privatize water services may have reduced access to clean water.[10] Overall, despite the bank's multisectoral approach, key bank actors functioned independently, with few strategies to foster collaboration.

Health Reform Prescriptions, Structural Adjustment, and Weakened Health Systems

Neoliberal policies prescribed by the World Bank, the IMF, and rich Western governments in the 1980s and 1990s affected public health perhaps even more than the bank's health projects. World Bank and IMF loan conditions required reduced overall public-sector spending, resulting in the deterioration of health systems in many low- and middle-income countries.

The World Bank entered the contested area of health policy in earnest in 1987, promoting user fees to shift "from health services that cater to the rich to those which cater to the poor."[11] The bank was not alone in promoting user fees: through the Bamako Initiative, endorsed by African health ministers, the WHO and UNICEF endorsed user fees—with exemptions for the poorest people—with the revenue to be retained locally.[12] The agencies argued that user fees would merely offset public subsidy of primary care for the wealthy without undermining universality. Yet subsequent research revealed that user fees posed major barriers to health care access.[13]

The bank's *World Development Report 1993: Investing in Health* marked the zenith of its global health influence, promoting reforms meant to improve equity, efficiency, and effectiveness. The report advocated a three-pronged approach: (1) fostering an improved health environment, including girls' education; (2) focusing on essential services, reduced tertiary care, decentralization, and the contracting out of services; and (3) promoting diversity and markets, including private health insurance and competition among private and public actors.

The report introduced the idea of essential health packages, including a narrow set of public health services (e.g., immunization, AIDS prevention, micronutrients, deworming, and tobacco control) and clinical services (e.g., STD and TB treatment, care for sick children, prenatal and delivery care, and family planning).[14] Many health advocates, such as those in the People's Health Movement, remain suspicious of the bank's "essential services" approach, seeing it as unduly narrow. Advocates similarly object to the bank's support for the private health sector, fearing that user fees and out-of-pocket expenses create a "poverty trap."[15]

Although such bank-promoted policies as user fees have since fallen out of favor, others continue to hold sway, including essential health packages, cost-effectiveness, and decentralization. Notably, the 1993 report introduced the disability-adjusted life year (DALY) as a measure of disease burden by combining premature death with loss of healthy life years. Today, DALYs represent a central tenet of cost-effectiveness analysis, which remains controversial.

The World Bank and the IMF required states to implement these favored policies as loan conditions. Structural adjustment programs drove economic reforms toward fiscal discipline and neoliberal policies, including reduced government spending, deregulation, privatization, consumption taxes, and trade liberalization.[16] IMF and World Bank loans had outsized influence, signaling to other donors whether governments were committed to responsible macroeconomics. With loan conditionality, the World Bank and the IMF held the power to unlock—or effectively block—other financing.

In their pursuit of deficit reductions, the bank and the IMF treated spending for armaments or prestige projects the same as spending for health and education, even though the latter would address immediate needs and have long-term economic payoffs. With governments choosing how to allocate the cuts, health ministries—traditionally weak entities—often lost out.

Reams of evidence suggest that neoliberal policies—reduced government spending, user fees, and public sector wage caps—had a devastating impact on public health. Health systems fell into disrepair, with health facilities becoming devoid of human resources and medicines, and infrastructure literally crumbling. Researchers found that user fees markedly reduced access to health care for the poor, whereas health service utilization would soar when fees were removed. In a 2010 speech, Margaret Chan summed up the harms: "User fees punish the poor. They are inefficient. They encourage people to delay seeking care until a condition is . . . far more difficult and expensive to treat. And when people do pay out of pocket for care, financial ruin can be the result."[17] Exemptions for the poor, moreover, rarely worked in practice. Hiring restrictions resulted in health worker unemployment, undermining capacity. In Tanzania, for example, only one in six health graduates joined the public health workforce from 1995 to 2005.[18]

Nonetheless, the World Bank and the IMF defended structural adjustment programs, arguing that the programs did not reduce health spending and worsen health but instead resulted in improved health and education.[19] And defenders of these policies argue that given the importance of economic growth to long-term poverty reduction, structural adjustment programs are "pro-poor."[20] Today officials schooled in neoliberal policies still impose fiscal austerity, resulting in underfunded health sectors.

Yet the consensus outside of the Washington Consensus is that these programs often eroded national health capacities, to devastating effect—although it would be a mistake to blame structural adjustment for all health system woes. As discussed earlier in this chapter, reduced revenue from falling commodity prices and spiraling debt repayment obligations also contributed (see Box 5.3).

To the Present: The World Bank Today

Today many of structural adjustment's most severe policies have been moderated. The World Bank has largely backed away from user fees.[21] Wage bill ceilings are now rare, and the bank now promotes increased health spending.[22] With these policy shifts, the bank's historically contentious relationship with civil society is improving. World Bank involvement with civil society grew in the mid-1990s as the bank hired civil society specialists and developed participation plans of action. By

BOX 5.3 Debt and Debt Relief

A spike in oil prices in the 1970s started a cascade of events ending with the travesty of poor countries spending less on health than on servicing their debts. Oil-rich countries deposited their earnings in Western banks, which were quick to offer generous loans to non-oil-producing states. In the late 1970s, wealthy countries raised interest rates and increased domestic agricultural subsidies. The result was a toxic mix of lower prices for Africa's agricultural exports—and hence lower revenue—and exploding debt service obligations. At the close of the 1990s, Tanzania was spending more than twice as much servicing its debt as on health care, while Zambia's debt service payments were nearly four times its health budget. All told, sub-Saharan African countries spent $15.2 billion in servicing debt to wealthy nations in 1998.[1]

Jubilee 2000, an international coalition in over forty countries, called for cancelation of third world debt by the dawn of the millennium. Advocacy for debt cancellation resulted in the 1996 Heavily Indebted Poor Countries (HIPC) Initiative, the Enhanced HIPC Initiative in 1999, and the G8's 2005 Multilateral Debt Relief Initiative. These initiatives established processes for successively reducing debt owed to wealthy creditors.

Building on earlier initiatives, the initial HIPC Initiative increased the level of bilateral debt relief available—and for the first time provided multilateral debt relief. To qualify, countries would have to implement structural adjustment programs, a requirement that slowed debt relief.

The 2005 G8's Multilateral Debt Relief Initiative proposed that the World Bank, the IMF, and the African Development Bank fully cancel the debt owed them by eligible HIPC countries—a proposal that the multilaterals accepted. By that time, most G7 countries had already canceled 100 percent of the bilateral debt of HIPC countries.[2]

Debt service levels are now far lower. Among the thirty-six HIPC countries that received debt relief by 2011, debt service payments had decreased to 5 percent of their revenue, down from 22 percent in 1999. Yet even after all of the initiatives, payments that could be used to improve the public's health instead flow to wealthy countries and Northern-based institutions. In 2008 the Jubilee USA Network, a successor to the Jubilee 2000 campaign, identified twenty-four low-income countries not part of the HIPC Initiative that required debt cancelation to meet the MDGs.[3]

NOTES

1. Kwesi Owusu et al., *Through the Eye of a Needle: The Africa Debt Report—A Country by Country Analysis* (London: Jubilee 2000 Coalition, 2000).

2. United Nations Economic Commission for Africa (UNECA), Economic and Social Council, *An Overview of Africa's Debt in the Context of the Highly Indebted Poor Countries (HIPCs) Initiative* (Addis Ababa: UNECA, Economic and Social Council, 1997).
3. World Bank, *HIPC Heavily Indebted Poor Countries Initiative: MDRI Multilateral Debt Relief Initiative*, prepared for spring 2012 meetings, http://siteresources.worldbank.org; Jubilee USA Network, *Transition Recommendations* (Washington, DC: Jubilee USA Network, 2008).

2009, 81 percent of its projects involved civil society.[23] In conjunction with its annual meetings, the bank holds civil society policy forums and offers scholarships to help representatives of developing countries attend.

Still, many in civil society remain distrustful, as evidenced by Oxfam's critique of the bank's support for private-sector health care. Gender Action, a World Bank and IMF watchdog group, criticizes the bank for failing to promote gender equity, such as making loans to mining projects in the Democratic Republic of Congo (DRC) that failed to address that nation's rampant gender-based violence, as well as the adverse health effects of privatizing mining enterprises.[24]

The 2012 election of Jim Kim as World Bank president represented a watershed. For the first time, one of civil society's own—a cofounder of Partners In Health and leader of the WHO's 3 by 5 treatment initiative—filled the bank's top position. Although still concerned about its policies, civil society began to view the bank more favorably. The new president's remarks at the 2013 World Health Assembly were emblematic of the bank's new tone, with Kim embracing "the grand spirit of Alma-Ata" and universal health coverage, and calling user fees "unjust and unnecessary."[25] Further, he has committed the bank to working to end absolute poverty in the world by 2030.[26]

Jim Kim's election marked a milestone in another respect: it reflected the growing economic strength—and political muscle—of developing countries and more equal South-North partnerships. Although Kim, the American nominee, was victorious, his election marked the first competitive elections for World Bank president—a position that had traditionally been chosen by the United States. He received a strong challenge from Nigeria's finance minister, Ngozi Okonjo-Iweala, who captured the votes of South Africa and Brazil. Okonjo-Iweala stressed the need for a "more open, transparent and merit-based" process to avoid "contributing to a democratic deficit in global governance."[27]

Transition and Lessons

The era of the World Bank's global health dominance offers important lessons. Technical and analytical expertise is important, but it is not value-neutral. Technical guidance and support are quite different when provided by an institution that has a right-to-health mission as opposed to an economic mission. Multisector capacities can expand an institution's potential for leadership, but that potential may go unrealized unless the sectors work collaboratively. Institutional power that extends beyond the health sector, such as the World Bank's connection to ministries of finance and its ability to leverage through loan conditions, greatly enhances its impact—but like any form of power, it can be exercised for good or ill.

The bank's neoliberal policies drew the ire of nonstate actors, including civil society and academics. However, these actors would have an increased role amid the proliferation of multistakeholder institutions and partnerships that is a defining feature of the next—and current—phase of global health institutions.

Phase Three: The Era of Partnerships

The loss of confidence in the WHO and doubts about the World Bank's effectiveness created space for the current era of global health institutions, led by multistakeholder partnerships. Broader concerns about inefficiencies in, and tensions among, UN agencies also drove these vast changes in global health architecture. UN agencies themselves recognized the need for partnerships to respond to the growing scope and complexity of the challenges they faced.[28] New sources of funding, chiefly from the Bill & Melinda Gates Foundation, emerged to give major new partnerships early financial backing.

Globalization has reshaped the institutional structure, revealing our interconnectedness, our common destiny, and the imperative of shared responsibility. The UN Millennium Declaration (2000) states that "in addition to our separate responsibilities to our individual societies, we have a collective responsibility to uphold the principles of human dignity, equality and equity at the global level."[29] The MDGs put AIDS, tuberculosis, and malaria, along with maternal and child mortality, at the center of the development agenda. This in turn catalyzed new institutional structures, including the Global Fund; the GAVI Alliance; Stop TB; Roll Back Malaria; and the Partnership for Maternal, Newborn and Child Health.

Globalization has also increased the recognition of how health hazards in one part of the world—e.g., an uncontained epidemic, a lax food safety regime—can exacerbate risks in another part of the world. Similarly, the globalization of culture and transnational corporations fans the spread of NCDs. These phenomena have elevated global health on political agendas, creating a complex landscape in which it is difficult for any single actor to dominate, and institutions are required to seek greater collaboration and inclusiveness.

Political leaders are not the only powerful actors affected by these vast changes. Philanthropists (e.g., Bill and Melinda Gates) and celebrities (e.g., Bono) have also been drawn to the field, seeking to leverage their resources and fame to save lives. Meanwhile, transnational corporations exert their influence—for good or bad—on health, in sectors ranging from pharmaceuticals to food and energy. Private industry has been thrust into this space as consumers demand healthier products and improved corporate responsibility.

The rise of NGOs also helps define this new era of partnerships. National democratization movements have spread to global institutions, with a demand for civil society participation. Meanwhile, bilateral development agencies began channeling significant funding through NGOs. Globalization strengthened transnational civil society movements, which focused on global social justice issues such as debt relief, structural adjustment, trade, and health inequalities.

The centrality of the AIDS movement, with its advocacy, networks, and community-based support, cannot be overstated (see Chapter 10). The AIDS movement's trailblazing strategies ushered in an era of civil society action, including partnerships that focused on maternal health (the White Ribbon Alliance for Safe Motherhood), tobacco control (the Framework Convention Alliance), and noncommunicable diseases (the NCD Alliance).

The AIDS pandemic was central to institutional development in another vital way: it was the trigger for unprecedented increases in global health funding. This funding, along with the social and economic effects of AIDS in all spheres of life, led to new institutions and programs, such as the Global Fund, UNAIDS, PEPFAR, and UNITAID, as well as a heightened focus on results and accountability. However, the flow of foreign funds to prevent and treat HIV/AIDS and the proliferation of AIDS projects also revealed—and contributed to—weaknesses in the global health architecture, presenting daunting challenges of fragmentation, neglected priorities, and unsustained funding.

This era is also characterized by a new set of principles. Governments realized that they had to do better to achieve the MDGs, with increased—and more effective—health financing. Reporting and other grant requirements were unduly burdening countries. And assistance often did not align with developing countries' priorities, while its unpredictability undermined countries' ability to effectively utilize aid.

To address these weaknesses, new principles emerged from a UN-driven process that was catalyzed by the 1995 Agenda for Development report from UN Secretary-General Boutros Boutros-Ghali and that culminated in the 2002 Monterrey Consensus on Financing for Development.[30] The principles that were agreed to in Monterrey, Mexico, have further evolved through periodic High-Level Forums on Aid Effectiveness, held in Rome (2003), Paris (2005), Accra (2008), and Busan (2011).[31]

The Paris Principles (contained in the 2005 Paris Declaration on Aid Effectiveness) cover five areas: (1) country ownership, meaning that countries establish their own strategies; (2) alignment, with development partners supporting country strategies and using local systems; (3) harmonization, meaning that development partners coordinate with each other and simplify their procedures; (4) results, with an emphasis on achieving measurable health improvements; and (5) mutual accountability, with countries and partners being accountable to one another.[32]

The Accra and Busan forums expanded and improved upon these principles, continuing an evolution toward recognizing developing countries as equal—and indeed, lead—partners in the development relationship, in charge of their own fates. The Accra Agenda for Action emphasized inclusiveness among all partners, along with capacity building. The Busan Partnership Agreement included South-South cooperation and highlighted the role of civil society, parliaments, and business. Most significantly, the Busan agreement represented a major shift in focus, from aid effectiveness—with its inherent division of the world into aid givers and aid receivers—to development cooperation.

I turn now to the hallmark feature of this third phase of global health institutions—namely, public-private partnerships—and will focus on the two partnerships that provide the most financing and innovations in governance: the Global Fund and the GAVI Alliance. Next, I will examine the impact of philanthropy, and the questions this raises, through a case study of the Gates Foundation. Finally, I will look at how global health institutions, new and old, are responding to contemporary dynamics and demands, including the growing force of civil society and the need for greater alignment with country priorities.

Defining Global Health Partnerships

Collectively, states continue to have a major influence on global health through their control of intergovernmental organizations such as the WHO and the World Bank. Their bilateral development agency funding represented two-thirds of total international health assistance in 2010.[33]

Although states remain powerful actors, the new global health landscape is increasingly influenced by partnerships—formally defined as "collaborative and formal relationship[s] among multiple organizations in which risks and benefits are shared in pursuit of a shared goal."[34] Behind this common definition lies extensive variety in composition and purpose, with diverse areas of focus and functions, such as "research and development, technical assistance and health service/system support, advocacy, coordination, and finance."[35] Many global health partnerships have close relationships with the WHO. Their governing boards include representatives from governments and intergovernmental agencies, but also from civil society, foundations, the private sector, and academia. A decade into the twenty-first century, there were more than one hundred global health partnerships.[36]

Not all global partnerships include for-profit representation—and even when they do, corporate representatives sometimes lack voting rights on governing boards. Still, partnerships often have corporate representatives on their boards, outnumbering representatives from NGOs and foundations. Furthermore, board members are disproportionately male and from the global North.[37]

Global health partnerships have often sought technical expertise, resources, and support from multiple stakeholders. For example, innovations in vaccines, medicines, and diagnostics require the collaboration of pharmaceutical companies to identify needs, ensure funding, and develop incentives. Addressing the problem of health worker migration and retention requires engaging health professionals, academics, and educators, as well as civil society, to increase political will.[38]

The Global Fund to Fight AIDS, Tuberculosis, and Malaria

At the turn of the millennium, the urgency and complexity of the AIDS pandemic signaled a need for innovations in governance, leading to the creation of the largest new global health financier: the Global Fund to Fight AIDS, Tuberculosis and Malaria. Despite persistent funding struggles, the Global Fund has proved to be a bold innovator, particularly with its embrace of civil society. It has also evolved to better align its funding with country strategies and is beginning to expand its scope to include country priorities beyond these three diseases.

History, Operations, and Results

The Global Fund was formed in response to an immense funding shortfall for HIV/AIDS programs at the turn of the twenty-first century. Although calls for AIDS treatment in poorer countries were becoming louder, funds were almost nonexistent. Prodded by advocates, the international community took a series of steps in 2000–2001 that culminated in the creation of the Global Fund. First, wealthy governments injected new urgency into HIV/AIDS funding at the 2000 G8 Summit in Okinawa, Japan. In April 2001 African heads of state held a summit in Abuja, Nigeria; there, UN Secretary-General Kofi Annan proposed "the creation of a Global Fund, dedicated to the battle against HIV/AIDS and other infectious diseases" and called for a "war chest" of $7 billion–$10 billion per year. The United States made the first pledge, $200 million, the following month. In June 2001 the UN General Assembly Special Session on HIV/AIDS endorsed the creation of a "global HIV/AIDS and health fund." The G8 Summit in July 2001 announced "a new Global Fund to fight HIV/AIDS, malaria and tuberculosis." The Global Fund began operations the following year, approving its first set of grants in April 2002.[39]

The Global Fund was established as an independent Swiss foundation. The decision to locate the fund outside the UN system was deliberate, reflecting concerns about UN bureaucracy, rivalries among UN agencies, and the political problems that the UN would have in turning down funding requests from its own members. Originally administered through the WHO, the Global Fund became autonomous in 2009.

During its first decade, the fund operated on a round system. Initially twice a year, and later annually, the fund would issue a call for proposals from low-income countries. Under the fund's demand-based model, country applicants were free to choose the interventions and the level of funding, as long as the proposals were technically sound and responded to country health needs—for example, focusing on marginalized populations in which the epidemics were concentrated. The Technical Review Panel (TRP), comprised of scientific experts, reviewed the proposals and issued recommendations to the board.

The Global Fund has been at the leading edge of results-based financing. Grant applications must include measurable targets for outcomes. Although grants were awarded for a five-year period, the board reviewed performance after two years, releasing additional funds only if there was adequate performance. In practice, the board denied continued funding only rarely, until an upsurge in denials began in mid-2010. If reports demonstrated poor performance, the fund's Secretariat could require corrective action and more frequent reporting.[40] Results-based financing has now become common in global health partnerships as well as in bilateral programs.

The shift to results-based financing raises the question of which outcomes should be measured. Do prominent numerical targets (e.g., the number of people on AIDS medication) divert attention from outcomes that are more difficult to measure, such as adherence to treatment or reduced stigma? Does a narrow focus on several diseases undermine the opportunity to address other challenges, such as child and maternal mortality or health system strengthening? The Global Fund has become attentive to these risks and has developed policies on both of those health priorities.

The fund's results have been impressive. By the end of 2012, a decade after providing its first grants, 4.2 million people in Global Fund–supported programs were receiving AIDS treatment. In addition, the fund had financed 310 million malaria prevention bed nets, treatment for 290 million cases of malaria, and detection and treatment of 9.3 million cases of tuberculosis. By its own calculations, through 2011 the fund had saved 8.7 million lives, having approved a cumulative $22.9 billion in grants to 151 countries. The fund has been a dominant global financier: it is the leading international funder for fighting tuberculosis and malaria—including providing 82 percent of international funds for tuberculosis programs in 2012 and 50 percent of funds for malaria programs in 2011—and is a major funder of AIDS programs.[41]

Civil Society and Governance

The Global Fund's progressive governance has served as a model for other institutions.[42] Its board comprises multiple constituencies—governments and nonstate actors, Northern and Southern representatives. Among its innovations, the fund's engagement with civil society warrants special attention. Three of the twenty voting board members are from NGOs: one representing communities living with the fund's target diseases, the second from a developing country, and the third from a developed country. The board also includes representatives from foundations and the private sector, with the remaining fifteen seats being held by representatives of governments (including major funders as well as governments from defined geographical regions). Multilateral organizations (e.g., the WHO, UNAIDS, and the World Bank) are nonvoting board members.

The Global Fund uses this inclusive approach in its local governance structure—in particular, through country coordinating mechanisms (CCMs). These multisector, multistakeholder committees develop Global Fund proposals, including soliciting input from community organizations and nominating "principal recipients" (grant recipients that disperse funds to stakeholders). CCMs also oversee grant implementation and ensure that grants are linked to national health programs.

The Global Fund requires CCMs to include members of communities living with the target diseases. Their own constituencies choose civil society and private sector representatives, not the government. The Global Fund considers it vital that at least 40 percent of CCM members be from nongovernmental constituencies. Further ensuring meaningful civil society engagement, CCMs must also document the role of "key populations"—such as women, men who have sex with men, migrants, sex workers, and injection drug users (IDUs)—in developing proposals.[43] In practice, however, the operation of CCMs has been variable, with problems in the areas of transparency, engagement, and gender inclusiveness.

An external review by the International Treatment Preparedness Coalition found that representatives from civil society "made notable contributions" and were treated as equal partners in some countries, but were often less influential than other representatives—either because they were reluctant to challenge government officials, lacked adequate knowledge, or simply were not treated as equals. This failure to harness the energy of civil society is not insurmountable. The coalition recommended several strategies, including capacity building of civil society, performance indicators to hold civil society representatives accountable, and separate civil society meetings to inform and empower their CCM representatives.[44]

Recognizing that countries might not adequately represent the needs of marginalized populations, the Global Fund permits non-CCM applications from NGOs. The fund also permits non-CCM proposals from failing states, such as those without a legitimate government, in conflict, or facing a humanitarian crisis.

Two innovations have deepened the fund's support for civil society. One is dual-track financing, whereby CCMs nominate both a governmental and nongovernmental principal recipient.[45] A second innovation is community systems strengthening (CSS)—activities designed to strengthen communities, ranging from service delivery to advocacy. Clusters of activity include partnerships; capacity building; service delivery; and planning, monitoring, and evaluation.

The Global Fund's approach raises fundamental questions about how best to support civil society engagement. To what degree does compliance with formal guidelines ensure meaningful involvement? Should the international community view national processes that lack genuine community participation as illegitimate? If so, how can institutions best identify inadequate engagement, and what should be the consequence? Finally, how can institutions ensure the input of disadvantaged groups such as indigenous peoples and persons with disabilities? In its 2012 reorganization, the Global Fund disbanded a six-person civil society support team in the Secretariat, devolving its functions to country-level teams. Will moving these functions to the national level foster civil society leadership or dilute it?[46]

Equity and Human Rights

Even as it grapples with these questions, the Global Fund's civil society engagement demonstrates a commitment to equity. In its 2011 round of grant approvals (which was ultimately canceled), the fund said it would "systematically include equity considerations into performance-based funding decisions." Also in 2011, the Global Fund broke its funding into two pools, "general" and "targeted," with 10 percent of funding allocated for the targeted pool, largely to address concentrated epidemics. Much of this funding is likely to target marginalized groups.[47] In 2008–2009 the fund developed highly regarded strategies on gender equality and on meeting the needs of sexual and gender minorities—though it has been criticized for insufficiently incorporating the needs and realities of women in the HIV pandemic into its monitoring and evaluation process.[48] Global Fund rounds in 2008 to 2010 saw successful proposals that addressed stigma and human rights. As part of its 2012–2016 strategic plan, the fund elevated human rights to one of five strategic objectives.[49]

The Paradox of Transparency, a Crisis, and a Transformation

In January 2011 the Associated Press reported on corruption uncovered by the fund's inspector general with the sensationalist headline "Fraud Plagues Celebrity-Backed Global Health Fund," claiming that the fund "sees as much as two-thirds of some grants eaten up by corruption." Yet only a minuscule part of the fund's portfolio was at issue—grants to four countries. Even the worst grants—for Mauritania, where two-thirds of funding disappeared through fake receipts and other fraud—had a total value of less than $8 million.[50]

The Global Fund's self-policing processes actually had worked. Internal mechanisms—an independent local fund agent in each country—uncovered the corruption. The fund investigated and took measures to recover misappropriated funds and stop corruption. The fund's inspector general announced the findings, and the fund had issued a news release the previous month stating that it had suspended two grants to Mali and terminated another. The fund also reported that it was placing grants from some countries, including Mauritania and Djibouti, under special scrutiny. In Mali, as a result of the fund's investigations, fifteen people were arrested and the health minister resigned. Mauritania and Zambia also launched criminal investigations.[51]

Paradoxically, the fund's commitment to transparency spurred another crisis: Sweden, Germany, and Ireland suspended payments to the fund. The fund's highly visible response to restore confidence included the forced resignation of Executive Director Michel Kazatchkine, who has now been replaced by Mark Dybul, former head of PEPFAR. The fund also announced financial safeguards and established an independent, high-level panel to propose improved financial controls and oversight. The fund accepted the panel's sweeping recommendations, which covered not only financial safeguards but also broader reform, such as streamlining grant processes, improving grant management, and revising governance.[52]

The fund's commitment to change bore fruit. Funders, including Germany, returned. Sweden, the first country to suspend Global Fund contributions, actually increased its contribution. Other funders, including Japan and the United Kingdom, provided new donations or accelerated existing ones.[53]

Following the panel's report, the fund adopted a five-year strategy that incorporated major structural changes to enhance grant management and impact. These changes include rebalancing staff from headquarters to the field, expanding country teams, and assigning three-quarters of the fund's approximately 600 staff to grant management. Special units will focus on high-disease-burden countries in Africa and Asia. The restructuring extended all the way up to the pinnacle of the organization, creating a new position of general manager.

The Challenges Ahead: Funding, Scope, and Emerging Economies

The persisting challenge of funding At its October 2010 replenishment conference (a periodic meeting of Global Fund contributors to pledge support), the fund sought $13 billion–$20 billion for 2011–2013—the lower figure to continue programs at the current pace, the higher figure to accelerate progress on the MDGs. Though the conference came only one month after countries pledged to provide "adequate funding" during the 2010 United Nations MDG Summit, pledges totaled only $11.7 billion.[54] Three years later, the Global Fund sought $15 billion for 2014–2016.[55]

The inadequate pledges, along with the global economic crisis and the corruption revelations, led the board to cancel Round 11 in November 2011, a month after its launch. Although the fund developed a transitional funding mechanism to maintain existing programs, countries would not be able to fund new programs. Within a year, however, the fund's reforms had mobilized several countries to resume and even increase their contributions, enabling plans for limited new funding in 2013. In mid-2013, the board approved the first three grants worth $622 million under a new funding model, explained below.[56]

In 2002, civil society proposed an "equitable contributions framework" to stave off what would become an annual funding struggle. The framework would have applied a common approach to funding by linking assessed contributions to global financing needs combined with national economic strength. The initial framework assumed that the private sector would donate $1 billion of an annual $10 billion needed, with the remaining $9 billion to be divided among the forty-eight countries rated "high" on the United Nations Development Program's Human Development Index.[57]

Although it was never adopted, the framework spurred advocates to demand enhanced financing from their governments; it also offered a model for a reimagined "Global Fund for Health," discussed later in this chapter. The fund's financing strategy through 2016 emphasizes "rapidly-industrializing middle-income countries and newly-industrialized or resource-rich economies," along with innovative funding mechanisms, corporate partnerships, and private donors.[58]

The fund is also seeking to ensure that its grants add to, rather than supplant, domestic health funding (the "additionality" principle). Recognizing the challenge of enforcing this principle, in 2011 the fund implemented a cofinancing policy in which a certain proportion of the budget for national disease programs had to come from domestic budgets, with progressively higher amounts based on a country's income category. The policy also required domestic disease spending and overall health spending to rise annually.

Aligning with country processes and strategies The Global Fund's approach has been an advance over traditional foreign assistance. Countries—often with health ministries in the lead—would apply for grants based on their needs, filling domestic funding gaps. As part of this needs-based approach, the fund did not limit demand or cap funding requests. This was a quantum improvement over donors funding standalone projects based on their own priorities. Yet the fund targets only three diseases, whereas countries must meet the full spectrum of health needs. In addition, the fund's round system of financing was disconnected from national budget cycles, and it burdened health ministries and partners with filling out lengthy, complex forms.

The Global Fund has sought to respond to shortcomings in aligning with country needs and processes. It now offers information sheets and tool kits to help applicants develop proposals. Civil society organizations, most prominently Aidspan, also developed guidance.[59] A technical service industry grew around the fund to assist in grant writing.

The Global Fund's 2012–2016 strategy represents a dramatic break from the round system, which is being replaced with an iterative process to better align with national processes, increase predictability, and speed grant disbursement. Under this new funding model, the fund will provide applicants with an indicative amount of funding for which they are eligible over a three-year period, though countries may also receive additional incentive funding to reward high-impact, well-performing programs. This will feed into a country dialogue that CCMs will use to develop a concept note for its funding request. Technically sound proposals will then form the basis of grant negotiation, leading to disbursement-ready grants awaiting only Board approval. Proposals that raise technical concerns, rather than being rejected, will be returned for revision and resubmission. Although this approach is new to the fund, the World Bank and other development agencies use similar processes.[60]

In the interest of aligning funding with national processes, applications should be based, wherever possible, on robust national strategic plans, developed through an inclusive, evidence-based process. Countries may still apply, however, in the absence of such a strategy.

Despite calls to expand its scope, the Global Fund's core focus is still on three diseases. The fund has progressed to include funding for health system strengthening and for maternal and child health. Applicants, however, must show how these resources would expand services to fight AIDS, tuberculosis, or malaria. Some countries, for example, have received funds to train new health workers, improve primary care, and collect health information.

Civil society advocates far more dramatic reform, notably a Global Fund for Health—i.e., expanding the current fund's scope to cover comprehensive health needs, or at least to fully incorporate the health-related

MDGs. A primary global financier could build on existing fund modalities, including inclusive governance. What makes this approach politically fraught is the problem of the existing fund's shortfalls. Expanding the fund's scope without assurances of sustainable funding could reduce support for the three diseases it currently targets, with grave consequences.[61]

Emerging economic powers Many formerly lower-income countries now have rapidly growing economies, with greater resources to devote to domestic health needs. The Global Fund board came under heavy criticism for making China—the world's second largest economy—the fund's fourth largest grant recipient. China has received Global Fund grants worth more than $830 million, yet it had provided only $16 million in contributions to the fund at the height of the controversy, a level that since increased to $30 million for pledges through 2013.[62]

In 2011 the board tightened eligibility requirements, limiting funding for middle-income countries while prioritizing funding for marginalized populations. Yet many advocates felt that these limits went too far, actually threatening marginalized populations. Without robust support, they argued, would countries like China and Vietnam continue harm-reduction programs for injection drug users? Would across-the-board limits on middle-income country funding undermine support for areas of greatest need? Countries with extremely high HIV burdens (e.g., South Africa, Nigeria, and India) are in the middle-income category.

In 2012 the board established a new approach to allocating funds, prioritizing countries with the highest disease burdens and the least ability to pay. It also called for investments in higher-income countries with lower disease burdens to target "most-at-risk" (marginalized) populations, such as IDUs.

The GAVI Alliance

Launched two years before the Global Fund, the GAVI Alliance—originally known as the Global Alliance for Vaccines and Immunizations—has faced similar challenges. It too endeavors to raise and effectively spend billions of dollars on a particular set of health challenges—vaccine-preventable diseases—with results measured in lives saved and children immunized. Yet the differences are significant as well. While the Global Fund addresses diseases mediated by social determinants, GAVI is more narrowly focused on ensuring the supply and delivery of vaccines tailored to the needs of developing countries. From their origins to their operations, the contrasts and congruencies between GAVI and the Global Fund are instructive.

GAVI's origins are atypical in that a private organization, the Gates Foundation, was at the heart of its formation. The Gates Foundation's keen interest in technology, cost-effectiveness, and measurable impact drove its investment in vaccination, a low-cost technology with proven potential to save millions of lives. The foundation, along with the World Bank, the WHO, and UNICEF, sought to refocus global support for vaccines as wealthier countries shifted their dollars elsewhere (e.g., to HIV/AIDS). In the late 1990s, nearly 30 million children in developing countries had not received basic vaccines, and newer vaccines were mostly unavailable. With the Gates Foundation's initial pledge of $750 million in 1999, the four institutions and other partners launched GAVI in 2000.[63] As with the Global Fund, an intergovernmental organization (UNICEF) initially hosted GAVI, and like the Global Fund, GAVI later became an independent Swiss foundation.[64] GAVI was founded with a threefold mission, geared toward low-income countries: expand basic vaccination coverage; accelerate vaccine use after its introduction in richer countries; and stimulate research.

From its founding through 2011, GAVI estimated that it had helped save more than 5.5 million lives and was on track to save 4 million more by 2015. Its vaccination programs had reached 370 million children. Hepatitis B vaccinations rank as one of GAVI's greatest successes, with coverage expanded in low-income countries from 17 percent in 2000 to 74 percent by 2009. Investments in vaccinations against measles, *Haemophilus influenzae* type b (Hib) (which causes meningitis and pneumonia), pertussis, and yellow fever had each saved more than 100,000 lives. GAVI has also supported vaccination against polio, pneumococcal disease, and rotavirus. The proportion of children in low-income countries receiving the basic childhood vaccine combination DPT3 (diphtheria-tetanus-pertussis) increased from 60 percent to 65 percent at GAVI's founding to 79 percent by 2012. Overall, GAVI commitments totaled $7.9 billion by mid-2012.[65]

GAVI supports countries in expanding coverage through its immunization support services, targeting infrastructure, including health worker training, vehicles, and a strengthened cold chain to keep vaccines at the proper temperature. GAVI supports safer injection practices, including auto-disposable syringes to prevent health workers from inadvertently transmitting diseases by reusing syringes. Ninety percent of the seventy-one countries receiving GAVI injection safety support reported that GAVI funding was critical to injection safety practices beyond immunization.[66]

GAVI also expands distribution of new and underused vaccines in low-income countries, which represents the bulk of its funding, nearly 84 percent through May 2012.[67] Initially focused on vaccines for Hepatitis B, Hib, and yellow fever, the vaccines available through this funding stream by 2012 had also come to include measles rubella, measles second dose, Meningococcal A conjugate, pneumococcal, and rotavirus. GAVI also supports human papillomavirus (HPV) vaccinations for girls to protect against cervical cancer, as well as the pentavalent vaccine, a conjugate vaccine combining DPT, Hepatitis B, and Hib.

In 2011 the highest country demand was for rotavirus vaccines to protect against a leading cause of diarrheal deaths (more than 450,000 per year) and for pneumococcal vaccines to protect against the bacteria that are the chief cause of pneumonia (responsible for more than 500,000 child deaths every year) and meningitis.[68] Prerequisites for applying for most new and underused vaccines are at least 70 percent DPT3 coverage and a policy to ensure sufficient immunization infrastructure. Funding, typically for four to five years based on a country's multiyear plan, is for the vaccines themselves and cash grants for dissemination (e.g., training, campaigns, and social mobilization).

Consistent with contemporary thinking, GAVI has established a funding stream for health system strengthening. GAVI encourages proposals on community and district-level systems required to deliver vaccines, in particular on the health workforce; drugs, equipment, and infrastructure; and organization and management. Support is tied to national health strategies, ranging from one to five years. Through 2010 GAVI committed $568 million to fifty-three countries for health system support.[69] Beyond immunization coverage, the support has also strengthened maternal and child health services.

Innovative Financing: Advance Market Commitments and the International Finance Facility for Immunization

Along with direct support for vaccination coverage, GAVI aims to reform the global market by reducing vaccine prices, ensuring adequate supply, and catalyzing vaccine development to meet the needs of poorer countries. By aggregating demand, improving predictability, and increasing funding, GAVI has incentivized manufacturers—especially in developing countries, where GAVI vaccine suppliers increased from one in 2000 to seven in 2010. With more companies entering the field, there has been increased competition and declining prices. Most dramatically, Hepatitis B vaccines fell from $0.56 to $0.18 per dose from 2000 to 2010, while pentavalent vaccine prices fell 29 percent from 2007 to 2011. By expanding the vaccine market, GAVI has also encouraged tiered pricing, where companies sell the same vaccine at a lower cost in low-income countries.[70]

GAVI strives to reform the vaccine marketplace through innovative financing. Its Advance Market Commitment (AMC) is designed to correct inherent weaknesses in the market, whereby manufacturers are dissuaded from investing in research on diseases found primarily in developing countries because of unpredictable markets. The AMC guarantees funding for these vaccines, spurring a market and catalyzing research and development as well as sufficient manufacturing capacity. Through the AMC, the pneumococcal vaccine costs GAVI $7.00 per dose initially, and $3.50 thereafter, a reduction of more than 90 percent compared to high-income country prices. GAVI estimates that by 2030 the AMC for pneumococcal vaccines will save seven million lives.[71]

The International Finance Facility for Immunization (IFFIm) is GAVI's other innovative financing mechanism. Established in 2006, the IFFIm works by selling bonds on capital markets, backed by long-term donor commitments to pay bondholders. Thus, GAVI receives up-front funding from bond purchasers, while donors pay back the bondholders over many years. The AMC ensures a long-term, predictable supply of vaccines, while the IFFIm provides both immediate and long-term funding for GAVI.

The IFFIm has proved a major source of funding, allowing GAVI to triple its average annual expenditure. From 2006 to 2011, the IFFIm raised $3.6 billion from bond sales—nearly half of GAVI's total funds—even as IFFIm donors paid only $600 million. Ten governments—chiefly the United Kingdom and France, but also South Africa and Brazil—had made legally binding commitments. The twenty-year-plus commitments are unprecedented for an aid agency.[72] An IFFIm-like mechanism to front-loading funds could benefit other global health financers (e.g., the Global Fund), covering financial gaps today, while emerging economies, with their rapid growth, cover larger shares tomorrow.

GAVI is on firmer financial footing than the Global Fund, in part due to the IFFIm, and in part due to its significantly lower funding requirements. The cost-effectiveness and measurable life-saving impact of vaccines make GAVI a particularly attractive investment. A 2011 pledging conference secured $4.3 billion in commitments through 2015, exceeding GAVI's $3.7 billion target.[73]

GAVI's Institutional Design: Comparisons with the Global Fund

Governance structures GAVI's governance structures share with the Global Fund a commitment to partnerships, but with details befitting GAVI's origins and mission to spur innovation. GAVI's four founding institutions—the Gates Foundation, the WHO, the World Bank, and UNICEF—have permanent board membership. With an eye toward harnessing innovation, the board includes vaccine industry seats, along with a health research and technical institute. One civil society representative holds a board seat, as do ten governments, evenly divided between developed and developing countries. Drawing on a feature common to corporate boards (and sensitive to being the rare global health board with voting privileges for corporations), GAVI's board includes nine individuals unconnected to its work, lending fundraising and other skills while embedding independent scrutiny within the board.

At country level, GAVI and the Global Fund have coalesced around a multishareholder model. GAVI requires an interagency coordinating committee (ICC) or similar health coordinating body to sign off on funding proposals. Unlike the Global Fund's CCMs (whose three diseases required new structures), ICCs typically predate GAVI. They are not subject to extensive guidelines on composition, as are CCMs.

The institutions take similar approaches to reviewing proposals. Like the TRP, GAVI's two independent review committees (IRCs)—one for new proposals and one for monitoring—are comprised of independent experts, providing legitimacy while helping ensure the quality of work. GAVI applications have a higher success rate than the Global Fund's, which may be attributable to the complexity of AIDS compared with vaccines, the IRC's discretion to give conditional approvals, and the IRC's considerable feedback for new proposals.

Finance GAVI has been a global health leader in innovative financing, even beyond the AMC and IFFIm. In 2011 GAVI launched a matching fund, whereby the United Kingdom's Department for International Development and the Gates Foundation offered to match donations from corporations, foundations, and their employees, customers, and business partners.

In addition, GAVI has been rigorous in its performance reviews. The IRC has been far more prepared than the Global Fund to find inadequate country performance, recommending against continued funding for 45 of 176 renewal requests in 2011.[74] Performance also affects how much funding countries receive. At the heart of GAVI's financing model is a basic formula: the more children covered, the more funds a country receives. After an initial investment for immunization support services, countries received $20 for every additional child to be immunized with DPT3. Better performance translates into more funds.

GAVI's health system funding is partially linked to performance as well. In 2011 GAVI's board decided that it would divide cash grants (as compared to direct procurements for vaccines and safe injection equipment) into two components: a fixed amount and a performance-based sum. Performance-linked grants require states to meet targets based on improved immunization coverage and equity. As with vaccine funding, health system support is capped, based on a country's birth cohort and per capita income.

GAVI's performance-based model and restrictive funding guidelines stand in contrast to the Global Fund's longstanding demand-driven funding, reflecting their different origins and missions. The Global Fund was developed chiefly to respond to health emergencies, making sustainability a lower priority initially. By contrast, GAVI funds the basic health services, and its cofounders included a bank and a foundation, making longer-term financing and ways to leverage GAVI's own funds an early concern. Under its new financing model, whereby a formula adjusted for qualitative factors will determine funding allocation, the Global Fund has moved closer to GAVI's approach. This comes as the global response to HIV/AIDS has transitioned from the emergency phase to a sustained response.

By strictly defining the confines of its support, GAVI is well positioned to predict its own financing needs while limiting its overall funding requirements. GAVI ensures country buy-in and puts states on the path toward national self-sufficiency by requiring government cofinancing, determined as a function of national income. The board can suspend a grant that is in default for more than a year until a country pays its cofinance share, although compliance is high. By late 2011 only the Democratic Republic of Congo (DRC) had yet to meet its 2010 cofinancing requirements. GAVI's Secretariat did not suspend the DRC's grants due to special circumstances but said it would not approve new grants until the DRC met its funding share.[75]

Are GAVI's financing restrictions good for global health? They preclude countries from receiving funds they might genuinely need, particularly for strengthening health systems, and may slow the introduction of new vaccines. At the same time, by setting clear expectations, GAVI gains consistent government buy-in while enhancing long-term sustainability. The Global Fund, by contrast, struggles with some governments that rely on international AIDS financing without significant domestic contributions—though it recently addressed this issue in its 2011 co-financing policy.[76]

Eligibility The number and nature of eligible countries also shape GAVI's finances. Only low-income countries are eligible for GAVI funding. By contrast, Global Fund grants can go to middle-income countries, although with increased restrictions.

The logic behind the different approaches can be traced to the nature and cost of the health threats each financer faces. The cost of fighting AIDS, particularly funding for treatment, can be substantial, whereas middle-income countries should be able to finance basic health services such as vaccines. Further, domestic politics may preclude funding marginalized populations, requiring an international response.

GAVI's eligibility limits contribute to its financial stability. The Global Fund struggles with adequate long-term financing. By contrast, GAVI's eligibility criteria can decrease the number of funding applicants. Economic growth often propels poorer states into the middle-income category, making them ineligible for GAVI funding. By 2013, of the seventy-three countries initially eligible for GAVI funding, seventeen were no longer eligible.[77]

Accountability In a world where there is intense competition for funds as well as countries still plagued by corruption, GAVI and the Global Fund are both committed to preventing and responding to corruption. Both organizations will suspend grants that are being misused, and may terminate a grant if corruption or other misuse is confirmed. Countries are required to keep careful records of how they expend funds. Under its 2009 Transparency and Accountability Policy, GAVI assesses a country's financial controls before initiating funding, addressing weaknesses and regularly assessing grant operations. GAVI recipients must conduct annual financial audits. The Global Fund, meanwhile, works with a local fund agent in each country to verify audits and investigate suspected misuse of funds.

The performance-based approach of both organizations adds a layer of accountability. Both agencies require misappropriated money to be returned, and both publicly report grant suspensions. GAVI instituted a transparency policy on reporting suspended grants in 2011.[78] GAVI's rules, like the Global Fund's, help prevent, detect, and respond to misuse.

There is one significant distinction between the approaches GAVI and the Global Fund take to corruption. Although the Global Fund may terminate a grant entirely, GAVI continues to fund vaccines even when it suspends cash grants for system support since GAVI funds UNICEF directly to purchase vaccines.

Civil society Civil society has had a major role in the Global Fund from the beginning, due to its advocacy for creating the fund and the AIDS movement's historic social mobilization. By contrast, with its funding initially channeled exclusively to UNICEF and governments, GAVI had limited civil society engagement at its outset. This is changing, however, as it becomes clear that community support is essential for vaccination programs. In recent years, GAVI has piloted mechanisms that engage civil society organizations in service delivery (immunizations, child health care, and health system strengthening), raising community awareness, and outreach to remote populations.[79] Broadening eligibility in 2012, the GAVI board decided that NGOs could receive funding directly, primarily through health systems funding.[80] GAVI's civil society constituency developed a fifteen-member steering committee in 2010 and established a civil society forum, engaging civil society in its advocacy and fundraising efforts.[81]

Foundations: Reaching New Heights

Foundations have long had a historic role in global health, none deeper than that of the Rockefeller Foundation, founded in 1913 by the oil magnate John D. Rockefeller. Global health was a core area of its work supporting malaria and yellow fever research, developing medical systems in China as well as the China Medical Board, and financing medical schools—all in its first decade.[82] The Rockefeller Foundation would later support the work of agronomist Norman Borlaug, whose innovations led to high-yield varieties of wheat and rice that sparked the Green Revolution. Today the foundation advocates for universal health coverage and supports health system strengthening, including using mobile phones, laptop computers, and other information technologies in the emerging field of eHealth.

The Rockefeller Foundation's century of funding is testament to the impact that an entrepreneur with a vision can have on global health. Its work has at times been controversial: in the late 1970s, the foundation mobilized UNICEF and the World Bank behind selective primary health care only a year after the Alma-Ata Conference.[83]

The Bill & Melinda Gates Foundation

No private foundation today has greater influence or resources than the Bill & Melinda Gates Foundation, founded in 1994 by the cofounder of Microsoft. Melinda Gates shares in the foundation's leadership, as does Warren Buffett, following his 2006 pledge of $31 billion in annual installments. In 2012 the foundation's assets exceeded $37 billion.[84]

Of the $26 billion the foundation had distributed by September 2011, more than $15 billion was for global health, with much of the rest going to education in the United States and to international development. Of the $3 billion allocated in 2011 alone, $2 billion went to global health.[85]

The foundation makes grants based on the potential for impact on neglected or underfunded diseases that burden developing countries. In 2011 one-third of its global health funding was for polio and vaccines and 30 percent for HIV and other infectious diseases, with the rest for family health, policy and advocacy, and research and development.[86] The foundation supports tobacco control in Africa, India, and China as well as major HIV programs in the two Asian giants.[87]

Like those of the World Bank and bilateral aid agencies, the foundation's grants extend beyond health care to nutrition, clean water and sanitation, and agricultural development (nutritious and productive staple crops, data collection, and research, as well as improving smaller farmers' access to markets). The foundation's work reflects its penchant for technical solutions, such as supporting nutrient-fortified crops.

Filling a Niche: Innovation

The Gates Foundation epitomizes the role of foundations in innovation, emphasizing that it is "passionate about the potential for innovation to transform global health at every level. Innovation in basic science may lead to big breakthroughs, but equally important is innovation in how we deliver affordable and effective health tools to those who need them."[88] The foundation has invested heavily in research for drugs and vaccines against HIV, malaria, and tuberculosis.

Its penchant for cost-effectiveness has driven support for the Health Metrics Network to improve health program evaluation and for vaccines against childhood diseases such as pneumonia and diarrhea. In 2010 the foundation pledged $10 billion for vaccine research, development, and delivery, seeking to catalyze additional funding to scale up vaccine coverage in developing countries to 90 percent of children under five, which could save an additional 7.6 million lives by the end of the decade.[89]

As an independent organization, free from political pressures that constrain governments, the foundation is able to make long-shot investments. Its Grand Challenges in Global Health, launched in 2003, promoted a variety of key innovations, such as vaccines that do not require refrigeration, needle-free vaccine delivery, and abatement of disease-transmitting insects.[90]

The foundation followed this initiative with Grand Challenges Exploration grants. Winning projects have included low-power microwaves to kill malaria-transmitting mosquitoes.[91] The foundation also launched a contest to develop a "next generation" of low-cost toilets that do not require piped water or electrical or sewer connections and transform human waste into useful resources. First prize went to a solar-powered toilet that generated electricity.[92]

The foundation's R&D investments are yielding results. For example, a $70-million grant in 2001 jump-started the Meningitis Vaccine Project to develop a vaccine against the form of meningococcal meningitis responsible for most meningitis epidemics in Africa.[93] Children in several West African states began receiving the vaccine in late 2010.

Filling a Niche: Taking the Long View

One of the foundation's top priorities is polio eradication.[94] Successful eradication would not only end a disease that once caused paralysis in hundreds of thousands of children annually, but would also be less expensive than controlling the disease over the long run. Less than a quarter-century in, the eradication effort has reduced cases by 99 percent, saving 250,000 lives and preventing 5 million cases of paralysis.[95] Only two other diseases, smallpox and the "cattle plague" rinderpest, have been eradicated.

The foundation invested $358 million in polio eradication in 2011, more than for any other disease. It joined Rotary International as the main nongovernmental funder of the Global Polio Eradication Initiative, with the two groups collectively contributing nearly as much as the G8 countries in 2012–2013.[96] The foundation's investments in polio highlight its focus on innovation, including improved surveillance systems, a better vaccine, and new drugs should polio reemerge.

Final eradication has encountered obstacles in the three remaining endemic countries in 2013, in the form of distrust about vaccine safety and violence in Nigeria, Afghanistan, and Pakistan, including murders of polio workers. The polio virus has also been imported into previously polio-free countries, including, in 2012/2013, Somalia, Kenya, Niger, and

Chad—part of the "wild poliovirus importation belt" from West Africa to the Horn of Africa. The Syrian civil war created the conditions for polio outbreaks in 2013. Despite these setbacks, the number of polio cases fell to a record low (223) in 2012. India was declared polio-free in January 2012.[97]

Beyond Niches: Leveraging Influence through Partnerships and Advocacy

The Gates Foundation seeks to maximize impact by finding niches that yield major benefits, as with research and polio eradication. Another strategy is to leverage investments of other actors, including support for partnerships such as GAVI and the Global Fund. In 2012 the foundation issued a legally binding $750 million promissory note through 2016 to help the Global Fund through its greatest financial challenge.[98]

Also in 2012 the Gates Foundation launched—along with the WHO, the World Bank, other aid agencies, and health ministries—the largest coordinated effort ever undertaken to control five neglected tropical diseases and eliminate or eradicate five others by 2020. The foundation solicited pharmaceutical companies, which will donate billions of doses of drugs and share compounds with the Drugs for Neglected Diseases initiative, a public-private partnership to facilitate drug development.[99]

Beyond partnerships, the foundation supports NGOs (e.g., the ONE Campaign) that advocate for global health reform and greater government funding. The foundation aims to raise the profile of global health and demonstrate its successes, especially in the United States—for example, by funding the 2005 PBS series *Rx for Survival* and the multimedia initiative *Living Proof Project: U.S. Investments in Global Health Are Working*.[100]

Private Influence: Critiques of the Gates Foundation

The Gates Foundation's power raises serious questions about governance and accountability. How much influence is appropriate for a handful of wealthy individuals who represent no constituency and are not formally accountable? The foundation's modus operandi of leveraging partnerships and funding the WHO gives it outsized influence over the global health agenda not only through its own resources, but also by influencing other actors. Its earmarked voluntary contributions of more than $466 million for the WHO's 2010–2011 budget represented nearly 10 percent of the agency's entire revenue, making the Gates Foundation the largest contributor after the United States.[101] This funding affects how the WHO uses its staff, which partners it funds, and possibly even its recommendations.

In 2007 the head of the WHO's malaria department, Dr. Arata Kochi, expressed concern that the Gates Foundation pressured the WHO to support a particular malaria intervention—intermittent preventive treatment for infants—despite doubts among scientists, a charge the foundation denied. Dr. Kochi observed that by dominating research funding, the foundation could skew research in the direction it favored, reducing the independence of the scientific process.[102]

The Gates Foundation's health priorities are all immensely important. But even as the foundation is at the cutting edge, notably absent is funding for injuries, NCDs (other than tobacco control), mental health, and health systems. Is the Gates Foundation doing the world a service by ensuring that family health, food security, clean water and sanitation, and the eradication of infectious diseases are advanced, or is it impeding funding and advocacy for NCDs and health systems? And does its focus on technological solutions divert attention from more structural drivers of inequality?

The fact that the Gates Foundation is directly accountable to so few people—Bill and Melinda Gates, joined by Warren Buffett in 2006, are its only trustees—amplifies questions about its influence. To broaden the voices guiding the foundation, it has established an advisory panel of global health luminaries and seeks external review of grants.

The immense assets of the Gates Foundation give it another form of influence, in supporting private companies. A 2007 *Los Angeles Times* investigation revealed that the foundation invested heavily in companies responsible for pollution, including the oil companies responsible for toxic air pollution in Nigeria's Delta region. As one local doctor put it, "We're smokers here . . . but not with cigarettes." The *LA Times* asserted, "Gates Foundation investments—totaling at least $8.7 billion, or 41% of its assets—have been in companies that countered the Foundation's charitable goals or socially concerned philosophy." The foundation also invests heavily in pharmaceutical companies—despite criticism that their advocacy for strong intellectual property protection impedes access to medicines. Its support for beverage and food giants (e.g., Coca-Cola and Kraft) ignores their intense marketing of sugary beverages and unhealthy foods.[103]

Despite adverse publicity, the foundation has declined to change its investment policies. While the foundation reports that Bill and Melinda Gates have "defined areas in which the endowment will not invest, such as companies whose profit model is centrally tied to corporate activity that they find egregious," the only specific example is tobacco. The foundation did follow the lead of several universities to divest from companies connected with the genocidal government in Sudan.[104]

Should foundations be held to the same standards of good governance as public entities? Other premier institutions such as the Global Fund and GAVI post grant proposals online, whereas the Gates Foundation does not. With its limited transparency and participation in its decision making, the foundation requires reform. How can global governance capture the immense resources and ingenuity of towering figures such as Bill Gates, Bill Clinton, and Michael Bloomberg (see Box 5.4) while ensuring that they do not skew priorities or divert attention from the underlying drivers of inequality?

The significance of these questions deepens with the "Giving Pledge," asking billionaires to donate at least 50 percent of their wealth to charity. As of 2013, the number of families signing the pledge had surpassed one hundred.[105] What funds will they put toward global health?

BOX 5.4 More Niches for Foundations

The Clinton Foundation and HIV/AIDS

A year after its 2001 launch, the Clinton Foundation formed the Clinton Health Access Initiative (CHAI) to lower AIDS treatment costs. Whereas Bill Gates tackled disease through his wealth, President Clinton—like President Jimmy Carter through the Carter Center—used the weight of his former office and relationships. CHAI helped to dramatically lower antiretroviral (ARV) prices for first-line medications[1] through bulk purchases and accurately predicting ARV demand, while enabling manufacturers to secure raw materials at reduced prices and use improved production methods. The initiative also encouraged new companies to manufacture ARVs, increasing competition.[2]

In 2005 few HIV-infected children in developing countries were being treated—only one in forty, compared with one in eight adults. CHAI expanded pediatric AIDS treatment by increasing health worker training, collaborating with pharmaceutical companies, and intervening in the pediatric AIDS drug market, lowering costs and increasing access. Between 2005 and 2011 the number of children on AIDS treatment in CHAI countries had increased more than thirtyfold.[3]

CHAI has followed the trend toward a broader health system focus. In 2010 it separated from the Clinton Foundation to become the Clinton Health

Access Initiative. While continuing its work on treatment access, CHAI strengthens health systems, increases the supply of trained health workers, and expands testing and drugs for malaria and tuberculosis.

Bloomberg Philanthropies: Tobacco Control

Former New York mayor and entrepreneur Michael Bloomberg is making his greatest global health mark in tobacco control, through his Bloomberg Philanthropies. An initial $125 million pledge in 2006 from the Bloomberg Family Foundation, the main funding vehicle of Bloomberg Philanthropies, to launch a global campaign encompassed prevention and cessation, surveillance, and policy reform.[4]

In 2007 the foundation joined forces with the WHO to expand tobacco control policies, contributing $375 million to "monitor tobacco use and prevention policies, protect people from tobacco smoke, offer help to quit tobacco use, warn about the dangers of tobacco, enforce bans on tobacco advertising, promotion, and sponsorship, and raise taxes on tobacco." This initiative focused on fifteen countries—including Russia, China, India, Brazil, and Mexico—in which two-thirds of all smokers live. As the tobacco industry moved to oppose antismoking laws, in 2012 the foundation pledged $220 million to support lower-income countries in developing antismoking policies and litigation against Big Tobacco. This next phase of Bloomberg Philanthropies' fight against tobacco will focus on five low- and middle-income countries with particularly high levels of tobacco consumption: Bangladesh, China, India, Indonesia, and Russia.[5]

NOTES

1. "HIV/AIDS," Clinton Foundation, http://www.clintonfoundation.org/our-work/clinton-health-access-tinitiative/programs/hivaids (accessed 10/10/13).
2. "Business Approach," Clinton Health Access Initiative, http://www.clintonhealthaccess.org/about/stories/business-approach (accessed 10/10/13).
3. "Pediatric Aids," Clinton Foundation, http://www.clintonfoundation.org/our-work/clinton-health-access-initiative/programs/pediatric-aids (accessed 10/10/13); WHO, *Global HIV/AIDS Response: Epidemic Update and Health Sector Progress towards Universal Access* (Geneva: WHO, 2011), 162.
4. Diane Cardwell, "Bloomberg Donating $125 Million to Anti-Smoking Efforts," *New York Times*, August 15, 2006, http://www.nytimes.com/2006/08/15/nyregion/15cnd-bloom.html.
5. Bloomberg Philanthropies, *Accelerating the Worldwide Movement to Reduce Tobacco Use* (New York: Bloomberg Philanthropies, 2011); Michael Bloomberg, "Bloomberg Philanthropies Commits $220 Million to Fight Tobacco Use," March 22, 2012, http://www.mikebloomberg.com/index.cfm?objectid=3A9E3B81-C29C-7CA2-F32D-97DE06EC82C7; "Tobacco Control," Bloomberg Philanthropies, http://www.bloomberg.org/initiative/tobacco (accessed 10/10/13).

Principles of Good Governance and Aid Effectiveness

How have older institutions such as the WHO, the World Bank, and bilateral agencies responded to the shift to country-ownership and inclusive partnerships—far from the traditional government-to-government, donor/recipient paradigm? We saw earlier how the WHO's reform process is searching for greater inclusiveness (see Chapter 4) and how the World Bank is engaging civil society. The WHO and the World Bank are also part of a larger collaborative of health agencies, the Health Eight (see Box 5.5). Bilateral agencies are conforming to principles of aid effectiveness and good governance. The International Health Partnership (IHP+) is the most significant collaborative effort to date, explicitly drawing on the Paris Principles.

International Health Partnership (IHP+)

Governments from the developed and developing world joined with global health institutions (e.g., the WHO, the Global Fund, and GAVI)

BOX 5.5 **The Health Eight (H8)**

From catalyzing aid effectiveness to sparking new partnerships, the MDGs will leave an immense institutional imprint. The MDGs also led to a collaborative of leading global health institutions known as the Health Eight (H8). Formed in 2007 to reach the MDGs, the H8 consists of the WHO, the World Bank, UNICEF, UNFPA, UNAIDS, the Global Fund, GAVI, and the Gates Foundation. The H8 serves as a forum for joint advocacy and sharing lessons. It has called for the G8 to prioritize the MDG health agenda[1] and to increase investments in health information "to better monitor and evaluate progress and performance."[2] While embracing collaboration, the group has shunned transparency, not sharing its agenda and issuing few public statements.[3] In so doing, the H8 risks engendering distrust and being viewed as an elite club making decisions behind closed doors.

NOTES

1. World Health Organization (WHO), "G8 Urged to Act on Food Crisis and Health," *Bulletin of the World Health Organization* 86, no. 7 (2008): 497–576.
2. Health Metrics Network, "Health Information 'Tribes' Unite behind Bangkok Call to Action," February 5, 2010, http://www.who.int/healthmetrics/news/weekly_high lights/ghif_2010_call_to_action/en/index.html.
3. Sandi Doughton, "Global-Health Stars Converge on Seattle," *Seattle Times*, June 17, 2009, http://seattletimes.com/html/health/2009348027_healthdavos17m0.html.

and the Gates Foundation in 2007 to form the International Health Partnership, and soon became an umbrella for several other health initiatives, and was dubbed IHP+. Its goal is to make health assistance more effective by improving donor coordination and alignment with national plans and processes while elevating support for health systems. While not guaranteeing funds to fully implement national health plans—a point of NGO criticism—IHP+ aims to increase health funding indirectly by demonstrating its effectiveness. Reflecting the growing strength of civil society, the IHP+ incorporated NGO representatives into its loose governing structures.

Central to the IHP+ is that all partners should support a single national health strategy, avoiding duplication, fragmentation, and high transaction costs while fostering national leadership. Funders commit to coordinate in support of national strategies, for example by sharing a single results framework. This goal resulted in the most tangible IHP+ initiative, the Joint Assessment of National Strategies (JANS) process, under which the host government, civil society, and development partners collectively review national health strategies. JANS could improve quality and give partners the confidence to directly align their support.[106] Good governance principles such as effectiveness and efficiency, transparency and inclusion, financial management, equity, and high-level political commitment infuse the evaluations.[107]

How has the IHP+ fared? The growing number of partners—from twenty-six initially to fifty-nine by mid-2013, including thirty-three developing countries[108]—indicates that countries see benefits to participating. In 2012 an independent consortium, IHP+Results, reported significant progress in country ownership, but less in aid effectiveness.[109]

Phase Four: Tomorrow's Global Health Institutions

The complexity and multiplicity of global health institutions are here to stay. Yet the evolution of institutions also demonstrates the inevitability of change. Whether that change will stifle progress toward global health with justice (e.g., through funding cuts, unhealthy competition, and siloed programs) or advance it (e.g., through enhanced resources, innovation, and impact) depends on governments, their constituencies, and advocates. As geostrategic power blocs shift, the dynamic tension between the global South and the global North could assume new forms. Will this dynamic benefit all or chill progressive reform?

The Rising Tide of Emerging Economies: Shifting Power, New Opportunities, and New Perils

Few changes have greater implications for institutions than the rising tide of newly powerful states—both economically and politically. As states in Africa, Asia, and Latin America transition from low- to middle-income status, they continue to have pressing health needs despite their expanding resources. At the same time, they have new-found influence over the governance and direction of institutions as they vie with high-income states for control over the global health agenda.

The 70 percent of poor people living in middle-income countries have vast health needs.[110] Even with greater economic wherewithal, these countries are unable to fully meet the demand for health services. How should institutions respond? Should they, like GAVI, concentrate solely on the poorest countries? Or, following the policy of the Global Fund, should funding be available, but with stricter requirements, for middle-income countries as well? Is there a risk that, without international funding, middle-income states will neglect marginalized populations?

Economic growth and a desire for a spot on the world stage are leading the BRICS and other emerging economies to exert greater political influence. Bilateral foreign assistance is not new to the BRICS countries, but it is rising. China, for example, has sent health workers abroad since 1963—more than 21,000 in the past half-century—and its malarial control work in Africa dates back three decades.[111] But in the first decade of the twenty-first century, China vastly expanded its malaria control efforts. Beyond discrete health programs, China has exerted influence in Africa by building infrastructure (e.g., roads, bridges, hospitals) while drawing on the continent's natural resources to fuel its own domestic industrialization.

Characteristic of the transition to donor status, disbursing billions of dollars, middle-income countries are creating or expanding bilateral development agencies, including the Brazilian Cooperation Agency, the Mexican Agency for International Development Cooperation, the Indian Agency for Partnership in Development, and the South African Development Partnership Agency.[112]

Emerging states have also contributed to global institutions, but often too little relative to their economic capacity. Russia has contributed more than $200 million to the Global Fund, while Brazil delivers most development assistance through multilateral institutions. Margaret Chan has encouraged middle-income countries to allocate more resources to the WHO's budget and programs. Although middle-income states have yet to make a major commitment to multilateral assistance, they nonetheless want to help steer the direction of major institutions.

Innovative Financing

If twentieth-century global health was effectively financed out of state treasuries—whether given bilaterally or multilaterally—twenty-first-century global health must find creative ways to increase resources. Will the number of innovative financing mechanisms for health, such as GAVI's AMC and the IFFIm, grow? Advocates have pressed for new sources of revenue, whether through taxes on air travel and financial transactions, or through increased levies on cigarettes, alcoholic beverages, and even sugary drinks. As the AMC demonstrates, innovative financing can not only raise needed funds, but also drive innovations. Might future innovative financing have effects beyond the level of funds available? Could such funds be designed to encourage inventive ways to reach marginalized populations, increase accountability, or address other governance shortcomings?

Will these new funding sources ease the struggle for resources that has plagued institutions such as the WHO and the Global Fund? If they do, will advocates' calls for a Global Fund for Health move closer to reality? Will health financiers move to new areas of health funding—from AIDS and infectious diseases to injuries, mental health, and NCDs? Might funding pivot to health systems and deeper socioeconomic determinants? Will the goal of international health financing move even slightly, from overall reductions in morbidity and mortality to narrowing unconscionable disparities? And will resources shift to civil society, with an emphasis on democracy building and human rights?

A dimmer funding scenario is possible. Will long-term budget austerity in North America and Europe lead to scarcer international health assistance? Will new funding sources go to reducing deficits and to other priorities—even ones critical to health, such as combating climate change?

Anarchy versus Order in the Global Health Landscape: Toward a Global Fund for Health?

Scholars lament the deep fragmentation in the global health landscape. While the WHO Constitution enshrines the agency as the "directing and coordinating authority on international health work,"[113] the agency has not lived up to that expectation. At the same time, David Fidler famously characterized global health governance as "architecture amidst anarchy."[114]

Two future scenarios seem possible, with the debate over a Global Fund for Health epitomizing the disparate visions. Such a fund would guide the field toward two sought-after goals: pooling funding to build sustainable health systems and aligning international assistance with national health strategies. This is the direction in which institutions and partnerships are already moving, albeit slowly. Pooled funding would promote universal health coverage and integrated health programming. A major pooled global health funder would be better positioned to guide stakeholder cooperation around a single set of country-led priorities.

Opposition to a Global Fund for Health rests largely on a realpolitik conception of global health. If donor states could not directly trace the health impact to feed back to their electorates or direct resources to their own priorities, or even to their own NGOs, would the political community cut back on funding? And in a world of scarcity, would existing actors balk at a monolithic agency taking the lion's share of funding? History rejects the idea that existing institutions would agree to take a back seat. No major global health institution in recent history has closed or merged.

What seems at least possible is a compromise between these two visions. While there might be a *primary* global health funder, there surely will not be a *single* funder. The global health landscape may become more orderly, with greater alignment, but its diversity is likely to remain—and with good reason. Global health is a complex endeavor. Its ambit ranges from health systems to clean water and nutritious food. It is structured through dynamic programs and institutions with multiple layers. It spans multiple sectors, including agriculture, energy, trade, transportation, and the environment. No single institution has the capacity or expertise to direct a massive global health enterprise.

Questions and Opportunities

While current trends give clues to future directions—even more diversity of actors, greater respect for country-led approaches, more inclusiveness—major questions remain. Will there be a Global Fund for Health, with increasing proportions of assistance channeled through such a fund? Or will countries seek to control most of their own funding, leading to perhaps a more robust approach, similar to that taken by IHP+? Will states continue to give primarily tied funding to the WHO, weakening its ability to direct its own course?

Perhaps of even greater consequence, how will global health institutions interact with other regimes, such as investment, trade, and migration? Multiple regimes become increasingly important to health as globalization, development, and climate change shape health outcomes everywhere. Meanwhile, deep connections between key social issues (e.g., education, employment, and social security) and health highlight the importance of cross-sector engagement. Echoing the power transition from the G8 to the G20 in international affairs, might the H8 expand to become an H20, encompassing institutions in other regimes?

Amid the uncertainties are also new opportunities. The Paris Principles and their successors, including the Busan Partnership Agreement and its shift from aid to development cooperation, could transform global health institutions. Beyond realizing these principles, global health institutions could go beyond combating discrete diseases toward genuine assurance of the conditions in which people can be healthy—e.g., sanitation, hygiene, clean water, nutritious food, and vector control. And they could gain a renewed focus on justice, with its attention to the needs of the poor and disadvantaged. To achieve "smarter" funding, better coordination, country ownership, and equity, global health institutions will need improved governance: transparency, monitoring, evaluation, and accountability. And to achieve all of these goals they will need to embrace civil society—not only in their governance, but also as catalysts for resources and new ideas. These are the opportunities that global health architects—from international civil servants to community health advocates—must seize.

PART III

International Law and Global Health

HAVING EXAMINED HEALTH INEQUITIES in a globalized world and the key global health institutions, I now turn to the core sources of law in global health. The method of development in Part III reflects the definition of global health law developed in Chapter 3. First, Part III describes the two major WHO normative treaties. The International Health Regulations (IHR), discussed in Chapter 6, manage the worldwide response to rapidly emerging health threats of international concern, such as pandemic influenza. Dating back to the mid-nineteenth century, the IHR represent the primary global strategy for "health security." The WHO's most recent treaty is devoted to tobacco use—the single most preventable cause of premature death globally. The Framework Convention on Tobacco Control (FCTC), dealt with in Chapter 7, requires both supply- and demand-side policies to prevent tobacco-related diseases such as cancer, cardiovascular disease, and respiratory diseases.

Chapter 8 examines the international human rights law regime—both the right to health and a variety of "health-related" rights, such as the right to food, water, and life itself. As the right to health is a central element of this book's thesis, the chapter systematically explores the interconnections between health and human rights. It draws attention to the well-understood deficiencies in the precision of human rights norms, as well as the deficits in monitoring, compliance, and accountability. Yet, consistent with this book's approach, the chapter shows how the right to health could be more robust, paving the way for meaningful improvements in health and in health justice.

Part III concludes with a consideration of the contentious relationship between trade and health in Chapter 9. The adverse health effects of trade liberalization are among the most persistent and deeply felt global health narratives. The emergence of neoliberalism, often associated with the World Bank, was profoundly unpopular within civil society. This narrative holds, with good reason, that trade and intellectual property (IP) protection benefit primarily the global North, weakening health systems in the South. The World Trade Organization (WTO) forms the architecture for the modern trade system, which wealthy countries and multinational corporations fiercely defend. This political and philosophical division is marked by the idea that trade "raises all boats" by fueling prosperity versus the idea that trade disadvantages the weak, while IP protection makes essential medicines unaffordable for the poor. The truth, of course, is somewhere in between these two extremes, but there is a growing recognition that lower-income countries do not get a fair deal. The WTO has responded by asserting the right of sovereign states to enact public health laws, together with so-called TRIPS flexibilities in the Doha Declaration on IP. The fact that the Doha Round of trade talks has been in stalemate shows that the North/South divide remains politically charged.

CHAPTER 6

The International Health Regulations

Responding to Public Health Emergencies of International Concern

THE WORLD HEALTH ASSEMBLY (WHA) adopted the revised International Health Regulations (IHR) on May 23, 2005—the only international rules governing global health security.[1] The assembly's historic vote came at a time when public health, security, and democracy became intertwined, addressed at the highest levels of government. Former UN Secretary-General Kofi Annan envisaged the IHR as moving humanity toward a "larger freedom."[2]

What were the critical factors that galvanized states to create international rules to govern global health security?

Traditionally, public health powers resided in sovereign states. Political leaders, however, came to realize that states acting in isolation could not control the spread of infectious diseases, as trying to stop health threats at the border proved futile. Instead, states could better protect their populations through early detection of health hazards and containment at their source.

Prompt identification and control of diseases required both national and international action. Domestically, all states had to develop a sound public health system for surveillance and response. Absent a national public health infrastructure, diseases would escape detection and move swiftly in international traffic and along international trade routes. Global health security also required a well-coordinated international network of information, surveillance, and response.

None of this could happen unless states and the international community gained the capacity for rapid and effective action. At all levels, successful detection and response could only be achieved with well-trained scientists, well-equipped laboratories, and interoperable data systems. Capacity building, of course, requires considerable resources, and international law is characteristically weak in mobilizing technical assistance and economic investment.

There were other key insights that drove states to devise international rules to improve global health security. States have core interests not only in health, but also in international trade and commerce, as well as personal freedoms. Historically, rapidly spreading infectious diseases instilled deep fear, precipitating overreaction, and even prejudice against "the other." The usual targets of discrimination were foreigners, particularly the poor, living in overcrowded countries where infectious diseases were endemic.

In response to deep-seated fear of dreaded diseases, states often imposed restrictions on travel and trade, irrespective of their effectiveness. The states where outbreaks occurred, in turn, were reluctant to notify the international community due to concerns about commerce, tourism, and national prestige. This led to a vicious cycle of disease emergence, failure to report, and economic ramifications.

Disease epidemics also drove governments to act against their own residents, as well as international travelers, through compulsory powers such as testing, treatment, and quarantine. Although coercive powers were sometimes necessary, they were often ineffective or disproportionate to the risk. And in many cases, states acted out of animus toward disfavored groups, particularly immigrants. At the turn of the twentieth century, for example, health officials quarantined only Chinese Americans during a plague outbreak in San Francisco, prompting a federal court to rule that officials operated with an "evil eye and an unequal hand."[3]

What emerged was a growing recognition of the delicate balance between health security on the one hand and trade and human rights on the other. National law could not ensure an effective and balanced approach, thus driving the need for transnational solutions. The result is that the IHR has become arguably the most important global health treaty of the twenty-first century, with the WHO at the center of the governance regime. What made all this politically possible was the advent of frightening emerging infectious diseases, notably SARS and avian influenza. It is thus unsurprising that in 2009 the so-called swine flu (H1N1) pandemic became the first, and to date the only, officially declared public health emergency of international concern.

Antecedents to the IHR (2005)

Historians trace modern international infectious disease law to ten European Sanitary Conferences, with the first meeting in Paris in 1851. Powerful states sought protection against external health threats, notably "Asiatic" cholera from the Near and Middle East. As global commerce brought dreaded diseases to their shores, European leaders resolved to devise international legal solutions.

Delegates failed to agree on an international treaty in Paris,[4] but European states negotiated multiple conventions to address the transboundary effects of infectious diseases during the late nineteenth and early twentieth centuries:[5] in 1892 the first International Sanitary Convention (ISC) focused on quarantine for cholera; the second convention, held in 1897, was restricted to plague;[6] the ISC was extended in 1926 to smallpox and typhus; and a separate ISC for aerial navigation—addressing the public health impact of transnational air-travel—was adopted in 1933.[7]

European leaders realized that, in order to reach their objectives, they required a well-prepared, "neutral agency" so that the conventions would not become a "dead letter."[8] By 1907 the Rome Agreement created the Office International d'Hygiène Publique (OIHP) based in Paris, entrusting the OIHP with the ISC. Notably, the raison d'être of the earliest international health organizations was the administration of infectious disease treaties.

International infectious disease law, therefore, grew out of a perceived security imperative for powerful countries. What seemed most important was self-protection against external threats rather than improving health within poor countries. However misconceived, the perception persists that disease threats originate in the global South, requiring international law to prevent their spread to affluent regions.

The WHO Constitution: Extraordinary Power to Negotiate Regulations

The WHO Constitution empowers the World Health Assembly to adopt regulations concerning "sanitary and quarantine requirements and other procedures designed to prevent the international spread of disease" (art. 21; see Chapter 4). The WHA's regulatory authority is unique in international law, designed to simplify and encourage international agreement. WHO regulations automatically enter into force and are binding on all member states except those that notify the director-general of their decision to opt out within a limited period of time (art. 22). Although state ratification is not required as a matter of international law, implementation through domestic law or policy may be necessary to give the IHR full effect.

From the International Sanitary Regulations to the International Health Regulations

On May 25, 1951, the fourth Health Assembly adopted the International Sanitary Regulations (ISR), replacing the ISC. The ISR covered six reportable diseases: cholera, plague, epidemic (louse-borne) typhus, relapsing fever, smallpox, and yellow fever. Its avowed aim was "to ensure the maximum security against the international spread of disease with minimum interference with world traffic," imposing state obligations to notify the WHO of disease outbreaks and to maintain public health capacities at national borders to protect against disease entry and exit.

In 1969 the twenty-second WHA renamed the ISR to become the International Health Regulations (IHR 1969), excluding louse-borne typhus and relapsing fever, and leaving only cholera, plague, smallpox, and yellow fever. For the remainder of the twentieth century, the IHR remained much the same. The twenty-sixth assembly (1973) amended the IHR in relation to cholera. In 1981 the thirty-fourth assembly excluded smallpox in view of its global eradication. By the time the forty-eighth assembly (1995) called for revision of the IHR, it applied only to cholera, plague, and yellow fever.

This period of marginalization and stagnation in international health law was associated with complacency, as many developed countries mistakenly believed the era of infectious diseases to be over—even as such diseases continued to ravage Africa, Asia, and Latin America. It was also a time of weariness with international organizations and international treaties in particular.

Revision Process for the IHR (2005)

International complacency turned to a sense of urgency as a confluence of events raised infectious diseases to the realm of high politics in the late twentieth century.[9] In 1995 the WHA resolved to revise the IHR in response to frightening outbreaks of cholera in Peru, plague in India, and Ebola hemorrhagic fever in Zaire. During this time, the world was also facing one of the great pandemics, AIDS, as well as the looming threats of avian influenza, Marburg hemorrhagic fever, and bioterrorism. The potentially drastic economic and security consequences of these public health threats made it politically difficult to oppose an ambitious reform of international infectious disease law.

The IHR (1969) proved inadequate to meet these challenges. Perhaps the IHR's greatest weakness was its limited applicability. The regulations applied to only three diseases (cholera, plague, and yellow fever)—the same diseases discussed at the 1851 Paris Conference. In addition, the regulations covered mostly sanitary measures at national borders, de-emphasizing action throughout a country's territory.

Even for diseases to which the regulations applied, notification systems for outbreaks frequently broke down. States often failed to report fully and promptly, fearing loss of tourism, trade, and national prestige. The simple act of reporting could trigger excessive reactions from other countries, such as travel or trade restrictions. Importantly, many lower-income countries lacked surveillance needed for the early detection and management of health hazards. Compliance with IHR obligations remained a persistent concern, particularly the requirement that measures interfere with world traffic as little as possible.

Noncompliance was also attributable to poor monitoring and enforcement. While the IHR (1969) established a dispute settlement procedure, the WHO had no powers to resolve disagreements. Nor did the WHO take action to identify or publicize noncompliance.

Negotiations to revise the IHR continued for over a decade. But political will was galvanized in the face of two frightening outbreaks: severe acute respiratory syndrome (SARS) in 2003, followed by the first probable human cases of highly pathogenic Influenza A (H5N1) in Thailand a year later. As Fidler argued, SARS represented "the coming-of-age of a governance strategy for infectious diseases more radical than any previous governance innovation in international relations."[10] Political leaders urgently had to rethink global cooperation as they reached agreement on the revised regulations only days before the 2005 WHA (Figure 6.1).

The International Health Regulations (2005)

The IHR (2005)—containing sixty-six articles organized into ten parts, with nine annexes—is among the world's most widely adopted treaties, with 196 states parties, including all WHO member states, Liechtenstein, and the Holy See.[11] The IHR are legally binding on the entire government, not a particular ministry, and states parties are bound by all of its provisions. The rules expand WHO jurisdiction beyond a

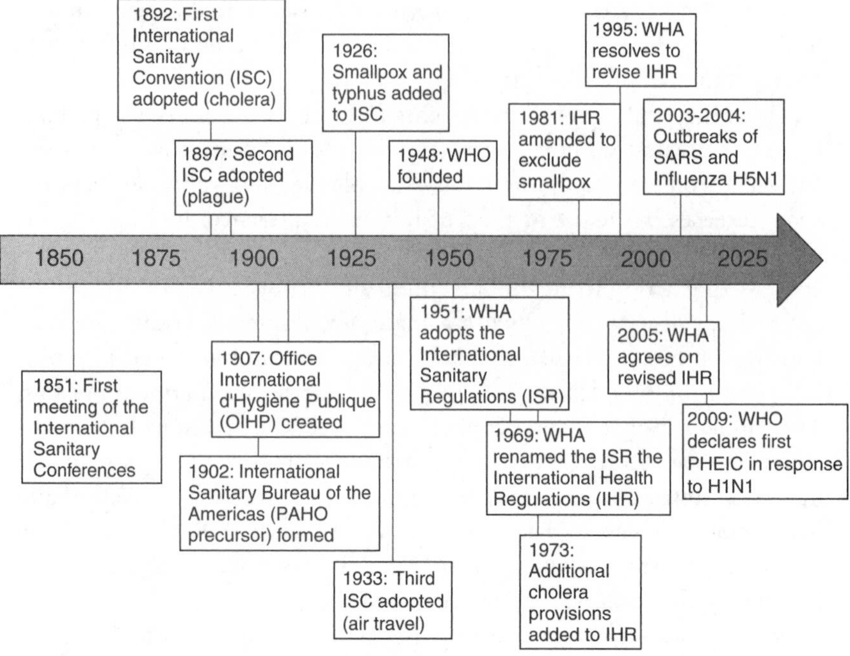

Figure 6.1 **International Health Regulations: Timeline of major milestones**

narrow band of infectious diseases to the entire spectrum of public health risks of international importance. The IHR focus on global preparedness, ranging from surveillance and capacity to response and border control. The cumulative effect could transform the WHO's role and stature in international law and establish a coherent global preparedness framework.[12]

Principal Purpose

The purpose of the IHR is "to prevent, protect against, control and provide a public health response to the international spread of disease . . . commensurate with and restricted to public health risks, and which avoid unnecessary interference with international traffic and trade" (art. 2). The IHR act at the national and international level to provide (1) ongoing surveillance and response within countries and at their borders, and (2) coordinated and proportionate global detection and control of transnational threats. Above all, the IHR's success depends on building capacity in all countries—with a network of international support—to detect, assess, notify, and respond.

Balancing Dynamic

The IHR (2005) craft a delicate balancing dynamic of health security, trade, and human rights, entailing difficult tradeoffs among the three interests.

International trade The regulations capture the balance between health and trade by underscoring a state's "sovereign right to legislate and to implement legislation in pursuance of their health policies" while upholding the regulations' purpose (art. 3(4)). Health measures cannot be more restrictive of trade and human rights than needed to avert or reduce the risk. State action, moreover, must be rooted in scientific evidence (art. 43(2)).

By calibrating health, science, and trade interests, the IHR resonate with international trade law, which also recognizes the state's right to restrict trade for health purposes, but limits this right to ensure that restrictions are necessary (see Chapter 9).[13] Both health and trade law view disease control as embedded in an international system that facilitates economic activity through globalized markets. Finding ways to balance public health and economic activity has become an enduring feature of global governance.

Human rights The IHR balance not only health with trade, but also health with human rights.[14] States parties must have "full respect for the dignity, human rights and fundamental freedoms of persons," guided by the UN Charter and the WHO Constitution. The IHR have "universal application for the protection of all people of the world" (art. 3), and health measures must be applied in a transparent and nondiscriminatory manner (art. 42).

The IHR safeguard the human rights of international travelers. States parties must "treat travelers with respect for their dignity, human rights, and fundamental freedoms and minimize any discomfort or distress," including treating them with courtesy and respect. States must consider the individual's gender as well as sociocultural, ethnic, or religious concerns, and provide adequate food, water, accommodation, baggage protection, medical treatment, and communication for quarantined or isolated travelers (art. 32). The emphasis on human dignity may suggest that international human rights law, such as the Siracusa Principles, is relevant in interpreting and implementing the IHR (see Chapter 8). That is, human rights principles should be applied where there is uncertainty in the IHR.

Commerce: Trade and Travel

Consider risk of interfering with international traffic when determining if an event is a public health emergency. (Art. 12)

No ship or aircraft shall be prevented from calling at a port of entry for public health reasons unless the point of entry is unable to apply health measures. (Art. 28)

Unless otherwise authorized, goods in transit without transshipment that are not live animals will not be subject to IHR health measures or detained for public health purposes. (Art. 33)

Health measures shall not be more restrictive to international traffic than reasonably available alternatives that would achieve the appropriate level of health protection. (Art. 43)

States implementing additional health measures that significantly interfere with international traffic shall provide WHO with rationale and relevant scientific information. (Art. 43)

Public Health: Scientific Methodologies

Determination of a public health emergency of international concern based on scientific principles, available scientific evidence, and other relevant information. (Art. 12)

Determination of whether to implement health measures based on scientific principles and available scientific evidence of risk to health. (Art. 43)

Consultation between states impacted by an emergency and states implementing health measures to clarify scientific information and public health rationale underlying implemented health measures. (Art. 43)

Human Rights

HR implementation shall be with full respect for the dignity, human rights and fundamental freedoms of persons. (Art. 3)

No IHR medical examination, vaccination, prophylaxis, or health measure will be performed on travelers without prior informed consent, except as otherwise noted. (Art. 23)

States shall minimize discomfort or distress from IHR measures by treating all travelers with courtesy and respect and taking into consideration gender, sociocultural, ethnic, or religious concerns of travelers. (Art. 32)

Health measures pursuant to the IHR shall be applied in a transparent and non-discriminatory manner. (Art. 42)

Health information collected or received under the IHR referring to an identifiable person shall be kept confidential and processed anonymously, unless otherwise mentioned. (Art. 45)

Figure 6.2 **The IHR balancing dynamic: Commerce, public health, and human rights**
Adopted from WHO, *International Health Regulations*, 2nd ed. (Geneva: World Health Organization, 2005).

The IHR's balancing dynamic, then, includes scientific methodologies, the flow of trade and travel, and respect for human rights. In each of these realms there are hard trade-offs: Can countries take action to safeguard the public's health in the face of scientific uncertainty? How much interference with economic freedom should be tolerated in the name of health? When should personal autonomy, privacy, or liberty yield for the sake of the population's health and safety (Figure 6.2)?

Scope: An All-Hazards Approach

As explained earlier in this chapter, the IHR (1969) applied only to a few infectious diseases whose spread was historically associated with trade and travel. The regulations now encompass a broad spectrum of health hazards of international concern, irrespective of their origin or source—whether biological, chemical, or radio-nuclear (Table 6.1). Since the hazard's source is immaterial, the WHO possesses jurisdiction for events that are naturally occurring, accidental, or intentional.[15] Depending on the severity (e.g., a new strain that is highly transmissible, pathogenic, or drug-resistant) and the international ramifications, the IHR may apply to risks arising from numerous sources:

1. *Persons*—e.g., SARS, MERS, novel influenza, polio, Ebola
2. *Goods, food, water, or animals*—e.g., botulism, bovine spongiform encephalopathy, cryptosporidiosis
3. *Vectors*—e.g., plague, yellow fever, tularemia
4. *The environment*—e.g., radio-nuclear releases, chemical spills, or other contamination such as anthrax.

This "all-hazards" approach embodies a conceptual shift. While trade calculations determined the old IHR's scope, health risks define the ambit of the revised IHR. The result is greater legitimacy, flexibility, and adaptability. This expanded public health approach is found throughout the IHR. Reporting health events, handling epidemiological data, making WHO recommendations, and limiting national health measures all apply across the full spectrum of health risks. The expanded scope creates a more demanding framework than previous versions of the IHR.

Table 6.1 **IHR Scope: Article 1 Definitions**

Surveillance: "the systematic ongoing collection, collation and analysis of data for public health purposes and the timely dissemination of public health information for assessment and public health response as necessary."

Disease: "an illness or medical condition, irrespective of origin or source, that presents or could present significant harm to humans."

Event: "a manifestation of disease or an occurrence that creates the potential for disease."

Public health risk: "a likelihood of an event that may affect adversely the health of human populations, with emphasis on one which may spread internationally or may present a serious and direct danger."

Public health emergency of international concern (PHEIC): "an extraordinary event which is determined: (i) to constitute a public health risk to other States through the international spread of disease and (ii) to potentially require a coordinated international response."

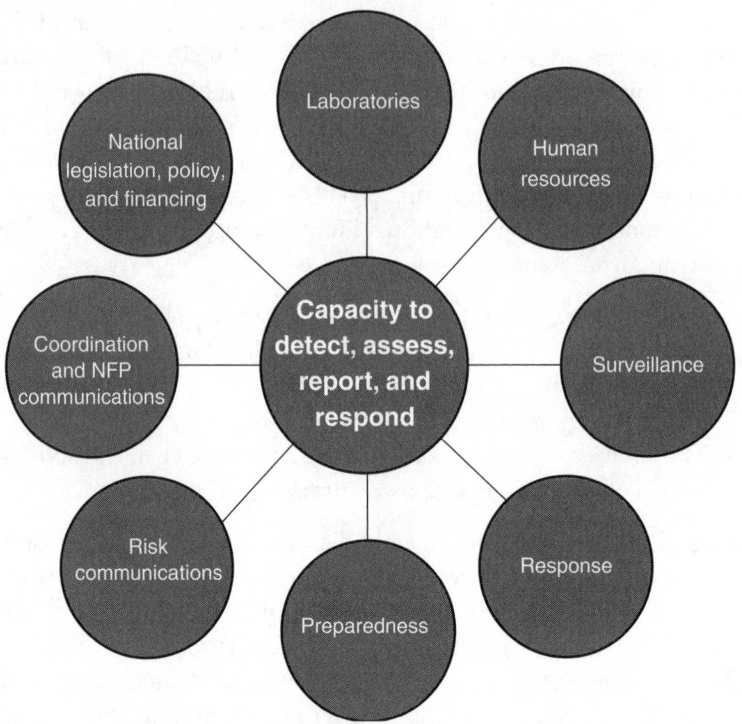

Figure 6.3 **IHR core capacities**

National Preparedness Capacities

Preparedness is vital to health security—both domestic and global. States parties have the duty to develop, strengthen, and maintain public health capacities to detect, assess, notify, and report events (art. 5(1), annex 1). They must also be able to respond promptly and effectively to an array of risks.[16] Capacities must be operational at the national and subnational levels, as well as at borders,[17] constituting "a blueprint for a comprehensive, fully-integrated, public health emergency detection and response system."[18]

The WHO has identified several core IHR capacities (Figure 6.3):[19]

1. *National legislation, policy, and financing.* States parties must have an adequate legal framework that may require the enactment of laws or regulations to implement IHR obligations (e.g., expanding the list of notifiable diseases) and safeguarding rights (e.g., privacy or informed consent) (Box 6.1).

BOX 6.1 The Role and Importance of National Legislation

Although not expressly required by the IHR, national health legislation can institutionalize and strengthen the IHR's performance. Because the IHR encompass risks arising from multiple sources, they influence a range of government sectors, such as public health, environment, border security, food safety, agriculture, animal health, nuclear-chemical, justice, and transportation. In assessing the adequacy of legal structures, states should consider an equally broad range of laws and regulation.

States parties have discretion on whether, and how, to implement IHR standards, depending on the legal system, domestic policies, and sociopolitical context. As of 2010 approximately half of states parties had amended legislation to fulfill IHR obligations.[1] Some states annex the IHR's text or incorporate the regulations by reference into domestic law. Other states use nonbinding instruments (e.g., guidelines and resolutions).

NOTE

1. Rebecca Katz and S. Kornblet, "Comparative Analysis of National Legislation in Support of the Revised International Health Regulations: Potential Models for Implementation in the United Sates," *American Journal of Public Health* 100, no. 12 (2010): 2347–2353.

2. *National focal points.* States parties must establish a national focal point (NFP) accessible at all times, tasked with transmitting urgent communications to WHO IHR contact points and acting as a communication channel (art. 4). IHR focal points establish "a global network that improves the real-time flow of surveillance information from the local to the global level and also between state parties."[20] Virtually all states have identified NFPs.
3. *Notification (reporting).* States parties must monitor health hazards occurring within their territories and notify the WHO within twenty-four hours of all events that may constitute a public health emergency of international concern (PHEIC) (art. 6). Annex 2 provides a decision instrument to guide states parties in determining whether an event constitutes a PHEIC.
4. *Planning and risk communication.* States should develop emergency plans for responding to health threats. Risk communication encompasses processes for defining risks, identifying hazards, assessing vulnerabilities, and promoting community resilience. It takes into account "social, religious, cultural, political, and

economic [factors], as well as the voice of the affected population."[21]

5. *Public health infrastructure.* Public health preparedness requires a skilled health workforce, data systems, laboratories, and cross-sector coordination.

The IHR's success depends on well-functioning infrastructure—a prerequisite many states parties are unable to satisfy. A health system with capabilities for surveillance, laboratories, and response requires substantial resources. Novel pathogens can present technical difficulties even for the most scientifically advanced countries.

The WHO review committee on IHR functioning during the 2009 H1N1 pandemic stressed that many states parties lacked core capacities and were not on a path to fulfill their IHR obligations. By 2011 states parties began to make "fair progress" for surveillance, response, laboratories, and zoonotic events. However, most reported low capacities in human resources and for chemical and radiological events.[22] The D-G's report to the WHA in May 2012 expressed concern about poor capacity and planning for radiological events following the Fukushima nuclear plant disaster in Japan.[23]

The IHR lack detailed strategies for capacity building. The regulations oblige states parties to utilize existing structures and resources to meet capacities (annex 1). Although the regulations require the WHO to assist states parties, the IHR do not allocate any funds for this purpose. The duties placed on the WHO, moreover, do not address the organization's own resource shortages (see Chapter 4). The IHR similarly require states parties to provide financial and technical resources, but the obligations are nonbinding or weak, requiring compliance only "to the extent possible" (arts. 13(5), 44(1)). The IHR's silence on how to meet the economic demands of capacity building poses a serious problem for which the regulations offer no apparent answer.

The 2009 IHR review committee made several proposals to address this issue: (1) establish a "global health emergency workforce" mobilized as part of a sustained response in countries that request assistance; (2) create a $100 million contingency fund for health emergencies for surge capacity, to be released during a PHEIC; and (3) modernize strategies for implementing IHR capacity building. Galvanizing political will for more resources, however, will remain a major challenge.

Notification of PHEIC within a State's Territory: The Decision Instrument

States parties must assess events within their territories to determine their obligation to notify the WHO. The NFP must report to the WHO within twenty-four hours by "the most efficient means of communication available" all events that may constitute a PHEIC (art. 6). Similarly, states parties must inform the WHO of any unexpected or unusual event that may constitute a PHEIC, irrespective of origin or source (art. 7) (Table 6.2).

***Table* 6.2 Surveillance, Notification, and Information Sharing: State Party Responsibilities (Articles 5–9)**

- *Surveillance Capacity*
  - Develop core capacity to detect, assess, and report events.
- *Within Territory*
  - Assess events using decision instrument (Figure 6.4).
  - Notify the WHO of event that may constitute a PHEIC.
  - Inform the WHO of unexpected or unusual public health event irrespective of origin or source that may constitute a PHEIC.
  - Notify the WHO, through the NFP, within twenty-four hours of assessment.
  - *Ongoing duty:* Provide the WHO with health information on notified event.
  - *Events not requiring notification* (i.e., due to insufficient information): Keep the WHO advised through NFP and consult on health measures.
- *Outside Territory*
  - As far as practicable, inform the WHO within twenty-four hours of a health risk that may cause international disease spread manifested by exported or imported human cases, vectors, or contaminated goods.
- *Unofficial Sources of Information*
  - The WHO must use epidemiological principles to assess reports from unofficial sources.
  - The WHO may keep source confidential only if duly justified.
  - The WHO must inform state party, consult, and seek verification before taking action.
  - State party, when the WHO requests, must verify event and provide information within twenty-four hours.

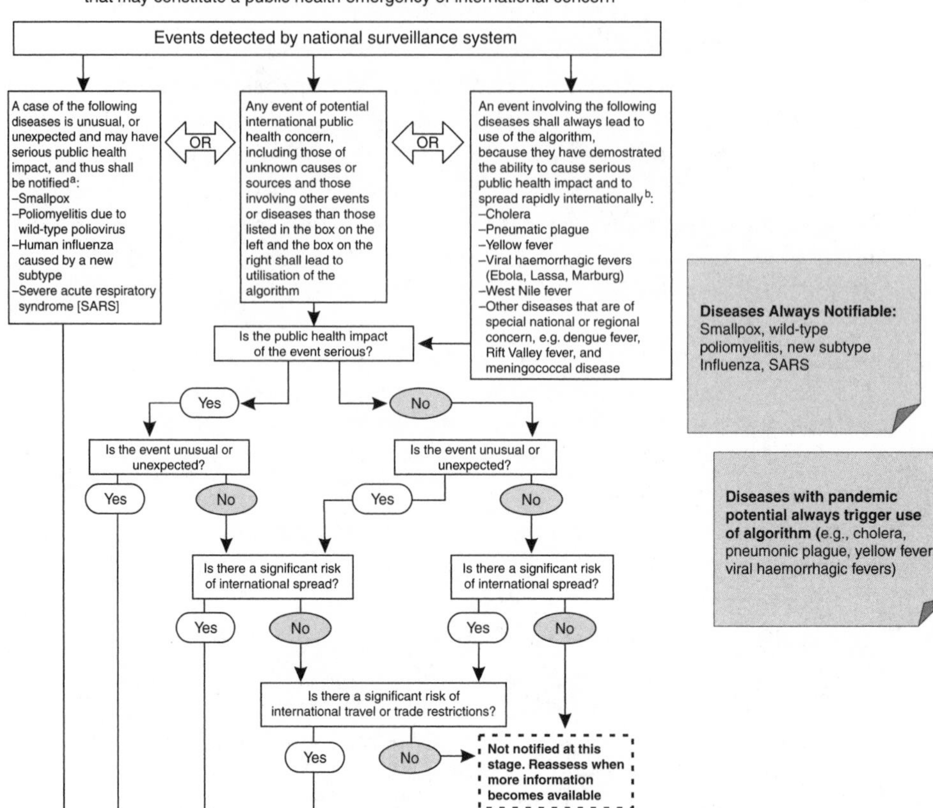

Figure 6.4 **IHR decision instrument for determining Public Health Emergencies of International Concern (PHEIC)**

Source: WHO, *International Health Regulations*, 2nd ed. (Geneva: World Health Organization, 2005), annex 2.

Annex 2 provides a "decision instrument" to determine which events rise to the level of a PHEIC (Figure 6.4).[24] The instrument requires states parties to *always* notify the WHO of any case of specified diseases with well-established global impact: smallpox, poliomyelitis due to a wild virus, human influenza with a novel subtype, and SARS.[25]

The instrument also provides a list of pandemic-prone diseases that automatically trigger assessment under the algorithm. Diseases such as cholera, pneumonic plague, yellow fever, and viral hemorrhagic fevers have been demonstrated to have serious health impacts with potential for international spread. Beyond listed diseases, health officials must utilize the instrument for any event of potential international public health concern, including those of unknown causes or sources. The IHR's algorithm requires states to report events fulfilling two or more of four situational criteria: (1) serious public health impact, (2) unusual or unexpected event, (3) significant risk of international spread, and (4) significant risk of international travel or trade restrictions. For example, the emergence of a novel coronavirus, such as MERS, appears to fit squarely within at least two of these categories, triggering a duty to notify the WHO.

Although the decision instrument is simple to apply for listed diseases, it lacks specificity and detailed guidance for many others.[26] Most NFPs view the instrument as prioritizing acute and novel infections exhibiting rapid international spread. However, there are reasonable grounds for thinking that longer-term, chronic threats can also rise to the level of a PHEIC, such as pan-resistant strains of known diseases.[27] For example, extensively drug-resistant strains of tuberculosis or staphylococcus aureus could fulfill at least two annex criteria: a serious public health impact and a significant risk of international spread. However, for enduring diseases that are common, such as AIDS or malaria, it would make little sense to require states to report new cases.

Declaration of a PHEIC The director-general has the exclusive power to declare a PHEIC (art. 12). While states parties are required to report disease events that *may* constitute such emergencies, the D-G makes the final determination of a PHEIC. Although the D-G must consult with states parties in whose territories disease events are occurring, she is not bound to follow their views. Thus, a state's refusal to cooperate does not bar WHO action. A PHEIC is an extraordinary event, and the D-G therefore sparingly exercises her power to declare such an emergency. To date, the D-G has made only one PHEIC determination under the IHR (2005)—pandemic Influenza A (H1N1). Although the D-G convened an Emergency Committee in 2013 to evaluate MERS, she has thus far declined to declare it a PHEIC (see Chapter 4).

Ongoing duty to inform The WHO does not automatically publish IHR notifications, but rather initiates a dialogue with the notifying party on steps needed for further assessment, investigation, and potential responses. States have an ongoing obligation to provide the WHO with "timely, accurate and sufficiently detailed public health information" about the notified event and the support needed (art. 6(2)).

Nonnotifiable events States may keep the WHO advised and consult on appropriate health measures regarding events not determined to be a PHEIC. This situation might arise, for example, when the decision instrument could not be completed due to insufficient scientific data (art. 8).

Events outside a State's Territory

Even for public health risks *outside* their territory, states parties must, where practicable, inform the WHO within twenty-four hours of public health risks that may spread internationally as manifested through humans, vectors, or contaminated goods (art. 9(2)).

Unofficial Sources of Information: Confidentiality of Sources

Globalization has significantly decreased the state's ability to control the flow of information, and thus its prospects of keeping major health hazards hidden from scrutiny. The old IHR, which limited WHO data gathering to official state reports, seemed antiquated in a globalized world. The SARS outbreaks, moreover, vividly illustrated the critical importance of nongovernmental sources of information.

The IHR (2005) explicitly empower the WHO to take into account unofficial sources, such as NGOs, independent scientists, and social networks or news reports in print and electronic media (art. 9). Harnessing new information technologies for surveillance has been at the heart of the WHO's Global Outbreak Alert and Response Network (GOARN)—a collaboration of institutions and networks that pool human and technical resources for the rapid identification, confirmation, and response to outbreaks of international importance (Box 6.2).

The WHO's access to nongovernmental information, its authority to request verification from states, and its power to share information with the international community (arts. 9, 10) increase incentives for state compliance. Given the rapid speed of information dissemination, the WHO will likely gain access to data through state or nonstate sources. The lesson for states may be that transparency and cooperation offer the best path to minimizing the health and economic consequences of epidemics.

The IHR, however, have a potentially serious flaw. The WHO is permitted to maintain the confidentiality of the source "only where it is duly justified" (art. 9(1)). This prima facie requirement to disclose the source of nongovernmental information might deter nonstate actors from informing the WHO of emerging public health threats. Authoritarian regimes, for example, could punish scientists or civil society groups for conveying information without state permission. The IHR provide no guidance as to the circumstances under which the WHO could keep nonstate information sources confidential. Making explicit the WHO's responsibility to protect nonstate actors from sanctions would insulate the organization from the political ramifications of failing to disclose the identity of sources.

Confidentiality of Personally Identifiable Health Information

States parties must keep personally identified or identifiable patient information confidential and all such information must be "processed anonymously as required by national law" (art. 45(1)). While many states and regions, including the United States and the European Union, have data protection laws, others do not. These varying domestic standards have the potential to weaken the IHR's privacy mandate, as well as to create considerable global inconsistency in privacy protection.

States may disclose personal data where "essential" to assess or manage a health risk. However, even if personal data are disclosed, states parties must follow fair information practices. The data disclosed must be relevant and not excessive; accurate and current; processed fairly and lawfully; and kept no longer than necessary. The WHO must also, as far as practicable, provide individuals with their personal data in an intelligible form, with the opportunity to correct inaccuracies (art. 45).

WHO Recommendations

The IHR empower the WHO to make standing and temporary recommendations to states parties (Table 6.3). These powers enable the organization to provide leadership on the most effective health measures from scientific and public health perspectives while balancing health security with human rights and international travel and trade.

Advisory committees The IHR require the D-G to establish committees—selected from the IHR Expert Roster and other experts—to advise her regarding IHR functions and powers:

Table 6.3 Declarations and Recommended Health Measures: WHO Director-General Responsibilities

- Definitions (art. 1)
  - *Health measure:* Procedures applied to prevent the spread of disease or contamination; a health measure does not include law enforcement or security.
  - *Standing recommendation:* Nonbinding WHO advice (art. 16) for specific ongoing public health risks regarding appropriate health measures for routine or periodic application needed to prevent or reduce the intentional spread of disease and minimize interference with international traffic.
  - *Temporary recommendation:* Nonbinding WHO advice (art. 15) on a time-limited, risk-specific basis, in response to a PHEIC to prevent or reduce the international spread of disease and minimize interference with international traffic.
- *Declarations* (art. 12)
  - D-G has authority to declare a PHEIC using decision instrument (Figure 6.4) based on
    - information received, particularly from state party where event occurred
    - emergency Committee advice
    - scientific information and principles
    - risk assessment: to health, international spread, interference with international traffic
- *Temporary Recommendations* (art. 15)
  - D-G *must* issue nonbinding temporary recommendations after declaring a PHEIC
    - for state party experiencing the PHEIC or other states parties
    - regarding persons, baggage, cargo, containers, conveyances, goods, and/or postal parcels
    - to reduce international spread of disease and avoid unnecessary interference with international traffic
    - three-month, renewable time limits
- *Standing Recommendations* (art. 16)
  - D-G *may* issue nonbinding standing recommendations of health measures for routine or periodic application
    - applied to states parties regarding persons, baggage, cargo, containers, conveyances, goods, and/or postal parcels for specific ongoing health risks
    - to prevent or reduce international spread of disease and avoid unnecessary interference with international traffic
- *Criteria for Temporary or Standing Recommendations* (art. 17)
  - Views of states parties directly concerned
  - Advice of Emergency Committee or Review Committee
  - Scientific principles and evidence

Table 6.3 (continued)

- Risk assessment
- International standards and institutions

- *Allowable Health Measures* (arts. 42–43)
  - States parties may adopt health measures in accordance with national and international law to achieve same or greater level of health protection than WHO recommendations, except that such measures *must* be
    - no more restrictive of international traffic and trade or personally intrusive than reasonable alternatives
    - transparent and nondiscriminatory
  - States parties must base health measures on scientific principles, scientific evidence, and available information.

- *The Emergency Committee* advises the D-G (a) whether an event constitutes a PHEIC (b) on the termination of a PHEIC; and (c) whether to make, modify, extend, or terminate temporary recommendations (art. 48).
- *The Review Committee* advises the D-G on (a) IHR amendments; (b) standing recommendations; and (c) the functioning of the IHR (art. 50).

Temporary recommendations If the D-G declares a PHEIC, she must issue nonbinding, temporary recommendations on the most appropriate ways for states to respond (art. 15). The IHR impose time limits for temporary recommendations and permit the D-G to modify or extend them as conditions change, such as when a PHEIC has ended.[28] Temporary recommendations can cover domestic health measures regarding persons, baggage, cargo, containers, goods, and postal parcels to prevent or reduce the international spread of disease and avoid unnecessary interference with traffic.

Standing recommendations The D-G may issue nonbinding, standing recommendations on domestic health measures for ongoing public health risks to prevent or reduce the international spread of disease and avoid unnecessary interference with international traffic (art. 16). Standing recommendations can apply to the same broad range of health hazards as temporary recommendations.

Criteria for health measures Article 19 provides criteria that the D-G must follow when making, modifying, or terminating temporary or standing recommendations. She must consider (a) the views of the applicable advisory committee, states directly concerned, and international organizations; (b) scientific principles and evidence; (c) international standards and instruments; and (d) international organizations. Health measures must be no more restrictive of international traffic and trade, or intrusive to persons, than reasonable alternatives based on a risk assessment.

Recommended health measures Article 18 contains examples of health measures that the WHO can make for (a) persons (e.g., medical examinations, vaccination, contact tracing, isolation, and exit screening) and (b) baggage, cargo, containers, conveyances, and goods (e.g., review of manifest and routing, inspections, safe handling, seizure and destruction, and refusal of departure or entry).

The IHR permit states parties to apply health measures that achieve the same or a greater level of health protection than the WHO recommends (art. 43(1)). However, health measures must be based on scientific principles, available scientific evidence, or relevant WHO guidance, and cannot be more restrictive of international traffic or more intrusive to persons than reasonably available alternatives (art. 43(1)(2)). All health measures under the IHR must be applied in a transparent and nondiscriminatory manner (art. 42).

International Travelers

As discussed earlier, the IHR balance the human rights of international travelers with the legitimate public health objectives of states parties. The IHR safeguard travelers' autonomy, bodily integrity, and liberty, requiring the least intrusive or restrictive health measure necessary to achieve the public health objective. This reflects human rights values embedded in the Siracusa Principles that public health powers must be proportionate to the risk involved and must conform with national law (see Chapter 8.)

Health measures on arrival or departure States parties may require international travelers to (1) provide information concerning their destination and itinerary and (2) submit to a noninvasive medical examination (art. 23(1)).

Medical examinations, vaccinations, and other health measures States parties may not subject an international traveler to an invasive medical examination, vaccination, or other health measure without the traveler's prior express informed consent or that of his/her parent or guardian (art. 23(3)).[29] Travelers must be informed of any health risk associated with these health measures, which must also conform to established national or international safety standards (art. 23).

If the traveler refuses to consent, a state party may deny entry. If necessary to control an *imminent* public health risk, the state may compel the traveler to submit to a medical examination, a vaccination, or an established health measure to prevent the spread of disease (e.g., isolation or quarantine) (art. 31(2)).

Public health observation A "suspect" traveler potentially exposed to infection who is placed under "public health observation" can continue an international voyage only if he/she does not present an imminent health risk (art. 30).

Compliance and Enforcement

States parties often violated the old IHR by failing to report notifiable diseases and unnecessarily restricting travel and trade. The revised IHR sought to promote greater state compliance. Yet the regulations grant the WHO few, if any, explicit powers to monitor state performance, impose sanctions, or provide incentives—"the most important structural shortcoming of the IHR."[30] Instead, the IHR rely on global norms and transparency, as civil society and the international community hold states accountable for evidence-based decisions.

Article 56 does provide a voluntary dispute settlement process between states parties on the IHR's interpretation or application. States parties should first seek to resolve the dispute through negotiation, mediation, or conciliation. If they are unable to reach agreement, the parties may refer the dispute to the D-G. At any time a state party can consent in writing to compulsory binding arbitration. If a dispute arises between the WHO and a state party, the matter must be submitted to the WHA.

International cooperation will be a crucial factor in the IHR's success. Experience during the H1N1 pandemic suggests variable state compliance. The H1N1 notifications by Mexico and the United States in April 2009 conformed to IHR requirements.[31] Nevertheless, many states violated the

D-G's temporary recommendations to refrain from "clos[ing] borders or restricting international traffic and trade."[32] Governments advised citizens against travel to North America; screened or quarantined international travelers; and banned pork imports from the United States, Canada, and Mexico. The World Bank estimated that the economic cost of the pandemic ranged from 0.7% to 4.8% of GDP, with Mexico suffering the greatest burden.[33]

Compatibility with Other International Legal Regimes

Since it imposed duties on the WHO and states parties that overlap with those of other institutions and legal regimes, the IHR have to harmonize different responsibilities. The IHR accomplish this task by stating that their provisions, wherever possible, should be interpreted to be "compatible" with other international agreements. To underscore this point, the IHR state that their provisions "shall not affect the rights and obligations of any state party deriving from other international agreements" (art. 57).

WHO Roles and Multisectoral Relationships

The IHR affirm the WHO's leadership in global outbreak alert and response, giving the organization major responsibilities in governing global health security. The IHR grant the D-G the power to coordinate international surveillance, declare a PHEIC, ensure core public health capacities, act as an information hub (receiving state reports and disseminating data), and make recommendations to states parties (Table 6.4). The D-G and WHO Contact Points seek external advice from the Emergency Committee, coordinate with other competent organizations, and communicate with NFPs and relevant government ministries (Figure 6.5).

The WHO has a vital role in collaborating with multiple entities while coordinating their activities—transnational and national, state and non-state, public and private.[34] The IHR's expanded all-hazards approach—biological, chemical, and radio-nuclear—means that the WHO must engage with international organizations not traditionally regarded as having health responsibilities, many of which operate within distinct legal regimes, such as trade, human rights, food safety, security, and air and sea transport. The WHO committee on IHR functioning stressed the links between the WHO, the World Organization for Animal Health (OIE), and the FAO given the importance of animals and food in human health and disease.

Table 6.4 **The WHO's Major Responsibilities under IHR (2005)**

- Coordinate global surveillance and assessment of significant public health risks and disseminate public health information to states parties.
- Determine whether particular events constitute a PHEIC (with advice from external experts) (arts. 12, 48, 49).
- Develop and recommend temporary and standing recommendations under articles 15 and 16.
- Provide direct support to states parties by
  - supporting states in assessing and strengthening their core public health capacities for surveillance and response at designated ports of entry
  - mobilizing financial resources to support developing countries in strengthening such core public health capacities
  - providing technical assistance to states
- Monitor and evaluate implementation of IHR (2005) and adopt technical guidelines to address evolving needs.

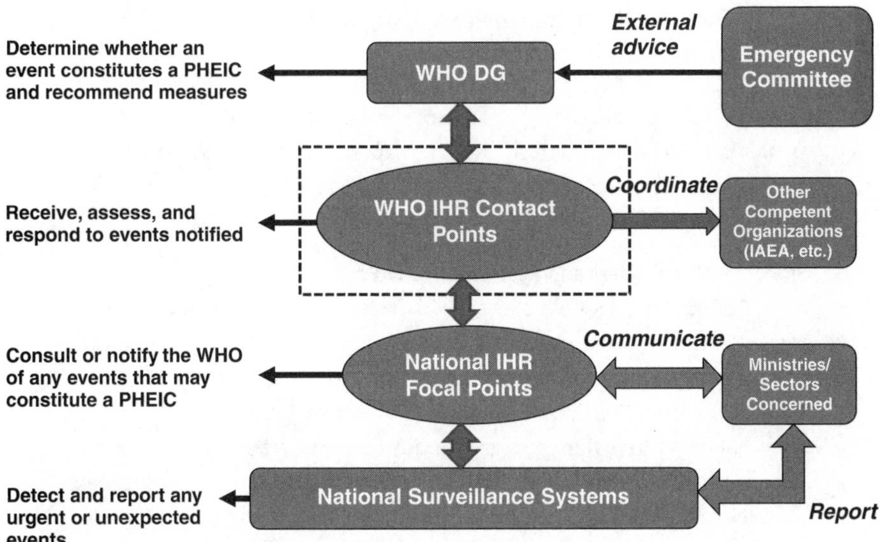

Figure 6.5 **WHO communication flow**

The IHR expressly require the WHO to cooperate with other international organizations. The WHO must coordinate activities if notification or verification is primarily within an international organization's competence (art. 14). The WHA specified a range of international organizations with which the WHO must engage, including the UN, FAO, OIE, International Atomic Energy Agency, International Civil Aviation Organization, and International Maritime Organization.[35] The WHO may share health information with international organizations as well as states parties (art. 11). In making or terminating IHR recommendations, the D-G must consider relevant international standards and instruments (art. 17).

The WHO's global health security mandate reaches across sectors and disciplines. To enhance its ability to manage the global scope of health risks, the organization has established technical partnerships with scientists, academics, and NGOs (Box 6.2).

In a multilateral, multi-organization, multi-network environment, international cooperation is needed to protect global health security. The IHR authorize or require communication and collaboration across international organizations while supporting coordination with other international regimes. The regulations designate the WHO as the governing institution to accomplish these objectives. How the WHO can successfully

BOX 6.2 The WHO's Technical Partnerships for Outbreak Alert and Response

No single institution or country has all of the capacities necessary to respond to international public health emergencies caused by exposure to lethal pathogens, radiation, or toxic chemicals. To ensure preparedness and response, the WHO has formed various technical partnerships.

Global Outbreak Alert and Response Network (GOARN)

In April 2000 the WHO established GOARN as a "technical collaboration of existing institutions and networks who pool human and technical resources for the rapid identification, confirmation and response to outbreaks of international importance."[1] GOARN is a resource network for surveillance and response, aiming to provide technical support to states; investigate and characterize events and assess risks; and support national outbreak preparedness. GOARN has developed Guiding Principles for International Outbreak Alert and Response, and established operational protocols to standardize field logistics, security, and communications for rapid mobilization.

Chemical Incident Alert and Response System (ChemiNet)

In 2002 the WHO established ChemiNet—sometimes referred to as GOARN's "chemical arm"—to assist countries in investigating and responding to chemical events.[2] ChemiNet—a network of institutions, laboratories, WHO collaborating centers, poison centers, and academics—mitigates incidents of chemical origin of international concern through early detection, assessment, and verification; rapid and effective response; and long-term preparedness and capacity building.

Radiation Emergency Medical Preparedness and Assistance Network (REMPAN)

Established by the WHO in 1987, REMPAN now constitutes a network of forty medical and research institutions "specializing in diagnosis, monitoring, dosimetry, treatment, and long-term follow-up of radiation injuries, acute radiation syndrome, internal contamination and other radio-pathology."[3] REMPAN provides emergency assistance to people overexposed to radiation; facilitates long-term care and follow-up of radiation accident victims; and conducts research in radiation medicine and emergency medicine epidemiology.

Response Assistance Network (RANET)

Although RANET is not a formal WHO technical partnership, it fits within the IHR's broad mission. RANET is designed to assist states parties to the Convention on Assistance in Case of a Nuclear Accident or Radiological Emergency. RANET's purposes are to strengthen the IAEA's capability to provide advice and coordinate assistance and to promote emergency preparedness for nuclear or radiological emergencies/incidents.[4]

NOTES

1. "Global Outbreak Alert and Response Network," WHO, http://www.who.int/csr/outbreaknetwork/en/ (accessed 10/10/13).
2. "WHO Global Chemical Incident Emergency Response Network (ChemiNet)," WHO, http://www.who.int/environmental_health_emergencies/ChemiNet3.pdf (accessed 10/10/13).
3. "WHO/REMPAN Collaborating Centres and Liaison Institutions," WHO, http://www.who.int/ionizing_radiation/a_e/rempan/en/ (accessed 10/10/13).
4. "IAEA's Response System," International Atomic Energy Agency (IAEA), http://www-ns.iaea.org/tech-areas/emergency/iaea-response-system.asp (accessed 10/10/13).

coordinate multiple entities, and whether it has the resources to do so, remain daunting challenges. Although technical partnerships are vital, neither the WHA nor states parties have provided the resources needed for the WHO to carry out its broad mandate.

Lessons Learned from the H1N1 Pandemic

The IHR (2005) represent a landmark in global governance, with their three-pronged strategy on health security, international trade, and human rights. The 2009 Influenza (A) H1N1 pandemic offered the first, and still the only, significant test of the IHR's effectiveness.[36] The high-level WHO review committee on IHR functioning found that the regulations provided effective governance of the pandemic, but also identified structural weaknesses.[37]

During the H1N1 pandemic, the WHO spoke with an authoritative voice, gained substantial cooperation, and acted as a hub for strategy and communications. Many states were well prepared, implementing national influenza plans devised during ongoing avian flu outbreaks. Mexico and the United States notified the WHO promptly and cooperated fully. Overall, the IHR improved global governance as the novel virus inexorably spread.

The pandemic also revealed fault lines in global health governance. The WHO made science-based recommendations that states avoid the use of trade sanctions, travel restrictions, and coercive public health powers. Yet, as discussed earlier, many states disregarded WHO advice, curtailing travel to North America, banning pork products, and screening or quarantining international travelers. Egypt took the drastic measure of culling the country's estimated 400,000 pigs, perhaps motivated by prejudice against the Coptic Christian minority (the primary consumers of pork).[38]

The WHO also learned lessons. The D-G structured daily press briefings around the 2009 WHO Pandemic Influenza Phases—even though the IHR contain no reference to pandemic phases. The D-G announced the progression through all six pandemic phases. This risk communication strategy did not allay public fears or dispel confusion, and perhaps contributed to overreaction. As the pandemic rapidly spread, ministries of health became overwhelmed by the WHO's weekly case counts and ongoing requirements to report new cases.

More important, the pandemic influenza phases had a significant deficiency—the organization focused only on the international spread of disease without accounting for whether it caused serious illness or death. Fortunately, H1N1 was not highly pathogenic in most populations. But this fact did not influence the WHO's pandemic phase progression. On June 10, 2013 the WHO issued interim guidance in response to criticism of its 2009 Pandemic Influenza Preparedness and Response report, revising the global influenza phases and uncoupling national actions from global phases. The interim guidance further encompasses ethical considerations, a whole-of-society approach, business continuity planning, and parameters for core severity indicators.[39]

Trustworthiness is the WHO's most crucial attribute. However, some stakeholders questioned the organization's objectivity, expressing concern that it hewed to the interests of pharmaceutical companies. Whether or not this critique was fair, the perceptions were fueled by the lack of transparency in making recommendations. Its decision not to disclose IHR Emergency Committee membership and the absence of rigorous conflicts of interest rules undermined the organization's credibility.

Beyond objectivity and transparency lies the challenge of building capacity in lower-income countries. The IHR, and the WHA itself, have made clarion calls for technical support and resources for preparedness. But funding for capacity building is voluntary, and the WHO lacks the resources or power to incentivize states to fulfill their international responsibilities.

Perhaps the greatest challenge for the WHO is to ensure the rapid deployment and fair distribution of vaccines and antiviral medications. Although the D-G placed vaccine development and equitable allocation high on her agenda, major impediments remain. Due to market forces and technical limitations, timely development and delivery of vaccines are fraught with uncertainty. Rich countries with ample purchasing power are also likely to gain a disproportionate share of scarce therapeutics. The WHO's Influenza Sharing Agreement (see Chapter 4), moreover, imposed no obligation on states to ensure a fair share of therapeutic benefits. To close the health gap, the WHO, in partnership with states and industry, should negotiate agreements to equitably allocate vaccines and medicines (see Chapter 12).

Going forward, the WHO and states must work to find innovative ways to disseminate timely pertinent information to governments, scientists, and the public; restore trust through transparency and management of conflicts of interest; build capacity for preparedness domestically and globally; and encourage compliance, including conforming to WHO recommendations and devoting resources for surveillance and response. Above all, the principles of shared responsibility and social justice require equitable allocation of life-saving therapeutics to benefit everyone, and particularly the world's poorest people.

The IHR's seminal achievement constitutes only the starting point for global health security. The hard work of making this transformative vision efficacious for individuals, states, and the international community now begins.

CHAPTER 7

The Framework Convention on Tobacco Control

The Global Response to Tobacco

PUBLIC HEALTH HISTORIANS will look back in amazement at the sheer devastation wrought in our age by a single agricultural product. Tobacco claimed 100 million lives in the twentieth century—a death toll comparable to the combined casualties of the two world wars. To this day, a half-century after researchers demonstrated that smoking causes cancer, heart disease, and respiratory disease,[1] tobacco remains the leading cause of preventable death.[2]

Tobacco, both combustible and smokeless (see Box 7.1), kills more people than AIDS, tuberculosis, and malaria combined—nearly 6 million people every year—and this is expected to rise to 8 million by 2030. Half of the 1 billion smokers living today will die of tobacco-related diseases.[3] And these data do not begin to describe the disability and suffering among smokers, along with the immeasurable psychological, social, and economic toll on families and communities. For every person who dies as a result of smoking, twenty more suffer from serious and painful chronic disease.[4] What is most disturbing is that most of the suffering and early deaths are concentrated among the poor, the less educated, and racial minorities.[5] Tobacco and poverty result in a vicious cycle of ill health and diminishing resources, as spending on tobacco represents a daily drain on funds needed for food, housing, and health care.

As alarming as these statistics are, the death rates would be much higher were it not for the aggressive regulatory response in developed countries. In the United States, for example, the proportion of the adult population that smoked cigarettes declined from 42 percent in 1965 to 19.3 percent in 2010.[6] The remaining cohort comprises the heavier, more

BOX 7.1 The Heterogeneity of Smokeless Tobacco

Smokeless tobacco products allow individuals to consume tobacco, orally or nasally, without combustion. Oral products are placed on or in the lip, cheek, gums, or mouth and chewed or sucked (often called "dipping"). Fine tobacco powder mixtures are usually inhaled and absorbed in the nasal passages. Smokeless tobacco has been used for thousands of years in South America and Southeast Asia. Over time the products have gained popularity, posing a significant challenge in global tobacco control.

There are now over twenty-five different types of smokeless tobacco products used worldwide, including commercial and homemade formulations, with the product type and level of use varying by geographic region. In North America the most common products are chewing tobacco and snuff, with an adult smokeless tobacco prevalence of 3.5 percent. In Scandinavia, particularly Sweden, the most common form is snus, which is consumed orally. Approximately 20 percent of the Swedish adult males use snus daily, and the average user keeps snus in the mouth for eleven to fourteen hours per day. In India smokeless tobacco is used by more than a quarter of all adults and accounts for the majority of tobacco users. The most common products are gul, a paste sold in toothpaste-like tubes, and chewing tobacco mixtures. Use of smokeless tobacco products, particularly Toombak, a locally made mixture of tobacco and bicarbonate, has a high adult prevalence in African countries.

Despite bans on the import and sale of smokeless tobacco in some forty countries, global use and marketing is increasing. In 2010, 710,211 tons of smokeless tobacco products were consumed, a dramatic increase from 2000 levels. There has been a significant growth in "dual use" of cigarettes and smokeless tobacco products, accounting for 15 percent of tobacco users in India and Bangladesh and around 10 percent of tobacco users in Thailand and Egypt. Large global cigarette companies have entered the smokeless tobacco market, promoting such products as extensions of their cigarette brands.

Most smokeless tobacco products have toxic constituents, such as nitrosamines and nicotine, with most posing health risks. However, the magnitude of those risks remains controversial, particularly the extent to which smokeless tobacco presents a safer alternative to cigarettes and other tobacco combustion. Further complicating this picture is the variability in regulating smokeless tobacco, with some states regulating it poorly or not at all.

Although most tobacco control advocates reject the use of smokeless tobacco as a harm reduction strategy for nicotine addiction, results from Sweden reveal low cancer rates, as snus has largely supplanted cigarette smoking among men. Neither the WHO Scientific Advisory Committee nor the Framework

Convention on Tobacco Control Secretariat has endorsed smokeless tobacco as an effective means of harm reduction, expressing concern about unproven benefits along with potential for harm, including a false perception of safety and encouraging dual use.[1]

Electronic cigarettes (e-cigarettes) have also gained popularity, with global sales rising by as much as 30 percent. The Centers for Disease Control (CDC) reported that e-cigarette experimentation and use more than doubled among U.S. middle and high school students during 2011–2012, resulting in an estimated 1.78 million students having used the product.[2] E-cigarettes are battery-powered devices that use a water-based solution to simulate cigarette smoke, delivering vaporized nicotine. The industry markets e-cigarettes for use in places where smoking is banned—a sort of end run around smoke-free laws. They are marketed as a safer alternative to cigarettes, although the health risks remain uncertain. More worrying still, the tobacco industry promotes e-cigarettes as ultra-cool, with celebrity endorsements and stylized images reminiscent of tobacco's heyday, as well as targeting young people with sweet and fruity flavors. The *New York Times* depicted the fashionable image of e-cigarettes:

> In the shadow of the Arc de Triomphe, a line spilled onto the sidewalk of a trendy new boutique. . . . But this was no temple of gastronomy. It was one of scores of electronic cigarette shops springing up in Paris and across Europe and the U.S. Inside the boutique, shoppers can choose from 60 flavors of nicotine liquid—including Marlboro and Lucky Strike flavors.[3]

Some countries, including Australia, Brazil, and Mexico, have banned the sale and/or importation of e-cigarettes, while others regulate various aspects of their use. However, there is still significant debate over whether e-cigarettes should be treated as smoking-cessation aids or heavily regulated as tobacco products.[4]

The U.S. Food and Drug Administration (FDA) is empowered to regulate e-cigarettes if they are marketed for therapeutic purposes.[5] In April 2011 the FDA announced its intent to issue new rules that treat e-cigarettes as tobacco products for the purposes of the Family Smoking Prevention and Tobacco Control Act 2009, thus submitting them to tighter restrictions.[6] Some U.S. states have also implemented, or are considering, new regulations for e-cigarettes (particularly bans on sales to minors), but the FDA could create comprehensive rules that would benefit public health across the country.[7]

NOTES

1. World Health Organization (WHO), *Scientific Advisory Committee on Tobacco Products Regulation's Recommendation on Smokeless Tobacco Products* (Geneva: WHO, 2003); Conference of the Parties to the WHO Framework Convention on Tobacco Control (FCTC), Fourth Session, *Control and Prevention of Smokeless Tobacco Products and Electronic Cigarettes: Report by the Convention Secretariat*, FCTC/COP/4/12 (Punta del Este, Uruguay, September 15, 2010).
2. Centers for Disease Control and Prevention (CDC), "Notes from the Field: Electronic Cigarette Use among Middle and High School Students—United States, 2011–2012," *Morbidity and Mortality Weekly Report* 62, no. 35: 729–730.
3. Liz Alderman, "E-Cigarettes at a Crossroads," *New York Times*, June 13, 2013, B1.
4. Nathan K. Cobb and David B. Abrams, "E-Cigarette or Drug-Delivery Device? Regulating Novel Nicotine Products," *New England Journal of Medicine* 365, no. 3 (2011): 193–195.
5. "Electronic Cigarettes (E-Cigarettes)," U.S. Food and Drug Administration (FDA), http://www.fda.gov/newsevents/publichealthfocus/ucm172906.htm.
6. "'Tobacco Products' Subject to the Federal Food, Drug, and Cosmetic Act, as Amended by the Family Smoking Prevention and Tobacco Control Act," Office of Information and Regulatory Affairs, http://www.reginfo.gov/public/do /eAgendaViewRule?pubId=201210&RIN=0910-AG38 (accessed 9/20/13).
7. Tobacco Control Legal Consortium, *Citizen Petition Asking the U.S. Food and Drug Administration to Assert Jurisdiction over and Regulate All Tobacco Products*, September 6, 2013, http://www.publichealthlawcenter.org/sites/default/files /resources/tclc-fdacitizenpetition-menthol-2013.pdf, 11.

deeply addicted smokers, with the poor and vulnerable suffering inequitably. The mentally ill, for example, smoke at a 70 percent higher rate, consume a third of cigarettes, and die an average of 25 years earlier than the general population. Is this unequal distribution acceptable? Could antismoking strategies have reached a point of diminishing returns? If so, how could government reenergize the fight for a tobacco-free society?[7]

Faced with decreased demand in the developed world, Big Tobacco has turned its formidable lobbying and marketing prowess to poorer countries, using free trade and intellectual property rights to gain access to foreign markets, and taking advantage of lax regulatory environments to ply its addictive wares. Using marketing campaigns linking cigarettes to glamorized images of Western culture, Big Tobacco has stimulated demand: every day, 80,000–100,000 people take up smoking in low-resource countries. Women and children are major targets of opportunity for an unscrupulous industry.[8]

If historical trajectories in developed countries are indicative, it will be decades before already strained health systems in lower-income countries face the full brunt of spiking rates of cancer, diabetes, heart disease, and respiratory disease. Of the world's 6 million tobacco-related deaths, 80 percent occur in low- and middle-income countries. If consumption remains constant, and given population growth, a billion lives will be lost to smoking in the twenty-first century.[9]

While globalization has unleashed Big Tobacco on the developing world, the WHO, governments, and civil society are now organizing a systematic response. The future is not cast in stone, and it is surely possible to attenuate this global public health disaster.

In this chapter, I first explore the inexorable rise of cigarettes in the twentieth century, tracing the scientific evolution, Big Tobacco's dishonesty and deceit, and the social mobilization of organized medicine and civil society. I then turn to the most innovative international health treaty ever adopted by the World Health Assembly (WHA): the Framework Convention on Tobacco Control. Next, I discuss the titanic struggle against Big Tobacco in national and international forums—pitting trade and investment treaties against the human rights to life, health, and a clean environment. The chapter concludes with a discussion of nascent global campaigns for a tobacco "endgame." Is this even feasible given the explosion in smoking in poor countries, and, if so, what are the strategies that could end the Great Tobacco Pandemic?

From Scientific Discovery and Industry Obfuscation to Social Mobilization

Cigarette smoking was uncommon during the nineteenth century, and even socially unacceptable. Reformers issued prescient but (at the time) unsubstantiated warnings about the health risk of "coffin nails," linking smoking to criminality and moral degeneracy. The U.S. government played to this sentiment, introducing a cigarette "sin tax" in 1898, while several states prohibited the sale of tobacco.[10] From there, the cigarette began an astonishing rise and fall in the developed world, through the twentieth century.

With the advent of mass production and modern marketing, cigarettes gained popularity—as a momentary reprieve in the trenches of the Great War and in crowded, regimented industrial workplaces. At the pandemic's peak in the developed world at midcentury, ubiquitous and slick marketing had established the cigarette as an accoutrement of the good life, managing at once to symbolize adulthood and youthfulness, masculine brawn and feminine refinement, the working man and the Hollywood starlet.

Meanwhile, evidence began to emerge—from laboratory mice, postmortems of smokers' lungs, and epidemiological monitoring—linking cigarettes to cancer, cardiovascular disease, and respiratory disease. Weaning the public from an extremely addictive product, however, took decades, as the tobacco industry waged a war of disinformation and relentless political lobbying. The story of the Great Tobacco Pandemic can be traced along three narratives: scientific advancement proving the unimaginable harms; Big Tobacco's dishonesty, denials, and secrecy; and sustained social mobilization that stemmed the tide only to see it resurface in the developing world.

Scientific Evolution

At the turn of the twentieth century, lung cancer was so uncommon as to be a medical oddity. With the advent of the milder flue-cured tobacco in cigarettes, smokers began inhaling deeply, exposing their lungs to carcinogens. And as the population began to smoke heavily in the early twentieth century, tobacco-related diseases began to surge. It is astonishing, in retrospect, that there was lasting medical uncertainty regarding the health risks. *Scientific American* in 1933 encapsulated the flawed, short-term thinking: "Any substance so widely and commonly used as the cigarette cannot be as dangerous and deleterious as the propaganda of the more fanatical 'no-tobacco' advocates might lead one to infer."[11]

By midcentury, half the U.S. adult male population used tobacco, averaging a staggering pack a day per smoker. This was so despite early groundbreaking studies demonstrating the suffering and early death of smokers.[12] U.S. Surgeon General Luther Terry's seminal report on smoking released on January 11, 1964, was undoubtedly the turning point. Terry recalled two decades later that the report "hit the country like a bombshell. It was front page news and a lead story on every radio and television station in the United States and many abroad."[13]

The surgeon general's report concluded that smokers had a 70 percent increase in mortality, with a tenfold increased risk for lung cancer; heavy smokers had a twentyfold increased risk. Public attitudes and policy began to shift: 44 percent of Americans believed smoking caused cancer in 1958, but a decade later 78 percent held this view. In 1965 Congress required all cigarette packages to carry a health warning, and in 1970 it banned radio and television advertisements.

Big Tobacco's Denial, Stalling, and Misinformation

Early cigarette ads made outlandish health claims—for example, that "more doctors smoke Camels"—and urged people to "reach for a Lucky instead of a sweet." As evidence of the hazards of smoking mounted, companies vied to portray their brands as the healthiest, claiming that their filtered or mentholated cigarettes were safer and contained less tar. Companies marketed "light" and "extra-light" cigarettes by the late 1960s, a deceptive practice that continues to this day in many countries. Big Tobacco also engineered low-tar and filtered cigarettes to increase nicotine levels—a sinister manipulation to keep customers addicted.

In 1953 Big Tobacco executives issued a "frank statement to cigarette smokers," promising to address health concerns. While insisting that the "products we make are not injurious to health," the executives committed to further research, creating the Tobacco Industry Research Committee (TIRC). The industry spent an astounding $200 on marketing its addictive product for every $1 spent on "research." Yet the TIRC was far from a scientific enterprise, as it obfuscated and diverted attention from the true health hazards of tobacco use.

Beyond disingenuous research, Big Tobacco's propaganda machine sowed public doubt: industry insiders were delighted, for example, by exit surveys showing that their 1972 propaganda film, *Smoking and Health*—shown to hundreds of thousands, including high school students—eased viewers' concerns about the hazards.[14] While stoking uncertainty, the industry also presented smoking as a personal choice, arguing that regulation was unnecessary beyond ensuring that individuals were informed of the "debate" over cigarette safety.

Big Tobacco privately recognized the health risks, as internal communiqués have since revealed, but carried its public denials to farcical lengths. The high-water mark for its deceit may have been in 1994 when tobacco CEOs testified to the U.S. Congress under oath that they believed smoking was neither addictive nor carcinogenic.[15] As its stalling campaign faltered and high-income countries enacted effective regulations, the industry turned its marketing aptitude to the developing world, hoping to addict a new generation of children and adolescents.

Intense Social Mobilization

Grave challenges to the public's health rarely are overcome through scientific advancements alone, as we have learned from the AIDS movement. Social mobilization is needed to bring about change from the bottom up: disseminating information, supporting communities at risk, and galvanizing pressure on governments to act.

Among public health crises, tobacco politics presented unique challenges. Unlike campaigns to eradicate polio or smallpox, the antismoking movement was at war with a multinational industry with deep pockets and a vested interest in perpetuating the crisis. As well, there was a widespread misperception that the harms of smoking were self-inflicted and therefore not a matter of public concern.

Big Tobacco's counterpropaganda lost any shred of credibility on May 12, 1994, when a whistle-blower at Brown and Williamson's law firm disclosed 10,000 pages of internal industry documents. The "Tobacco Papers," along with documents unearthed in litigation (see Box 7.2), uncovered the industry's unscrupulous practices of concealing its product's toxicity and addictiveness, targeting children and adolescents, and manipulating nicotine levels.[16]

BOX 7.2 **Three Waves of United States Tobacco Litigation**

Successes in tort litigation against Big Tobacco were long in coming: cigarette makers had fended off lawsuits since the mid-1950s, mainly from persons with lung cancer. It was not until the late 1990s that Big Tobacco first paid out damages. In the first wave of litigation, dating from 1954 to 1973, the industry's core defense was to deny the evidence linking cigarettes to disease. In the second wave of litigation, from 1983 to 1992, the defense tactic shifted to emphasize that smokers knowingly assumed the health risks of lighting up.

In November 1998, at a high-water mark of the third wave, forty-six states reached a $206 billion Master Settlement Agreement with four leading tobacco companies, to be paid over twenty-five years. In addition to the payments, the agreement required the industry to restrict marketing, disband front groups, and release documents disclosed in litigation. The third wave of litigation also saw individual plaintiffs succeeding against Big Tobacco, with lawsuits drawing upon the so-called Tobacco Papers—documents revealing the industry's long-term deceit and obfuscation.

From a public health perspective, perhaps the most important effect of tobacco litigation was to transform public and political perceptions about risk and responsibility in smoking, making clear what manufacturers knew, how they concealed this knowledge, and how they manipulated consumers. This spurred regulation and litigation in other countries and became a catalyst for the Framework Convention on Tobacco Control.

The lawsuits and media coverage fueled by the Tobacco Papers reinvigorated social movements. Professional organizations joined the fray (e.g., the American Cancer Society and the International Union against Cancer), allied with skillful civil society groups such as Tobacco-Free Kids. Powerful philanthropists, including the Bloomberg and Gates foundations, stepped in with a huge influx of resources for tobacco control in the United States and globally.

By the late 1990s, most industrialized states had adopted strong regulatory measures and saw tobacco consumption plummet. As the industry shifted its attention to unregulated markets in the developing world, the need for international cooperation became clear, with the WHO as the obvious locus for global leadership.[17]

The Framework Convention on Tobacco Control

In May 1995 the World Health Assembly asked the director-general to report on "the feasibility of developing an international instrument, such as guidelines, a declaration or an international convention on tobacco control to be adopted by the United Nations."[18] By this time tobacco had become a worldwide pandemic, the evidence of harm was abundant, and a detailed picture of Big Tobacco's strategy of denial and obfuscation was understood.

International cooperation became essential given the globalization of tobacco products and marketing, and the industry's aggressive pursuit of new markets in Africa, Asia, eastern Europe, and Latin America. Cross-border advertising rendered domestic bans ineffective, while a growing tide of illicit trade in tobacco products undermined taxation and other tobacco control policies. Normally, it would have been nearly impossible to gain worldwide consensus around a global health treaty. But the tobacco industry—even with all of its political influence and economic clout—was widely reviled. What emerged was a period of social action and political resolve that would lead to a landmark global health treaty.

The Framework Convention on Tobacco Control (FCTC) was nevertheless politically contentious, taking a decade to draft and negotiate (see the FCTC Time Line at www.fctc.org).[19] It took a vast civil society movement, with the creation of the Framework Convention Alliance in 1998; champions in the halls of government; and the arduous work of NGOs, researchers, and trial attorneys who uncovered the full extent of Big Tobacco's disinformation.

The WHA adopted the FCTC by consensus in 2003,[20] and it was opened for signature on June 16, 2003. By the end of the signature period twelve months later, 168 states had signed, making the FCTC one of the most widely and rapidly embraced treaties in United Nations history.[21] The convention entered into force on February 27, 2005, creating binding norms for demand reduction, supply reduction, and information/resource sharing. As of 2013 there were 177 states parties covering 88 percent of the world's population, with two densely populated countries conspicuously missing—Indonesia and the United States.[22]

The FCTC achieved three great advances in tobacco control, demonstrating the power of international law. First, the convention spurred cooperative action, overcoming classic collective-action problems such as cross-border advertising and the illicit tobacco trade. Second, the convention—through its negotiation and ongoing Conference of the Parties (COP)—formed a "social hub" where civil society and governments could convene for support, information exchange, and advocacy. Third, the convention built international consensus around social norms (tobacco as socially unacceptable), scientific facts (the incontrovertible harms to smokers and those exposed to environmental smoke), and the public health imperatives (placing tobacco control high on the global political agenda).

The convention's Secretariat must report regularly on global progress in FCTC implementation. Its 2012 report estimates the average rate of implementation for all substantive articles, across all member states, at 56 percent. Nearly 80 percent of the 159 countries that submitted implementation reports since 2007 strengthened tobacco control following ratification.[23] As with so many metrics, however, the appearance of overall progress masks serious disparities. For example, China—the world's largest producer and consumer of tobacco—has shown "an alarming lack of progress on tobacco control,"[24] while India has been slow in implementing key FCTC provisions, such as smoke-free environments and health education. Court challenges have also thwarted efforts to ban smoking in theaters.[25]

The Framework Convention–Protocol Approach

Although it is frequently stated that the FCTC is the WHO's first treaty, the Nomenclature Regulations and the International Health Regulations (IHR) actually preceded it. The Vienna Conventions on the Law of Treaties define a treaty as a binding agreement between states (or between states and international organizations) intended to create legal rights and duties. Agreements negotiated by international organizations with treaty-making powers, such as the WHO's IHR, are included within the definition.

The FCTC, however, is the only treaty adopted under article 19 of the WHO Constitution, which grants the WHA the power to "adopt conventions or agreements" by a two-thirds vote. WHO members must "take action" by accepting or rejecting the convention within eighteen months, giving reasons for their decision (art. 20). States parties must report annually on "action taken" toward implementation (arts. 20, 62). As explained in Chapter 4, this is a powerful mechanism, highly unusual in international law.

The framework convention–protocol approach is a powerful tool for transnational social movements to safeguard health and the environment; one example is the UN Framework Convention on Climate Change with its Kyoto Protocol. Under this model, states create a binding accord using an incremental process with key normative standards, information sharing, and ongoing monitoring. More stringent obligations can be subsequently created through protocols.

The FCTC provides the blueprint for a global mesh of systematic and integrated national tobacco control policies. The framework-protocol approach has the advantage of considerable flexibility, allowing states parties to decide critical issues at the level of specificity that is currently politically feasible, deferring consideration of more complex or contentious issues to later protocols. It also allows parties to negotiate guidelines and protocols in response to newly emerging issues. Further, it creates a bottom-up process of social mobilization, as illustrated by civil society engagement in the FCTC Alliance.

Its principal disadvantage is that the framework often establishes broad principles without specificity and enforcement; the FCTC's norms are sometimes vaguely worded and lack strong accountability mechanisms. The other disadvantage—the difficulty of negotiating subsequent protocols—has already materialized.

Objective and Guiding Principles

The FCTC's declared objective is to "protect present and future generations from the devastating health, social, environmental and economic consequences of tobacco consumption and exposure to tobacco smoke by providing a framework for tobacco control . . . to reduce continually and substantially [its] prevalence" (art. 3). The convention's guiding principles include informing the public about health hazards, building political support, facilitating international cooperation, and promoting civil society engagement (art. 4).

The FCTC's "general obligations" outline broad strategies for achieving these aims, requiring states parties to develop, implement, and periodically update comprehensive, multisectoral national tobacco-control strategies, with national coordination and effective regulations. States parties are required to cooperate with each other and with international organizations, for example, by sharing information and raising resources for effective implementation of the convention (art. 5). The convention sets only minimum requirements, encouraging states parties to impose stricter policies (art. 2(1)) and to enter bilateral or multilateral agreements (art. 2(2)).

Public Health, Human Rights, and Trade: Synergy or Tension?

While the IHR call for a "balancing dynamic" between public health, trade, and human rights (Chapter 6), the FCTC prioritizes public health, emphasizing states' rights "to protect public health" (preamble). The IHR primarily stress civil and political rights (e.g., individual dignity, autonomy, and privacy), whereas the FCTC emphasizes socioeconomic rights, affirming the WHO Constitution's primary norm: "the highest attainable standard of health is one of the fundamental rights of every human being" (preamble).[26] The FCTC, therefore, finds synergies between public health and human rights.

In the FCTC, however, the relationship between health and trade is more equivocal. The convention does not include an explicit trade provision, as the states parties were unable to reach agreement. Some wanted a clear expression of "health over trade" in the text, while others countered that this would invite "disguised protectionism" and create a precedent whereby states forgo their prior treaty obligations.[27]

Although it lacks formal legal force, the FCTC Conference of Parties adopted the Punta del Este Declaration on November 29, 2010, reiterating states parties' "firm commitment to prioritize the implementation of health measures designed to control tobacco consumption." States parties asserted their sovereign "right to define and implement national public health policies" under the FCTC, "including regulating the exercise of intellectual property."[28]

The political compromise of not explicitly prioritizing health over trade would become problematic, as battles are now being waged under trade and investment treaties between industry and public health. Meanwhile, Big Tobacco is litigating in domestic courts—arguing that public health should not trump economic interests. The FCTC, moreover, has not been as effective in influencing trade and investment regimes as it could have been. Although the convention encourages states parties to implement measures beyond those required, it also stipulates that domestic regulation must be "in accordance with international law"—presumably including trade and investment agreements (art. 2(1)).

Institutional Arrangements: The COP and the Framework Convention Alliance

The Conference of the Parties (COP) is the governing body of the FCTC, comprised of all parties to the convention. The COP's mandate is to review and promote the treaty's implementation through the adoption of protocols, annexes, and amendments to the convention (art. 23). The COP aims at consensus, but where this is unattainable, decisions may be adopted by a two-thirds majority of the parties in attendance. The COP plays a critical role: setting normative standards, disseminating information, and mobilizing international cooperation and resources.[29] The COP met annually for its first three years (in Geneva, Bangkok, and Durban) before scheduling biannual meetings (in Punta del Este and Seoul). The WHO hosts the COP's Secretariat, which supports the states parties in fulfilling their treaty obligations (art. 24).

The COP is empowered to create subsidiary entities, such as the Intergovernmental Negotiating Body (INB) on a Protocol on Illicit Trade in Tobacco Products, and guidelines/recommendations for working groups (art. 23). In 2012 the COP adopted its only protocol to date—a protocol on illicit trade that has the force of international law. The protocol opened for signature in January 2013; as of September 2013, twenty-three countries had signed the protocol.[30]

Under framework conventions, states often prefer the adoption of guidelines rather than protocols, because they create "softer" norms. Article 7 requires the COP to propose implementation guidelines on articles 8–13 (nonprice measures), but it has gone further. As of 2013 the COP had adopted seven guidelines covering provisions in eight of the convention's articles: 5.3 (fighting vested interests), 8 (environmental tobacco smoke), 11 (packaging and labeling), 12 (education and public awareness), 13 (advertising and promotion), and 14 (tobacco dependence and cessation). The COP has also issued partial guidelines on tobacco ingredients and disclosures (arts. 9, 10). Guidelines do not have the force of law but provide advice to states parties, containing normative standards that can exceed those in the convention.

The Framework Convention Alliance, although not a formal FCTC organ, is a global network of more than 350 NGOs that had marked influence in negotiating the FCTC and the illicit trade protocol, and it continues to be a potent advocate. The alliance demonstrates the power of social movements to hold governments to account in fulfilling their treaty obligations.

Protecting Public Health from Big Tobacco's Vested Interests

The FCTC demonstrated mistrust of Big Tobacco by requiring states parties to set tobacco control policies without interference from "commercial and other vested interests" (art. 5(3)). The preamble warns states to be alert to industry subversion of national policies—an admonition that turned out to be prescient.

Responding to civil society advocacy, the COP 3 (i.e., the third regular session of the COP) adopted guidelines to address the "fundamental and irreconcilable conflict between the tobacco industry's interests and public health policy interests." States parties are urged to (1) limit and ensure the transparency of interactions with the tobacco industry, including state-owned industry and individuals or front groups for the industry; (2) refuse the industry or its conduits preferential treatment; (3) avoid conflicts of interest within government; and (4) denormalize activities that the industry characterizes as "socially responsible."[31] Unlike other industries implicated in public health (e.g., food or energy), Big Tobacco is not a genuine stakeholder with any rightful claim to participate in policy making.

Demand Reduction: Preventing and Reducing Tobacco Consumption and Exposure

Tobacco is the only lawful product that kills up to half of its consumers when used as intended.[32] It not only kills smokers (and non-smokers), but also often causes prolonged suffering from diseases such as lung cancer or emphysema. The classic public health approach to all harmful products is to influence behavior to avoid or diminish the risks by (1) preventing individuals, especially children and adolescents, from ever taking up the habit, and (2) helping smokers to reduce their dependence or, preferably, to quit entirely. Accordingly, the FCTC requires states parties to adopt demand reduction strategies: tax, price, and nonprice measures.

Taxing and pricing Tax and price policies can be highly effective in preventing and reducing tobacco use. The higher the price—whether through taxation, tariffs, or sales practices—the greater the reduction in smoking, and this is particularly true for low-income consumers such as children and adolescents. Although states retain sovereignty over taxation, the FCTC encourages (1) taxing and pricing guided by health objectives, and (2) restricting or prohibiting the sale or importation of tax- or duty-free tobacco products by international travelers (arts. 6(1)(2)). States must report tobacco tax rates and consumption trends to the COP (arts. 6(3), 21).

Environmental exposure: A 100 percent smoke-free environment Tobacco demand reduction policies diverge from the classic public health paradigm by targeting "self-regarding" behavior. Tobacco primarily harms smokers themselves, which enabled the industry for decades to claim that the state should not interfere with personal autonomy. Big Tobacco disingenuously framed—and still frames—smoking as a "right" and a "freedom." Although this libertarian argument still has political traction in some countries, it fails on its own terms: the majority of smokers take up the highly addictive habit in adolescence, at a stage when they are unable to make rational and informed judgments about the dangers of smoking.

The idea that tobacco control was paternalistic, however, was turned on its head with the realization that smoking was "other regarding." Environmental tobacco smoke (ETS) is hazardous to everyone exposed, especially those with prolonged involuntary exposures (e.g., in airplanes, bars, and restaurants).[33] Infants and children are at particular peril when constantly exposed to toxic fumes in their family homes and vehicles.

Accordingly, the FCTC requires that states parties protect against ETS in workplaces, public transport, and indoor public places (art. 8). Many states have enacted countrywide clean indoor air acts, which prohibit smoking in most, or all, enclosed public places. Some cities have gone further, restricting outdoor smoking (e.g., at beaches, parks, and shopping areas).[34] Other laws ban smoking in vehicles with children but do not cover smoking in the home, which is their principal place of exposure. Overall, smoke-free laws reduce smoking, enhance air quality, and support longer and healthier lives.[35]

In 2007 the COP 2 issued more ambitious guidelines on ETS, covering all indoor workplaces, indoor public places, and public transport, as well as outdoor public places "as appropriate."[36] National legislation should create a 100 percent smoke-free environment, recognizing there is no safe level of exposure; engage civil society to support smoke-free laws;

and create mechanisms to enforce, monitor, and evaluate the legislation.[37] Contrary to tobacco and service industry claims, 100 percent smoke-free laws do not have an adverse economic effect on bars, restaurants, and places of entertainment.[38] When given the choice, most people want to socialize and work in places where the air is fresh and clean.

Tobacco ingredients In April 1994 six major American tobacco companies disclosed a list of cigarette ingredients that had long been kept a secret: 4,000 chemical compounds, forty-three of which are recognized carcinogens and many of which are poisonous, including carbon monoxide, nitrogen oxides, hydrogen cyanides, and ammonia. The chemicals released when burning tobacco are hazardous to smokers and to those who breathe secondhand smoke.[39] Carcinogens in the body spike at the first puff. "The chilling thing . . . is just how early the very first stages of the process begin—not in 30 years but within 30 minutes of a single cigarette."[40]

The FCTC charges states parties to ensure that manufacturers and importers disclose the contents and emissions of tobacco products, including on packaging, so that the public is aware of their toxic constituents (arts. 10 and 11). The COP 4 issued partial guidelines, with a view to establishing full guidelines for sampling, testing, and measuring noxious ingredients to ensure uniformity and scientific rigor (art. 9).[41]

Packaging and labeling Tobacco companies use packaging not only to inform consumers about product details (e.g., brand, price, contents) but also to attract them (e.g., by using color, images, sales messages). Package designs are alluring, associating smoking with glamorous, healthful pursuits. Teens, women, and racial minorities are often targeted.

States parties must ensure that packages and labels are not false, misleading, deceptive, or likely to convey an erroneous impression. For example, labels such as "low tar," "light," "ultra light," or "mild" falsely imply that these cigarettes are less hazardous than those without such labels. States parties must also ensure that packages and labels contain health warnings. National authorities must sign off on a rotation of large, clear warnings, occupying at least 30 percent of the display area (preferably more than 50 percent). The label may include vivid images that graphically convey the harms of smoking (art. 11(1)). The COP 3 guidelines recommend larger warnings with images; bans on logos, colors, and brand images; display of toxic contents; and penalties for industry noncompliance.[42]

Big Tobacco vigorously opposes laws that require lurid depictions on their packages of the harm caused by smoking, claiming that "mandated gruesome images (smoke coming out of a tracheotomy hole, rotting teeth, cadavers) convey no new information."[43] But graphic health warnings do convey a clear message that truthfully depicts the horrors of smoking. The industry protests against graphic warnings precisely because vivid images are effective in reducing smoking. And the industry wants it both ways, insisting that their glamorous cigarette package images are a form of free expression, whereas the government's vivid warnings have no informational value. Big Tobacco is now using international trade and investment agreements to sue states for enacting "plain packaging" legislation in compliance with their FCTC obligations (see the section titled "The Australia Plain-Packaging Case" later in this chapter).

Advertising, Promotion, and Sponsorship

Cigarette advertisements are replete with text and images associating smoking with healthy, adventuresome, glamorous lifestyles. These messages mislead the public, implying that health warnings are exaggerated. Tobacco campaigns, moreover, appeal to multiple demographics: fitness, wealth, and power for men; slimness, emancipation, and sophistication for women; and youthful vigor, sexual attraction, and independence for adolescents.

Enticing children For Big Tobacco to remain profitable, it must recruit new smokers to replace those who quit or die. Since long-term smoking characteristically begins at a young and suggestible age—and because those who start early in life become the heaviest smokers—this is the target market. For decades, Big Tobacco lured children by linking its brands to cartoon characters, giving away cool clothing and free cigarettes, and sponsoring sports, music, film, and fashion. A study conducted in 1991 found that more children recognized Joe Camel than Mickey Mouse. What is worse, Big Tobacco has redeployed in developing countries tactics now banned in Europe and North America.[44] And in highly regulated countries, the industry has turned to social media such as Facebook to engage young audiences, inviting them to shape and vote on marketing campaigns.[45]

Attracting girls and women It did not escape the notice of Big Tobacco that half its potential market—girls and women—rarely smoked at the midpoint of the twentieth century. (And in many lower-income countries today, relatively few women smoke.) By 1968 the Altria Group (formerly Philip Morris) launched Virginia Slims (also sold as "super-slims," "light," and "ultra-light"), with the slogan "You've come a long way, baby." In the 1990s, ad campaigns morphed into "It's a woman thing" and "Find your voice"—as if smoking were a symbol of feminine power. More recently, R. J. Reynolds, eager to push its Camel brand among women, introduced Camel No. 9, signaling its buyers with subtle cues like its colors, a pink fuchsia and a minty teal; its slogan, "Light and luscious"; and the flowers surrounding cigarette packs in magazine ads. As the *New York Times* put it, "The next time R. J. Reynolds Tobacco asks smokers to walk a mile for a Camel, watch how many of them are in high heels."[46]

Targeting minorities Whereas smoking was once a fashion statement among the professional and moneyed classes, it is now gravitating to the poor and less educated.[47] Tobacco companies—noticing the growth potential—are pushing menthol-flavored cigarettes in urban minority communities with price discounts and signage, hip-hop music, and cultural edginess. R. J. Reynolds's Uptown brand—introduced during Black History Month in 1989—boldly targeted African Americans, featuring black models and urban nightlife: "Uptown, the place, the taste." Remarkably, the Family Smoking Prevention and Tobacco Control Act, signed by President Barack Obama in 2009, bans flavored cigarettes but exempts menthol pending a Food and Drug Administration (FDA) review (see the section titled "Indonesia–U.S. Clove Cigarettes Case" later in this chapter). Mentholated cigarettes are particularly popular among African Americans.

The FCTC requires states parties to comprehensively ban all tobacco advertising, promotion, and sponsorship (art. 13(2))—including radio, television, print, and electronic media ads (art. 13(4)(e)). During FCTC negotiations, politically influential countries such as the United States objected to a total advertising ban, claiming that this would violate freedom of expression (Box 7.3). Consequently, the FCTC allows states parties to "act in accordance with constitutional principles," which can undermine tobacco control policies.

Even where constitutional protections preclude a ban, states parties still must restrict advertising, promotion, and sponsorship (art. 13(3)). Minimally, states parties must prohibit messages that are false, misleading, or deceptive; require health warnings; restrict incentives (e.g., free samples); and mandate industry disclosure of expenditures on advertis-

BOX 7.3 The United States Commercial Speech Doctrine: Conflating Money with Speech

During FCTC negotiations, the United States insisted that the duty to ban advertising should not violate freedom of expression under national constitutional principles. The U.S. Supreme Court has ardently defended commercial speech, overturning government restrictions on the advertising of tobacco and alcoholic beverages.[1]

In *Lorillard Tobacco Co. v. Reilly* (2001), the Supreme Court struck down comprehensive state advertising regulations that banned outdoor advertising near playgrounds or schools and imposed point-of-sale restrictions such as requiring shops to place ads higher than five feet. "The broad sweep of the regulations," said the Court, "indicates that the Attorney General did not carefully calculate the costs and benefits associated with the burden on speech imposed."[2]

Tobacco Companies Fume over FDA Rule

In 2009 President Obama signed the historic Family Smoking Prevention and Tobacco Control Act (FSPTCA), empowering the FDA to regulate tobacco.[3] In a direct rebuke to the Supreme Court, the FDA issued a 2010 rule similar to the one struck down in *Lorillard*, with broad restrictions on advertising and promotions. Big Tobacco immediately challenged the FSPTCA and the FDA rule as a violation of free speech. R. J. Reynolds protested that "the law severely restricts the few remaining channels we have to communicate with adult tobacco consumers."[4]

The Sixth Circuit U.S. Court of Appeals upheld the FSPTCA's directive of "color graphics depicting the negative health consequences of smoking" on cigarette packets, reasoning that Big Tobacco has learned to circumvent marketing bans. "We return to where we began—the lack of consumer awareness of tobacco's serious health risks resulting from the decades-long deception."[5]

The U.S. Court of Appeals for the District of Columbia, however, struck down the FDA rule requiring "in-your-face" images covering half the packet, front and back—diseased lungs, gnarly, rotting teeth, and a smoker's corpse—with the warnings "Smoking can kill you" and "Cigarettes cause cancer."[6] The court said that the government could compel only "purely factual and uncontroversial disclosures," and only to directly advance a valid state objective. The graphic warnings, the Court found, were designed to "evoke emotion," and the FDA presented not a "shred of evidence" of the labels' effectiveness in reducing smoking prevalence.

With conflicting appellate decisions, it appeared that the matter was destined for the U.S. Supreme Court. The prospects of success for the government were not bright: in 2011 the Court found that commercial speech restrictions are subject to "heightened scrutiny" if based on who the speaker is and the content of the message—which is what tobacco advertising regulations aim to do.[7] Anticipating a possible defeat, in March 2013 the government chose not to seek Supreme Court review, sending the FDA back to the drawing board to devise a new set of warning labels.[8] At the time of writing this book, the FDA was researching new graphic warning labels that would effectively deter smokers and would-be smokers, but which could also withstand constitutional challenge.[9]

NOTES

1. *44 Liquormart, Inc. v. Rhode Island*, 517 U.S. 484, 516 (1996); *Rubin v. Coors Brewing Co.*, 514 US 476, 489–91 (1995).
2. *Lorillard Tobacco Co. v. Reilly*, 533 U.S. 525, 561–71 (2001).
3. Family Smoking Prevention and Tobacco Control Act of 2009, Pub. L. No. 111–31, 123 Stat. 1776 (codified at 21 U.S.C. § 387 et. seq.).
4. Ronald Bayer and Matthew Kelly, "Tobacco Control and Free Speech: An American Dilemma," *New England Journal of Medicine* 362, no. 4 (2010): 281–283.
5. *Discount Tobacco City & Lottery, Inc. v. United States*, 674 F.3rd 509 (6th Cir. 2012), 84.
6. *R. J. Reynolds Tobacco Co. v. U.S. Food and Drug Administration*, 696 F.3rd 1205 (D.C. Cir. 2012).
7. *Sorrell v. IMS Health, Inc.*, 131 S. Ct. 2653, 2664 (2011).
8. Jennifer Corbett Doorsen, "FDA Scraps Graphic Cigarette Warnings," *Wall Street Journal*, March 19, 2013, http:// online.wsj.com/news/articles/SB10001424127887323639604578370874162067966.
9. John D. Kraemer and Sabeeh A. Baig, "Analysis of Legal and Scientific Issues in Court Challenges to Graphic Tobacco Warnings," *American Journal of Preventive Medicine* 45, no. 3 (2013): 334–342.

ing, promotion, and sponsorships (art. 13(4)). States parties are encouraged to go beyond these minimal obligations (art. 13(5)).

Cross-border advertising—via television, radio, and the Internet—is an ongoing concern, as it undermines state sovereignty over public health. The FCTC requires states parties to ban or restrict cross-border advertising; cooperate in the development of technologies; and consider a protocol for international collaboration (art. 13(6, 7, 8)). In 2010 the COP reported that only approximately 35 percent of states reported a total advertising ban, including across borders.[48]

Although the COP has yet to negotiate a protocol on cross-border advertising, it issued guidelines in 2010 recommending an expert committee and a website dedicated to information exchange on this topic. The guidelines advise states on enacting and enforcing a comprehensive ban

promotion, and sponsorship (within constitu-
elines also elaborate on the meaning of a "com-
; an "indicative" (nonexhaustive) list of banned
ntraditional" techniques such as retail displays,
s to retailers, and corporate "social responsibil-

The FCTC requires states parties to strengthen
zards of tobacco using all available communi-
ation, training (e.g., of health and community
engagement (e.g., public and private actors).
s should address the adverse health, eco-
ects of tobacco products (art. 12). The COP
the effectiveness of education and training,
ee, universal access to accurate and truth-
with special emphasis on priority populations.[50]

Dependence and cessation Most of the FCTC's demand reduction strategies aim to prevent smoking initiation, ideally making the habit inconvenient, unattractive, and socially undesirable. But smokers are not to blame, and the aim should not be punishment—most smokers began as children, and many are heavily addicted to nicotine. It is vital to do everything possible to help current smokers quit or at least reduce their reliance on tobacco.

Consequently, states parties must develop comprehensive guidelines and adopt effective measures to promote tobacco cessation and treatment for dependence (e.g., counseling and nicotine replacement). Although long-term success rates of smoking cessation therapies remain low, behavioral and pharmaceutical interventions can be cost-effective.[51] Evidence-based support and treatment programs must have a broad reach, extending into schools, health care facilities, and workplaces. Such programs should be accessible and affordable to all (art. 14).

Supply Reduction: Illicit Trade, Minors, and Viable Alternatives

Tobacco is the most hazardous drug sold lawfully in the world—more dangerous than many drugs that are banned and criminalized. The FCTC does not call for a worldwide prohibition on tobacco products, but rather aims to reduce supply using three measures: eliminating illicit trade in tobacco, banning sale to minors, and supporting viable alternatives for tobacco workers and sellers.

Illicit trade The illicit trade in tobacco products—smuggling, bootlegging, unlawful manufacturing, and counterfeiting—is a global problem linked to organized crime through well-established distribution channels.[52] "It's a way of getting cheap, illegal cigarettes into the hands of young people, poor people, people who are in a vulnerable position. The finance from the trade . . . gets into the hands of organizations which will use to finance other crime—human trafficking, drug trafficking, weapons trafficking, and even worse." Low manufacturing costs and high profit margins from tax evasion make the illicit market attractive. In 2009 illicit trade was estimated at 11.6 percent of global cigarette consumption (657 billion cigarettes) and 16.8 percent in lower-income countries.[53]

For governments worldwide, illicit trade is a major fiscal and public health challenge. It costs states vast tax revenues that could be used for tobacco control—estimated at $30 to $50 billion per annum. Developing countries bear the brunt of lost revenues—20 percent or more of the cigarette market is illicit in many lower-income states.[54] Beyond forgone revenues, illicit trade stimulates demand through reduced prices, with black market cigarettes often 30 percent to 50 percent cheaper than legal products.[55] Illicit traders can sell at affordable prices, circumvent age limits, and evade health regulations such as warnings labels.

Big Tobacco proclaims its opposition to illicit trade: "We fully support regulators, governments and international organizations such as the World Customs Organization, the World Trade Organization, World Health Organization and European Union in seeking to eliminate all forms of illicit tobacco trade. We would like to see all our markets free of it."[56] Yet the industry itself has been engaged, directly and indirectly, in cigarette smuggling. For example, in 2008 two Canadian tobacco giants paid a $1.15 billion settlement after pleading guilty to tax evasion for supplying cigarettes to a contraband scheme.[57] Despite its complicity in crime, Big Tobacco lobbies aggressively to undermine tobacco control policies, arguing that "ever greater taxes" fuel the black market.

Anti-illicit trade policies must be multifaceted, combining licensing and regulation, fiscal/taxation policy, detection technologies, border security, law enforcement, and public awareness campaigns. The FCTC requires states parties to develop a tracking and tracing system to secure the distribution chain. States parties must ensure that all unit packets are marked to assist officials in determining the product's origin, such as "Sales only allowed in [name of country]" (art. 15(2)). To eliminate illicit trade, states parties must monitor cross-border tobacco trade, both gathering and sharing data; impose penalties and create remedies; confiscate contraband and proceeds; and cooperate in investigations and prosecutions (art. 15(4, 5, 6)).

Transnational organized crime markets are global in scale, requiring a coordinated international response. To facilitate this, the COP created the INB in July 2007 (open to all states parties) to draft a protocol on the illicit trade in tobacco products. The INB, after nearly five years of negotiation, proposed a draft protocol at its fifth session in Geneva in April 2012,[58] adopted by the COP 5 in Seoul, Korea in November 2012. The illicit trade protocol will enter into force when forty countries ratify it—a process expected to take two years (Box 7.4).

Sales to minors The UN Convention on the Rights of the Child requires states parties to protect children from tobacco and ensure that children's

BOX 7.4 Protocol on Illicit Trade in Tobacco Products

The first FCTC protocol aims to eliminate illicit trade in tobacco products, in accordance with FCTC article 15. The protocol's negotiations were contentious, with civil society insisting on adequate funding for lower-income countries. Although the protocol does not have an enforceable funding mechanism, it calls for technical assistance, financial support, capacity building, and international cooperation (arts. 3, 4).

Securing the Supply Chain

Part III of the protocol secures the tobacco supply chain by licensing and tracking all key actors in the chain: farmers, manufacturers, wholesalers, transporters, and retailers. All actors must conduct due diligence by monitoring sales, identifying customers, and reporting to national authorities (art. 7). To further secure the supply chain, states parties must, within five years, establish a global tracking and tracing regime and a global information sharing focal point (art. 8). To ensure accountability, supply chain actors must maintain accurate records (art. 9) and take security measures such as reporting suspicious activities and cross-border cash transfers (art. 10). The protocol is applicable to electronic and Internet sales as well as to customs-free zones and duty-free sales (arts. 11–13).

Offenses: Law Enforcement

Part IV of the protocol requires states parties to make illicit trade unlawful, ensure liability for unlawful conduct, and ensure effective and proportionate sanctions (arts. 14–16). Seized contraband may be destroyed and lost taxes recouped (arts. 17–18). The protocol authorizes investigative techniques such as electronic surveillance and undercover operations (art. 19).

Counterfeiting: Declining to Protect Intellectual Property

The Framework Convention Alliance achieved a victory at INB-5 when the negotiating body dropped all references to "counterfeit" from the protocol. The WHO should not protect tobacco companies' intellectual property rights through the force of international law.[1] As the Brazilian delegate to INB-5 put it, this protocol should not "give the false impression that we are here to protect trademarks of the tobacco companies."[2] Beyond the decision to cut references to "counterfeit" products, the preamble states, "This Protocol does not seek to address issues concerning intellectual property rights."

International Cooperation

Part V of the protocol contains strategies to ensure international cooperation. States parties must share relevant information (e.g., seizures and tax evasions) and respond to information requests by states parties with good justification (arts. 20, 21). Data exchanged are subject to national privacy laws (art. 22). International assistance extends to training, technical assistance, and scientific or technological cooperation as well as to criminal investigations (arts. 23, 24). States parties must "afford one another the widest measure of mutual legal assistance in investigations, prosecutions and judicial proceedings" (art. 29).

NOTES

1. Jonathan Liberman, "Combating Counterfeit Medicines and Illicit Trade in Tobacco Products: Minefields in Global Health Governance," *Journal of Law, Medicine and Ethics* 40, no. 2 (2012): 326–347.
2. Conference of the Parties to the WHO FCTC, Intergovernmental Negotiating Body on a Protocol on Illicit Trade in Tobacco Products, Third Session, Verbatim Records of Plenary Meetings, FCTC/COP/INB-IT/3/VR4, June 29, 2009, 93.

interests take precedence over those of the industry. The FCTC specifically requires states parties to prohibit sales to minors. States have various regulatory tools at their disposal, such as a low minimum age for purchase; restrictions at the point of sale (e.g., prominent notices of age limits and hiding cigarette displays); bans on smoking near schools; and bans on flavored cigarettes, vending machines, and youth marketing (art. 16).

Economically viable alternatives Although there is widespread hostility to tobacco corporations, the FCTC does provide a safety net for tobacco farmers, workers, and individual sellers. Article 18 asks parties to promote economically viable alternatives for individuals whose livelihoods would be jeopardized as the tobacco industry declines (art. 17).

International Cooperation and Information Exchange

A core objective of the FCTC is to facilitate national, regional, and international cooperation. States parties must promote and coordinate research on the determinants and consequences of tobacco use and exposure; track the magnitude, patterns, causes, and effects of tobacco use and exposure; and ensure the exchange of scientific, technical, socioeconomic, commercial, and legal information (art.20(1,2)). The FCTC stresses the need for progressive realization of national surveillance systems and statutory/regulatory databases (art.20(3,4)). And it requires state party reporting on treaty implementation to the COP (art. 21).

As the FCTC makes clear, effective tobacco control must be systematic, multisectoral, and scientifically rigorous. Consequently, a major challenge lies in building financial and technical capacities in lower-income countries. Although there is no funding mechanism, the convention urges states parties to develop, transfer, and acquire the necessary technology, knowledge, skills, and expertise (art. 22).

The FCTC's Future Effectiveness

The FCTC represents a momentous achievement in global health governance to prevent and reduce the worldwide scourge of tobacco use and exposure. The convention boasts at least three bold innovations. First, it creates legally binding obligations to develop systematic, multisectoral tobacco control policies. The duties it imposes cover the full spectrum of strategies: demand reduction, supply reduction, and technical/scientific/informational exchanges.

Second, the convention actively promotes international cooperation in an age when tobacco markets (both legal and illicit) are emphatically global. No state, acting alone, can protect its population from tobacco because the supply chain—from agriculture and manufacturing to marketing and promotions—is international, with routes and connections everywhere.

Finally, the FCTC has spurred bottom-up social mobilization, evidenced by the energy and influence of the Framework Convention Alliance. The incremental process of framework conventions can spur civil society to drive implementation and reform, holding governments to account.

Certainly, the FCTC faces multiple challenges. Typical of the framework convention–protocol approach, the FCTC contains few concrete standards that countries must meet. It is vulnerable to the critique that it uses "hortatory rather than legal statements, soft rather than hard law, [without] self-executing requirements, leaving treaty implementation solely at the discretion of individual states."[59] The FCTC employs nonobligatory terminology throughout: "recognize," "consider," "guidelines," "endeavor to," and "without prejudice to the sovereign right of the Parties." The solution to this shortcoming is to specify more rigorous obligations through protocols. But the contentious five-year negotiations on the illicit trade protocol show how arduous a task this will be.

A further challenge is the most familiar in international law, which is to ensure that states possess the capacity for implementation. The Great Tobacco Pandemic is going through an epidemiological transition, where the burdens are moving from the rich to the poor, both within and among states. This transition is willfully fueled by Big Tobacco, which aggressively targets the poor and seeks markets in densely populated low- and middle-income countries. The only sure response is to build national capacities to stand up to Big Tobacco through regulated markets, evidenced-based interventions, information disclosure, and public education.

Capacity building should be the joint responsibility of lower-income countries and the international community. The COP 4 issued partial guidelines recommending domestic financing options, including designated tobacco taxes, licensing and product registration fees, and financial penalties for noncompliance.[60] The COP, however, has failed thus far to devise a coherent strategy for international assistance, which is essential for the FCTC's success.

At the time of the FCTC's adoption, the rate of smoking in high-income countries was already abating—a result of a decades-long campaign of law and social transformation. The same dynamic could occur in lower-income countries as they follow the FCTC's strategies.

The Tobacco Wars: Globalization, Investment, and Trade

Smoking is shifting from industrialized to developing countries, spurred by rising incomes, trade liberalization, and intensive marketing. Losing customers in highly regulated markets, Big Tobacco has gone global, redeploying tactics in poorer countries that are prohibited in Europe and North America—cartoon characters, free cigarettes, games, and sponsorship. High-income states, moreover, often aid and abet domestic manufacturers and advertisers in exporting tobacco to the developing world (Box 7.5).

Big Tobacco is co-opting domestic and international law—investment and trade treaties—to shamelessly challenge state tobacco control policies. It has spent mightily to turn the law on its head: where once courts were used as a tool for justice and health, the industry is using the law as

BOX 7.5 "Developing World Lung Cancer: Made in the USA"

High-income states often adopt a double standard: strictly regulating tobacco at home but pressuring lower-income countries to open their markets to imported cigarettes.[1] In 1997 U.S. Senator John McCain asked, "We want to stop American kids from smoking—so why don't we seem to care as much about Asian or African kids?"[2] He was referring to U.S. policies undermining tobacco control in lower-income countries.

American trade policy promotes expansion of the industry's overseas markets. Nearly every trade and investment treaty negotiated by the United States reduces tariffs on tobacco exporters and protects U.S. tobacco companies' overseas manufacturing and investments. The United States has also turned a blind eye to unscrupulous marketing in poorer countries.

Even after President Clinton issued an executive order in 1991 barring federal agencies from promoting the sale or export of tobacco products, little has changed. President Obama signaled his intention to end tobacco industry protection, but in negotiations on the Trans-Pacific Partnership (TPP), the U.S. government rescinded a "safe harbor" provision that would have protected a state's sovereignty over its tobacco control laws. The then New York City Mayor, Michael Bloomberg, rebuked President Obama, calling it "a colossal public health mistake" that will "severely tarnish" his public health legacy.[3]

Global leadership in tobacco control requires an array of strategies:[4]

- *Global health diplomacy.* The president's Global Health Initiative should partner with lower-income countries to reduce smoking. A demonstrable commitment to tobacco control would improve America's prestige and influence.
- *FCTC ratification.* The United States would send a powerful signal of its global engagement by ratifying the FCTC and building developing-world capacity for treaty implementation.
- *Trade and investment.* The United States should negotiate or renegotiate trade and investment treaties to remove favorable treatment for Big Tobacco, exempting it from any benefit. The Justice Department should support states that are resisting tobacco industry litigation.
- *Resources for global tobacco control.* Tobacco control in lower-income countries is underfunded. The United States should seek a G20 commitment to institute a surtax on tobacco products, with the revenues devoted to a dedicated WHO fund for FCTC implementation.

- *Technical assistance.* The United States could help states in need with the skills required for tobacco control—surveillance, customs, tax, regulatory reform, and program evaluation.

NOTES

1. The title of this box is quoted directly from Thomas Bollyky, "Developing-World Lung Cancer," *Atlantic*, May 24, 2011, http://www.theatlantic.com/health/archive/2011/05/developing-world-lung-cancer-made-in-the-usa/239398/.
2. Ibid.
3. Michael R. Bloomberg, "Why Is Obama Caving on Tobacco?," *New York Times*, August 22, 2013, http://www.nytimes.com/2013/08/23/opinion/why-is-obama-caving-on-tobacco.html.
4. Thomas J. Bollyky and Lawrence O. Gostin, "The United States' Engagement in Global Tobacco Control: Proposals for Comprehensive Funding and Strategies," *Journal of the American Medical Association* 304, no. 23 (2010): 2637–2638.

a sword to strike down strict tobacco regulation. Its goal is to "chill" governments by imposing punitive costs (in defending suits and paying damages) and delaying implementation of national policies. The unmistakable signal is that if a government goes too far in tobacco control—even if mandated under the FCTC—the industry will take a toll on the public purse by embroiling ministries of health and justice in protracted litigation.

Investment Treaties: Should Big Tobacco Gain the Fruits of Its Investments?

There are over 2,500 bilateral investment treaties (BITs) worldwide, as well as investment chapters in multilateral free trade agreements. Capital exporting states often enter into agreements to safeguard the private economic interests of citizens and corporations investing in lower-income states. A BIT sets the terms and conditions for foreign investments.

Expropriation of property Most investment treaties prohibit expropriation of the property of a national contracting party unless the state has a sound public purpose and acts in a nondiscriminatory manner. Even where these requirements are met, states must compensate the foreign investor for expropriating property. Although sound tobacco regulation does not "take" private property directly, the industry claims that such regulation amounts to an indirect expropriation.

A regulation does not trigger an obligation to compensate the industry if it is enacted within the state's legitimate powers, with a sound public purpose, on a nondiscriminatory basis, and uses means proportionate to the aims.[61] Tobacco control laws are squarely within the state's powers to protect the public's health and safety. As the law applies to all tobacco products (domestic and foreign), it is generally applicable and nondiscriminatory. To the extent that the law is consistent with FCTC obligations, it is internationally recognized as commensurate with valid public health objectives.

Thus, lawfully enacted tobacco controls, supported by scientific evidence and for a compelling public health purpose, cannot be regarded as an expropriation of property. Given the legitimacy of such laws and their widespread adoption, any determination that they deprive tobacco companies of their "reasonable expectation" for investment returns appears misplaced.

Dispute resolution Investment treaties often provide a dispute resolution system administered by the International Centre for the Settlement of Investment Disputes. Private investors gain recourse to international arbitration rather than having to sue in the host state's court system. This contrasts with the WTO system, whereby only member states—not private companies—have standing.

Big Tobacco has challenged historic public health reforms in Australia and Uruguay, claiming that tobacco control laws diminish the fruits of their investments. The true "fruits" of tobacco investments, however, are the suffering and early death of the population, accompanied by massive health care costs. Governments have a sovereign power to enact laws to prevent these human and economic harms. Indeed, FCTC parties have a duty to enact strict tobacco control laws. In negotiating investment treaties, states could not have envisaged that such treaties would be used to undercut vital public health reforms.

The Uruguay Graphic Warnings and Differentiated Branding Case

In March 2010, Philip Morris (Switzerland), a subsidiary of International PMI, launched binding international arbitration seeking damages from Uruguay under the Switzerland-Uruguay Agreement on the Promotion and Protection of Foreign Investments. The request for arbitration invoked three provisions of the agreement, requiring the parties (1) not to obstruct the use and growth of investments through unreasonable or discriminatory measures; (2) not to expropriate property except for a public purpose and upon payment of compensation; and (3) to treat claimants' investments fairly and equitably. The agreement also requires the parties to generally respect international commitments, notably WTO intellectual property obligations.

The case hinges on three aspects of Uruguay's tobacco packaging laws, requiring that 80 percent of the surface area of packages be devoted to health warnings; that government-mandated graphic images be used; and that single brands not be marketed in multiple forms, such as expanding a popular brand like Marlboro to a family of "regular," "light," and "mild" products (that is, "differentiated" branding).

As a party to the FCTC, Uruguay was entitled and obligated to impose strict rules for packet labeling and branding. In the Punta del Este Declaration, the COP rallied to Uruguay's defense, asserting its "right to define and implement national public health policies."[62] As one international tribunal put it: "Trade in tobacco products has historically been the subject of close and extensive regulation, a circumstance that should have been known . . . from extensive past experience in the tobacco business. An investor entering an area traditionally subject to extensive regulation must do so with awareness."[63]

State-mandated health warnings are common in every region, reinforced by the FCTC. Research suggests that large and graphic health warnings are effective in reducing tobacco use.[64] Uruguay was similarly justified in curtailing differential branding as misleading because it conveys the illusion of less-harmful alternatives. Reacting to state bans on deceptive labels such as "light" or "mild," Big Tobacco now is using a color-coding ploy, such as gold (signaling "light") or green (signaling menthol). It is well within a state's power to prohibit devious marketing to sell a lethal product.

The proceedings against Uruguay consist of two separate stages. First, Uruguay filed a preliminary challenge as to whether the tribunal had jurisdiction regarding Philip Morris' claims.[65] The tribunal heard arguments on these jurisdiction issues in early 2013, and in July of that year decided that it did have jurisdiction, enabling the tribunal to make a decision on the merits of the case.[66] This second stage in the hearing is likely to take place toward the end of 2014 or in early 2015, and a decision may not be reached for two or three years.[67]

The Australia Plain-Packaging Case

Advocates who have followed Big Tobacco's combative tactics were unsurprised by its attack on Uruguay. More surprising was a challenge to a powerful state with a long history of strict tobacco regulation. Australia became the first country to enact a plain packaging law, which requires tobacco products to be sold in unadorned packets with graphic health warnings.[68] Under the law, the only way to distinguish among brands is by the product name in a standard drab-brown color, position, font size, and style. But Australian cigarette packets are anything but plain. Rather, they bear a rotation of grotesque images luridly depicting the true horrors of smoking, such as a mouth riddled with cancer, an eyeball vacant and blind, and a child breathless and bedridden. (In Brazil, cigarette packets display images of dead fetuses, hemorrhaging brains, and gangrenous feet.)

Australia realized that Big Tobacco used cigarette packets to circumvent advertising bans. The packets delivered a commercial message through vibrant colors, soft texture, and alluring images, and signaled that the brand would give smokers an enjoyable experience. Every time a smoker reached for a cigarette, she would advertise the brand to family, friends, and bystanders. Further, eye-catching packaging encourages young people to try cigarettes.

Fearful that plain packaging would cascade worldwide, Big Tobacco unleashed a ferocious attack on the Australian government. (States such as Canada, New Zealand, and the United Kingdom are currently considering 100-percent plain packaging, although the United Kingdom recently announced that it would delay such measures until the impact of the Australian ban has been established.) The industry's multimillion-dollar mass-media campaign intimated that plain packaging was a paternalistic tool of the "nanny state" that would mire government in litigation at great taxpayer expense. The industry claimed that the law represented a "slippery slope" that would dictate the packaging of alcoholic beverages and unhealthy food. To spite the government and addict more smokers, British American Tobacco slashed the price of cigarettes.

Politically, tobacco companies began to contribute large sums to the (then) opposition Liberal Party. Tobacco interests created and funded front organizations to engage in grassroots advocacy ("astroturfing"), ostensibly on behalf of small-business owners.

Big Tobacco's self-serving campaign was so transparent that it only worsened its public standing. One cartoonist captured the blatant sophistry, with a tobacco lawyer pleading, "My client's business will die a painful and lingering death and he deserves compensation!"[69]

Hours after Australia passed its plain packaging law, Big Tobacco filed a panoply of legal cases: in the High Court of Australia; in investment treaty arbitration; and, later, in the World Trade Organization through state conduits.

The High Court of Australia A consortium of powerful companies (British American Tobacco, Imperial Tobacco, Japan Tobacco, and Philip Morris) sought compensation in the High Court of Australia, alleging that plain packaging violated section 51 of the constitution, which requires that the government's acquisition of property be undertaken "on just terms." (Many countries have similar provisions, such as the U.S. ban on taking property without just compensation.) The plain packaging mandate restricts tobacco companies' rights to use their trademarks, thus reducing their property value. However, the High Court ruled in 2012 that there was no "acquisition" of private property because the government neither uses tobacco trademarks nor obtains a proprietary benefit.[70] The High Court's decision cleared the path for bans on brand marks and logos to take effect from December 2012, along with other restrictions on the design of retail tobacco packaging. Although it is too soon to determine the impact of plain packaging on tobacco use, emerging evidence suggests that it makes cigarettes less appealing and increases smokers' desire to quit.[71]

Investment Treaty arbitration In November 2011, Philip Morris Asia (PMA) gave notice of a dispute under the Hong Kong–Australia Bilateral Investment Treaty.[72] As Mitchell and Studdert observed, "In a remarkable move, this Hong Kong–based subsidiary of the Philip Morris conglomerate purchased a 100% stake in Philip Morris [Australia] only months before the legislation was introduced."[73] Philip Morris Asia claimed that Australia's plain packaging law expropriated its investments and intellectual property without compensation; treated the company inequitably and unfairly; impaired its investments; violated the WTO Agreement on Trade-Related Aspects of Intellectual Property Rights (the TRIPS Agreement) and the Agreement on Technical Barriers to Trade (the TBT Agreement); and violated the Paris Convention for the Protection of Industrial Property.[74]

Although plain packaging may interfere with investors' property, it is a proportionate measure to achieve a fundamental public purpose. Moreover, given Australia's progressively stricter tobacco regulation over the years, PMA could not have had a legitimate expectation that it would have full use of its trademarks. As of 2013 the investment dispute case had not been decided. However, Australia has vowed not to negotiate further treaties providing economic benefit to tobacco companies or permitting binding international arbitration.

WTO dispute Private companies are not WTO members and thus lack standing to file a dispute. But that did not stop Big Tobacco from actively soliciting and financing Ukraine to file a dispute, even though Ukraine has no tobacco exports to Australia and, therefore, no clear economic interest. Following Ukraine's lead, Honduras, the Dominican Republic, and Cuba joined the attack on Australia, filing similar WTO complaints.[75] The TRIPS Agreement grants a trademark owner the exclusive right to prevent others from using identical or similar signs without the owner's consent. Although plain packaging may deny tobacco companies the ability to freely use their trademarks, it does not prevent them from registering their trademarks or refusing permission to others to use those marks. The TRIPS Agreement, moreover, states that trademarks must not be "unjustifiably encumbered." Plain packaging, however, is fully justified as a valid public health measure sanctioned by the FCTC.

In a show of solidarity, the European Union and several states (e.g., Brazil, Canada, Norway, and Uruguay) joined Australia in the consultations.[76] This demonstrates global recognition that plain packaging laws are valid public health measures. As of 2013 the WTO dispute body had not decided the Australian plain packaging dispute, as Ukraine asked the WTO to suspend the adjudication process in November 2012. Ukraine recently reactivated its request for adjudication, and in September 2013 Honduras requested that the WTO establish an adjudication panel to hear the dispute, meaning that it will now proceed.[77]

Big Tobacco's actions against Australia reflect a global trend of the continued use of litigation by the tobacco industry to delay, thwart, or water down countries' tobacco-control policies, particularly in Asia. For example, in June 2013 Philip Morris, along with other tobacco companies, filed suit against the Thai government over its planned increase in the size of graphic health warnings from 55 to 85 percent of cigarette pack covers.[78]

Indonesia–U.S. Clove Cigarettes Case

In 2009 the U.S. Family Smoking Prevention and Tobacco Control Act (FSPTCA) prohibited all flavored cigarettes but exempted menthol flavoring pending an FDA review. Indonesia brought a WTO complaint, claiming discrimination under the TBT Agreement (see Chapter 9). Although all cigarettes pose serious health risks, Indonesia argued that clove cigarettes (mostly imported from Indonesia) and menthol cigarettes (mostly produced in the United States) were "like products." On April 4, 2012, the WTO Appellate Body (AB) upheld a panel's ruling that the U.S. ban was discriminatory. Using a test that balances public health regulation with protection against trade discrimination, the AB found that "both menthol and clove mask the harshness of tobacco" and thus have the same product characteristics.[79]

What is most worrying about the clove cigarettes case was that the WTO trampled on a historic public health law fashioned after years of political compromise—as all democratic institutions must compromise. Menthol cigarettes already constitute a large domestic market share, whereas clove flavoring would have been a virtually new entry into the U.S. market. With so many Americans addicted to menthol cigarettes, Congress feared that a total ban would cause suffering, strain the health system, and drive illicit trade. The AB sent a subtle message that limited exemptions, reached in political compromise, could trigger "like treatment" claims under trade rules. This could constrain a government's ability to make important but incremental advancements in public health law.

The AB did seek to ease states' concerns: "We do not consider that [any WTO agreement should] be interpreted as preventing Members from devising and implementing public health policies generally and tobacco-control policies in particular. . . . Moreover, we recognize the importance of Members' efforts in the World Health Organization on tobacco control."[80]

WTO law required the United States to conform to the AB's ruling within a "reasonable period of time"—in this case by July 2013. The United States indicated that it would comply with the AB's decision, and bring its actions into conformity with the TBT Agreement within the given timeframe. It began this process by taking a number of measures toward regulating menthol cigarettes. Specifically, the FDA published an Advanced Notice of Proposed Rule Making concerning menthol cigarettes,[81] and released a preliminary scientific evaluation on the health effects of menthol cigarettes, finding they negatively affected smokers' attempts to quit.[82]

However, Indonesia argued that the United States failed to comply with the AB's ruling within the allotted time, requesting the right to suspend tariff concessions.[83] As of September 2013, the WTO had agreed to send the matter to arbitration.[84]

The Tobacco Endgames: Toward a Tobacco-Free World

The stunning successes of the tobacco control movement in the developed world offer an inspiring model of what might be done to eradicate the "brown plague" worldwide.[85] In the space of decades, vast changes in law and culture transformed cigarette smoking from being ubiquitous to a point where advocates are envisioning the endgame—to bring smoking prevalence to near-zero levels. Endgame strategies, moreover, must be attentive to social justice so that steep reductions are achieved across all socioeconomic groups and across all regions. It will not be easy, but it is perhaps the most vital global health challenge of our time.

Tobacco control has focused intensely on reducing demand through antismoking campaigns, taxation, clean air laws, package labeling, and restrictions on marketing, promotions, and sponsorships. An endgame strategy must push these reforms still further—extending clean air bans to multi-occupant apartments and outdoor public places; requiring plain packaging and larger, graphic warnings; and banning all advertising, especially to children, focusing on misleading labels such as "light" or "mild."[86] In short, governments must denormalize smoking so that the behavior is personally and socially unappealing and unacceptable.

What sets endgame strategies apart is the focus on the supply side of the tobacco market—rendering cigarettes a lawful but intensely regulated product. The FCTC contains only two supply-side strategies: banning sales to minors and curtailing illicit trade. However, the International Conference on Public Health Priorities in the 21st Century: The Endgame for Tobacco (held in New Delhi, India, in September 2013) identified additional pressure points in the supply chain, ranging from manufacturing to the point of sale, where governments could stifle the cigarette market.[87] When doing so, governments will also need to be aware of moves by tobacco companies to expand smokeless tobacco markets to offset declining cigarette sales.

Tobacco companies perpetuate sales through the product's highly addictive character. Marketing and peer pressure lure young people into experimenting with tobacco, and by the time they grasp the existential threat, they are chemically dependent. Most adults who began smoking as adolescents wish they had never taken up the deadly habit. There is no reason why states ought to permit an addictive and dangerous consumer product to remain on the market.

Governments could pursue a constellation of endgame strategies, with the aim of achieving near-zero tobacco use over time: reducing nicotine content, increasing the smoking age, licensing smokers, controlling all tobacco marketing, setting sales quotas, and/or banning commercial sales.

Reducing nicotine content States could require companies to reduce nicotine content gradually, to below the threshold of addiction.[88] If tobacco were no longer addictive, young people could experiment, but most would give it up over time. Evolving the product over time to nonaddictive levels entails an intergenerational trade-off: younger generations will be saved from the trap of addiction, but already addicted smokers could increase their toxic exposures as they compensate for lower nicotine levels (e.g., deeper inhalation and increased smoking). This requires expansion of cessation and nicotine replacement therapies as well as political courage to transform social expectations.[89]

Increasing the legal age of sale Governments could also gradually increase the legal age for buying tobacco products. For example, in October 2013, New York City raised the legal age of purchase from eighteen to twenty-one years. Singapore and Australia are considering gradually phasing out cigarette sales by changing minimum-age restrictions from "above eighteen" to "born before 2000."[90] With rigorous enforcement, and tight control of the illicit market, younger generations would be saved from a lifetime of smoking. Over time, the increasing-age strategy would transform culture so that younger people never want to smoke. As with all endgame strategies, it will be important to implement a suite of complementary interventions, with substantial public financing, monitoring, and compliance.[91]

Licensing smokers The state could require smokers to obtain a license to purchase tobacco. To obtain a license, the smoker would have to demonstrate full knowledge of its addictive and hazardous qualities as well as pay a licensing fee annually. To incentivize smokers to quit, the state could offer to refund the cumulative license fee with interest if the individual relinquished the license by a certain age. This comports with data showing that individuals who give up smoking by middle age have life expectancies similar to those of nonsmokers.[92]

Controlling tobacco marketing As regulators worldwide struggle to tamp demand, the tobacco industry has been cagey and unrelenting in its marketing, resorting to practices that are immoral, if not illegal, in a bid to addict a new generation of buyers. It has not escaped the industry's notice that children are its future customers, prompting a move to social media such as Facebook, Myspace, and Twitter.[93]

This game of cat and mouse between public health and Big Tobacco must end. In the future, all tobacco messages should be handled exclusively by a public agency with a public health mandate. Such an agency would enjoy a monopsony as a "middleman" between tobacco producers and retailers, working toward its own obsolescence by pursuing branding and marketing strategies that drive sales down.[94] The only information about tobacco that consumers should receive should concern health, addiction, and cessation. Any information apart from this is bound to mislead.

Setting a quota (the "sinking lid") Even more ambitious is a "sinking lid" strategy, whereby regulators incrementally limit the amount of tobacco available for commercial sale, eventually to zero. For example, the government could set a quota on the number of cigarettes sold each year, diminishing over a ten-year time horizon. As supply dwindles, the price of tobacco will be driven upward toward its real social cost. High prices will incentivize smokers to quit and deter younger people from taking up the habit.

Banning commercial sales The most far-reaching endgame strategy would simply ban the commercial sale of cigarettes.[95] If states were to pursue this goal, advocates would have to think through a series of hard questions, such as how to phase out tobacco sales and over what time frame, and how to curb illicit trade. Just as important is how to mobilize social and political support for phasing out the industry.

In 2004 Bhutan became the first (and currently only) country to ban cigarettes, allowing limited import for personal use only. Thus far, the country has a relatively low smoking prevalence (10 percent among adult men, although it is higher among boys).[96]

Against charges of paternalism, endgame proponents point to myriad laws that already prohibit the commercial sale of hazardous goods and services, from asbestos to unsafe automobiles. When cigarettes are looked at as a drug like any other, talk of a ban seems less radical: there is near-universal agreement that if cigarettes were introduced today, regulators would never approve them for commercial sale.

What gives some segments of the public pause about endgame strategies is the failure of alcohol prohibition in the 1920s and the destructive "war on drugs" waged since the 1970s.[97] There are, however, crucial distinctions between tobacco endgames and alcohol or illicit drugs. First, endgame strategists propose that the addictive component of tobacco, nicotine, remain accessible in safer forms (e.g., nicotine replacement therapies). Second, endgame strategists seldom advocate criminal prohibitions on smoking per se. Suppliers are the targets, not smokers. Third, endgame strategies would be initiated only when smoking prevalence sinks to a tipping point, such as less than 10 percent.[98] At that point, smoking would have become so socially objectionable that the public will accept rigorous endgame strategies.

History has shown the tobacco industry to have a kind of in-built response mechanism. As smoking prevalence is reduced in high-income states, the industry preys on those less advantaged, intensifying marketing to the less educated and to lower-income countries. As endgame strategies are rolled out at the national level, global governance for health must be strengthened—from the FCTC with ever more stringent protocols through to agriculture and trade—to ensure that the developing world does not feel the blowback of the last blasts in the war against Big Tobacco.

CHAPTER 8

Health and Human Rights

Human Dignity, Global Justice, and Personal Security

ANIMATED BY THE BELIEF that health is a right, not a privilege to be purchased, AIDS advocates from South Africa and India to Latin America took to the courts to argue that human rights obligate government to provide AIDS medications—and they won. In India, the right to food has served up cooked meals to millions of schoolchildren. A regional human rights commission catalyzed the transformation of Paraguay's mental health system from institutionalization to community care. In Colombia, where unsafe abortions are a leading cause of maternal death, the highest court demanded the legalization of abortions to protect women's health. And an Indian court prohibited smoking in public places to safeguard the right to life. Social movements are now turning to the right to health to demand universal health care, clean water, sanitation, and tobacco control.

Human rights law, with its central tenet of the inherent and equal dignity of all people, is uniquely positioned to catalyze progress toward global health equity. Human rights protections expressly afford everyone the right "to the enjoyment of the highest attainable standard of physical and mental health."[1] This and other socioeconomic rights extend from health care and public health to the social determinants of health, such as water, sanitation, nutrition, housing, education, and employment. Human rights promote civic engagement and political accountability, and can even transform power dynamics, stimulating governments to meet the health needs of even the most marginalized people.

Human rights are universally accepted. Virtually all states have ratified one or both foundational human rights treaties—the International

Covenant on Economic, Social and Cultural Rights (ICESCR) and the International Covenant on Civil and Political Rights (ICCPR). All countries have ratified at least one treaty recognizing the right to health.[2]

The glaring health inequalities pervasive today testify to the still unmet potential of international human rights law. The majority of people who need AIDS treatment still do not have it; malnutrition in sub-Saharan Africa and the Indian subcontinent stubbornly persists. Health equity is the great unmet challenge of the health and human rights movement in our time.

Human rights are routinely and often flagrantly violated, and enforcement is weak. Socioeconomic rights are hedged by such broad stipulations as allowing for progressive realization within maximum available resources (ICESCR, art. 2). Authoritative interpretations that precisely structure these obligations are lacking. Human rights can be in tension with other international legal regimes, such as trade and intellectual property. Yet there is no established hierarchy of regimes or ultimate arbiter.

State sovereignty, politics, and power stand as even greater barriers. Human rights set boundaries on political leaders—what they may not do (e.g., restrict the right to vote or freedom of expression) and what they must do (e.g., invest in health and education). Governments may neglect the needs of the disadvantaged because the latter wield little political power. Human rights demand accountability, but political leaders may resist.

Even liberal democracies have interests that compete with respect for human rights, such as national security, trade, economics, and geopolitical influence. And to the extent that human rights oblige wealthy countries to provide financial and technical support beyond their borders to advance the realization of rights in other countries, budget constraints and competing domestic priorities often stand in the way.

Yet pathways toward improved health through human rights can be found. At the international level, the ICESCR now includes an Optional Protocol to monitor violations and enforce rights. The UN Committee on Economic, Social and Cultural Rights' (CESCR) General Comment 14 and UN special rapporteur reports—although not legally binding—clarify state obligations and offer benchmarks for compliance. Civil society holds governments accountable and litigates right-to-health cases.

This chapter defines the field of health and human rights (its history, doctrine, and case law), explores the power of social movements as champions of health rights, and proposes strategies to build on progress.

Health and Human Rights: From Tension to Synergy

As World War II ended and the unspeakable atrocities of the German Third Reich came to light, delegates of fifty nations signed the United Nations Charter. The UN symbolized a new world order, with its charter reaffirming "fundamental human rights" and the "dignity and worth of the human person."[3] On December 10, 1948, the UN General Assembly adopted without dissent the Universal Declaration of Human Rights (UDHR), commencing an era of human rights under the rule of international law.

Human rights law challenged a prevailing prewar notion of state sovereignty and noninterference in domestic affairs. Although national sovereignty remains robust, the essential premise of human rights—that every person possesses fundamental rights that governments may neither bestow nor deny—rejects the idea. Human rights law expressly confers rights on individuals against their own state. And when states fail to meet their own responsibility to protect their populations from genocide, war crimes, crimes against humanity, or ethnic cleansing the "responsibility-to-protect" norm requires international action.[4]

The origins of the health and human rights movement are comparatively recent, beginning in earnest only with the pioneering work of the late Jonathan Mann early in the AIDS pandemic. At the time, the prevailing view was that individual-centered human rights conflicted with community-oriented public health, as coercion is sometimes exercised to safeguard population health.[5] AIDS advocates' opposition to compulsory testing and criminal prosecutions shifted the paradigm to one viewing health and human rights as mutually reinforcing. The field of health and human rights was born.

Jonathan Mann and colleagues offered a three-part framework to capture the relationship between health and human rights, showing how the two together could advance human welfare.[6] First, health policies could burden human rights, as when quarantines deprive individuals of their freedoms. Second, human rights violations could harm health, even beyond obvious cases such as torture. Discrimination that keeps girls from school, for example, can increase maternal and child mortality. Third, health and human rights are mutually reinforcing. The rights to information, education, nutrition, and social security, for example, safeguard health, and healthy people are better able to participate in the political process and exercise rights of citizenship.

Social movements have taken health and human rights to new heights, with the emergence of AIDS advocacy in the 1980s, from ACT UP in the

United States to the Treatment Action Campaign in South Africa. The disability rights and women's rights communities, too, have become powerful forces. Civil society across the world is organizing around health and human rights. It has successfully linked health rights to concrete interventions, such as the right to AIDS treatment and to tobacco control.

Civil/Political Rights and Economic/Social/ Cultural Rights: A Double Standard

Scholars sometimes frame civil and political rights as "first generation" and economic, social, and cultural rights as "second generation." Despite the unity and equal status of human rights in the UDHR, international treaties reflect this divide. The ICCPR demands immediate state compliance, while the ICESCR is progressively realizable. The collective nature of socioeconomic rights, the progressive realization, and connection to resources meant that they would not be as rigorously enforced. The second generation of rights—although of equal value—has in practice been relegated to secondary status.

Cold war politics further entrenched the division, with the West championing civil and political rights and the Soviet bloc supporting economic, social, and cultural rights. Even as the West triumphed in that ideological conflict, the purported lesser status of economic, social, and cultural rights still lingers. It was only with civil society advocacy that the African Union health strategy for 2007 to 2015 framed the right to health as enforceable.[7] And almost exactly sixty years after the UDHR was adopted, the United States called the right to health an "ultimate goal, not an immediate entitlement."[8]

It is often argued that civil and political rights—sometimes inaccurately termed "negative" rights to designate that they entail freedom from government action—should be attended to first, as they require no positive action or resource commitments from government. Yet the idea that civil and political rights impose no affirmative state obligations, while socioeconomic rights impose costs on societies, is vastly oversimplified. Civil and political rights require state action and resources. Free and fair elections require a census, voter registration, voting machines, ballot counting, and election commissions—and possibly public financing. Fair trials require a trained judiciary, legal assistance, and enforcement. By contrast, the duty not to discriminate in the right to health is immediate, without major cost, and readily enforceable.

International Human Rights Law: The Foundations

Human rights law's potential to improve health derives from its worldwide recognition, with near-universal adoption of its principal treaties, together with declarations, principles, and other nonbinding instruments. The main body of human rights law is comprised of the UN Charter and the International Bill of Human Rights (an informal name given to the UDHR, ICCPR, ICESCR, and their Optional Protocols) as well as "core treaties" safeguarding special populations and proscribing flagrant abuses (Box 8.1 and Table 8.1).

The United Nations Charter and Institutions

The UN Charter is the cornerstone of modern international law. Its preamble articulates the international community's determination "to reaffirm faith in fundamental human rights, [and] in the dignity and worth of the human person." Through the charter, a binding treaty, UN member states pledge to promote "universal respect for, and observance of, human rights and fundamental freedoms for all without distinction as to race, sex, language, or religion" (arts. 55, 56).

The charter affirms human rights as one of the central tenets of the United Nations. Arguably, the centrality of human rights in the charter affords human rights a privileged status over other legal regimes if they conflict—for example, if trade or investment treaties were used to limit a state's power to protect its population's health.

The charter established the Economic and Social Council (ECOSOC) as the principal organ to coordinate the UN's economic and social work. In 1946 ECOSOC created the Commission on Human Rights, which the General Assembly later replaced with the Human Rights Council (Box 8.2). ECOSOC also created the Office of the UN High Commissioner for Human Rights (OHCHR) in 1993. The OHCHR coordinates and strengthens UN human rights activities, supporting special rapporteurs, building human rights capacity of member states, and engaging civil society. The High Commissioner is the principal UN official with responsibility for human rights.[9]

The Universal Declaration of Human Rights

The UDHR built upon the promise of the UN Charter by identifying specific rights and freedoms. The UDHR was the international community's first enunciation of "a common standard of achievement for all

BOX 8.1 Core Human Rights Treaties: Race, Gender, Children, and Persons with Disabilities

The UN has designated nine "core" human rights treaties, which guard against discrimination, protect special populations, and proscribe flagrant human rights crimes (Table 8.1). The UN has also negotiated many other treaties, guidelines, principles, and declarations that affect health, including the suppression of human trafficking, the humane treatment of prisoners, and protection of indigenous people.

Racial and Gender Discrimination

The International Convention on the Elimination of All Forms of Racial Discrimination (ICERD) and the Convention on the Elimination of All Forms of Discrimination against Women (CEDAW) prohibit any distinction, exclusion, or restriction that has the "purpose or effect" of limiting human rights based on race, color, descent, or national or ethnic origin (ICERD), or of limiting the rights of women (CEDAW).[1] States must take measures to eliminate discrimination, including repealing customs or practices that discriminate against women. Both treaties permit affirmative action to achieve equality and equal enjoyment of rights.

ICERD requires equality before the law in "public health, medical care, social security and social services" (art. 5). CEDAW proscribes discrimination in the right to health, including with respect to family planning and access to health services in rural areas. The CEDAW treaty monitoring body has called for "a comprehensive national strategy to promote women's health throughout their lifespan."[2]

The Rights of the Child

The Convention on the Rights of the Child (CRC) proscribes discrimination against and protects the rights of children.[3] The CRC is the most widely adopted human rights treaty, ratified by all UN members except the United States, Somalia, and South Sudan. The CRC requires states to ensure the healthy development of the child by recognizing a right to play and promoting the "physical and psychological recovery" of child victims of exploitation, torture, and armed conflict (art. 39).

The CRC guarantees children the right to the highest attainable standard of physical and mental health and requires states to "strive to ensure that no child is deprived of his or her right of access to such health care services" (art. 24). States should reduce infant and child mortality, combat disease and malnutrition, and abolish harmful traditional practices.

In 2013 the Committee on the Rights of the Child issued General Comment 15 on the right to health, focusing on children in disadvantaged situations; the best interests of the child; and a holistic approach to health, including universal access to quality primary health services and responding to the underlying determinants of health. The general comment recognizes actions across sectors required to fulfill children's right to health, from ensuring that macroeconomic policies do not compromise children's health to investing in road safety and safe public spaces as well as regulating the marketing and availability of unhealthy foods.[4]

The Rights of Persons with Disabilities

The Convention on the Rights of Persons with Disabilities (CRPD) safeguards the full and equal enjoyment of human rights for persons with disabilities. Adopted in 2006 and coming into force in 2008, the treaty has a far-reaching impact, as 1 billion people live with some form of disability.[5] The CRPD's primary principles are equality, nondiscrimination, autonomy, and full participation in society. States must prohibit public and private discrimination, increase access to technologies, and combat prejudice. States must enable people with disabilities to live independently and fully participate in society.

The CRPD requires the same access to health care for people with disabilities as the rest of the population, mandating health services to prevent further disabilities, educating health personnel, and prohibiting health and life insurance discrimination. The CRPD also requires rehabilitation services and affords the right to an adequate standard of living.

NOTES

1. United Nations General Assembly (UNGA), "Convention on the Elimination of All Forms of Discrimination against Women" (1979), entered into force September 3, 1981; UNGA, "International Convention on the Elimination of All Forms of Racial Discrimination" (1966), entered into force January 4, 1969.
2. UN Committee on the Elimination of Discrimination against Women, General Recommendation No. 24, "Women and Health," UN Doc. A/54/38/Rev.1, chap. 1 (1999).
3. UNGA, "Convention on the Rights of the Child, 1989" (1989), entered into force September 2, 1990.
4. UN Committee on the Rights of the Child, General Comment No. 15, "The Right of the Child to the Enjoyment of the Highest Attainable Standard of Health," UN Doc. CRC/C/GC/15, February 15, 2013, art. 24.
5. UNGA, "International Convention on the Protection and Promotion of the Rights and Dignity of Persons with Disabilities" (2006), entered into force May 3, 2008; World Health Organization (WHO) and World Bank, *World Report on Disability* (Malta: WHO, 2011).

peoples and all nations" to promote human rights, which are the "highest aspiration of the common people" (preamble).

The UDHR is pivotally important in state-centric international law because it calls upon not only states but also "every individual and every organ of society" to secure the universal observance of human rights. Toward this end, it stresses "teaching and education to promote respect for these rights and freedoms" (preamble).[10]

The Universal Declaration is not a treaty, but rather a UN General Assembly resolution that generally lacks the formal force of law. Nevertheless, international lawyers widely regard its key provisions as binding—either because the UDHR gives effect to rights guaranteed in the charter or because it has gained the status of customary international law.

The UDHR delineates a basic set of rights that would later be incorporated into treaties. The declaration affords equal status to both civil and political rights (e.g., freedoms of expression, religion, and assembly; prohibitions against torture, slavery, and arbitrary detention; and rights to equal protection and public trials) and social, economic, and cultural rights (e.g., rights to social security, work, education, and an adequate standard of living). Article 25 is particularly important for global health:

> Everyone has the right to a standard of living adequate for the health and well-being of himself and of his family, including food, clothing, housing and medical care and necessary social services, and the right to security in the event of unemployment, sickness, disability, widowhood, old age or other lack of livelihood in circumstances beyond his control.

The cold war's political divisions made it impossible for the international community to unify around a single human rights treaty. It took nearly two decades to adopt two separate treaties (1966), the ICCPR and the ICESCR, and another decade before they entered into force (1976). By 2013 the ICCPR had 167 parties, including the United States, while the ICESCR, which the United States has signed but not ratified, had 161.[11]

The end of the cold war enabled the international community to reassert the unity of human rights, returning full circle to the UDHR's conception of a single set of universal rights, without hierarchies among them. Although not binding, the Vienna Declaration and Program of Action, adopted in 1993, affirms that "all human rights are universal, indivisible and interdependent and interrelated" (para. 5).[12]

The International Covenant on Economic, Social, and Cultural Rights

Article 12 of the ICESCR enunciates the definitive formulation of the right to health: "the right of everyone to the enjoyment of the highest attainable standard of physical and mental health." Article 11 captures key determinants of health: the right to "an adequate standard of living . . . including adequate food, clothing and housing, and to the continuous improvement of living conditions," as well as freedom from hunger. The ICESCR further guarantees labor rights, social insurance, child protection, education, shared scientific benefits, and participation in cultural life.

The ICESCR recognizes that resource limitations may impede states from fully realizing socioeconomic rights. Consequently, states are not required to fully implement all such rights immediately—although the prohibition on discrimination does have immediate effect. Rather, states must "take steps, individually and through international assistance and cooperation, especially economic and technical, to the maximum of [their] available resources, with a view to achieving progressively the full realization" of rights in the ICESCR (art. 2). The most authoritative interpretation of the treaty clarifies the elements of progressive realization:

1. *Expeditious progress.* States must make steady progress, moving "as expeditiously and effectively as possible towards" full realization. The "nonretrogression" principle states that any deliberately retrogressive measures must be "fully justified" by "the totality of rights."[13]
2. *Maximum available resources.* States must realize rights to the "maximum of [their] available resources." If resource constraints render it impossible to comply fully with its obligations, the state has the "burden of justifying" that it has made every effort to use all available resources "as a matter of priority."[14]
3. *International cooperation.* States must cooperate toward achieving ICESCR rights, and those "in a position to do so" must provide economic and technical assistance. (See also UN Charter, arts. 55–56.)[15]
4. *Minimum core obligation.* Although not stated in the ICESCR, states have "a minimum core obligation to ensure, at the very least, minimum essential levels of each of the rights."[16]

The latitude offered by the principle of progressive realization does not render ICESCR rights unenforceable. As with other flexible legal standards, court decisions, national laws, practice, and scholarship gradually draw out its specific, enforceable implications. Civil society and academics are developing metrics to inform courts whether states are spending the "maximum of their available resources."[17]

The ICESCR has only a single relatively weak accountability mechanism, requiring states to report on progress to the ECOSOC. The ECOSOC, in turn, created the CESCR, which reviews reports and makes recommendations to states. The CESCR also issues "general comments" to further clarify the ICESCR, notably General Comment 14 on the right to health.

An Optional Protocol negotiated in 2008 (applicable only to states that ratify it) establishes a process for adjudicating specific rights violations. Upon entering into force in May 2013 following ratification of a tenth state, individuals or groups are empowered to submit complaints about rights violations to the CESCR. Complainants must first exhaust domestic remedies and demonstrate harm or that their complaint "raises a serious issue of general importance" (art. 4). The CESCR then would draw conclusions and make recommendations.

The Optional Protocol provides the CESCR with additional tools, such as the power to conduct on its own initiative confidential investigations of "grave or systematic violations" (through an "inquiry procedure"). It also allows states to report that another state has not met its obligations ("interstate communications"), after which the CESCR can seek a "friendly solution" and issue a report.[18]

The International Covenant on Civil and Political Rights

The ICCPR requires states "to respect and to ensure" civil and political rights (art. 2(1)) without regard to available resources or progressive realization. It safeguards the freedom of expression, opinion, religion, conscience, assembly, and movement; freedom from slavery, torture, and arbitrary detention; and rights to privacy, equal protection, asylum from persecution, and free elections.

Demonstrating the connections between purportedly separate categories of rights, the ICCPR protects cultural rights of minorities, the freedom to join labor unions, and the right to life—rights that could be classified as economic, social, and cultural.

Although the right to life in article 6 focuses on the death penalty and arbitrary deprivation of life, its basic statement—"Every human being has the inherent right to life"—also encompasses health-related rights. The ICCPR treaty monitoring body, the Human Rights Committee, said that the right to life "should not be interpreted narrowly." States

BOX 8.2 The Human Rights Council

The Human Rights Council is an intergovernmental body responsible for promoting and protecting human rights around the globe, including by making recommendations, responding to human rights emergencies, and holding thematic discussions. In 2006 it supplanted the Commission on Human Rights, which was viewed as ineffective and politically motivated. The Human Rights Council reviews all UN member states' human rights records through a new procedure, the Universal Periodic Review. In a measure of accountability, the General Assembly can suspend any of the Council's forty-seven member states for gross human rights violations.[1]

NOTE

1. UNGA, Resolution 60/251, "Human Rights Council," March 15, 2006.

parties should "take all possible measures to reduce infant mortality and to increase life expectancy," especially eliminating malnutrition and epidemics.[19]

Like the CESCR, the Human Rights Committee reviews state implementation and issues general comments. The first ICCPR Optional Protocol establishes a complaints procedure, allowing individuals to petition after they have exhausted domestic remedies. The committee established a special rapporteur to strengthen accountability.[20]

The ICCPR and ICESCR accountability mechanisms are not sufficiently robust—a concern common to human rights treaties (Box 8.1 and Table 8.1). Their committees do not issue binding decisions, but rather views and recommendations. The CESCR can recommend interim measures to prevent irreparable harm, but states are not required to comply, only to give them "urgent consideration." Similarly, the Human Rights Committee can merely inform states "whether interim measures may be desirable to avoid irreparable damage to the victim."[21] The CESCR's self-initiated inquiries of severe violations, for which there is no ICCPR equivalent, are confidential, eviscerating their potential for civil society advocacy. States parties declare whether they agree to the inter-state communications and inquiry procedures and may withdraw consent.[22]

Legitimate Limits on Rights and Freedoms: The Siracusa Principles

When is it permissible to limit a human right to protect the public's health? The UDHR permits limitations to ensure "respect for the rights

Table 8.1 **The Core International Human Rights Instruments and Their Monitoring Bodies**

Charter of the United Nations

The International Bill of Human Rights

Universal Declaration of Human Rights 1948

International Covenant on Economic, Social and Cultural Rights 1966

Optional Protocol to the International Covenant on Economic, Social and Cultural Rights

International Covenant on Civil and Political Rights 1966

Optional Protocol to the International Covenant on Civil and Political Rights

Second Optional Protocol to the International Covenant on Civil and Political Rights, aiming at the abolition of the death penalty

There are nine core international human rights treaties, each with a committee of experts to monitor implementation. Some treaties have optional protocols on specific concerns.

	Treaty	Date of Adoption	Monitoring Body
ICERD	International Convention on the Elimination of All Forms of Racial Discrimination	21 Dec. 1965	CERD
ICCPR	International Covenant on Civil and Political Rights	16 Dec. 1966	CCPR
ICESCR	International Covenant on Economic, Social and Cultural Rights	16 Dec. 1966	CESCR
CEDAW	Convention on the Elimination of All Forms of Discrimination against Women	18 Dec. 1979	CEDAW
CAT	Convention against Torture and Other Cruel, Inhuman or Degrading Treatment or Punishment	10 Dec. 1984	CAT
CRC	Convention on the Rights of the Child	20 Nov. 1989	CRC
ICRMW	International Convention on the Protection of the Rights of All Migrant Workers and Members of Their Families	18 Dec. 1990	CMW

Table 8.1 (continued)

	Treaty	Date of Adoption	Monitoring Body
CRPD	Convention on the Rights of Persons with Disabilities	13 Dec. 2006	CRPD
CPED	International Convention for the Protection of All Persons from Enforced Disappearance	20 Dec. 2006	CED
OP-ICESCR	Optional Protocol to the International Covenant on Economic, Social and Cultural Rights	10 Dec. 2008	CESCR
OP1-ICCPR	Optional Protocol to the International Covenant on Civil and Political Rights	16 Dec. 1966	HRC
OP2-ICCPR	Second Optional Protocol to the International Covenant on Civil and Political Rights, aiming at the abolition of the death penalty	15 Dec. 1989	HRC
OP-CEDAW	Optional Protocol to the Convention on the Elimination of Discrimination against Women	10 Dec. 1999	CEDAW
OP-CRC-AC	Optional Protocol to the Convention on the Rights of the Child, on the involvement of children in armed conflict	25 May 2000	CRC
OP-CRC-SC	Optional Protocol to the Convention on the Rights of the Child, on the sale of children, child prostitution, and child pornography	25 May 2000	CRC
OP-CAT	Optional Protocol to the Convention against Torture and Other Cruel, Inhuman or Degrading Treatment or Punishment	18 Dec. 2002	CAT
OP-CRPD	Optional Protocol to the Convention on the Rights of Persons with Disabilities	12 Dec. 2006	CRPD

and freedoms of others" and to meet "the just requirements of morality, public order and general welfare in a democratic society" (art. 29(2)). No individual or state may "perform any act aimed at the destruction of any of the rights and freedoms" (art. 30). These limits are also incorporated into the ICCPR and the ICESCR.

The ICESCR and the ICCPR diverge in permissible limitations of rights. The ICCPR guarantees certain rights that are so essential that no state may deny them even in a public health emergency. These nonderogable entitlements include the rights to life, freedom from slavery and torture, and freedom of thought, conscience, and religion.

The ICCPR, however, allows states parties to curtail other civil and political rights in an officially proclaimed public emergency that "threatens the life of the nation" (art. 4). States must not discriminate and can limit rights only to the "extent strictly required by the exigencies of the situation" (art. 4). Rights that may be limited include the right to public hearings, freedom of expression, peaceful assembly, association, and movement. States can constrain these rights only if the limitation is (1) prescribed by law, (2) enacted within a democratic society, and (3) necessary to achieve public order, public health, public morals, national security, public safety, or the rights and freedoms of others.

The Siracusa Principles on the Limitation and Derogation of Provisions in the ICCPR (1984) is an important interpretive instrument for measuring valid human rights limitations.[23] Echoing the ICCPR, they require that limitations be (1) prescribed by law, (2) based on a legitimate objective, (3) strictly necessary in a democratic society, (4) the least restrictive and intrusive means available, and (5) not arbitrary, unreasonable, or discriminatory. Public health may be grounds for personal restraint solely to deal with "a serious threat to health." The state's purpose must be to prevent disease or injury or provide care for the sick or injured (para. 25).[24]

It is far more difficult to find legitimate restrictions on economic, social, and cultural rights. The ICESCR permits "such limitations as are determined by law only in so far as this may be compatible with the nature of these rights and solely for the purpose of promoting the general welfare in a democratic society" (art. 4). Arguably, valid limitations on the right to health include only measures necessary for the public's health.

Do Human Rights Make a Difference?

Does human rights law actually change people's lives for the better? Human rights can change norms and improve lives, informing public officials about their duties and catalyzing social movements. The impact of human rights law, not only international law but also human rights as incorporated into national constitutions and laws, can range from shaping the contours and basic expectations of society to specific judicial decisions advancing human rights. A twenty-country study in 1999–2000 found substantial legislative and judicial changes attributable to international human rights law.[25]

At the same time, states frequently flagrantly violate their human rights commitments. Researchers found treaty compliance to be a low priority. Beyond a broader failure to comply, states often are late in submitting reports, fail to distribute treaty body reports domestically, and disregard recommendations. However, despite its weaknesses, monitoring gives civil society an opportunity to submit "shadow reports" and to highlight state violations.

UN human rights institutions can also draw attention to pressing public health problems. The Human Rights Council, for example, has issued resolutions on safe drinking water, climate change, and discrimination based on sexual orientation.[26]

The Right to the Highest Attainable Standard of Health

There is no single universally agreed-upon interpretation of the right to health. Yet human rights treaties, national constitutions, and courts all draw upon the singular idea expressed in the WHO Constitution, reiterated in article 12 of the ICESCR, guaranteeing "the right of everyone to the enjoyment of the highest attainable standard of physical and mental health." Article 12 specifies state obligations to reduce stillbirths and infant mortality; promote healthy child development; improve environmental and industrial hygiene; prevent and treat epidemic and endemic diseases; and assure medical services in the event of sickness.

General Comment 14 on the Right to the Highest Attainable Standard of Health

General Comment 14 offers the most definitive interpretation of the right to health, even though it is not legally binding.[27] In it, the CESCR identifies rights and freedoms that are "integral components of the right to health," such as food, housing, life, education, privacy, and access to information. The CESCR captures public health services and the underlying determinants of health, such as safe and potable water; sanitation; safe and nutritious food; housing; occupational and environmental health; and health information and education (Box 8.3). Even this broad conception may be constrained, as many additional factors influence health, such as gender equality, employment, and social inclusion.

BOX 8.3 The Rights to Food, Water and Sanitation, and Housing

The UDHR (art. 25) and the ICESCR (art. 11) both recognize the rights to food and housing as necessary for an adequate standard of living. The right to food includes having nutritious and safe food that is sustainably available, economically and geographically accessible, and culturally acceptable.[1] The right to housing extends beyond shelter to include affordability, tenants' rights, protection from the elements, habitability, physical safety, cultural adequacy, and access to common resources (e.g., safe drinking water and sanitation) and to employment, health services, and schools.[2]

The International Bill of Human Rights does not expressly recognize the rights to water and sanitation, but the CESCR has determined that they are necessary for an adequate standard of living and inextricably linked to the rights to health and life. The right to water includes its availability, quality, and accessibility for all, including vulnerable populations, and requires that water of good quality remain available for and accessible to future generations. The right to sanitation includes sufficient facilities that are hygienic and safe, accessible, affordable, and culturally acceptable.[3] The UN General Assembly in 2010 recognized "the right to safe and clean drinking water and sanitation as a human right essential for the full enjoyment of life."[4]

NOTES

1. United Nations General Assembly (UNGA), "International Covenant on Economic, Social and Cultural Rights (ICESCR)" (1966), entered into force January 3, 1976, art. 11; UNGA, Resolution 65/220, "The Right to Food," April 5, 2011, para. 1; UN Committee on Economic, Social and Cultural Rights (CESCR), General Comment No. 12, "The Right to Adequate Food," UN Doc. E/C.12/1999/5, May 12, 1999; UN Economic and Social Council (ECOSOC), *Report by the Special Rapporteur on the Right to Food, Mr. Jean Ziegler,* UN Doc. E/CN.4/2001/53, February 7, 2001.
2. CESCR, General Comment No. 4, "The Right to Adequate Housing," UN Doc. E/1992/23, December 13, 1991.
3. CESCR, General Comment No. 15, "The Right to Water," UN Doc. E/C.12/2002/11, January 20, 2003; Catarina de Albuquerque, *Report of the Independent Expert on the Issue of Human Rights Obligations Related to Access to Safe Drinking Water and Sanitation,* UN Doc. A/HRC/12/24, July 1, 2009.
4. UNGA, Resolution 64/292, "The Human Right to Water and Sanitation," July 28, 2010. The Convention on the Rights of the Child (art. 24) and the Convention on the Elimination of All Forms of Discrimination against Women (art. 14) both expressly recognize the right to water.

The right to health contains four "interrelated and essential elements," which encompass health care, public health, and the underlying determinants of health (General Comment 14, para. 12). Health goods, services, and facilities must be (1) *available* in sufficient quantity; (2) *accessible* to everyone without discrimination, including being affordable and geographically accessible; (3) *acceptable,* including ethically, culturally, and with respect for privacy; and (4) of *good quality* and scientifically appropriate.

General Comment 14 offers key principles: (1) *equality and nondiscrimination* (nondiscriminatory access to health services); (2) *participation* (meaningful public engagement in health policy); and (3) *accountability* (government must be answerable to the public on its implementation of the right to health).

States must respect, protect, and fulfill the right to health. States respect the right to health by not interfering with people's ability to realize this right, such as discrimination in state-provided health services. States must protect people from violations of the right to health by third parties, such as when private practitioners discriminate against vulnerable patients. Finally, states must fulfill the right to health by taking affirmative "actions that create, maintain and restore the health of the population," such as by universal coverage (para. 37). State violations can occur through omission (e.g., failing to protect against private discrimination) and commission (e.g., public sector discrimination).

The right to health requires states to meet "minimum core obligations," including primary health care (para. 43). Core obligations include health facilities, goods, and services; nutritious and safe food; basic shelter, housing, sanitation, and safe and potable water; essential drugs; and equitable distribution of health facilities, goods, and services. Obligations of comparable priority to the "minimum core" include reproductive, maternal, and child health care; prevention, treatment, and control of epidemic and endemic diseases; education and health information; and health care worker training on health and human rights (para. 44).

States must adopt a scientifically sound public health strategy and plan of action, including measurable indicators and benchmarks—devised and periodically reviewed using a participatory and transparent process. Finally, developed countries must provide international assistance and cooperation, especially economic and technical assistance, to enable developing countries to fulfill their obligations.

Challenges in advancing the right to health include more precise definitions of ICESCR obligations and more effective tools for monitoring, implementatation, and enforcement. These challenges require careful thinking and catalyzing concerted action—tasks central to the mandate of the UN Special Rapporteur on the Right to Health.

UN Special Rapporteur on the Right to Health

Shortly after issuing General Comment 14, the Human Rights Commission established the Special Rapporteur on the right of everyone to the enjoyment of the highest attainable standard of physical and mental health. The commission charged the rapporteur with developing a global dialogue, reporting on the right's status throughout the world, and making recommendations to realize this right. The rapporteur is empowered to hear individual complaints and can invite the government to respond, seek information, and, where appropriate, recommend steps to redress a violation.

Paul Hunt was the first special rapporteur (2002–2008), followed by Anand Grover (2008–2014). They have investigated and reported on broad public health concerns (e.g., health systems, essential medicines, and health worker migration) and the needs of vulnerable populations (e.g., indigenous peoples, persons with disabilities, sex workers, and drug users). The rapporteurs have undertaken country visits on such issues as maternal mortality in India and neglected tropical diseases in Uganda.[28] The Human Rights Council's 2010 renewal of the special rapporteur's mandate focused on older persons and the Millennium Development Goals, as well as AIDS, health systems, gender, and disabilities.[29]

Regional Human Rights Systems

Africa, Europe, and the Americas have regional human rights treaties, along with commissions and courts to promote compliance. Regional human rights charters principally safeguard civil and political rights, including the right to life. The African Charter on Human and Peoples' Rights is the only regional treaty to expressly incorporate the right to health, while the American Convention on Human Rights does so indirectly. Although the European Convention on Human Rights protects only civil and political rights, the European Social Charter (a distinct treaty with more limited enforcement) includes the rights to health and medical and social assistance (Box 8.4).[30]

The Inter-American Court has the most dynamic right to health litigation, though the Court has yet to support a claim under article 26, which guarantees economic, social, and cultural rights due to its interpretation of the article's progressive realization requirement.[31] Instead, the Court's right-to-health decisions hinge on the American Convention's right-to-life guarantee. The Court construes this right to encompass the conditions

BOX 8.4 Regional Human Rights Systems and the Right to Health

African Charter on Human and Peoples' Rights

The African Charter guarantees everyone the right to enjoy the best attainable state of physical and mental health, requiring states parties to protect the health of people and to ensure medical attention when they are sick.

American Convention on Human Rights

The American Convention requires states parties to progressively realize the economic, social, educational, scientific, and cultural rights implicit in the Charter of the Organization of American States. The charter supports the right to health by safeguarding human potential through modern medical science and by ensuring proper nutrition, housing, and urban conditions for a healthful, productive, and full life.

The Optional Protocol of San Salvador to the American Convention guarantees everyone the right to health, understood to mean the enjoyment of the highest level of physical, mental, and social well-being. States parties agree to recognize health as a public good and, particularly, to adopt primary health care, health care services for all, universal immunization, prevention and treatment of disease, health education, and measures to meet health needs for those at highest risk. The protocol also includes the right to a healthy environment and the right to the nutrition needed to enable the highest possible level of physical, emotional, and intellectual development.

European Social Charter

The European Social Charter requires states to take appropriate measures to ensure the effective exercise of the right to health, including social and medical assistance to sick persons who lack adequate resources.

necessary for life, including access to health services. In 1999 the Court held that the right to life requires that no person "be prevented from having access to the conditions that guarantee a dignified existence" and that states must "guarantee the creation of the conditions required" for fulfilling this basic right.[32]

The Court has extended its right-to-life jurisprudence in three cases involving indigenous communities in Paraguay pertaining to access to drinking water, food, and sanitation and to health protection (especially for children, the elderly, and pregnant women).[33] These cases required the state to take reasonable protective measures when authorities knew about a situation posing an immediate and certain risk to life.

The African Commission on Human and Peoples' Rights has issued significant right-to-health rulings,[34] finding that Nigeria had violated the rights to health and housing for failing to require (or even permit) health and environmental impact studies for oil exploration. The commission also held that The Gambia failed "to take the concrete and targeted steps . . . to ensure that the right to health [of persons with mental illness] is fully realized without discrimination"[35] (Box 8.5).

The European Court has used civil and political rights to protect health. For example, the failure to provide immediate treatment to a person injured while being arrested constituted inhuman and degrading treatment, as did a state's denial of treatment for a seriously ill prisoner and a mentally ill patient.[36] More novel was the Court's determination that health professionals violated this right by denying a woman prenatal

BOX 8.5 A Focus on Vulnerable Populations

A common thread in right-to-health jurisprudence in the Americas and Africa is the state's responsibility for vulnerable groups. The Inter-American Court first recognized the right to life in a case involving street children[1] and expanded this right to protect dispossessed indigenous people. The Court issued historic orders on the right to health and dignity of people with mental disabilities,[2] a population that is also the focus of a major African Commission right-to-health ruling. The Inter-American Court has held that states must provide detainees with necessary medical assistance and an adequate supply of water.[3]

This focus on marginalized populations is consistent with the human rights principle of nondiscrimination. As regional human rights courts enforce right-to-health obligations, vulnerable populations are an appropriate starting point. A next step would be to extend their rulings to demand access to health services and to underlying determinants of health for all marginalized populations.

NOTES

1. *Case of the "Street Children" (Villagrán-Morales et al.) v. Guatemala,* Inter-Am. Ct. H.R. (Ser. C) No. 63 (1999).
2. *Ximenes-Lopes v. Brazil,* Inter-Am. Ct. H.R. (Ser. C) No. 149 (2006). Further, the Inter-American Commission issued precautionary measures to protect against life-threatening conditions in a psychiatric institution in Paraguay; Allison Hillman, "Protecting Mental Disability Rights: A Success Story in the Inter-American Human Rights System," *Human Rights Briefs* 12, no. 3 (2005): 25–28.
3. Matter of the Persons Deprived of Liberty in the "Dr. Sebastião Martins Silveira" Prison in Araraquara, São Paulo (Brazil), Order of the Inter-American Court of Human Rights of September 30, 2006 (provisional measures); *Vélez Loor v. Panamá,* Inter-Am. Ct. H.R. (Ser. C) No. 218 (2006), cited in Organization of American States and Inter-American Court of Human Rights, *Annual Report of the Inter-American Court of Human Rights 2010* (San Jose, Costa Rica: Organization of American States, 2011).

genetic testing, which prevented her from having a legal abortion.[37] By contrast, the Court has denied claims of inhuman or degrading treatment when the state deported sick people to countries where care is available, even if unaffordable.[38]

The Right to Health in National Constitutions

Early constitutions, such as the U.S. Constitution (1789), guaranteed only civil and political rights; socioeconomic rights came later. Chile's 1925 constitution was the first to include a right to health, with others following. After World War II, guarantees of the right to health became more common, and are increasingly adopted in modern constitutions. Today, over two-thirds of the world's constitutions, more than 130, guarantee health rights. Most of these grant an explicit right to health, such as "the highest attainable standard of physical and mental health," "health protection," "health care," "health security," or "health and medical care."[39] Some also guarantee determinants of health such as clean water, nutrition, and housing. In some cases, national constitutions incorporate human rights treaties into domestic law (Box 8.6).

BOX 8.6 Salient Examples of the Constitutional Right to Health

National constitutions offer a rich array of health rights. Salient illustrations from Latin America and Africa include the following:

The Constitution of Bolivia, adopted in 2009, protects the right to health, promoting policies to improve quality of life and collective well-being and to provide universal access to health care (arts. 35–36). The state has an "irrevocable obligation" to provide sustainable health services as a "supreme function and primary financial responsibility" (art. 36). The constitution guarantees public participation in decision making (art. 40) and prioritizes generic medicines through domestic production and importation, without intellectual property restrictions (art. 41).

The Constitution of Brazil, adopted in 1988, declares health a "right of all and a duty of the State," with social and economic policies to reduce risk and provide for universal and equal access to health services (art. 196). All states within the federation must invest annually in public health under a prescribed formula (art. 198).

The Constitution of the Dominican Republic, adopted in 2010, provides a comprehensive right to health, encompassing health services, access to clean water, better food, sanitation, quality medicines, and free hospitalization (art. 61).

The Constitution of Ecuador, adopted in 2008, designates water as an essential and nonderogable right (art. 12), while nutritious food should be produced locally (art. 13). Article 32 guarantees health determinants such as water, food, education, sports, work, and social security. Governing principles include equity, universality, solidarity, interculturalism, and quality, with a gender and generational approach.

The Constitution of Kenya, adopted in 2010, guarantees the right "to the highest attainable standard of health," including reproductive and other health services as well as rights to housing, sanitation, nutritionally adequate food, safe water, social security, and education (art. 43). No one may be denied emergency medical treatment.

The Constitution of South Africa, adopted in 1996, guarantees health care services, food and water, social security, and housing. The state must progressively realize these rights within available resources (secs. 26–27), though no one may be refused emergency medical treatment.

Litigating the Right to Health

Civil society has used national litigation to catalyze policy reform and give greater texture and meaning to the right to health. National courts adjudicate the right to health under statutes, constitutions, and treaties incorporated into domestic law. They address underlying determinants of health through the rights to food, water, and housing or through the right to health or to life. India's Supreme Court called the right to life

> the most precious human right . . . which forms the ark of all other rights [and] must therefore be interpreted in a broad and expansive spirit. . . . [It] includes the right to live with human dignity and all that goes along with it, namely, the bare necessaries of life such as adequate nutrition, clothing and shelter, [and encompasses] such functions and activities as constitute the bare minimum expression of the human self.[40]

Whatever the route, national litigation demonstrates the justiciability of health rights despite their progressive nature and budgetary implications. As South Africa's Constitutional Court stated, many entrenched civil and political rights "give rise to similar budgetary implications without compromising their justiciability." The fact that socioeconomic rights "almost inevitably give rise to such implications does not seem to us to be a bar to their justiciability."[41] Judicial enforcement can help break the second-class status of socioeconomic rights, giving expression to the ideal that "all human rights are universal, indivisible, interrelated, interdependent and mutually reinforcing."[42]

Health Services and Medicines: The AIDS Movement at the Forefront

The most successful national litigation has involved access to essential services and medicines. A systemic review in 2003–2004 found seventy-one access-to-medicines cases in twelve low- and middle-income countries, with fifty-nine succeeding.[43] Dig deeper and include the right to life, and the number of cases soars. Most cases occur in a small set of countries such as Brazil and Colombia, with thousands of cases determining whether a medicine or service should be covered by national health packages.

Echoing the formative impact of the AIDS movement, antiretroviral drugs have been at the leading edge of court decisions. In *Minister of Health v. Treatment Action Campaign (TAC)* (2002), South Africa's Constitutional Court held that government limits on public sector provision of nevirapine (which significantly reduces perinatal transmission) to eighteen pilot sites was unreasonable and hence unconstitutional. The state had to progressively realize the rights of mothers and infants to essential health services.[44]

Latin American courts also focused on antiretroviral therapy. The Venezuelan Supreme Court required the state to provide HIV treatment and to develop social awareness campaigns. The Argentine Supreme Court similarly found that the "right to health falls within the right to life . . . the first natural right of the individual," directing the government to provide HIV treatment.[45]

In India in 2003, NGOs asked the Supreme Court to require free and equitable access to antiretroviral medications based on the rights to health and life. Within months the government offered free AIDS drugs for people in six high-incidence states. In 2010 the Court ordered the government to provide free second-line AIDS treatment.[46]

AIDS-related cases extend beyond antiretroviral medication. The Canadian Supreme Court determined that a health ministry decision that would have forced a medically supervised injection site in Vancouver to close—heightening drug users' risk of contracting HIV and hepatitis C—violated the right to life in the Canadian Charter of Rights and Freedoms.[47]

Underlying Determinants: Food, Water, and Housing

Judicial decisions are increasing access to human needs such as food, water, and housing. A landmark right-to-food case initiated in India in

2001, *People's Union for Civil Liberties (PUCL) v. Union of India,* yielded far-reaching interim rulings, one finding that the government violated the right to life by failing to use huge food stocks to alleviate hunger: the "very existence of life" for families below the poverty line is endangered by the failure to provide "requisite aid."[48]

In November 2001 the Supreme Court of India held that state nutrition programs were legal entitlements, requiring cooked midday meals for primary school children. In later orders, the Court set standards and timetables for state action on subsidized grain, maternal and child health, and food for the homeless and rural poor. High-ranking officials could be held responsible for starvation deaths. The case triggered a right-to-food campaign to educate the public and mobilize action.[49]

Although water is also needed for survival, it has not produced sweeping court rulings equivalent to *PUCL.* Yet in a variety of contexts courts have recognized this right. In India, the right to water and sanitation often are tied to environmental protection, such as the right to "pollution free water and air for full enjoyment of life."[50] The High Court of the Indian state of Kerala found that "sweet water" is a component of the right to life. In 2009 the Indian Supreme Court required scientific research to find alternative water sources, such as seawater and wastewater conversion.[51] Botswana's Court of Appeals drew upon the UN right to drinking water resolution to protect the water rights of an indigenous community living in the Kalahari Desert. Nepal's Constitutional Court said that clean water is needed to protect life, property, and liberty.[52]

Despite an express constitutional right to "sufficient food and water," the South African Constitutional Court in *Lindiwe Mazibuko v. City of Johannesburg* found no immediate state duty to provide a specific amount of water, only the duty to take reasonable measures within its resources. City policy to provide households six kiloliters of free water monthly was not unreasonable. The Court stated, "A measure will be unreasonable if it makes no provision for those most desperately in need," stressing that government "may not ignore the needs of the most vulnerable."[53]

Resource constraints have tempered the duty to provide housing to the poor. In *Government of the Republic of South Africa v. Grootboom* (2000), the South African Constitutional Court held that the right to "adequate housing" did not require ensuring housing immediately for everyone, but only to the extent resources that were available. However, the state's housing plan was unconstitutional because it failed to reach people "in desperate need."[54] In India, the Supreme Court said the right to life includes the duty "to provide shelter to the poor and indigent." But it also adopted a progressive realization approach, deferring to the political branches to set the housing budget. Indian courts have, however, begun to set minimum core obligations for the right to housing, requiring large cities to provide night shelters with basic facilities and prohibiting the demolition of shelters.[55]

Combating Tobacco: The Primacy of the Right to Health

The Framework Convention on Tobacco Control (FCTC) sparked a flood of domestic regulations to reduce the overwhelming health burden resulting from tobacco use, such as restricting advertising, banning sponsorship of sporting events, requiring plain packaging and graphic warnings, and prohibiting smoking in public places (see Chapter 7). The tobacco industry has challenged tobacco control laws under the theory that health and safety laws interfere with their right to free expression and economic freedom.[56]

Courts have relied on the rights to health, life, and a safe environment in upholding tobacco control laws. The Colombia Constitutional Court upheld a complete ban on tobacco advertising and sponsorship, ruling that the public's right to health far outweighs the reduced value of commercial speech in the marketplace.[57] Marketing a commercial product—particularly one that is singularly harmful—is not the same as political, artistic, or social expression. Similarly, in upholding a public smoking ban, Peru's Constitutional Court rejected industry claims of free enterprise, invoking the right to health and classifying the FCTC as a "human rights treaty."[58]

Courts have also invoked human rights to safeguard the expansion of state protections against tobacco. The Constitutional Court of Costa Rica used the right to health to require a state institution to relocate a designated smoking area that threatened the right to health of workers. The High Court of Kerala also held that smoking in public places violated the constitution's rights to life and "pollution-free air," and ordered a statewide ban on smoking in public places. More recently, the Mexican Supreme Court appeared receptive to the civil society claim that the right to health required a complete public indoor smoking ban, but dismissed the lawsuit on procedural grounds.[59]

Fulfilling the Potential of Human Rights Litigation

Courts hearing right-to-health cases face a common set of problems. Should socioeconomic rights be treated similarly to civil and political rights? To what extent is the right to health immediately enforceable?

What resources must governments devote to the right to health? Underlying these questions is one of institutional competence. Because budget choices are complex, involving trade-offs among competing public goods, should courts defer to the political branches?

Consider the different judicial approaches to deference in South Africa and Brazil. In *Soobramoney v. Minister of Health (Kwazulu-Natal)* (1997), the South African Constitutional Court held that the right to health did not require the state to provide dialysis for a patient with chronic renal failure. To hold otherwise, said the Court, "would make substantial inroads into the health budget . . . [which] would have to be dramatically increased to the prejudice of other needs which the state has to meet."[60]

The Brazilian courts have used a more individualistic lens, routinely granting litigants the right to medicines that the state has not chosen to provide free of charge. Consequently, the state is spending an increasing proportion of its health budget on court-ordered medical expenses. Arguably, court-ordered health spending crowds out higher-priority health needs.[61]

The judiciary may lack the legitimacy to make resource allocation decisions that undermine democratically determined priorities. But at some point, government's failure to provide essential health services must be actionable if the right to health is to have meaning. The judiciary could push harder for the right to health without overreaching into the political realm in at least three ways. First, it could invoke an immediate state obligation to spend the maximum available resources. If the budget clearly underfunds health vis-à-vis competing expenditures, the courts could redress the imbalance. Second, the courts could insist on minimum core obligations, stressing the need for at least prevention, primary care, and essential needs. Third, the courts could pay special attention to the needs of the most vulnerable. Thus, if health budgets leave society's poorest people without care, courts would be well positioned to intervene.

Not only must courts be bolder in human rights rulings, they also need to be attentive to the difficulties of enforcement. Poor implementation is part of the reason that India's right-to-food case has extended for more than a decade. In *Grootboom,* the landmark South African right-to-housing case, the seemingly victorious Irene Grootboom died "still homeless and penniless."[62] Realizing the right to health requires the cooperation of all branches of government. Here too, courts could fashion creative remedies, with the Inter-American Court serving as a model. In *Xákmok Kásek Indigenous Community v. Paraguay,* the Court demanded specific, time-bound action, involving experts and community members to develop the remedy.[63]

Realizing the right to health through litigation also requires better-trained lawyers sharing knowledge about innovative strategies. A comprehensive global health and human rights database opens up new possibilities for cross-border learning.[64] Civil society will be most effective in realizing the potential of litigation when integrating it into broader advocacy efforts.

Overall, fundamental reform requires a multipronged strategy encompassing human rights litigation, political advocacy, public education, and social mobilization—reminiscent of the successes of the AIDS movement.[65] This comprehensive approach could strengthen social, legal, and political counterweights to competing political and economic interests. It would improve participation, enhance accountability, prioritize equity, expand legal frameworks, and amplify the voices of the most marginalized. Capturing the synergies among multiple human rights strategies and creating bold governance that effectively reinforces rights holds promise for improving global health and narrowing the health inequalities that so tarnish the world today.

CHAPTER 9

Global Health, International Trade, and Intellectual Property

Toward a Fair Deal for the Global South

THE INTERNATIONAL TRADE in goods and services is pervasive, traversing both political and geographic boundaries. The movement of products, services, and knowledge along routes of trade is the engine that drives economies, but it is also the means by which disease is spread and cultures homogenize. Trade provides countries with resources and technological advances to which they would not otherwise have access. It opens markets not only to life-saving products such as vaccines and medicines, but also to life-threatening products such as tobacco or asbestos. Trade agreements also can make essential medicines so expensive that they are out of reach for the poor. Trade in services can reallocate expertise to where it is needed while draining another area of its human capital. International trading systems can (for better or worse) change the way states engage in commerce and protect the health and well-being of their inhabitants.

Increased trade liberalization, a driving force behind globalization, brings new opportunities and challenges for global health. Increased trade in health-related goods, services, and people (e.g., patients and professionals) offers myriad benefits for the public's health. The trade system, for example, by reducing tariffs, can improve the quality of, and lower the price for, health-related goods and services. To those who embrace capitalism and competitive markets, trade is the answer to many socioeconomic problems, including challenges in health and development.

Although free trade advocates believe that trade liberalization will lift the prospects of the poor as well as the rich, there remain deep concerns that the trade system favors the North while impeding development and health in the South—leaving the poor in no better, and perhaps worse, shape economically. The global rich benefit from trade liberalization and particularly from international protection of intellectual property. However, poorer countries—which may lack scientists, entrepreneurs, investment, and industrial capacity—are often left behind.

For those concerned with equity, there is a fear that trade liberalization places the interests of rich countries and multinational corporations ahead of the health and lives of the world's poor. As former UN Secretary-General Kofi Annan put it, the reality of the international trading system does not match the rhetoric. "Instead of open markets, there are too many barriers that stunt, stifle and starve. Instead of fair competition, there are subsidies by rich countries that tilt the playing field against the poor. And instead of global rules negotiated by all, in the interest of all, and adhered to by all, there is too much closed-door decision-making, too much protection of special interests, and too many broken promises."[1]

The goal from a global health perspective is to achieve the efficiencies of trade liberalization while also advancing health equity. There is no reason why the international community cannot do both—lowering barriers to trade while ensuring that the global South is an active partner, prospering in a global system. International trade rules, in other words, must ensure that low-resource countries receive equal benefits, with their populations having affordable access to health-related goods and services.

Currently, the governance of these interlinkages depends on a complex and overlapping web of international, regional, and bilateral rules. The World Trade Organization (WTO) serves as the multilateral organization for trade, but its decisions significantly affect global health. Together, WTO agreements form a rule-based system within which members must operate. Some agreements provide rule "flexibilities" that can be exercised to safeguard the public's health. Other agreements allow countries to restrict trade for the purposes of protecting health, while at the same time barring trade discrimination.

Beyond the WTO, a "spaghetti bowl" of bilateral and regional free trade agreements (FTAs) has formed.[2] These separately negotiated trade agreements often weaken health protections or flexibilities built into the WTO's multilateral treaties.

Trade rules, even when they take health into account, are primarily designed to facilitate trade, which is why the World Health Organization must be a counterbalancing voice to the WTO. Indeed, the WHO has developed a body of international laws and policies that influence trade, including the International Health Regulations (IHR) and the Framework

Convention on Tobacco Control (FCTC), as well as nonbinding resolutions such as the Global Code of Practice on the International Recruitment of Health Personnel.

Tensions and confusion about this disjointed assortment of rules remain a serious concern. Although free trade supporters claim that WTO rules provide adequate flexibilities to protect health, public health proponents decry the organization's trade-biased nature. WTO supporters counter that such measures are necessary to ensure that states are not improperly utilizing public health as a subterfuge for trade protectionism. All in all, a satisfactory balance between economic prosperity and health protection remains an elusive goal.

This chapter elucidates the complex relationship between health and trade through a review of international laws and institutions that govern the intersection between the two domains. As the relationship between health and trade continues to evolve, it is critical for the public health community to understand the trade system and to actively shape its rules to safeguard health and promote justice.

The World Trade Organization

Origins of the WTO

The 1920s and 1930s were marked by a breakdown in multilateral trade as countries implemented protectionist trade policies in efforts to insulate themselves from spreading economic decline. The trauma of World War II sparked a desire to enhance economic cooperation as the United States emerged from a sustained period of isolation.[3]

The framework for the modern world trade system draws its origins from a conference held at Bretton Woods in 1944. The conference established the key pillars of the international economic system through the formation of the International Monetary Fund and the International Bank for Reconstruction and Development (the original institution of the World Bank Group) and recognized the need for a complementary International Trade Organization (ITO). An agreement known as the Havana Charter sought to provide the ITO with a broad mandate and a dispute settlement process. Despite the charter's popularity, the ITO never came to fruition.

The failure of the ITO, however, did not end aspirations for a multilateral trade agreement on tariff reductions. This agreement emerged in the form of the General Agreement on Tariffs and Trade (GATT 1947). Though the GATT was initially envisioned as a specialized agreement of the ITO, it morphed into an interim governing agreement for international trade.[4] The GATT, which originated in 1947 and was superseded by the GATT 1994, is designed to liberalize trade by reducing tariffs (e.g., import and export duties) and nontariff trade barriers (e.g., import quotas, licensing, and misuse of health and safety measures). Under the auspices of the GATT, the contracting parties agreed to hold periodic multinational negotiations ("rounds").

Over time, the GATT evolved into a complicated "GATT à la carte" whereby an array of codes (e.g., sanitary and phytosanitary measures, technical barriers to trade) emerged and functioned as stand-alone plurilateral treaties with varying country membership. The GATT successfully lowered tariffs, but its effectiveness was limited by the lack of a formal institution and enforcement. Nevertheless, GATT membership grew as developing countries joined. Developed countries took an interest in expanding the trade system beyond goods (as covered by the GATT) into other areas, such as services and intellectual property protection. The complexity of the GATT system brought renewed interest in a unified trading system with a broader mandate and increased membership.

Developing countries, however, were wary of a multilateral trading system and, as a result, the possibility of a multilateral trade organization became strategically tied to what has been termed "the Grand Bargain"—an "implicit deal" during the Uruguay Round (1986–1994) whereby the global North would incorporate trade agreements in services, intellectual property, and investment as well as create a new world trade organization with the ability to enforce decisions, while the global South would gain access to the North's markets in agriculture and labor-intensive manufactured goods.[5]

The creation of the WTO was formulated as a "single undertaking," meaning that accession to the WTO would require accepting "all the obligations of the massive treaty complex." Developing countries, however, accepted WTO membership "without a full comprehension" of the profoundly transformative new trading system, which would require "major upgrading and change in the institutional infrastructure of many or most Southern countries" as well as legal expertise and resources to deal with the WTO's "litigious and evidentiary-intensive dispute settlement system."[6]

The WTO was established on January 1, 1995, at the conclusion of the Uruguay Round, with the objective of "raising standards of living, ensuring full employment, . . . and expanding the production of and trade in goods and services, while allowing for the optimal use of the world's resources [for] sustainable development . . . [and ensuring] that developing countries . . . secure a share in the growth in international trade."[7]

Notwithstanding these lofty intentions, nearly two decades later there remains bitter controversy over the effects of trade on health, the environment, and economic development for the poor.

WTO Composition and Structure

The WTO, based in Geneva, has a membership of 159 countries, covering over 90 percent of global trade; 34 members are least developed countries (LDCs), with another 9 LDCs seeking to join.[8] The WTO's governance structure is comprised at the highest level of a Ministerial Conference followed by a General Council, a Dispute Settlement Body (DSB) (Box 9.1), a Trade Policy Review Body (TPRB), and an individual council for each of the WTO's substantive three agreements: GATT, Trade-

BOX 9.1 WTO Dispute Settlement Body

A member that believes it has been injured by another member's violation of WTO obligations or, while not violating WTO obligations, deprives it of the benefits to which it believes it is entitled, can seek redress before the Dispute Settlement Body (DSB). The WTO's DSB is one of the most powerful mechanisms in international law due to its nearly unparalleled "mandatory exclusive jurisdiction and virtually automatic adoption of dispute settlement reports." It is one of the "most prolific international dispute settlement systems" given its record of 467 disputes from 1995 through September 2013.[1]

The dispute settlement process begins with consultations and mediation between the parties, aimed at reaching a mutually agreeable solution. If a solution cannot be reached within sixty days, the DSB convenes a panel to hear the case. Panel decisions can be appealed to the Appellate Body (AB), a standing body of seven members with expertise in law and international trade. Decisions of the AB, which are rendered by panels of three of the seven members, become final and binding unless the DSB unanimously decides otherwise. The DSB is also charged with monitoring the implementation of rulings. If the complainant wins the dispute, the respondent is expected to follow the ruling within a determined time period. "Mutually acceptable" compensation (in the form of tariff concessions) may be required on an interim basis if the respondent fails to act. If the losing party does not comply, the complainant can request that the DSB authorize it to impose trade sanctions upon the respondent.

NOTE

1. "Chronological List of Disputes Cases," World Trade Organization (WTO), http://www.wto.org/english/tratop_e/dispu_e/dispu_status_e.htm (accessed 9/30/13).

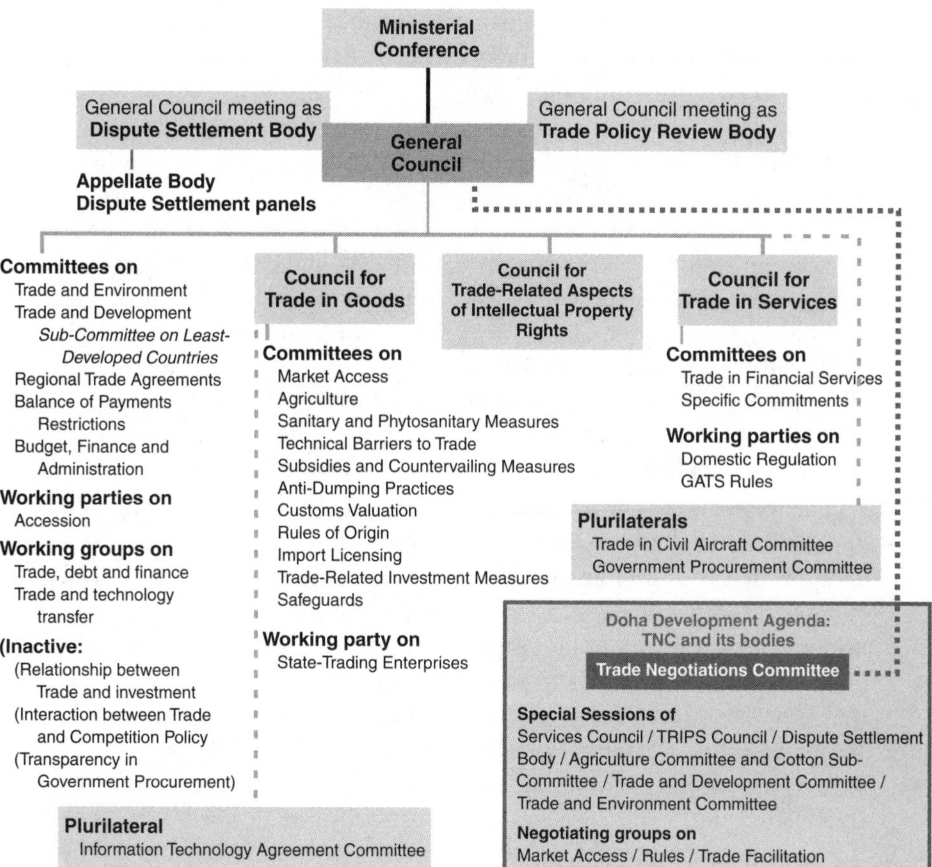

Figure 9.1 **WTO organization chart**

Source: "WTO Organization Chart," World Trade Organization (WTO), http://www.wto.org/english/thewto_e/whatis_e/tif_e/org2_e.htm (accessed 10/4/13).

Related Aspects of Intellectual Property Rights (TRIPS), and General Agreement on Trade in Services (GATS). An array of specialized committees and working parties address particular topics (Figure 9.1).

The Ministerial Conference, attended by all members, meets at least biennially and is authorized to make decisions "on all matters under any of the [WTO] Multilateral Trade Agreements."[9] The Ministerial Conference's powers include adopting interpretations of and amendments to WTO agreements; approving state accessions to the WTO; and appointing the WTO director-general. When this chief body is not in session, the General Council is charged with the Ministerial Conference's functions along with the management of the WTO's regular operations (e.g., approval of budget and financial regulations). Participation in the General Council is open to any WTO member, and the council typically meets at least every two months. The General Council also serves as the DSB and TPRB.

All members are permitted to attend, intervene, and introduce motions at the WTO. Under the WTO's governing structure, decisions typically are made by consensus—that is when no state vetoes the proposed decision.[10] Developing countries express concern that consensus decisions often involve "deference to economic power," with vetoes likely only when "important national, economic or other interests are at stake."[11] Although WTO law provides that a majority or supermajority of members make decisions, when consensus cannot be reached, voting rarely occurs.

Civil society criticizes WTO decision making for being "undemocratic, non-transparent and accountable to none."[12] Most important, the WTO process marginalizes developing countries. Given the WTO's customary approach of consensus, developing countries find it difficult to veto a decision that is widely accepted by more influential members. Powerful countries, for example, can leverage the practice of "green room" meetings whereby a group of developing countries are invited for a private informal negotiation and the agreed outcome is brought before the entire body for consensus. Formal meetings of WTO members usually accept drafts that emerge from green room caucuses. This process can stifle opposition, as developing countries fear retaliation by more powerful members.[13]

Developing countries face additional barriers to participating fully and on equal terms. Many cannot attend WTO meetings due to a lack of resources—for instance, many developing-country members do not have a Geneva mission and instead participate remotely or are represented by missions or embassies elsewhere in Europe. Furthermore, many developing countries have been declared "inactive" for not paying their assessed WTO contributions, effectively preventing them from chairing any WTO body.[14] Oxfam concludes that the WTO fails in "representational democracy," creating a power imbalance in favor of wealthy members.[15]

Coalitions have been used by developing countries to enable effective representation. For example, the Group of 77, established at the UN Conference on Trade and Development (UNCTAD) in June 1964, serves as the largest coalition of developing states. The G20 Group of Developing Countries (distinct from the G20 major economies) provides another prominent example of a coalition. More recently, developing countries have also turned to issue-based coalitions, which often incorporate developed country members. There have been notable gains through this approach, such as the "Café au Lait" coalition (led by Colombia and Switzerland) and the Cairns Group of agricultural exporting nations. The success of the coalitions, however, is uncertain due to conflicting loyalties and potential instability. The Advisory Center on WTO Law offers developing countries legal advice, support, and training.

International organizations such as the WHO and the Food and Agriculture Organization (FAO) have observer (or ad hoc observer) status in specific WTO councils and committees. For instance, the WHO holds observer status in the Ministerial Conferences and on the Agreement on Sanitary and Phytosanitary Measures (SPS Agreement) and Agreement on Technical Barriers to Trade (TBT Agreement) Committees as well as ad hoc observer status on the Council for Trade in Services and the TRIPS Council. Likewise, the WTO has held observer status at the World Health Assembly, the FCTC negotiations, and the joint WHO-FAO Codex Alimentarius Commission.

Civil society similarly has a vested interest in the WTO. The Marrakesh Agreement (1994) called upon the WTO to make "appropriate arrangements for consultation and cooperation with nongovernmental organizations," and in 1996 the General Council adopted guidelines to clarify its relations with NGOs.[16] In the WTO's early years, the organization was criticized for not fully engaging civil society by institutionalizing relationships or giving NGOs a meaningful voice. The WTO's problems of unequal access, shallow relations, and limited reciprocity in civil society dialogue reduced transparency and accountability.

The WTO has since sought to improve NGO relations and, thus far, arrangements with civil society have taken the form of permitting attendance at Ministerial Conferences and issue-specific symposia. The WTO also provides briefings to NGOs and circulates NGO position papers to members.

Underlying Principles of WTO Agreements

Before turning to the WTO's agreements and their health impacts, it is important to understand two underlying principles: most favored nation (MFN) and national treatment—designed to prevent discrimination between trading partners and avert trade protectionism. MFN prohibits a WTO member from discriminating between other countries, while national treatment prohibits a member from discriminating against another member in its internal rules and practices. (Box 9.2 discusses WTO public health cases, illustrating these principles.)

The MFN principle (GATT art. I, TRIPS art. 4, and GATS art. II) requires WTO members not to unjustifiably discriminate among their trading

BOX 9.2 WTO Cases Applying International Trade Principles to Public Health

The intersection between international trade and public health is critically important to global governance for health, particularly as WTO dispute resolution bodies decide an increasing number of claims with profound public health implications. Chapter 7 described how several states, including Ukraine and Honduras, have requested WTO dispute consultations in relation to Australia's tobacco plain-packaging legislation. Philip Morris has also challenged this legislation under a bilateral investment treaty between Australia and Hong Kong.

In May 2012 the United States requested that the WTO establish a panel to hear a dispute concerning measures taken by India to restrict the importation of certain agricultural products—primarily poultry—from countries where low pathogenic avian influenza has been identified.[1] The United States claims that these restrictions are inconsistent with India's obligations under the SPS Agreement and the GATT 1994, significantly impair trade, are not based on international guidelines, and have no scientific basis.[2] Given that the U.S. request for a panel tests several provisions in the SPS Agreement, "the dispute may help shape interpretation of the agreement and have flow-on effects for measures to protect public health."[3]

The claims discussed above had not been concluded at the time of this writing. However, the WTO Appellate Body (AB) has made it clear in previous rulings that health concerns are relevant in interpreting and applying the basic principles of international trade:

EC-Canada Asbestos Case (2001)

In the EC-Canada asbestos case, the AB upheld a French regulation prohibiting the manufacture, domestic sale, and import of asbestos-containing products.[4] The AB stressed that health is "important to the highest degree" and noted strong scientific evidence that asbestos fibers were toxic, whereas similar fibers were not. Based on this distinction, it held that products containing asbestos were not "like" similar products containing other fibers. Therefore they could properly be excluded without violating national treatment obligations. In addition, France's import ban was found to be necessary to protect human life, and no reasonably available alternative measures were identified. Consequently, the ban was found to conform to the health exception contained in GATT art. 20(b).

Indonesia–U.S. Clove Cigarettes Case (2012)

The Indonesia–U.S. clove cigarettes case, discussed in Chapter 7, arose under the Technical Barriers to Trade (TBT) Agreement. Embodying both national treatment and MFN principles, the TBT Agreement requires members to ensure that "in respect to technical regulations, products imported from . . . any Member shall be accorded treatment no less favourable than that accorded to like products of national origin and to like products in any other country" (art 2.1). It also prohibits technical regulations that are "more trade-restrictive than necessary to fulfill a legitimate objective, [including] the protection of human health or safety" (art. 2.2).

Indonesia brought a complaint against the United States for banning the sale of clove cigarettes while failing to ban menthol cigarettes. Although any cigarettes pose serious health risks, Indonesia argued that the clove cigarette ban was more trade restrictive than necessary and that banning clove cigarettes (mostly imported from Indonesia) but not mentholated cigarettes (mostly produced in the United States) was discriminatory.

On September 2, 2011, the WTO panel rejected Indonesia's claim that the measure was more trade restrictive than necessary to protect health under article 2.2. Although the panel found that the ban was a valid public health measure, it held that the United States violated the nondiscrimination principle. Clove and mentholated cigarettes were found to be "like" products under article 2.1, and the treatment of imported clove cigarettes was found to be "less favorable" than treatment of domestic mentholated cigarettes.[5]

The United States appealed the decision under article 2.1, but Indonesia did not cross-appeal the decision under article 2.2. On April 4, 2012, the AB upheld the panel's finding that the U.S. ban on all flavored cigarettes except menthol was discriminatory, reasoning that the TBT Agreement's "likeness" principle should be interpreted consistently with the approach under the GATT: "a determination about the nature and extent of a competitive relationship between and among the products at issue."[6] Thus, the AB followed the approach in the EC-Canada asbestos case whereby "divergent risks posed by the same products are relevant only to determining the competitiveness of the products."[7]

With respect to the less favorable treatment claim, the AB balanced the right to regulate with the obligation not to discriminate. The AB focused on whether the difference in treatment stemmed solely from legitimate regulatory distinctions between product categories. Using this balancing test, it found that both menthol and clove mask the harshness of tobacco and thus have the same product characteristics. As described in Chapter 7, the Unites States agreed to implement the AB's ruling by implementing further restrictions on mentholated cigarettes. However, Indonesia challenged the United States's compliance with the AB's ruling and sought authorization to suspend tariff concessions.

Brazil–European Community Retreaded Tires Case (2007)

The European Community challenged Brazil's import prohibition on retreaded tires, together with the exemption from the import ban granted to MERCOSUR countries (Argentina, Brazil, Paraguay, and Uruguay). [8] The retreaded tire import restriction had public health validity (stockpiles of tires collect water, creating a mosquito habitat, and burning tires causes pollution). However, the MERCOSUR exemption resulted in the import ban being applied in a manner that constituted arbitrary or unjustifiable discrimination and a disguised restriction on trade, in contravention of the "chapeau" of GATT, article 20.

NOTES

1. WTO, *India—Measures concerning the Importation of Certain Agricultural Products, Request for the Establishment of a Panel by the United States*, WT/DS430/3 (May 14, 2012).
2. Mission of the United States, Geneva, "Statement by the United States at the May 24, 2012, DSB Meeting," May 24, 2012, http://geneva.usmission.gov/2012/05/24/statement-by-the-united-states-at-the-may-24-2012-dsb-meeting/.
3. Benn McGrady, "More on the US–India Dispute concerning Avian Influenza," *O'Neill Institute Trade, Investment and Health Blog*, May 25, 2012, http://www.oneillinstitutetradeblog.org/.
4. WTO Appellate Body, *European Communities—Measures Affecting Asbestos and Asbestos-Containing Products*, WT/DS135/AB/R (March 12, 2001), para. 172.
5. WTO, *United States—Measures Affecting the Production and Sale of Clove Cigarettes*, Panel Report, WT/DS406/R (September 2, 2011).
6. WTO, *United States—Measures Affecting the Production and Sale of Clove Cigarettes*, Report of the Appellate Body, WT/DS406/AB/R (April 4, 2012).
7. Benn McGrady, "Tobacco Product Regulation and the WTO: Appellate Body Report, US–Clove Cigarettes" (O'Neill Institute, briefing paper, April 9, 2012).
8. WTO, *Brazil—Measures Affecting Imports of Retreaded Tyres*, Report of the Appellate Body, WT/DS332/AB/R (December 3, 2007).

partners. That is, each member must treat goods and services from a member no less favorably than goods and services imported from another country, whether or not that country is a member. A benefit granted to one country, therefore, must be granted to all WTO members in regard to "like" products.[17] For example, if a country offers a lower customs tariff on cigarettes for one country with which it trades, this lower tariff must be applied to cigarettes from any WTO member unless an exemption applies, such as in the case of a free trade area.

The national treatment principle (GATT art. III, TRIPS art. 3, and GATS art. XVII) generally requires members to provide the same treatment of other members' goods, services, and service suppliers as they give to their own. It prohibits discrimination in taxes and regulations between domestic goods and services and those from another member.[18] Hence, WTO members must not treat imported goods less favorably than like domestic goods. A country, for example, may restrict pesticide use on fruit because of health risks. However, if that country applies the pesticide regulation to imported fruit but not domestic fruit, the policy could violate WTO rules. The risk to consumers would be the same irrespective of the fruit's country of origin. The national treatment principle applies not only to measures that openly discriminate against imported goods, but also to measures that are neutral on their face but have the effect of discriminating against imported goods or are applied in a discriminatory manner.

National treatment is applied differently under various WTO agreements. Under the GATT, national treatment applies only once a product has entered the domestic market. This means that a customs duty can be imposed on an import even though "like" local products do not carry the same charge. In contrast, under the GATS, national treatment applies only to those service sectors and particular conditions that have been specified by a member's schedule of commitments and have not been included on the MFN list of exemptions. (The GATS schedule of commitments and MFN exemptions are discussed later.) Under TRIPS, national treatment requires that foreigners not be treated any less favorably than nationals with regard to the protection of intellectual property.

Nondiscrimination principles prompt concerns of interference with states' sovereign rights to protect the health and safety of their inhabitants. However, general exceptions exist in WTO agreements for the protection of human, animal, or plant life or health, while still requiring that countries do not arbitrarily or unjustifiably discriminate between countries where the same conditions prevail or adopt measures as a subterfuge for discrimination. The WTO agreements generally require that health measures be no more trade-restrictive than necessary.

WTO Trade Rounds and Key Agreements

Multilateral trade agreements have been reached through a series of nine trade rounds, which date back to the GATT's inception; they include the Geneva Round (1947), the Annecy Round (1949), the Torquay Round (1950–1951), the Geneva Round (1955–1956), the Dillon Round (1960–1961), the Kennedy Round (1963–1967), the Tokyo Round (1973–1979), the Uruguay Round (1986–1994), and the Doha Round (2001–present day). The WTO, along with the GATT 1994, GATS, TRIPS, and TBT/SPS agreements, was established at the conclusion of the Uruguay Round. The Doha "Development" Round has undergone a series of Ministerial Conferences, but the negotiations stalled in 2008 largely due to ongoing North/South tensions. Periodic attempts have been made to revive discussion, including an "absolute deadline" of December 31, 2011—since missed.[19] In September 2013, the new WTO director-general, Roberto Azevêdo, called the resumption of trade talks his "first priority."[20]

WTO Agreements in Relation to Health

The complex interactions between health and trade rules are centrally important to global governance for health. The WTO agreements must ensure a fair balance between health and trade while also lifting countries from poverty and ill health. This section explores WTO agreements in relation to health and country disputes over their application.

The Free Trade in Goods and the Protection of Health and Safety

While the free trade in goods can bring benefits to countries, it can also spread health and safety hazards widely and rapidly (see Chapter 2), sometimes requiring states to restrict the trade of goods to protect human, animal, or plant health and life. However, when not justified by safety concerns, such restrictions can act as disguised nontariff barriers that improperly disrupt trade. The TBT Agreement and the SPS Agreement govern health and safety concerns. The challenge in applying these agreements is to protect health without unduly obstructing trade or resorting to trade protectionism.

The GATT

As explained earlier, the GATT deals with trade in goods, constraining states from imposing measures that distort trade.[21] Although the GATT prohibits discrimination according to MFN and national treatment obligations, article 20 allows discrimination by WTO members when "necessary to protect human, animal or plant life or health." However, the actions taken cannot constitute "arbitrary or unjustifiable discrimination between countries . . . or a disguised restriction on international trade."

The lack of clarity has provoked tense trade disputes. For example, in the Thailand-Cigarettes case, the United States disputed Thailand's import restrictions and taxes on foreign cigarettes.[22] Thailand responded that U.S. cigarettes contained "chemicals and other additives . . . [that] might make them more harmful to human health than Thai cigarettes." The WHO said that there was no scientific evidence to prove that foreign cigarettes were more harmful than Thai cigarettes; American cigarettes, however, were easier to smoke (due to additives and flavoring), leading to the false impression that they were safer.[23]

The panel determined that Thailand's act violated the GATT and that its import restrictions were not "necessary" under article 20(b). The panel believed that Thailand could have protected the public's health without discriminating against foreign cigarettes. However, the panel upheld Thailand's Tobacco Act advertising ban because it applied to all cigarettes.

The TBT Agreement

Under the original GATT, nondiscrimination was the only constraint imposed on technical regulations governing products. However, the nondiscrimination provision was insufficiently nuanced to distinguish between states pursuing legitimate objectives, such as health, and states pursing illegitimate protectionist objectives. During the Tokyo Round, some members agreed to a Standards Code, which subjected regulations to a "least restrictive means" test. Where possible, states were required to use preexisting performance standards and to adopt international standards. Remaining issues, including the omission of requirements for scientific evidence, prompted further negotiations during the Uruguay Round, culminating in the TBT Agreement and the closely linked SPS Agreement.

The TBT Agreement, which applies to regulations governing "product characteristics or their related processes or production methods" (annex 1, para. 1), permits trade restrictions for "legitimate objectives," namely, for the protection of: (1) human health or safety, (2) animal or plant life or health, (3) the environment, or (4) for national security requirements.[24] It also requires that such barriers—often in the form of technical requirements such as product standards, testing, or certification procedures—not create unnecessary obstacles to trade or be more severe than needed to accomplish their legitimate purposes.

In addition, states must comply with the principles of MFN and national treatment. The TBT Agreement obliges members to base measures on "relevant" international standards, but states may establish their own standards. The WTO and the WHO state that members may depart from international standards if their application would be "an ineffective or inappropriate means for the fulfillment of the legitimate objectives pursued, for instance because of fundamental climatic or geographical factors or fundamental technological problems."[25] Common TBT measures pertaining to health include pharmaceutical packaging, cigarette labeling, and regulation of nutrition claims.

The SPS Agreement

The SPS Agreement originated from concerns about the trading system's limited ability to prevent protectionist nontariff trade barriers with respect to agriculture. Members feared that human, animal, or plant health might be used as an excuse to obstruct trade. The SPS Agreement makes it "more difficult for countries to shelter domestic industries behind restrictive health regulations or to disguise protectionist strategies under the cloak of health regulations."[26]

From a public health perspective, SPS measures can be used for food safety or for protection from plant-related or animal-borne (including zoonotic) diseases. Sanitary measures often take the form of food safety standards, while phytosanitary measures may involve import prohibitions to protect plant health. The goods involved typically include food products, agricultural commodities, live animals (e.g., livestock, aquatic animals, and wild animals), and horticultural products (including natural vegetation). An SPS measure, for example, could limit pesticide residue in food or mandate product fumigation.

The SPS agreement permits states to restrict trade for the protection of humans, animals, and plants from contaminants, toxins, additives, pests, diseases, or disease-causing organisms. To harmonize safety standards across WTO members, the SPS encourages states to base measures on standards, guidelines, and recommendations issued by international organizations, such as the Codex Alimentarius Commission (Box 9.3). If a state adopts a trade measure that deviates from international standards, article 5 requires that the measure be based on assessment of the risk to human, animal, or plant life or health. The assessment must take into account scientific evidence as well as economic factors. However, it need not follow the majority scientific view. If a state adopts a trade measure that deviates from international standards, it will have to show that a health risk warrants a higher level of protection.

WTO members must also ensure that SPS measures "are applied only to the extent necessary to protect human, animal or plant life or health" and aim to "minimize negative trade effects." In other words, states must

BOX 9.3 Codex Alimentarius Commission: Risk Assessment and the Precautionary Principle—Case Study on Labeling Genetically Modified Foods

The FAO and the WHO created the Codex Alimentarius Commission in 1963 to develop food standards and guidelines, such as codes of practice under the Joint FAO/WHO Food Standards Program. The main purposes of the codex are to protect consumer health, ensure fair trade practices, and coordinate food safety standards. Codex guidance is not mandatory, but its adoption by states could reduce the threat of WTO legal challenges.

States, for example, have often been in tension regarding the safety of genetically modified (GM) foods, sometimes provoking trade disagreements. Some countries, such as the United States, contend that GM foods cannot be differentiated from other foods. To others, such as the European Union, labeling enables consumers to make informed choices. In 2011 the Codex Alimentarius Commission issued landmark guidance to approve labeling of GM foods, which could provide a safe harbor for states that adopt labeling requirements. The codex standard states that "risk managers should take into account the uncertainties identified in the risk assessment and implement appropriate measures to manage these uncertainties."[1] This expression of the precautionary principle specifically encompasses food labeling.

NOTE

1. Codex Alimentarius Commission, "Principles for the Risk Analysis of Foods Derived from Modern Biotechnology," CAC/GL 44–2003, para. 18.

ensure that SPS measures do not present "an unnecessary, arbitrary, scientifically unjustifiable, or disguised restriction" upon trade.[27]

SPS disputes often turn on the quality of scientific evidence. For example, in the EC-Hormones case, the WTO panel found in favor of the United States and Canada in their dispute over the European Union's ban on the importation of beef treated with any one of six growth hormones—which was largely supported by EU consumers. Although Codex Alimentarius standards existed for five of the six hormones, the European Community (EC) did not apply these standards, instead defending its ban on the grounds of more stringent measures based on scientific evidence. The dispute panel, affirmed by the Appellate Body,[28] found that the measures were not based on a risk assessment.

High-quality scientific evidence, of course, is the gold standard for health and safety regulations. However, there is often no scientific consensus, and states have to act under circumstances of scientific uncertainty. Should states be permitted to adopt the "precautionary principle," erring on the side of public health and safety?

The deep tensions between health and trade, as illustrated by the China-Poultry case (Box 9.4), remain a multifaceted problem, which only increases the fissure between the global North and South. Powerful countries may insist that developing countries accept their products even in the face of genuine health concerns, such as the United States challenging Thailand's cigarette import ban. As developed countries open their doors to products from resource-poor countries, they are demanding more stringent safety standards to satisfy domestic consumers. This can place a substantial and disproportionate strain on poorer countries, which often lack the infrastructure and resource capacity to implement and enforce foreign safety standards.

BOX 9.4 WTO Dispute over the Importation of Poultry from China into the United States

In 2006 the U.S. Department of Agriculture's Food Safety Inspection Service (FSIS) determined that China's meat and poultry processing standards were sufficient to permit importation. However, Congress later prohibited the FSIS from using public funds to implement the rule, effectively banning Chinese poultry imports. Advocates of the ban pointed to regulatory deficiencies in China, including inconsistent control over food processing plants, inadequate enforcement, and deficient testing for bacteria and residues. The ban stayed in effect until November 2009.

China challenged the funding ban, alleging breaches in complying with the GATT 1994 MFN requirement and a lack of scientific evidence or risk assessment to support the ban under the SPS Agreement. A WTO panel on September 29, 2010, found that the U.S. refusal to apply normal approval procedures for Chinese imported poultry constituted arbitrary and unjustifiable discrimination.[1] The panel also found that there was "no scientific evidence, risk assessment, or other justification for treating Chinese poultry products differently from those of other WTO Members." The outcome of this dispute indicates that trade restrictions for public health purposes must be justified by ongoing scientific assessment.

NOTE

1. WTO, *United States—Certain Measures Affecting Imports of Poultry from China*, Panel Report, WT/DS392/R (October 25, 2010); Renee Johnson and Geoffrey S. Becker, *China–U.S. Poultry Dispute* (Congressional Research Service, 2010).

At the same time, divergent regulatory standards among WTO members raise concerns for developed and developing countries alike. Greater harmonization of health and safety standards could relieve trade tensions but will require better partnerships in setting international standards as well as technical and capacity support in implementing harmonized standards.

Trade in Health Services

The trade in health services is recognized to have direct and indirect public health implications. Health services are experiencing increased mobility due to technological innovations (e.g., telemedicine and e-commerce) as well as medical tourism and health worker migration. Regulatory reforms in traditionally state-run service sectors (e.g., hospitals, sanitation, and water) have opened the doors to privatization and, thus, transnational corporate involvement. These changes can better meet consumer demands and achieve efficiencies in health services. Service providers stand to benefit from the economic potential of tapping new markets. In particular, some developing countries, such as India, hold a comparative advantage given their ability to provide high-quality services at low cost.

Trade proponents commonly cite foreign direct investment, technology transfer, and development as expected benefits of trade liberalization in services. Despite these benefits, some fear that public health in developing countries will suffer from an imbalance in the allocation of health resources (such as hospitals and personnel), favoring the wealthy as opposed to the domestic poor and rural areas.[29]

The General Agreement on Trade in Services

The GATS seeks to liberalize trade in services. The agreement was part of the "single undertaking" required by the WTO. The GATS has two major parts. The first part imposes general obligations, including the MFN principle (GATS art. II) and transparency and notification obligations (GATS art. III). The ability to protect human, animal, and plant life is governed by GATS article XIV. The GATS general obligations potentially apply to all service sectors, with the exception of "any service supplied in the exercise of governmental authority."[30] To qualify for the government exemption under GATS, services must be "supplied neither on a commercial basis, nor in competition with one or more service suppliers."[31] The GATS categorized the numerous services into four defined modes: cross-border supply (mode 1), consumption abroad (mode 2), commercial

Table 9.1 **The Four Service Modes of GATS**

GATS Service Modes	Health Service Example
Mode 1: Cross-border supply of services	• Diagnosis or treatment services via telecommunications (i.e., telemedicine)
Mode 2: Consumption of services abroad	• Movement of patients from one country to another for treatment (i.e., medical tourism)
Mode 3: Commercial presence	• Establishment of or investment in hospitals by foreign owners
Mode 4: Presence of natural persons/movement of natural persons	• Services by health workers in one country who are nationals of another country

Adapted from WTO and WHO, *WTO Agreements and Public Health: A Joint Study by the WHO and the WTO Secretariat* (Geneva: WTO, 2002).

presence (mode 3), and presence of natural persons (mode 4). Table 9.1 illustrates the GATS modes in relation to health services.

The second part of the GATS is the schedule of specific commitments undertaken by each member. These schedules are comprised of specific market access and national treatment commitments on a "sector-by-sector and mode-of-supply basis" following a negotiations process.[32] Such commitments can take one of three general forms: full commitment (i.e., no limitations in terms of market access and national treatment), partial commitment (i.e., some restrictions, conditions, and/or other measures), or no commitment (i.e., unbound). As of January 2013, forty-seven members (mainly developing and transitional countries) had made commitments in the area of health-related and social services.[33] The vast majority of commitments are restricted to hospital services and, more specifically, to modes 2 (consumption abroad) and 3 (commercial presence). To the extent that countries make commitments regarding the supply of other health and social services, they can be quite limited. For example, Belize limits commitments to services supplied by epidemiologists; Guinea limits them to training centers for persons with disabilities. Only a small number of low-income countries have made health-related GATS commitments, among them Cambodia, the Gambia, Malawi, and Zambia.

The GATS legal structure, however, is unique in its emphasis on "progressive liberalization" in the trade of services. This means that members have the opportunity to periodically negotiate new commitments and open existing commitments to renegotiation. Thus it is likely that the health services and trade relationship will be "most significantly shaped by the on-going and subsequent efforts" in GATS negotiations on specific commitments. It is vital that health ministries, despite not having played an active role in GATS negotiations during the Uruguay Round, be proactive about their responsibilities. The fact that GATS allows states to establish specific commitments grants them substantial "choice, discretion, and flexibility" in managing the liberalization of health services trade for the protection of health.[34]

GATS negotiations began in 2000 but have not proceeded smoothly. In 2001 GATS negotiations were included as part of the WTO's contentious Doha Round, and states were asked to submit their requests and offers of commitments. These negotiations struggled with missed deadlines and "low-quality" offers among the few that made submissions. The GATS negotiations have made slow progress as part of the Doha Round, which has been plagued by troubles involving the agricultural trade negotiations.

Even if the negotiations resume, serious concerns remain about how increased liberalization in health services will affect health and development. Fears about "brain drain" (due to health worker migration) and the sidelining of poor populations (due to health services privatization) have led to questions about how to ensure access and equity. It is worth noting that the preamble to the GATS explicitly "recognizes the rights of members to regulate the supply of services within their territories." Unfortunately, this could pose a major challenge for developing countries if they lack the regulatory capacity to carry out such measures.

Protection of Intellectual Property Rights and Public Health Implications

Intellectual property (IP) protection gives creators incentives to generate ideas to benefit society. However, by giving creators exclusive rights to exploit their inventions, designs, or other ideas, IP protection can make products unaffordable—which is why IP rights are so politically contentious. To entrepreneurs, IP protection is indispensable to scientific innovation and the long-term public good. Biotechnology companies claim that exclusive rights to new drugs or vaccines are needed to recoup the high costs of research and development. IP protection can, however, make medicines prohibitively expensive for the world's poorest people. Advocates believe that it is intolerable when countless people die of AIDS or other treatable diseases out of respect for the IP rights of private companies. As part of the "single undertaking," negotiated during the Uruguay Round, TRIPS was introduced into the multilateral trading system. Ideas and knowledge have emerged as a key part of international commerce, and powerful corporate interests have sought to safeguard new inventions in global markets.

The TRIPS Agreement

Before the Uruguay Round, states could effectively set their own IP policies, with approximately fifty countries offering no patent protection for pharmaceutical products, such as Brazil, India, and Mexico. The TRIPS Agreement (art. 27), however, required patents to be granted in all fields of technology without exclusion, so that patenting of pharmaceutical products became nearly universal. TRIPS established minimum levels of IP protection that governments must afford to rights holders, thus ensuring uniformity and bringing national policies under international rules with a dispute settlement system.

The central mission of TRIPS is to protect and enforce IP rights for "the promotion of technological innovation and . . . the transfer and dissemination of technology, to the mutual advantage of producers and users of technological knowledge and in a manner conducive to social and economic welfare" (art. 7). Members, however, may adopt measures necessary to protect public health and nutrition, and to promote the public interest in sectors of vital importance (art. 8(1)). Whether TRIPS achieves a fair balance between IP and health has been the subject of bitter dispute.

There has been intense debate over the TRIPS Agreement's effects on developing countries. Some poor countries currently lack the systems of education, manufacturing, and marketing to innovate effectively and therefore gain the benefits of IP protection. To these nations, TRIPS may afford little advantage because they possess few patentable products. At the same time, TRIPS can make it difficult to produce or purchase affordable generic medications that people need desperately. Some economists estimate that a $60 billion per year transfer from poor to rich countries would occur if TRIPS were fully implemented—caused mainly by increased patent and royalty payments as well as higher prices.[35]

TRIPS affords protection of IP rights, including trademarks, copyrights, and designs. Of these rights, patent protection is perhaps the most important in matters of health. The agreement requires a patent life for inventions of at least twenty years (art. 33). Patent protection is granted for both products (e.g., medicines) and processes (e.g., methods of producing chemical ingredients for medicines) in all fields of technology. To qualify for a patent, an invention must be "novel," be an "inventive step" (i.e., not obvious), and have "industrial application" (i.e., be useful) (art. 27).

The TRIPS Agreement contains significant "flexibilities" that can be exercised to protect public health. The Doha Declaration emphasized members' rights to grant compulsory licenses (e.g., for generic medicines) and determine the grounds upon which such licenses can be granted; determine what constitutes a national emergency or conditions of extreme urgency; and establish their own regime for exhaustion of IP rights (which enables states to engage in parallel importation).

A compulsory license is a legal vehicle whereby a government grants to itself or a third party the right to produce or import a patented product without authorization of the patent holder (art. 31). Compulsory licenses are subject to a number of conditions, including the following: (1) the government must first attempt to negotiate a voluntary license from the rights-holder on reasonable commercial terms; (2) the government need not seek a voluntary license in a national emergency or other urgent circumstance; (3) adequate remuneration must be paid to the rights-holder, taking into account the economic value if a compulsory license is issued; and (4) the compulsory license must be "predominantly for the supply of the domestic market."

Parallel importation involves the import of "products marketed by the patent owner . . . or with the patent owner's permission in one country and imported into another country without the approval of the patent owner."[36] If a country adopts the principle of exhaustion of IP rights, the patent holder cannot prohibit or otherwise condition the resale of a patented product to a third country. This allows countries to import patented pharmaceuticals at the lowest available international price. TRIPS stipulates that the "exhaustion" of IP property rights cannot be contested under the WTO (art. 6).

The TRIPS Agreement contains flexibilities beyond the Doha Declaration. Members are free to determine the implementation of TRIPS within their own legal system (art. 1)—for example, by setting a high bar for novelty and inventiveness, thus reducing the problem of evergreening patented medicines (extending patents through new uses, forms, and combinations). TRIPS also allows certain exclusions from patentability, such as diagnostic, therapeutic, and surgical methods (art. 27.3(a)), and limited exceptions to the exclusive rights conferred by a patent. TRIPS flexibilities should enable countries to fashion a TRIPS-compliant IP regime that serves health, social, and economic purposes.

Nonetheless, developing countries have found it difficult to exercise TRIPS flexibilities due to the treaty's complexity and political pressure from developed countries and pharmaceutical companies. Many developing countries previously did not have domestic IP protections in place, and there was often a political expectation to implement TRIPS swiftly despite a lack of technical capacity and resources. (Box 9.5 discusses an important case, *Novartis v. Union of India,* in which the Supreme Court of India denied the pharmaceutical company Novartis's claim for patent protection of a lucrative cancer drug.)

BOX 9.5 ***Novartis v. Union of India:*** **TRIPS Implementation, Industry Power, and Generic Drugs**

India—sometimes called the "pharmacy of the developing world"—supplies much of the developing world's demand for affordable generic drugs.[1] In April 2013 the Supreme Court of India ruled against the drug company Novartis on its claim for a patent on the lucrative and widely used cancer drug Gleevec—the culmination of a high-profile, seven-year legal battle. In denying Novartis's claim, the Court affirmed that India's standard for patentability exceeds that of the United States or the European Union. In the United States, companies can often extend patent life simply by tweaking a drug's formula or dosage (known as "evergreening"), but the Court ruled that India's patent laws require more: it is not enough that a new compound is different—the modification must also improve patient treatment.[2]

The Court's reasoning was narrow. To comply with TRIPS, India began granting drug patents in 2005, but only for drugs created after 1995. In 1993 Novartis patented Gleevec's original chemical form. But the Court found that Novartis did not prove that Gleevec offered "enhanced or superior efficacy" as required under India's 2005 patent law. Gleevec can cost $70,000 annually in the United States, whereas Indian generic versions cost about $2,500 a year.

Despite the narrow reasoning, the *Novartis* decision could have far-reaching implications. Multinational pharmaceutical companies seek strong patent protections in emerging economies, particularly given declining revenues in Europe and North America.[3] India is the world's leading supplier of generic drugs, exporting $10 billion worth of generic medicines annually, while India and China together produce more than 80 percent of the active ingredients used in pharmaceuticals manufactured in the United States. A ruling in Novartis's favor could have altered the global landscape in regard to access to medicines. The Court's ruling could spur pharmaceutical companies to focus on genuine innovation rather than evergreening existing patents. It could also embolden other emerging economies (e.g., Argentina, Brazil, the Philippines, and Thailand) as they debate domestic IP regulation and its compatibility with their TRIPS obligations. At the same time, developed countries are seeking stricter IP protection in bilateral and regional trade agreements, such as the Trans-Pacific Partnership the United States is negotiating.

Finally, the decision illustrates a growing recognition among governments and civil society that access to affordable medicines is an issue that reaches far beyond its historical roots in HIV/AIDS. The increasing burden of NCDs in developing countries, along with the high price of treatment, suggests a central role for drugs like Gleevec in future debates.[4]

NOTES

1. Amy Kapczynski, "Engineered in India: Patent Law 2.0," *New England Journal of Medicine* 369, no. 6 (2013): 497–499.
2. *Novartis v. Union of India,* Civil Appeal Nos. 2706–2716 of 2013 (April 1, 2013), available at http://judis.nic.in/supremecourt/imgs1.aspx?filename=40212.
3. Eva von Schaper, "Drugs for Indian Poor Spark Pfizer Anger at Lost Patents," *Bloomberg,* March 27, 2013, http://www.bloomberg.com/news/2013-03-27/drugs-for-indian-poor-spark-pfizer-anger-at-lost-patents.html
4. Thomas J. Bollyky, "Access to Drugs for Treatment of Noncommunicable Diseases," *PLoS Medicine* 10, no. 7 (2013), doi: 10.1371/journal.pmed.1001485.

More critically, the devastation caused by the AIDS pandemic brought the shortcomings of TRIPS into stark relief. Patented drugs cost anywhere from three to fifteen times their generic equivalents. Developing countries could not afford to pay the high costs of combination drug therapy—even when civil society pressured pharmaceutical companies to lower them. As a result, the international community became more sensitive to public health concerns, lessening support for the stringent IP demands of industrialized countries.

This was apparent with the 2001 passage of the Doha Declaration on the TRIPS Agreement and Public Health, which reaffirmed the use of TRIPS flexibilities and stated that "the Agreement can and should be interpreted and implemented in a manner supportive of WTO members' right to protect public health and, in particular, to promote access to medicines for all" (Doha Declaration, para. 4) (see Box 9.6). While the Doha Declaration has been widely praised as a victory for developing countries, the growing developed country practice of negotiating "TRIPS-plus" free trade agreements has undermined the Doha Declaration. For example, the United States has negotiated many bilateral and regional

BOX 9.6 The Doha Declaration on TRIPS and Public Health

To ensure greater access to life-saving medications for resource-poor countries, the WTO Ministerial Conference promulgated the Declaration on the TRIPS Agreement and Public Health in November 2001.[1] The declaration explicitly recognized the public health problems facing resource-poor countries, especially AIDS, tuberculosis, and malaria, stating that TRIPS "can and should be interpreted and implemented in a manner supportive of WTO members' right to protect public health and, in particular, to promote access to medicines for all." It reaffirmed members' rights to use, "to the full," all TRIPS flexibilities for that purpose.

Countries with manufacturing capacity, such as Brazil, India, and Thailand, can make generic medications, yielding dramatic health benefits. Brazil, for example, reduced AIDS deaths by 50 percent over a four-year period. Governments manufacturing generic drugs have faced intense pressure from the United States and pharmaceutical companies to respect existing patents. Indeed, in 2001, thirty-nine drug companies sued the South African government to block the production of generic anti-HIV drugs on the grounds that it breached patent protection. The suit was dropped when the public and NGOs protested vehemently.[2]

The Doha Declaration, however, left an important problem unresolved. It recognized that "WTO Members with insufficient or no manufacturing capacities in the pharmaceutical sector could face difficulties in making effective use of compulsory licensing." For example, countries with manufacturing capacity (e.g., India and Canada) could not help by exporting generic drugs because of the TRIPS requirement that compulsory licenses be primarily to supply the domestic market. The TRIPS Council was charged with finding "an expeditious solution to the problem" (Doha Declaration, para. 6).

A decision was nearly reached in December 2002 when 143 out of 144 countries agreed to a waiver that would allow developed countries to export generic drugs made under compulsory license to countries that lacked the manufacturing capacity. The United States was the sole dissenter but eventually joined the agreement in August 2003, under specified conditions. In December 2005, WTO members reached an agreement to change the temporary waiver to a permanent measure. However, amending compulsory licensing provisions will require the approval of two-thirds of WTO members before it becomes effective.

Thus far, the export system has been used only once, by Rwanda and Canada in 2008; however, the process was "complicated and time consuming."[3] More than a dozen countries and the EU have now changed their domestic laws to allow medicines to be manufactured under compulsory license for export.

NOTES

1. WTO, *Ministerial Declaration on the TRIPS Agreement and Public Health*, WT/MIN(01)/DEC/2, 41 I.L.M. 746 (2002).
2. Pat Sidley, "Drug Companies Withdraw Law Suit against South Africa," *British Journal of Medicine* 357, no. 7293 (2001): 1011; "South Africa's Moral Victory," editorial, *The Lancet* 357, no. 9265 (2001): 1303.
3. Lisa Mills and Ashley Weber, "A One-Time-Only Combination: Emergency Medicine Exports under Canada's Access to Medicines Regime," *Health and Human Rights* 12, no. 1 (2010): 109–122, quotation from p. 118.

FTAs to implement a U.S.-type IP regime.[37] TRIPS-plus provisions can undermine the ability of developing countries to protect health beyond the already restrictive levels required by TRIPS itself.

The message of the Doha Declaration and its aftermath is that international trade rules should not serve as a major barrier to access essential drugs. Many problems remain, however, such as poor health care infrastructure, making it difficult to deliver medicines to a large population and to provide medical supervision. In retrospect, many developed countries genuinely believed that creating incentives for innovation would help the poor. But the net effect of trade rules has been to impede access to affordable treatments for the world's most vulnerable people.

International Health Agreements with Implications for Trade

The WHO's laws and policies could have a major impact at the intersection of trade and health. Chapters 6 and 7 discussed the WHO's International Health Regulations (IHR 2005) and FCTC. Here I consider how they overlap with WTO agreements. This raises questions about the precedence of different international legal regimes and how conflicts should be resolved.[38] These are not sterile legal problems. If global health treaties fail to gain traction in the hierarchy of international law, then other regimes could effectively eviscerate their impact.

Framework Convention on Tobacco Control

Given concerns about trade liberalization's ability to stimulate tobacco consumption, along with the possibility of WTO nontariff barrier restrictions on public health regulations, the FCTC's interaction with trade laws has emerged as a vital consideration. The FCTC's strategies for demand reduction (e.g., pricing, taxation, and regulation of contents, disclosures, and labeling) and supply reduction (e.g., illicit trade and sales to minors) raise questions about compliance with WTO law.

Cases such as U.S–Clove Cigarettes and Australia–Tobacco Plain Packaging illustrate complaints that can arise when states attempt to implement the FCTC (see Chapter 7). Yet WTO panels are supposed to safeguard the right to protect the public's health if the state conforms to international standards.

The FCTC does not clearly specify parties' obligations in relation to trade law. Although the FCTC preamble states that governments will give priority to public health, it does not specify what health should take priority over. Article 2 is the conflicts clause, but it merely authorizes member states to adopt measures beyond those required by the convention, provided they are "consistent" with international law. States may enter bilateral or multilateral agreements on tobacco-related matters that are "compatible" with convention obligations. Yet the FCTC does not specify what might be consistent or compatible.

In the absence of an FCTC provision addressing conflicts with earlier treaties, the general rule is that the later treaty prevails. However, another rule is that the treaty with "greater specificity" prevails. The "last-in-time" and "specificity" rules suggest that the FCTC should prevail over earlier, less-explicit trade-related agreements despite the FCTC being silent on this issue. However, if one of the disputing parties is not a party to the FCTC, the treaty to which both disputants are parties will govern their legal relations.

International Health Regulations

Infectious disease could have serious repercussions for international trade. For example, the EU's 1997 decision to restrict fish importation from Africa following outbreaks of salmonella and cholera resulted in an economic loss of more than $332 million. Trade and travel restrictions due to the 2003 SARS outbreak created an even larger economic burden, estimated at $40 billion. The World Bank estimates that a severe influenza pandemic could cost the global economy as much as 4.8 percent of global GDP.[39]

The 2005 IHR revisions redressed the 1969 IHR's weaknesses, including concerns about "unduly restrictive travel and trade measures."[40] The revised IHR state that public health responses must "avoid unnecessary interference with international traffic and trade" (art. 2), and if a measure causes significant interference, states must provide "the public health rationale and relevant scientific information" (art. 43).

The IHR 2005 was drafted to complement WTO law, as a contextual reading illustrates. Article 43 of the IHR reflects the SPS criteria: health measures should be no more restrictive of trade than necessary to protect health, measured by available scientific evidence of risk, and based on international standards. Similarly, "by calibrating health and trade interests, the IHR resonate with international trade law . . . which also recognizes the state's right to restrict trade for health purposes but limits this right to ensure that restrictions are necessary."[41]

Although the IHR may be supportive of trade, compliance with IHR could have trade consequences. Public health measures taken in response to IHR notifications can violate WTO obligations—in particular, obligations under the SPS Agreement (which covers diseases transmitted by means of animals or plants or products). Countries seeking to reduce transborder disease spread may restrict trade (e.g., by banning certain imports) in the early days of a rapidly emerging infectious disease before the etiology and response become clear. In such cases, which treaty obligation should prevail—the IHR or WTO agreements? And under which institutional framework should disputes be resolved? WTO disputes are resolved through a well-structured dispute settlement system. The IHR, on the other hand, simply urges parties to "settle the dispute through negotiation or any other peaceful means of their own choice." If the dispute still remains unresolved, the parties may bring it before the WHO director-general (IHR art. 56). The result of a dispute, therefore, depends on which regime takes precedence.

The 2009 Influenza H1N1 pandemic suggests that states may prefer to rely on the WTO rather than the WHO in resolving disputes regarding "excessive" health measures. Influenza H1N1, which was not highly pathogenic, prompted numerous country responses ranging from travel advisories to import restrictions on pork products. These actions were taken despite WHO guidance that such measures were unnecessary. In response, some exporting countries raised the issue in the WTO's SPS Committee, pointedly citing an FAO, WHO, and World Organization for Animal Health finding that "influenza viruses are not known to be transmissible to people through eating processed pork or other food products derived from pigs."[42] Notably, the IHR has not been recognized as an international standard under the SPS Agreement.

Overall, if the IHR is to play a greater role in governance, it will need to overcome the perception—and in some cases the reality—that there are "substantial economic disincentives to reporting and responding to public health threats."[43] This could be achieved, for example, through compensation to those suffering economic losses due to compliance with the IHR and other WHO recommendations.

The Doha Development Round and the Future of the WTO

The WTO faces an array of daunting challenges, perhaps threatening its legitimacy. The Doha Development Round has been marked by stalled trade negotiations, although the new D-G has promised to reinvigorate negotiations. Meanwhile, a proliferation of bilateral and regional free trade agreements has emerged in parallel, which could make a multilateral trade organization appear less relevant. The emerging economies of China, Brazil, and India have also influenced WTO power. Such impacts on the trading system can have profound repercussions for global health and development.

The Doha Development Round

Developing countries felt that the Uruguay Round promoted the interests of the rich and was unfair in its distribution of benefits and burdens. Intense media attention and mass protests magnified the discontent of the world's poor. Development and global equity emerged as prime political issues, resulting in the Zanzibar Declaration, which proposed a "development agenda" for the WTO's 2001 Doha Ministerial Conference.[44]

The Doha Round, highlighted by the Doha Ministerial Declaration, aimed to "better integrate developing countries into the global trading system," giving them "a trade-fueled boost."[45] The Ministerial Conference also adopted the Doha Declaration on TRIPS and Public Health, regarded as a key developing-country achievement. Beyond IP negotiations, the Doha Round covers multiple trade issues, including agriculture, services, nonagricultural market access, the environment, special and differential treatment for developing countries, and fairer implementation of existing agreements.

Domestic subsidies and market access for agricultural products emerged as major points of contention, as did the call for special and differential treatment (SDT) for developing countries. There remains broad agreement that developing countries should be afforded SDT. However, developing countries view Doha as a mandate for action to rectify the marked imbalance of rights embedded in the single-package system. Developed countries take a distinctly different view of SDT as simply designed to integrate developing countries into the multilateral trading system.[46] In the course of over a decade, the Doha Round stalled over the conflicting interests of the South and the North. Clearly, political will is necessary if the Doha Round is to reach a successful conclusion.

The WTO's Precarious Future

Prior to the Uruguay Round, developing countries lacked the political and economic power necessary to move the negotiations in their favor. The strategy of coalitions boosted their power through the sheer force of numbers. For example, at the Cancun WTO Ministerial Conference in 2003, the Group of 20 (G20) developing countries drove agricultural market liberalization, including the reduction of European Commission (EC) and U.S. subsidies.

At the same time, Brazil, China, and India are changing WTO power dynamics. The election of a Brazilian, Roberto Azevêdo, as the new director-general of the WTO in May 2013 is indicative of the evolving global political landscape. With the economic difficulties faced by the West in recent years, the emerging economies have pushed their agendas forward. This power shift has been a significant contributor to the changing priorities of the Doha Round. A successful conclusion of the round requires the emerging powers to assume ownership of the outcome. The WTO's continued vibrancy, in many ways, depends on their leadership and support.

Another significant challenge to the WTO and the Doha Round has emerged in the form of regional and bilateral FTAs, which have been negotiated in rapid succession. Since they are negotiated outside WTO auspices, FTAs could undermine developing country interests. The United States, for example, has FTAs with twenty countries. The North American Free Trade Agreement (NAFTA) covers trade with Canada and Mexico; meanwhile, the United States is also negotiating a Trans-Pacific Partnership (TPP) Agreement, with major implications for trade and health.[47]

The emergence of FTAs has serious implications for the WTO and the global trade system. First, FTAs enable powerful countries to lock developing countries into agreements that could not be achieved during WTO negotiations. This dynamic, referred to as TRIPS-plus, is evidenced in bilateral and regional FTAs. TRIPS-plus agreements often incorporate stronger IP protection than those in TRIPS, such as lengthier patent durations, limitations on compulsory licensing, and data exclusivity. Health advocates express deep concern about TRIPS-plus provisions because they extend the period in which pharmaceutical companies can charge monopoly prices and block cheaper generic medicines from entering the market.

Second, FTAs transform North-South negotiating dynamics. Under the WTO, smaller countries could form like-minded coalitions to negotiate on more equal terms. Outside the WTO, however, developing countries lose their ability to leverage coalitions to achieve favorable terms.

Third, FTAs can reduce global welfare and disrupt development. They can also lower economic efficiency, as preferential market access negotiated under FTAs can block the most efficient suppliers. With country resources and energy invested in FTA negotiations, states have less capacity and political will to address the Doha Round's development agenda. Similarly, once FTAs afford market access, powerful states may lose interest in serious WTO negotiations.

Although FTAs purportedly have the same trade liberalization objective as the WTO, they pose a challenge to the WTO's future. To remain relevant, the WTO will have to find ways to overcome the paralysis that afflicts multilateral negotiations and demonstrate its comparative advantage. One area in which the WTO has an advantage is dispute settlement. However, under current rules, WTO panels and the Appellate Body do not have the jurisdiction to hear intra-FTA disputes. WTO reform, for example, could set parameters for FTAs as well as empower WTO panels and the Appellate Body to hear disputes arising from FTAs.

The WTO also faces challenges by international organizations seeking to broaden their mandates. The WHO has expanded its mandate to include the intersection of international health and trade,[48] and its two main treaties (the IHR and FCTC) explicitly encompass aspects of trade and health. Beyond these two treaties, WHO resolutions have potential trade implications, such as the Global Strategies on Diet, Physical Activity and Health (2004) and Public Health, Innovation and Intellectual Property (2008–2009). The WHO Global Code of Practice on the International Recruitment of Health Personnel (2010) aims to govern trade in health services. Although the WHO has received both praise and criticism for its fledgling efforts in nontraditional areas such as trade, there remain serious questions as to whether the agency has the capacity, expertise, and power to tackle new roles and functions.

In a postmillennium era, the WTO's future appears far from stable. The historical reasons behind its establishment no longer hold the same resonance, as developed countries aggressively seek alternative forums for trade negotiations and the original power imbalances shift to emerging economies with uncompromising demands. The WTO's ability to lead its members to embrace development and justice in the global trade system is critical to its future. High on its agenda must be affordable access to essential vaccines and medicines, marked reductions in agricultural subsidies, states' sovereignty to safeguard domestic public health, and counteracting the corrosive effects of FTAs.

The Balance between International Health and Trade

At first glance, it might appear that there is an antagonistic relationship between the objectives of health and trade. Yet success in both fields depends on mutually beneficial arrangements. A fair and vibrant trade system would raise everyone's standard of living, which would benefit global health and development. At the same time, a healthy population is more creative and productive, which bodes well for trade and investment. All countries will be inclined to participate in the ideals of trade liberalization if they feel that their population's health and welfare are high priorities.

At the same time, multiple issues sit at the intersection of these two realms, ranging from patented medicines and international commerce during public health emergencies to the migration of health workers. These critical issues, and many more, cannot be solved in isolation from either trade or health, but require a coordinated approach. Just as there is a need for robust health protection in WTO agreements, so too would WHO treaties and global strategies and codes benefit from trade input. The siloed manner in which the WTO, the WHO, and their respective member states have operated must evolve into mutual respect and collaboration.

Most importantly, the extant challenges require a marked shift in mentality. The dogged pursuit by the WTO and powerful states of trade liberalization without sufficient concern for health justice threatens to alienate states and drive members toward negotiations outside the WTO. This will only result in worse outcomes for, and alienation of, developing countries, further undermining the development-themed Doha Round. Transparency, collaboration, and civil society engagement at the WTO are preferable to bilateral and regional FTA negotiations. All in all, public health and global justice must remain at the forefront of the WTO's agenda, while the WHO must develop the political and economic power, as well as the expertise and mandate, to become a major force at the intersection of international trade and global health.

PART IV

On the Horizon

The Quest for Global Social Justice

GLOBAL HEALTH WITH JUSTICE is the animating theme of this volume. In the final part of the book, I use a series of penetrating case studies as a lens to examine the content and processes of global health equity. These case studies all have two vital features in common: (1) they tell gripping stories of prominent health threats of worldwide significance that demand substantial public attention (and *action*); and (2) they illustrate the social, economic, and political factors that have driven major reforms—whether those factors have been positive (e.g., social mobilization) or negative (e.g., industry obfuscation). (Other parts of the book discuss cases with similar features, notably Chapter 7 on the tobacco pandemic.)

Part IV begins with Chapter 10's case study of arguably the most salient and compelling global health threat: the AIDS pandemic. Its importance is reflected not only in the devastation it has wrought, but also in the stunning technological and political progress fueled by civil society activism. Chapter 11 describes a dramatic case of social injustice—the international migration of health workers from poor to richer countries, thus sapping vital human resources in the developing world. This chapter also tells the story of an innovative "soft" law agreement to resolve the inequity—the WHO Code of Practice on the International Recruitment of Health Personnel.

The final two cases in Part IV focus on pandemic threats—both infectious and noncommunicable. Rapidly moving novel influenzas are vitally important to global health security; consequently, Chapter 12 should be read in conjunction with Chapter 6 on the International Health Regulations.

Chaper 12 also contains a proposal for a global insurance scheme to ensure fairer distribution of scarce vaccines and antiviral medications. The final case, in Chapter 13, discusses the "coming storm" of noncommunicable diseases. The forces of globalization (see Chapter 2) are fueling an epidemiological transition from infectious to chronic diseases—particularly in low- and middle-income countries. Because NCDs—including cancer, cardiovascular disease, and diabetes—are driven by lifestyle factors such as poor diet, tobacco use, and lack of physical activity, they require a different set of behavioral interventions.

The final chapter in this book takes a step back and asks three questions that are fundamental to achieving global health with justice. If we could achieve it, what would a state of genuine global health look like? What would global health embedded in a just world look like? And what would it take to actually achieve our vision of global health equity? My answer to the first question is to give greater preference to the "upstream" causes of ill health, such as public health and socioeconomic determinants. The answer to the second question is to embed justice in the environment in which everyone lives, and also to distribute public goods equitably, with particular attention to the least advantaged. The answer to the third—and most difficult—question borrows from a series of "high-minded" reform proposals offered by civil society and academics. This entails good governance, sustainable funding, research and development, affordable access to essential health technologies, and a "new deal" for global health, such as that found in a proposed Framework Convention on Global Health.

CHAPTER 10

"Getting to Zero"

Scientific Innovation, Social Mobilization, and Human Rights in the AIDS Pandemic

THERE IS NO STORY in global health as transformative, awe-inspiring, and yet as tragic as the AIDS pandemic. The disease was unknown only a generation ago—a medical curiosity among young gay men in New York and San Francisco in June 1981. Within a few short years, AIDS could be found on every continent, enveloping the world to become one of the most devastating pandemics in human history—causing untold human suffering, social disintegration, and economic destruction.

The human immunodeficiency virus (HIV) is a rare retrovirus that insidiously attacks the immune system, triggering opportunistic infections and ultimately killing its host. In the early days of the pandemic, public health officials relied on prevention strategies devised for other sexually transmitted diseases (STDs): testing, counseling, education, condoms, and partner notification. Newly diagnosed persons had a median survival period of six to eight months, their weakened immune systems making them vulnerable to rare cancers, pneumonias, chronic fatigue, and horrific wasting until death ensued. HIV spreads from person to person through behaviors that are universal: sex, needle injection, even childbirth. Over time it embeds itself in society's most oppressed populations—drug users, sex workers, sexual minorities, and the poorest of the poor—creating often-impenetrable sociopolitical and economic barriers to prevention and treatment.

In the early days, the sociopolitical response was, at best, denial, ignorance, and silence—President Reagan did not utter the word "AIDS" in public until 1986. At worst, the response was social marginalization, discrimination, and punishment—blaming people for their own suffering and criminalizing them for their behavior. The fear, pain, and despair faced by persons living with AIDS and their loved ones cannot be overstated.

By 2010 UNAIDS announced a goal that was once unimaginable: *Getting to zero*—zero new infections, zero AIDS-related deaths, and zero discrimination. At the 2012 International AIDS Conference—held in the United States for the first time in twenty-two years, because the United States restricted entry of persons living with HIV between 1990 and 2010[1]—then Secretary of State Hillary Clinton called for an *AIDS-free generation.* To be sure, these high hopes provoked a skeptical response, with experts saying the goal was unrealistic and open-ended—what exactly is the definition of "zero" or "AIDS-free," and which generation are we talking about? But stepping back from perennial debates about aspiration tempered by realism, it is impossible not to marvel at the technological advances that enabled global health leaders to say the unthinkable—that we may one day see the end of the scourge of AIDS.

The technological advances that made all this possible include, first and foremost, antiretroviral treatments, so that a newly diagnosed twenty-five-year-old today can expect to live another fifty years on treatment. But it also includes combination prevention, which extends well beyond traditional methods of testing, counseling, condoms, and education (although these remain vital). Research has shown remarkable reductions in HIV transmission from male circumcision, preexposure prophylaxis (PrEP), and antiretroviral therapy (ART). At the 2011 International AIDS Conference, scientists announced a jaw-dropping 95 percent-plus reduction in sexual transmission among heterosexual couples adhering to ART ("treatment as prevention").

What if it were possible to reach every person at risk, or already infected, with these powerful interventions? What if the next discovery could empower women to protect themselves, such as with a vaginal microbicide, which is on the horizon?[2] Given the political will, isn't it imaginable that the international community could "get to zero"?

How did all these technological advances come about, and why did this particular disease forge a pathway toward unprecedented scientific discoveries? Very sadly, science has not been able to match these technological advances for most global health challenges—not mental illness, cancer, or tuberculosis. It has been said that these are all highly complex, multifactorial diseases, while AIDS is not. But this is far from the truth. AIDS is one of the most complicated and stubbornly persistent diseases the world has ever known.

AIDS is a socially mediated disease; public perceptions are tainted by prejudices toward sex workers, drug users, and the lesbian, gay, bisexual, and transgender (LGBT) community. This often leads to stigmatization and inaction, as evidenced with mental illness and tuberculosis. Yet the sociopolitical dimension of AIDS had the opposite effect, galvanizing perhaps the greatest social mobilization around a health crisis that the world has seen. From the AIDS Coalition to Unleash Power (ACT UP) and Lambda Legal Defense in the United States to the Treatment Action Campaign (TAC) in South Africa, courageous individuals and organizations have literally transformed the politics of AIDS—turning neglect and derision into empowerment and social action.

This vast social mobilization was targeted not only at fighting the social dimensions of this disease—with poignant calls for dignity, nondiscrimination, and justice. It was perhaps principally about access to medicines. AIDS campaigns had crisp clarity, appealing to a basic sense of social justice: the rich have access to life-sustaining medicines while the poor do not. This message resonated both in developed countries (where the poor often were denied access to antiretroviral medication) and developing countries (where most people could not afford a life-saving pill that the majority of those in the developed world could access).

The access-to-medicines campaigns brought AIDS advocates to pursue solutions beyond the health sector. Activists directly attacked the prevailing trade liberalization paradigm, which protects intellectual property, and asserted the higher priority of the right to health. In South Africa the TAC successfully challenged the government's restrictions on access to perinatal treatment before the Constitutional Court. At the international level, the AIDS movement energized the World Health Organization to take access to medicines seriously, prompting campaigns such as the WHO's 3 by 5 Initiative. It forced the World Trade Organization to change course, introducing Doha Declaration flexibilities to soften a harsh intellectual property regime (see Chapter 9).

This social mobilization also unleashed unprecedented resources in global health—new funding for biomedical research, vaccines, and treatment. Moreover, social mobilization around AIDS literally transformed global health governance. It fundamentally altered the foreign assistance of the most powerful countries (e.g., PEPFAR in the United States, and UNITAID, formed by Brazil, Chile, France, Norway, and the United Kingdom). For the first time, the major powers began to frame an infectious disease as a national security threat, addressed at the highest political levels at the G8. Social mobilization drove the United Nations' response, prompting the first high-level summit ever held on a health issue to be devoted to AIDS.[3] The General Assembly also formed a new umbrella agency to fight AIDS and coordinate UN work—UNAIDS. A novel public-private partnership emerged, outside the UN/WHO structure, to generate and pool resources—the Global Fund to Fight AIDS, Tuberculosis and Malaria.

Although the international community has rallied to fight AIDS, fierce debates have raged within the movement. Initially, advocates worried that traditional public health strategies such as testing and reporting would undermine privacy or foster discrimination. At the same time, policy makers debated which interventions—and in what combination—were most effective. And then there was the divisive issue of cost-effectiveness. Could governments afford expensive interventions such as lifetime treatment with antiretrovirals? If not, how could the benefits be fairly allocated among the large population of persons at risk or living with HIV? And should the same level of resources devoted to AIDS be made equally available for other pressing health conditions, such as child/maternal health, injuries, or NCDs? These battles ensued within both domestic health sectors and foreign health assistance budget debates. They remain topics of lively debate.

This chapter begins with a deeper discussion of AIDS as a socially mediated disease before turning to the vast social mobilization that is a defining feature of the AIDS response. It moves to the most urgent message of AIDS campaigns: universal access to treatment. It then explores the AIDS movement's transformative impact on global governance for health. The chapter ends by examining the dramatic scientific innovations, along with the controversies they have wrought. Is it possible to imagine the end of the AIDS pandemic? How can we temper grand aspirations with hard realities?

The Social Construction of AIDS

The historian Charles Rosenberg wrote, "Disease necessarily reflects and lays bare every aspect of the culture in which it occurs."[4] The social and cultural values that came to define the AIDS pandemic vividly illustrate Rosenberg's insight.[5] The historic and ongoing marginalization of persons most deeply affected by AIDS—men who have sex with men (MSM), injection drug users (IDUs), sex workers (including children), prisoners, and migrants—makes the AIDS movement's vast social mobilization all the more remarkable.[6] Simply put, AIDS is a disease of "economic and gender inequalities and weakened social cohesion" (Box 10.1).[7]

BOX 10.1 The Demographics of the AIDS Pandemic

AIDS is one of the most destructive pandemics in human history, having infected more than 60 million people since the disease was first identified in 1981 and costing nearly half of them their lives.[1] In 2012 an estimated 35.3 million people were living with HIV, including 2.3 million newly infected that year. The large number of people living with HIV reflects not only the scale of the pandemic, but also the immense contribution of antiretroviral therapy (ART) in keeping people alive longer.[2]

Although the pandemic is far from over, progress in prevention and treatment has been dramatic, with a 50 percent decline in new HIV infections in twenty-six countries between 2001 and 2012.[3] And by 2012, AIDS-related deaths had dropped by 30 percent since peaking in 2005, following progressive expansion of ART.[4]

The aspiration of universal treatment, however, remains out of reach. In 2012 9.7 million people in low- and middle-income countries were receiving ART, representing 61 percent of all those eligible for treatment under 2010 WHO guidelines. However, under updated 2013 WHO guidelines, which made more people eligible for treatment, ART coverage in low- and middle-income countries represented only approximately 34 percent of the 28.3 million people eligible that year.[5] And among marginalized groups such as injection drug users, the percentage of eligible individuals on treatment is disproportionately small (e.g., in China, 14.7 percent of those receiving ART are IDUs, but IDUs make up 38.5 percent of persons living with HIV in China).[6]

Sub-Saharan Africa continues to be the epicenter of the pandemic, accounting for 70 percent of new infections in 2012.[7] Still, the rate of progress in preventing AIDS is encouraging; since 2001 the number of new HIV infections among adults in sub-Saharan Africa has declined by 24 percent. The Caribbean has experienced an even more pronounced decline of 49 percent since 2001.[8] Sadly, while the annual infection rates continue to decline in these countries, AIDS is resurgent in other regions. The Middle East and North Africa, for example, have seen rates of annual infection rise after a period of stabilization. New HIV infections have also been on the rise in Eastern Europe and Central Asia, despite declines in Ukraine.[9]

The 2013 UNAIDS report identified major challenges in preventing new infections and scaling up HIV services. Key among these was ensuring increased prevention coverage among IDUs, particularly given the persistently high HIV rates in this population.[10] Other critical barriers included gender inequalities, violence against women and girls, and HIV-related stigma and discrimination, including restrictions on freedom of movement, as well as punitive laws. These obstacles must be addressed if we are to reach the target of zero new infections, zero AIDS-related deaths, and zero discrimination.

NOTES

1. World Health Organization (WHO), *A New Health Sector Agenda for HIV/AIDS: Global Health Sector Strategy on HIV/AIDS: 2011–2015* (Geneva: WHO, 2011).
2. Joint United Nations Programme on HIV/AIDS (UNAIDS), *Global Report: UNAIDS Report on the Global AIDS Epidemic* (Geneva: UNAIDS, 2013), 4.
3. Ibid.
4. UNAIDS, "UNAIDS Reports a 52% Reduction in New HIV Infections among Children and a Combined 33% Reduction among Adults and Children Since 2001," September 23, 2013, http://www.unaids.org/en/resources/presscentre/pressreleaseandstatementarchive/2013/september/20130923prunga/.
5. UNAIDS, *Global Report*, 6.
6. Richard H. Needle and Lin Zhao, *HIV Prevention among Injection Drug Users: Strengthening U.S. Support for Core Interventions* (Washington, DC: Center for Strategic and International Studies, 2010).
7. UNAIDS, *Global Report*, 12.
8. Ibid.
9. Ibid.
10. Ibid., 5–6.

"Know Your Epidemic"

Before its Getting to Zero campaign, UNAIDS urged countries and communities to "know your epidemic." The key idea was that the characteristics of AIDS vary depending on the locale, requiring well-targeted interventions. While some communities are engulfed in generalized epidemics affecting wide cross-sections of the population, others see concentrations in vulnerable groups, such as injection drug users, gay men, or sex workers. Public health strategies, therefore, must be up to date and adapted to evolving patterns of transmission. Interventions that are effective in one community (e.g., young women in Africa) will be ineffective in others (e.g., IDUs in eastern Europe).

Notwithstanding these variations, the common link is that many risk factors are socially mediated, associated with the most emotive symbols in society: sex, blood, prostitution, and drug use. Although HIV is transmitted by individual behaviors, these are structured by the relationships within which individuals are embedded.[8] Social networks can fuel the spread of HIV in marginalized communities[9] but can also be a crucial source of support for their members.

The gay community The common perception in the West is that AIDS is primarily a "gay disease," in part because the first reported cases were in gay men in California and New York. The gay community was also among the first affected in Australia and western Europe. The media initially referred to AIDS as "gay compromise syndrome" or GRID (gay-related immune deficiency).[10] Negative stereotypes fueled social ostracization, discrimination, and violence. States often made gay sex a crime, with harsh penalties for sexual transmission of HIV. In a hostile environment, gay men kept their sexuality hidden, driving the epidemic underground.[11] "The dominant feature of this first period was silence, . . . [the disease] spread unchecked by awareness or preventive action."[12]

Aside from self-identified gay men, AIDS strongly affects the broader group of men who have sex with men but who do not necessarily identify as gay or bisexual. In North America and western Europe, there has been a resurgence of HIV among MSM, particularly young men. High infection rates are also found in sub-Saharan Africa—for example, nearly 20 percent of new infections in Senegal and 15 percent of those in Kenya and Rwanda are linked to unprotected sex between men.[13]

Stigma, discrimination, and violence make the already enormous task of preventing and treating HIV even more challenging. A particularly distressing illustration occurred in Uganda in 2011 when the gay rights campaigner David Kato was beaten to death, causing openly gay men to fear for their lives.[14] A further challenge to the safety of the LGBT community in Uganda is a bill (which was before parliament at the time of writing this book) that would broaden criminalization of same-sex relationships and introduce severe penalties for individuals and organizations that support gay rights.[15] In South Africa, twenty-three homophobic murders were reported between April 2010 and February 2012.[16] In 2013 gay rights activists reported an upsurge in homophobic vigilantism in Russia (particularly against LGBT teenagers), following the introduction of a law that banned "propaganda" promoting nontraditional sexual relationships among young people.[17]

Injection drug users Sharing contaminated injection equipment places millions of drug users at high risk of HIV and other blood-borne infections (e.g., hepatitis B and C). To maximize their dose, IDUs often "draw back the plunger of the syringe to fill the barrel with blood and then re-inject the blood," flushing out any residue of the drug before passing it on to a needle-sharing partner—a process called booting.[18]

Although needle sharing is often part of the drug ritual, risk behavior is fueled by state policy creating an artificial scarcity of sterile equipment.

Illicit drug use is unlawful almost everywhere, driving the behavior underground. States frequently restrict the sale of injection equipment in pharmacies, and many even block needle exchange programs that are proven to be highly effective.[19]

In the absence of harm reduction, an injection-driven epidemic can accelerate quickly, rising from negligible levels to over >50 percent in only a few years. Once it takes hold among injection drug users, HIV can spread to sexual partners and (through childbirth) to newborns. Drug users are among the most marginalized people in society. They are criminalized by the state and often denied protection against discrimination and violence. An estimated 75 percent of IDUs live in developing countries, with little access to services. UN Secretary-General Ban Ki-moon has condemned the "virtual neglect of this most-at-risk population."[20]

Injection drug use is the major route of HIV transmission in eastern Europe, Southeast Asia, the Middle East, and the southernmost portion of Latin America. The percentage of AIDS cases attributed to injection drug use in some countries is astounding—for example, 83 percent in Russia and 72 percent in Malaysia.[21] The social and economic costs are staggering—measured in increased crime, domestic violence, and homelessness.

Sex workers As with MSM and IDUs, sex workers worldwide are disproportionately affected by AIDS. In Asia, sex work is the "single-most powerful driving force" in the AIDS epidemic.[22] Although the degree of disempowerment varies across regions and societies, female sex workers are deeply vulnerable. Male transgender sex workers are in a similarly precarious position. The risk for sex workers is compounded by the interplay with drug and alcohol use, complicating targeted interventions. Policy makers fail to appreciate the sheer breadth of the challenge because these activities are hidden, making it difficult to track or intervene in the epidemic.

Female sex workers often have very high rates of infection, indicating that condoms are not routinely used—a by-product of the profoundly unequal bargaining power between sex workers and their clients. Male clients may offer to pay more to have sex without using a condom, simply refuse to use a condom, or sexually assault the woman. As participants in an underground trade, without recourse to legal protection, sex workers are faced with the impossible choice of accepting the risk or forgoing a livelihood—their meager pay is desperately needed for their own survival as well as that of their children.

Beyond sex work, criminal enterprises traffic vulnerable children and women for sex, often without serious risk of arrest or prosecution. The lives of these children and women are utterly destroyed by this modern-day form of slavery. They are held captive, assaulted, and frequently left to die of AIDS by brutal men often twice their age.

Prisoners Prisoners are under the supervision of the state, so it is remarkable that incarceration is such a profound risk factor for HIV and other sexually transmitted or blood-borne infections. Yet HIV is rampant in prison systems worldwide. In many low- and middle-income countries, HIV prevalence among prisoners exceeds 10 percent.[23] Similar infection rates can be found in large urban prisons in high-income countries.[24]

Many states exhibit an unjust and counterproductive neglect of AIDS in prisons. Unprotected (often forcible) sex and injection drug use are endemic in many incarcerated populations—as prison authorities turn a blind eye to these prohibited activities. Governments actually block crucial harm reduction programs, such as the distribution of condoms and sterile injection equipment to inmates. Prison systems often do not screen prisoners for HIV infection or provide treatment for those living with HIV/AIDS. When released from incarceration, men often spread HIV infection to their wives and other sexual or needle-sharing partners.

Migrants Migrants face multiple challenges of language, culture, and legal status. Facing violence and oppression, they are deeply vulnerable to infection, with limited access to health care. As UNAIDS observed, "Being mobile in and of itself is not a risk factor for HIV infection. It is the situations encountered and the behaviors possibly engaged in during mobility or migration that increase vulnerability and risk regarding HIV/AIDS."[25]

The overlap of risk behaviors among migrants, particularly paid sex, contributes to the increased prevalence. In China, young rural-to-urban male migrants have been identified as the "tipping point" for the AIDS epidemic, as they "play a crucial role in broadening social and sexual networks."[26] In the Middle East and North Africa, returning refugees often are infected with HIV, transmitting the virus to their unknowing sexual partners.[27] Undocumented migrants are less likely to seek testing and treatment, which fuels sexual and perinatal HIV transmission throughout society.

Social Mobilization: The Vast Potential of Civil Society

In the face of despair and social ostracization, brave advocates across the globe fought back. Taking to the streets, canvassing parliaments, and spearheading litigation, civil society achieved remarkable success—not only in fighting AIDS, but also in forging a pathway for broader health rights activism. Initially forced into isolation, persons living with HIV/AIDS and their loved ones formed grassroots networks. They built support systems to care for the ill and passionately campaigned for scientific research, equal rights, and equitable access to treatment. From organic networks among Cambodian women, to advocacy groups in Uganda, South Africa, and Singapore, to gay rights organizations in the United States and Europe, the AIDS movement changed the world.

Vito Russo, a gay activist in the late 1980s, viewed AIDS as a test of community resolve, revealing the transformative power of the movement: "When future generations ask what we did in this crisis, we're going to have to tell them that we were out here today. Someday the AIDS crisis will be over. And when that day comes, there will be people alive on this earth—gay people and straight people, men and women, black and white—who will hear the story, that once there was a terrible disease and that a brave group of people stood up and fought, and in some cases gave their lives, so that others might live and be free."[28]

Innovative Advocacy Strategies

Larry Kramer, the American playwright and LGBT rights activist, argued that indifferent governments and a fearful public allowed the pandemic to unfold.[29] There is truth in Kramer's claim, evidenced by the halting and inadequate response by governments, whose leaders often fell silent, denying the magnitude—and even the scientific causes—of an unprecedented public health crisis.

President George H. W. Bush (1989–1993) responded dismissively to protests outside his summer home in Kennebunkport, Maine, in 1991: AIDS activists "were here because they could get disproportionate television coverage . . . because the President happened to be at his ancestral home." Casting implicit blame on those suffering from the disease, he said, "Here's a disease where you can control its spread by your own personal behavior."[30] (How ironic that his son would create PEPFAR—the largest national program in history to combat a single disease.) Perhaps no one epitomized hostility more than Senator Jesse Helms, who called homosexuality "deliberate, disgusting, revolting."[31]

From this apathy and homophobic enmity, the AIDS community rose up, quite literally, to fight for their lives. AIDS campaigns made an impact on every front—research, security, trade, and social justice.

The Human Face of AIDS

A key strategy of the AIDS movement was to put a human face on the disease. Humanizing people living with HIV/AIDS began to shift public attitudes from negative stereotypes toward compassion. The following powerful stories transformed public attitudes in America:

The NAMES Project AIDS Memorial Quilt was first displayed in 1987 on the National Mall in Washington, DC and became a powerful symbol. The quilt had 1,920 panels, each representing a person who had died from AIDS, and covered a space larger than a football field. Half a million people visited the quilt during its inaugural weekend. Only a year later, the quilt had quadrupled in size, and by 1996 it covered the entire National Mall. Through humanizing messages, the public came to see persons living with HIV/AIDS as friends and lovers, mothers and fathers, sons and daughters.

Ryan White's story is well known in America. Ryan contracted HIV from a blood transfusion needed to treat his hemophilia. When he was diagnosed in 1984 at age thirteen, his school in Kokomo, Indiana, barred him from attending. Ryan's words lay bare the constant violation of his dignity: "Discrimination, fear, panic, and lies surrounded me—spitting on cookies, urinating on bathroom walls, restaurants threw away my dishes. . . . My school folders were marked FAG and other obscenities. . . . I was not welcome anywhere. People would get up and leave so they would not have to sit anywhere near me. Even at church, people would not shake my hand."[32] Activists used Ryan's moving story to push for the Ryan White CARE Act to enhance treatment access for low-income persons.

Arthur Ashe's story resonated worldwide. In 1992 this beloved tennis star disclosed that he had AIDS, contracted from a blood donation during cardiac surgery. Ashe devoted the last year of his life to public awareness, including a speech to the UN General Assembly. Seeing a world-class athlete die of AIDS vividly demonstrated that the disease could touch anyone.

Magic Johnson's story shocked America. When Johnson (a basketball star) announced in 1991 that he had contracted HIV from unsafe sex, it moved public opinion beyond the division between the "innocent" and the "blameworthy." It dawned on the public that universal human behaviors could transmit infection. Johnson became a role model among African Americans. As AIDS became more widespread, celebrities such as U2's Bono, the late Princess Diana, and Elton John joined the fight, offering not only their names, but also a valuable brand for advocacy and fund-raising.

Scientific Literacy: Born of Necessity

Before the era of AIDS, consumers were rarely invited into the halls of power. Advocacy was usually through surrogates, with well-intentioned charitable workers campaigning for their favorite cause. That all changed with AIDS, as persons living with the disease came to the forefront of the struggle. They not only demanded to be present when key decisions were taken, but came armed with scientific knowledge about the virus, prevention, and treatment. The exceptional literacy of activists became a hallmark of the movement. At every turn they were as knowledgeable as—and sometimes better informed than—the researchers and government officials on whose work their lives depended.

In the United States, advocacy groups such as ACT UP and Lambda Legal Defense Fund drew on the expertise of their members and supporters—often highly educated gay men. AIDS advocates did their homework, winning respect and a seat at the table. Anthony Fauci of the National Institutes of Health observed, "It became very clear that you weren't going to mess with these people."[33] AIDS advocacy moved beyond merely observing government decision making to strongly influencing it, often driving the research agenda.

Once treatment became a scientific reality, activists—notably South Africa's Treatment Action Campaign—mobilized around "treatment literacy" to empower people to claim their rights. The TAC's Mark Heywood argued, "Treatment literacy is the base for both self-help and social mobilization. Armed with knowledge about HIV . . . people can become their own advocates, personally and socially empowered."[34] Treatment literacy entailed not just scientific knowledge, but political activism as well.

Civil Disobedience and Bold Confrontation

On the eve of the twenty-fifth anniversary of the founding of ACT UP, David France wrote, "the gay ghetto was a tinderbox by March 1987. . . . Along Christopher Street [NYC] you could see the dazed look of the doomed, skeletons and their caregivers alike. . . . Then the posters appeared. . . .

Overnight, images bearing the radical truism SILENCE = DEATH appeared all over lower Manhattan. The fuse was set. . . . Just like that, a new, grassroots-direct-action movement congealed—ACT UP."[35]

A characteristic feature of AIDS activism—and the hallmark of ACT UP—was its irreverence for political power structures, both scientific and political. Advocates did not make polite requests, but rather demanded to be heard, to be in the room, and to shape decisions that affected their communities deeply. Borrowing from the American Black Power movement of Malcolm X and Stokely Carmichael, AIDS activists took an aggressive stance against a fearful and indifferent society.

With their bold assertiveness, AIDS activists pierced the icy political silence. Acts of protest and civil disobedience ranged from a "die-in" on Wall Street (chaining dying activists to the New York Stock Exchange) to a shutdown of FDA headquarters to confrontation with the Catholic hierarchy for opposing condoms ("Stop the Church"). (Echoes of the tension between religion and health reemerged in 2005; paraphrasing then UNAIDS head, Peter Piot's retort to the pope, "You do God, UNAIDS will do science.") The campaign United in Anger vividly revealed the outrage, as ACT UP proclaimed, "Government has blood on its hands." The chant "Act up, fight back, fight AIDS" resounded across America and the world.

As effective treatments emerged, social movements began pressing for access. In South Africa the TAC engaged in civil disobedience, but also in sophisticated legal and political advocacy. Borrowing from the anti-apartheid movement, the TAC demanded that the government honor the constitution's guarantee of the right to health services. The TAC clashed with powerful institutions—for example, when its members occupied a Queenstown hospital, police fired a barrage of rubber bullets.

Litigation and Political Lobbying

While civil disobedience and confrontation garnered public attention, advocates also exercised their political and legal rights. In South Africa, the TAC brought the most celebrated right-to-health case before the Constitutional Court. President Mbeki, who refused to accept HIV as the causative agent of AIDS, limited nevirapine (which reduces mother-to-child HIV transmission) to pilot sites, severely restricting access to treatment by pregnant women.

On the day of the hearing in *Minister of Health v. Treatment Action Campaign,* 5,000 people marched to Johannesburg demanding the right to treatment.[36] Siding with AIDS advocates, the Constitutional Court ruled that the policy violated the constitutional duty (contained in section 27) to "take reasonable measures within its available resources, to progressively achieve the right to health." The case showed the world that litigation could enhance treatment access, providing an inspiring model for integrating political and legal action.

Beyond treatment access, decriminalizing same-sex relationships became a rallying cry of the movement. Advocates lobbied governments, arguing that these laws were discriminatory and discouraged testing and counseling. Although many states still have such laws on the books (sometimes making same-sex acts punishable by the death penalty),[37] litigation and political lobbying have had a measure of success. The Delhi High Court in 2009 ruled that a 150-year-old law outlawing "carnal intercourse against the order of nature" violated the Indian Constitution. Many states have also repealed these draconian laws, among them Fiji in 2010 and Chile in 2012. Beyond national-level action, AIDS advocates persuaded the UN General Assembly in 2011 to recommend that states review laws adversely affecting the "effective and equitable delivery of HIV services."[38]

Advocates have made considerable strides in reducing stigma and discrimination, particularly in western Europe, North America, and countries such as Belarus, Brazil, India, Namibia, and South Africa.[39] In Brazil, activists won court battles for nondiscrimination, including the right to serve in the military and to collect retirement and disability benefits. The Lambda Legal Defense won the first HIV/AIDS discrimination case in the United States in 1983,[40] and by 1990 AIDS activists helped secure the passage of the landmark Americans with Disabilities Act (ADA).

Emulating these successes, activists in other regions are fighting for antidiscrimination laws—particularly in sub-Saharan Africa, which often has been resistant to change. These efforts are critical in countries with deep-rooted homophobia; for example, Nigerian activist Thaddeus Ugoh described how village elders proclaimed in 2011 that persons living with HIV and their families would be expelled under the threat of being burned alive.[41]

Social Support Networks

The AIDS movement sent a message that if government refused to support their loved ones, they would provide the care. In Uganda, AIDS activists formed an indigenous support network known as the AIDS Support Organization (TASO) in 1987, unified by common experiences of adversity. TASO began informally but has evolved into an organization providing counseling, medical care, and social support for 100,000 people annually, enrolling 40,000 clients on ARTs since 2004. In China, where the governmental response continues to lag, the Lingnan Health Center, located in Guangzhou and run largely by gay volunteers, is providing testing, counseling, and care. Le, a gay man, shied away from the state-run HIV clinic, fearing reproach, but "here we're all in the same community, so there's less to worry about."[42]

Similar activism emerged in diverse parts of the world, tailored to local needs. In Cambodia, marginalized communities (e.g., MSM and sex workers) established local grassroots organizations, subsequently forming the Cambodian Alliance for Combating HIV/AIDS, a coordinating NGO with a powerful voice.[43] In Ukraine, female sex workers mobilized for their rights as well as to advocate for prevention.[44] In Singapore, citizens founded Action for AIDS (AfA) in 1988, operating the first HIV testing facility.[45] AfA adopted multipronged strategies, engaging in traditional support (e.g., home counseling and treatment access), but also media outreach and political lobbying.

AIDS advocacy has moved from local and national action to regional and global mobilization. The Global Network of Persons Living with HIV (GNP+) coordinates international advocacy, with regional and national networks of people living with HIV. Other global and regional networks include the International Community of Women Living with HIV/AIDS, which improves the lives of women through advocacy. The Global Forum on MSM and HIV advocates for health and human rights, and the International AIDS Society comprises health professionals advocating for scientific research.

Legacies of AIDS Activism

AIDS transformed all activism, and it is a rare movement today that does not draw on the AIDS movement's courage and novel strategies. As early as 1992, NIH Director Bernadine Healy said, "AIDS activists have led the way, . . . [creating] a template for all activist groups."[46] A leading AIDS scientist put it succinctly: "Having our patients or our research subjects ask—or demand—to have an active voice in what we do and how we do it may be challenging, time-consuming, and even unpleasant. . . . It is also undeniably right."[47]

Across the spectrum of NGOs—from mental illness and disabilities to diabetes, cancer, and heart disease—advocates have been emboldened in their social and political activism, with consumers in the vanguard. Breast cancer advocates credited AIDS activists with "showing us how to get through to government."[48] "We've had it with politicians and physicians and scientists who 'there, there' us with studies and statistics and treatments that suggest the disease is under control."[49]

Where once there were telethons seeking charitable donations, today there are walks, runs, and marches in which advocates control the narrative. The "Occupy" campaign (protesting economic inequalities) drew its inspiration from the AIDS movement. Political lobbying became increasingly sophisticated. Through its multipronged approach, the AIDS movement transformed modern advocacy, demanding ramped-up investment, time-bound targets, monitoring, and accountability.

Governing the AIDS Pandemic: Global AIDS Institutions in the New Millennium

By the dawn of the new millennium, social mobilization finally brought major reform to global health forums. AIDS was suddenly on the agenda at the World Economic Forum, the G8 summit, the Africa Development Forum, and the United Nations. These pivotal events set in motion a period of remarkable institutional reform that continues to shape global AIDS policy as well as the wider global health landscape.

During this period of reform, thinking shifted from framing AIDS as a health issue to one with broader geostrategic ramifications. Millennium Development Goal 6 ("Combat HIV/AIDS, malaria and other diseases") thrust AIDS to the forefront of development. Even more transformative, political leaders began viewing AIDS as a security threat—in terms of both human security and international peace (Box 10.2). In January 2000 the UN Security Council called AIDS in Africa a security threat—the first time the council dealt with a health issue under the UN Charter. Later that year, the Security Council directed the Secretary-General to focus on AIDS prevention and education for peacekeepers, recognizing that soldiers both contract and transmit HIV.[50]

Building on the Security Council resolution, the General Assembly held a special session on HIV/AIDS in June 2001—the first UN high-level summit devoted to health.[51] The session—driven by social mobilization—became a crucial turning point. Although not legally binding, the special session's Declaration of Commitment on HIV/AIDS became the symbol of a new political will. The declaration set out ambitious and measurable goals, including national AIDS strategies, holding states politically accountable. The most controversial aspect of the special session was ac-

BOX 10.2 HIV/AIDS as a Security Threat

By the late 1990s, with HIV spreading at alarming rates and no plan for expanding treatment access, the pandemic threatened to destroy "the very fiber of what constitutes a nation: individuals, families and communities; economic and political institutions; military and police forces."[1] The high infection rates among the young, mobile, and educated were particularly concerning, as these were the future leaders needed to keep states stable and productive. The impact of AIDS on social and economic progress could fuel violent conflict and humanitarian catastrophes, threatening national stability and international security as conflict spread across borders and forced mass migrations. HIV infection in militaries and peacekeeping forces could undermine the capacity to respond. It was in this context that the UN Security Council in 2000 held its historic session on HIV/AIDS as a security threat.[2]

Although combination prevention and treatment averted the most catastrophic security scenarios, AIDS continues to threaten human security in the hardest hit regions. Reframing AIDS as a security threat also shaped the "securitization" of global health, with a sharper focus on "smart power"—i.e., health assistance as a vital diplomatic tool.

NOTES

1. International Crisis Group (ICG), *HIV/AIDS as a Security Issue* (Washington, DC: ICG, 2001), 1.
2. UNAIDS, *The Responsibility of the Security Council in the Maintenance of International Peace and Security: HIV/AIDS and International Peacekeeping Operations* (Geneva: UNAIDS, 2011).

cess to treatment. Although the declaration urged treatment expansion, it failed to establish specific commitments.

What became clear from the special session was that genuine progress was impossible without an unprecedented increase in financial resources. As Peter Piot, then head of UNAIDS, said at the Durban Conference in 2000, "We need billions, not millions, to fight AIDS in this world. We can't fight an epidemic of this magnitude with peanuts." Global AIDS expenditures had already grown from under $300 million in 1996 to $1.3 billion in 2000,[52] but even this amount paled in comparison to the need. UNAIDS estimated that it would cost $3 billion for even a basic response to AIDS in Africa, with $10 billion more annually to make treatment access a global reality.

The international community realized that investments on this scale would require innovative funding mechanisms. Existing humanitarian assistance was insufficient, and a vast influx of funds would require new governance structures to oversee the distribution and effective use of resources. By the time of the UN special session, international negotiations had already begun on a novel funding mechanism, which eventually became the Global Fund to Fight AIDS, Tuberculosis and Malaria (the Global Fund). The Global Fund commenced operations in 2002, forever altering the institutional landscape. The fund's creation catalyzed institutional reform, ushering in a transformative phase of governance characterized by public-private partnerships (see Chapter 5).

Putting AIDS at the Center of Global Health Institutions

Global AIDS institutions have been critical to treatment expansion, with significant funding and technical expertise. Beyond treatment access, AIDS institutions have played key roles in monitoring and analyzing the pandemic while supporting prevention. Equally important, AIDS institutions have provided a transformative model for global health governance. Reflecting the dynamics of the social mobilization that spawned them, global AIDS institutions included civil society and persons living with AIDS in their governance structures. AIDS institutions also implemented key principles of aid effectiveness and good governance, particularly by shifting from a donor/recipient "aid" dynamic to one of country ownership /equal partnership.

UNAIDS

The development of AIDS institutions reflected both the unprecedented response needed and the crosscutting nature of the disease. The UN system saw the need for a focused, multisectoral response, creating the Joint United Nations Programme on HIV/AIDS (UNAIDS) in 1996 to coordinate six agencies: the WHO, UNICEF, UNDP, UNFPA, UNESCO, and the World Bank. The World Food Program, the UN Office on Drugs and Crime, UN Women, and the International Labor Organization joined as cosponsors in later years.

While not a funding agency, UNAIDS ensures that resources are well spent—making the money work. The agency works with partners for better coordination across diverse programs and sponsors at the country level, allowing governments to harmonize their activities under a single national AIDS framework, a single AIDS coordinator, and a single country-level monitoring and evaluation system (known as the "Three Ones").

UNAIDS mobilizes political will and financial and technical resources, unites stakeholders, develops strategies and evidence, and supports inclusive country leadership. It publishes annual state of the epidemic reports and periodic evaluations of available funding compared to needs. UNAIDS offers technical support to build capacity at country level and promotes human rights, particularly combating discrimination and protecting women, girls, and sexual minorities.[53]

Under Executive Director Peter Piot and his successor, Michel Sidibé, leadership has been at the center of the UNAIDS mission, working closely with civil society. In an early example of AIDS governance charting innovation, UNAIDS was the first UN agency with NGO representation on its governing board. The Program Coordinating Board (PCB) includes five regional NGO representatives and people living with HIV/AIDS, three of whom are from the global South, although only governments have PCB voting rights.[54] UNAIDS played a crucial role in political mobilization, particularly in ensuring the success of the UN special session. Its mission affirms the agency's priority of "speaking out in solidarity with the people most affected by HIV in defense of human dignity, human rights and gender equality."[55]

UNAIDS has responded to earlier criticisms by advocating for human rights and the empowerment of marginalized populations; revising downward the overly high estimates of HIV/AIDS prevalence; and emphasizing prevention as well as treatment.[56]

The Global Fund to Fight AIDS, Tuberculosis, and Malaria

Chapter 5 provides a detailed account of the innovative structure, history, and ongoing challenges of the Global Fund, an institution that has shaped the global health landscape, leading innovations in public-private governance and injecting extensive resources to fight three key diseases.

The resources mobilized and channeled through the fund's performance grants to country-owned programs have vastly scaled up prevention and treatment. Although the Global Fund focuses on three diseases, AIDS constitutes the bulk of its work: in its first decade, more than half of approved funding ($12.4 billion) went to HIV/AIDS programs across 147 countries. Global Fund financing accounted for 21 percent of international HIV/AIDS funding in 2009.

Without Global Fund support, the increase in treatment access would never have been possible. By 2010 the Global Fund supported services for nearly half the people worldwide receiving ART. The Global Fund's work in enhancing treatment access has lowered AIDS mortality rates.

Treatment has not been the Global Fund's sole focus. The fund, for example, meets nearly half the global need for perinatal prophylaxis: by mid-2012, 1.5 million pregnant women had received ARTs to prevent mother-to-child transmission. Global Fund grants also support HIV testing and counseling, condom distribution, male circumcision, and community-based prevention for at-risk populations.[57]

PEPFAR

President George W. Bush created the President's Emergency Plan for AIDS Relief (PEPFAR) in 2003; it would become the world's largest bilateral program to combat a single disease, allocating $18.8 billion in its first five years. Reflecting its inception shortly after the Monterrey Consensus, PEPFAR viewed states not as funding recipients, but rather as partners. Accountability for results was at the heart of PEPFAR, with defined targets for 2008, known as "2-7-10"—treating 2 million people, preventing 7 million new HIV infections, and providing care to 10 million. The treatment goal took center stage and was achieved.[58] On World AIDS Day in 2011, with PEPFAR already treating nearly 4 million people, President Obama announced an increase of the treatment goal to 6 million people by the end of 2013—a goal PEPFAR was on target to reach, supporting more than 5 million people on treatment through September 2012.[59]

Partnership Frameworks between PEPFAR and developing-country partners became central to its second phase, beginning with a 2008 reauthorization. Vital principles governed these frameworks, such as country ownership and government-led plans; sustainability, supplementing and not supplanting national AIDS funding; flexibility in recognizing different country contexts; accountability, including for budgeting and expenditures; integration, to strengthen health systems and maximize impact; and monitoring and evaluation, with measurable goals and concrete commitments. By 2013 PEPFAR had signed Partnership Frameworks with more than twenty countries.

PEPFAR also embraced a multilateral approach often absent in U.S. foreign assistance, notably by partnering with the Global Fund. Beyond being the fund's largest contributor, PEPFAR funded technical assistance to improve implementation of Global Fund grants, recognizing that often both Global Fund and U.S. bilateral funding treated the same individuals (e.g., the Global Fund provided ART resources, while bilateral funds paid staff salaries).

For all its good work, PEPFAR has been the subject of valid criticism. PEPFAR did not fully incorporate good governance and aid effectiveness in its early days. Country plans were not made public until several years after its launch, and information on individual grants remains undisclosed. Politically motivated restrictions for organizations that work with sex workers or implement needle exchange programs (now revoked) significantly undermined country ownership. The higher pay of PEPFAR programs drew health workers away from local health facilities, worsening a critical shortage (see Chapter 11). PEPFAR often developed its own supply chains and information systems rather than strengthening national systems.

In June 2013 the Supreme Court held that PEPFAR's "antiprostitution" loyalty pledge violated the freedom of expression of U.S. organizations that receive government funds for work in combating AIDS overseas.[60] This pledge required grant recipients to adopt a policy explicitly opposing commercial sex work and was a particularly controversial aspect of PEPFAR, as it risked alienating vulnerable sex workers and undermining relationships between international organizations and the local community.[61]

As PEPFAR matured, focusing more on sustainability and health system strengthening, it increasingly used national health systems to expand the reach of HIV programs. Its congressional mandate, revised in 2008, aimed to train and retain 140,000 new health workers.[62] When President Obama announced his Global Health Initiative (GHI) in 2009, PEPFAR remained a distinct program. The GHI seeks to better integrate PEPFAR programs into broader efforts to strengthen health systems, supporting work on malaria, tuberculosis, child/maternal health, reproductive health, family planning, and neglected tropical diseases.

A 2013 Institute of Medicine (IOM) report acknowledged PEPFAR's "remarkable progress," and that its efforts had "saved and improved the lives of millions of people"; however, it also said that "substantial unmet needs remain for all services and programs," particularly for children and adolescents.[63] The IOM recommended that PEPFAR focus more strongly on prevention strategies with clear target outcomes, accompanied by monitoring mechanisms, including in the areas of patient retention and treatment adherence. The IOM concluded that PEPFAR needed to transition from funding services to supporting the sustainable delivery of HIV/AIDS programs by partner countries themselves. Although countries such as Mozambique will remain reliant upon PEPFAR services for the immediate future, other states have begun this transition process. For example, PEPFAR signed a five-year plan with South Africa in 2012 that detailed how the government would take over PEPFAR programs.[64]

UNITAID

While the Global Fund has been a major international financier, smaller multilateral partnerships such as UNITAID have also been established.

Brazil, Chile, France, Norway, and the United Kingdom formed UNITAID in 2006 to decrease the price and increase the supply of medicines and diagnostics for AIDS, tuberculosis, and malaria.

UNITAID is the first global health institution to be funded primarily through a so-called innovative financing mechanism, namely, a tax levied by participating countries on all outgoing flights. Participating countries set the level of the tax. Some 65–70 percent of UNITAID's funding comes from the airline tax, which as of 2012 was implemented by ten of UNITAID's twenty-nine member states. The rest of the budget comes from member contributions, the majority to date from France. In its first five years, UNITAID raised $2 billion.

UNITAID combines "pooling of large-scale drug procurement, bulk volume price negotiation, and support for speedier [WHO] prequalification of medicines." These efforts have decreased the cost of medicines, achieving 80 percent price reductions in pediatric formulations for HIV/AIDS and 60 percent price reductions for second-line HIV medications.[65] UNITAID also contributed to another governance innovation, partnering with the WHO, UNAIDS, and the Global Fund to create the Medicines Patent Pool (Box 10.3) to negotiate with AIDS medicine patent

BOX 10.3 **The Medicines Patent Pool**

Though civil society had advocated for the creation of a patent-sharing body since 2002, the Medicines Patent Pool (MPP) did not come into being until July 2010, when UNITAID committed to five years of funding. Under the scheme, HIV drug patent holders license their patents to the MPP, which in turn sublicenses them to generic manufacturers. The pool acts as a one-stop shop for generic manufacturers seeking multiple licenses to produce HIV treatments—lowering the transaction costs of negotiating with each patent holder and encouraging new players by reducing the uncertainty of entering the market. By fueling competition among generic drug makers, the MPP aims to lower prices and increase affordability, making drugs more accessible in developing countries. The pool encourages innovation for new, more effective treatment formulations by generic companies.[1] In addition to negotiating and partnering with companies, the MPP has created a comprehensive database of HIV drug patents.

NOTE

1. Medicines Patent Pool (MPP), *Stimulating Innovation, Expanding Access, Improving Health: Annual Report 2010–2011* (Geneva: MPP, 2012).

holders to increase access. UNITAID also helped create the Millennium Foundation for Innovative Financing for Health, which mobilizes private-sector support for innovative financing. Looking ahead, key challenges for UNITAID include expanding its funding base, broadening its range of partners, responding more quickly to market needs, improving project selection to contribute to price reductions, and better alignment with national planning processes.[66]

All Institutional Hands on Deck: The Impact of Other Key Actors

The vital work of AIDS institutions complements long-standing international institutions with broader mandates. Ultimately, the AIDS response could not be separated from global health and development more broadly. Many international institutions had to deal with AIDS to accomplish their own missions.

Following the formation of UNAIDS, the WHO struggled to define a clear role as constructive tensions emerged between the two agencies. The WHO evolved to establish an important niche, providing technical guidance on treatment and combination prevention. In 2002, just as the treatment expansion was gaining momentum and quality control rose in importance, the WHO published its first list of recommended HIV medicines and the first edition of its treatment guidelines for resource-limited settings.[67]

In the same year, the WHO assumed lead responsibility for HIV treatment within UNAIDS, with WHO Director-General Gro Harlem Brundtland announcing its 3 by 5 Initiative—to have 3 million people on ART by the year 2005. This was a vital initiative, as the 2001 Declaration of Commitment failed to set a measurable target for expanding access. Although the goal was not met, 3 by 5 became a major political tool. Today, the WHO is implementing its Global Health Sector Strategy on HIV/AIDS for 2011–2015, leveraging the AIDS response into sustainable health systems.[68]

The UN has continued to focus on AIDS at the highest political levels. Following the 2001 special session, the General Assembly held high-level meetings in 2006 and again in 2011, each giving rise to political declarations—reaffirming past commitments and affirming new ones. The 2011 declaration committed to "having 15 million people on antiretroviral treatment by 2015," emphasizing prevention.[69] The Security Council continues to view AIDS as a security threat, adopting a 2011 resolution calling on states to reinforce their work on prevention in

BOX 10.4 Global Commission on HIV and the Law

In July 2010, UNDP, with the support of UNAIDS, launched the Global Commission on HIV and the Law—comprising leaders representing all regions, including former heads of state and legal, human rights, and HIV experts. Fernando Henrique Cardoso, former president of Brazil, chaired the commission.

The commission's report, released in July 2012, found that punitive laws hinder HIV responses, waste resources, and undermine human rights. The report urged governments to base laws on public health and human rights, including banning discrimination and repealing laws that criminalize risk behaviors (e.g., same-sex relationships, sex work, and injection drug use). The report asked states to use the law to end violence against women and to resist international pressure to prioritize trade over health.[1] The commission's report reinforces the 2011 Political Declaration on HIV and AIDS, whereby UN member states pledged to review their national laws for adverse impacts on HIV and to create legal and social environments that promote effective policy.

NOTE

1. Global Commission on HIV and the Law, *HIV and the Law: Risks, Rights, and Health* (New York: UNDP, 2012).

peacekeeping missions.[70] In 2010 the UN sponsored a Global Commission on HIV and the Law (Box 10.4).[71]

At the same time, the World Bank has continued its work on AIDS as a major challenge for economic development. Since 2000 the bank has made investments in sub-Saharan Africa through the Multi-Country HIV/AIDS Program (MAP), which funds antiretroviral procurement as part of comprehensive AIDS programming (Box 5.2).

Large philanthropic foundations have also been deeply engaged in the AIDS pandemic. Most important, the Gates Foundation had committed over $2.5 billion to the response by 2012, including $1.4 billion to the Global Fund, while supporting research in such areas as vaccines and antiretrovirals as a form of prevention. The Gates Foundation has also helped scale up national responses in several countries, including India and China.[72] Also, the Clinton Health Access Initiative, established by former U.S. president Bill Clinton has helped reduce the cost of life-saving HIV medicines to around $100 to $200 per person per year in many countries.[73]

Building an Institutional Response for the Future: Challenges Moving Forward

The inroads that have been made into slowing, and even reversing, the devastating death march of AIDS would not have been possible without the emergence of powerful institutions. It is impossible to overstate the importance of new institutions in mobilizing resources and sharing scientific expertise.

AIDS institutional reform holds lessons for broader global health governance, including the critical importance of partnerships with diverse stakeholders, country ownership, and equitable access to technologies. Nevertheless, the AIDS institutional landscape poses major challenges. For lower-income states, program fragmentation and the need to maintain relationships with, and report to, multiple institutions can be onerous—at its worst hampering service delivery. This makes the UNAIDS initiative on coordination and harmonization all the more important.

Sustainability will also remain a major challenge, particularly in times of economic uncertainty, as evidenced by difficulties in replenishing the Global Fund. Despite the significant treatment scale-up, universal access remains a distant goal. Moreover, for the foreseeable future—without a vaccine or cure—persons living with HIV will need treatment for life, and some will acquire drug-resistant infections. The new institutional architecture will be vital as AIDS transitions to a chronic disease—facilitating sustainable assistance, while governments move to self-supported programs.

Leveraging the AIDS response to support the broader health agenda remains the greatest challenge. The unprecedented outpouring of political will, celebrity attention, and resources to fight AIDS has also sparked debate about the broader health system, including the equally compelling claims for ramping up the response to injuries, NCDs, and mental illness. What seems clear is that the current focus on health systems, tropical diseases, and maternal mortality might not even be occurring without the legacy of AIDS political mobilization. The AIDS pandemic is at a turning point. Advocates understand the need to broaden efforts to a wider global health agenda, but the entrenched institutional architecture may be resistant to change.

How will it be possible to mobilize massive global support beyond discrete, compelling diseases? Will powerful countries like the United States shift to a diffuse goal of, say, health system strengthening or sanitation? Will civil society become passionate about broader systemic goals, and will elected leaders go along? The AIDS movement will powerfully shape global health even while it faces a perilous future.

Science and Policy: The Ethical Allocation of Scarce Resources

Scientific and policy innovations have progressed so dramatically that an "AIDS-free generation" can now be seriously discussed. This sentiment was almost unthinkable even as recently as a decade ago, when AIDS was accelerating globally and the idea of universal treatment was considered wildly unrealistic. The story of the remarkable evolution from rudimentary medicine to today's advances is multifaceted, involving science, law, and policy—with intense ethical challenges.

Traditional Public Health Measures

Early in the pandemic, with no treatment available, public health officials focused on monitoring, prevention, and palliative care, primarily using the traditional STD tools of testing, counseling, reporting, and partner notification. Public information campaigns urged behavior change, primarily safer sex and fewer sexual partners. But standard STD interventions met with fierce resistance from communities at risk, who were concerned about autonomy, privacy, and discrimination. Policy makers debated the idea of "AIDS exceptionalism"—was AIDS distinct from other diseases, raising special human rights concerns? The tensions between public health and civil liberties took center stage in the political battles over screening, named reporting, and partner notification.

HIV Screening: Opt-In or Opt-Out Testing?

The evolution of HIV screening is emblematic of the tensions between public health and civil liberties. Although testing remains controversial, it was even more so before the advent of effective treatment—an HIV test was not just another medical test, given the dire social and health consequences of a diagnosis.

Where medical interventions offered scant benefit, AIDS advocates resisted testing. Policy makers proposed a variety of testing programs ranging from mandatory (e.g., for prisoners, immigrants, and health care workers) to routine, either on an opt-in or opt-out basis. Although most standard blood tests were performed as an opt-out, AIDS advocates urged legal safeguards. HIV-specific legislation often required pre- and post-test counseling, informed consent, and strict confidentiality.[74] The result was greater civil liberties protection, but at the price of making testing more expensive.

Policy debates were transformed by the advent of new treatment regimes, with public health officials urging routine testing—in effect, challenging AIDS exceptionalism itself. Would legal barriers to HIV testing result in fewer individuals knowing their HIV status, and could well-intentioned safeguards have the unintended effect of perpetuating stigma? It was in this context that the WHO called for a dramatic scale-up in testing.[75] In the late 1990s, Dr. Kevin De Cock (who directed the WHO's Department of HIV/AIDS from 2006 to 2009) argued that it was time to routinize testing by dismantling the strict safeguards—"what was once protection of individual rights may now represent negligent practice and missed opportunities for prevention."[76]

This debate had particular resonance in Africa, where countless individuals living with HIV did not know their serological status. Activists in Botswana, for example, supported opt-out testing, which was implemented in 2004.[77] Still, there remained strong opposition from many human rights activists who argued that an "informed right of refusal" in an opt-out setting would inadequately safeguard civil liberties. This raised the deeper question of whether a Northern-centric conception of informed consent and confidentiality should prevail in Africa.

Bowing to the imperative of widespread, cost-effective screening, an opt-out paradigm with safeguards for voluntariness is on the rise today. Testing offers a pathway to treatment and, in turn, prevention. The WHO, UNAIDS, and the CDC all now support routine opt-out HIV screening,[78] although country approaches still vary. The ethical discourse has changed so markedly that in 2013 historians declared an "end to the debate" over routine HIV testing.[79]

Named HIV Reporting

Without privacy assurances, persons at risk might not come forward for testing and counseling, imperiling their own and the public's health. The critical problems were what status should be reportable to the health department (HIV, AIDS, or both), and with what information (individual names, coded/unique identifiers, or anonymous).

When AIDS first emerged, many countries approached it in the same way as other infectious diseases, requiring health workers and labs to notify public health agencies. Named reporting would generate the most accurate epidemiological picture of the epidemic—modes of transmission, groups at highest risk, and the incidence and prevalence of disease.

By 1983 every U.S. state, Australia, and Denmark had made AIDS reportable by name. In Canada, some provinces made AIDS reportable, while others did not. The Netherlands, France, Great Britain, and Sweden used voluntary systems of anonymous or coded reporting.

There was, however, a major public health flaw in AIDS reporting. It failed to give a true epidemiologic picture of the current state of the epidemic, but rather offered a snapshot of prevalence a decade earlier. Because it took the disease roughly ten years to progress from HIV infection to AIDS, tracking AIDS status was a weak predictor of current and future trends. However, when health officials moved to adopt HIV reporting, this provoked fierce resistance, with advocates arguing that named HIV reporting represented an unjustifiable intrusion on privacy.[80] They argued, moreover, that name-based reporting would deter at-risk persons—fearful of the risks to privacy—from coming forward for testing and counseling.

As an alternative, advocates urged anonymous HIV reporting or notification with unique identifiers but without names. Although many jurisdictions adopted this approach, the public health community expressed concern that unique identifiers would result in duplicate reporting.[81] As with screening, opposition to named HIV reporting subsided, especially when public health officials sought to link infected individuals to treatment. New York State offered this rationale when adopting named HIV reporting in 2000, as well as pointing to studies showing that it would not deter individuals from testing.[82] Since the mid-1990s, there has been a marked trend toward HIV case reporting, either by name (in most U.S. states) or by unique identifiers (in Australia and much of Europe).

Partner Notification

Partner notification entails notifying the sexual and/or needle-sharing partners of persons infected with HIV, with three primary methods: source referral (patients are encouraged to voluntarily disclose the exposure to their partners, referring them for testing or treatment), provider referral (health professionals notify the patient's partners, while maintaining patient's anonymity), and conditional or contract referral (health professionals notify sexual partners if the patient does not, trying to maintain anonymity).

Concerns over partner notification were the same as for testing and reporting: without privacy safeguards, individuals would be subjected to stigma and discrimination. Partner notification, however, raises unique ethical questions in that it aims explicitly to protect the public's health without conferring a benefit for patients. This pitted two values against each other: patient privacy versus the partner's right to know.

There were major problems in implementing provider and conditional referral. Could, for example, a patient be forced to disclose the names of his or her sexual partners, and how is it even possible to maintain anonymity? To strike a balance between privacy and public health, UNAIDS and the WHO encourage "ethical partner counseling." Under this approach, patients would be counseled to notify their partners, but health professionals, considering the public's health, would be empowered to notify partners without the patient's consent. Source patients are to be provided legal and social supports to protect them from repercussions of notification.[83]

Harm Minimization

Once basic research identified the cause of AIDS and the primary modes of transmission, harm minimization—or harm reduction—emerged as a critical policy tool. Counseling and education encouraged safer sexual behaviors, leading to PEPFAR and UNAIDS campaigns touting the ABCs of prevention: abstinence (abstaining or delaying first sexual contact); being safer (remaining faithful to one's partner or reducing the number of partners); and condom use (correct and consistent wearing of condoms).[84] With abstinence and faithfulness being controversial and hard to implement, condom use became the quintessential harm minimization approach for sexual transmission. AIDS organizations now view the male latex condom as the single most efficient, available prevention technology.[85]

Even more controversial were harm reduction strategies to reduce needle-borne transmission. Quite early in the pandemic, researchers identified needle and syringe exchanges as highly effective at reducing HIV transmission without increasing drug use.[86] Australia led the way in 1985 as the first country to officially adopt a national drug and HIV harm reduction strategy.[87] The continued low level of HIV infection among injection-drug users in Australia, and among other early adopters of needle exchange, demonstrated the marked success of harm reduction. In states or areas that failed to develop harm reduction (e.g., the United States and eastern Europe), HIV spread rapidly among IDUs and through them to their sexual partners and infants. The roadblocks were based not on science or even resources, but on political ideology.

Remarkable Scientific Transformation: A Journey from Despair to a Hopeful Future

From our current perspective, it is easy to forget that at the beginning of the pandemic, scientists did not even know the identity of the infectious agent causing a rare immunodeficiency. Rapid scientific advancement was needed to implement even basic public health measures, such as laboratory-based testing to identify infected individuals and screening the blood supply. In 1984, three years after the first AIDS reports, the human immunodeficiency virus was identified, followed the next year by the first licensed test. Following from these early advances, research has revealed the HIV disease process, developed major new therapies, and designed methods of prevention.

Antiretroviral Technology: From Treatment to Combination Prevention

Research enabled scientists to discover key targets for antiretroviral therapies and then highly effective multidrug regimens. Treatment transformed the outlook for persons living with HIV from almost certain death to a manageable chronic condition. Critically, the treatment revolution led not only to vast improvement in human lives, but also to crucial vehicles for prevention and public health. Beyond the success of preventing perinatal transmission, the two key public health breakthroughs are treatment as prevention and pre-exposure prophylaxis:

- *Treatment as prevention:* In 2011 the randomized clinical trial HPTN 052 demonstrated that early initiation of ART by infected individuals in a long-term, heterosexual, serodiscordant relationship (i.e., where one partner is infected and the other is not) could reduce transmission to an uninfected partner by 96 percent.[88] The WHO subsequently revised its treatment guidelines in 2013, recommending that HIV infected persons be started on ART much earlier.[89] Despite the potential for stemming the pandemic, treatment as prevention still faces multiple hurdles, including testing and initiating early treatment in hard-to-reach populations. Under previous WHO guidelines, seven million people who were eligible for ART failed to receive treatment and the new guidelines will widen that gap even further (see Box 10.1).[90] Success also requires full compliance with treatment regimens, which itself can be challenging. Above all, there is the political challenge of mobilizing resources—not only for universal access to ART, but also to treat those with drug-resistant infections.

- *Preexposure prophylaxis (PrEP):* In 2010 clinical trials provided the first clear evidence of the effectiveness of preexposure prophylaxis—a daily oral dose of antiretroviral drugs given to uninfected individuals reduced the risk of acquiring HIV through sex by 44 percent among MSM. In 2011 the Partners PrEP study found a 75 percent risk reduction among heterosexual serodiscordant couples who adhered to tenofovir/emtricitabine combination treatment,[91] whereas a CDC study reported a 62 percent reduction in risk.[92] By July 2012 the FDA approved Truvuda (tenofovir/emtricitabine) for preexposure prophylaxis for anyone "at high risk of HIV infection and who may engage in sexual activity with HIV-infected partners," opening the way for PrEP as a tool of prevention.[93] A 2013 study of injection drug users in Bangkok showed that taking tenofovir reduced IDUs' risk of contracting HIV by almost 50 percent.[94]

The extraordinary success of research has brought a shift toward "combination prevention," defined as "rights-based, evidence-informed, and community-owned programmes that use a mix of biomedical, behavioural, and structural interventions, prioritized . . . to have the greatest sustained impact on reducing new infections."[95] Evidence-based prevention tools include PrEP, preventing perinatal transmission, universal treatment, and voluntary male circumcision (Box 10.5), in tandem with testing, counseling, condoms, harm reduction, and education.

These developments have shifted the discourse over AIDS exceptionalism. The issue now is not so much that public health and civil liberties are in tension, but rather that AIDS has captured a disproportionate amount of political attention and economic resources. The very success of the AIDS movement has sparked a debate about the ethical allocation of scarce resources.

Game-Changing Interventions: Discovering a Vaccine, a "Cure," and Effective Female Protection

Although there is much to celebrate in the incredible scientific advances of the last three decades, key breakthroughs remain elusive. There is broad scientific consensus that "getting to zero" requires an effective vaccine. Results from a 2009 trial in Thailand showed a 31 percent vaccine efficacy in preventing HIV infections. Although the vaccine conferred only modest protection, the results are seen as "proof of concept," instilling new hope

BOX 10.5 Voluntary Male Circumcision

Compelling scientific evidence has demonstrated the effectiveness of male circumcision (MC) to prevent female-to-male HIV transmission (by approximately 60 percent). The WHO and UNAIDS recommend safe, voluntary MC as an important prevention strategy for men in areas with high HIV prevalence and low levels of MC.[1]

Despite the evidence of high cost-effectiveness, MC has deep cultural, religious, and human rights overtones. As it entails cutting of the penis, MC may be viewed with suspicion, particularly if proposed by outsiders. Challenges of privacy and informed consent remain hard to overcome. Should young boys be permitted to consent (or assent) to MC? Should parents have the right to circumcise male newborns? Importantly, there is currently no evidence that MC will benefit women directly, although lowering HIV prevalence would almost certainly benefit women as well as men.

Beyond ethical quandaries, there are logistical difficulties in implementing MC. Weak health systems, difficulty in reaching marginalized populations, and the scarcity of skilled health personnel undermine population-based scale-up.[2]

NOTES

1. WHO and UNAIDS, *New Data on Male Circumcision and HIV Prevention: Policy and Programme Implications* (Montreux: WHO/UNAIDS, 2007).
2. Lawrence O. Gostin and Catherine A. Hankins, "Male Circumcision as an HIV Prevention Strategy in Sub-Saharan Africa: Sociolegal Barriers," *Journal of the American Medical Association* 300, no. 21 (2008): 2539–2541.

for a game-changing intervention.[96] Recent work at Oregon Health and Science University reignited hope of an AIDS vaccine. In this study 16 rhesus monkeys infected with simian immunodeficiency virus were given an experimental vaccine, which protected nine of them from the effects of the virus and apparently "cleared" them of infection.[97]

The 2012 International AIDS Conference also saw renewed optimism toward a cure, with the report of the "Berlin patient"—who was cured of the infection after a bone marrow transplant from a donor carrying the genetic variant providing resistance to HIV.[98] In June 2013 researchers reported another two cases of individuals who had undergone bone marrow transplants and appeared to be virus-free once their antiretroviral drugs were stopped.[99] While bone marrow transplants will never be practical for large numbers of people, genetically based HIV treatment could emerge. On March 3, 2013, researchers announced that an HIV-infected infant treated aggressively with antiretrovirals thirty hours after birth had no detectable viral levels at one month of age.[100] If confirmed, this case could transform treatment for newborns, providing hope for the estimated 330,000 HIV-infected infants in the developing world. Finding a cure would close a critical innovation gap, removing the need for arduous lifelong treatment regimes.

Another potentially game-changing innovation would be a female-controlled prevention method, such as an effective vaginal microbicide gel. In 2010 the clinical trial CAPRISA 004 showed that a coitally dependent 1 percent tenofovir gel was 39 percent effective in reducing the risk of contracting HIV during sex.[101] The option of taking preventive measures without their partner's agreement or knowledge would give women greater autonomy over their sexual health.

At the same time, scientists will be pressed to overcome the problems associated with current treatment regimes, such as drug resistance, chronic adverse effects, and the need for more easily administered and cost-effective formulations. These breakthroughs, of course, require continued investment in research while addressing many pressing needs not only for HIV/AIDS, but in global health more broadly.

On World AIDS Day 2012, then Secretary of State Hillary Clinton, unveiling her blueprint for an AIDS-free generation, said that realistically, global AIDS has yet to reach a tipping point at which the annual increase in new patients being treated exceeds the number newly infected.[102] Until that point is reached, the international community will have to accelerate combination prevention to reach all persons at risk for, or infected with, HIV.

Ethical Allocation of Scarce Resources

Even with considerable global funding devoted to HIV/AIDS ($7.86 billion in foreign assistance in 2012),[103] resources remain scarce, requiring agonizing decisions on how to allocate life-saving interventions: Who should receive treatment when all cannot access it? Should priority go to research, prevention, or treatment? And, ultimately, should AIDS receive a higher priority than other health threats? These are life-and-death questions for millions of people, and there is no consensus on the right answers.

Treatment

In July 2013 UNAIDS, joined by the WHO, PEPFAR, the Global Fund, and other partners, launched the Treatment 2015 initiative, which aims to ensure that the world reaches the target of 15 million people on ART by 2015, as a stepping stone toward providing universal access to treatment.[104] The initiative provides a framework for expediting the scaling-up of treatment, intensifying efforts in delivering treatment to key settings and population groups, and innovation in program planning and service delivery.

As of 2012 an estimated 9.7 million people in low- and middle-income countries were on ART, an increase of 1.6 million over 2011.[105] However, under the WHO's 2013 treatment guidelines, this figure represents only 34 percent of people eligible for treatment in 2013 (see also Box 10.1).[106] As the region with the highest burden of HIV, sub-Saharan Africa has seen major progress, although there is a long way to go (approximately 60 percent of eligible people in treatment in 2012). Treatment coverage is even lower in eastern Europe and Central Asia (30 percent) and in the Middle East and North Africa (20 percent).[107] Despite drastic reductions in drug prices, the cost of second-line treatments remains high—up to $6,000 per month in developed countries.

Although resources have risen, drug scarcity is a fact of life, and will be for the foreseeable future. Without a major decrease in HIV incidence, competition for treatment resources will only become more intense. While the global community cannot even meet current treatment needs, there will be additional calls for treatment expansion—for example, expanding PrEP. The future portends ever-increasing strains on existing drug resources in a time of fiscal austerity.

In a resource-constrained world, allocation decisions rest on multiple factors: the level of immune dysfunction that triggers treatment initiation; treatment costs (first- or second-line); and the use of ARTs for prevention or treatment. In allocating resources, which population groups, countries, and regions deserve priority: those with the greatest number of HIV-infected persons, those with the lowest treatment coverage, or those where the most people can be reached at the lowest cost? These are excruciating choices, as they often determine who will live when everyone cannot.

PrEP

Allocative decisions become even more challenging when considering medication for otherwise healthy populations under PrEP. Because PrEP does not require a partner's permission, moreover, it is especially valuable for those disempowered in their sexual relationships, such as sex workers or those at risk of rape or under pressure to have sex.

Despite its undeniable benefits, wide-spread scale-up of PrEP is unlikely given that it is prohibitively expensive. Further, questions remain about whether it is ethical to advise healthy individuals to take lifelong medication with potential adverse effects and drug resistance. PrEP is unlikely to be a population-wide intervention, but will be targeted to high-risk groups within a combination prevention strategy. For example, PrEP could be offered to the HIV negative partners of individuals infected with HIV, until the HIV positive partner has effectively suppressed the virus using ART.[108]

Ethical Values

Given vexing ethical tensions, what values ought to guide resource allocation decisions? Although finding an optimal solution will never be possible, epidemiological and comparative cost-effectiveness could maximize lives saved: which interventions work best, in what combination, and at what cost? Would nonbiological interventions and/or PrEP provide more benefit than treatment at less cost? Would treatment as prevention induce resistance to first-line drugs, requiring expensive second- or third-line pharmaceuticals?

Values beyond cost and benefit are equally critical. Should priority be given to those already in treatment because it would be a hardship to discontinue their medication? Or are all treatment-eligible individuals equally deserving of a fair chance for treatment? Should priority be given to the most marginalized populations, such as MSM, IDUs, or sex workers, recognizing their compounding disadvantages? The answers to these ethical questions will evolve over time, based on science and community preferences.

The Place of AIDS in Global Health

The AIDS movement is at an inflection point due to the interplay of key health and economic determinants—the global financial downturn, tight foreign aid budgets, and intense resource competition. AIDS is only one of multiple health threats, requiring deeper, more complex strategies for ethical allocation of resources. What position should AIDS hold within the broader spectrum of global health priorities—for example, maternal/child health, injuries, NCDs, and mental health? Although AIDS funding is shifting to include broader health systems, it is still a vertical program. Is the flattening out of AIDS funding enough to meet the demands of multiple health constituencies?

Unquestionably, the AIDS movement has had dramatic success, which has redounded to the benefit of global health. AIDS advocates moved global health onto the international agenda; the historic level of political engagement would have not been possible without the movement.

Diverse constituencies dealing with health issues ranging from cancer and obesity to alcohol and tobacco have learned from the AIDS response.

Global health should build upon the successes of the AIDS movement—mobilize new resources, energize civil society, and demand political accountability. In the end, it will be self-destructive to pit one health constituency against another, forced to make do in the face of dire need. As the AIDS movement finds its way in a changing world, it will have to advocate for broader health system reform, perhaps even reconceptualizing AIDS institutions to broaden their mandate.[109]

Reflecting Back, Looking Forward

So much has happened in the years since AIDS first emerged. Whereas once an HIV diagnosis was a death sentence, today patients can live long and full lives. But some things have remained constant—even as the sociocultural perceptions of AIDS have changed fundamentally, it remains a highly stigmatized disease. Remnants of discrimination can be seen everywhere, from the testing of health care workers and segregation of prisoners to travel restrictions and criminalization.

While AIDS advocates will continue to demand universal treatment access, the reality of scarce resources and competing priorities will stand as major obstacles. The global health framework is transforming to one in which no single disease takes precedence—in the way that AIDS arguably has done. Already, the vertical disease-specific paradigm is shifting—if not to a perfect horizontal system, then at least to a "diagonal" paradigm that leverages AIDS programs to meet a wider range of health needs.

Still, even with these looming changes, the contributions of the AIDS movement to global health are almost immeasurable.[110] It ushered in an era of unprecedented scientific achievement, changed the paradigm for social mobilization, and altered global health's institutional architecture and basic values. AIDS even critically informed contemporary principles of global engagement, such as partnerships, country ownership, and accountability for results. Whereas once international assistance was measured by money donated, it is now about lives saved. AIDS brought global health to the world political stage, raising consciousness about security, trade, intellectual property, and human need. In short, AIDS forever changed the way we think about health, culture, and politics.

CHAPTER 11

The International Migration of Health Workers

A Troubling Example of Global Injustice

THE DEEP AND ENDURING INEQUITIES between North and South, rich and poor, present myriad global health challenges. But one of the most vivid illustrations of global health injustice may be the international migration of health workers.[1] Highly skilled workers emigrate every day, leaving their countries devoid of crucial human resources. Professional search firms actively recruit health workers. Others migrate of their own accord in search of a better life. The search for a better life, however, is often thwarted by exploitation and discrimination in their destination countries. In view of the appalling shortages of health workers in low-income countries, global health advocates call active recruitment a crime,[2] and the World Health Organization calls human resource shortages "a crisis in health"[3] and the "the most serious obstacle" to realizing the right to health.[4]

This stunning injustice has mobilized social action in the form of the Global Health Workforce Alliance—a multisectoral partnership dedicated to advocating for and implementing solutions to the global workforce shortage.[5] It has also spurred innovative governance in the form of the WHO Code of Practice. Even so, the brain drain persists, taking its toll on health systems and human lives in the world's poorest countries.

This chapter offers an analysis of the rights and obligations of the major stakeholders—source countries, destination countries, and health workers. It also explores innovative governance solutions for workforce development and for narrowing glaring regional disparities. Before exploring solutions, it is important to understand the magnitude of the health workforce crisis, together with the drivers of international migration.

Human Resource Inequalities: Magnitude of the Health Crisis

The world is experiencing a grave human resource shortage in the health sector. In 2006, the WHO estimated that 4.3 million additional health workers were required to meet the health-related Millennium Development Goals, with 1.5 million needed in Africa alone. Even this alarmingly high figure underestimates global human resource needs because the WHO only accounted for shortages in fifty-seven countries that miss the minimalist target of 2.28 doctors, nurses, and midwives per 1,000 in the population.

In states with "critical shortages," many people go without health services because there are simply too few professionals to meet vast health needs. There is also an uneven distribution of workers between rural and urban areas, wealthy and poor communities, and public- and private-sector health services. The dearth of health workers has contributed to high levels of suffering and illness, with dire health effects for people who cannot access needed services. The actual magnitude of the problem far exceeds the WHO estimate, which does not account for the added burdens on health systems from HIV/AIDS and NCDs. Nor does the WHO fully factor in the shortages that emerging economies, and even developed countries, are experiencing.

Given these limitations in WHO statistics, the global human resource shortage is in reality much greater than 4.3 million health workers. And the shortage includes more than physicians and nurses, extending to health workers across the spectrum, such as midwives, pharmacists, dentists, laboratory technicians, health administrators, and community health workers.

The human resource crisis affects both developed and developing countries, but the global poor suffer disproportionately, not only because they have a smaller health care workforce, but also because their needs are so much greater. Of the fifty-seven countries with critical shortages, thirty-nine are in Africa, which has 25 percent of the world's disease burden but only 3 percent of the world's health workers and 1 percent of the world's health financing. In stark contrast, the Region of the Americas, which has only 10 percent of the global disease burden, has an estimated 37 percent of the world's health workers and 50 percent of the world's health financing.[6]

This disparity in resources is evident across the globe, where rich countries have far more health workers to deal with a considerably lower disease burden. The extreme imbalance is illustrated by nurse-to-population ratios ten times higher in North America and Europe than in Africa, Southeast Asia, or South America. Migration exacerbates this disparity: more than half of registered nurses have emigrated from low-

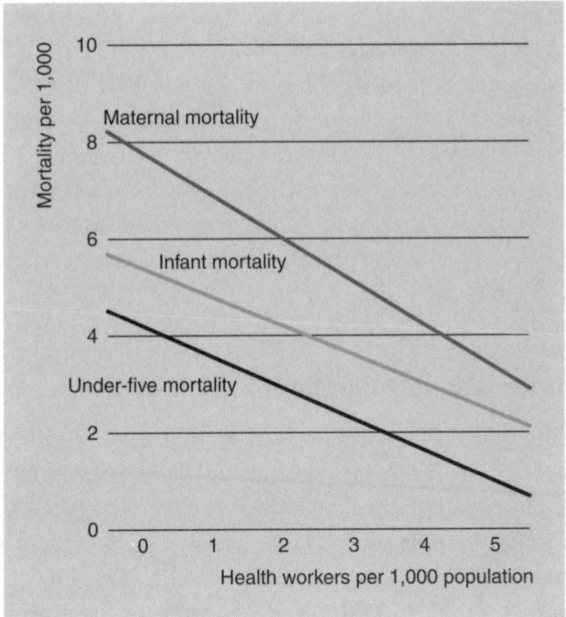

Figure 11.1 **Health worker density and maternal/child mortality**
Source: Joint Learning Initiative (JLI), *Human Resources for Health: Overcoming the Crisis* (Washington, DC: JLI, 2004), 26.

and middle-income states such as Ghana, Malawi, Swaziland, and the Philippines.

Several kinds of migration are occurring simultaneously: internal migration from rural to urban areas and from the public to the private sector, and international migration from low- and middle-income countries to high-income countries.[7] The overall pattern—both domestic and transnational migration—disadvantages societies that are already at the margins.

These sterile numbers mask the human tragedy: without an adequate health workforce, people have fewer opportunities for prevention, treatment, and pain relief. Human resource deficits cause many deaths among those who would have survived had they had decent health care. Multiple studies, even when controlled for poverty, show that lack of access to health workers is directly related to negative health outcomes, ranging from patient injury, disease, and cross-infection to early death.[8] Maternal, infant, and child survival increases with the density of health workers (Figure 11.1). Beyond harming patients, worker shortages lead to increased violence against staff, as patients become frustrated by the waiting and lack of care.[9]

Although multiple factors contribute to weak health systems (e.g., financing, training, and management), health services cannot be delivered effectively without a skilled workforce. There is little point, for example, in foreign delivery of drugs and medical equipment if there are insufficient skilled professionals to serve the people. The drivers of human resource deficits are multifaceted and complex, but not so complex that they cannot be understood and acted upon. The factors that produce health workforce shortages are not the same in all countries, but many are common across nations.

Drivers of International Migration

Understanding the confluence of factors that cause health workforce shortages is critical in designing solutions. As one would expect, there is no single cause, but rather manifold complex causes that combine to produce a global shortage: population growth, aging societies, high disease burdens, and increased purchasing power for health services.

Although it is tempting to think of resource shortages as homegrown (e.g., insufficient education, training, and resources), the reality is that richer countries intensify the problem by relying on migrating workers to meet their escalating human resource needs.[10] This boundary crossing is expected in a globalized world, but that does not mean that the resulting inequalities are ethical or that solutions cannot be found.

National Self-Sufficiency

This cross-border problem is seen most clearly when rich countries meet their escalating demand for human resources through the migration of workers from poorer countries rather than through investing in a domestic health workforce. For example, an estimated 18 percent of doctors and 11 percent of nurses in OECD countries[11] and 75 percent of both doctors and nurses in oil-rich Middle East countries are foreign expatriates.[12] High-income countries claim to have severe worker shortages, and, of course, politicians strive to satiate public demand for more health care. But in reality, rich countries have the luxury of vast human resources compared to those in poorer states.

Few countries have policies for, and pathways toward, national self-sufficiency. They have not planned, trained, and invested in enough health workers, with the result that many rely on foreign-trained professionals. They have not been willing to make the hard choices to task shift (e.g., nurses and community workers conducting certain tasks offered exclusively by doctors) or to train enough professionals to work in neglected areas, such as primary care, mental health, and in rural settings. Investment in human resources remains chronically insufficient.[13] In 2011 the WHO urged states to educate and sustain a health workforce with skills to meet their population's needs.[14]

National self-sufficiency applies to all countries, rich or poor, but some states will not have sufficient capacity to build an adequate health workforce, which requires sustainable investments in education and retention. International assistance—whether through multilateral agencies (e.g., the World Bank), public-private partnerships (the Global Fund), or states (e.g., PEPFAR)—should make health workforce development a priority.

Critics argue that national self-sufficiency is an outmoded model in a globalized world—even a form of trade protectionism. However, an unfettered market cannot ensure adequate numbers and types of health workers migrating in and out of countries. There is no "happy merry-go-round" with a fair distribution of human resources coming from and going to countries to meet all health needs. The reality is that poor countries have no human resource surplus in which to trade, and they will rarely attract skilled foreign workers.

The United States, for example, absorbs a huge foreign trained workforce, but few U.S. workers emigrate to close gaps in other countries. A free market will inevitably result in worsening inequities, with rich states profiting from inexpensive foreign-trained workers and poor states suffering from an ever-dwindling supply of trained professionals. Policies of national self-sufficiency and equitable distribution, however, would ameliorate shortages in all regions while reducing glaring inequalities.

Push Factors: Why Health Workers Want to Leave Home

Why would a health worker want to leave her home, family, and country to go to a faraway and unfamiliar place? A major reason is the "push" of an environment that makes clinical practice unrewarding. Salaries in developing countries are often very low, below the threshold of a living family wage. Workers may have to wait months to receive even meager wages, sapping their motivation and driving them toward more rewarding pursuits. Health workers cannot imagine a brighter future in their home country if they lack mentorship, advanced training, and career development.

Facilities in lower-income countries are often overcrowded and sometimes unsanitary, with scarce supplies of drugs and equipment, making it hard to provide quality patient care. In Zimbabwe, for example, nurses work without gloves or essential medicines, and food for patients is rationed.[15] Patients are less likely to recover and more likely to die, making the workplace stressful and demoralizing. In underserved rural areas, workplace conditions may be still worse, with weak infrastructure (e.g., housing, utilities, and police). Patients are not the only ones jeopardized by poor conditions; health workers also incur risks of blood-borne diseases (e.g., HIV and hepatitis) and infectious diseases (e.g., TB, staphylococcus, and hemorrhagic fevers) due to inadequate safety protocols and protective equipment. Beyond occupational risks, violence in the health sector instills fear among workers.

Professional and workplace push factors are often exacerbated by political, economic, or social conditions, as well as high crime, social unrest, or war. There is a universal human desire to escape poverty and live a more peaceful and prosperous life. Migrating to a rich country can enable workers to settle debts, provide for their extended families, and ensure quality education for their children.

Pull Factors: The Promise of a Better Life

Specialized training in richer countries affords health professionals opportunities that did not exist for their parents. Skilled workers are drawn by the allure of decent wages, with enough for a comfortable life and to remit to their families back home. They desire a place to work that is clean, safe, and well equipped so that they can provide high-quality care. They have ambitions for career advancement, with opportunities for higher qualifications. And they want a community that is secure and stable—a humane environment in which to raise their children.

Even though most workers have a wide choice of destinations, they often prefer countries with colonial ties, offering compatibility of language and culture together with social support networks. For example, three times as many English-speaking Caribbean community–trained nurses work abroad—primarily in Canada, the United Kingdom, and the United States—than in the region itself, with 30 percent of nursing positions in the region remaining vacant.[16]

Health worker skills, moreover, are transferable in a globalized world. And they are prized by rich countries, which are all too willing to grant visas, ensure placements, offer generous incentives, and smooth the transition to a new country. In a globalized world, health workers become a cog in a dynamic trade system that has always favored the global North.

Given a wide confluence of push/pull factors (Table 11.1), the human resources crisis is deepening, and the solutions are complex.

International Recruitment of Health Workers

International recruitment services have escalated, responding to increased demand for health workers—mostly nurses. Half the migrant nurses entering the United States are actively recruited, with many coming from Africa or other disadvantaged regions. In 2007, 267 U.S.-based firms recruited foreign-educated nurses, including five publicly traded firms.[17] Northern-based recruiters maintain an active presence in seventy-four countries. Recruitment is a lucrative business, with profits as high as $50,000 per nurse placement.

Recruiters often smooth a worker's entry into the destination country. For example, companies provide visa and immigration processing, credentialing, travel, food, and accommodation—even test preparation and language or acculturation training. Recruitment strategies include

Table 11.1 **Push/Pull Factors That Influence Health Workers to Migrate**

Push Factors	
Low and unreliable remuneration	Unrewarding and unsafe workplace
Poverty and economic hardship	Crime and violence
War and civil unrest	Political instability
Desire for a better life	Few opportunities for career advancement (education and training)
Pull Factors	
Strong demand for health workers in destination country	Migration policy: visas, placements, incentives
Active recruitment: encouragement for, and assistance with, relocation	Globalization: movement of information, services, and people around the world
Promise of better pay, conditions, and opportunities for professional advancement	Training, career enhancement, and professional status
Promise of better life for self and family, including remittances to family back home	Colonial/language/cultural ties between source and destination countries

touring workshops, media advertising, text messaging, personal e-mails, and alluring Internet sites.

Recruiters sometimes engage in predatory practices such as denying workers the right to obtain a copy of their contract, altering contracts without consent, and retaining passports or resident cards. Firms can charge up-front or back-end fees and may require buy-out or punitive breach fees in the event a health worker wishes or needs to resign before the end of the contract. Recruiters may also threaten workers with deportation if they break their contracts. These coercive tactics can be exploitive of workers who feel compelled to remain in the host institution.

Migrant workers report a wide variety of indignities and unfulfilled promises once they reach their destination: failure to provide clinical orientation; assignment to undesirable tasks below their skill level; demands to work overtime without differential pay; and substandard housing.[18] Beyond the workplace, harsh police practices and neighbors who resent foreigners can make life unpleasant for migrant workers.

Global Justice: Balancing the Interests of Source Countries, Destination Countries, and Health Workers

Global justice requires a fair allocation of benefits and burdens for source countries, destination countries, and health workers. In source countries, health workers serve essential needs, and losing skilled workers can render the health system dysfunctional. From an economic perspective, migration, in effect, represents an inherently unjust cross-subsidy from poor to wealthy states, as source countries invest in the training and education of health workers who then leave to work abroad.

Developed countries have human resource needs as well. Their perceived health shortages drive them to attract foreign-trained staff. In a globalized world, they see the trade in professional services as legitimate. However, even though rich countries have a responsibility to ensure an adequate health workforce for their populations, they should not deprive poorer countries of the same opportunities to serve their people. International law requires states not to undermine the right to health in other countries. Yet it is a rare situation in which recruitment by a wealthy country does not deprive a poorer country of a vitally important resource.

Health workers themselves possess human rights and cannot be tied to an impoverished life at home with grim prospects. They are entitled to escape denigrations of their dignity arising from workplace dangers and the inability to provide their families with a decent living. Moreover, liberty of movement is an indispensable condition for the free development of a person.[19] International law guarantees freedom of movement and residence within the person's state, as well as the right to leave and to return to his or her country.[20] Responses to the global health worker shortage must respect the human right to migrate, irrespective of the adverse effects on the source country.

When workers do choose to migrate, they retain fundamental rights to dignity, freedom from exploitation, and fair treatment. A variety of international treaties safeguard worker rights, including safe working conditions, free expression and association, trade union membership, protection against violence, and nondiscrimination.[21] States not only must respect workers' rights, they must also prevent and, if necessary, remedy, the inhumane and unequal treatment of migrant workers by the private sector.

The complexity of balancing the competing rights and interests of host countries, source countries, and health workers in furtherance of justice requires effective governance. It is unrealistic to expect that human resource disparities can be resolved in the absence of a transnational framework that fairly balances the interests of all parties.

Global Governance: The WHO Code of Practice

As evidence documenting the unfairness of health worker migration mounted, stakeholders began to negotiate a variety of governance mechanisms to rein in the worst abuses. Stakeholders most often adopted "soft," nonbinding instruments, such as professional guidelines and codes of practice on international recruitment. Some countries or regions adopted bilateral or multilateral agreements governing migration between signatory states (Boxes 11.1a, 11.1b).

Most instruments are voluntary, without monitoring and enforcement, but a few have more formal status, characteristic of harder law. The United Kingdom Code of Practice, for example, "strongly advises" employers to adhere to the code, and requires recruitment agencies supplying the National Health Service (NHS) to conform. Among its provisions, the code proscribes active recruitment in developing countries unless a government-to-government agreement supports recruitment activities.[22]

The South Africa/United Kingdom Memorandum of Understanding takes a different form but also has features of harder law. The memorandum states that the parties "shall" exchange information and expertise as

BOX 11.1a National, Bilateral, and Regional Codes of Practice and Memoranda on Health Worker Migration

Representative examples of national, bilateral, and regional codes of practice and memoranda of understanding include the following:

- Commonwealth Code of Practice for International Recruitment of Health Workers[1]
  Adopted in May 2003 by Commonwealth Health Ministers, the code applies the principles of transparency, fairness, and mutuality of benefits to health worker recruitment activities among Commonwealth countries and to relations between recruiters and recruits.
- United Kingdom Code of Practice for NHS Employers[2]
  In 2001 the UK Department of Health introduced a code of practice for international recruitment for National Health Service employers (updated in 2004). The code requires NHS employers not to actively recruit from low-income countries without source country agreement, and to use only recruitment agencies in compliance with the code.
- South Africa/UK Memorandum of Understanding on Reciprocal Educational Exchange of Healthcare Personnel[3]
  In 2003 the UK and South Africa signed a Memorandum of Understanding in which the parties agreed to formulate a plan for technical assistance, ethical recruitment, partnerships between hospitals, and time-limited placements of health workers trained in South Africa.
- Pacific Code of Practice for Recruitment of Health Workers[4]
  Adopted in 2007 by WHO Western Pacific Region member states, the code's guiding principles are (1) a fair balance between rights and duties of source countries, destination countries/institutions, health workers, and recruiting agencies; and (2) respecting the principles of transparency, fairness, and mutuality of benefits.

NOTES

1. *Commonwealth Code of Practice for the International Recruitment of Health Workers* (May 18, 2003); The Commonwealth, *Companion Document to the Commonwealth Code of Practice for the International Recruitment of Health Workers* (London: Commonwealth Health Ministers, May 18, 2003).
2. *Code of Practice for the International Recruitment of Healthcare Professionals* (United Kingdom Department of Health, December 2004).
3. *Memorandum of Understanding between the Government of the United Kingdom of Great Britain and Northern Ireland and the Government of the Republic of South*

Africa on the Reciprocal Educational Exchange of Healthcare Concepts and Personnel (October 2003)

4. *Pacific Code of Practice for Recruitment of Health Workers and Compendium*, Seventh Meeting of Ministers of Health for Pacific Island Countries (Port Vila, Vanuatu, March 12–15, 2007).

BOX 11.1b **Professional Organization Voluntary Codes of Practice and Strategies on Health Worker Migration**

Examples of codes, guidelines, and strategies by professional associations:

- AcademyHealth, Voluntary Code of Ethical Conduct for the Recruitment of Foreign-Educated Nurses to the United States[1]
  In 2008, following multiyear negotiations among diverse stakeholders, AcademyHealth unveiled its code, which sets voluntary standards for fair and transparent recruitment, the cultural and clinical orientation of foreign-educated nurses, and "best practices" to minimize or eliminate harm to source countries.
- European Federation of Public Service Unions (EPSU) and European Hospital and Healthcare Employers' Association (HOSPEEM) Code of Conduct on Ethical Cross-Border Recruitment and Retention in the Hospital Sector[2]
  ESPU and HOSPEEM agreed to the code in 2008, with the aim of promoting ethical practices in cross-border recruitment of health workers as well as stopping unethical practices. Governing principles include transparency, justice, and equity.
- International Council of Nurses, The Global Nursing Shortage: Priority Areas for Intervention[3]
  In 2006 the ICN called on national and global partners to engage in interventions in five priority areas, one of which was health worker migration and the maldistribution of health workers within countries.
- World Medical Association Statement on Ethical Guidelines for the International Recruitment of Physicians[4]
  Adopted by the WMA General Assembly in 2003, the statement recommends ethical doctor recruitment, with three guiding principles: justice, cooperation, and autonomy.

NOTES

1. "International Recruitment of Foreign-Educated Nurses: Consensus on Ethical Standards of Practice," Academy Health, http://www.academyhealth.org (accessed 9 /30/13); Alliance for Ethical International Recruitment Practices, *Voluntary Code of Ethical Conduct for the Recruitment of Foreign-Educated Health Professionals to the United States* (September 2008, rev. April 2011) (this document was formerly titled Voluntary Code of Ethical Conduct for the Recruitment of Foreign-Educated Nurses to the United States, September 2008).
2. European Federation of Public Service Unions (EPSU) and European Hospital and Healthcare Employers' Association (HOSPEEM), *EPSU-HOSPEEM Code of Conduct and Follow Up on Ethical Cross-Border Recruitment and Retention in the Hospital Sector* (April 7, 2008).
3. International Council of Nurses and Florence Nightingale International Foundation, *The Global Nursing Shortage: Priority Areas for Intervention* (Geneva: International Council of Nurses, 2006).
4. World Medical Association (WMA), "WMA Statement on Ethical Guidelines for the International Recruitment of Physicians," 54th WMA General Assembly (Helsinki, Finland, September 2003)

well as formulate a plan for South African professionals to be educated and practice in the U.K. Notably, it provides for settlement of disputes through "amicable" negotiation.[23]

The governance tools described in Boxes 11.1a and b were critical to the development of the WHO Global Code of Practice on the International Recruitment of Health Personnel adopted in May 2010, marking only the second time in history that the WHO has invoked its constitutional power to make member state recommendations (art. 23). (The WHO first used its article 23 powers in 1981 when it adopted the International Code of Marketing of Breast-Milk Substitutes.) Member states negotiated the code over many years, with the participation of stakeholders and civil society.[24] Margaret Chan called the code a "gift to public health, everywhere."[25]

Objectives and Scope: Articles 1 and 2

The code sets out principles and practices for the ethical international recruitment of health personnel; provides guidance for establishing or improving the legal and institutional framework, including bilateral and multilateral agreements; and promotes international cooperation (art. 1). It is designed as an inclusive framework that views human resources as integral to health system strengthening. It is global in scope, offering guidance to states, in cooperation with public and private stakeholders such as health workers, recruiters, employers, professional associations, and nongovernmental organizations (art. 2).

Guiding Principles: Article 3

The code's guiding principles extend beyond international recruitment by expressing the values of universal access to health care, health system strengthening, fair labor practices, and good governance (e.g., transparency, monitoring, and reporting), paying special attention to the needs of resource-poor countries:

- Health is fundamental to the attainment of peace and security, requiring full cooperation. Governments can fulfill their responsibility for the public's health only by ensuring adequate health and social services.
- Migration can contribute to health system strengthening if properly managed, but international principles and coordination are needed to mitigate adverse effects in developing countries and to safeguard health worker rights.
- States should attend to the specific needs of developing countries. High-income countries should, to the extent possible, provide technical and financial assistance for health system strengthening, including health personnel.
- States should take into account the human right to health in source countries but should not limit health workers' freedom to migrate.
- International recruitment should be conducted in accordance with the principles of transparency, fairness, and sustainability of health systems.
- States should ensure fair labor practices, including nondiscrimination.
- States should strive, to the extent possible, to create a sustainable health workforce, with workforce planning, education, training, and retention strategies to reduce the need to recruit.
- Collection and sharing of national and international data are vital to achieving the code's objectives.
- States should facilitate circular health worker migration, so that skills and knowledge can benefit both source and destination countries.

Responsibilities, Rights, and Recruiting Practices: Article 4

Although WHO member states adopted the code, it makes recommendations to a broader group of stakeholders, such as health workers, professional organizations, and recruiters—urging them to cooperate with national regulations and guidelines. Recruiters and employers should respect migrating workers' legal responsibilities in their home country, such as fair contracts for continuing service. (Workers themselves should disclose their contractual obligations.) States and stakeholders have an ethical duty to be transparent, so that workers can make timely and informed decisions regarding the benefits and risks of migration.

States should require recruiters and employers to observe fair and just recruitment and contractual practices, ensuring that migrant workers—whether temporary or permanent—are not subject to illegal or fraudulent conduct. Hiring, promotion, and remuneration should be based on objective criteria, such as qualifications, skills, and experience. States and stakeholders should conform to the international principle of equality of treatment with domestically trained workers in all terms of employment and conditions of work. The "equality" principle includes workplace orientation, professional education, qualifications, and career progression. All workers have the right to a safe and hygienic workplace.

Health Workforce Development and Health Systems Sustainability: Article 5

Reflecting the potential benefits of migration to all parties, destination and source countries should collaborate to sustain and promote human resource development and training. Governments should discourage active recruitment from countries facing critical shortages. The code should guide states entering into bilateral, regional, or multilateral arrangements designed to promote transnational cooperation and coordination. These agreements should build capacity in destination countries (e.g., technical assistance, technology, and skills transfer) for health worker retention, training, and return; regulatory frameworks; and professional exchanges and health facility "twinning."

Recognizing the importance of a competent workforce to sustainable health systems, states should build and maintain human resources to meet all domestic needs, paying attention to underserved communities. Governments should reduce geographical maldistribution of workers by supporting their retention in underserved areas, such as through education, financial incentives, regulation, and social or professional support.

The Code acknowledges the goal of national self-sufficiency, urging states to meet human resource needs with nationally trained workers. Consequently, states should scale up training and education, using well-planned curricula. The Code asks states to adopt a multisectoral approach to strengthen health systems, continuously monitor the health labor market, and coordinate all stakeholders.

Data Gathering, Research, and Information Exchange: Articles 6 and 7

Formulation of effective policies and plans on the health workforce requires a sound evidence base. Consequently, states should strengthen research and information systems, including data gathering on worker migration and its impact on the health system. The collection, analysis, and translation of accurate data should inform workforce policies and planning. The WHO is charged with the task of collaborating with international organizations and states to ensure that comparable and reliable data are generated and collected (art. 6).

The code contains innovative guidance to promote states' conformance through the exchange of information, nationally and internationally, on health worker migration and health systems through public agencies, academic institutions, professional organizations, multilateral bodies, and nongovernmental organizations. The code gives states a "soft" charge to progressively establish and maintain updated databases of laws and regulations on worker migration, as well as personnel data to support national workforce policy and planning. States are asked to provide these data to the WHO Secretariat every three years, as well as to designate a national authority responsible for information exchange and code implementation. The national focal point should communicate with member states, international bodies, and the WHO Secretariat, submitting reports and other data to the Secretariat. The WHO is charged with compiling and publishing a register of designated national authorities (art. 7).

Code Implementation: Article 8

In addition to information exchange, the code adopts creative methods for state and stakeholder conformance. To increase awareness, states should publicize and implement the code; incorporate the code into applicable laws and policies; consult with stakeholders in decision-making processes and activities; maintain updated records of authorized recruiters; promote good recruiting practices; and assess the magnitude of active international recruitment from countries facing critical shortages. Although it applies only to member states, the code urges all stakeholders to fully adhere to, cooperate with, and promote the code's guiding principles.

Monitoring and Institutional Arrangements: Article 9

States should periodically report to the WHO Secretariat the measures taken, results achieved, difficulties encountered, and lessons learned in implementing the code. The director-general is charged with keeping under review the code's implementation based on national reporting and other competent sources. To hold the Secretariat accountable, the D-G must periodically report to the Health Assembly on the code's effectiveness in achieving its stated objectives, with recommendations for improvement. Consistent with other code provisions, the D-G shall (1) support the information exchange system and the network of national authorities; (2) develop guidelines and make recommendations on practices and procedures on measures specified by the code; and (3) liaise with the United Nations, the International Labor Organization (ILO), the International Organization for Migration, other multilateral agencies, and nongovernmental organizations to support code implementation. The code asks the Health Assembly to periodically review the code's relevance and effectiveness, considering it a "dynamic text" to be updated as needed.

Partnerships, Technical Collaboration, and Financial Support: Article 10

Perhaps the hardest aspect of global health governance is ensuring that states have the capacity to implement the code's provisions. The code, like many other international instruments, lacks specificity and dedicated resources. States and stakeholders should collaborate to strengthen capacity to implement the code. The code also urges international organizations, donor agencies, and financial or development institutions to provide technical and financial support for implementation and health system strengthening in countries experiencing critical workforce shortages. In a special appeal to disease-specific programs (e.g., AIDS, TB, and malaria), the code urges more support for health system strengthening, including health worker development.

Ensuring adequate capacity remains a critical challenge. As of 2013 the code's implementation was uneven, and strongly correlated with states' wealth. Of the 51 progress reports the WHO received, 70 percent came from a single, affluent region (Europe). In total the reports represented "more than 80% of the world's population living in destination countries, but only . . . a minority of source countries."[26]

Innovative Global Health Governance?

The opening words of Article 2 put it simply: "The Code is voluntary." Throughout its text, the code bows to state prerogatives ("should," "encouraged," if "compatible" with national law or policy) and resource constraints ("progressive realization" or "to the extent possible"). In the vital area of capacity building, all the Health Assembly could do was implore richer actors and funding agencies to step up support for workforce development.

Given the reluctance of traditional state powers to ratify a binding treaty and world economic retrenchment, the soft diplomacy of a code represented a signal achievement.[27] As a soft instrument, it imaginatively adopted the forms characteristic of harder law: state monitoring, information exchange, and reporting; designation of a national authority; and a timetable for implementation. Where it could be prescriptive, the code mandates WHO's Secretariat and the Health Assembly to continually monitor and improve the code's "dynamic" text and to keep worker migration on the political agenda.

The code also contains vulnerabilities. Its text stresses throughout that international migration is good for all parties—source as well as destination countries. This may be accurate, but only if the benefits are truly shared. In reality, powerful states and stakeholders may not equitably share benefits and burdens, leaving vulnerable countries without redress. The code could give no assurances of equitable distribution.

Noticeably absent are specific targets with benchmarks of progress; clear indicators of success; sustainable funding to build capacity; incentives for compliance (or penalties for transgressions); fair and effective dispute resolution; and pathways for negotiating stronger international agreements. Despite its flaws, the code stands as a major achievement for the WHO—a well-crafted nonbinding instrument that used patient diplomacy to garner the unanimous approval of member states. At the very least, the code serves as a foundation on which states and stakeholders can build and adapt to build the health workforce, strengthen health systems, and contribute to economic development. The great unanswered question is whether the code can do enough to end one of the most glaring examples of global health injustice.

CHAPTER 12

Pandemic Influenza

A Case Study on Global Health Security

INDONESIA SENT SHOCK WAVES around the world in December 2006 when its minister for health, Siti Fadilah Supari, announced the decision to refuse to share samples of avian influenza A (H5N1) with the WHO's Global Influenza Surveillance Network (since renamed the Global Influenza Surveillance and Response System, or GISRS). The international virus-sharing system provides vitally important virus samples and genetic sequence data needed to develop effective vaccines targeted to prevailing influenza strains. Invoking sovereign ownership of a virus isolated in its territory, Indonesia justified the move on grounds that the WHO had failed to ensure equitable access to the benefits arising from use of the samples, notably vaccines.[1]

Indonesia's decision revealed fissures within the international community. Many developing countries and advocates for health justice strongly backed Indonesia's claim for fair access to medicines and vaccines.[2] At the same time, many high-income countries condemned Indonesia's actions, arguing that it placed the world's health at grave risk.[3]

It was five years before the WHO was able to broker a compromise to ensure continued operation of the global surveillance network. The World Health Assembly adopted a novel agreement in May 2011 known as the Pandemic Influenza Preparedness Framework for the Sharing of Influenza Viruses and Access to Vaccines and Other Benefits (the PIP Framework).[4]

The Indonesian controversy and the ensuing governance response threw into the spotlight the imperative of cooperation in global preparedness for seasonal and pandemic influenza. It also highlighted the deeply political nature of global governance for health. Health security is not only a public health imperative, but also a matter of social justice. Imagine if a pandemic of highly pathogenic influenza rapidly spread around the world. Australia, Europe, and North America—where many vaccine companies reside—might have ample vaccines, but lower-income countries might not. If disease and death engulfed the poor, but the rich remained relatively unscathed, a sense of deep anger and distrust would damage international cooperation in multiple spheres—not only in health, but also in trade, climate change, and arms control.

Perhaps few other threats engage the public's imagination the way pandemic influenza does, from time to time dominating political attention and capturing health security resources. Responding to the threat of novel influenza therefore raises profound questions about what research can be conducted and published, whether countries must share virus samples, how to build capacity for surveillance and response, and, most fundamentally, how to achieve global health with justice—a fair distribution of life-saving vaccines and antiviral medications in the early stages of a pandemic.

Before exploring these intriguing issues, this chapter offers a history and explanation of seasonal and pandemic influenza as well as therapeutic and public health countermeasures. Following this brief background, the chapter turns to the PIP Framework as a potentially innovative form of global governance, as well as the WHO's role in pandemic planning and response—a topic also covered in Chapters 4 (WHO) and 6 (International Health Regulations, or IHR). Next, the chapter covers the relationship between influenza preparedness and national security, including the controversy surrounding influenza research and publication—pitting the value of security against scientific freedom. The chapter ends with a discussion of this book's central theme of global health with justice, using vaccine development and just distribution of benefits as a lens to better understand the imperative of ethical allocation of scarce resources.

A Short History and Description of Influenza

Influenza is a zoonotic disease (transmitted between, or shared by, animals and humans) causing illness that is usually mild but can be life-threatening. It is a complex disease ranging from seasonal variations that traverse the globe, but kill a relatively small number of those infected, to novel forms that periodically threaten to overrun the world, causing higher rates of infection and sometimes being substantially more fatal.

These two types of influenza—seasonal and novel—are interlinked, requiring a holistic response.

Influenza Viruses: Constant Adaptation and Change

There are three types of influenza viruses, characterized as influenza A, B, and C. Influenza A infects humans as well as birds and some mammals (e.g., swine, horses, aquatic birds, and domestic poultry), whereas influenzas B and C are mostly restricted to humans. (Influenza C is not a significant human pathogen.) Influenza A viruses—the type of influenza of pandemic concern—are further classified into subtypes, identified by differences in virus surface molecules that are the human immune system's primary targets—hemagglutinin (H) and neuraminidase (N)—giving rise to the now widely recognized nomenclature of H1N1, H5N1, and so on.

Influenza viruses are adaptive, constantly evolving to form new strains, with vital public health implications: exposure to one viral strain does not ensure an effective immune response to others if there have been significant changes to viral surface proteins, and the emergence of influenza of a different subtype will sometimes cause severe disease because the immune system will not be able to respond effectively. New strains emerge through relatively limited genetic mutations (antigenic drift) against which immune responses are only partially effective; a more severe problem arises when different viruses simultaneously infect a host cell, allowing "reassortment" of virus genes and the development of entirely new subtypes (antigenic shift).

Seasonal Influenza: An Ongoing Global Burden

Every year the world experiences seasonal influenza epidemics driven by the virus' constant evolution while circulating among populations. Influenza viruses spread rapidly from human to human through airborne transmission via respiratory tract secretions and aerosols. The viruses also have a short serial interval (the mean interval between disease onset in two successive patients is two to four days), and infectivity is highest early in the illness, all aiding easy transmission. In temperate regions, seasonal influenza epidemics typically occur in colder weather—often migrating from the Southern winter to the Northern Hemisphere.[5]

Although political attention is often devoted to novel, highly pathogenic influenza, seasonal epidemics cause considerable illness and death.

Influenza infects 5–15 percent of the global population each year, killing 250,000–500,000 people and causing severe illness in millions more.[6] Infants, the elderly, and persons with co-morbid conditions are at greatest risk. The annual morbidity, mortality, and economic losses are onerous in many middle- and lower-income countries that lack the vaccines, antiviral drugs, and health systems to prevent and treat infections.[7]

Pandemic Influenza: A Health Security Challenge

Against the backdrop of constantly circulating, highly adaptive viruses, there remains a threat that a novel strain with pandemic potential will emerge. Humans often have little immune response to a novel influenza virus, enabling it to spread rapidly and possibly cause widespread illness and death. Given the transboundary threat of novel influenza, it requires well-coordinated global surveillance and response mechanisms.

There are three essential prerequisites for influenza pandemics: the existence of a novel virus; its ability to infect humans; and efficient human-to-human transmission.[8] The greatest public health fear is that a normally circulating, highly virulent animal strain will "jump" to humans, becoming capable of efficient human-to-human transmission. Aquatic birds are a natural reservoir of influenza A, but swine provide a more likely site for viral reassortment, as they can be co-infected with human and avian subtypes.

The emergence of pandemic influenza is more than a hypothetical possibility. Historically, the world has experienced three or four influenza pandemics per century, with at least ten pandemics over the last three centuries. The notorious 1918 "Spanish" flu (H1N1) resulted in between 20 million and 50 million deaths (Box 12.1); the 1957 "Asian" flu (H2N2) resulted in 1–2 million deaths; and the 1968 "Hong Kong" flu (H3N2) resulted in 700,000 deaths. In 1976 a novel H1N1 swine influenza emerged, causing political upheaval, but without mass casualties.[9]

Three novel influenza strains have had a particularly high profile in recent years, triggering national and global mobilization: (1) avian influenza A (H5N1), which thus far has been primarily a zoonotic disease contained among bird populations, with occasional cross-species transmission to humans; (2) influenza A (H1N1) (known colloquially, but incorrectly, as swine flu), which triggered the first, and to date only, public health emergency of international concern under the IHR; and (3) influenza A (H7N9), which emerged in China in 2013, triggering intense global surveillance to grasp the virus's ability to spread and its pathogenicity.

BOX 12.1 The Devastation of the 1918 Spanish Flu

In the early months of 1918, as World War I raged, another killer emerged. Known as Spanish flu—resulting from Spain's openness about its severity—this avian influenza strain ranks with the plague of Justinian and the Black Death as among the most destructive pandemics in history, ultimately causing more deaths than all the twentieth-century wars combined. Although its origin is unknown,[1] Spanish flu was first reported in March 1918 in the United States.[2] It then spread rapidly along travel and trade routes.[3] The virus was especially virulent, and it infected about half the world's population. Unlike most influenza, which typically burdens children and the elderly, Spanish flu was deadly for young, healthy adults, exacerbating its socioeconomic impact. And it killed quickly—with 25 million dead in the first twenty-five weeks. It took twenty-five *years* for AIDS to claim an equal number of lives.

Governments responded haphazardly to the unfolding crisis. The United States required reporting and many states and localities restricted public gatherings (e.g., instituting school closures); San Francisco required people to wear masks. Some island nations, including Australia and Madagascar, imposed maritime quarantines.[4]

Fears of another Spanish flu fuel political attention. A retrospective look at Spanish flu offers constructive lessons even though there is only an inchoate understanding of the effectiveness of early twentieth-century infectious disease measures. Researchers found an association between early and sustained application of certain countermeasures (e.g., school closures) and the delayed onset of the disease—supporting the use of personal hygiene and social distancing to complement modern biological interventions.[5]

The effect of the Spanish flu was so severe that the average life span in countries hardest hit was depressed by ten years. The worst fears of the international community would be the emergence of a flu strain with the same transmissibility and virulence. An H1N1 virus with genetic features that made it both highly transmissible and highly virulent caused the 1918 flu pandemic.[6] To date, no known influenza virus has shared all of these features—usually trading off virulence for transmissibility or vice versa—but the possibility of such a virus emerging keeps the international community on high alert.

NOTES

1. Edward D. Kilbourne, "Influenza Pandemics of the Twentieth Century," *Emerging Infectious Diseases Journal* 12, no. 1 (2006): 9–14.
2. Howard Markel et al., "Nonpharmaceutical Interventions Implemented by US Cities during the 1918–1919 Influenza Pandemic," *Journal of the American Medical Association* 298, no. 6 (2007): 644–654.

3. Jeffery Taubenberger and David Morens, "1918 Influenza: The Mother of All Pandemics," *Emerging Infectious Diseases Journal* 12, no. 1 (2006): 15–22.
4. World Health Organization (WHO) Writing Group et al., "Nonpharmaceutical Interventions for Pandemic Influenza, National and Community Measures," *Emerging Infectious Diseases Journal* 12, no. 1 (2006): 88–94.
5. Markel et al., "Nonpharmaceutical Interventions Implemented by US Cities."
6. Taubenberger and Morens, "1918 Influenza: The Mother of All Pandemics."

Avian Influenza A (H5N1): Animal Health and a Looming Human Threat

Although highly pathogenic avian influenza (HPAI) was first identified in the late nineteenth century, the HPAI H5N1 strain currently circulating the globe originated in Guandong Province, China, in 1996. This strain remains highly lethal, both to birds and people, although it has infected relatively few of the latter. The story of its spread highlights the linkage between animal and human health as well as the need for global preparedness.

The first human HPAI H5N1 infection was reported in Hong Kong in 1997, and for the next few years there emerged a slow, steady stream of reports of animal-to-human H5N1 transfer in Southeast Asia, most likely by intense contact with poultry—for example, in backyard poultry flocks or live bird markets, or by consuming uncooked poultry. In 2003–2004 significant outbreaks of HPAI H5N1 occurred in avian populations in Southeast Asia; more cases of human infection were reported. Large poultry populations were culled, causing economic loss and nutrition problems for poor farmers who relied on the animals as a source of protein.[10] By 2006 the virus had spread beyond Southeast Asia, becoming endemic in avian flocks.[11]

Even more ominous than the geographic spread were cases of human-to-human transmission. In Thailand, a mother contracted the virus from her sick child, and in Indonesia, one extended family had seven fatalities. Whether H5N1 was evolving or surveillance was simply better is unknown, as is the evolutionary process by which the virus could acquire human-to-human transmission capability.

The spike in human cases captured political and media attention. In an address to the 2007 Pacific Health Summit, WHO Director-General Dr. Margaret Chan called for participants to "maintain vigilance [and] maintain preparedness activities. Influenza pandemics are recurring events, and the threat has not diminished. If you put a burglar in front of a locked door with a sack full of keys and give him enough time, he will get in. Influenza viruses have a sack full of keys and a bag full of tricks."[12]

States devised pandemic influenza preparedness plans, while media hype drove private and public stockpiling of antiviral medications such as Tamiflu. Culling of avian populations continued, and additional countermeasures were employed, including bans on live bird markets, "poultry zones" to reduce cross-contamination, and improved surveillance.[13] International cooperation also increased. By 2008 global spending on avian influenza was estimated at $1.68 billion.[14] The UN Food and Agricultural Organization (FAO) worked with at-risk countries to build capacity, share information, and develop regional networks.

HPAI H5N1 remains an ongoing public health threat. As of October 8, 2013, 641 people had contracted the virus, with 380 deaths.[15] The true case fatality rate, however, is unknown. Milder H5N1 infections likely have gone undetected or unreported. Sixty countries have reported outbreaks in domestic poultry, wild birds, or both. The constant threat of a human H5N1 pandemic continues to drive global influenza preparedness strategies.

Influenza A (H1N1): A Pandemic Enveloping the Globe with Relatively Mild Disease

A novel strain of influenza A (H1N1) spread rapidly through Mexico in March and April 2009. Although colloquially called swine flu, H1N1 is a "quadruple reassortant" virus with two genes from flu viruses that normally circulate in pigs, avian genes, and human genes. Similar to seasonal influenza, it is highly transmissible from person to person—a necessary precondition for a pandemic. Illness ranges from mild to severe, with most people recovering without treatment. Children and pregnant women are at higher risk, as well as those with co-morbidities (e.g., diabetes, asthma, and kidney disease). Unlike with seasonal influenza, the elderly do not appear to be at increased risk, perhaps due to immunity from distantly related viruses.

The 2009 H1N1 outbreak provided the first test of the pandemic influenza plans formed in response to H5N1. By the time the WHO was notified of the emerging infection on April 12, 2009, geographical containment was not feasible (although influenza's transmissibility and short generation time always made containment unlikely), leading the agency to call for mitigation of disease spread. On April 25, 2009, the director-general declared a public health emergency of international concern under the IHR.[16] The same day, the D-G recommended that "all countries should intensify surveillance for unusual outbreaks of influenza-like illness and severe pneumonia," but did not recommend trade or travel restrictions.[17] However, many countries issued travel advisories and warnings, screened air passengers, quarantined suspected cases, and initiated trade restrictions on pork (see also Chapter 6). States also used "social distancing," such as canceling public events, closing schools, and shutting down mass transportation.[18]

On June 11, 2009, the WHO raised the alert level to a full-blown pandemic, indicating widespread geographic distribution. By July 16, 2009, the WHO said that further spread was inevitable and therefore eliminated most country reporting responsibilities. By the time H1N1 fully emerged in the Northern Hemisphere (autumn 2009), a human vaccine already had been developed. By August 2010, when the transition from pandemic to post-pandemic period was announced, approximately 12,500 people had died in the U.S.[19] Although there were 18,500 laboratory-confirmed deaths reported worldwide from April 2009 to August 2010, a 2012 study estimates that fatalities from H1N1 during this period were fifteen times higher than this figure, in other words between 151,700 and 575,400.[20] More than 214 countries reported confirmed cases of the disease, underscoring its global scope. However, a disproportionate number of deaths occurred in Southeast Asia and Africa, where access to prevention and treatment resources were more limited.[21]

A retrospective review on March 10, 2011, concluded that "the world is ill-prepared to respond to a severe influenza pandemic . . . with tens of millions at risk of dying." The report criticized the WHO's "needlessly complex" definition of a pandemic, which had six alert levels based on the virus's geographical spread, not its severity. (As discussed later, the WHO updated its guidance on pandemic phases in 2013.)[22] A lesson from the twenty-first century's first influenza pandemic was the need for flexibility in preparedness, as predicting the form or consequences of the next pandemic is fraught with difficulty.

Influenza A (H7N9): Global Mobilization around an Evolving Health Threat

The threat of novel influenza reemerged when China reported a new strain in 2013. Influenza A (H7N9) is a serotype that normally circulates among avian populations, with some H7 variants occasionally infecting humans. In the past, H7 viruses have been concerning, both because they tend to be more likely to be highly pathogenic and because they have a history of human-to-human transmission. For example, an outbreak associated with infected poultry in the Netherlands in 2003 infected at least 89 people, killed one, and involved human-to-human transmission.[23]

Most H7N9 infections to date have been from poultry, with no sustained human-to-human transmission. The early case fatality rate exceeded 20 percent, making it a lethal influenza strain.[24] Although not easily transmissible between humans, a 2013 study suggests that the H7N9 virus has the potential to be so, as the virus attaches to both the upper and lower respiratory tracts in humans—a trait uncommon in other avian influenza viruses.[25] The viral characteristics render this novel threat concerning: most humans have not been exposed to H7N9 and therefore lack immunity. As of November 6, 2013, the WHO had confirmed 139 cases of avian influenza A(H7N9), including 45 deaths.[26]

The WHO has recommended a high level of alert, preparedness, and response for the H7N9 virus, while the U.S. Centers for Disease Control (CDC) prepared viral seed strains to begin the vaccine development process. In September 2013 the FAO issued a warning about the H7N9 and H5N1 influenza viruses,[27] and launched two emergency regional projects aimed at containing the spread of H7N9 in the Asian region.[28] Critical questions are already emerging: Are the WHO, the CDC, China, and the international community responding effectively? Does H7N9 pose a risk of pandemic influenza? What lessons can be learned from past outbreaks (e.g., SARS, H5N1, H1N1) as well as from the newly circulating SARS-like novel coronavirus (MERS-CoV)?

Influenza Preparedness and Response: Therapeutic and Public Health Countermeasures

The ongoing threat of a virulent flu strain unleashed in a globalized world fans public fear and galvanizes political will. The political dynamics of preparedness are complex, with critical relationships between seasonal and pandemic influenza. Influenza countermeasures include surveillance, preventing animal-human interchange, vaccines, antivirals, and public health interventions.

Global Influenza Surveillance

The surveillance system allows global tracking of the spread and evolution of seasonal influenza viruses, particularly the emergence of novel strains. Global surveillance, in partnership with national monitoring, provides a critical link between seasonal and pandemic preparedness. The WHO's

GISRS collects influenza samples, which are analyzed by a national influenza center and then sent to a WHO collaborating center or reference laboratory for advanced analysis. Beyond traditional surveillance, the emerging (still experimental) field of digital epidemiology employs computational methods to monitor disease spread—culling data from novel sources, including cellphone records, blog posts, tweets, and flight data.[29]

Global surveillance forms the backbone of vaccination strategies. The scientific community has an ongoing need for virus samples and sequencing information to formulate vaccines targeted to prevailing circulating viral strains. Using these data, the WHO's surveillance network, in collaboration with industry, develops a vaccine against the most likely seasonal influenza strains each year. This system also facilitates vaccines against novel emergent strains (Box 12.2). Surveillance and vaccines, therefore, are intimately linked through international virus sharing, which demonstrates the importance of global governance.

Therapeutic Countermeasures

Population-based vaccination is the primary method used to contain seasonal influenza in high-income countries. Although vaccination is essential, it has not eliminated significant morbidity and mortality. Vaccination campaigns do not reach a critical mass of the public for several reasons: (1) lack of coverage—for example, only about 60 percent of U.S. health care workers are vaccinated annually;[30] (2) unreliable vaccine production—in some years, vaccination supplies have been disrupted; and (3) variable efficacy—although efficacy is high in healthy adults (70–90 percent), it is lower in at-risk populations, such as the elderly. Efficacy can be further reduced if the vaccine strain incompletely matches the influenza strains in circulation that year.

Vaccination strategies for a pandemic influenza strain are even more fragile (Box 12.3). A considerable lag time occurs between emergence of the strain and completion of scientific testing of a candidate vaccine. Just as important, there is limited global vaccine production capacity, which will cause almost inevitable shortages, particularly in lower-income countries.

Despite significant morbidity and mortality, poor states do not invest adequately in influenza vaccines due to competing health burdens and limited budgets. International assistance has not filled the gap, posing a problem of global health justice, as people in the global South die of vaccine-preventable diseases. Further, even when vaccine manufacturers or high-income countries donate influenza vaccines, fragile health systems in

BOX 12.2 Global Surveillance and Vaccine Production

The global influenza surveillance system gathers virus samples and sequence information needed to design and manufacture vaccines. Vaccine formulation must contain an antigen that elicits a protective immune response—either inactivated virus or live attenuated virus (a virus that is genetically altered to reduce pathogenicity, but is not destroyed), with inactivated virus most common. Most production is still based on viral growth in embryonated chicken eggs, an old technology that does not result in high vaccine yields. Viruses in vaccine production therefore must be modified for efficient growth in chicken eggs, using either classical genetic reassortment or patented reverse genetics technology. The viral strains selected and modified for vaccine production are called seed viruses. Newer technologies allow culturing seed viruses in mammalian cell lines to overcome the limits of egg-based production, but access to these technologies is not widespread.[1]

Because a universal vaccine protective against all influenza strains remains elusive, vaccines must be targeted to circulating seasonal strains, which is why surveillance is critical to vaccine production. Based on GISRS surveillance, the WHO coordinates scientific recommendations about seasonal vaccines—one targeted to the Northern Hemisphere and the other to the Southern Hemisphere. The emergence of a pandemic strain would trigger a similar process for vaccine production.[2]

Until the 2011 PIP Framework, the WHO released virus samples and sequence information to vaccine manufacturers free of charge. The PIP Framework introduced cost sharing, whereby industries using GISRS viruses must make annual partnership contributions, collectively amounting to half the surveillance system's costs (art. 6.14.3).

NOTES

1. Alan W. Hampson, "Vaccines for Pandemic Influenza: The History of Our Current Vaccines, Their Limitations and the Requirements to Deal with a Pandemic Threat," *Annals of Academy of Medicine* 37, no. 6 (2008): 510–517.
2. WHO, "Influenza Vaccines: WHO Position Paper," *Weekly Epidemiological Record* 80, no. 33 (2005): 279–287.

low-income countries (combined with legal and regulatory requirements) make it difficult to ensure timely access to vaccines for populations in low-resource countries.[31]

Antiviral medications (such as oseltamivir [Tamiflu] or zanamivir [Relenza]) can be used to treat those who develop influenza or to reduce the risk of infection among those exposed to the virus. Antiviral medications

BOX 12.3 The Factors at Play in Pandemic Vaccine Shortages

In the event of a pandemic, vaccinating populations with little immune protection against viral infection will be essential. Demand will soar, with vaccine shortages virtually certain. In such a scenario, all countries will be affected, but lower-income countries will bear the greatest burden. Price is a significant factor, but nonprice factors also disadvantage the poor:

Vaccine design, production, and registration A considerable time lag will occur between identifying a pandemic strain and designing an effective vaccine. Although pressure to produce the vaccine rapidly will be immense, safety and effectiveness must be ensured. Once seed viruses have been developed, testing, licensing, and approval are also necessary. By the time a vaccine is ready, the pandemic will have spread rapidly, stimulating even higher demand. To illustrate this point, it took twenty weeks between isolating the 2009 H1N1 virus and deployment of the first vaccines. By that time the virus had spread globally.

Intellectual property rights Vaccines are technological packages subject to input, product, and process patents. The prospect of wild-type virus itself being patented causes public concern. Although most countries would not allow a patent on wild-type virus isolates, they could allow patents on viral genetic sequences or on genetically engineered viral variations. Companies may also seek patents on new technologies, such as tissue culture virus production or reverse genetics technology. Any point in the vaccine pipeline where companies can exert IP rights could restrict access. Intellectual property management, therefore, is critical for global justice.[1]

Production capacity The lack of demand for seasonal vaccines outside of developed countries limits vaccine capacity, representing a crucial limiting factor in producing a pandemic vaccine. Although global vaccine capacity increased from 876 million doses in 2009 to 1.42 billion doses in 2011, it remains well below pandemic demand. Avian H5N1 influenza is particularly problematic, as the virus is virulent to chicken eggs, returning low yields. As of 2011, the seven largest vaccine companies (producing 64 percent of available supplies) were all located in wealthy countries. Thus, even if lower-income countries can obtain IP rights, they may lack the ability to produce domestically.

Prepurchase agreements High-income countries often have contracts with industry to secure pandemic vaccine supplies, exacerbating shortages for countries without such agreements. The 2009 H1N1 pandemic demonstrated that once richer countries have signed agreements, it is difficult to persuade them to give up their secured supplies.[2]

Multiple stakeholders Vaccine production brings together multiple stakeholders, including state-owned laboratories, private research facilities, pharmaceutical companies, and international agencies. Creative governance is needed to coordinate diverse stakeholders, which have varied interests and motivations. Overall the global governance system needs to develop pathways to ensure sustainable and ample capacity of influenza vaccines, together with a system for fairly allocating the benefits to all countries.

NOTES

1. World Intellectual Property Organization, "Patent Issues Related to Influenza Viruses and Their Genes" [and Annex] (working paper, October 19, 2007).
2. Adam Kamradt-Scott and Kelley Lee, "The 2011 Pandemic Influenza Preparedness Framework: Global Health Secured or a Missed Opportunity?," *Political Studies* 59, no. 4 (2011): 831–847.

impede viral reproduction in infected individuals, and if taken within forty-eight hours of symptom onset can reduce the severity and duration of influenza. Antivirals, however, are only partially effective; they must be administered shortly after symptom onset, and their intermittent use can lead to drug-resistant strains.

Preventing Animal-Human Interchange

The complex interplay of pathogens among animals and humans informs prevention and response. Monitoring and controlling influenza in wild and domestic animal populations can reduce the reservoir of infection. Global surveillance, however, does not systematically track animal health, and international law does not effectively control animal pathogen interchange. Limiting close contact between animals and humans can prevent animal-to-human transmission. States, for example, can regulate poultry farms, migratory poultry workers, and live bird markets, and can cull diseased animals, with closures of live bird markets being particularly effective.[32] Health and safety regulations, however, require states to have enforcement capacity, while also ensuring the livelihood of poor farmers.

Trade disputes can also flare up when states regulate animal-human interchange. The United States, for example, brought a WTO dispute in response to India's ban on poultry from states with low pathogenic avian influenza. The United States claimed that India's decision was protectionist and without the requisite scientific evidence (see Box 9.2, Chapter 9).[33]

Table 12.1 **Influenza Countermeasures—Balancing Public Benefits and Private Rights**

Countermeasure	Example	Public Benefits	Private Rights Potentially Affected
Surveillance	• Screening • Reporting • Contact tracing • Monitoring	• Essential data • Early warning • Transmission • Incidence response	• Privacy • Fair information practices
Animal-human interchange	• Occupational health • Quarantines • Culls	• Protect animal health • Prevent "species jump" to humans	• Farmer livelihood • National economy • International trade
Community hygiene	• Hand washing • Respiratory hygiene • Personal protective equipment (PPE)	• Reduce transmission in families and the community	• Minimal but requires behavior changes
Hospital infection control	• Hand washing • PPE • Health care worker vaccination	• Reduce transmission among patients, health care workers and their families/communities	• Collective bargaining agreements • Health care worker autonomy • Freedom of religion and conscience
Decreased social mixing	• Close public places • Cancel public events • Restrict mass transit	• Slow spread of infection in public settings	• Free association • Free commerce
Border controls (entry/exit)	• Screening/reporting • Health alerts • Passenger data • Travel advisories • Hygiene • Inspection • Pest extermination	• Prevent cross-border spread of infectious disease	• Freedom to travel • International trade
Isolation and quarantine	• Home • Hospital • School • Workplace • Institutional setting • "Shelter in place"	• Separate the infected or exposed from the healthy	• Freedom of movement • Personal health and livelihood • Nondiscrimination
Medical countermeasures	• Vaccines • Antiviral agents (Tamiflu or Relenza)	• Prophylaxis • Reduced infectiousness • Treatment	• Bodily integrity • Fair allocation to the disadvantaged • Intellectual property • Business and trade

Adapted from Lawrence O. Gostin, "Public Health Strategies for Pandemic Influenza: Ethics and the Law," *Journal of the American Medical Association* 295, no. 14 (2006): 1700–1704.

Public Health Powers

After identifying an emergent pandemic strain, states can utilize a range of nontherapeutic tools. Public health countermeasures, used in combination, include community hygiene (e.g., hand washing, respiratory etiquette), social distancing (e.g., closure of schools, workplaces, and mass transit, and cancellation of public events), hospital infection control (e.g., gloves, masks), border controls (e.g., travel restrictions), and isolation or quarantine (see Table 12.1).

In utilizing their public health powers, states must balance public health with civil liberties—for example, by ensuring that limits on liberty (e.g., isolation, quarantine, and travel restrictions) are justified. Personal restraint requires rigorous safeguards, including risk assessments, safe and habitable environments, procedural due process, less restrictive alternatives, and nondiscrimination.

The PIP Framework: A Novel Compact for Virus Sharing and Access to Benefits

The global circulation of constantly evolving influenza viruses and the cross-border spread of novel strains necessitates global collaboration. To guide states, the WHO published a pandemic preparedness plan (last updated in 2009)[34] and guidance on risk management in June 2013.[35] The 2013 guidance, based on a review of the H1N1 pandemic,[36] recommends only four pandemic stages, which are uncoupled from actions at the country level. Using principles of emergency risk management, the WHO encourages member states to develop flexible preparedness plans commensurate with an assessment of national levels of risk.[37]

The WHO also issued the Global Action Plan (GAP) for Influenza Vaccines in 2006.[38] The GAP aimed to increase vaccine supplies by promoting seasonal vaccine use, raising production capacity, and urging research and development. The GAP II, issued in July 2011, broadened the plan, encompassing surveillance and regulation.[39] However, inadequate financing and pandemic fatigue may impede implementation.

The Indonesian withdrawal from the global influenza surveillance system in 2007, however, required the WHO to go beyond technical guidance. The power dynamics behind the PIP Framework were unusual because Indonesia had something to leverage to gain access to benefits: virus samples critical to global system functioning.[40] The unique agreement aims to change an unfair status quo whereby lower-income countries were expected to share viruses and then rely on ad hoc charitable donations. Brokering the PIP Framework proved arduous, spanning five years, as rich states were eager to secure virus sharing but reluctant to give up sovereign control over vaccines and antivirals. The PIP Framework and the IHR are the two international agreements that now form the foundation of WHO pandemic preparedness.

The PIP Framework secured for the first time a prior agreement for multijurisdictional surveillance and sharing of benefits. The agreement highlights critical compromises among stakeholders. It is nonbinding, or "soft law," as the WHO declined to exercise its treaty-making authority. Member state commitments under the Framework have no legal force. The PIP Framework applies only to "H5N1 and other influenza viruses with human pandemic potential," and expressly excludes seasonal influenza or other non-influenza pathogens (art. 3). The PIP Framework's narrow scope limits the WHO's ability to redress inequities in seasonal influenza or non-influenza emerging infections (see, for example, the discussion of MERS-CoV in Box 4.3, Chapter 4).

The PIP Framework has two distinct parts: (1) The main body sets out nonbinding member state commitments and directions to the WHO's D-G and Secretariat; and (2) the annexes incorporate the standard material transfer agreement (SMTA) (annexes 1, 2) as well as terms of reference for the advisory group (annex 3), existing and future WHO GISRIS laboratories (annex 4), and WHO collaborating centers for influenza (annex 5). This novel structure aims to harmonize the interests of stakeholders—state and private laboratories, governments, and industry—to accomplish the framework's two central tenets: (1) a transparent system of international virus sample sharing, and (2) access to benefits derived from the surveillance system.

Member States' Commitments and the WHO's Responsibilities

The PIP Framework creates a range of roles and responsibilities for the WHO, member states, the private sector, and other key stakeholders in facilitating the sharing of influenza viruses and increasing access to pandemic influenza vaccines.

Virus sharing system (art.5) Member states agree to provide "PIP Biological Materials" (including wild-type virus samples and viruses modified as candidate vaccine viruses) to GISRS laboratories. By providing materials, states consent to their onward transfer and use, governed by the standard material transfer agreements (annexes 1, 2). States may share materials bilaterally, provided they are also supplied to GISRS as a priority. To increase transparency, genetic sequence data and analyses should be shared with the originating state and GISRS laboratories. The handling of genetic sequence data, however, remains controversial, with the D-G charged to consult with an advisory group to resolve this sensitive issue. The D-G also must consult with the advisory group on a traceability mechanism designed to electronically track the movement of PIP biological materials into, within, and out of GISRS—although the D-G has authority to modify the tracking requirement during a pandemic emergency.

The PIP Framework therefore formalizes international virus sharing and clarifies the rights and obligations of parties, envisaging that biological materials will be shared within the WHO's GISRS network of laboratories for surveillance and vaccine development, as well as being shared outside the network. Although the framework does not impose a legal obligation to share virus samples, its norms should encourage state cooperation.

Benefits-sharing system (art.6) Member states agree to work with the WHO to ensure surveillance and risk assessment; benefits to states, prioritizing antivirals and vaccines to lower-income countries according to health needs; and technical capacity, including expanded vaccine production. State responsibilities, however, are cast in aspirational terms:

- *Provision of candidate vaccine viruses:* GISRS labs must provide candidate vaccine viruses upon request to manufacturers, as well as to labs in the originating state and other member states.
- *Capacity building:* States with advanced laboratory, surveillance, and regulatory capacity should assist developing countries upon request.
- *Pharmaceutical stockpiling:* The D-G is charged to work with stakeholders to develop stockpiles of antivirals and vaccines. Importantly, states made no commitment to contribute to stockpiles, but only to urge manufacturers to respond.
- *Access to vaccines:* In the interpandemic period, states should urge vaccine manufacturers to set aside a portion of each production cycle for stockpiling and/or use by developing countries, and work with the WHO and industry to ensure adequate vaccine supplies at tiered prices, including during a pandemic.
- *Technology transfer:* Member states should work with the WHO to implement the GAP to increase vaccine supplies, including (1) building production facilities in developing and/or industrialized

countries; and (2) urging manufacturers to transfer technology on vaccine, diagnostic, and pharmaceutical production, consistent with domestic and international law. States seeking technology should study the burden of seasonal influenza and, where appropriate, incorporate seasonal vaccination into national plans.

Private Sector Commitments: A Governance Innovation

The truly creative aspect of the PIP Framework is its private-sector engagement. Manufacturers are crucial to vaccine development, but international agreements rarely include private parties. The WHO resolved this dilemma through SMTAs, which are model contracts with prenegotiated terms governing virus sample transfers within the GISRS laboratory network (SMTA 1/annex1) and to entities outside of that network (SMTA 2/annex 2). Through SMTA 2, private entities receiving PIP biological materials, such as vaccine manufacturers, make binding commitments about the terms of virus sharing. Although they exist within a nonbinding PIP Framework, SMTAs, when signed, are legally enforceable private contracts between the WHO and virus sample recipients.

The SMTA 2 represents the most meaningful method for advancing equity.[41] Under these contracts, private companies agree to make contributions to the WHO, providing benefits to developing countries in exchange for access to PIP biological materials that support industry research and development. Recipients of materials make specific monetary and in-kind commitments, including donating vaccines or pharmaceuticals to WHO stockpiles, offering products at affordable prices to developing countries, and making intellectual property rights available (Box 12.4).

In addition to SMTA 2 commitments, the PIP Framework also asks companies receiving samples to make monetary contributions to the WHO. Historically, the WHO provided industry with virus samples free of charge. The PIP Framework, however, has a sustainable financing mechanism requiring companies using GISRS to make an annual partnership contribution, with the funds used to improve influenza preparedness and response—for example, disease burden studies, laboratory and surveillance capacity, access, and effective deployment (art. 6 (14)). The annual contributions must be equivalent to 50 percent of GISRS running costs, with the advisory group determining the breakdown between private contributors. In May 2013 the WHO released a distribution of partnership agreement among companies.[42]

BOX 12.4 **SMTA 2 Benefit-Sharing Commitments (Annex 2)**

The SMTA 2 requires companies to select two commitments from six benefit-sharing options in the model contract: (1) donating at least 10 percent of pandemic vaccine production to the WHO; (2) reserving at least 10 percent of pandemic vaccine production at affordable prices for the WHO; (3) donating a predetermined, but unspecified, minimum number of antiviral courses to the WHO; (4) reserving a predetermined, but yet unspecified, minimum number of antiviral courses at affordable prices to the WHO; (5) granting licenses to manufacturers in developing countries on mutually agreed, fair terms (including affordable royalties) on technology, know-how, product, and processes under patent; (6) granting royalty-free, nonexclusive licenses to industry or the WHO for pandemic influenza vaccines, adjuvants, antivirals, and diagnostics, with the WHO permitted to sublicense them to developing country manufacturers.

The WHO showed initiative by inviting the private sector into the negotiating process, but what incentives do companies have to sign SMTAs? Industry's main incentive is not so much related to pandemic influenza (which occurs irregularly), but to ensuring the sustainability of the global surveillance system that is necessary for producing seasonal vaccines that generate consistent profits. By the May 2013 World Health Assembly, two years after the PIP Framework's adoption, only one vaccine manufacturer had signed an SMTA 2. Negotiations with other manufacturers are ongoing, but until SMTAs are signed, GISRS labs will continue to fulfill requests for biological materials with the understanding that recipients will discuss SMTAs going forward.[43] To ensure success of the PIP Framework, the WHO will have to speed up implementation and ensure transparency regarding funding and distribution of vaccines.

The promise of SMTAs should not overshadow the fact that states have failed to make meaningful commitments to enhance global health justice. States did not even make "soft" voluntary pledges of vaccines. This missed opportunity is the PIP Framework's central weakness. Although the agreement's stated objective is a "fair, transparent, equitable, efficient, effective system" that places virus sharing and benefits "on an equal footing," in reality it secured the norm of virus sharing while providing only weak benefit sharing in return. The PIP Framework will likely fall short in meeting vaccine demand during a pandemic, and it provides no guidance on equitable rationing during scarcity. Given the sovereign interests of powerful countries, this outcome may not be surprising, but it remains disappointing. Equitable access to countermeasures remains a pressing issue of global health justice.

Dual Use Research of Concern: Influenza in an Age of Biosecurity

For centuries, influenza has been a constant force of nature—a periodic inevitability over which humans have little control. But influenza in the modern era of biosecurity is fraught with concern about human manipulation and release of an extremely dangerous pathogen.[44] Might it be possible, for example, to alter the genetic materials in influenza A (H5N1) to transform this already highly lethal virus into one that is also easily transmissible from human to human? Should scientists have the freedom to engage in "dual use research of concern" (legitimate research that could be misused to pose a biologic threat), and should journals have the right to publish the results?

Finding the appropriate balance between scientific innovation, freedom, and openness, on the one hand, and biosecurity, on the other hand, is fraught with difficulty. Modern conceptions of the scientific enterprise encapsulate key normative principles—exploration and discovery, scientific freedom, and the open dissemination of ideas.

Balanced against the norm of scientific freedom is the imperative of biosecurity and biosafety. Scientific supervision has many facets, such as pathogen handling and transfer, laboratory safety and security, research oversight, and restraints on publishing. In the wake of the 2001 anthrax attacks, for example, the United States established the National Science Advisory Board for Biosecurity (NSABB) to provide guidance and oversight of "dual use research of concern."

Basic research into the genetic makeup and capacity for mutation of influenza viruses is critical for increasing understanding of human transmission; viral evolution in animals, particularly aquatic birds and swine reservoirs; and the drivers of seasonal influenza strains. Influenza remains unpredictable, constantly throwing up new and unexpected developments. Scientists, for example, reported an avian influenza strain that had evolved to infect seals, killing 162 harbor pups in the autumn of 2011.[45] Basic research, however, can be deeply controversial, such as the CDC's reconstruction of a 1918 Spanish flu strain in 2005. The agency sought to identify genetic changes that allowed the deadly strain to move from birds to humans, acquiring human-to-human transmission capabilities.[46]

The simmering debates over regulation of influenza research came to a head in December 2011 when the NSABB requested that scientists redact their articles due for publication in the journals *Nature* and *Science*.[47] The journals were about to report on laboratory-mutated H5N1 strains that had acquired mammal-to-mammal transmission in ferrets (a common animal model for human influenza). The NSABB expressed concern with "the methodological details that could enable replication of the experiments by those who would seek to do harm."[48] In January 2012 scientists agreed to a voluntary moratorium on research that endows H5N1 with new properties such as the ability to transmit between mammals.[49] (The voluntary moratorium ended in early 2013.) Research had not been suspended in such a manner since 1976 in the face of safety concerns about recombinant DNA.[50]

A politically charged debate ensued with two ideas in tension. Scientists supporting greater oversight of research and publication cited the grave public safety risks—either the escape of the virus from unsecured laboratories or replication of the experiment by bad actors. Dual use research could be undertaken not only by reputable scientists in secure labs, but perhaps also by amateurs in "garage" labs.

Scientists supporting unfettered scientific freedom stressed the value of basic research, arguing that naturally occurring pandemic strains pose a greater threat than bioterrorism. The value of effectively weaponizing H5N1, moreover, is relatively small (e.g., terrorists could not control the virus's indiscriminate spread).[51] In any event, censorship would not work in an information age, with the Internet rapidly disseminating methods and results.

In April 2012, a month after the WHO came out in support of full publication,[52] the NSABB agreed to publication with more limited redaction of the text.[53] Although *Nature* and *Science* published the papers in May–June 2012,[54] the future of research oversight remains unresolved.

Other countries have taken more stringent steps. Many states restrict the export of products or technical information that pose a risk to national security, including items that could lead to the proliferation of weapons of mass destruction. In order to submit their publication to *Nature,* the Erasmus researchers in one of the controversial H5N1 papers had to apply for (and were granted) an export license from the Dutch government. The government argued that the license was required by European Union rules that aim to prevent the spread of nuclear, chemical, and biological weapons, including by restricting access to dangerous strains of influenza and information about them.[55] The researchers also had to receive an export license to discuss certain details of the research at WHO meetings.[56]

Erasmus challenged the government's decision in a Dutch district court. However, in September 2013 the court upheld the application of export license regulations to scientific information under certain circumstances.[57] In some countries, this would likely run afoul of freedom of expression guarantees.[58]

In March 2012 the U.S. government published a federal policy on "dual use research of concern" that requires funding agencies to assess their research portfolios and, as necessary, impose risk mitigation measures.[59] In February 2013 the government proposed amendments to the policy establishing institutional review and oversight requirements for certain categories of life sciences research at federally funded institutions.[60] At the same time, the United States created a framework requiring even more stringent review of H5N1 "gain-of-function" studies—such as research that renders HPAI H5N1 viruses transmissible among mammals by respiratory droplets.[61]

Clearly, no single country should have unilateral authority to strike the appropriate balance between science and security. Even though the United States funds a great deal of dual use research, decisions about regulatory oversight affect every country, requiring global solutions. Nonetheless, there are few, if any, binding international rules applicable to lawful but potentially dangerous scientific research. There remains an urgent need for a meaningful international consensus on governing this politically charged research activity.

Global Health Justice: The Imperative of Innovative Governance

Consider this tragic scenario: A virulent novel influenza strain spreads rapidly throughout the globe. It might be a lethal avian influenza that acquires the capability of sustained human-to-human transmission. Or it might be a seasonal virus that acquires greater virulence through an unexpected reassortment. Although states would deploy public health countermeasures, only an effective vaccine could avoid an ensuing global catastrophe.

The most likely outcome would be that affluent countries in the global North would gain access to the vaccine, while the global South had to wait. The reason this scenario is realistic is that most vaccine producers do business in Europe, North America, and Australia. Affluent states have already forged understandings with industry for "first-refusal" purchase agreements, and wealthier countries also have the wherewithal to purchase costly vaccines. Poorer countries could be devastated—not only due to vaccine shortages, but also because their people are more vulnerable due to co-morbid conditions and overstretched health systems.

The WHO stockpiles would be a small drop in the ocean of what is needed, with minimal impact. The poor would die as the pandemic ravaged communities with no immune protection to the novel strain. The world would face the unconscionable situation where the rich were protected while the poor would die, unable to access those same life-saving resources.

An influenza pandemic, therefore, raises a critical problem of distributive justice—how to fairly allocate scarce life-saving resources. Extant global health governance is inadequate: the PIP Framework was never intended as a robust redistributive mechanism, but rather as a diplomatic resolution of a political impasse. It is also unrealistic to believe that ad hoc reactive agreements during an unfolding crisis would work, as heads of state will find it politically infeasible to give up secured supplies of life-saving vaccines. The Obama administration's decision to delay delivery of its vaccine donation pledges during the 2009 H1N1 pandemic until most at-risk Americans had been immunized highlights the political dilemma.

A preexisting, binding international agreement to secure equitable vaccine access is essential to global health security. A mutual responsibility framework offers the only viable solution, with benefits shared equitably. Devising a political solution is fraught with difficulty, but could take the form of a social insurance system, with tiered pricing based on national income. Suppose states created advance agreements to buy into an insurance scheme that guaranteed a fair share of available global vaccine supplies. In essence, governments would purchase "vaccine policies" to protect against future losses from a pandemic. Operating like classic insurance, the scheme would spread the risk across all income groups. Vaccine producers would also have to be parties to the fund to ensure the production and distribution of adequate supplies.

If the vaccine pool were viable, the advantages of global health security would far exceed the economic costs. Although it may appear counterintuitive, powerful countries would have a vested interest in negotiating an equity scheme. Imagine the geopolitical ramifications of a pandemic that divided the world. The blatant injustices of a pandemic could thwart international relations on matters of vital concern—for example, arms control, climate change, and trade. Whether the venue is the G-77 or the United Nations, the traditional powers rely on cooperative relations with emerging economies. For their part, vaccine companies have an interest in correcting market failures to ensure a more stable demand for vaccines.

The mutual interests shared among stakeholders could create a pathway for advancing global health justice. The question then becomes whether stakeholders will recognize their enlightened self-interest and act decisively before the next pandemic, or whether they will take their chances in the ongoing battle between nature and science.

CHAPTER 13

The "Silent" Pandemic of Noncommunicable Diseases

GLOBAL HEALTH GOVERNANCE has historically focused on infectious diseases—with good reason, as pathogens have taken an enormous human toll, and still do. This is slowly changing, with the emergence of a broadened concern for primary care and health system strengthening. Yet a further broadening—indeed a qualitative transformation—is now desperately needed to ameliorate the underlying risk factors that fall outside the traditional health care sector. The precipitous rise of noncommunicable diseases (NCDs) worldwide requires fundamental shifts in behavior, habit, and culture. No country can succeed on its own, as globalized forces drive the underlying causes of NCDs.

NCDs accounted for 65 percent of global death in 2010, the vast preponderance due to four conditions: cardiovascular disease, cancer, respiratory disease, and diabetes.[1] The conventional wisdom conceives of NCDs as a First World problem, but this is starkly belied by current data: 80 percent of the 35 million people who die annually from NCDs live in low- and middle-income countries. The death toll is projected to rise by 17 percent over the next decade unless meaningful steps are taken urgently. A meta-analysis in 2012, for example, showed a *quintupling* of diabetes in rural areas of low- and middle-income countries.[2] With the exception of Sub-Saharan Africa, NCD mortality now exceeds that of communicable, maternal, perinatal, and nutritional conditions combined.[3] It is predicted that by 2030, NCDs will be the leading cause of death in every region of the world.[4]

The juxtaposition of stick-thin poverty alongside obesity is vividly depicted by N. R. Kleinfield: "The conventional way to see India is to inspect the want—the want for food, the want for money, the want for life. . . . But in a changing India, it seems to go this way—make good money and get cars, get houses, get servants, get meals out, get diabetes."[5]

Conventional wisdom errs as well in supposing that rising NCD rates are simply the by-product of an aging population. Although aging is a powerful contributing factor (especially affecting rapidly aging societies, such as China, India, and Japan), more than half of the global NCD burden is borne by those under the age of sixty.

The suffering and early deaths from NCDs, and the disproportionate burden in lower-income countries, will only grow. And these chronic maladies will interact with existing health challenges in poorer countries, not only creating the double burden of hunger alongside obesity, but also in other ways—in coping with infectious diseases and injuries that still plague the developing world. Poor countries still bear the burden of AIDS, malaria, tuberculosis, and tropical diseases, while more than 90 percent of deaths from unintentional injuries occur in lower-income countries.[6]

Beyond their direct impact on well-being and longevity, NCDs take a toll on development through rising health care costs and lost productivity. The cumulative costs of NCDs are projected to be $47 trillion from 2011 to 2030, with mental illnesses accounting for more than one-third of the cost; some $21.3 trillion (45 percent) of this total will be borne by low- and middle-income countries.[7] This is a low-end estimate. Other economic models calculate the costs at far higher levels. These costs manifest themselves in downward spirals of poverty, for individuals and families, as people living with NCDs may find themselves unable to work or faced with ruinous medical expenses.

The moral tragedy lies in the fact that much of this suffering and early death is preventable, and at reasonable cost. Although longer life spans partly explain the increased burden of NCDs, human behavior plays a central role: unhealthy diets, sedentary lifestyles, smoking, excessive alcohol consumption, poor oral health, and stressful occupations account for more than two-thirds of all new NCD cases. These behavioral risk factors contribute to underlying chronic conditions in the NCD trajectory, such as hypertension (high blood pressure), high cholesterol, and elevated blood glucose (see the NCD flow chart, Figure 13.1).

The complex interplay of primary risk factors, intermediate physical conditions, and NCD progression can be demonstrated by examining the role of obesity in NCDs (Box 13.1). Although behavioral risk pre-

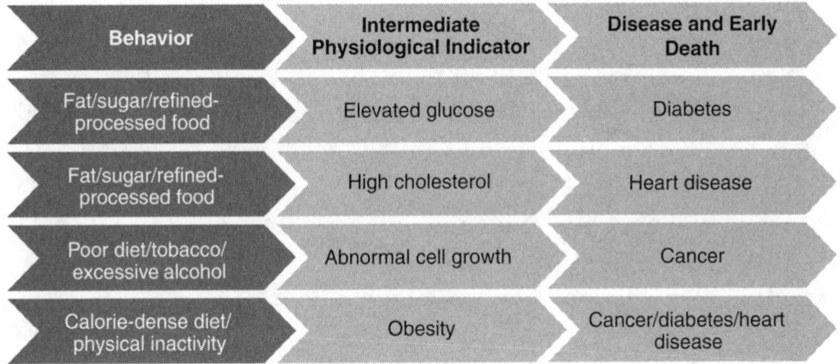

Figure 13.1 **NCD flow chart: Disease progression**

vention is preferable, there are also highly effective, low-cost pharmaceuticals to treat the intermediate stages of chronic disease, such as low-dose aspirin (anticoagulant), beta-blockers (blood pressure), and statins (cholesterol).

Although we often categorize infectious and noncommunicable diseases separately, there is a complex interplay between them. NCD risk factors exacerbate infectious diseases (e.g., smoking increases death rates from tuberculosis); pathogens cause cancer (e.g., HPV is the major cause of cervical cancer); and infectious disease therapies can increase the risk of NCDs (e.g., antiretroviral regimens raise the risk of heart disease). Worldwide, one out of every six cancers is caused by treatable or preventable infections. Infection-related cancers are far more prevalent in the developing world than in the developed (23 percent of cancers versus 7 percent, respectively)—owing to low rates of vaccination (e.g., human papillomavirus vaccine to prevent cervical cancer), inadequate cancer screening, and lack of antimicrobial treatments.[8] This picture requires global health leaders to rethink their strategies and priorities.

A problem as complicated and consequential as NCDs requires the engagement of national governments, the international community, and all of society. This chapter discusses governance strategies at the national and international levels, spanning sectors (e.g., agriculture, trade, transportation, and the environment) and engaging diverse stakeholders (e.g., multilateral organizations, states, civil society, philanthropists, and industry). But before setting out in search of solutions, it is worth trying to understand the failings to date.

BOX 13.1 Obesity

The complex interplay among risk factors underlying chronic conditions and NCD progression is best illustrated through the causes and impact of obesity, which is rising precipitously worldwide. Obesity can be understood as an underlying chronic, often co-morbid, condition—although it is also a serious health concern in its own right.

High-caloric diets and physical inactivity increase body weight to an unhealthy level. For many people, gaining weight reinforces behavioral risk factors—for example, overweight individuals find physical activity more difficult, so they are less likely to exercise,[1] and the body progressively craves more sugar and fat in response to high-sugar, high-fat diets, making unhealthy eating habits hard to break.[2] The end result of this vicious cycle often is obesity, which contributes to NCD progression.

Obesity markedly increases the risk of NCDs, particularly cardiovascular diseases, diabetes, and cancers (especially esophageal and colon cancer in men and endometrial, gallbladder, and postmenopausal breast cancer in women). Overweight and obesity are also associated with other illnesses, such as osteoarthritis, infertility, asthma, and sleep apnea.[3]

The global statistics are staggering, with the WHO projecting 1.5 billion overweight individuals by 2015.[4] The number of obese people more than doubled globally from 1980 to 2008.[5] However, there are significant regional variations in the prevalence of obesity—from 2 percent in Bangladesh to more than 60 percent in some Pacific Island nations.[6] The pandemic among young people is a grave concern because it foretells a future that is bleak for the child, her family, and her society. An estimated 170 million children globally are overweight or obese, including more than 25 percent of all children in some countries, more than double the obesity rates of a decade ago.[7] There is also an epidemiologic shift taking place in lower-income countries. Diabetes prevalence in rural parts of low- and middle-income countries, for example, has risen dramatically over the past twenty-five years, increasing from 1.8 percent (1985–1989) to 8.6 percent (2005–2010).[8] This trend has major implications for the public's well-being and the economic viability of developing countries.

Because of its link to behavioral risk factors and its role as a co-morbid condition, reducing obesity rates is often a central tenet of NCD prevention and control. The *Lancet*, for example, has called for a Framework Convention on Obesity Control to stem the tide of NCDs.[9]

NOTES

1. Tara Parker-Pope, "Exercise Advice Often Ignores Jiggle Factor," *New York Times*, November 13, 2007, F5.

2. Bonnie Spring et al., "Abuse Potential of Carbohydrates for Overweight Carbohydrate Cravers," *Psychopharmacology (Berl)* 197, no. 4 (2008): 637–647.
3. Y. Claire Wang et al., "Health and Economic Burden of the Projected Obesity Trends in the USA and the UK," *The Lancet* 378, no. 9793 (2011): 815–825.
4. World Health Organization (WHO), "The World Health Organization Warns of the Rising Threat of Heart Disease and Stroke as Overweight and Obesity Rapidly Increase," September 22, 2005, http://www.who.int/mediacentre/news/releases/2005/pr44/en/.
5. Mariel M. Finucane et al., "National, Regional, and Global Trends in Body-Mass Index since 1980: Systematic Analysis of Health Examination Surveys and Epidemiological Studies with 960 Country-Years and 9.1 Million Participants," *The Lancet* 377, no. 9765 (2011): 557–567; Goodarz Danaei et al., "National, Regional, and Global Trends in Fasting Plasma Glucose and Diabetes Prevalence since 1980: Systematic Analysis of Health Examination Surveys and Epidemiological Studies with 370 Country-Years and 2.7 Million Participants," *The Lancet* 378, no. 9785 (2011): 31–40.
6. Finucane et al., "National, Regional, and Global Trends in Body-Mass Index since 1980."
7. Boyd A. Swinburn et al., "The Global Obesity Pandemic: Shaped by Global Drivers and Local Environments," *The Lancet* 378, no. 9793 (2011): 804–814.
8. Christopher K. Hwang et al., "Rural Diabetes Prevalence Quintuples over Twenty-Five Years in Low- and Middle-Income Countries: A Systematic Review and Meta-analysis," *Diabetes Research and Clinical Practice* 96, no. 3 (2012): 271–285.
9. "Urgently Needed: A Framework Convention for Obesity Control," editorial, *The Lancet* 378, no. 9793 (2011): 741.

The Quiet Growth of a Pandemic

The past half-century has seen momentous accomplishments in global health: the eradication of smallpox, the triumph of polio vaccination, and unimagined success in curbing the HIV/AIDS pandemic. On the face of it, the challenge of NCDs would appear comparatively manageable—the risk factors are well understood, and there are promising strategies to mitigate them. Yet, to date there is no global fund for chronic diseases, no major foundation championing the cause, scant discussion within the G8/G20, and NCDs are not a target of the UN's Millennium Development Goals (MDGs). What explains this inaction? How could the global community fail to notice, and act on, such a momentous health crisis? (As we will see, the international community has only recently become engaged at the highest political levels.)

Challenges in Social Mobilization

Recent history has shown social mobilization to be a key driver of fundamental change and innovation in global health. Vocal and organized civil society movements drove vast policy changes around AIDS, breast cancer, and tobacco control. Their demands had such simplicity and clarity that they rallied communities with unadorned and poignant messages: Red ribbons symbolize the poor dying of AIDS who could be saved by a pill widely available to the well-off. Pink ribbons symbolize mothers dying of breast cancer when medical research could find a cure. A uniquely evil industry has concealed the fact that tobacco kills and must be stopped.

By contrast, the demands of NCD activist groups such as the NCD Alliance (Box 13.2) do not fit neatly on a placard. In fact, the alliance is badly splintered. Yes, diabetes, cancer, cardiovascular disease, and respiratory disease activists all want to reduce the four risk factors, but how? The alliance's "ask" is unclear, and sometimes conflicting. The difficulty stems partly from the multifactoral causation of NCDs. As explained below, reducing the burden of NCDs will require complementary strategies across multiple sectors. Even if the challenge of coherent messaging could be overcome, would the target audience be apparent? The agents of change (e.g., government, industry, and the media) are as loosely affiliated as the consumer groups.

In solving the NCD crisis, the primary focus will need to be on prevention as opposed to pharmacomedical treatment after the fact (Box 13.3). But prevention for the next generation lacks the political urgency of

BOX 13.2 **The NCD Alliance**

The campaign for a UN high-level summit on NCDs began in May 2009, and by the following May the NCD Alliance was formed. Spearheaded by four international professional groups—the International Diabetes Federation, the World Heart Federation, the Union for International Cancer Control, and the International Union against Tuberculosis and Lung Disease—the NCD Alliance uses targeted advocacy and outreach to ensure that NCDs are recognized as a major cause of poverty, a barrier to economic development, and a global emergency. The alliance builds the evidence base for NCDs and their solutions, produces policy position statements, convenes expert working groups, and lobbies governments for effective action.

BOX 13.3 NCD Risk Factors: Primary, Secondary, and Tertiary Prevention

The hazardous effects of behavioral risk factors on NCDs, and the metabolic and physiological conditions that mediate their effects, have been well established.[1] Social policies to ameliorate NCDs rely on several levels of intervention. *Primary prevention* protects individuals from developing an illness in the first place.[2] In NCD prevention, this means reducing the main behavioral risk factors for these diseases, namely poor diet (overconsumption of calories, saturated fats, sugar, and sodium), physical inactivity, smoking, and excessive alcohol use.[3]

Secondary prevention focuses on stopping or slowing the progression of disease by relatively inexpensive treatments, such as beta-blockers (blood pressure), statins (cholesterol), aspirin (anticoagulant), and regular screening.[4]

Finally, if such efforts fail to prevent serious chronic diseases, *tertiary prevention* focuses on more expensive management and treatment of the disease to help maintain a reasonable quality of life. Therapy can include insulin for diabetes, chemical or radiologic therapy for cancer, surgery for heart disease, and stroke rehabilitation programs.[5] For advanced disease, pain management and hospice care can improve quality of life.

NOTES

1. Majid Ezzati and Elio Riboli, "Behavioral and Dietary Risk Factors for Noncommunicable Diseases," *New England Journal of Medicine* 369, no. 10 (2013): 954–964.
2. "Primary, Secondary and Tertiary Prevention," Institute for Work and Health, http://www.iwh.on.ca/wrmb/primary-secondary-and-tertiary-prevention (accessed 10/4/13).
3. Although high salt intake is correlated with hypertension and cardiovascular disease, there is insufficient evidence to conclude that lowering sodium to recommended levels below 2,300 mg/day reduces all-cause mortality; low sodium intake may even increase health risks in some populations. Institute of Medicine (IOM), *Sodium Intake in Populations: Assessment of Evidence* (Washington, DC: National Academies Press, 2013).
4. National Public Health Partnership (NPHP), *The Language of Prevention* (Melbourne: NPHP, 2006).
5. David L. Katz and Ather Ali, *Preventive Medicine, Integrative Medicine and the Health of the Public* (Washington, DC: Institute of Medicine of the National Academies, 2009).

treatment strategies that save identifiable lives today. The strategies outlined in what follows will pay out their dividends over decades. From the vantage point of today, the beneficiaries are largely statistical people—for example, the cohort of adults entering middle age decades from now experiencing reduced rates of adult-onset diabetes, stroke, and heart disease thanks to public health interventions on diet, exercise, tobacco, and alcohol.

The four diseases represented by the NCD Alliance have come to the forefront of policy debates at the UN and the WHO as well as nationally. But it is vital to stress that other NCDs, notably mental illness, cry out for the world's attention.[9] By deemphasizing mental illness, we risk splintering within the NCD movement. This risk has been especially apparent as the mental health movement has struggled for a prominent voice in NCD policy and action (Box 13.4).

BOX 13.4 **Mental Illness: A Global Tragedy**

The vision—"no health without mental health"—speaks to the universal value of mental health in emotional and social wellbeing.[1] Yet, Becker and Kleinman have shown how historically it has been treated in the opposite way, with a cavernous divide between physical and mental health—in resources, political commitment, and human compassion.[2]

Mental illness is invisible: often it does not reveal its chemical composition in a blood test, and it cannot be viewed as a body lesion. However, its effects are unmistakable. It causes debilitating anguish that pushes human beings to withdraw from society; it forces families into caretaking roles; and it prompts societies to find resources for treatment and to develop strategies to compensate for lost human capital. Biological, socioeconomic, and environmental factors all contribute to mental illness.

About 10 percent of the global burden of disease is attributed to neuropsychiatric disorders, accounting for 28.2 percent of all years lived with disability—mostly due to the chronically disabling nature of bipolar disorder, schizophrenia, anxiety, dementia, and substance use.[3] Stressors such as poverty and social exclusion contribute to the 20 percent of adolescents who experience mental illness each year.[4] The economic burdens associated with mental illness exceed those associated with cardiovascular disease, cancer, chronic respiratory disease, and diabetes—the four other main categories of NCDs.[5] Mental illness is exacerbated by natural disasters, forced migrations, and war, and its prevalence can increase twofold in the wake of such upheavals.[6]

Although often viewed as a discrete health concern, mental illness can significantly affect the course and outcome of co-morbid chronic conditions such as cancer, heart disease, diabetes, and AIDS. Individuals with untreated mental illness are at heightened risk for unfavorable disease outcomes resulting from unhealthy behaviors, noncompliance with prescriptions, and diminished immune functioning. Their rate of tobacco use far exceeds that of other populations.

The pervasiveness and persistence of mental disability across the globe demand a commensurate response. Global health resources are urgently required to prevent and treat mental disabilities. Yet resources are sparse, and there is a major health service gap in most countries. Worldwide, countries spend less than $2 per person annually on mental health. Countries that contain almost half of the world's population, including China and India, have one psychiatrist or less for every 200,000 people.[7]

The deficits in mental health services are especially acute in poorer countries: 76–85 percent of persons with severe mental illness in low- and middle-income countries have no access to mental health treatment. This compares with 35–50 percent in high-income countries—but coverage is still too low to meet the population's mental health needs.[8] While most low-income countries include psychotropic agents on their list of essential medicines, these medications are not available at all primary health care facilities in 85 percent of these countries. When combined with other treatment expenses, the high cost of psychotropic agents relative to income creates a further barrier to treatment in poorer countries.[9]

Addressing treatment inequities requires building clinical capacity in low-income countries (which suffer from a deficit of mental health clinicians), developing new models of treatment that are tailored to diverse socio-cultural settings, and enhancing research on global mental health, combined with the political will to elevate mental health to a more prominent position in national and global health agendas.

However, the "most basic cultural and moral barrier to the amelioration of global mental health problems continues to be the enormously negative, destructive, and almost universal stigma that is attached to mental illnesses."[10] Stigmatization further diminishes society's willingness to address mental health head on and discourages sick individuals from seeking whatever care is available. In a major step, the 2013 WHA adopted a comprehensive mental action plan for 2013–2020, emphasizing the human rights of people with mental disabilities and the urgent need for mental health law reform (see Box 4.4, Chapter 4).[11] Whether these actions can reverse the legacy of neglect and marginalization of global mental health is yet to be seen.

NOTES

1. WHO European Ministerial Conference, *Mental Health: Facing the Challenges, Building Solutions* (Geneva: WHO, 2005).
2. Anne E. Becker and Arthur Kleinman, "Mental Health and the Global Agenda," *New England Journal of Medicine* 369, no. 1 (2013): 66–73, quotation from p. 66.
3. Christopher J. L. Murray et al., "Disability-Adjusted Life Years (DALYs) for 291 Diseases and Injuries in Twenty-One Regions, 1990–2010: A Systematic Analysis for the Global Burden of Disease Study 2010," *The Lancet* 380, no. 9859: 2197–2223; Theo Vos et al., "Years Lived with Disability (YLDs) for 1,160 Sequelae of 289 Diseases and Injuries, 1990–2010: A Systematic Analysis for the Global Burden of Disease Study 2010," *The Lancet* 380, no. 9859 (2012): 2163–2196.
4. WHO, *Adolescent Mental Health: Mapping Actions of Nongovernmental Organizations and Other International Development Organizations* (Geneva: WHO, 2012).
5. David E. Bloom et al., *The Global Economic Burden of Noncommunicable Diseases: A Report by the World Economic Forum and the Harvard School of Public Health* (Geneva: World Economic Forum, 2011), 32.
6. "Fact File: 10 Facts on Mental Health, Fact 4," WHO, http://www.who.int/features/factfiles/mental_health/mental_health_facts/en/index3.html (accessed 10/4/13).
7. WHO, *Mental Health Atlas 2011* (Geneva: WHO, 2011).
8. WHA, Resolution WHA65.4, "Global Burden of Mental Disorders and the Need for a Comprehensive, Coordinated Response from Health and Social Sectors at the Country Level: Report by the Secretariat," March 16, 2012.
9. Becker and Kleinman, "Mental Health and the Global Agenda," 70.
10. Ibid., 70–71.
11. WHA, Resolution WHA66.8, "Comprehensive Mental Health Action Plan 2013–2020, World Health Assembly," May 27, 2013.

The "Nanny" State: The Politics of Paternalism

Social and political action is constrained by political tensions about how far government should go in pursuit of public health. Prevention strategies often invite charges of state paternalism, which can be a major political liability. New York City's then mayor, Michael Bloomberg, unveiled a plan in 2012 to limit the serving size of sugary soft drinks, immediately earning the nickname Nanny Bloomberg. *USA Today* cautioned, "bans don't sit well with grown-ups."[10] Similarly, the antitobacco movement floundered for decades, as the decision to smoke was treated as a matter of personal choice, not of public concern. It was only when the dangers of secondhand smoke came to light (as well as the deceptive and manipulative tactics of the tobacco industry), that the social movement gained momentum.

Government action often stalls in the face of charges of paternalism, but these claims are often unfounded. Like secondhand tobacco smoke, NCDs have an enormous impact on third parties, for example by consuming scarce health care resources and driving families into poverty. Just as there is a valid public interest in assuring that citizens are educated and thereby able to contribute to the common good, so too there is a valid public interest in the prevention of chronic diseases.

Many NCD risk factors, moreover, are facilitated by physiological and/or psychological influences (even dependence), which robs individuals of a truly unconstrained choice. Nicotine is widely understood to be highly addictive, but so too are alcohol, sugar, and fats, which are marketed aggressively by the food industry.[11] At the same time, habits are formed at a young age, with industry often targeting children and adolescents in promotions for unhealthy food, tobacco, and alcohol. Young people thereby develop a taste for unhealthy products before they have formed the ability to reason and assess information and advertising.

The antipaternalism objection, moreover, rests on a perverse assumption—namely, that the status quo, with its rising NCD rates, is itself the product of individual choices, freely made. The reality, of course, is that myriad collective decisions made by governments and private interests shape the menu of options available to individuals, determining the price and availability of nutritious foods, the accessibility of recreation places, and the provision of safe paths to walk and bike to school or work. There is no avoiding government influence over behavior. The question is only whether that influence will advance or detract from the ability to lead a healthy lifestyle.[12]

Calls for a laissez-faire approach to NCD risk factors are especially galling from the standpoint of health justice because it is the poor who bear the brunt of government inaction, as they often lack the financial means and leisure time needed to prepare healthy foods, exercise, have regular medical checkups, and so on.

Policy Myths and Misunderstandings

The lack of social mobilization has allowed myths about NCDs to go unchallenged in the halls of power. Some of these myths were discussed earlier, such as the view that NCDs affect only the elderly and the affluent; that they are products of personal choice and therefore beyond the proper reach of government; and the fatalistic assumption that the problem is insolubly complex.

Policy makers often assume that their pursuit of economic development will bring improved health as a by-product. That assumption, although true in many respects, is tenuous in the case of NCDs, which may be exacerbated by development, as urbanization leads to increased reliance on cars and less green space for recreation, and rising incomes lead to increased consumption of tobacco, alcohol, and highly processed, calorie-laden foods. Globalization of trade and investment—a favored strategy for economic development—facilitates the supply and marketing of unhealthy consumer goods. As a senior Chinese health official once told me, "How is it possible to tell people who were once dirt poor that they should not eat butter, cream, and meat now that they can afford to live like those in the West?"

A Daunting Challenge for National and Global Governance

The situation is dire but not hopeless. Given the political and societal will, much can be done to stem the tide of NCDs. At the domestic level, as I describe in the next section of this chapter, the options range from tax incentives and public-private partnerships to more direct forms of regulation (e.g., labeling and bans on trans fats). Yet domestic initiatives are doomed to fail without international cooperation. Many NCD risk factors are, in a very real sense, communicable through channels of global trade. They move from wealthy nations to developing nations, facilitated by global trade agreements and the marketing and export of cigarettes, alcohol, and highly processed foods. Billions of people have seen their physical, cultural, and nutritional landscape drastically altered by forces of globalization that lie mostly beyond their control. In the third section of this chapter, I explain how global forces could be marshaled as a force for health.

One way or another, the private sector will need to be engaged in the search for sustainable solutions. Although the antitobacco movement rightly demands that Big Tobacco be denied any role in policy formulation, the food industry will need to be engaged in the battle against NCDs, subject to rigorous conflict of interest rules. The need for food industry engagement as part of a lasting solution remains a daunting challenge: experience with tobacco suggests that entrenched industries will fight reforms tooth and nail, and that has certainly occurred with the food, beverage, and alcohol industries.

Domestic Law and Regulation as a Tool for Preventing NCDs

National governments—and their counterparts at the state and local level—will of necessity be the primary actors in the battle against NCDs, as they alone possess the sovereign authority to implement legal and regulatory measures and to coordinate comprehensive NCD prevention programs. Indeed, governments are obligated under international human rights law to promote the highest attainable standard of health, within the resources at their disposal (see Chapter 8). What does this obligation require, concretely, by way of action on NCDs? There is no one-size-fits-all governance solution, as interventions must be tailored to the particular needs of a population and optimized within resource constraints. Next, I survey key interventions, ranging from surveillance to direct regulation. Table 13.1 categorizes the domestic interventions needed to create the conditions for healthy people, healthy places, and healthy societies.

NCD Surveillance

Although infectious disease surveillance is well accepted, monitoring of chronic diseases remains controversial. New York City, for example, has drawn controversy with its diabetes surveillance program, which includes mandatory laboratory reporting of glycated hemoglobin, guidance for physicians in managing patients with poor glycemic control, and advice to patients about diabetes management. Civil libertarians vehemently opposed surveillance, arguing that it interfered with patient privacy, clinical freedom, and the doctor-patient relationship. Patients can opt out of receiving health department advice, but not reporting.[13]

Despite the controversy, monitoring NCD incidence and prevalence is essential if governments are to be held accountable for health outcomes. Moreover, there is good reason to question the traditional outlook that views infectious diseases as a legitimate public health concern, whereas NCDs fall within the privity of the doctor-patient relationship. As explained, NCD risk factors are not entirely matters of individual choice, and their impact is not entirely self-regarding.

Full Health Disclosures

Consumers often make poor product choices because they lack clear, comprehensible information. Consider the bewildering way in which much food is marketed: "low fat" claims mask products that are high in sugar and sodium, "low sodium" masks high calorie foods, "zero trans fats" masks products high in saturated fats, and so forth. Hidden sugars,

Table 13.1 Domestic Strategies: Healthy Lifestyles, Places, and Societies

Domain	Goal	Intervention	Example
Healthy lifestyles	Optimal nutrition	Agricultural production	Food and agricultural policies, economic incentives to produce healthier foods
		Food manufacturing, processing, and distribution	Regulation of food manufacturers and retailers
		Disincentives for buying and selling unhealthy food	"Fat taxes"
		Marketing unhealthy foods	Restrictions on marketing to children
		Nutritional information disclosure and education	Providing government nutritional guidelines, improving package labeling, menu labeling
		Direct regulation	Banning unhealthy ingredients (such as trans fats)
		Public-private partnership	Voluntary targets for nutritional values
	Physical activity	Incentives for exercise	Subsidies for physical exercise and organized activities
		Flexible spending accounts	Corporate allowances for fitness activities
		Monitoring of community physical activity	Public health surveillance of NCD prevalence
Healthy places	Nutritious dietary options in neighborhoods, schools, and workplaces	Access to affordable, healthy foods	Mobile farmers' markets, zoning of unhealthy fast-food restaurants
		Healthy foods in schools, workplaces, etc.	Soda bans in school vending machines, nutritional audits of cafeterias, healthy food procurement policies
		School/childcare curricula and programs	Body mass index surveillance, nutrition education

Table 13.1 (continued)

Domain	Goal	Intervention	Example
	Places to walk, recreate, and play	Workplace/education settings and programs	Organized activities, fitness memberships, physical activity strategies
		Urban land use and planning	Attractive, accessible, safe public places and paths
		Tax incentives for building design	Businesses incorporating building designs that promote physical activity
		Transportation	Mass transit and safe routes
		Health impact assessments	Consultation with affected communities, public health evaluations
Healthy societies	Social justice	Antidiscrimination laws	Proscribing health-status discrimination
	Access to services	Services to support life functions of ill individuals	At-home support services
		Encouraging prevention and treatment	Metabolic screening; counseling
		Monitoring disease in the community	Surveillance through body mass index reporting

fats, and sodium pervade most processed foods in ways that consumers would not expect. Even "health" foods such as most yogurt, peanut butter, and soy milk are loaded with sugar.

To remedy this obfuscation, governments can compel industry to disclose the truth about its products by requiring clearer food package labeling, health warnings, and nutritional information on restaurant menus. The United Kingdom Food Standards Agency developed a voluntary "traffic light" system that is visible and simple to follow. From June 2013, traffic light labeling was included in the food "pledges" agreed to by U.K. food manufacturers and retailers under the Responsibility Deal—a novel form of public–private partnership involving the U.K Department of Health, industry groups, and non-government organizations.[14]

Beyond labeling, government can conduct health education campaigns with bold targets for healthier populations. Finland has implemented a

BOX 13.5 A Multisectoral Approach to Promoting Physical Activity—São Paulo, Brazil

A *Lancet* study in 2012 found that inactivity caused 9 percent of premature mortality, or more than 5.3 million of the 57 million deaths that occurred worldwide in 2008. If inactivity could be reduced by 25 percent, more than 1.3 million deaths could be averted annually.[1]

Brazil's Agita São Paulo program adopts a multisectoral approach to promoting physical activity. *Agita* is a Portuguese verb meaning to move the body, but it also evokes changing the way one thinks and becoming a more active citizen. The program's simple message is targeted to students, workers, and the elderly: adopt an active lifestyle by undertaking thirty minutes of moderate physical activity daily. The program builds public-private partnerships to promote physical activity, including targeting "mega-events" such as Carnival. Since Agita began in 1996, São Paulo residents have become more aware of the message and have increased their levels of exercise.[2] Following its success, Agita has expanded to other areas in Brazil and Latin America, with the WHO characterizing it as a model for the promotion of physical activity.[3]

NOTES

1. I-Min Lee et al., "Effect of Physical Inactivity on Major Noncommunicable Diseases Worldwide: An Analysis of Burden of Disease and Life Expectancy," *The Lancet* 380, no. 9838 (2012): 219–229.
2. Sandra Mahecha Matsudo et al., "The Agita São Paulo Program as a Model for Using Physical Activity to Promote Health," *Pan American Journal of Public Health* 14, no. 4 (2003): 265–272.
3. Sandra Mahecha Matsudo et al., "Physical Activity Promotion: Experiences and Evaluation of the Agita São Paulo Program Using the Ecological Mobile Model," *Journal of Physical Activity and Health* 1, no. 2 (2004): 81–97.

comprehensive campaign to reduce dietary salt intake, the leading cause of hypertension. Originally named the North Karelia Salt Project after the region where the program began in the late 1970s, it later expanded nationally. The campaign combined health education on salt and hypertension, daily dietary salt intake targets, voluntary food industry salt reductions, compulsory warning labels for high-salt products, and monitoring through dietary salt surveys every five years.[15] By 2002 daily population salt intake had reduced from 12g per person to 9g, making a significant contribution to declines in blood pressure and cardiovascular disease.[16] (For an innovative Brazilian approach to physical activity, see Box 13.5.)

Not only do these policies enable the lay public to make informed choices, they also drive food manufacturers to develop healthier products. What company would want to display four prominent red lights on its packaging, or a legislated high-salt warning label? Food labeling and nutritional educational campaigns are entirely consonant with concerns for personal autonomy, as they empower people to make informed choices.

Regulation of Marketing and Promotions

Many governments already limit advertising of cigarettes and, to a lesser extent, alcoholic beverages—for example, proscribing advertising to children and adolescents (though in virtually every country, more could be done, such as on plain packaging of cigarettes or visible warnings on alcoholic beverages). But the food industry—which spends $10 billion annually to market its products in the United States alone—has escaped comparable regulation. The bulk of industry spending is to promote unhealthy foods, such as sweetened beverages, sugary cereals, candy, and highly processed foods with added sugar, fats, and sodium.[17] Advertising is ubiquitous, spanning television, radio, and the print media to the Internet and "advergames," where food is promoted in fun video games.[18] The industry sometimes adopts ineffectual voluntary measures to stave off regulation—often at the encouragement of national governments.[19]

As many parents can attest, relentless food advertisements achieve their intended effect—prompting children to nag their parents for french fries, soft drinks, sugary breakfast cereals, candy, and so on. Governments can help parents steer their children toward healthy dietary habits. In 1980 Québec banned fast-food advertisements targeting children (as part of a broader advertising ban), reducing annual spending on fast-foods by an estimated $88 million. The province now boasts Canada's lowest childhood obesity rate. Moreover, healthier eating habits, once ingrained in childhood, are carried into adult life.[20]

Limits on advertising remain politically contentious, in some countries implicating the constitutional right to commercial free speech. Certainly the public supports regulation of misleading messages directed toward young people. Evidence from Australia and the United States suggests that there is widespread support for restrictions on promotional techniques that the food industry uses to exploit children's vulnerability to commercial messaging, for example, "premium offers" in which companies give away a free toy or other item with a food purchase.[21] Yet industry pushes the idea that its ads are alluring, not misleading, and directed toward adults rather than children. Whatever the intent, an increasing body of evidence shows that advertising of unhealthy foods influences children's (and adults') food preferences, as well as their actual purchasing and consumption choices and in turn their diet-related health.[22] It is simply not possible to change habits and culture without significantly reducing the aggressive marketing of foods that literally make people ill over time.

Incentives and Disincentives for Health

Government can disincentivize the consumption of unhealthy products by making them more expensive. Tobacco and alcohol taxes, for example, have proved effective in reducing consumption, especially among young people who typically lack as much disposable income as adults. The WHO has proposed so-called fat-taxes as a proactive response to a food industry and consumer culture that increasingly promote unhealthy foods as the cheapest, tastiest, and most readily accessible option.[23]

As expected, critics allege that taxes on unhealthy foods (as recently introduced in Mexico), are paternalistic, and also regressive, as poor people are the primary consumers. For these reasons, economic measures that seek to discourage unhealthy consumption choices often are unpopular and therefore politically difficult. As an obesity prevention measure, Denmark introduced a tax on foods that are high in saturated fats in 2011. However, the Danish government abolished the tax after just one year (and without formal evaluation of its impact), citing concerns that it had pushed up food prices for consumers and companies and put jobs at risk. It is reasonable to assume that the immense political power of the food industry also played a role in the decision to discontinue the tax.[24]

Again, it is instructive to contrast this to the regulation of cigarettes, where there is greater support for state intervention. Politicians rarely argue that cigarette taxes are paternalistic—not in serious debate, at least—as it is widely acknowledged that taxes serve merely to internalize the full social costs of smoking. On the "regressive" charge, notice that cigarette taxes are often praised as progressive precisely because the deterrent effect becomes stronger as one moves down the income scale.[25]

Unlike cigarettes—for which cessation is the best option—government can take steps to increase incentives to produce, sell, and consume healthier foods, for example, by subsidizing fresh fruits and vegetables at the level of the farm, retailer, or school. (In leading food-producing states in Europe and North America, a first step would be to cease subsiziding unhealthy foods such as high-fructose corn syrup or cane sugar—but again, government faces the formidable lobbying power of the agricultural industry).

Optimize the Built Environment for Health

Individual choices are not made in isolation, but reflect the environment in which people live. The built environment may facilitate or inhibit healthy lifestyles. Government's job is to make healthy lifestyles the easier, or default, option rather than, as at present, the harder choice. Poor urban and rural areas are often devoid of opportunities to eat well, lacking supermarkets, farmers' markets, and gardens to cultivate food. Cities are often inundated with cheap, intensely marketed fast-food, such as that sold by McDonald's, KFC, and Dunkin' Donuts—enticing options for overworked parents feeding families on a limited budget. Government can provide incentives for retailers to sell nutritional food and can enact zoning ordinances to limit fast-food outlets.

Cities and rural environments can present challenges for physical activity. By designing green spaces, playgrounds, sidewalks, and paths for easy walking, hiking, and biking, local government can do a great deal to encourage people to get outside and lead more vigorous lives. Limiting or discouraging motor vehicles in city centers can similarly facilitate pedestrian traffic and make the air cleaner for walkers and bicyclists. London, for example, introduced a "congestion tax" that sharply reduced motor vehicle use. Supporting mass transit and ensuring safe routes for people to walk to school, work, and shops are essential to a healthy community. In this way, public health is closely aligned with the environmental movement.

To improve the built environment and encourage citizen participation, governments could require health impact assessments as a condition of new development. By requiring developers to take health into account, this would at least formalize a process for ensuring that health is on the agenda. Consultation with communities in the planning process would ensure that citizens become actively engaged in shaping the neighborhoods in which they live.

Target the Places Where People Live, Learn, and Work

Of course, efforts to promote healthy built environments cannot be limited to public spaces. It is vital that these strategies be designed with accessibility in mind—reaching people where they live, play, learn, and work. Most adults spend a majority of their waking hours at work, so these settings should be conducive to healthy eating and activity. Employers could offer healthy snacks and lunches, fitness memberships, organized activities, and recreation. They could make stairways a more attractive alternative to an elevator. Similarly, children spend most of their day in school, and their habits are formed in the early years of life. Schools should provide children with nutritious food, ban sugary drinks and salty snacks in vending machines, restrict school-based promotion of unhealthy foods (e.g., through food company sponsorship of sports events), and provide opportunities for physical activity (e.g., recreation during recess and physical education). Government can support these initiatives through tax incentives or more direct regulatory interventions.

Direct Regulation

Although incentives and voluntary approaches are more politically palatable than direct regulation, there is also a role for the latter. Some products are so hazardous to health that they should be removed from the market. The U.S. National Academy of Sciences, for example, concluded that artificial trans fats provide no benefit to health and are unsafe at any level of consumption.[26]

In 2003 Denmark became the first country to set an upper limit on the percentage of industrially produced trans fat allowable in foods. New York City later restricted the sale of products containing trans fat in restaurants,[27] and many cities have followed suit. New York's ban has been a clear success—restaurants have lowered trans fat levels without raising prices or substituting a commensurate rise in saturated fats.[28] The U.S. Food and Drug Administration, moreover, requires trans fat levels to appear on food labels but allows less than 0.5 gram of trans fat to be labeled trans-fat free. In 2013, the FDA proposed a ban on trans fats, recognizing that even 0.5 gram of trans fat per serving is unhealthy, particularly when consumers are eating multiple servings during the course of a day.

However, in many cases direct regulation of food products faces significant public and political animosity, due to distrust of government and ideologies supporting individual free choice, as well as arguments that such interventions lack evidence of effectiveness.[29] In 2013, for example, a New York appellate court upheld an industry association challenge to Bloomberg's ban on super-sized sodas, described above.[30]

Marshaling a Transnational Response

Infectious diseases are widely recognized as an international concern because they readily transcend borders—a point underscored by the worldwide adoption of the International Health Regulations. At first sight,

NCDs seem to be characteristically a national concern—and, as explained, domestic law and policy must be a primary locus of intervention. However, NCD risk factors have exhibited the same propensity as infectious diseases to travel from state to state and region to region—the result of the globalization of travel, marketing, and culture.

The processes of globalization have led to a harmonization of behaviors, spreading high-risk behaviors in the process.[31] Thus, for example, the industrialization of food manufacturing, along with the globalization of trade in food, has led to the displacement of traditional diets in favor of a dietary convergence around processed, high-sugar, high-salt, high-fat foods.[32] (The displacement of traditional diets powerfully explains why obesity has become such a serious health concern among indigenous peoples.) The result is that many low-resource countries have experienced a growth in obesity simultaneously with under-nutrition, due to changes in diet, food availability, and lifestyle known as the "nutrition transition."[33] The health effects are further exacerbated by urbanization, often linked to increased reliance on cars, polluted air, and fewer options for physical activity.

Globalization also shapes power dynamics in health politics, as large multinationals exert influence, often thwarting public health initiatives. Transnational tobacco companies, for example, have aggressively exploited growth opportunities in developing countries to promote their products using techniques that are more heavily regulated in high-income countries.[34] The alcohol industry is just as globalized as the tobacco industry, creating comparable problems for national regulation.[35] Alcohol companies also jealously defend the right to market their products, portraying them as sexy, adventurous, and sporty. Regulation of the food industry is more complex given that food is one of life's necessities. But the industry has ubiquitously marketed foods that are highly processed, fat-laden, sweetened, and full of sodium.

Apart from simply marketing their wares, industries can distort the research base. A meta-analysis found a systematic bias in industry-funded research, with studies supported by the food and beverage industry four to eight times more likely to yield findings congenial to their sponsors than studies done by independent bodies. Similarly, evaluations of voluntary food industry initiatives undertaken or sponsored by the industry demonstrate high levels of compliance with voluntary programs.[36] Yet independent research finds much higher levels of noncompliance, for example, one study of the Spanish code on food advertising to children (the PAOS Code) found that almost half (49.3 percent) of television advertisements from participating companies did not comply with the code.[37]

Industry stymies regulation by lobbying politicians and public officials. More insidiously, industry groups at times infiltrate the national policy-making processes; for example, the global alcohol producers' front group, the International Center for Alcohol Policies, has been actively involved in developing alcohol-control policies in Botswana, Lesotho, Malawi, and Uganda. The alcohol industry has also created "social aspect organizations" in Europe, North America, and the emerging markets of Asia and Africa. The industry funds these organizations to promote (ineffective) consumer education messages, while hiding their real function, which is to influence political sentiment and public opinion toward the industry.[38] Influenced by its most dominant company, Ireland even celebrates "Arthur's Day" (devoted to the famous Guinness brew master), bringing swarms of inebriated young people to the bars every September 26th.

Tobacco, alcohol, and food companies spend significant resources on appeals to the public, urging individual choice and industry self-regulation.[39] They also employ corporate social responsibility strategies that enhance their reputation, but can damage the public's health. For example, the tobacco industry undertakes philanthropy and youth anti-smoking programs that aim to improve companies' images, while obscuring poor environmental and labor practices, and undermining governments' tobacco control efforts.[40] Beer companies promote, "drink responsibly" messages while using sexy imagery to market their products to adolescent men. Industry cleverly cultivates a wholesome corporate image to neutralize public health warnings and stave off government regulation, thus enabling them to continue with their core business of marketing unhealthy products to consumers—increasingly those in lower-income countries.[41] PepsiCo has come under significant criticism for its "Performance with Purpose" program, as the company promotes healthier "Good-for-You" products while simultaneously marketing unhealthy "Fun-For-You" products such as Pepsi-Cola, Doritos corn chips, and Lay's potato chips.[42] Researchers have revealed a "playbook" of corporate tactics that is shared between the three industries, including influencing research, lobbying government, and marketing unhealthy products to children and young people.[43]

Such is the impact of globalization that no country—rich or poor—can effectively tackle NCDs without the support and cooperation of the international community. The complexity of NCDs, however, presents a serious challenge in forging a unified and comprehensive global response. NCDs comprise a basket of diseases, implicating risk factors that span multiple sectors of economies and societies. For each risk factor there is often conflict between public health, on the one hand, and commercial and trade interests, on the other. Furthermore, viable solutions necessarily implicate not only public actors but also a host of private actors, including industry, civil society, the media, and academia.

Effective global governance therefore requires a multifaceted approach that simultaneously shapes global norms, institutions, and processes. It requires building domestic capacity in lower-income countries that lack resources and technical capabilities.[44] Multinational companies promoting cigarettes, alcohol, and unhealthy foods have resources at their disposal that far surpass those of many lower-income countries.

To effectively counterbalance these forces, states require the wherewithal to educate their population, encourage healthier behaviors, and regulate the private sector. Global health governance has an indispensable role to play.[45] While the WHO and the UN have, at long last, raised the profile of NCDs (see below), the real work lies ahead. Soft and hard legal instruments must create norms; set priorities; provide guidance on the most cost-effective interventions; set achievable targets with benchmarks, monitoring, and accountability; coordinate activities; and provide a strong mandate for national action. Global governance, of course, is not only about health, but also about justice. With the burden of NCDs so inequitably distributed, a major objective must be to reduce health inequalities.

The WHO's Global Strategies

Until comparatively recently, the global response to NCDs has been weak. As the world health leader, the WHO is best placed to steer international action but has instead focused most of its attention and resources on infectious diseases.

The WHO's leadership on tobacco control was solidified with the adoption in 2003 of the Framework Convention on Tobacco Control, which provides a blueprint for supply and demand reduction at the national level (see Chapter 7). That was the organization's only use of hard law to control an NCD risk factor. Its response to diet, physical activity, and alcohol has involved soft-norm development, but with too few clear targets, resources, or consequences for noncompliance.

The World Health Assembly (WHA) has adopted a series of global strategies covering NCD prevention and control (2000); diet, physical activity, and health (2008); and the harmful use of alcohol (2010).[46] In 2008 the WHA adopted the 2008–2013 Action Plan for its global strategy on NCDs;[47] in May 2013 it adopted an updated Global Action Plan for the Prevention and Control of Noncommunicable Diseases 2013–2020, following the UN's 2011 high-level meeting on NCDs (discussed in the section titled "The UN High-Level Summit and Its Aftermath" below).[48] In 2010 the WHA adopted recommendations on the marketing of foods and nonalcoholic beverages to children,[49] and the WHO later released an implementation framework to assist member states in developing policies in accordance with these recommendations.[50] The WHO has also fostered NCD coalitions such as the Global NCD Network (NCDnet)[51] and the Global Alliance for the Prevention of Obesity and Related Chronic Diseases (NGOs that coordinate strategies on diet and exercise).[52]

The WHO global strategies demonstrate member state support for NCD prevention and treatment, but without hard norms, achievable targets, sufficient resources, and accountability. For nonbinding instruments to succeed, they need to be backed by implementation tools, funding to build capacity, and effective monitoring and compliance.

WHO global strategies have been lacking in all these respects,[53] but further development of soft norms could foster compliance. Scholars, for example, have proposed a WHO/UNICEF Global Code of Practice on the Marketing of Unhealthy Foods and Beverages to Children, which sets out minimum standards, timetables, and ongoing monitoring.[54] Measures to prevent the marketing of junk food and alcohol to young people could draw global support, given the vulnerability of children and the vast scale of the health threat.

The UN High-Level Summit and Its Aftermath

The decade of WHO governance on NCDs, which relied on global strategies, failed to raise NCDs to the same high profile and impact as global initiatives around HIV/AIDS. But hopes were raised by a General Assembly agreement to host a high-level meeting on NCDs in September 2011. This was only the second health topic ever discussed at a UN high-level summit. The first, on AIDS, changed the world, galvanizing social and political action around a historic pandemic.[55] But the NCD summit was different—more notable for its fragmentation, indecisiveness, and infighting than for social and political mobilization.[56]

The General Assembly did adopt the Political Declaration on the Prevention and Control of Non-communicable Diseases, a sixty-five-point document cataloguing many of the global challenges and calling for an all-of-government/all-of-society response.[57] Broadly speaking, the Political Declaration recommends preventive measures, health system strengthening, international cooperation, research and development, and monitoring and evaluation of progress.

The Political Declaration, however, is short on specifics or implementation, asking member states to develop national action plans by 2013, guided by voluntary targets subsequently issued by the WHA in May 2012. The WHA set a global target of a 25 percent reduction in premature mortality from NCDs by 2025—the so-called 25×25 campaign. Setting abstract and distant targets is the easy part, as experience with climate change has shown. The hard part is establishing specific, near-term targets, monitoring progress against clear benchmarks, and ensuring compliance.

The WHA adopted the Global Action Plan for the Prevention and Control of NonCommunicable Diseases in May 2013, with improved voluntary global targets, including (1) a 25 percent relative reduction in the overall mortality from cardiovascular diseases, cancer, diabetes, or chronic respiratory diseases; (2) at least a 10 percent relative reduction in the harmful use of alcohol; (3) a 10 percent relative reduction in the prevalence of physical inactivity; (3) a 30 percent relative decrease in population-level salt intake; and (4) a 30 percent relative reduction in tobacco use by persons over 15 years of age.[58]

Still, these are all voluntary, nonbinding targets—a feature that has been the focus of many critiques of the Political Declaration. The UN Special Rapporteur on the Right to Food, Olivier De Schutter, for example, promptly complained of a missed opportunity for firm action to end farm subsidies for nonnutritious foods or to curtail the marketing of junk food to children worldwide.[59] What was conspicuously absent from the Political Declaration and WHA resolutions was effective global governance with the power to steer global health action.

The Political Declaration came at a time of economic crisis, which curtailed enthusiasm in Europe and North America for a response commensurate with the scale of the health threat. There were few promises for global resources or dramatic new initiatives along the lines of the Global Fund or PEPFAR. But without political will and an injection of resources, lower-income countries will not be able to do enough to educate the public, alter the built environment, treat the sick, and regulate the private sector. The Political Declaration meekly calls on member states to investigate funding options and to think about innovative financing mechanisms—but states made no financial commitments. Likewise, the Political Declaration stresses the importance of North-South cooperation but takes no steps to set it in motion.

Ambitious, long-term targets and slogans can play an important role in raising consciousness—the campaign to eradicate smallpox worked to a target date, and more recently the 3 by 5 Initiative (3 million people on antiretroviral therapy by 2005) was an inspiring benchmark for the AIDS movement. The 25x25 target, however, is ambitious even by comparison to those lofty campaigns, and there is no clear pathway to get there.

The challenge grows more daunting by the day, as the key risk factors of smoking, alcohol, unhealthy diet, and physical inactivity are rising, while at the same time the global population ages. Notably, there are limits on what can be achieved through preventive measures in the space of thirteen years. A good portion of the target 25 percent reduction will need to be achieved through treatment rather than prevention: for example, through screening, individuals at high risk for cardiovascular disease can be identified and put on a multidrug regimen, preventing 18 million deaths in lower-income countries over the coming decade.[60] But such promising interventions will require dramatic increases in funding, full engagement of pharmaceutical companies, low-cost and effective diagnostics, and buy-in from ministries of finance, trade, customs, and transportations.

Despite the need for urgent action, wealthy member states balked at labeling NCDs an "epidemic," fearing this would open the door to cheaper medications, which pharmaceutical companies were actively resisting. Beyond low-cost, accessible medications, curbing the NCD pandemic will require determined action to prevent the primary behavioral risk factors.[61] There is no other way to make a dramatic, sustainable impact than by transforming habit and culture. Box 13.6 illustrates the problem of weak global governance to reduce the harmful use of alcohol.

Looking Beyond the WHO: The Need for Total Global Engagement

Just as domestic governments need to adopt an all-of-government/all-of-society approach, so too must global institutions look beyond the WHO to a more expansive view of governance. In short, there is a need for total global engagement, encompassing agriculture, trade, development, and human rights. The private sector is a vital part of the problem, and of the solution, but corporate regulation must operate at the global as well as the national level, and be closely supervised by international organizations.

An elaborate network of bilateral, regional, and global agreements governs foreign investments, trade, and intellectual property. The world

BOX 13.6 Alcohol and Global Governance

Globally, alcohol consumption is the third biggest risk factor for disease and disability. Alcohol plays a role in causing sixty types of disease and injury, including at least seven types of cancer, cirrhosis of the liver, heart disease, neuropsychiatric disorders, diabetes, and unintentional and intentional injuries (e.g., car crashes, assaults, suicides, murders, and spousal or child abuse). About 2.5 million people die each year from alcohol-related disease or injury.[1] Achieving global norms has been arduous in the face of varying cultural acceptance of alcohol and determined industry opposition. In 1979, and then again in 1983, the WHO urged members to adopt alcohol policies.[2] It was not until 2010 that the WHA adopted the Global Strategy to Reduce the Harmful Use of Alcohol, which outlined ten action areas ranging from preventing drunk driving to restricting marketing. The strategy called for banning unlimited-drinks specials, enforcing a minimum age limit, and enacting licensing restrictions for new drivers. These recommendations are nonbinding, and there are no priorities or implementation assistance.

A global debate has ensued over the extent to which the alcohol industry should be a partner in alcohol harm prevention initiatives, and the extent to which it is similar to, or different from, the tobacco industry. Unlike the FCTC, the global alcohol strategy envisages a role for the private sector, including through self-regulation. However, some public health advocates argue forcefully against cooperation with the alcohol industry, which has been complicit in the personal and social destruction caused by its products.[3] For example, scholars have urged the WHO to negotiate a Framework Convention for Alcohol Control, while others prefer nonbinding instruments.[4] But despite the immense human toll caused by excessive alcohol use, there is scant indication that the WHO will adopt more effective governance strategies.

NOTES

1. WHO, *Global Status Report on Alcohol and Health* (Geneva: WHO, 2011); "Management of Substance Abuse: Alcohol," WHO, http://www.who.int/substance_abuse/facts/alcohol/en/ (accessed 10/4/13).
2. WHO, *Global Status Report.*
3. Anna B. Gilmore, Emily Savell, and Jeff Collin, "Public Health, Corporations and the New Responsibility Deal: Promoting Partnerships with Vectors of Disease?," *Journal of Public Health* 33, no. 1 (2011): 2–4.
4. Devi Sridhar, "Health Policy: Regulate Alcohol for Global Health," *Nature* 482, no. 7385 (2012): 302; Allyn L. Taylor and Ibadat S. Dhillon, "An International Legal Strategy for Alcohol Control: Not a Framework Convention—At Least Not Yet," *Addiction,* 108, no. 3 (2013): 450–455.

trade system, for example, requires lower-income countries to open their markets to foreign goods, which has fueled the spread of tobacco, alcohol, and processed foods. The inconsistencies in global governance are evident. How can voluntary WHO guidelines and global strategies compete with the binding norms that support trade liberalization? Global governance for health (GGH) must empower lower-income countries to exercise their sovereign authority to protect the health of their populations. Whether strong governance requires reform of the world trade system or a counterweight of binding health norms, the central point is that extant GGH is ineffectual.

At the same time, international development assistance must become more robust and expansive, with considerably more economic support and technical assistance for states dealing with the multiple burdens of infectious diseases, NCDs, and injuries. Symptomatic of the lack of political attention, the MDGs do not mention NCDs despite their palpable impact on poverty, health equity, and economic stability.[62] Although access to medicines for NCDs is formally a part of the MDGs, official reporting has, year after year, ignored targets; thus, for example, the lost opportunity to prevent cardiovascular disease has gone largely unnoticed. While great strides have been made in ensuring equitable access worldwide to antiretroviral drugs for HIV, gaping disparities remain for NCD medicines.[63] NCD treatment has become the new focus for international disputes over medicine access and affordability in the developing world, including issues of intellectual-property protection.[64]

A positive outcome of the high-level meeting was the mainstreaming of NCDs into agency planning and programming throughout the UN system and the integration of chronic diseases into country work plans (known as national development assistance frameworks).[65] What would an innovative post-2015 development framework look like?[66] Unless we set bold targets and create a concrete plan for their achievement, aging populations and worsening diet and lifestyle will conspire to create a grave crisis over the coming decades, consuming scant health resources at a magnitude measured in trillions of dollars.[67]

The Status Quo Is Unacceptable

The NCD crisis is largely of our own making, reflecting individual and societal choices, and can be reversed only through concerted national and global action. The past century has seen inspiring achievements in public health, though perhaps none has required such a broad, multisectoral response as reversing the dominant trend of obesity, sedentary lifestyles, and self-destructive behaviors through tobacco use and excessive consumption of alcoholic beverages.

For those who argue that all this human suffering and economic toll is only a matter of personal choice, family responsibility, and the free market, the answer is that the status quo is simply unacceptable. Make health the easier choice rather than being agonizingly difficult. Reveal the suffering of individuals, families, and whole societies caused by the crushing burden of NCDs. And refuse to accept the unconscionable health inequalities between the rich and the poor—both within and among nations.

CHAPTER 14

Imagining Global Health with Justice

THE SCOPE AND COMPLEXITY of global health law—its expanse of hard and soft norms, its proliferation of institutions, and its often opaque processes—can be overwhelming, making it difficult to form an inspiring and unified vision for the future. Mired in this complexity, the international community defines success disease by disease—without a clear picture of what fundamental reform would actually look like. If readers agree with this book's aspiration of global health with justice, then answering three simple questions may help pierce the haze.

First, what should global health look like? That is, given optimal priority-setting, funding, and implementation, to what level of health should we aspire, and with what provision of health-related services? Properly reenvisioned, I will argue, global efforts should be directed toward universal assurance of the essential conditions for health: population-level strategies drawn from the tool box of public health; fully affordable, accessible, and high-quality health care for all; and a wide range of policies beyond the health sector to address the social determinants of health.

Second, what would global health with *justice* look like? Global health seeks to improve all the major indicators of health, such as infant mortality and life expectancy. Global health with justice, however, requires that we look beyond improved health outcomes for the population as a whole. Although overall population health is vitally important, justice requires a significant reduction in health disparities between the well-off and the poor. Societies that achieve high levels of health and longevity for most, while the poor and marginalized die young, do not comport with social justice. Global health with justice demands that society embed fairness into the environment in which people live and equitably allocate services, with particular attention to the needs of the most disadvantaged.

Third, what would it take to achieve global health with justice? That is, once we clearly state the goal and meaning of global health with justice, what concrete steps are required to reach this ambitious objective? This raises fundamental challenges, intellectually and operationally, as the response cannot be limited to dedicating ever-greater resources to health, but must also involve improved governance—at the country and international level and across multiple sectors. The hard work entails setting clear but bold targets, monitoring progress, and ensuring accountability for results. Good governance is critical because it is a rare society that has a healthy population amid governing institutions that are corrupt, nonresponsive, or uncaring.

Posing these three elementary questions to arrive at a vision of global health with justice, of course, oversimplifies a field that is fraught with tensions and trade-offs. I have tried to convey the complexity and nuances of global health—its legal instruments and governance structures—throughout the book. But I want to end by imagining a more ideal future for world health, with bold proposals to get there. After thinking about these three basic questions, I turn to an idea for innovative global governance for health—a Framework Convention on Global Health (FCGH). In this final section, I will also canvass related high-minded ideas for global health reform that could overcome the stubborn persistence of health inequalities still found in the world today.

What Should Global Health Look Like?

The very idea of promoting health for all on a global scale is relatively new, and the international community is still finding its footing. Historically, states prioritized global health security in their international health dealings, primarily on grounds of self-interest. The earliest international health treaties in the nineteenth century sought to protect Europe against cholera, plague, and yellow fever spreading from Africa and Asia. The International Health Regulations, which governed the response to influenza A (H1N1), are the lineal successor to these European treaties. However, a more ambitious, encompassing, and proactive vision is needed to meet today's most urgent challenge: assuring the health of all people—not only the well-off, but also the disadvantaged.

In the twentieth and early twenty-first centuries, countless institutions emerged to promote global health. The World Health Organization's constitution best captures the high hopes of the post–World War II era in its vision for global health: "complete physical, mental, and social well-being." Yet this vision is generalized—offering no concrete guidance on how to achieve its lofty goal. The WHO, moreover, has not taken leadership to fulfill its expansive constitutional mission and is mired in an economic crisis (see Chapter 4).

What would a genuine state of global health look like? There are few satisfying answers in today's global health landscape. For the most part, states and stakeholders have dwelled on important but narrow goals, such as eradicating specific diseases (e.g., polio), reaching treatment targets (e.g., access to HIV antiretrovirals), or expanding capacities (e.g., the health workforce). Global health partnerships are broadening their mandates to health system strengthening but still operate largely in silos devoted to particular illnesses (e.g., AIDS) or interventions (e.g., vaccinations).

To many, the primary aim of global health remains—even to this day—to reduce health threats that traverse national borders, such as emerging infectious diseases. The vast resources and political attention given to SARS and novel influenzas illustrate the continued priority given to global health security. Although security is important, the deepest global health challenges have little to do with cross-border threats. The primary challenge is to significantly reduce the enduring and unconscionable burdens of endemic disease and early death among the world's poor.

A bold vision for global health should aim to dramatically reduce morbidity and premature mortality across the full span of health threats. In the end, of course, what matters are the outcomes: longer, healthier lives for everyone. But a meaningful vision for global health must specify the means as well as the ends; it must articulate the health-related goods and services that every human being may rightfully expect. The global health movement of today, mired in combating specific diseases, lacks this kind of holistic vision.

Assuring the Conditions in Which People Can Be Healthy

No government or institution—not even those with unlimited resources—can guarantee complete physical and mental well-being. What governments *can* be held accountable for is assuring the conditions in which people can be healthy. Individuals are embedded in built and natural environments that determine their well-being in fundamental ways. They are dependent upon government to ensure the provision of health services to prevent and treat injury and illness. They depend on basic socioeconomic foundations for a healthy, productive, and fulfilling life. What, then, are the essential conditions in which people can be healthy? Put simply, three conditions of life would give everyone a fairer opportunity for good health: (1) public health services on a population level; (2) health care services to all individuals; and (3) the socioeconomic determinants that undergird healthy and productive lives.

Public Health Services: A Population-Based Perspective

The first condition needed for good health is the provision of public health services—that is, services not allocated to particular individuals, but rather provided to the population as a whole. Classical population-based services include hygiene and sanitation, potable water, clean air, vector abatement, injury prevention, health education, and tobacco and alcohol control. Conceived more broadly, they include built environments conducive to good health, such as green spaces for recreation, walking and bike paths, access to nourishing foods, safe vehicle and road design, and environmental controls. Public health requires surveillance, data systems, and laboratories to monitor health within the community. In short, governments must provide all the goods and services needed for a safe and healthy life in a well-regulated society.

Most public health services offer low-technology solutions to ill health and early death. Erecting and maintaining an adequate public health infrastructure has long been a fact of life in the developed world. In robust democracies, people do not tolerate living in filthy and chaotic environments that breed disease and expose individuals to horrific injuries in their daily lives. The progressive and sanitary movements revolted in horror at the squalor, filth, and unsafe conditions of the Industrial Revolution. In the nineteenth century, great public health figures devoted their lives to sanitary reform, including Louis-René Villermé in France, Lemuel Shattuck in the United States, Edwin Chadwick in England, and Rudolf Virchow in Germany. Each of these campaigners stressed the devastating effects of urbanization, industrialization, and poverty on morbidity and premature mortality.[1] Once basic public health reforms are implemented, they quickly come to be seen as a baseline requirement for a functioning society—their widespread or sustained disruption is treated as a crisis.

What seems remarkable is that modern conceptions of global health rarely focus on fundamental public health services. What rich countries take for granted in their domestic policies they rarely prioritize in international health assistance. Governments in lower-income states—in part responding to the inducements of global aid—also focus attention and resources on specific diseases and high-technology solutions. What health and development partners forget is to provide the basics of good health—an environment that is clean, safe, and conducive to living a healthy life. If there were a single message I could convey to global health leaders, it would be to first attend to the task of building a habitable, safe environment.

Universal Health Coverage

The second essential condition for good health is the provision of health care services to all individuals, increasingly an expectation of every society, with a moral mandate that is not new but becomes ever "stronger as clinical progress continues to accelerate in developed societies."[2] Comprehensive health care coverage includes clinical prevention (e.g., testing, counseling, and vaccinations), medical treatment for injury and disease, and supportive care for those who are suffering. These services range from primary care to emergency and specialized services, through to rehabilitation and pain relief. Universal health coverage aims to make all vital health care services available, affordable, and accessible to the entire population—poor/rich, physically and mentally able/disabled, and urban/rural. Effective health systems require health care facilities (e.g., clinics, hospitals, nursing homes), human resources (e.g., doctors, nurses, and community workers), and essential medicines to serve the full range of needs within the population.

Universal health coverage is particularly beneficial to the poor, who otherwise may forgo care due to resource constraints. Consequently, key health metrics such as infant and maternal mortality and life expectancy tend to be improved as societies move toward universal health coverage.[3] The introduction of user fees or enrollment obstacles can easily undo the benefits to the poor, however, allowing the middle and upper classes to capture an ostensibly public system. Where countries opt for mixed public-private arrangements, well-to-do classes often stream into the private system, leaving an underfunded public system as a safety net for the poor. Likewise, a lack of comprehensiveness (e.g., offering coverage only for in-patient care) undermines the effectiveness of universal coverage and leaves individuals impoverished from having to pay out-of-pocket costs.

More broadly, gains from universal health coverage are easily undone through failings in governance. Health systems must, therefore, guard against the debilitating effects of corruption and poor management, fostering better public sector administration and provider accountability with the rollout of universal coverage.[4]

The growing emphasis on universal health coverage arises, in part, in response to shortcomings of disease-specific initiatives. There is a palpable futility in efforts to save lives through antiretrovirals or bed nets if survivors then face a fusillade of other largely avertable threats—for example, maternal mortality, diarrheal diseases, or cervical cancer. This sense of futility is not a license for inaction. Rather, preventive and therapeutic efforts must be expanded and rationally prioritized to address the health of the whole person (or the whole population, as public health advocates prefer to say).

Achieving universal health coverage requires systematic and inclusive planning; engaging affected communities; training, education, and good career prospects for the full cadre of health professionals; adequate funding that is predictable and sustainable over the long term; and governance that is honest, transparent, and accountable for the health of the population.

Universal health coverage is within the means of most low- and middle-income countries. Ghana, for example, has financed a universal, single-payer system through consumption taxes, with revenues earmarked for the National Health Insurance Scheme. Although legitimate concerns exist about the impact of consumption taxes on the poor, the Ghanaian experience suggests that the tax can be structured as a progressive financing mechanism.[5] External funding remains an indispensable gap-filler for states that lack the capacity to meet the full spectrum of national health needs.

Socioeconomic Determinants of Health

The third essential condition for good health is the assurance of socioeconomic determinants that undergird healthy and productive lives, "the full set of conditions in which people live and work."[6] Key underlying determinants include education, income, housing, employment, social inclusion, and gender/racial/ethnic equality. Socioeconomic factors influence health through a wide variety of causal pathways. The underlying (or upstream) determinants just mentioned are linked to more direct (or downstream) risk factors such as smoking, exposure to air pollution, endangerment at home and in the workplace, addiction, and stress.[7] Having a functioning social safety net for every inhabitant is the hallmark of solidarity and should be seen as foundational to the global health system.

The dramatic rise in life expectancy in high-income countries over the past century has been primarily the result of improved socioeconomic determinants, along with public health services, as opposed to breakthroughs in clinical medicine.[8] Even in high-income countries with systems of universal health care, the distribution of disease and early mortality continues to be strongly patterned on socioeconomic factors.[9] The groundbreaking Whitehall studies of British civil servants in the 1960s revealed that lower social status, with the stress and reduced control over one's life that this entails, is a major risk factor for ill health. As *The Economist* acutely observed, "Cardiac arrest—and, indeed, early death from any cause—is the prerogative of underlings."[10] In the United States, white adults with at least sixteen years of education outlive black adults with less than twelve years of education by a dozen years (2008 data).[11]

Addressing the socioeconomic determinants of health can set in motion a virtuous cycle, yielding long-term benefits for development as individuals are enabled to thrive in their work and family lives as well as their health.[12] Effective interventions require action beyond the governmental health sector, and indeed beyond government—requiring both an "all-of-government" and "all-of-society" strategy. If the health sector is to play a leading role, it needs to mobilize and coordinate this inclusive societal response.

The WHO has proclaimed the importance of social determinants, notably in the Marmot report in 2008, which found that the conditions in which people are born, grow, live, work, and age powerfully affect their health. In the 2011 Rio Declaration on the Social Determinants of Health, world leaders made commitments on five action areas: governance for health and development; participation in policy making and implementation; reorienting health systems toward reducing inequities; global governance and collaboration; and monitoring and accountability.[13] Regrettably, the declaration established no new resource commitments to support social determinants in developing countries. The specifics (and effectiveness) of monitoring and accountability mechanisms remain to be seen.

Although all three essential conditions for good health—health care, public health, and socioeconomic determinants—call for distinct investments and governance strategies, taken as a whole they are mutually reinforcing. Thus, for example, population-level prevention marshaled under the banner of public health will ease the strain of injuries and disease epidemics on health care systems. Conversely, universal health coverage will advance public health—notably through clinical prevention, immunizations, and improved access for the poor.[14] Finally, investments in public health and universal health care will advance the social determinants of health by easing the financial burdens of health care on individuals and families. In turn, improving socioeconomic determinants will strengthen social cohesion and empower disadvantaged populations to demand responsiveness from their government.

A country's ability to provide these essential conditions of health is of course partly a function of its overall level of development. Yet population health and broader development do not move in lockstep, as evidenced by the fact that countries with comparable levels of per capita GDP show highly divergent life expectancies, such as the poor-health outcomes in the United States relative to OECD states.[15] Accordingly, health outcomes are not primarily dictated by inexorable forces of global economics, but rather reflect policy choices made by governments, and are thus susceptible to domestic and international pressures for improvement.[16]

Setting Global Priorities: A Thought Experiment

Among the three essential conditions for good health, global health actors have focused intently on the provision of health care, often neglecting or deemphasizing the other two major conditions for health and well-being. Even when leaders focus on health care services, they tend to take a narrow perspective. Rather than devoting resources to broadly strengthening health systems, efforts are often targeted at particular diseases, such as AIDS, tuberculosis, and malaria. Or inordinate resources are marshaled in response to rapidly emerging infectious diseases (e.g., novel influenzas) or bioterrorism (e.g., anthrax). The enduring burdens of injuries, mental health conditions, and noncommunicable diseases are often left behind in the political struggle—notwithstanding their immeasurable toll on health and well-being.

This disease-specific focus remains, but global health actors are now starting to expand into health system strengthening. Major actors such as the Global Fund and PEPFAR have incorporated health systems into their funding and programs,[17] while the WHO has promoted the idea of universal health coverage, which is also influencing thinking on the post-2015 UN sustainable development agenda.

It is too early to predict whether the recent trend toward health systems is only the latest global health fashion, or whether it will have sustaining power. Given the lessons of history (from Alma-Ata onward), there is ample reason for skepticism about whether the international community will make the necessary investments to fully achieve universal health coverage. But even if global health leaders did give serious and sustained attention to health system development, two essential conditions of health would remain largely unaddressed: public health and the socioeconomic determinants of health.

Does this tacit prioritization of medical care make sense, given finite resources? To get some purchase on this question, consider a thought experiment loosely modeled on the political philosopher John Rawls's "veil of ignorance." Suppose—without knowing your life's circumstances (young/old, rich/poor, healthy/ill/disabled, or living in the global South or global North)—you were forced to choose between two stark options for the future of global health.

Under option one, provision of health care would be strongly prioritized. You could see a health care professional whenever you wanted to, attend high-quality clinics and hospitals, and gain access to advanced medicines. This scenario would achieve the ideal of universal health coverage but would be highly oriented toward medical care—leaving gaps in population-level public health services and the social determinants of health. Universal health coverage would best serve the interests of individuals already ill and suffering, but it would have limited impact in preventing illness, injury, and early death.

Under option two, scarce resources would be directed primarily toward population-level prevention strategies. As a result, everyone would live in an environment in which they could turn on the tap and drink clean water; breathe fresh, unpolluted air; live, work, and play in sanitary and hygienic surroundings; eat safe and nourishing food; be free from infestations of malarial mosquitoes, plague-ridden rats, or other disease vectors; not be exposed to tobacco smoke or other toxins; and not live in fear of avoidable injury or violence. This scenario would make unsparing use of public health measures but would offer no assurance of medical treatment.

Blinded to your life's circumstances, and facing these stark options, there are compelling reasons for choosing option two—and I believe most people would prefer to live in a safe, habitable environment. If the day-to-day circumstances of your life do not allow for the maintenance of good health, medical treatments cannot fill the gap. Health care operates primarily *after* one sustains an injury or develops a disease, and even following a successful medical outcome, patients will return to the same unhealthy and hazardous conditions. It is better to live in an environment that significantly lowers health risks—*preventing* exposures to pathogens, toxins, vermin, and treacherous conditions. Unfortunately, the world's poorest countries are at times the worst offenders in this regard, investing in expensive tertiary care or genomic research while neglecting elementary public health measures.

Historically, the greatest strides in combating disease and extending life expectancy have been achieved through population-level interventions. In his seminal study of population health in England, for example, Thomas McKeown found that improved standards of living, nutritional gains, and infectious disease control were primarily responsible for the major declines in mortality. Modern historians have also stressed the relative importance of sanitation[18] and of government's vital role in ensuring the socioeconomic determinants of health.[19] The twentieth century witnessed miraculous scientific achievements in clinical medicine, but the payoff in saved lives has been primarily through population-based public health. Given the choice between high-technology solutions and raising a family in wholesome, clean, and safe conditions, I believe the decision is clear.

While clinical interventions deliver benefits primarily at later stages of life, investments in public health are essential in guarding against threats that arise in infancy, childhood, and adolescence. Life expectancy is dragged down in the developing world in large part due to childhood deaths owing to elementary gaps in public health: undernutrition, unsafe water, raw sewage, exposure to disease-bearing pests, suboptimal breast-feeding, and vitamin A and zinc deficiencies.[20] A selling point of public health interventions, then, is that they effectively address health needs upstream in a human life span.

The same reasoning applies to the maladies that afflict the developed—and already much of the developing—world. When investments in tobacco control targeting adolescents succeed, health risks are drastically mitigated for a lifetime. And so it is with a whole range of public health investments. For example, there is a window in childhood where malnutrition can be ruinous to cognitive development, imposing a setback with lifelong effects. Likewise with the problem of childhood overweight, with evidence showing that healthy eating and physical activity habits in childhood will be carried on through adulthood.[21]

The public is often scandalized by stories of inaccessible or inadequate medical care or failure to make available a particular medicine or technology. This is due in part to media attention to the latest scientific breakthroughs and the visibility of a sympathetic patient denied treatment. Public health, however, is concerned with creating broad environmental and behavioral changes for the masses, such as the many children saved by access to potable water. In focusing attention on heroic medical treatments, it often goes unnoticed that the sixty-year-old heart attack patient or diabetes sufferer is above all a victim of government's chronic underinvestment in proven prevention strategies.

Underinvestment in public health is especially apparent in the developing world. While inhabitants of high-income countries continue to take public health services for granted (even though population health receives only a fraction of health spending), those in lower-income countries still often live in crude, unsafe, and filthy environments. Visit most major cities in the developing world and you will experience the insecurity felt from consuming contaminated food and water, being bitten by infected mosquitoes, driving on chaotic roads in rickety cars and buses, working in perilous sweatshops, being exposed to raw, untreated sewage, or breathing fumes belching from unregulated vehicles and industrial factories. The essential corrective to these hazardous conditions is to prioritize population-level strategies, using well-understood, relatively low-cost interventions.

Despite the manifest benefits of healthy built and natural environments, structural factors often push governments toward discrete, disease-based health care over broader public health infrastructure. Driven by domestic political pressures and international donors to show clear, measurable near-term benefits, governments often underinvest in public goods whose benefits accrue over the long term. The problem manifests itself in many public sector services that affect health, such as roads, mass transit, schools, electricity, and clean energy.

Beyond the pressure to deliver short-term results, governments face a "rescue imperative," which often drives political leaders to spend disproportionately on specialized medical and emergency services. Whether it is a little girl in a well or a mother with advanced breast cancer, identifiable lives have faces, names, and stories that are politically compelling. It is much harder to mobilize resources for the statistical lives that might be saved over the long term through population-level strategies.

Consider the effectiveness of even the most prominent humanitarian relief effort. The international community poured $8 billion into Haiti—one of the world's least developed countries—in the aftermath of the devastating 2010 earthquake. Yet, years after the crisis, despite billions of dollars in reconstruction aid, the most obvious, pressing needs—potable water, sanitation, safe/stable housing, and electricity—remained unmet. Only a fraction of the aid disbursed went to building a public health infrastructure, with the lion's share going to current programs, medicines, and a teaching hospital. With all the goodwill and money pouring in, international officials were determined to transform not only an intractably poor country, but also an ineffectual humanitarian relief system. But weak governance, donors' pet projects, and the continuation of the aid-business-as-usual, undercut those lofty goals.[22]

Even though public health investments are hard to achieve, they are well worth the expenditure of economic and political capital. The health of a population can never be realized when interventions are medically based and primarily directed at individuals. Rather, the building blocks of public health must be in place before a society can effectively realize the benefits of strong health care systems. The public health approach, therefore, would likely bring us a long way toward the goal of markedly improved global health, but it would do more than that: it would embed justice in the environment in which everyone shares, rich and poor alike. Global health *with justice* is the subject to which we now turn.

What Would Global Health with Justice Look Like?

Looking at aggregate metrics, the international community has made remarkable progress in global health over the past half century. Global life expectancy increased from forty-seven years in 1955 to sixty-eight in 2010. The global infant mortality rate per 1,000 live births was 148 in 1955 and has dropped to 43 today.[23] Yet amid these positive overall trends, deep inequities persist. As we have seen, progress in global health often conforms to a distributional pattern: advancements accrue to the well-off first and trickle down to disadvantaged populations slowly, if at all. We have seen this pattern emerge with virtually every major challenge—AIDS, tobacco, injuries, and so on.

Is this distributional pattern of health acceptable, provided there is continuing improvement in overall outcomes? The first point to clarify is that inequitable distribution of health is by no means a necessary precondition of aggregate improvements. Economic inequalities—which are deeply intertwined with health disparities—are sometimes rationalized on grounds that promoting equity would slow overall growth, leaving everyone worse off. It may be comforting for those privileged by current arrangements to explain away global health inequalities along similar lines. Or high-income governments may be so proud of their concrete measures of success in foreign assistance (e.g., persons in treatment, eradication of disease, or lives saved) that they do not stop to ask whether the benefits accrue to all equitably.

Whatever the merits in economics or politics, these rationalizations of inequality are implausible when carried over to global health.[24] Whether inequality is good for economic growth—and this is a doubtful proposition[25]—it is demonstrably bad for health. In international comparisons, countries with more equal wealth distribution have higher life expectancies regardless of per capita GDP. The same phenomenon exists within countries. In the United States, for example, states with the largest health disparities have the slowest increases in life expectancy. In short, there is no reason to fear that the promotion of health equity will drive down aggregate health outcomes, as the evidence is quite to the contrary: justice, it turns out, is "good for your health."[26]

Embedding Justice in Human Ecology

Given the reality of limited resources, there is an implicit trade-off between a society's investment in state-of-the-art medical interventions, on the one hand, and investments in population-level health strategies, on the other. In the developed world, the United States offers an extreme example of this trade-off: at once a world leader in cutting-edge medical technology, while trailing much poorer countries in population health metrics (e.g., infant mortality and longevity)[27]—spending only 1–2 percent of health dollars on public health.[28] At the same time, the United States has one of the world's highest levels of economic inequality. The problem is not how much the United States spends—no country spends more on health per capita. It is rather a question of skewed priorities and a severe, and worsening, underinvestment in population-level prevention strategies. As the Institute of Medicine observes, the United States "spends extravagantly on clinical care but meagerly on other types of population-based actions that influence health more profoundly than medical services, . . . taking a growing toll on the economy and society."[29] On average, social expenditures outside health care in OECD countries is double their health care spending; in the United States, by contrast, health care spending exceeds non–health care social spending.[30]

The stakes in this trade-off are much higher in the developing world, where many live at the very margins of survival for lack of basic necessities. At least in the United States, inhabitants—rich or poor—for the most part can drink clean water, use flushing toilets, eat uncontaminated food, remain free of malaria-infected mosquitoes, and rely on reasonable health and safety regulations at work, at home, and in consumer products. The same cannot be said for the masses in many lower-income countries, or for that matter in powerful emerging economies such as Brazil, Indonesia, or Thailand.

Earlier we saw that investments in public health yield tremendous benefits in improved health outcomes. What is less often understood is that such investments will generally have the added benefit of promoting equity in the *distribution* of health. When countries invest in genuinely public goods—such as water supply systems, sanitation, sewage systems, safe roads, vector abatement, and pollution control—the benefits will, for the most part, accrue to rich and poor alike. The key point is that when government embeds healthy and safe conditions within the environment (not simply allocating services to particular individuals or groups), all human beings who live in that setting will benefit—simply by the fact that they inhabit the same space.

Viewed in this way, the primary manifestations of justice in global health may look rather mundane. Justice in health is not primarily realized by delivering heroic medical interventions or through courtroom victories vindicating an individual's right to some particular therapy. Rather, justice will primarily be embedded in features of day-to-day life that are often taken for granted: the tap flowing clean water, the toilet that flushes, the neighborhood market selling affordable nourishing food, public sanitation controlling the spread of disease, well-regulated industries, and so on.

Adopting this perspective involves, in part, a broadened understanding of the institutional actors responsible for promoting and protecting global health justice. While national governments, and particularly their ministries of health, must bear primary responsibility, it is clear that a host of other actors have a vital role to play.

To begin, given the wide range of factors implicated in public health and the socioeconomic determinants of health, it is imperative that all ministries of government coordinate in the protection and promotion of health. In recent years, across many countries, we have seen the gradual adoption of a "health-in-all-policies" (HiAP) approach within government.[31] The trend reflects the recognition that health outcomes are largely determined by policies falling outside the traditional portfolio of health ministries. For example, a government scheme of cash transfers to low-income populations, frequently with conditions attached, are demonstrating positive health effects in areas as diverse as HIV infection rates and childhood illness.[32] The HiAP approach is a kind of process innovation: governments commit to routinely assessing the health impact of policy initiatives, with a view to promoting optimal health outcomes. When effectively implemented, the HiAP strategy achieves many of the foundational principles of good governance discussed in Chapter 3—civic engagement, transparency, and accountability for the health impacts of government action and inaction.

However, responsibility cannot rest with government alone, requiring an all-of-society strategy. As we have seen with tobacco control and HIV/AIDS, political institutions often fail to initiate action, or make progress, without the prodding of social movements. And as we saw in the discussion of NCDs, efforts to build a healthier world are bound to fail without the engagement of the private sector and the media, whose decisions shape the health landscape in myriad ways, ranging from dietary options and physical activity to workplace safety. And when the private sector fails to transform toward healthier and safer products, governments have a responsibility to regulate their activities.

Many of the basic conditions of health are beyond the power of national governments to fully control—even where they have enlisted cooperation from all of society. As explored in previous chapters, globalization drives multiple risk factors: infectious diseases through travel and trade; NCDs through urbanization, trade in tobacco, and the harmonization of marketing and cultures; and injuries and illness stemming from global supply chains for consumer products. Just as at the national level, international actors must consciously prioritize health among competing norms (e.g., trade and development). The international community, moreover, has an obligation to provide financial and technical support to assist poorer countries in securing the essential conditions of health for all.[33]

This picture of *what justice in global health looks like* entails a fundamental shift in our understanding of the right to health. The right to health must be conceived primarily as a collective right, imposing obligations on governments, and in turn implicating all of society. There remains an important role for safeguarding individual rights and the rights of vulnerable groups, but the implementation of broader public health measures is a precondition for securing these more targeted rights. This is the population-based approach, which brings the benefits of improved health for all with an embedded form of social justice.

All of this considerably complicates the conventional picture of rights holders and correlative duty bearers. With so many actors at the table, and such diffuse obligations, how do we establish order out of the chaos? That question will be explored in the final section of this chapter, on achieving global health with justice, which sketches the institutions, monitoring, and enforcement mechanisms needed to achieve the vision of global health with justice.

Correcting Barriers to Access

As indicated, investments in public health tend, broadly speaking, to promote equity by default—insofar as these are mostly nondivisible, nonexcludable goods and services, their benefits flow to all. It will not suffice, however, to simply invest in public health and trust that everyone will benefit. There will often be barriers to access, particularly for disadvantaged groups or those in either crowded inner cities or remote rural villages.

In some cases, barriers exist in the literal sense. The homeless may be denied access to benefits of public water systems—the dignity of a private, safe space in which to bathe or urinate. For those living in remote regions, or simply outside of urban centers, distance may be a barrier to public health interventions (e.g., vaccination campaigns). For persons with disabilities, services may be accessible only with appropriate accommodations. Where interventions take the form of information and knowledge, language, culture, or illiteracy may block access.

These examples reflect comparatively straightforward and foreseeable accessibility barriers. Often, problems of accessibility are detected only after the fact, as surveillance reveals that a given group is experiencing outcomes or risk exposures that lag behind the population as a whole. It remains an open question, for example, why disadvantaged socioeconomic groups have seen limited benefit from tobacco control or why they have vastly higher rates of diabetes, tuberculosis, and HIV/AIDS.

Challenges related to accessibility are solved, ultimately, through adherence to principles of good governance. Interventions must be carefully vetted and monitored on an ongoing basis for their effectiveness at reaching vulnerable populations. The objective is to identify and eliminate financial and nonfinancial barriers and to ensure that public health interventions are of uniformly high quality—reaching all people wherever they live. Michael Marmot and colleagues have offered the concept of "proportionate universalism," with actions that are "universal, but with a scale and intensity that is proportionate to the level of disadvantage," meaning the most intense actions are "likely to be needed for those with greater social and economic disadvantage."[34] The active participation of marginalized communities in policy-making processes is invaluable in detecting and effectively resolving barriers to access.

Equitable Allocation of Scarce Goods and Services

Although I have highlighted the efficacy and the in-built equity of population-level strategies, the dilemma of allocating scarce resources cannot be avoided altogether. Putting aside the broad question of access to health care, allocative challenges may arise in the context of prevention services targeted to populations—as with the rollout of "treatment-as-prevention" strategies to combat HIV/AIDS, the distribution of vaccines for novel and seasonal influenzas, or in disaster preparedness and relief. Notice, for example, the neglect of the most disadvantaged in the aftermath of Hurricane Katrina in the United States. Instructing everyone to evacuate or store up on food and water may seem egalitarian until one considers that the poor, elderly, and disabled do not have the means.

There is no template solution to these allocative dilemmas; what bears emphasizing again is the importance of accountable, transparent, and participatory governance. In the face of public health threats, marginalized populations are especially reliant on government as a provider of last resort. While disadvantaged groups are the least equipped to secure health services, the stressors of poverty and stigma create a heightened risk of injury and disease. It stands to reason that government must be especially accountable to these groups. In practical terms, this special accountability is achieved through advance scrutiny of allocative decisions to assess their impact on vulnerable populations, followed by monitoring their actual impact. In the interests of transparency, accountability, and participation, representatives of affected groups should have a seat at the table as this process plays out.

How Do We Achieve Global Health with Justice?

To this point, I have loosely outlined what justice in global health might look like, particularly from the perspective of those less advantaged. In so doing, I have pressed for a shift in priorities, toward increased investment in upstream population-level strategies. In this last section, I want to explore what all of this might require on the level of governance, nationally and globally.

As the concept is broadly defined in this book, global governance for health concerns the rules, norms, institutions, and processes that shape the health of the world's population. By now it should be clear that I conceptualize governance as dynamic and normative. My aim is not to detachedly describe the workings of global health, but to explore how those workings might be actively reorganized and steered, with a view to ensuring all human beings the opportunity for a long and healthy life.

I have put forth a number of suggestions, including a suite of prevention strategies to contain the NCD crisis, a global insurance scheme for influenza vaccines, and WHO reform. Here, I will explore six current initiatives that target major challenges facing the field: global health leadership, good governance, sustainable financing, equitable priorities in scientific research, equitable access to the fruits of innovation, and a "new deal" for global health, such as through a Framework Convention on Global Health.

Proposals in this field must be tempered with a heavy dose of humility. The global health landscape has undergone drastic transformations. We have only an inchoate grasp of what is possible now and in the coming years. Over the past half century, the movement has rallied around divergent visions: the initial optimism for the "highest attainable standard of health"; a more tangible vision of primary health care (starting with Alma-Ata in 1978, reaffirmed in 2008); various disease-specific targets; and the MDGs, along with the emerging post-2015 sustainable development agenda. These were, and remain, noble visions, reflecting the best intentions and understandings of deeply committed advocates and leaders. Our task in arriving at a new vision for global health is to learn from past experiences, adapting global governance to both new and enduring challenges.

At the same time, today's global health landscape is increasingly complex, populated by more than one hundred organizations, often with competing programs and priorities. Trying to schematize this landscape—organizing institutions, norms, and processes into a clear hierarchy—would be impossible. This complexity is now a fact of life, and the architecture of global governance must embrace it rather than pursue easy answers. This need not mean acquiescing to fragmentation and inefficiency, which has a cost in human lives. But it does advise that we tread cautiously when exploring fundamental restructuring.

Global Health Leadership: Rationalizing a Fragmented System

Improved leadership is needed to champion health in international affairs, coordinate diverse stakeholders, and set priorities to advance global health with justice. Although the WHO has been the subject of legitimate criticism, no rival organization is better suited to undertake this leadership role. Private and nongovernmental organizations lack the breadth of the WHO's membership and its democratic accountability to member states. Other international institutions (e.g., the World Bank, UNAIDS, and the Global Fund) play a major role, but none possesses the WHO's broad health mandate.

The very idea of the WHO steering a coherent path for global health—rationalizing the behavior of fragmented actors—did not seem far-fetched when the organization was established in 1948, its constitution entrusting the agency to "act as the directing and coordinating authority on international health work." The WHO does not have the legal powers or political and economic clout to fully harmonize disparate activities. But it does have the legitimacy (and mandate) to become an effective convener, mediator, and negotiator. Through its authority to set norms, advise member states, and convene global stakeholders, it can help guide global health activities toward country ownership, a clearer set of priorities, and increased harmonization of disparate activities.

Models for improved coordination already exist, albeit on a smaller scale. The Three Ones initiative spearheaded by UNAIDS committed AIDS funders to harmonize their efforts—working under one national action framework, one national coordinating body, and one country-level monitoring and evaluation system.[35] The H4+—comprising the WHO, UNFPA, UNICEF, and the World Bank—coordinate work on maternal and child health,[36] while the Health 8 (H8) increase harmonization among seven multilateral organizations and the Gates Foundation.[37] Meanwhile the World Bank, the GAVI Alliance, and the Global Fund collaborate on health system strengthening.[38]

The leadership challenge, of course, grows more complicated as goals are broadened to encompass the essential conditions of health and as the number of actors multiplies. Historically, the WHO's leadership has been undermined by factionalism and distrust among member states, along with competition from other international institutions vying for money and influence.[39] No matter how savvy and effective the WHO's leadership may be, successful coordination of global health will fail without buy-in from stakeholders: unless states adequately fund the organization with un-tied resources and give the Secretariat political support, the WHO will not be able to succeed.

One way to assert leadership would be for the WHO to launch negotiations for a comprehensive global health accord with itself at the helm. Later, I discuss such an international agreement—whether in the form of a treaty-based FCGH such as Ban Ki-moon[40] and Michel Sidibé[41] support, or a softer normative "framework for global health," as proposed by Margaret Chan.[42]

Good Governance: The Values of Stewardship

If gaping health disparities are ever to be resolved, this will require a shift in mind-set—with assurance of the essential conditions of health seen as a matter of basic justice. Global solidarity is difficult to kindle and quickly extinguished by perceptions of corruption and dishonesty. Thus a grand vision for global health must be accompanied by an abiding commitment to good governance.

I have laid out in Chapter 3 what I take to be the underlying, universal values of good governance: honesty, transparency, participatory deliberation, efficiency, and accountability. Apart from its inherent worth in building open and honest institutions, adherence to values of good governance is directly linked to improved health outcomes.[43] Genuine transformations in population health require stakeholders to act with integrity, adopt open processes, engage civil society as partners, manage efficiently, set targets, monitor outcomes, and subject themselves to processes of accountability.

Inculcating these values into the workings of institutions and governments, however, will require creative solutions. Settling upon workable solutions will require negotiation, but several possibilities exist. The international community could agree on a hard or soft accountability norm, with monitoring through a code of practice or convention such as an FCGH. Another option would be to create an incentive system, so that certain financial assistance from the international community is tied to national accountability reforms. If the latter, it will be important to ensure that a country's population does not further suffer as a result of its government's failure to govern well.

The assumption throughout this book has been that national governments bear primary responsibility for the health of their domestic populations, drawing on the support and assistance of the global community. But the values of good governance extend beyond government. Arguably, one of the major missteps in global health of recent decades arose as international bodies imposed strict conditions on governments in the developing world (e.g., the World Bank and its structural adjustment programs) while remaining blithely optimistic about the efficiency and accountability of the private sector. And international organizations themselves often were inscrutable, accepting little genuine input from communities that had the most to gain (or lose) from the policies adopted.

Sustainable Financing Scalable to Needs: Toward a Global Fund for Health

Perhaps the most enduring and difficult challenge in global health is to ensure that programs and activities are financed in ways that are predictable, sustainable, and scalable to health needs. The most pressing resource needs are in low- and middle-income countries that lack the full capacity to ensure the conditions in which people can be healthy. As explained throughout this volume, capacity building is not a code for ever-increasing foreign assistance. The mutual responsibility approach places a primary duty on states to meet their inhabitants' health needs, but also creates a residual duty on the international community to assist—with technical advice, resources, and respect for country ownership.

Lower-income governments are not alone in needing sustainable financing. International institutions also require the economic wherewithal to fulfill their missions. The most obvious illustration is the WHO itself, plagued by restricted and unstable funding, with resources wholly incommensurate with the global health challenges it faces.[44] International assistance for health requires both bilateral and multilateral funding—directly to countries and to international organizations.

At present, the global health space is roughly divided among several leading institutions, among them the WHO, setting norms and offering technical guidance; the Global Fund, harnessing and dispersing resources for three diseases; and the GAVI Alliance, playing a similar role for childhood immunizations. If assuring the essential conditions of health is to become the major objective in global health reform, this will require agencies to move out of their silos. To this end, one might imagine a Global Fund for Health overseeing the collection and disbursal of funds to support the three conditions for healthy populations: health care systems, public health measures, and social determinants—with precedence given to the underlying conditions of health.[45]

Is it necessary to establish a new institution to oversee funding for the essential conditions of health? There would certainly be risks involved in broadening the Global Fund's mandate to support the essential health conditions rather than targeted diseases, even beyond the question of whether necessarily increased funding for the Global Fund would accompany a more expansive mandate. Governments—the Global Fund's principal financiers—are less likely to provide support for broad systemic changes that fail to capture the public's imagination. Beyond these political liabilities, established institutions such as the Global Fund specialize in delivering services for a discrete set of health conditions. Any far-reaching extension of their mandate would entail a shift in priorities and a broadening of their expertise. Plainly there are risks associated with institutional transformations of this sort, which must be weighed against the costs of continuing with the status quo. At any rate, whether built on new or preexisting infrastructures, global health reform will require reliable and well-resourced institutions, with the broad mandate to raise adequate funds to ensure the conditions for healthy people living in healthy communities.

Harnessing Innovation: An R&D Treaty

While targeting risk factors is essential—more so as one moves upstream in the disease pathway—there is also a need to harness the creativity of scientists, engineers, architects, and other innovators to develop life-saving and life-enhancing technologies. More pointedly, the global governance system must find ways to encourage innovations to address the major causes of injury and diseases, particularly among the disadvantaged.

Global health advocates have critiqued current incentive structures for research and development (R&D) for failing to adequately address the health needs of developing countries. The existing system of intellectual property and privatized research creates incentives for health technologies that can be patented and sold at a high profit. There is little financial incentive for research into diseases that primarily burden the poor, who cannot afford companies' patented products. As a result, the poor suffer and die for lack of effective diagnostics, medicines, and vaccines.

The severity of this imbalance is captured in the widely discussed "10/90" gap—the notion that only 10 percent of worldwide expenditure on health research and development is devoted to the problems primarily affecting the poorest 90 percent of the world's population. A 2004 report critiqued this analysis, saying that "neglected" diseases constitute a relatively small health burden in lower-income countries.[46] Nevertheless, the profit incentive does militate toward inventions that are lucrative—high-margin products for which the global rich will pay a high price. It is symptomatic of this dynamic that pharmaceutical companies often pour resources into marketing "me-too" drugs—products having therapeutic qualities similar to those of an already marketed drug. In 2013 the Supreme Court of India, for example, ruled that Novartis could not patent the lucrative cancer drug Gleevec because it did not possess "enhanced or superior efficacy" over previous formulations (see Box 9.5, Chapter 9).[47]

In an effort to address this market failure—and to provide incentives for research based on health needs rather than profitability—the WHO created the Consultative Expert Working Group on Research and Development (CEWG).[48] The 2012 CEWG report urged the WHO to negotiate a global health treaty to enhance R&D, primarily to meet the needs of developing countries. The key mechanisms would include obligations to (1) invest a certain percentage of national income in R&D, including devoting a small portion to a new multilateral pooled funding system; (2) augment the innovative capacity of developing countries; and (3) transfer technology to developing countries and expand their access to scientific knowledge. A critical principle underlying the report was to delink the costs of R&D from the prices of the drugs.[49]

Initial reaction to the report was favorable, with even pharmaceutical companies offering preliminary support, recognizing that the treaty could infuse new resources into the R&D pipeline without infringing on intellectual property rights.[50] However, high-income countries resisted the accord, concerned about incurring a legal obligation to expend resources while relinquishing control over the proposed pooled funding system. Moreover, these countries saw little benefit to their own citizens.[51] Although the prospects of an R&D treaty appear dim in the near term, the CEWG advanced the international dialogue about the importance of scientific innovation and the role of international law in addressing global health disparities.

Equitable Access to the Fruits of Innovation: A "Health Impact" Fund

If R&D is to truly benefit developing countries, the poor must have equitable access to the fruits of innovation. There are many medical technologies that would be of major value everywhere—for example, medication for cholesterol, diabetes, cancer, neglected tropical diseases, or AIDS, TB, and malaria. But too often these medicines are priced out of the reach of the poor. A mechanism is needed to stimulate investment in high-impact drugs that actually reach the poor. Civil society and academics have offered a number of important proposals to make essential medicines more affordable, among them the Medicines Patent Pool (see Box 10.3, Chapter 10).

Thomas Pogge and Aidan Hollis have proposed an innovative reform—a Health Impact Fund (HIF) to create a market-based scheme to develop and distribute medications that reduce the global burden of disease.[52] States and stakeholders would contribute to the fund, with funding distributed to biotechnology and pharmaceutical companies that fulfill a large unmet need, as measured by a standardized unit such as the DALY. Patent holders would register new medicines or new uses of existing medicines with the fund, thereby agreeing to distribute the drug worldwide at cost. The HIF, in return, would give an annual reward to companies based on their measurable contribution to overall health outcomes. Registrants would remain eligible for reward payments for ten years from the time of marketing approval, after which they would agree to generic manufacturing. The HIF would act as a corrective to the perverse incentives of the existing intellectual property system.

Toward a New Deal in Global Governance for Health

Global governance for health is at a defining moment: the WHO is facing a budgetary shortfall, the proliferation of actors has fragmented the system, and a disease-specific focus has diverted resources from a broad range of health services. At the same time, the United Nations is deliberating over its post-MDG agenda. Global health resources could have far greater impact with more effective governance and institutional structures. "Put more directly, today and every day, people will die and lives will not be improved because of the way global health is governed and implemented."[53] With all these transformations in global health, this is an opportune time to implement major reforms aimed at achieving global health with justice.

What is needed is a new deal for global health, just as the Bretton Woods system of monetary management revolutionized commerce and finance in the mid-twentieth century, creating the International Monetary Fund and the World Bank. Mark Dybul, Peter Piot, and Julio Frenk have proposed a Bretton Woods–style agreement to transform global health governance.[54] With the newly emergent G20 taking a lead, this new deal would change the global health architecture to foster genuine partnerships and mutual responsibility for health. Whether or not the G20 will take up this formidable challenge is an open question; in recent years global health has not made its agenda, crowded out by financial crises and trade.

To achieve a more integrated health system, the global health architecture must move to a more cohesive model for financing and service delivery. As discussed earlier, a new Global Fund for Health could become the primary global health financier. At the same time, a new deal would have to rationalize the activities of diverse global health actors so that they strive for common goals and synergistic planning and programs.

A global architectural model successfully used in other contexts is a framework convention–protocol approach (Table 14.1). The Framework Convention on Tobacco Control (FCTC) offers proof of concept in the health sphere, while the UN Framework Convention on Climate Change (with its Kyoto Protocol) exists in the environmental sphere. While creating binding international law, the framework/protocol approach is incremental, allowing states parties to continually deepen their normative obligations. First, parties negotiate broad "framework" principles, which leave a degree of latitude for states to craft their own domestic laws. More complex or controversial issues can then be resolved through future negotiation of specific protocols. This governance dynamic, starting

Table 14.1 The Framework Convention–Protocol Approach

Definition—A binding treaty using an incremental process whereby states negotiate a framework with key normative standards. More stringent obligations can be subsequently created through protocols. The Framework Convention on Global Health (FCGH) would create fair terms of international cooperation and clear national obligations grounded in the right to health. It would aim to solve the defining global health issues of our time in a more systemic and integrated way, advancing global justice with its dual imperatives of domestic and global health equity.
Current models—The framework/protocol approach has become an important strategy of transnational social movements to safeguard health and the environment. The Kyoto Protocol to the UN Framework Convention on Climate Change sets specific levels for greenhouse gas emissions. The WHO Framework Convention on Tobacco Control sets global standards for reducing the demand for, and supply of, tobacco.
Institutional structures—The FCGH envisions linkages between existing institutional structures and newly created ones: a Secretariat, possibly hosted by the WHO, the Conference of Parties (implementing FCGH duties and drafting protocols), an Intergovernmental Panel on Global Health (facilitating and evaluating scientific research on innovative solutions), and a high-level Intersectoral Consortium on Global Health (placing health on the agendas of multiple sectors).
Advantages—The framework convention–protocol approach is flexible, allowing states to agree to politically feasible obligations, saving contentious issues for later protocols. It enables a bottom-up process of social mobilization for health and health justice.

with open-ended negotiations and leading to firm action by countries, is sometimes termed "the power of the process."[55] The end result, ideally, would help set priorities and coordinate diverse stakeholders, implemented with genuine partnerships and deliberative participation.

The perceived success of the FCTC has led to calls for the WHO to negotiate framework conventions targeting other major risk factors—notably on alcohol, which bears important similarities to tobacco (ubiquity, addictiveness, transnational trade, inequities in the resulting disease burden, harm to third parties, and vehement industry opposition).[56] From the public health perspective advocated in this chapter, the central appeal of these recent initiatives lies in their targeting of upstream risk factors.

Although there has been enthusiasm for building on the FCTC precedent, the framework/protocol approach requires perseverance. For one thing, the sheer investment of time and resources involved in negotiating a framework convention can be daunting—at least if the FCTC is a guide. A decade elapsed from the time that the World Health Assembly first asked the D-G to explore the feasibility of a tobacco treaty in 1995 to its ratification in 2005, and another seven years passed before the adoption of its first protocol in late 2012. And as its key architects have explained, FCTC negotiations had the benefit of fortuitous circumstances: as it was the first treaty of its kind, negotiations were able to proceed mostly under the radar of the tobacco industry. The alcohol industry will no doubt learn from this mistake and strenuously oppose any treaty process from the outset.[57]

Framework Convention on Global Health (FCGH)

A proposal with which I have been deeply involved would employ the framework/protocol model toward a more ambitious end, engaging the global community in an ongoing dialogue to arrive at concrete commitments and accountability mechanisms for honoring the right to health and reducing health inequities.[58] A global coalition of civil society and academics—the Joint Action and Learning Initiative on National and Global Responsibilities for Health (JALI)[59]—has initiated an international campaign to advocate for a Framework Convention on Global Health (FCGH).[60]

UN Secretary-General Ban Ki-moon has issued a clarion call for the FCGH: "Let the AIDS response be a beacon of global solidarity for health as a human right and set the stage for a future United Nations Framework Convention on Global Health."[61] In a similar vein, the head of UNAIDS, Michel Sidibé, and his colleague Kent Buse ask, "What better way to [advance health and dignity] than by rekindling our common interest in the right to health?" They called for "unprecedented social and political mobilization towards a framework convention on global health."[62]

The FCGH would reimagine global governance for health, offering a new vision. Although creating a bold global health treaty is an enormous undertaking, it could begin as a soft, nonbinding instrument—something WHO Director-General Margaret Chan has referred to as a "framework for global health."[63] (Table 14.2 describes the key modalities of an FCGH.)

An FCGH would cover in a structured way the major global health challenges discussed in this volume:

Table 14.2 **A Framework Convention on Global Health—Objectives and Modalities**

Objective	FCGH Modalities
Define state responsibilities for the health of their domestic populations	Establish domestic funding targets covering health care, public health, and the social determinants of health, with timelines for compliance. Establish responsibilities for enhancing health equity and ensuring participation in health-related decision making, and provide for accountability.
Define international responsibilities to provide sustainable funding	Establish a global health financing framework to ensure reliable funding. Equitably apportion responsibilities according to resource capacities and health needs.
Define the right to health to meet health needs and reduce global health disparities	Establish agreed-upon definitions for "universal coverage" and "health equity" and right to health standards such as maximum available resources. Strengthen commitments under WHO codes of practice and global strategies, such as reducing health worker recruitment in developing countries with personnel shortages. Update the right to health for a globalized world, including the responsibility to regulate transnational corporations vis-à-vis their health impacts.
Ensure that policies in key domains (e.g., trade, agriculture, environment) promote health and health equity	States commit to a health-in-all-policies approach. The WHO is charged with engaging with and coordinating multiple sectors.
Create innovative financing mechanisms for health	States commit to innovative financing for health, such as a tax on financial transactions, unhealthy foods, and alcoholic beverages.
Improve empirical monitoring of progress and setbacks in implementing the right to health	Establish standardized methods of data gathering and benchmarks for measuring progress on health outcomes and health equity.
Promote sound models of global governance for health	States commit to good governance (e.g., transparency, engagement, and accountability) and mechanisms to effectuate its principles. The WHO to lead a health-focused multisectoral consortium.
Promote strong global health leadership	Strengthen the WHO with sustainable funding, expertise to develop evidence-based innovative solutions, and normative authority to implement those solutions.

- *The right to health*—providing more specificity on its normative obligations, including defining the goods and services to which everyone is entitled under human rights law, with particular attention to the health needs of marginalized communities; enhancing understanding of this right and its incorporation into policy; and enabling people to more effectively claim their right to health.
- *Upstream priority setting*—ensuring that health priorities encompass prevention and assuring the conditions for health (e.g., systemic changes in public health and social determinants).
- *Mutual responsibility*—creating clear domestic and international responsibilities on states parties to ensure the health of their inhabitants, and a duty for wealthier states to build capacities in partnership with lower-income states.
- *Innovative financing*—harnessing resources for health, such as through taxes on air travel, financial transactions, and unhealthy foods.
- *Health in all policies*—encouraging governments to work with multiple ministries and societal stakeholders to assess health impacts and promote healthy activities.
- *Multisectoral engagement*—implementing the global governance for health strategy of engaging international sectors affecting health, such as trade, intellectual property, and the environment.
- *Good governance*—ensuring clear targets, monitoring outcomes, and establishing accountability for results through honest, transparent governance with the active participation of marginalized communities.

If the bold vision of a global health treaty does become a reality, it would enshrine the international value of "health for all, justice for all," empowering communities to claim the right to health domestically and internationally.[64]

Seizing the Moment for Global Health

I began, in the preface, by marveling at the world's growing awareness and concern for global health. Lest readers despair at the complexity and diversity of global health challenges, bear in mind that these are, in a very real sense, good problems to have. Better to be faced with the task of rationalizing the activities of disparate actors than to be faced with the indifference and disengagement that plagued global health for decades.

But this is certainly no time for complacency: the international community's concern for global health could dissipate as quickly as it formed. If the global health movement stalls in its progress, there is every reason to believe that affluent states, philanthropists, and celebrities will simply move on to another cause. And if they do, the vicious cycle of poverty and endemic disease among the world's least healthy people will continue unabated.

NOTES

GLOSSARY

ACKNOWLEDGMENTS

INDEX

Notes

1. Global Health Justice

1. World Health Organization (WHO), *World Health Statistics 2013* (Geneva: WHO, 2013), 58–59; WHO et al., *Trends in Maternal Mortality: 1990–2010* (Geneva: WHO, 2012), 19. The life expectancy at birth of high-income countries in 2011 was eighty years, compared with fifty-six years in sub-Saharan Africa.
2. Juan Garay, "Global Health (GH) = GH Equity = GH Justice = Global Social Justice: The Opportunities of Joining EU and US Forces Together," *Newsletter of the European Union of Excellence at the University of California, Berkeley* (Winter 2012).
3. United Nations Children's Fund (UNICEF) and WHO, *Progress on Drinking Water and Sanitation: 2012 Update* (New York: UNICEF, 2012), 2; UN Food and Agriculture Organization, *The State of Food Insecurity in the World 2012* (Rome: UN Food and Agriculture Organization, 2012), 8.
4. Vincent Navarro, "What We Mean by Social Determinants of Health," *Global Health Promotion* 16, no. 1 (2009): 5–16.
5. Organization for Economic Cooperation and Development (OECD), *The Paris Declaration on Aid Effectiveness: Ownership, Harmonisation, Alignment, Results, and Mutual Accountability* (Paris: OECD, 2005); *The Accra Agenda for Action: 2005/2008* (Paris and Accra: OECD, 2005, 2008); Global Fund to Fight AIDS, Tuberculosis and Malaria, "About the Global Fund," http://www.theglobalfund.org/en/about/ (accessed 10/10/12).
6. WHO, *World Health Statistics 2013*, 141.
7. Institute for Health Metrics and Evaluation, *Financing Global Health 2010: Development Assistance and Country Spending in Economic Uncertainty* (Seattle: University of Washington, 2010), 15–16. This international health assistance includes funding from governments and multilateral institutions, and accessible data on U.S. NGOs and foundations. The figure for 2010 represents a preliminary estimate.
8. David Stuckler and Martin McKee, "Five Metaphors about Global-Health Policy," *The Lancet* 372, no. 9633 (2008): 95–97.
9. Jennifer P. Ruger and Nora Y. Ng, "Emerging and Transitioning Countries' Role in Global Health," *Saint Louis University Journal of Health Law and Policy* 3, no. 2 (2010): 253–290.

10. African Union (AU), *Roadmap on Shared Responsibility and Global Solidarity for AIDS, TB and Malaria Response in Africa* (Addis Ababa, Ethiopia: African Union, 2012), 11.
11. UN Committee on Economic, Social and Cultural Rights (CESCR), General Comment No. 14, "The Right to the Highest Attainable Standard of Health," UN Doc. E/C.12/2000/4, August 11, 2000.
12. CESCR, General Comment No. 3, "The Nature of States Parties' Obligations (Art. 2 Para. 1 of the Covenant)," UN Doc. E/1991/23, December 14, 1990.
13. UN General Assembly (UNGA), "International Covenant on Economic, Social and Cultural Rights," (1966), entered into force January 3, 1976, art. 2.
14. UNGA, Resolution 64/292, "The Human Rights to Water and Sanitation," July 28, 2010.
15. WHO, *Everybody's Business: Strengthening Health Systems to Improve Health Outcomes: WHO's Framework for Action* (Geneva: WHO, 2007).
16. WHO, London School of Hygiene and Tropical Medicine, and South African Medical Research Council, *Global and Regional Estimates of Violence against Women: Prevalence and Health Effects of Intimate Partner Violence and Non-partner Sexual Violence* (Geneva: WHO, 2013), 2.
17. Michael Marmot, *The Status Syndrome: How Social Standing Affects Our Health and Longevity* (New York: Henry Holt and Company, 2004), 38–39.
18. WHO, *World Health Report: Health Systems Financing; The Path to Universal Coverage* (Geneva: WHO, 2010), 22.
19. WHO, *World Health Statistics 2013*, 140.
20. Organisation of African Unity, "Abuja Declaration on HIV/AIDS, Tuberculosis and Other Related Infectious Diseases," April 27, 2001.
21. AU Assembly, Declaration 1(XV), "Actions on Maternal, Newborn and Child Health and Development in Africa by 2015," July 27, 2010.
22. WHO, *World Health Statistics 2013*, 140.
23. Ministers of Finance and Ministers of Health of Africa, *Tunis Declaration on Value for Money, Sustainability and Accountability in the Health Sector* (Tunis, Tunisia: African Development Bank, 2012), 3.
24. Chunling Lu et al., "Public Financing of Health in Developing Countries: A Cross-National Systematic Analysis," *The Lancet* 375, no. 9723 (2010): 1375–1387.
25. Maureen Lewis, "Corruption and Health in Twenty-Two Countries in Developing and Transition Economies," presentation, Anti-Corruption Resource Center, http://www.u4.no/assets/themes/health/Corruption-and-Health-in-Developing-and-Transition-Economies.pdf (accessed 10/10/13); Taryn Vian et al., eds., *Anticorruption in the Health Sector: Strategies for Transparency and Accountability* (Sterling, VA: Kumarian Press, 2010); Jillian C. Kohler, *Fighting Corruption in the Health Sector: Methods, Tools, and Good Practices* (New York: United Nations Development Program, 2011).

26. José Tavares, "Does Foreign Aid Corrupt?," *Economics Letters* 79, no. 1 (2003): 99–106.
27. Norman Daniels, *Just Health: Meeting Health Needs Fairly* (New York: Cambridge University Press, 2008), 140–158; Jennifer Prah Ruger, "Global Health Governance as Shared Health Governance," in I. Glenn Cohen, ed., *The Globalization of Health Care: Legal and Ethical Issues* (New York: Oxford University Press, 2013), 384, 397–398.
28. George J. Schieber et al., "Financing Global Health: Mission Unaccomplished," *Health Affairs* 26, no. 4 (2007): 921–934.
29. WHO Commission on Macroeconomics and Health, *Macroeconomics and Health: Investing in Health for Economic Development* (Geneva: WHO, 2001), 92.
30. Millennium Development Goals (MDG) Africa Steering Group, *Achieving the Millennium Development Goals in Africa: Recommendations of the MDG Africa Steering Group, June 2008* (New York: UN Department of Public Information, 2008), 30–31.
31. Author's calculation based in part on Adam Wexler et al., *Donor Funding for Health in Low- and Middle-Income Countries, 2002–2010* (Washington, DC: Kaiser Family Foundation, 2013), 3.
32. Taskforce on Innovative International Financing for Health Systems, *More Money for Health, and More Health for the Money* (Geneva and Washington, DC: WHO and World Bank, 2009), 4.
33. "Fiscal Space and Sustainability: Towards a Solution for the Health Sector," in *High-Level Forum on the Health MDGs, November 14–15, 2005* (Paris: International Hospital Federation, 2005), ii.
34. Gorik Ooms et al., "Crowding Out: Are Relations between International Health Aid and Government Health Funding Too Complex to Be Captured in Averages Only?," *The Lancet* 375, no. 9723 (2010): 1403–1405.
35. Lawrence O. Gostin and Emily A. Mok, "Grand Challenges in Global Health Governance," *British Medical Record* 90, no. 1 (2009): 7–18; Devi Sridhar, "Seven Challenges in International Development Assistance for Health and Ways Forward," *Journal of Law, Medicine and Ethics* 38, no. 3 (2010): 459–469.

2. Globalized Health Hazards

1 Derek Yach and Douglas Bettcher, "The Globalization of Public Health I: Threats and Opportunities," *American Journal of Public Health* 88, no. 5 (1998): 735–738.
2. David P. Fidler, "The Globalization of Public Health: Emerging Infectious Diseases and International Relations," *Indiana Journal of Global Legal Studies* 5, no. 1 (1997): 11–51.
3. Rafael Lozano et al., "Global and Regional Mortality from 235 Causes of Death for Twenty Age Groups in 1990 and 2010: A Systematic Analysis for the Global Burden of Disease Study 2010," *The Lancet* 380, no. 9859 (2012): 2095–2128.

4. Kate E. Jones et al., "Global Trends in Emerging Infectious Diseases," *Nature* 451, no. 7181 (2008): 990–993.
5. Stephen S. Morse, "Factors in the Emergence of Infectious Diseases," *Emerging Infectious Diseases* 1, no. 1 (1995): 7–15.
6. David M. Morens et al., "The Challenge of Emerging and Re-emerging Infectious Diseases," *Nature* 430, no. 6996 (2004): 242–249.
7. Institute of Medicine (IOM), *Microbial Threats to Health: Emergence, Detection, and Response* (Washington, DC: National Academies Press, 2003), 53–148.
8. Laurie Garrett and Scott Rosenstein, "Missed Opportunities: Governance of Global Infectious Diseases," *Harvard International Review* 27, no. 1 (2005): 64–69.
9. David P. Fidler and Lawrence O. Gostin, *Biosecurity in the Global Age: Biological Weapons, Public Health, and the Rule of Law* (Palo Alto, CA: Stanford University Press, 2008), 23–54.
10. WHO, *Cities and Public Health Crises* (Lyon, France: WHO Press, 2009), 4.
11. Norwegian Directorate of Health, *Migration and Health—Challenges and Trends* (Oslo: Norwegian Directorate of Health, 2009), 15.
12. Mary E. Wilson, "Travel and the Emergence of Infectious Diseases," *Emerging Infectious Diseases* 1, no. 2 (1995): 39–46.
13. Centers for Disease Control and Prevention, "Swine Influenza A (H1N1) Infection in Two Children—Southern California, March–April 2009," *Morbidity and Mortality Weekly Report* 58 (April 24, 2009): 400–402. Although the first H1N1 cases were thought to emerge from Mexico, arguably two earlier laboratory-confirmed cases were reported in California.
14. An interactive step-by-step tool for tracking events of the H1N1 epidemic, *H1N1 Timeline: Meeting the Challenge,* is available at http://www.flu.gov/blog/2010/01/timeline.html.
15. William B. Karesh et al., "Wildlife Trade and Global Disease Emergence," *Emerging Infectious Diseases* 11, no. 7 (2005): 1000–1002.
16. William B. Karesh and Robert A. Cook, "The Human-Animal Link," *Foreign Affairs* 84, no. 4 (2005): 38–50. More than 60 percent of known infectious diseases are capable of infecting both humans and animals, with most diseases originating in animals and crossing the species barrier to humans.
17. IOM, *Sustaining Global Surveillance and Response to Emerging Zoonotic Diseases* (Washington, DC: National Academies Press, 2009), 1.
18. Jones et al., "Global Trends," 991. Twenty-one percent of EID events are caused by drug-resistant microbes.
19. Joseph Goldstein, "Woman from Texas Is Charged in Ricin Case," *New York Times*, June 8, 2013, A10.
20. Lozano et al., "Global and Regional Mortality," 2123; WHO, *2008–2013 Action Plan for the Global Strategy for the Prevention and Control of Noncommunicable Diseases* (Geneva: WHO Press, 2008), 5.
21. Abdesslam Boutayeb and Saber Boutayeb, "The Burden of Non-Communicable Diseases in Developing Countries," *International Journal for Equity in Health* 4 (January 2005), doi: 10.1186/1475-9276-4-2.

22. Oleg Chestnov, Shanthi Mendis, and Douglas Bettcher, "A Milestone in the Response to Non-communicable Diseases," *The Lancet* 382, no. 9891 (2013): 481–482.
23. World Health Assembly (WHA), Resolution WHA66.10, "Follow-Up to the Political Declaration of the High-Level Meeting of the General Assembly on the Prevention and Control of Non-communicable Diseases," May 27, 2013.
24. Derek Yach and Robert Beaglehole, "Globalization of Risks for Chronic Diseases Demands Global Solutions," *Perspectives on Global Development and Technology* 3, no. 1 (2004): 213–233.
25. N. R. Kleinfeld, "Modern Ways Open India's Door to Diabetes," *New York Times,* September 13, 2006, A1.
26. Geoffrey Rose, *The Strategy of Preventive Medicine* (Oxford: Oxford University Press, 1992), 135.
27. Etienne G. Krug et al., "The Global Burden of Injuries," *American Journal of Public Health* 90, no. 4 (2000): 523–526.
28. Mark Rosenberg, "Roads That Are Designed to Kill," *Boston Globe,* August 18, 2009, 13.
29. Lozano et al., "Global and Regional Mortality," 2109; Christopher J. L. Murray et al., "Disability-Adjusted Life Years (DALYs) for 291 Diseases and Injuries in Twenty-One Regions, 1990–2010: A Systematic Analysis for the Global Burden of Disease Study 2010," *The Lancet* 380, no. 9859 (2012): 2197–2223.
30. Richard A. Gosselin et al., "Injuries: The Neglected Burden in Developing Countries," *Bulletin of the World Health Organization* 87, no. 4 (2009): 246.
31. Alison Harvey et al., "Injury Prevention and the Attainment of Child and Adolescent Health," *Bulletin of the World Health Organization* 87, no. 5 (2009): 390–394.
32. United Nations General Assembly (UNGA), Resolution A/CONF.217/2013/L.3, "Final United Nations Conference on the Arms Trade Treaty, Draft Decision," March 27, 2013.
33. Christine Grillo, "A World of Hurt: Global Injuries," *Magazine of the Johns Hopkins Bloomberg School of Public Health* (Summer 2009) (quoting Adnan Hyder).
34. Margie Peden et al., eds., *World Report on Child Injury Prevention* (Geneva: WHO Press, 2008), 1.
35. R. Norton et al., "Unintentional Injuries," in *Disease Control Priorities in Developing Countries,* 2nd ed., edited by D. T. Jamison et al. (New York: Oxford University Press and World Bank, 2006), 737–754.
36. Margie Peden, "Global Collaboration on Road Traffic Injury Prevention," *International Journal of Injury Control and Safety Promotion* 12, no. 2 (2005): 85–91.
37. Ronald Labonté and Ted Shrecker, "Globalization and Social Determinants of Health: The Role of the Global Marketplace," pt. 2, *Globalization and Health* 3, no. 6 (2007): 1–17.

38. UNGA, "Convention on the Rights of the Child" (1989), entered into force September 2, 1990.
39. Adnan Hyder et al., "Childhood Drowning in Low- and Middle-Income Countries: Urgent Need for Intervention Trials," *Journal of Paediatrics and Child Health* 44, no. 4 (2008): 221–227.
40. Peden et al., *World Report on Child Injury Prevention,* 2.
41. WHO, *A WHO Plan for Burn Prevention and Care* (Geneva: WHO Press, 2008), 2–5.
42. Nicholas Kulish, "Deadly Kenyan Crash Underscores Traffic Safety Woes," *New York Times*, August 30, 2013, A4.
43. WHO, *Global Status Report on Road Safety 2013: Supporting a Decade of Action* (Geneva: WHO Press, 2013), 4.
44. Jim Yardly, "Recalling the Fire's Horror and Exposing Global Brands' Safety Gap: The Human Price," *New York Times,* December 7, 2012, A1.
45. Jim Yardly, "Tears and Rage as Hope Fades in Bangladesh," *New York Times,* April 29, 2013, A1.
46. International Labor Rights Forum (ILO), "Accord on Fire and Building Safety in Bangladesh," May 13, 2013.
47. Steven Greenhouse, "U.S. Retailers See Big Risk in Safety Plan for Factories in Bangladesh," *New York Times,* May 22, 2013, http://www.nytimes.com/2013/05/23/business/legal-experts-debate-us-retailers-risks-of-signing-bangladesh-accord.html.
48. ILO, "ILO Statement on Reform of Bangladesh Labor Law," July 22, 2013, http://www.ilo.org/global/about-the-ilo/media-centre/statements-and-speeches/wlms_218067/lang-en/index.
49. Human Rights Watch, "Bangladesh: Amended Labor Law Falls Far Short," August 29, 2013, http://www.hrw.org/news/2013/07/15/bangladesh-amended-labor-law-falls-short.
50. Jerry Davis, "Invitation to a Dialogue: Bangladesh Lessons," *New York Times,* May 8, 2013, A26.
51. World Trade Organization (WTO), *International Trade Statistics 2012*, 53, 61.
52. Walt Bogdanich, "Counterfeit Drugs' Path Eased by Free Trade Zones," *New York Times,* December 17, 2007, http://www.nytimes.com/2007/12/17/world/middleeast/17freezone.html.
53. Kathryn Senior, "Estimating the Global Burden of Foodborne Disease," *The Lancet Infectious Diseases* 9, no. 2 (2009): 80–81.
54. WHO, "Food Safety and Foodborne Illness, Fact Sheet No. 237," https://apps.who.int/inf-fs/en/fact237.html (accessed 10/10/13).
55. Julia A. Phillips, "Does 'Made in China' Translate to 'Watch Out' for Consumers? The U.S. Congressional Response to Consumer Product Safety Concerns," *Penn State International Law Review* 27, no. 1 (2008): 227–268.
56. Jonathan Liberman, "Combating Counterfeit Medicines and Illicit Trade in Tobacco Products: Minefields in Global Health Governance," *Journal of Law, Medicine and Ethics* 40, no. 2 (2012): 326–347.
57. Amir Attaran et al., "Why and How to Make an International Crime of Medicine Counterfeiting," *Journal of International Criminal Justice* 9, no. 2 (2011): 325–354.

58. William Burns, "WHO Launches Taskforce to Fight Counterfeit Drugs," *Bulletin of the World Health Organization* 84, no. 9 (2006): 689–690.
59. "Medicines: Spurious/Falsely-Labelled/Falsified/Counterfeit (SFFC) Medicines, Fact Sheet No. 275," WHO, http://www.who.int./mediacentre/fact sheets/fs275/en/.
60. Kathleen E. McLaughlin, "Fake Drugs Driving Ugandans Back to Witch Doctors," *Washington Post,* January 28, 2013, A6.
61. Council of Europe, "Convention on the Counterfeiting of Medical Products and Similar Crimes Involving Threats to Public Health," October 28, 2011, text corrected September 18–19, 2012. The convention is a multilateral treaty intended to prevent the public health threats of illegitimate drugs.
62. Ministry of Foreign Affairs of Japan, "Anti-Counterfeiting Trade Agreement," April 2010. This multilateral treaty creates a framework for international cooperation on enforcing intellectual property rights.
63. European Commission, "Statement by Commissioner Karel De Gucht on ACTA (Anti-Counterfeiting Trade Agreement)," European Union. February 22, 2012. The EU's vote to reject the ACTA was a final blow to the treaty.
64. Amir Attaran et al., "How to Achieve International Action on Falsified and Substandard Medicines," *British Medical Journal* 345, no. 7884 (2012): e7381.
65. IOM, *Countering the Problem of Falsified and Substandard Drugs* (Washington, DC: National Academies Press, 2013), 295–308.
66. WHA, Resolution WHA 65.19, "Substandard/Spurious/Falsely-Labelled/Falsified/Counterfeit Medical Products," May 26, 2012.
67. WHO, First Meeting of the Member State Mechanism on Substandard/Spurious/Falsely-Labelled/Falsified/Counterfeit Medical Products, "Proposed Programme of Work," September 17, 2012.
68. Christine A. Haller, "Made in China," *Journal of Medical Toxicology* 4, no. 2 (2008): 141–142.
69. Walt Bogdanich and Renwick McLean, "Poisoned Toothpaste in Panama Is Believed to Be from China," *New York Times,* May 19, 2007, A1.
70. Louise Story and David Barboza, "Mattel Recalls 19 Million Toys Sent from China," *New York Times,* August 15, 2007, A1.

3. Global Health Law in the Broader Currents of Global Governance for Health

1. Mark L. Rosenberg et al., *Real Collaboration: What Global Health Needs to Succeed* (Berkeley: University of California Press, 2009).
2. Lawrence O. Gostin, *Public Health Law: Power, Duty, Restraint,* 2nd ed. (Berkeley: University of California Press, 2008); Lawrence O. Gostin, ed., *Public Health Law and Ethics: A Reader,* 2nd ed. (Berkeley: University of California Press, 2010).
3. David P. Fidler, "The Future of the World Health Organization: What Role for International Law?" *Vanderbilt Journal of International Law* 31, no. 5 (1998); Allyn L. Taylor, "Making the World Health Organization Work: A Legal Framework for Universal Access to the Conditions for Health,"

American Journal of Law and Medicine 18, no. 301 (1992); Lawrence O. Gostin and Allyn L. Taylor, "Global Health Law: A Definition and Grand Challenges," *Public Health Ethics* 1, no. 1 (2008).

4. World Health Assembly (WHA), *Draft Comprehensive Mental Health Action Plan 2013–2020* (Geneva: World Health Organization [WHO], 2013), 17–18.
5. Gian L. Burci and Claude-Henri Vignes, *World Health Organization* (The Hague: Kluwer Law International, 2004), 141.
6. Jennifer S. Edge and Steven J. Hoffman, "Empirical Impact Evaluation of the WHO Global Code of Practice on the International Recruitment of Health Personnel (2010) on Government, Civil Society and Private Sectors in Australia, Canada, United Kingdom and United States of America" (paper presented at the Annual Meeting of the American Political Science Association, Seattle, Washington, September 1–4, 2011).
7. Kelli K. Garcia and Lawrence O. Gostin, "One Health, One World: The Intersecting Legal Regimes of Trade, Climate Change, Food Security, Humanitarian Crises, and Migration," *Laws* 1, no. 1 (2012): 4–38.
8. Ximena Fuentes Torrijo, "International Law and Domestic Law: Definitely an Odd Couple," *Revista Juridica de la Universidad de Puerto Rico* 77, no. 2 (2008): 484–485.
9. *Medellín v. Texas,* 552 U.S. 491 (2008). This Supreme Court decision found that a treaty is not binding domestic law unless Congress has enacted a statute implementing it or unless the treaty conveys an intention that it is self-executing.
10. WHA, Doc. A64/10, "Implementation of the International Health Regulations: Report of the Review Committee on the Functioning of the International Health Regulations (2005) in Relation to Pandemic (H1N1) 2009," May 5, 2011.
11. James N. Rosenau, "Governance in the Twenty-First Century," *Global Governance* 1, no. 1 (1995): 13–43.
12. Lawrence S. Finkelstein, "What Is Global Governance?," *Global Governance* 1, no. 3 (1995): 367–72.
13. David P. Fidler, *The Challenges of Global Health Governance* (New York: Council of Foreign Relations, 2010); Obijiofor Aginam, *Global Health Governance: International Law and Public Health in a Divided World* (Toronto: University of Toronto Press, 2005); Kent Buse et al., eds., *Making Sense of Global Health Governance—A Policy Perspective* (Basingstoke, UK: Palgrave Macmillan, 2009); Devi Sridhar and Lawrence O. Gostin, eds., "Innovations in Global Health in the New Political Era," special issue, *Global Health Governance* 2, no. 2 (Fall 2008/Spring 2009).
14. Julio Frenk and Surie Moon, "Governance Challenges in Global Health," *New England Journal of Medicine* 368, no. 10 (2013): 936–942.
15. David P. Fidler, "Global Health Governance: Overview of the Role of International Law in Protecting and Promoting Global Public Health, Discussion Paper No. 3" (working paper, WHO and London School of Hygiene and Tropical Medicine, Geneva, 2002).

16. David P. Fidler, "Architecture amidst Anarchy: Global Health's Quest for Governance," *Global Health Governance* 1, no. 1 (2007); Scott Burris, "Governance, Microgovernance and Health," *Temple Law Review* 77, no. 2 (2004): 335–361.
17. World Bank, *Managing Development: The Governance Dimension; A Discussion Paper* (Washington, DC: World Bank, 1991), 36–38.
18. Adam Nossiter, "U.S. Engages with an Iron Leader in Equatorial Guinea," *New York Times,* May 31, 2011, A4.
19. Taryn Vian, "Review of Corruption in the Health Sector: Theory, Methods and Interventions," *Health Policy and Planning* 23, no. 2 (2008): 83–94.
20. World Bank, "Six Questions on the Cost of Corruption with World Bank Institute Global Governance Director Daniel Kaufmann," http://go.worldbank.org/KQH743GKF1 (accessed 10/10/13).
21. *Glenister v President of the Republic of South Africa and Others,* 2011 3 SA 347 (CC).
22. Magnus Lindelow, Inna Kushnarova, and Kai Kaiser, "Measuring Corruption in the Health Sector: What We Can Learn from public expenditure tracking and service delivery surveys in Developing Countries," *in* Transparency International, *Global Corruption Report 2006: Corruption and Health* (Berlin: Transparency International, 2006), 29–33.
23. Organization for Economic Cooperation and Development (OECD), *Paris Declaration on Aid Effectiveness: Ownership, Harmonisation, Alignment, Results and Mutual Accountability* (Paris: OECD, 2005), 1–8; OECD, *Accra Agenda for Action* (Accra: OECD, 2008).
24. Abdallah S. Daar et al., "Grand Challenges in Chronic Non-communicable Diseases," *Nature* 450, no. 7169 (2007): 494–496.
25. Karen McColl, "Europe Told to Deliver More Aid for Health," *The Lancet* 371, no. 9630 (2008): 2072–2073.
26. Michael Marmot, "Working through the Issues of Global Governance for Health," *The Lancet* 374, no. 9697 (2009): 1231–1232. More than 37,000 international NGOs work in health and development.
27. Institute of Medicine (IOM), *The U.S. Commitment to Global Health: Recommendations for the Public and Private Sectors* (Washington, DC: National Academies Press 2009), 160.
28. David Bloom, "Governing Global Health," *Finance and Development* 44, no. 4 (2007): 31–35.
29. Laurie Garrett, "The Challenge of Global Health," *Foreign Affairs* 86, no. 1 (2007): 14–38.
30. Nirmala Ravishankar et al., "Financing of Global Health: Tracking Development Assistance for Health from 1990 to 2007," *The Lancet* 373, no. 9681 (2009): 2113–2124. Private foundations and NGOs contributed 30 percent of total global health aid in 2007.
31. OECD, "Aid to Poor Countries Slips Further as Governments Tighten Budgets," April 3, 2013.
32. George J. Schieber et al., "Financing Global Health: Mission Unaccomplished," *Health Affairs* 26, no. 4 (2007): 921–934.

33. WHO, *World Health Statistics 2013* (Geneva: WHO, 2013), 131–142.
34. Devi Sridhar and R. Batniji, "Misfinancing Global Health: A Case for Transparency in Disbursements and Decision Making," *The Lancet* 372, no. 9644 (2008): 1185–1191.

4. Fulfilling the Promise of the World Health Organization

1. Jack C. Chow, "Is the WHO Becoming Irrelevant?," *Foreign Policy Magazine,* December 8, 2010.
2. David P. Fidler, *The Challenges of Global Health Governance* (New York: Council of Foreign Relations, 2010), 1–2.
3. Declan Butler, "Revamp for WHO," *Nature* 47, no. 7348 (2011): 430–431.
4. World Health Organization (WHO), *The First Ten Years of the World Health Organization* (Geneva: WHO, 1958), 24.
5. John Charles, "Origins, History, and Achievements of the World Health Organization," *British Medical Journal* 2, no. 5600 (1968): 293–296.
6. Elizabeth Fee et al., "WHO at Sixty: Snapshots from Its First Six Decades," *American Journal of Public Health* 98, no. 4 (2008): 630–633; Wilbur A. Sawyer, "Achievements of UNRRA as an International Health Organization," *American Journal of Public Health* 37, no. 1 (1947): 41–58.
7. UN, "Charter of the United Nations," entered into force (1945) October 24, 1945, art. 55.
8. Thomas Parran and Frank G. Boudreau, "The World Health Organization: Cornerstone of Peace," *American Journal of Public Health* 36, no. 11 (1946): 1267–1272.
9. Frank P. Grad, "The Preamble of the Constitution of the World Health Organization," *Bulletin of the World Health Organization* 80, no. 12 (2002): 981–982.
10. WHO, "Constitution of the World Health Organization," (1984), entered into force April 7, 1948, preamble.
11. UN WHO Interim Commission, "Proceedings and Final Acts of the International Health Conference Held in New York from 19 June to 22 July 1946," *Official Records of the World Health Organization,* no. 2 (1946), 23–25.
12. Ibid., 23.
13. WHA, Resolution WHA44.30, "Prior Consideration of Proposals for Resolutions on Technical Matters by the Executive Board," 1991.
14. Marcel Tanner and Don de Savigny, "Malaria Eradication Back on the Table," *Bulletin of the World Health Organization* 86, no. 2 (2008): 82–82A.
15. WHA, Resolution WHA11.54, "Smallpox Eradication," June 12, 1958, 90.
16. WHA, Resolution WHA18.38, "Smallpox Eradication Programme," May 19, 1965, 24.
17. WHA, Resolution WHA33.3, "Declaration of Eradication of Smallpox," May 8, 1980, 164.
18. Donald R. Hopkins, "Disease Eradication," *New England Journal of Medicine* 368 (2013): 54–63.
19. Saad Omer et al., "Go Big and Go Fast: Vaccine Refusal and Disease Eradication," *New England Journal of Medicine* 368, no. 1 (2013): 1374–1375.

20. Gian Luca Burci and Claude-Henry Vignes, *World Health Organization* (The Hague: Kluwer Law International, 2004), 160–161.
21. WHA, Resolution WHA30.43, "Technical Co-operation," May 19, 1977.
22. Halfdan Mahler, "The Meaning of Health for All by the Year 2000," *World Health Forum* 2, no. 1 (1981): 5–12.
23. WHO Commission on Social Determinants of Health, *Closing the Gap in a Generation: Health Equity through Action on the Social Determinants of Health* (Geneva: WHO, 2008), 8.
24. Donald G. McNeil Jr., "Pakistan Battles Polio, and Its People's Mistrust," *New York Times,* July 21, 2013, http://www.nytimes.com/2013/07/22/health/pakistan-fights-for-ground-in-war-on-polio.html.
25. Global Polio Eradication Initiative, *Polio Eradication and Endgame Strategic Plan 2013–2018* (Geneva: WHO, 2013), 1.
26. Bernhard Schwartländer et al., "The Ten-Year Struggle to Provide Antiretroviral Treatment to People with HIV in the Developing World," *The Lancet* 368, no. 9534 (2006): 541–546.
27. Maria Ines Battistella Nemes et al., *Evaluation of WHO's Contribution to "3 by 5"* (Geneva: WHO, 2006), 83.
28. WHO, "Cumulative Number of Confirmed Human Cases for Avian Influenza A(H5N1) Reported to WHO, 2003–2013," http://www.who.int/influenza/human_animal_interface/EN_GIP_20130829CumulativeNumberH5N1cases.pdf (accessed 11/17/13).
29. WHO, "Pandemic Influenza Preparedness Framework for the Sharing of Influenza Viruses and Access to Vaccines and Other Benefits," May 5, 2011.
30. WHA, Resolution WHA35.10, "Regulations for Expert Advisory Panels and Committees," May 20, 2000.
31. WHO Expert Committee on the Selection and Use of Essential Medicines, *The Selection and Use of Essential Medicines: Report of the WHO Expert Committee, 2002* (Geneva: WHO, 2003), 14.
32. WHO, "Framework Convention on Tobacco Control" (2003) entered into force February 27, 2005.
33. Allyn L. Taylor, "Making the World Health Organization Work: A Legal Framework for Universal Access to the Conditions for Health," *American Journal of Law and Medicine* 18 (1992): 301–346; David P. Fidler, "The Future of the World Health Organization: What Role for International Law?," *Vanderbilt Journal of Transnational Law* 31, no. 5 (1998): 1079–1126.
34. Philippe Naughton, "Hillary Clinton Says 'Smart Power' Will Restore American Leadership," *Times*, January 13, 2009, http://www.thetimes.co.uk/tto/news/world/americas/article1999131.ece.
35. James A. Tobey, "Review of International Digest of Health Legislation, Vol. 1, No. 1," *American Journal of Public Health* 39, no. 11 (1949): 1484.
36. WHA, "The Future of Financing for WHO: World Health Organization: Reforms for a Healthy Future: Report by the Director-General," May 5, 2011; WHO Executive Board (EB), Special Session on WHO Reform, EB Doc. EBSS/2/2, "Reforms for a Healthy Future: Report by the Director-General," October 15, 2011.

37. U.S. Government Accountability Office, *World Health Organization: Reform Agenda Developed, but U.S. Actions to Monitor Progress Could Be Enhanced*, July 23, 2012. This GAO report recommended an assessment tool to monitor WHO progress on transparency and accountability.
38. Devi Sridhar and Lawrence O. Gostin, "Reforming the World Health Organization," *Journal of the American Medical Association* 305, no. 15 (2011): 1585–1586.
39. Berne Declaration et al., "NGO Letter on Conflicts of Interest, Future Financing, Reform, and Governance of the WHO," May 24, 2011.
40. WHO, "World Health Forum: Concept Paper," June 22, 2011.
41. WHO, "WHO Reform for a Healthy Future: An Overview," July 20, 2011.
42. Eric A. Friedman, "World Health Assembly 2011 Outcomes and United Nations AIDS Review Preview" (blog entry), O'Neill Institute for Global Health Law, June 7, 2011, http://www.oneillinstituteblog.org/world-health-assembly-2011-outcomes-and-united-nations-aids-review-preview/; Democratizing Global Health Coalition, "Letter to Member States of the WHO re: Concept Papers on the WHO Reform Process," June 30, 2011.
43. WHO Civil Society Initiative (CSI), "Principles Governing Relations with Nongovernmental Organizations."
44. Christophe Lanord, *A Study of WHO's Official Relations System with Nongovernmental Organizations* (Geneva: WHO, 2002), 4; Thomas Schwarz, "A Stronger Voice of Civil Society at the World Health Assembly?," Medicus Mundi International Network, June 2010.
45. WHO, *Policy for Relations with Nongovernmental Organizations: Note by the Director-General*, April 1, 2004; CSI, "Status of Proposal for a New Policy to Guide WHO's Relations with NGOs," http://www.who.int/civilsociety/relations/new_policy/en/index.html (accessed 10/10/13).
46. Gaudenz Silberschmidt et al., "Creating a Committee C of the World Health Assembly," *The Lancet* 371, no. 9623 (2008): 1483–1486.
47. David Stuckler et al., "Global Health Philanthropy and Institutional Relationships: How Should Conflicts of Interest Be Addressed?," *Public Library of Science Medicine* 8, no. 4 (2011): e1001020.
48. WHA, Doc. A66/7, "Proposed Programme Budget 2014–2015," April 19, 2013.
49. UK Department for International Development, "Multilateral Aid Review: Ensuring Maximum Value for Money for UK Aid through Multilateral Organizations," March 2011.
50. WHO, "Independent Formative Evaluation of the World Health Organization: Concept Paper," June 22, 2011.
51. U.S. Department of State, "Observations by the United States of America on 'The Right to Health, Fact Sheet No. 31,' " October 15, 2008.
52. WHA, Resolution WHAA64/4, "Reforms for a Healthy Future," May 5, 2011.
53. WHO, "Proposed Programme Budget 2014–2015"; Centers for Disease Control, "FY12 Budget Request Overview," http://www.cdc.gov/fmo/topic

/Budget%20Information/appropriations_budget_form_pdf/FY2013 _Budget_Request_Summary.pdf (accessed 10/10/13).

54. Declan Butler, "Agency Gets a Grip on Budget," *Nature* 498, no. 7452 (2013): 8–9.
55. Ibid., 9.
56. WHO, Resolution WHA60.11, "Medium-Term Strategic Plan 2008–2013," May 21, 2007, amended draft submitted January 2009, 58–59; WHO, "Proposed Programme Budget 2014–2015" (the actual figure is 77 percent voluntary contributions); Devi Sridhar and Ngaire Woods, "Trojan Multilateralism: Global Cooperation in Health" (working paper, Global Economic Governance Programme, University of Oxford, 2013).
57. Rafael Lozano et al., "Global and Regional Mortality from 235 Causes of Death for Twenty Age Groups in 1990 and 2010: A Systematic Analysis for the Global Burden of Disease Study 2010," *The Lancet* 380, no. 9859 (2012): 2095–2128; Christopher J. L. Murray et al., "Disability-Adjusted Life Years (DALYs) for 291 Diseases and Injuries in Twenty-One Regions, 1990–2010: A Systematic Analysis for the Global Burden of Disease Study 2010," *The Lancet* 380, no. 9859 (2012): 2197–2223.
58. WHO, WHA Doc. A66/50, "WHO Reform: Financing of WHO," May 13, 2013; Ikuma Nozaki, "WHO's Budgetary Allocation and Disease Burden," *The Lancet* 382, no. 9896 (2013): 937–938; Butler, "Agency Gets a Grip on Budget," 18–19.
59. Clive Mutunga et al., "Enhancing Cooperation between the Health and Climate Sectors," *Bulletin of the Atomic Scientists,* December 3, 2009.
60. Toni Johnson, "Backgrounder: The World Health Organization (WHO)," Council on Foreign Relations, last modified September 20, 2011, http://www.cfr.org/public-health-threats-and-pandemics/world-health-organization-/p20003.
61. WHO, WHA Doc A66/4, "Implementation of the International Health Regulations (2005): Report of the Review Committee on the Functioning of the International Health Regulations (2005) in Relation to Pandemic (H1N1) 2009: Report by the Director-General," May 5, 2011.
62. WHO, Sixty-Sixth World Health Assembly, Provisional Agenda Item 11, "WHO Reform: High-Level Implementation Plan and Report: Report by the Director-General," May 10, 2013.

5. Old and New Institutions

1. Gill Walt et al., "Mapping the Global Health Architecture," in Kent Buse et al., eds., *Making Sense of Global Health Governance: A Policy Perspective* (Basingstoke, UK: Palgrave Macmillan, 2009).
2. Mark Dybul et al., "Reshaping Global Health," *Policy Review,* no. 173 (2012), http://www.hoover.org/publications/policy-review/article/118116.
3. United Nations, *Monterrey Consensus on Financing for Development,* International Conference on Financing for Development (Monterrey, Mexico, March 18–22, 2002); Organization for Economic Cooperation and Development (OECD), *The Paris Declaration on Aid Effectiveness: Ownership,*

Harmonisation, Alignment, Results, and Mutual Accountability (Paris: OECD, 2005); *The Accra Agenda for Action* (Accra: 2005 and 2008), OECD; *Busan Partnership for Effective Development Co-operation,* Fourth High Level Forum on Aid Effectiveness (Busan: 2011).

4. Lesley Magnussen et al., "Comprehensive versus Selective Primary Health Care: Lessons for Global Health Policy," *Health Affairs* 23, no. 3 (2004): 167–176; WHO, *Declaration of Alma-Ata* (1978).
5. Marcos Cueto, "The Origins of Primary Health Care and Selective Primary Health Care," *American Journal of Public Health* 94, no. 11 (2004): 1864–1874.
6. Theodore M. Brown et al., "The World Health Organization and the Transition from 'International' to 'Global' Public Health," *American Journal of Public Health* 96, no. 1 (2006): 62–72.
7. Independent Evaluation Group, *Improving Effectiveness and Outcomes for the Poor in Health, Nutrition, and Population: An Evaluation of World Bank Group Support since 1997* (Washington, DC: World Bank, 2009), 105–107.
8. Devesh Kapur et al., *The World Bank: Its First Half Century,* vol. 1, *History* (Washington, DC: Brookings Institution Press, 1997).
9. Independent Evaluation Group, *Improving Effectiveness and Outcomes,* 15.
10. Sara Grusky, "Privatization Tidal Wave: IMF/World Bank Water Policies and the Price Paid by the Poor," *Multinational Monitor* 22, no. 9 (2001): 14–19.
11. Jennifer Prah Ruger, "The Changing Role of the World Bank in Global Health," *American Journal of Public Health* 95, no. 1 (2005): 60–70.
12. Valéry Ridde, "Is the Bamako Initiative Still Relevant for West African Health Systems?," *International Journal of Health Services* 41, no. 1 (2011): 175–184.
13. WHO, *The World Health Report 2008: Primary Health Care (Now More Than Ever)* (Geneva: WHO, 2008), 26–27.
14. World Bank, *World Development Report 1993: Investing in Health* (New York: Oxford University Press, 1993), 117–118.
15. Margaret Whitehead et al., "Equity and Health Sector Reforms: Can Low-Income Countries Escape the Medical Poverty Trap?," *The Lancet* 358, no. 9248 (2001): 833–836.
16. Mohammed Nuruzzaman, "The World Bank, Health Policy Reforms and the Poor," *Journal of Contemporary Asia* 37, no. 1 (2007): 59–72.
17. Margaret Chan, "The World Health Report 2010," keynote address, International Ministerial Conference on Health Systems Financing, Berlin, Germany, November 22, 2010.
18. Nils Gunnar Songstad et al., "Why Do Health Workers in Rural Tanzania Prefer Public Sector Employment?," *BMC Health Services Research* 12, no. 92 (2012): 1–12.
19. Masahiro Nozaki et al., "Are the Critics Right?" *Finance and Development* 48, no. 4 (2011): 50–52.

20. Anne O. Krueger, "Whither the World Bank and the IMF?," *Journal of Economic Literature* 36, no. 4 (1998): 1983–2020.
21. World Bank, *World Development Report 2004: Making Services Work for Poor People* (Washington, DC: World Bank, 2003), 71.
22. Marijn Verhoeven and Alonso Segura, "IMF Trims Use of Wage Bill Ceilings," *IMF Survey Magazine*, September 5, 2007, http://www.imf.org/external/pubs/ft/survey/so/2007/pol095a.htm.
23. "Civil Society: Background," World Bank, http://go.worldbank.org/PWRRFJ2QHo (accessed 10/10/13).
24. Anna Marriott, *Blind Optimism: Challenging the Myths about Private Health Care in Poor Countries,* briefing paper (Oxford, UK: Oxfam International, 2009).
25. Jim Kim, "Poverty, Health and the Human Future," address to the Sixty-Sixth World Health Assembly, Geneva, Switzerland, May 21, 2013.
26. Jim Yong Kim and Margaret Chan, "Poverty, Health, and Societies of the Future," *Journal of the American Medical Association* 310, no. 9 (2013): 901–902.
27. Lesley Wroughton, "World Bank Picks Health Expert Kim as President," *Reuters,* April 16, 2012, http://www.reuters.com/article/2012/04/16/us-worldbank-idUSBRE83F0XF20120416.
28. Kent Buse and Gill Walt, "Global Public-Private Partnerships: Part 1—A New Development in Health?," *Bulletin of the World Health Organization* 78, no. 4 (2000): 549–561.
29. UN General Assembly (UNGA), Resolution 55/2, "UN Millennium Declaration," September 8, 2000, para. 2.
30. United Nations, "Chronological History of the Financing for Development Process," http://www.un.org/esa/ffd/overview/chronology.htm (accessed 10/10/13).
31. United Nations, *Monterrey Consensus; Rome Declaration on Harmonisation* (Rome: February 2003); *The Paris Declaration, The Accra Agenda; Busan Partnership.*
32. "The High Level Fora on Aid Effectiveness: A History," OECD, http://www.oecd.org/dac/effectiveness/thehighlevelforaonaideffectivenessahistory.htm (accessed 10/10/13).
33. Adam Wexler et al., *Donor Funding for Health in Low- and Middle-Income Countries, 2002–2010* (Washington, DC: Kaiser Family Foundation, 2013).
34. WHO, "Partnerships," report by the Secretariat, World Health Assembly, WHO Doc. A62/39, April 30, 2009.
35. Kent Buse and Andrew Harmer, "Global Health Partnerships: The Mosh Pit of Global Health Governance," in Kent Buse et al., eds., *Making Sense of Global Health Governance: The Policy Perspective* (London: Palgrave Macmillan, 2009), 247.
36. Action for Global Health, *Aid Effectiveness for Health: Towards the Fourth High-Level Forum, Busan 2011; Making Health Aid Work Better* (Brussels: Action for Global Health, 2011), 8.

37. Sania Nishtar, "Public–Private 'Partnerships' in Health—A Global Call to Action," *Health Research Policy and Systems* 2, no. 5 (2004), doi:10.1186/1478-4505-2-5.
38. WHO, *World Health Report 2006—Working Together for Health* (Geneva: WHO, 2006).
39. Kofi Annan, "Africa: Abuja Summit, Annan Speech, 04/26/01," address to the Abuja Summit on HIV/AIDS, tuberculosis, and other infectious diseases, April 26, 2001; Declaration of Commitment on HIV/AIDS, UNGA Resolution s-26/2 (June 27, 2001), para. 90; "Communiqué," G8 Summit, Genoa, Italy, July 22, 2001, para. 15, http://www.g8.utoronto.ca/summit/2001genoa/finalcommunique.html (accessed 10/10/13).
40. Karanja Kinyanjui, "Global Fund's No-Go Decisions for Grant Renewals Are on the Rise," *Global Fund Observer,* April 20, 2012, http://www.aidspan.org/gfo_article/global-funds-no-go-decisions-grant-renewals-are-rise.
41. Global Fund to Fight AIDS, Tuberculosis and Malaria (Global Fund), *The Global Fund to Fight Aids, Tuberculosis and Malaria Fourth Replenishment (2014–2016): Update on Results and Impact* (Geneva: Global Fund, 2013); Global Fund, *Strategic Investments for Results: Global Fund Results Report 2012* (Geneva: Global Fund, 2012).
42. Gorik Ooms et al., "Financing the Millennium Development Goals for Health and Beyond: Sustaining the 'Big Push,'" *Globalization and Health* 6, no. 17 (2010), doi:10.1186/1744-8603-6-17.
43. Global Fund, *Guidelines and Requirements for Country Coordinating Mechanisms* (Geneva: Global Fund, May 12, 2011).
44. International Treatment Preparedness Coalition, *Making Global Fund Country Coordinating Mechanisms Work through Full Engagement of Civil Society: On-the-Ground Research in Argentina, Cambodia, Cameroon, India, Jamaica, Romania, and Uganda,* CCM Advocacy Report (San Francisco: International Treatment Preparedness Coalition, October 2008).
45. Global Fund, *Dual Track Financing Information Note* (Geneva: Global Fund, February 2013).
46. Angela Kageni, "New Structure at Global Fund Will Reduce Influence of Civil Society," *Global Fund Observer,* May 10, 2012, http://www.aidspan.org/gfo_article/new-structure-global-fund-will-reduce-influence-civil-society.
47. Global Fund, *Policy on Eligibility Criteria, Counterpart Financing Requirements, and Prioritization of Proposals for Funding from the Global Fund,* Twenty-Third Board Meeting, Geneva, Switzerland, GF/B23/14 Attachment 1 (May 11–12, 2011); Eric A. Friedman, *Guide to Using Round 10 of the Global Fund to Fight AIDS, Tuberculosis and Malaria to Support Health Systems Strengthening* (Cambridge, MA, and Washington, DC: Physicians for Human Rights, 2010).
48. Global Fund, *Global Fund Gender Equality Strategy* (Geneva: Global Fund, 2008); Global Fund, *The Global Fund Strategy in Relation to Sexual Orientation and Gender Identities* (Geneva: Global Fund, 2009); Michael

Wilkerson, AIDS-Free World, "An Open Letter to the Executive Director of the Global Fund to Fight AIDS, Tuberculosis and Malaria," July 29, 2013.

49. Global Fund, *The Global Fund Strategy 2012–2016: Investing for Impact* (Geneva: Global Fund, 2012).
50. Sarah Boseley, "Can the Global Fund Weather the Corruption Storm?," *Guardian*, January 28, 2011, http://www.theguardian.com/society/sarah-boseley-global-health/2011/jan/28/aids-infectiousdiseases.
51. Global Fund, "Global Fund Suspends Two Malaria Grants, Terminates TB Grant to Mali," December 7, 2010, http://www.theglobalfund.org/en/mediacenter/newsreleases/2010-12-07_Global_Fund_suspends_two_malaria_grants_terminates_TB_grant_to_Mali/; Global Fund, "Global Fund Statement on Abuse of Funds in Some Countries," January 24, 2011, http://www.theglobalfund.org/en/mediacenter/newsreleases/2011-01-24_Gobal_Fund_statement_on_abuse_of_funds_in_some_countries/.
52. Laurie Garrett, "The Global Fund: Can It Be Saved?," January 24, 2012, http://www.cfr.org/diseases-infectious/global-fund-can-saved/p27210.
53. Debrework Zewdie, "The Global Fund at Ten Years: Reflecting on Its Impact and Looking Forward to Challenges Ahead," speech to the Council on Foreign Relations, April 24, 2012, http://www.cfr.org/world/global-fund-ten-years-reflecting-its-impact-looking-forward-challenges-ahead/p28070.
54. UNGA, "Keeping the Promise: United to Achieve the Millennium Development Goals," UN Doc. A/RES/65/1, October 19, 2010.
55. Global Fund, "Global Fund Targets $15 Billion to Effectively Fight AIDS, TB and Malaria," April 8, 2013, http://www.theglobalfund.org/en/mediacenter/newsreleases/2013-04-08_Global_Fund_Targets_USD_15_Billion_to_Effectively_Fight_AIDS_TB_and_Malaria/.
56. Global Fund, "Global Fund Board Approves First Grants under New Approach to Funding," June 19, 2013, http://www.theglobalfund.org/en/mediacenter/newsreleases/2013-06-19_Global_Fund_Board_Approves_First_Grants_under_New_Approach_to_Funding/.
57. Tim France et al., "The Global Fund: Which Countries Owe How Much?," April 21, 2002, http://www.aidsmap.com/The-Global-Fund-which-countries-owe-how-much/page/1414201/.
58. Global Fund, *The Global Fund Strategy 2012–2016,* para. 81.
59. "Other Publications," Aidspan, http://www.aidspan.org/page/other-publications (accessed 10/10/13).
60. Global Fund, *Transition Manual for the New Funding Model of the Global Fund* (Geneva: Global Fund, 2013).
61. Gorik Ooms and Rachel Hammonds, "Correcting Globalisation in Health: Transnational Entitlements versus the Ethical Imperative of Reducing Aid-Dependency," *Public Health Ethics* 1, no. 2 (2008): 154–170; Giorgio Cometto et al., "A Global Fund for the Health MDGs?," *The Lancet* 373, no. 9674 (2009): 1500–1502.

62. Sharon LaFraniere, "AIDS Funds Frozen for China in Grant Dispute," *New York Times*, May 20, 2011, http://www.nytimes.com/2011/05/21/world/asia/21china.html?pagewanted=all; "Government Donors," Global Fund, http://www.theglobalfund.org/en/partners/governments/ (accessed 10/10/13).
63. "Origins of GAVI," GAVI Alliance, http://www.gavialliance.org/about/mission/origins/ (accessed 10/10/13).
64. "Institutional Timeline," GAVI Alliance, http://www.gavialliance.org/about/mission/institutional-timeline/ (accessed 10/10/13); "Governance and Legal Structures," GAVI Alliance, http://www.gavialliance.org/about/governance/legal-structures/ (accessed 10/10/13).
65. "GAVI's Impact," GAVI Alliance, http://www.gavialliance.org/about/mission/impact/ (accessed 10/10/13); "GAVI Facts and Figures," GAVI Alliance, http://www.gavialliance.org/library/publications/ (accessed 10/10/13).
66. Grace Chee et al., *Evaluation of the First Five Years of GAVI Immunization Services Support Funding* (Bethesda, MD: Abt Associates, 2007).
67. "What We Do," GAVI Alliance, http://www.gavialliance.org/about/mission/what/ (accessed 10/10/13).
68. "GAVI's Impact," GAVI Alliance.
69. "Health System Strengthening Support," GAVI Alliance, http://www.gavialliance.org/support/hss/ (accessed 10/10/13).
70. Aurélia Nguyen et al., *Market Shaping: Strategic Considerations for a Healthy Vaccine Marketplace* (Geneva: GAVI Alliance, May 26, 2011); "The Market-Shaping Goal," GAVI Alliance, http://www.gavialliance.org/about/strategy/phase-iii-(2011-15)/market-shaping-goal/ (accessed 10/10/13).
71. Tania Cernuschi et al., *Pneumococcal Advance Market Commitment: Lessons Learnt on Disease and Design Choices and Processes* (Geneva: GAVI Alliance, September 2011).
72. "About IFFIm: Overview," IFFIm, http://www.iffim.org/about/overview/ (accessed 10/10/13); GAVI Alliance, *GAVI Secretariat Response to the IFFIm Evaluation* (Geneva: GAVI Alliance, June 2011).
73. GAVI Alliance, "Donors Commit Vaccine Funding to Achieve Historic Milestone," June 13, 2011, http://www.gavialliance.org/library/news/press-releases/2011/donors-commit-vaccine-funding-to-achieve-historic-milestone-in-global-health/.
74. "Independent Review Committees," GAVI Alliance, http://www.gavialliance.org/support/apply/independent-review-committees/ (accessed 10/10/13).
75. GAVI Alliance, *Guidelines for Applications: New and Underused Vaccine Support* (Geneva: GAVI Alliance, August 31, 2012); "Country Commitment to Co-financing," GAVI Alliance, http://www.gavialliance.org/about/gavis-business-model/country-commitment-to-co-financing/ (accessed 10/10/13); Hind Khatib-Othman, "Country Program and Health System Support Update," presentation to GAVI Alliance Board Meeting (Dar es Salaam, Tanzania: GAVI Alliance, December 4–5, 2012).
76. UNAIDS, *Together We Will End AIDS* (Geneva: UNAIDS, 2012).
77. "Graduating Countries," GAVI Alliance, http://www.gavialliance.org/support/apply/graduating-countries/ (accessed 10/10/13).

78. "Transparency and Accountability Policy," GAVI Alliance, http://www.gavialliance.org/about/governance/programme-policies/tap/ (accessed 10/10/13). In a prominent case that led to the indictment of top-tier Sierra Leone Ministry of Health officials for corruption, GAVI found that half a million dollars had been misused. Adam Nossiter, "Sierra Leone's Health Care System Becomes a Cautionary Tale for Donors," *New York Times,* April 13, 2013, http://www.nytimes.com/2013/04/14/world/africa/sierra-leone-graft-charges-imperil-care-and-aid.html?pagewanted=all.
79. "Civil Society Organization Support," GAVI Alliance, http://www.gavialliance.org/support/cso/ (accessed 10/10/13).
80. GAVI Alliance, *Review of Decisions and Actions,* GAVI Alliance Board Meeting (Washington, DC: GAVI Alliance, June 12–13, 2012). United States Agency for International Development (USAID), "GAVI Phase II: What USAID Missions and Projects Need to Know," *Immunization Snapshots* 3 (July 2006).
81. GAVI Alliance, *The GAVI Alliance Strategy 2011–2015 and Business Plan* (Geneva: GAVI Alliance, 2011).
82. "Moments in Time: 1913–1919," Rockefeller Foundation, http://www.rockefellerfoundation.org/about-us/our-history/1913-1919 (accessed 10/10/13).
83. Marcos Cueto, "The Origins of Primary Health Care and Selective Primary Health Care," *American Journal of Public Health* 94, no. 11 (2004): 1864–1874.
84. "Warren Buffett," Bill & Melinda Gates Foundation, http://www.gatesfoundation.org/who-we-are/general-information/leadership/management-committee/warren-buffett (accessed 10/10/13); KPMG LLP, *Bill & Melinda Gates Foundation: Consolidated Financial Statements, December 31, 2012 and 2011* (Seattle: KPMG LLP, 2013).
85. Bill & Melinda Gates Foundation, *Bill & Melinda Gates Foundation Annual Report 2011* (Seattle: Bill & Melinda Gates Foundation, 2012).
86. Ibid.
87. "Tobacco Control: Strategy Overview," Bill & Melinda Gates Foundation, http://www.gatesfoundation.org/What-We-Do/Global-Policy/Tobacco-Control (accessed 10/10/13); "HIV: Strategy Overview," Bill & Melinda Gates Foundation, http://www.gatesfoundation.org/What-We-Do/Global-Health/HIV (accessed 10/10/13).
88. Bill & Melinda Gates Foundation, *Global Health Program Overview* (Seattle: Bill & Melinda Gates Foundation, 2010).
89. Bill & Melinda Gates Foundation, "Bill and Melinda Gates Pledge $10 Billion in Call for Decade of Vaccines," January 29, 2010, http://www.gatesfoundation.org/Media-Center/Press-Releases/2010/01/Bill-and-Melinda-Gates-Pledge-$10-Billion-in-Call-for-Decade-of-Vaccines.
90. "Grand Challenges in Global Health," Grand challenges, http://www.grandchallenges.org/Pages/Default.aspx (accessed 10/10/13).
91. Donald G. McNeil Jr., "Malaria Gets the Foil-in-a-Microwave Treatment," *New York Times,* August 22, 2011, http://www.nytimes.com/2011/08/23/health/23microwave.html.

92. Bill & Melinda Gates Foundation, "Bill Gates Names Winners of the Reinvent the Toilet Challenge," August 14, 2012, http://www.gatesfoundation.org/media-center/press-releases/2012/08/bill-gates-names-winners-of-the-reinvent-the-toilet-challenge.
93. "Funding," Meningitis Vaccine Project, http://www.meningvax.org/funding.php (accessed 10/10/13).
94. Bill & Melinda Gates Foundation, *2012 Annual Letter from Bill Gates* (January 2012).
95. Global Health Group and SEEK Development, *Progress against Polio: Winning the Fight against a Deadly Disease* (San Francisco and Berlin: Living Proof Project, 2009).
96. Bill & Melinda Gates Foundation, *Annual Report 2011;* "Financing," Global Polio Eradication Initiative, http://www.polioeradication.org/Financing.aspx (accessed 10/10/13).
97. "Importation Countries," Global Polio Eradication Initiative, http://www.polioeradication.org/Infectedcountries/Importationcountries.aspx (accessed 10/10/13); "Polio This Week—As of 18 September 2013," Global Polio Eradication Initiative, http://www.polioeradication.org/Dataandmonitoring/Poliothisweek.aspx (accessed 10/10/13); Bill & Melinda Gates Foundation, *2012 Annual Letter.*
98. Global Fund to Fight AIDS, Tuberculosis and Malaria, "The Global Fund Welcomes US$750 Million Promissory Note from the Bill & Melinda Gates Foundation," January 26, 2012, http://www.theglobalfund.org/en/media center/newsreleases/2012-01-26_The_Global_Fund_Welcomes_USD750_Million_Promissory_Note_from_the_Bill_Melinda_Gates_Foundation/.
99. "Hot Tropic: The World's Nastiest Illnesses Get Some Belated Attention," *Economist,* February 4, 2012, http://www.economist.com/node/21546005.
100. ONE, *ONE Annual Report 2011* (Washington, DC: ONE, 2012).
101. WHO, "Annex: Voluntary Contributions by Fund and by Donor for the Financial Period 2010–2011," WHA Doc. A65/29 Add.1, April 5, 2012.
102. Donald G. McNeil Jr., "Gates Foundation's Influence Criticized," *New York Times,* February 16, 2008, http://www.nytimes.com/2008/02/16/science/16malaria.html.
103. Charles Piller et al., "Dark Cloud over Good Works of Gates Foundation," *Los Angeles Times,* January 7, 2007, http://www.latimes.com/news/la-na-gatesx07jan07,0,2533850.story; Claudio Schuftan, "The New Philanthropies in World Health Affairs: Masters of Our Universe," September 2011, http://www.wphna.org/2011_sept_col_claudio.htm.
104. "Our Investment Philosophy," Bill & Melinda Gates Foundation, http://www.gatesfoundation.org/Who-We-Are/General-Information/Financials/Investment-Policy (accessed 10/10/13); Charles Piller, "Gates Foundation to Keep Its Investment Approach," *Los Angeles Times,* January 14, 2007, http://www.latimes.com/business/la-na-gates14jan14,0,1160032.story.
105. "The Giving Pledge," http://givingpledge.org/ (accessed 10/10/13).
106. Veronica Walford, *Joint Assessment of National Health Strategies and Plans: A Review of Recent Experience* (International Health Partnership+, 2010).

107. International Health Partnership+, *Joint Assessment of National Health Strategies and Plans, Joint Assessment Tool: The Attributes of a Sound National Strategy,* version 2 (2011).
108. "IHP+ Partners," IHP+, http://www.internationalhealthpartnership.net/en/ihp-partners/ (accessed 10/10/13).
109. IHP+Results, *Progress in the International Health Partnership and Related Initiatives (IHP+)*: 2012 Annual Performance Report (London and Johannesburg: Responsible Action UK and Re-Action!, 2012).
110. "Frequently Asked Questions," International Bank for Reconstruction and Development, http://web.worldbank.org/WBSITE/EXTERNAL/EXTABOUTUS/EXTIBRD/0,,contentMDK:21116492~menuPK:3126966~pagePK:64168445~piPK:64168309~theSitePK:3046012,00.html (accessed 10/10/13).
111. Global Health Strategies Initiatives, *Shifting Paradigm: How the BRICS Are Reshaping Global Health and Development* (New York, New Delhi, and Rio de Janeiro: Global Health Strategies Initiatives, 2012), 64.
112. Nishika Patel, "India to Create Central Foreign Aid Agency," *Guardian,* July 26, 2011, http://www.theguardian.com/global-development/2011/jul/26/india-foreign-aid-agency; Simon Allison, "South Africa: Charity Begins in Pretoria—Dirco's Plan to Get Humanitarian Assistance Right," *Daily Maverick,* September 5, 2012, http://www.dailymaverick.co.za/article/2012-09-05-charity-begins-in-pretoria-dircos-plan-to-get-humanitarian-assistance-right/.
113. WHO, "Constitution of the World Health Organization" (1946), entered into force April 17, 1948, art. 2(a).
114. David P. Fidler, "Architecture amidst Anarchy: Global Health's Quest for Governance," *Global Health Governance* 1 (January 2007).

6. The International Health Regulations

1. World Health Assembly (WHA), Resolution 58.3, "Revision of the International Health Regulations," May 23, 2005; David P. Fidler and Lawrence O. Gostin, "The New International Health Regulations: An Historic Development for International Law and Public Health," *Journal of Law, Medicine and Ethics* 34, no. 1 (2006): 85–94.
2. UN Secretary-General, UN Doc. A/59/2005, "In Larger Freedom: Towards Development, Security, and Human Rights for All: Report of the Secretary-General," March 21, 2005.
3. *Jew Ho v. Williamson,* 103 F.10, 24 (C.C.N.D. Cal. 1900).
4. Norman Howard-Jones, *The Scientific Background of the International Sanitary Conferences, 1851–1938* (Geneva: WHO, 1975); David P. Fidler, "From International Sanitary Conventions to Global Health Security: The New International Health Regulations," *Chinese Journal of International Law* 4, no. 2 (2005): 325–392; "International Sanitary Conferences," Harvard University Library, http://ocp.hul.harvard.edu/contagion/sanitaryconferences.html (accessed 10/10/13).
5. Each state had two delegates at the first convention, one political and the other medical—often at loggerheads. Medical delegates were not invited to subsequent conventions.

6. Julie Fischer et al., *The International Health Regulations (2005): Surveillance and Response in an Era of Globalization* (Washington, DC: Stimson Center, 2011).
7. "Origin and Development of Health Cooperation," WHO, http://www.who.int/global_health_histories/background/en/index.html (accessed 10/10/13).
8. Frank G. Boudreau, "International Health," *American Journal of Public Health* 19, no. 8 (1929): 863–879, quotation from p. 864.
9. David P. Fidler and Lawrence O. Gostin, *Biosecurity in the Global Age: Biological Weapons, Public Health, and the Rule of Law* (Palo Alto: Stanford University Press, 2008).
10. David Fidler, *SARS, Governance, and the Globalization of Disease* (Basingstoke, UK: Palgrave Macmillan, 2004).
11. "States Parties to the International Health Regulations (2005)" (as of March 16, 2013), WHO, http://www.who.int/ihr/legal_issues/states_parties/en/ (accessed 10/10/13). The IHR (art. 64) permit nonmember states to become parties as well.
12. Michelle Forrest, "Using the Power of the World Health Organization: The International Health Regulations and the Future of International Health Law," *Columbia Journal of Law and Social Problems* 33, no. 3 (2000): 153–179; Allyn L. Taylor, "Controlling the Global Spread of Infectious Diseases: Toward a Reinforced Role for the International Health Regulations," *Houston Law Review* 33, no. 5 (1997): 1327–1362.
13. World Health Organization (WHO) and World Trade Organization (WTO), *WTO Agreements and Public Health: A Joint Study by the WHO and the WTO Secretariat* (Geneva: WHO, 2002). See Craig Murray, "Implementing the New International Health Regulations: The Role of the WTO's Sanitary and Phytosanitary Agreement," *Georgetown Journal of International Law* 40, no. 2 (2009): 625–653.
14. Bruce Plotkin, "Human Rights and Other Provisions in the Revised International Health Regulations (2005)," *Public Health* 121, no. 11 (2007): 840–845.
15. Permanent Mission of the United States to the United Nations Office and Other International Organizations in Geneva, "Letter of IHR Reservation and Understanding," December 13, 2006.
16. Arts. 5(1), 13(1), annex 1. States, however, were not required to fulfill capacity obligations until 2012, and even then could obtain a two-year extension by submitting a justified need and an implementation plan to the WHO; in exceptional cases, states can request a further two-year extension that the D-G has the power to grant or deny (art. 5(2)).
17. States parties must designate "points of entry" (e.g., airports, ports, and ground crossings) that require core public health capabilities (arts. 20, 21).
18. Kumanan Wilson et al., "Strategies for Implementing the New International Health Regulations in Federal Countries," *Bulletin of the World Health Organization* 86, no. 3 (March 1, 2008): 215–220, quotation from p. 215.
19. WHO, *Checklist and Indicators for Monitoring Progress in the Development of IHR Core Capacities in States Parties* (Geneva: WHO, 2011).

20. Michael G. Baker and David P. Fidler, "Global Public Health Surveillance under New International Health Regulations," *Emerging Infectious Diseases* 12, no. 7 (July 2006): 1058–1065, quotation from p. 1060.
21. WHO, *Checklist and Indicators for Monitoring Progress in the Development of IHR Core Capacities in States Parties* (Geneva: WHO, 2011).
22. WHA, WHA Doc. 64/10 "Implementation of the International Health Regulations: Report of the Review Committee on the Functioning of the International Health Regulations (2005) in Relation to Pandemic (H1N1) 2009," May 5, 2011.
23. WHA, WHA Doc. A65/17 Add. 1, "Implementation of the International Health Regulations (2005): Report on Development of National Core Capacities Required under the Regulations," May 15, 2012.
24. WHO, *WHO Guidance for Use of Annex 2 of the International Health Regulations (2005)* (Geneva: WHO, 2008).
25. WHO, *Case Definitions for the Four Diseases Requiring Notification in All Circumstances under the International Health Regulations* (Geneva: WHO, 2005).
26. Thomas Haustein et al., "Should This Event Be Notified to the World Health Organization? Reliability of the International Health Regulations Notification Assessment Process," *Bulletin of the World Health Organization* 89, no. 4 (2011): 296–303.
27. WHO, *The Evolving Threat of Antimicrobial Resistance—Options for Action* (Geneva: WHO, 2012).
28. Temporary recommendations expire after three months but may be modified or extended for additional periods of up to three months. They may not continue beyond the second World Health Assembly after the D-G's initial determination of a PHEIC (art. 15(3)).
29. States parties cannot require travelers to undergo an invasive medical exam or vaccination as a condition of entry except in specified circumstances (art. 31(1)).
30. WHO, "Implementation of the International Health Regulations: Report of the Review Committee on the Functioning of the International Health Regulations (2005) in Relation to Pandemic (H1N1)," 13.
31. Rebecca Katz, "Use of Revised International Health Regulations during Influenza A (H1N1) Epidemic, 2009," *Emerging Infectious Diseases* 15, no. 8 (2009): 1165–1170.
32. See "Director-General Statement following the Fifth Meeting of the Emergency Committee," WHO, September 24, 2009, http://www.who.int/csr/disease/swineflu/5th_meeting_ihr/en/. Temporary recommendations issued on April 27, 2009, November 26, 2009, and February 24, 2010, contain similar guidance.
33. "The Economic Impact of Influenza A (H1N1)," TrendsUpdates, http://trendsupdates.com/the-economic-impact-of-influenza-a-h1n1/ (accessed 10/10/13).
34. Max Hardiman, "The Revised International Health Regulations: A Framework for Global Health Security," *International Journal of Antimicrobial Agents* 21, no. 2 (2003): 207–211.

35. WHA, "Revision of the International Health Regulations."
36. James G. Hodge Jr., "Global Legal Triage in Response to the 2009 H1N1 Outbreak," *Minnesota Journal of Law, Science and Technology* 11, no. 2 (2010): 599–628; Lance Gable et al., "Global Public Health Legal Responses to H1N1," *Journal of Law Medicine and Ethics* 39, supp. 1 (2011): 46–50.
37. WHO, "Implementation of the International Health Regulations: Report of the Review Committee on the Functioning of the International Health Regulations (2005) in Relation to Pandemic (H1N1)."
38. Rebecca Katz and Julie Fischer, "The Revised International Health Regulations: A Framework for Global Pandemic Response," *Global Health Governance* 3, no. 2 (2010), http://blogs.shu.edu/ghg/?attachment_id=379.
39. WHO, *Pandemic Influenza Risk Management: WHO Interim Guidance* (Geneva: WHO, 2013).

7. The Framework Convention on Tobacco Control

1. U.S. Department of Health, Education, and Welfare, *Smoking and Health: Report of the Advisory Committee of the Surgeon General of the Public Health Service* (Washington, DC: U.S. Public Health Service, 1964).
2. World Health Organization (WHO), *WHO Report on the Global Tobacco Epidemic, 2011: Warning about the Dangers of Tobacco* (Geneva: WHO, 2011).
3. "Tobacco: Fact Sheet N°339," WHO, http://www.who.int/mediacentre/factsheets/fs339/en/ (accessed 10/10/13).
4. "Tips from Former Smokers," Centers for Disease Control (CDC), http://www.cdc.gov/tobacco/campaign/tips/ (accessed 10/10/13); "Smoking and Tobacco Use: Fast Facts," CDC, http://www.cdc.gov/tobacco/data_statistics/fact_sheets/fast_facts/ (accessed 10/10/13).
5. "Adult Cigarette Smoking in the United States: Current Estimate," CDC, http://www.cdc.gov/tobacco/data_statistics/fact_sheets/adult_data/cig_smoking/ (accessed 10/10/13).
6. "Adult Cigarette Smoking in the United States: Current Estimate;" American Lung Association (ALA), *Trends in Tobacco Use* (New York: ALA, 2011).
7. Pam Belluck, "Smoking, Once Used to Reward, Faces a Ban in Mental Hospitals," *New York Times*, February 7, 2012, A1, A4.
8. John P. Pierce et al., "Camel No. 9 Cigarette-Marketing Campaign Targeted Young Teenage Girls," *Pediatrics* 125, no. 4 (2010): 619–626.
9. Michael Eriksen et al., *The Tobacco Atlas,* 4th ed. (Atlanta: American Cancer Society, 2012).
10. Richard Kluger, *Ashes to Ashes: America's Hundred-Year Cigarette War, the Public Health, and the Unabashed Triumph of Philip Morris* (New York: Vintage Books, 1997).
11. Allan Brandt, *The Cigarette Century: The Rise, Fall, and Deadly Persistence of the Product That Defined America* (New York: Basic Books, 2007), 114.
12. Mark Parascandola, "Public Health Then and Now: Cigarettes and the U.S. Public Health Service in the 1950s," *American Journal of Public Health* 91, no. 2 (2001): 196–205.

13. "The Reports of the Surgeon General: The 1964 Report on Smoking and Health," Profiles in Science, National Library of Medicine, http://profiles.nlm.nih.gov/ps/retrieve/Narrative/NN/p-nid/60 (accessed 10/10/13).
14. Robert N. Proctor, "The History of the Discovery of the Cigarette–Lung Cancer Link: Evidentiary Traditions, Corporate Denial, Global Toll," *Tobacco Control* 21, no. 2 (2012): 87–91.
15. Hearings on Regulation of Tobacco Products before the Subcommittee on Health and Environment (Part 1), 103rd Cong., 2nd Sess. (1994).
16. Stanton A. Glantz et al., "Looking through a Keyhole at the Tobacco Industry: The Brown and Williamson Documents," *Journal of the American Medical Association* 274, no. 3 (1995): 219–224.
17. Allyn L. Taylor, "An International Regulatory Strategy for Global Tobacco Control," *Yale Journal of International Law* 21, no. 2 (1996): 257–304.
18. World Health Assembly (WHA), WHA Resolution 48.11, "An International Strategy for Tobacco Control, May 12, 1995.
19. WHO, *History of the WHO Framework Convention on Tobacco Control* (Geneva: WHO, 2009); Ruth Roemer et al., "Origins of the WHO Framework Convention on Tobacco Control," *American Journal of Public Health* 95, no. 6 (2005): 936–938.
20. WHO, "Framework Convention on Tobacco Control" (2003), entered into force February 27, 2005.
21. Kate Lannan, "The WHO Framework Convention on Tobacco Control: The International Context for Plain Packaging," in Tania Voon et al., eds., *Public Health and Plain Packaging of Cigarettes* (Cheltenham, UK: Edward Elgar, 2012).
22. "Parties to the WHO Framework Convention on Tobacco Control," WHO, http://www.who.int/fctc/signatories_parties/en/ (accessed 10/10/13). President Bush signed the FCTC on May 10, 2004, but it has not yet been sent to the U.S. Senate for ratification.
23. WHO, *2012 Global Progress Report on Implementation of the WHO Framework Convention on Tobacco Control* (Geneva: WHO, 2012).
24. International Tobacco Control (ITC) Project and Office of Tobacco Control, China CDC, *ITC China Project Report: Findings from the Wave 1 to 3 Surveys (2006–2009)* (Beijing: China Modern Economic Publishing House, December 2012).
25. Rachel L. Schwartz et al., "World Tobacco Day 2011: India's Progress in Implementing the Framework Convention on Tobacco Control," *Indian Journal of Medical Research* 133, no. 5 (2011): 455–457.
26. The FCTC preamble mentions the right to health in three treaties: the International Covenant on Economic, Social and Cultural Rights; the Convention on the Elimination of All Forms of Discrimination against Women; and the Convention on the Rights of the Child.
27. Hadii M. Mamudu et al., "International Trade versus Public Health during the FCTC Negotiations, 1999–2003," *Tobacco Control* 20, no. 1 (2011): 1–10.
28. Conference of the Parties to the WHO FCTC, Fourth Session, *Punta del Este Declaration on the Implementation of the WHO FCTC,* FCTC/COP4(5) (Punta del Este, Uruguay, November 18, 2010).

29. Jonathan Liberman, "Four COPs and Counting: Achievements, Underachievements and Looming Challenges in the Early Life of the WHO FCTC Conference of Parties," *Tobacco Control* 21, no. 2 (2012): 215–220.
30. Parties to the Protocol to Eliminate Illicit Trade in Tobacco Products, United Nations Treaty Collection, http://treaties.un.org/Pages/ViewDetails.aspx?src=TREATY&mtdsg_no=IX-4-a&chapter=9&lang=en (accessed 10/10/13).
31. Conference of the Parties to the WHO FCTC, Third Session, *Guidelines for Implementation of Article 5.3 of the WHO Framework Convention on Tobacco Control,* FCTC/COP3(7) (Durban, South Africa, November 17–22, 2008).
32. Richard Doll et al., "Mortality in Relation to Smoking: 40 Years' Observations on Male British Doctors," *British Medical Journal* 309, no. 6959 (1994): 901–911.
33. *See* U.S. Department of Health and Human Services, *The Health Consequences of Involuntary Smoking: A Report of the Surgeon General* (Washington, DC: U.S. Public Health Service, 1986); "Fact Sheet: Secondhand Smoke and Cancer," National Cancer Institute, http://www.cancer.gov/cancertopics/factsheet/Tobacco/ETS (accessed 10/10/13).
34. WHO, Framework Convention on Tobacco Control, "Guidelines on Protection from Exposure to Tobacco Smoke," http://www.who.int/fctc/cop/art%208%20guidelines_english.pdf (accessed 10/10/13). The FCTC permits, as appropriate, smoking prohibitions in outdoor spaces (art. 8(2)).
35. W. C. Lippert and J. Gustat, "Clean Indoor Air Acts Reduce the Burden of Adverse Cardiovascular Outcomes," *Public Health* 126, no. 4 (2012): 279–285.
36. Conference of the Parties to the WHO FCTC, Second Session, *First Report of Committee A (Draft),* A/FCTC/COP/2/17 (Bangkok, July 4, 2007).
37. WHO, *Protection from Exposure to Second-Hand Tobacco Smoke: Policy Recommendations* (Geneva: WHO, 2007).
38. Benjamin Alamar and Stanton A. Glantz, "Effect of Smoke-Free Laws on Bar Value and Profits," *American Journal of Public Health* 97, no. 8 (2007): 1400–1402.
39. "Highlights: Tobacco Products," CDC, http://www.cdc.gov/tobacco/data_statistics/sgr/2000/highlights/tobacco/index.htm (accessed 10/10/13).
40. "Smoking 'Causes Damage in Minutes,' U.S. Experts Claim," *BBC News,* January 15, 2011, http://www.bbc.co.uk/news/health-12193602.
41. Conference of the Parties to the WHO FCTC, Fourth Session, *Partial Guidelines for Implementation of Articles 9 and 10 of the WHO FCTC,* FCTC/COP4(10) (Punta del Este, Uruguay, November 20, 2010) (adopting partial guidelines; as of 2013, the COP was circulating proposed guidelines).
42. Conference of the Parties to the WHO FCTC, Third Session, *Guidelines for Implementation of Article 11,* FCTC/COP3(10) (Durban, South Africa, November 22, 2008).
43. Dan Jaffe, "Letter to the Editor: Graphic Cigarette Warnings," *New York Times,* April 17, 2012, http://www.nytimes.com/2012/04/18/opinion/graphic-cigarette-warnings.html?_r=0.
44. Thomas Bollyky, "Developing-World Lung Cancer: Made in the USA," *Atlantic,* May 24, 2011, http://www.theatlantic.com/health/archive/2011/05/developing-world-lung-cancer-made-in-the-usa/239398/.

45. Becky Freeman and Simon Chapman, "Open Source Marketing: Camel Cigarette Brand Marketing in the 'Web 2.0' World," *Tobacco Control* 18, no. 3 (2009): 212–217.
46. Stuart Elliott, "R. J. Reynolds Introduces a Feminized Camel," *New York Times,* February 15, 2007, http://www.nytimes.com/2007/02/15/technology/15iht-adco.4605969.html.
47. World Bank, *Curbing the Epidemic: Governments and the Economics of Tobacco Control* (Washington, DC: World Bank, 1999).
48. Conference of the Parties to the WHO FCTC, Fourth Session, *Measures That Would Contribute to the Elimination of Cross-Border Advertising, Promotion, and Sponsorship,* Report of the Convention Secretariat, Decision FCTC/COP3(14) (August 15, 2010). *See* "Tobacco Advertising Directive (2003/33/EC)" (banning cross-border advertising in all media other than television).
49. Conference of the Parties to the WHO FCTC, Third Session, *Guidelines for Implementation of Article 13,* FCTC/COP3(12) (Durban, South Africa, November 22, 2008).
50. Conference of the Parties to the WHO FCTC, Fourth Session, *Guidelines for Implementation of Article 12 of the WHO Framework Convention on Tobacco Control,* FCTC/COP4(7) (Punta del Este, Uruguay, November 19, 2010).
51. Jonathan M. Samet and Heather Wipfli, "Unfinished Business in Tobacco Control," *Journal of the American Medical Association* 302, no. 6 (2009): 681–682.
52. Conference of the Parties to the WHO FCTC, Intergovernmental Negotiating Body on a Protocol on Illicit Trade in Tobacco Products, Fifth Session, "Draft Protocol to Eliminate Illicit Trade in Tobacco Products," FCTC/COP/INB-IT/5/5, April 4, 2012. The FCTC draft protocol defines illicit trade as "any practice or conduct prohibited by law and which relates to production, shipment, receipt, possession, distribution, sale or purchase, including any practice or conduct intended to facilitate such activity" (art. 2(6)).
53. Luk Joossens et al., "The Impact of Eliminating the Global Illicit Cigarette Trade on Health and Revenue," *Addiction* 105, no. 9 (2010): 1640–1649; Stephanie Nebehay, "WHO Brokers Deal to Stamp Out Tobacco Smuggling," *Reuters,* April 4, 2012, http://www.reuters.com/article/2012/04/04/us-tobacco-idUSBRE8330QZZ0120404 (quoting Ian Walton-George, INB chair).
54. Framework Convention Alliance, *How Big Was the Global Illicit Tobacco Trade Problem in 2006?,* prepared for the Second Session of the Conference of the Parties to the WHO FCTC (Bangkok, June 30–July 6, 2007) (estimating $40 billion–$50 billion in lost revenues); Luk Joossens et al., *How Eliminating the Global Illicit Cigarette Trade Would Increase Tax Revenue and Save Lives* (Paris: International Union against Tuberculosis and Lung Disease, 2009) (estimating more than $31 billion in lost revenues in 2007).
55. Luk Joossens and Martin Raw, "Strategic Directions and Emerging Issues in Tobacco Control: From Cigarette Smuggling to Illicit Tobacco Trade," *Tobacco Control* 21, no. 2 (2012): 230–234.
56. "Illicit Trade," British American Tobacco, http://www.bat.com/theman (accessed 10/10/13).

57. Canada Revenue Agency, "News Release: Federal and Provincial Governments Reach Landmark Settlement with Tobacco Companies," July 31, 2008, http://www.cra-arc.gc.ca/nwsrm/rlss/2008/m07/nr080731-eng.html.
58. WHO Framework Convention on Tobacco Control, Intergovernmental Negotiating Body, UN Doc. FCTC/COP/INB-IT/5/5 "Draft Protocol," April 4, 2012.
59. Benjamin Mason Meier, "Breathing Life into the Framework Convention on Tobacco Control: Smoking Cessation and the Right to Health," *Yale Journal of Health, Policy, Law and Ethics* 5, no. 1 (2005): 137–192, quotation from p. 149.
60. Conference of the Parties to the WHO FCTC, Fourth Session, *Partial Guidelines for Implementation of Articles 9 and 10 of the WHO FCTC.*
61. *Corn Products Int'l., Inc. v. The United Mexican States,* ICSID Case No. ARB(AF)/04/01, Decision on Responsibility, para. 87(j) (January 15, 2008), http://icsid.worldbank.org.
62. *FTR Holding v. Oriental Republic of Uruguay,* ICSID, Request for Arbitration, paras. 3–5, 77 (February 19, 2010), http://arbitrationlaw.com/library/ftr-holding-sa-philip-morris-products-sa-and-abal-hermanos-sa-v-oriental-republic-uruguay; Conference of the Parties to the WHO FCTC, Fourth Session, *Punta del Este Declaration on the Implementation of the WHO Framework Convention on Tobacco Control,* FCTC/COP4(5) (Punta del Este, Uruguay, November 18, 2010).
63. *Grand River Enterprises Six Nations, Ltd. v. United States of America,* ICSID Case No. ARB/10/5, Award, para. 154 (January 12, 2011) (rejecting Canadian tobacco company's challenge to the U.S. Master Tobacco Settlement under the North American Free Trade Agreement).
64. D. Hammond et al., "Effectiveness of Cigarette Warning Labels in Informing Smokers about the Risks of Smoking: Findings from the International Tobacco Control (ITC) Four Country Survey," *Tobacco Control* 15, no. S3 (2006): iii19–iii25.
65. "Uruguay Bilateral Investment Treaty Litigation," Philip Morris International, http://www.pmi.com/eng/media_center/company_statements/pages/uruguay_bit_claim.aspx (accessed 9/20/13).
66. "List of Pending Cases," International Center for Settlement of Investment Disputes, https://icsid.worldbank.org/ICSID/FrontServlet?requestType=GenCaseDtlsRH&actionVal=ListPending (accessed 9/20/13).
67. "Uruguay Bilateral Investment Treaty Litigation," Philip Morris International.
68. *Tobacco Plain Packaging Act 2011* (Cth) No. 148 (Austl.).
69. Attorney General Nicola Roxon, quoting cartoonist, public address, O'Neill Institute for National and Global Health Law, Georgetown University, May 17, 2012.
70. *JT International SA v. Commonwealth of Australia; British American Tobacco Australia Limited v. The Commonwealth* [2012], HCA 43.
71. Melanie A. Wakefield et al., "Introduction Effects of the Australian Plain Packaging Policy on Adult Smokers: A Cross-Sectional Study," *British Medical Journal Open* 3, no. 7 (2013), doi:10.1136/bmjopen-2013-003175.
72. Agreement for the Promotion and Protection of Investments, H.K.- Austl., September 15, 1993, 1748 U.N.T.S 385, entered into force October 15, 1993.

73. Andrew D. Mitchell and David M. Studdert, "Plain Packaging of Tobacco Products in Australia: A Novel Regulation Faces Legal Challenge," *Journal of the American Medical Association* 307, no. 3 (2012): 261–262.
74. Allyn Taylor, "Plain Packaging: Fighting the Chill of Investment Treaties," *Jurist,* December 7, 2011, http://jurist.org/forum/2011/12/allyn-taylor-tobacco-suit.php.
75. "As Nations Try to Snuff Out Smoking, Cigarette Makers Use Trade Treaties to Fire Up Legal Challenges," Fair Warning, http://www.fairwarning.org/2012/11/as-nations-try-to-snuff-out-smoking-cigarette-makers-use-trade-treaties-to-fire-up-legal-challenges/ (accessed 10/10/13).
76. "Australia—Certain Measures concerning Trademarks and Other Plain Packaging Requirements Applicable to Tobacco Products and Packaging," Dispute Settlement, DS434, http://www.wto.org/english/tratop_e/dispu_e/cases_e/ds434_e.htm (accessed 10/10/13).
77. Tom Miles, "Ukraine, Honduras Revive Tobacco Dispute with Australia at WTO," *Reuters,* September 13, 2013, http://www.reuters.com/article/2013/09/13/australia-tobacco-wto-idUSL5N0H91RQ20130913; World Trade Organization (WTO), "Items Proposed for Consideration at the Next Meeting of Dispute Settlement Body, http://www.wto.org/english/news_e/news13_e/dsb_agenda_25sep13_e.htm (accessed 9/20/13).
78. Warangkana Chomchuen, "Thai Court to Be Urged to Allow Larger Cigarette Warnings," *The Wall Street Journal*, September 17, 2013, http://blogs.wsj.com.
79. WTO, *United States—Measures Affecting the Production and Sale of Clove Cigarettes,* Report of the Appellate Body, WT/DS406/AB/R, April 2012.
80. Ibid., para. 235. The AB similarly reaffirmed TRIPS "flexibilities" to protect the public's health (para. 4).
81. "Menthol in Cigarettes, Tobacco Products; Request for Comments," 78 *Federal Register* 142 (July 24, 2013): 44484-44485.
82. "Preliminary Scientific Evaluation of the Possible Public Health Effects of Menthol versus Nonmenthol Cigarettes," Food and Drug Administration, July 23, 2013, http://www.fda.gov/downloads/ScienceResearch/SpecialTopics/PeerReviewofScientificInformationandAssessments/UCM361598.pdf.
83. WTO, *United States—Measures Affecting the Production and Sale of Clove Cigarettes*, Recourse to Article 22.2 of the DSU by Indonesia, WT/DS406/12, August 12, 2013.
84. "United States—Measures Affecting the Production and Sale of Clove Cigarettes: Current Status," WTO, http://www.wto.org/english/tratop_e/dispu_e/cases_e/ds406_e.htm (accessed 9/20/13).
85. Kenneth E. Warner and David Mendez, "Tobacco Control Policy in Developed Countries: Yesterday, Today, and Tomorrow," *Nicotine and Tobacco Research* 12, no. 9 (2010): 476–887.
86. Kenneth E. Warner and David Mendez, "Tobacco Control Policy in Developed Countries: Yesterday, Today and Tomorrow," *Nicotine and Tobacco Research* 12, no. 9 (2010): 876–887.
87. "International Conference on Public Health Priorities in the Twenty-First Century," Ministry of Health and Family Welfare, Government of India, http://www.endgameconference2013.in/ (accessed 9/23/13).

88. Neal L. Benowitz and Jack E. Henningfield, "Establishing a Nicotine Threshold for Addiction: The Implications for Tobacco Regulation," *New England Journal of Medicine* 331, no. 2 (1994): 123–125.
89. Coral Gartner and Ann McNeill, "Options for Global Tobacco Control beyond the Framework Convention in Tobacco Control," *Addiction* 105, no. 1 (2010): 1–3.
90. Deborah Khoo et al., "Phasing Out Tobacco: Proposal to Deny Access to Tobacco for Those Born from 2000," *Tobacco Control* 19, no. 5 (2010): 355–360; Andrew Darby and Amy Corderoy, "Bid to Ban Cigarettes for Anyone Born after 2000," *Sydney Morning Herald,* August 22, 2012, http://www.smh.com.au/national/bid-to-ban-cigarettes-for-anyone-born-after-2000-20120822-24liy.html.
91. George Thomson et al., "Ending Appreciable Tobacco Use in a Nation: Using a Sinking Lid on Supply," *Tobacco Control* 19, no. 5 (2010): 431–435.
92. Simon Chapman, "The Case for a Smoker's License," *PLoS Medicine* 9, no. 11 (2012): e1001342, doi:10.1371/journal.pmed.1001342.
93. Becky Freeman and Simon Chapman, "British American Tobacco on Facebook: Undermining Article 13 of the Global World Health Organization Framework Convention on Tobacco Control," *Tobacco Control* 19, no. 3 (2010): e1–e9, doi:10.1136/tc.2009.032847.
94. Ron Borland, "A Strategy for Controlling the Marketing of Tobacco Products: A Regulated Market Model," *Tobacco Control* 12, no. 4 (2003): 374–382; C. Callard et al., "Transforming the Tobacco Market: Why the Supply of Cigarettes Should Be Transferred from For-Profit Corporations to Non-Profit Enterprises with a Public Health Mandate," *Tobacco Control* 14, no. 4 (2005): 278–283.
95. Richard A. Daynard, "Doing the Unthinkable (and Saving Millions of Lives)," *Tobacco Control* 18, no. 1 (2009): 2–3; Robert N. Proctor, *Golden Holocaust* (Berkeley: University of California Press, 2012).
96. Michael S. Givel, "History of Bhutan's Prohibition of Cigarettes: Implications for Neo-Prohibitionists and Their Critics," *International Journal of Drug Policy* 22, no. 4 (2011): 306–310.
97. Peter Hanauer, "The Case against Tobacco Prohibition," *Tobacco Control* 18, no. 1 (2009): 3–4.
98. George Thomson et al., "What Are the Elements of the Tobacco Endgame?," *Tobacco Control* 21, no. 2 (2012): 293–295.

8. Health and Human Rights

1. United Nations General Assembly (UNGA), "International Covenant on Economic, Social and Cultural Rights (ICESCR)," UN Doc. A/6316 (1966), entered into force January 3, 1976, art. 12.
2. UN Treaty Collection, Status of Treaties, Chapter IV: Human Rights, treaties; UNGA, "International Covenant on Civil and Political Rights (ICCPR)" (1996), entered into force March 23, 1976.
3. UN, "Charter of the United Nations" (1945), entered into force October 24, 1945, preamble.

4. UNGA, Resolution A/60/1, "2005 World Summit Outcome Document," September 16, 2005, paras. 138–139.
5. To reconcile public health with human rights, scholars developed a "human rights impact assessment." Lawrence O. Gostin and Jonathan Mann, "Towards the Development of a Human Rights Impact Assessment for the Formulation and Evaluation of Health Policies," *Health and Human Rights* 1 (1994): 58–81; Lawrence O. Gostin, "Public Health, Ethics, and Human Rights: A Tribute to the Late Jonathan Mann," *Journal of Law, Medicine and Ethics* 29 (2001): 121–130.
6. Jonathan Mann et al., "Health and Human Rights," *Health and Human Rights* 1 (1994): 6–23.
7. African Union, *Africa Health Strategy 2007–2015*, CAMH/MIN/5(III) (3rd Sess. of the African Union Conference of Ministers of Health, Johannesburg, South Africa, April 9–13, 2007).
8. United States Department of State, "Observations by the United States of America on 'The Right to Health, Fact Sheet No. 31.' "
9. UNGA, Resolution 48/141, "High Commissioner for the Promotion and Protection of All Human Rights," December 20, 1993.
10. UNGA, Resolution 217A (III), "Universal Declaration of Human Rights," December 10, 1948, preamble, art. 26(2); ICESCR, art. 13.
11. UN Treaty Collection, Status of Treaties, Chapter IV: Human Rights, ICCPR, http://treaties.un.org/Pages/ViewDetails.aspx?mtdsg_no=IV-4&chapter=4&lang=en%23EndDec (accessed 9/30/13); UN Treaty Collection, Status of Treaties, Chapter IV: Human Rights, ICESCR," http://treaties.un.org/Pages/ViewDetails.aspx?mtdsg_no=IV-3&chapter=4&lang=en (accessed 9/30/13).
12. World Conference on Human Rights, "Vienna Declaration and Programme of Action," UN Doc. A/CONF.157/23, July 25, 1993.
13. UN Committee on Economic, Social and Cultural Rights (CESCR), General Comment No. 3, "The Nature of States Parties' Obligations," UN Doc. E/1991/23, December 14, 1990, para. 9.
14. CESCR, General Comment No. 14, "The Right to the Highest Attainable Standard of Health," UN Doc. E/C.12/2000/4, August 11, 2000.
15. CESCR, General Comment No. 3.
16. Ibid., para. 10.
17. Radhika Balakrishnan et al., *Maximum Available Resources and Human Rights: Analytical Report* (New Brunswick, NJ: Center for Women's Global Leadership, 2011).
18. UNGA, Resolution 63/117, "Optional Protocol to the International Covenant on Economic, Social and Cultural Rights," December 10, 2008, arts. 10–11.
19. UN Human Rights Committee, General Comment No. 6, "The Right to Life (Art. 6)," UN Doc. HRI\GEN\1\Rev.1, April 30, 1982, paras. 1, 5.
20. UN Human Rights Committee, General Comments Adopted by the Human Rights Committee, UN Doc. HRI/GEN/1/Rev.1 at 2, May 19, 1989; UNGA, Resolution 2200A (XXI), "Optional Protocol to the International

Covenant on Civil and Political Rights," entered into force March 23, 1976.

21. UNGA, "Optional Protocol to the ICESCR," art. 5; Human Rights Committee, "Rules of Procedure of the Human Rights Committee," UN Doc. CCPR/C/3/Rev.3, May 24, 1994, rule 86.
22. UNGA, "Optional Protocol to the ICESCR"; UNGA, "Optional Protocol to the ICCPR."
23. United Nations Commission on Human Rights, Siracusa Principles on the Limitation and Derogation Provisions in the International Covenant on Civil and Political Rights, UN Doc. E/CN.4/1985/4, September 28, 1984.
24. *Enhorn v. Sweden,* No. 56529/00 Eur. Ct. H.R. (2005) (relying on the Siracusa Principles to find that Sweden must use "less severe measures" before isolating a person infected with HIV).
25. Christof Heyns and Frans Viljoen, *The Impact of the United Nations Human Rights Treaties on the Domestic Level* (The Hague: Kluwer Law International, 2002).
26. UN Human Rights Council, Resolution 7/22, "Human Rights and Access to Safe Drinking Water and Sanitation," March 28, 2008; UN Human Rights Council, Resolution 7/23, "Human Rights and Climate Change," March 28, 2008; UN Human Rights Council, Resolution 17/19, "Human Rights, Sexual Orientation and Gender Identity," June 17, 2011.
27. CESCR, General Comment No. 14.
28. "Special Rapporteur on the Right of Everyone to the Enjoyment of the Highest Attainable Standard of Physical and Mental Health," http://www.ohchr.org/EN/Issues/Health/Pages/SRRightHealthIndex.aspx (accessed 9/30/13).
29. UN Human Rights Council, Resolution 15/22, "Right of Everyone to the Enjoyment of the Highest Attainable Standard of Physical and Mental Health," October 6, 2010.
30. Organization of African Unity, "African [Banjul] Charter on Human and Peoples' Rights" (1982), entered into force October 21, 1986; Organization of American States, "American Convention on Human Rights, O.A.S." (1969), entered into force July 18, 1978; Council of Europe "Convention for the Protection of Human Rights and Fundamental Freedoms" (1950), entered into force September 3, 1953. A protocol to the European convention recognized the right to education: Council of Europe "Protocol to the Convention for the Protection of Human Rights and Fundamental Freedoms" (1952), entered into force May 18, 1954; Council of Europe "European Social Charter" (1961), entered into force February 26, 1965; Council of Europe "European Social Charter" (revised) (1996), entered into force January 7, 1999.
31. James L. Cavallaro and Emily Schaffer, "Rejoinder: Justice before Justiciability: Inter-American Litigation and Social Change," *NYU Journal of International Law and Policy* 39 (2006): 345–383; *Case of the "Five Pensioners" v. Peru,* Inter-Am. Ct. H.R. (Ser. C) No. 98 (2003).

32. *Case of the "Street Children" (Villagrán-Morales et al.) v. Guatemala,* Inter-Am. Ct. H.R. (Ser. C) No. 63 (1999), para. 144; Steven R. Keener and Javier Vasquez, "A Life Worth Living: Enforcement of the Right to Health through the Right to Life in the Inter-American Court of Human Rights," *Columbia Human Rights Law Review* 40, no. 3 (2009): 595–624.
33. *Yakye Axa Indigenous Community v. Paraguay,* Inter-Am. Ct. H.R. (Ser. C) No. 125 (2005); *Sawhoyamaxa Indigenous Community v. Paraguay,* Inter-Am. Ct. H.R. (Ser. C) No. 146 (2006); *Xákmok Kásek Indigenous Community v. Paraguay,* Inter-Am. Ct. H.R. (Ser. C) No. 214 (2010).
34. The African Commission on Human and Peoples' Rights found a right to health violation in five cases through 2011: (1) *World Organisation against Torture, Lawyers' Committee for Human Rights, Jehovah Witnesses, Inter-African Union for Human Rights v. Zaire,* Comm. No. 25/89, 47/90, 56/91, 100/93 (March 1996); (2) *Amnesty International v. Mauritania,* Comm. No. 61/91 (May 11, 2000); (3) *The Social and Economic Rights Action Center and the Center for Economic and Social Rights v. Nigeria,* Comm. No. 155/96 (October 2001); (4) *D. R. Congo v. Burundi, Rwanda and Uganda,* Comm. No. 227/99 (May 2003); (5) *Purohit and Moore v. The Gambia,* Comm. No. 241/2001 (May 2003).
35. *The Social and Economic Rights Action Center and the Center for Economic and Social Rights v. Nigeria; Purohit and Moore v. The Gambia.*
36. *Hurtado v. Switzerland,* No. 17549/90 Eur. Ct. H.R. (1994); *Holomiov v. Moldova,* No. 30649/05 Eur. Ct. H.R. (2006); *Riviere v. France,* No. 33834/03 Eur. Ct. H.R. (2006).
37. *R.R. v. Poland,* No. 27617/04 Eur. Ct. H.R. (2011).
38. *N. v. The United Kingdom,* No. 26565/05 Eur. Ct. H.R. (2008).
39. Johannes Morsink, *The Universal Declaration of Human Rights: Origins, Drafting, and Intent* (Philadelphia: University of Pennsylvania Press, 1999); Eleanor D. Kinney and Brian Alexander Clark, "Provisions for Health and Health Care in the Constitutions of the Countries of the World," *Cornell International Law Journal* 37, no. 2 (2004): 285–355.
40. *Francis Coralie Mullin v. The Administrator, Union Territory of Delhi & Ors. (1981),* 2 S.C.R. 516 (India).
41. *In re Certification of the Constitution of the Republic of South Africa,* 1996 (4) SA 744 (CC) para. 78 (S. Afr.).
42. UNGA, Resolution 60/251, "Human Rights Council," March 15, 2006, preamble.
43. Hans V. Hogerzeil et al., "Is Access to Essential Medicines as Part of the Fulfillment the Right to Health Enforceable through the Courts?," *The Lancet* 368, no. 9532 (2006): 305–311.
44. *Minister of Health & Ors. v. Treatment Action Campaign (TAC),* 2002 (5) SA 721 (CC) (S. Afr.).
45. *Cruz del Valle Bermúdez & Ors. v. Ministerio de Sanidad y Asistencia Social,* Expediente No. 15.789, Sentencia No. 196 (Supreme Court of Venezuela), July 15, 1999; *Asociación Benghalensis v. Ministerio de Salud y Accion*

Social-Estado Nacional, A. 186. XXXIV (Supreme Court of Argentina), June 1, 2000.

46. "Docket: *Voluntary Health Association of Punjab (VHAP) vs. The Union of India and others,*" Human Rights Law Network, http://hrln.org/hrln/hiv-aids/pils-a-cases/205-docket-voluntary-health-association-of-punjab-vhap-vs-the-union-of-india-and-others.html (accessed 9/30/13).
47. *Attorney General of Canada v. PHS Community Services Society,* [2011] S.C.R. 44 (Supreme Court of Canada), September 30, 2011.
48. *People's Union of Civil Liberties (PUCL) v. Union of India,* Writ Petition (Civil) No. 196 of 2001 (Supreme Court of India), Supreme Court Order, May 2, 2003.
49. *People's Union of Civil Liberties (PUCL) v. Union of India,* Writ Petition (Civil) No. 196 of 2001 (Supreme Court of India), Supreme Court Order, November 28, 2001.
50. *Subhash Kumar v. State of Bihar & Ors.*, 1991 1 S.C.R. 5 (India).
51. *Attakoya Thangal v. Union of India,* A.I.R. 1990 Ker. 321 (India); *M. K. Balakrishnan & Ors. v. Union of India & Ors.*, Writ Petition (Civil) No. 230 of 2001 (Supreme Court of India), April 28, 2009.
52. *Matsipane Mosetlhanyane & Ors v. The Attorney General,* Civil Appeal No. CACLB-074-10 (Botswana Court of Appeals), January 27, 2011; *Sharma v. Nepal Drinking Water Corp.*, WP 2237/1990 (Constitutional Court, Nepal), July 10, 2001; "Constitution of the Kingdom of Nepal 2047 (1990)."
53. *Lindiwe Mazibuko & Ors. v. City of Johannesburg & Ors.*, CCT 39/09 (Constitutional Court of South Africa), October 8, 2009.
54. *Government of the Republic of South Africa & Ors. v. Grootboom,* 2000 (1) SA 46 (CC) (S. Afr.).
55. *Ahmedabad Municipal Corporation v. Nawab Khan Gulab Khan,* A.I.R. 1996 S.C. 152 (India); "Urban Homelessness," Supreme Court Commissioners, http://www.sccommissioners.org/Homelessness/homelessness.html (accessed 11/18/13).
56. Oscar A. Cabrera and Lawrence O. Gostin, "Human Rights and the Framework Convention on Tobacco Control: Mutually Reinforcing Systems," *International Journal of Law in Context* 7, no. 3 (2011): 285–303.
57. *Cáceres, Pablo J. v. Colombia,* Corte Constitucional [C.C.] [Constitutional Court], October 20, 2010, Sentencia C-830/10 (Colom.).
58. Peruvian Constitutional Tribunal, Jaime Barco Rodas, Unconstitutionality Claim of Article 3 of Law 28705, July 19, 2011.
59. Sentencia 14593, *Expediente: 08-012440-0007-CO* (Costa Rica Constitutional Court), September 23, 2008; *K. Ramakrishnan v. State of Kerala, A.I.R. 1999 Ker. 385 (India); Balderas Woolrich v. Mexico*, Amparo en Revisión 315/2010, Supreme Corte de Justicia de la Nación [Supreme Court] (2011).
60. *Soobramoney v. Minister of Health (Kwazulu-Natal),* 1997 (1) SA 765 (CC) (S. Afr.).
61. Octavio Luiz Motta Ferraz, "The Right to Health in the Courts of Brazil: Worsening Health Inequities?," *Health and Human Rights* 11, no. 2 (2009): 33–45.

62. Pearlie Joubert, "Grootboom Dies Homeless and Penniless," *Mail and Guardian*, August 8, 2008.
63. *Xákmok Kásek Indigenous Community v. Paraguay*.
64. The Global Health and Human Rights Database is a collaborative effort of the O'Neill Institute for National and Global Health Law at the Georgetown University Law Center and the Lawyers Collective (India), and is available at http://www.globalhealthrights.org.
65. Eric A. Friedman and Lawrence O. Gostin, "Pillars for Progress on the Right to Health: Harnessing the Potential of Human Rights through a Framework Convention on Global Health," *Health and Human Rights* 14, no. 1 (2012): 4–19.

9. Global Health, International Trade, and Intellectual Property

1. Kofi Annan, "Message to the Fifth Ministerial Conference of the WTO in Cancun," September 10, 2003, http://www.un.org/sg/statements/?nid=491.
2. Richard E. Baldwin, "Multilateralising Regionalism: Spaghetti Bowls as Building Blocs on the Path to Global Free Trade," *World Economy* 29, no. 11 (2006): 1451–1518, quotation from p. 1451.
3. Douglas Irwin, *The Genesis of the GATT* (New York: Cambridge University Press, 2008).
4. Peter Van den Bossche, *The Law and Policy of the World Trade Organization* (Cambridge: Cambridge University Press, 2008).
5. Amrita Narlikar, *The World Trade Organization: A Very Short Introduction* (Oxford: Oxford University Press, 2005), 25: Sylvia Ostry, "The Uruguay Round North-South Grand Bargain: Implications for Future Trade Negotiations," in Daniel L. M. Kennedy and James D. Southwick, eds., *The Political Economy of International Trade Law: Essays in Honour of Robert E. Hudec* (Cambridge: Cambridge University Press, 2002), 287.
6. John H. Jackson, *Sovereignty, the WTO, and Changing Fundamentals of International Law* (Cambridge: Cambridge University Press, 2006), 100.
7. World Trade Organization (WTO), "Marrakesh Agreement Establishing the World Trade Organization" (1994), entered into force January 1, 1995.
8. LDCs currently negotiating to join the WTO include Afghanistan, Bhutan, Comoros, Equatorial Guinea, Ethiopia, Liberia, Sao Tomé & Principe, Sudan, and Yemen. WTO, "Least-Developed Countries," http://www.wto.org/english/thewto_e/whatis_e/tif_e/org7_e.htm (accessed 9/30/13).
9. "Marrakesh Agreement," art. 4.
10. "Marrakesh Agreement," art. 9 (all decisions should be made by consensus "except as otherwise" or when a decision cannot be reached through consensus).
11. Van den Bossche, *Law and Policy*, 139.
12. Ibid., 138.
13. R. H. Steinberg, "In the Shadow of Law or Power? Consensus-Based Bargaining and Outcomes in the GATT/WTO," *International Organization* 56, no. 2 (2002): 339–374.
14. Constantine Michalopoulos, "The Developing Countries in the WTO," *World Economy* 22, no. 1 (1999): 117–143.

15. Kevin Watkins and Penny Fowler, *Rigged Rules and Double Standards: Trade, Globalization, and the Fight against Poverty* (Oxford: Oxfam, 2002).
16. "Marrakesh Agreement," art. 5; "Guidelines for Arrangements on Relations with Non-governmental Organizations," WTO, http://www.wto.org/english/forums_e/ngo_e/guide_e.htm (accessed 9/30/13).
17. WTO, "General Agreement on Tariffs and Trade" (GATT) (1994), entered into force April 15, 1994, art. 1.
18. The national treatment principle is not yet fully extended to trade in services; under the GATS, members may negotiate over which foreign services will be covered. Ellen Shaffer et al., "Global Trade and Public Health," *American Journal of Public Health* 95, no. 1 (2005): 23–24.
19. "Goodbye Doha, Hello Bali," *Economist,* September 8, 2012.
20. "Azevêdo Jump-Starts WTO Talks as Bali Ministerial Approaches," *Bridges Weekly Trade News Digest* 17, no. 30 (2013): 1–3.
21. John H. Jackson, *The World Trade Organization: Constitution and Jurisprudence* (London: Royal Institute of National Affairs, 1998), 22.
22. WTO, Panel Report, *Thailand—Restrictions on Importation of and Internal Taxes on Cigarettes,* BISD 37S/200 (November 7, 1990).
23. Tracey Epps, *International Trade and Health Protection: A Critical Assessment of the WTO's SPS Agreement* (Cheltenham: Edward Elgar, 2008), 205.
24. WTO, "Agreement on Technical Barriers to Trade" (TBT Agreement) (1994), entered into force January 1, 1995, art. 2.2.
25. TBT Agreement, art. 2.4.
26. WHO Secretariat and WTO Secretariat, *WTO Agreements and Public Health: A Joint Study by the WHO and WTO Secretariat* (Geneva: WTO, 2002), 34–35; Epps, *International Trade,* 4.
27. SPS Agreement, arts. 2.2, 5.4; WHO and WTO, *WTO Agreements and Public Health,* 35.
28. WTO, Appellate Body Report, *European Communities—EC Measures concerning Meat and Meat Products (Hormones),* WT/DS26/AB/R (January 16, 1998).
29. I. Glenn Cohen, *The Globalization of Health Care: Legal and Ethical Issues* (New York: Oxford University Press, 2013).
30. WTO, "General Agreement on Trade in Services" (GATS) (January 1995), entered into force January 1, 1995, art. 1; David Price et al., "How the World Trade Organisation Is Shaping Domestic Policies in Health Care," *The Lancet* 354, no. 9193 (1999): 1889–1892.
31. GATS, art. 1; Nick Drager and David P. Fidler, *GATS and Health Related Services: Managing Liberalization of Trade in Services from a Health Policy Perspective* (Geneva: WHO, 2004), 2.
32. Bernard Hoekman, "The General Agreement on Trade in Services: Doomed to Fail? Does It Matter?," *Journal of Industry, Competition and Trade* 8, nos. 3–4 (2008): 295–318.
33. "Schedules of Commitments and Lists of Article II Exemptions," WTO, http://www.wto.org/english/tratop_e/serv_e/serv_commitments_e.htm (accessed 9/30/13).

34. Drager and Fidler, *GATS and Health Related Services,* 1.
35. J. Michael Finger, *The Doha Agenda and Development: A View from the Uruguay Round* (Manila: Asian Development Bank, 2002); J. Michael Finger and Philip Schuler, eds., *Poor People's Knowledge: Promoting Intellectual Property in Developing Countries* (Washington, DC: World Bank and Oxford University Press, 2004).
36. WTO Secretariat, *TRIPS and Pharmaceutical Patents* (Geneva: WTO, 2006), 5.
37. Bipartisan Trade Promotion Authority Act, 19 U.S.C. § 3802(b)(4)(A)(i)(II) (2004).
38. World Health Assembly (WHA), "International Trade and Health," WHA59.26 Resolution, May 27, 2006 (urging member states to coordinate and develop coherence in their trade and health policies).
39. A. M. Kimball et al., "An Evidence Base for International Health Regulations: Quantitative Measurement of the Impacts of Epidemic Disease on International Trade," *Revue Scientifique et Technique (International Office of Epizootics)* 24, no. 3 (2005): 825–832; D. M. Bell, "Of Milk, Health and Trade Security," *Far Eastern Economic Review* 171, no. 8 (2008): 34–38.
40. Matthias Helble et al., "International Trade and Health: Loose Governance Arrangements across Sectors," in Kent Buse et al., eds., *Making Sense of Global Health Governance: A Policy Perspective* (New York: Palgrave Macmillan, 2009), 167.
41. David P. Fidler and Lawrence O. Gostin, "The New International Health Regulations: An Historic Development for International Law and Public Health," *Journal of Law, Medicine and Ethics* 34, no. 1 (2006): 85–94, quotation from p. 86.
42. "Members Discuss Trade Responses to H1N1 Flu," WTO, http://www.wto.org/english/news_e/news09_e/sps_25jun09_e.htm (accessed 9/30/13).
43. David M. Bell, "Of Milk, Health and Trade Security," in David A. Relman et al., eds., *Infectious Disease Movement in a Borderless World: Workshop Summary* (Washington, DC: Institute of Medicine, 2010), 235.
44. Least Developed Countries Trade Ministers, *Zanzibar Declaration,* WT/L/409 (August 6, 2001).
45. Joshua Meltzer, "The Challenges to the World Trade Organization: It's All about Legitimacy," *Brookings Institution Policy Paper* 2011–4 (2011): 1–18, quotation from p. 3; Daniel Altman, "Goodbye and Good Riddance: Why the WTO Could Soon Be Obsolete," *Newsweek,* February 20, 2011, http://www.thedailybeast.com/newsweek/2011/02/20/goodbye-and-good-riddance.html.
46. Seung Wha Chang, "WTO for Trade and Development Post-Doha," *Journal of International Economic Law* 10, no. 3 (2007): 553–570.
47. "Free Trade Agreements," Office of the United States Trade Representative, http://www.ustr.gov/trade-agreements/free-trade-agreements (accessed 9/30/13).
48. WHA, "International Trade and Health."

10. "Getting to Zero"

1. Lawrence O. Gostin et al., "Screening and Exclusion of International Travelers and Immigrants for Public Health Purposes: An Evaluation of United States Policy," *New England Journal of Medicine* 322, no. 24 (1990): 1743–1746. In 2010 the United States lifted restrictions on travel into the country for persons who are HIV-positive. See "U.S. Lifts Restrictions on Visas to HIV-Positive Travellers," *CNN*, January 5, 2010, http://www.cnn.com/2010/TRAVEL/01/04/us.hiv.visa/index.html.
2. Abdool Karim Q. et al., "Effectiveness and Safety of Tenofovir Gel, an Antiretroviral Microbicide, for the Prevention of HIV Infection in Women," *Science* 329, no. 5996 (2010): 1168–1174.
3. United Nations General Assembly (UNGA), Special Session on HIV/AIDS: Global Crisis—Global Action, New York, June 25–27, 2001.
4. Charles E Rosenberg, "Disease and Social Order in America: Perceptions and Expressions," *Milbank Quarterly* 64:Suppl (1986): 1–55.
5. Allan M. Brandt, "How AIDS Invented Global Health," *New England Journal of Medicine* 368, no. 23 (2013): 2149–2152.
6. Peter Piot et al., "The Global Impact of HIV/AIDS," *Nature* 410, no. 6831 (2001): 968–973.
7. Peter Piot et al., "Squaring the Circle: AIDS, Poverty, and Human Development," *PLOS Medicine* 4, no. 10 (2007): 1571–1575.
8. Douglas D. Heckathorn et al., "AIDS and Social Networks: HIV Prevention through Network Mobilization," *Sociological Focus* 32, no. 2 (1999): 159–179.
9. Samuel R. Friedman et al., "Sociometric Risk Networks and Risk for HIV Infection," *American Journal of Public Health* 87, no. 8 (1997): 1289–1296.
10. R. O. Brennan and D. T. Durack, "Gay Compromise Syndrome," *The Lancet* 318, no. 8259 (1981): 1338–1339.
11. Robert Klitzman and Ronald Bayer, *Mortal Secrets: Truth and Lies in the Age of AIDS* (Baltimore, MD: Johns Hopkins University Press, 2003).
12. Jonathan M. Mann, "AIDS: A Worldwide Pandemic," in M. S. Gottlieb et al., eds., *Current Topics in AIDS,* vol. 2 (London: John Wiley and Sons, 1989).
13. UNAIDS, *Global Report: UNAIDS Report on the Global Aids Epidemic 2010* (Geneva: UNAIDS, 2010), 30, 50.
14. Jeffrey Gettleman, "Ugandan Who Spoke Up for Gays Is Beaten to Death," *New York Times,* January 28, 2011, A4.
15. David Davidson, "LGBT Targets Don't Only Reside in Russia," *Huffington Post Blog*, August 16, 2013, http://www.huffingtonpost.com/daniel-davidson/lgbt-targets-dont-only-reside-in-russia_b_3762081.html.
16. "Twenty-Three Murders Logged Since April 2010 Due to Homophobic Hate-Crimes in South Africa up to February 28, 2012," FarmiTracker, March 1, 2012, http://www.boerentrepreneur.com/farmitracker/.
17. Alec Luhn, "Russian Anti-Gay Law Prompts Rise in Homophobic Violence," *Guardian*, September 1, 2013, http://www.theguardian.com/world/2013/sep/01/russia-rise-homophobic-violence.

18. Institute of Medicine (IOM), *Preventing HIV Transmission: The Role of Sterile Needles and Bleach* (Washington, DC: National Academy Press, 1995), 25.
19. Lawrence O. Gostin and Zita Lazzarini, "Prevention of HIV/AIDS among Injection Drug Users: The Theory and Science of Public Health and Criminal Justice Approaches to Disease Prevention," *Emory Law Journal* 46, no. 2 (1997): 587–696.
20. International Harm Reduction Development Program, *Harm Reduction Developments 2008: Countries with Injection-Driven HIV Epidemics* (New York: Open Society Institute, 2008), 13.
21. Ibid., 29, 52.
22. UNAIDS Commission on AIDS in Asia, *Redefining AIDS in Asia: Crafting an Effective Response* (New Delhi: Oxford University Press, 2008).
23. Kate Dolan et al., "HIV in Prison in Low-Income and Middle-Income Countries," *The Lancet Infectious Diseases* 7, no. 1 (2007): 32–41.
24. Ralf Jürgens et al., "HIV and Incarceration: Prisons and Detention," *Journal of the International AIDS Society* 14, no. 26 (2011): 1–17.
25. UNAIDS, *Population Mobility and AIDS: UNAIDS Technical Update* (Geneva: UNAIDS, 2001).
26. Na He et al., "HIV Risks among Two Types of Male Migrants in Shanghai, China: Money Boys vs. General Male Migrants," supplement, *AIDS* 21, no. S8 (2007): S73–S79; "HIV and AIDS in China," AVERT, http://www.avert.org/hiv-aids-china.htm (accessed 9/30/13).
27. World Health Organization (WHO) et al., *Global HIV/AIDS Response* (Geneva: WHO Press, 2011), 45.
28. Vito Russo, "Why We Fight," transcript, ACT UP, May 9, 1988, http://www.actupny.org/documents/whfight.htm.l.
29. Larry Kramer, *Reports from the Holocaust: The Story of an AIDS Activist,* rev. ed. (New York: St. Martin's Press, 1994).
30. George Bush, "The President's News Conference in Kennebunkport, Maine," transcript, September 2, 1991, George Bush Presidential Library and Museum, http://www.presidency.ucsb.edu/ws/?pid=19931.
31. Katharine Q. Seelye, "Helms Puts the Brakes to a Bill Financing AIDS Treatment," *New York Times,* July 5, 1995, http://www.nytimes.com/1995/07/05/us/helms-puts-the-brakes-to-a-bill-financing-aids-treatment.html.
32. Ryan White, "Ryan White's Testimony before the President's Commission on AIDS," transcript, 1988, http://en.wikisource.org/wiki/Ryan_White's_Testimony_before_the_President's_Commission_on_AIDS (accessed 9/30/13).
33. David France, "How to Survive a Plague," official trailer at 1:25, https://www.youtube.com/watch?v=ciuCg3Q7P_U (accessed 9/30/13).
34. Mark Heywood, "South Africa's Treatment Action Campaign: Combining Law and Social Mobilization to Realize the Right to Health," *Journal of Human Rights Practice* 1, no. 1 (2009): 14–36, quotation from p. 18.
35. David France, "Pictures from a Battlefield," *New York Magazine*, March 25, 2012, http://nymag.com/news/features/act-up-2012-4/.
36. *Minister of Health & Ors. v. Treatment Action Campaign* 2002 (5) SA 721 (CC).

37. Lucas Paoli Itaborahy, *State-Sponsored Homophobia: A World Survey of Laws Criminalising Same-Sex Sexual Acts between Consenting Adults* (Brussels, International Gay, Lesbian, Trans and Intersex Association, 2012).
38. *Naz Foundation v. Government of NCT of Delhi & Ors.*, 2009 160 *Delhi Law Times* 277 (India); UNGA, Resolution A/65/L, "2011 High-Level Meeting on AIDS, Draft Resolution," June 8, 2011.
39. UNAIDS, *Reducing HIV Stigma and Discrimination: A Critical Part of National AIDS Programmes: A Resource for National Stakeholders in the HIV Response* (Geneva: UNAIDS, 2007).
40. *People v. 49 W. 12 St. Tenants Corp.*, No. 43604/83 (N.Y. Sup. Ct. October 17, 1983) (noted in *Lambda Update,* February 1985).
41. Heather Murdock, "Nigerian HIV/AIDS Agency Seeks Anti-discrimination Law," *Voice of America,* July 10, 2012, http://www.voanews.com/content/nigerian_hiv_aids_agency_seeks_anti_discrimination_law/1382090.html.
42. Dan Levin, "Hope in China in a New Model for HIV Care," *New York Times,* January 3, 2013, A1.
43. Seng Sary, *Nature and Particularities of the Social Mobilization of Cambodian Women Living with HIV/AIDS in the Fight against the Epidemic* (Paris: National Agency for AIDS Research, June 2007–June 2009), 11.
44. L. I. Andrushcak and L. N. Khodakevich, "The Reduction of the HIV Vulnerability of Women Involved in the Sex Business in Ukraine through Social Mobilization and the Creation of Self-Support Networks," *Zhurnal Mikrobiologil, Epidemiologil, i Immunobiologil* 4 (July–August 2000): 118–119.
45. "About Us," Action for Aids, http://www.afa.org.sg/aboutafa.php (accessed 9/30/13).
46. Malcolm Gladwell, "Beyond HIV: The Legacies of Health Activism," *Washington Post,* October 15, 1992, A29.
47. Robert M. Wachter, *The Fragile Coalition: Scientists, Activists, and AIDS* (New York: St. Martin's Press, 1991), xiii.
48. Steven Epstein, *Impure Science: AIDS, Activism, and the Politics of Knowledge* (Berkeley: University of California Press, 1996), 348–349.
49. Susan Ferraro, "The Anguished Politics of Breast Cancer," *New York Times Magazine,* August 15, 1993, 25, http://www.nytimes.com/1993/09/12/magazine/l-the-anguished-politics-of-breast-cancer-064893.html.
50. UN Security Council (SC), Resolution 1308, UN Doc. S/Res/1308 (2000), July 17, 2000.
51. UNGA, Special Session on HIV/AIDS.
52. Lindsay Knight, *UNAIDS: The First Ten Years, 1996–2007* (Geneva: UNAIDS, May 2008), 181.
53. UNAIDS, "Evidence, Strategy and Results Department," http://www.unaids.org/en/ourwork/programmebranch/evidencestrategyandresultsdepartment/ (accessed 9/30/13); UNAIDS, "Prevention, Vulnerability and Rights Division," http://www.unaids.org/en/ourwork/programmebranch/evidencestrategyandresultsdepartment/preventionvulnerabilityandrightsdivision/ (accessed 9/30/13); UNAIDS, "Regional Support Teams," http://www.unaids.org/en/ourwork/regionalsupportteams/ (accessed 9/30/13).

54. UNAIDS, "Governance and Civil Society Involvement in the UN General Assembly," http://www.unaids.org/en/media/unaids/contentassets/documents/programmes/janbeagle/civilsociety/cs_B1L2_gov.pdf (accessed 9/30/13); UNAIDS, *Modus Operandi of the Programme Coordinating Board of the Joint United Nations Programme on HIV/AIDS (UNAIDS),* rev. ed. (Geneva: UNAIDS, 2011).
55. UNAIDS, "About UNAIDS," http://www.unaids.org/en/aboutunaids/ (accessed 9/30/13).
56. Pam Das and Udani Samarasekera, "What Next for UNAIDS?," *The Lancet* 372, no. 9656 (2008): 2099–2102.
57. Global Fund to Fight Aids, Tuberculosis and Malaria, *Strategic Investments for Impact: Global Fund Results Report 2012* (Geneva: Global Fund, 2012).
58. Office of the Global AIDS Coordinator, *Celebrating Life: The U.S. President's Emergency Plan for AIDS Relief; 2009 Annual Report to Congress* (Washington, DC: PEPFAR, 2009).
59. Office of the Global AIDS Coordinator, *PEPFAR Blueprint: Creating an AIDS-Free Generation* (Washington, DC: PEPFAR, November 2012), 2.
60. *Agency Int'l Dev. v. Alliance Open Soc'y Int'l, Inc.,* 570 U.S. (2013).
61. Lawrence O. Gostin, "PEPFAR's Antiprostitution Pledge: Spending Power and Free Speech in Tension," *Journal of the American Medical Association* 310, no. 11 (2013): 1127–1128.
62. Tom Lantos and Henry J. Hyde, United States Global Leadership against HIV/AIDS, Tuberculosis, and Malaria Reauthorization Act of 2008, H.R. 5501, 110th Cong. (2008).
63. Institute of Medicine (IOM), *Evaluation of PEPFAR* (Washington, DC: National Academies Press, 2013), 333.
64. Anita Slomski, "IOM Report Advises Shift in Focus for Next Phase of US AIDS Relief Program," *Journal of the American Medical Association* 309, no. 16 (2013): 1672–1673.
65. UNITAID, "How UNITAID Came About," http://www.unitaid.eu/en/about/-background-mainmenu-18/159 (accessed 9/30/13); UNITAID, "Pediatric HIV/AIDS Project," http://www.unitaid.eu/en/paediatrics (accessed 9/30/13); UNITAID, "Adult Second-Line HIV/AIDS Project," http://www.unitaid.eu/en/secondline (accessed 9/30/13); UNITAID, *Factsheet: Increasing Testing and Treatment Coverage for HIV/AIDS, TB, and Malaria Market Solutions* (Geneva: UNITAID, 2012).
66. UNITAID, *UNITAID Five Year Evaluation Summary* (Geneva: UNITAID, 2012), http://www.unitaid.eu.
67. WHO, *Scaling Up Antiretroviral Therapy in Resource-Limited Settings: Guidelines for a Public Health Approach* (Geneva: WHO, 2002).
68. WHO, *A New Health Sector Agenda for HIV/AIDS* (Geneva: WHO, 2011).
69. UNGA, Resolution 65/277, "Political Declaration on HIV and AIDS: Intensifying Our Efforts to Eliminate HIV and AIDS," June 10, 2011.
70. SC, Resolution 1983, June 7, 2011.

71. Global Commission on HIV and the Law, *Global Commission on HIV and the Law: Risks, Rights, and Health* (New York: United Nations Development Program, 2012).
72. "HIV Strategy Overview," Bill & Melinda Gates Foundation, http://www.gatesfoundation.org/What-We-Do/Global-Health/HIV (accessed 9/30/13).
73. "HIV/AIDS," Clinton Health Access Initiative, http://www.clintonhealthaccess.org/program-areas/HIV-AIDS (accessed 9/30/13).
74. Ronald Bayer and Claire Edington, "HIV Testing, Human Rights, and Global AIDS Policy: Exceptionalism and Its Discontents," *Journal of Health Politics, Policy and Law* 34, no. 3 (2009): 301–323.
75. WHO, *Increasing Access to Knowledge of HIV Status: Conclusions of a WHO Consultation, December 3–4, 2001* (Geneva: WHO, 2002).
76. Kevin M. De Cock and Anne M. Johnson. "From Exceptionalism to Normalization: A Reappraisal of Attitudes and Practice around HIV Testing," *British Medical Journal* 316, no. 7127 (1998): 290–293.
77. Centers for Disease Control and Prevention (CDC), "Introduction of Routine HIV Testing in Prenatal Care—Botswana 2004," *Morbidity and Mortality Weekly Report* 53, no. 46 (2004): 1083–1086.
78. UNAIDS and WHO, *UNAIDS/WHO Policy Statement on HIV Testing* (Geneva: WHO, 2004); Stuart Rennie and Frieda Behets, "Desperately Seeking Targets: The Ethics of Routine HIV Testing in Low-Income Countries," *Bulletin of the World Health Organization* 84, no. 1 (2006): 52–57; Bernard M. Branson et al., "Revised Recommendations for HIV Testing of Adults, Adolescents, and Pregnant Women in Health-Care Settings," *MMWR Recommendations and Reports* 55, no. 14 (2006): 1–17.
79. Ronald Bayer and Gerald M. Oppenheimer, "Routine HIV Testing, Public Health, and the USPSTF: An End to the Debate," *New England Journal of Medicine* 368, no. 10 (2013): 881–889.
80. UNAIDS, *The Role of Name-Based Notification in Public Health and HIV Surveillance* (Geneva: UNAIDS, 2000), 12.
81. Lawrence O. Gostin and James G. Hodge Jr., "The 'Names Debate': The Case for National HIV Reporting in the United States," *Albany Law Review* 61, no. 3 (1998): 679–743.
82. Lawrence O. Gostin, "'Police Powers and Public Health Paternalism: HIV and Diabetes Surveillance," *Hastings Center Report* 37, no. 2 (2007): 9–10.
83. UNAIDS and WHO, *Opening Up the HIV/AIDS Epidemic: Guidance on Encouraging Beneficial Disclosure, Ethical Partner Counselling, and Appropriate Use of HIV Case-Reporting* (Geneva: UNAIDS, 2000), 19–20.
84. UNAIDS and WHO, *2004 Report on the Global AIDS Epidemic* (Geneva: UNAIDS, 2004).
85. UNAIDS, "Condoms and HIV Prevention: Position Statement by UNAIDS, UNFPA and WHO," March 19, 2009, http://www.unaids.org.
86. Susan F. Hurley et al., "Effectiveness of Needle Exchange Programs for Prevention of HIV Infection," *The Lancet* 349, no. 9068 (1997): 1797–1800.
87. Andrew L. Ball, "HIV, Injecting Drug Use and Harm Reduction: A Public Health Response," *Addiction* 102, no. 5 (2007): 684–690.

88. Myron S. Cohen et al., "Prevention of HIV-1 Infection with Early Antiretroviral Therapy," *New England Journal of Medicine* 365, no. 6 (2011): 493–505.
89. WHO, "WHO Issues New HIV Recommendations Calling for Earlier Treatment," June 30, 2013, http://www.who.int/mediacentre/news/releases/2013/new_hiv_recommendations_20130630/en/.
90. "Realities in Global Treatment of H.I.V.," editorial, *New York Times,* July 25, 2013, http://www.nytimes.com/2013/07/25/opinion/realities-in-global-treatment-of-hiv.html.
91. Jared M. Baeten et al., "Antiretroviral Prophylaxis for HIV Prevention in Heterosexual Men and Women," *New England Journal of Medicine* 367, no. 5 (2012): 399–410.
92. Michael C. Thigpen et al., "Antiretroviral Preexposure Prophylaxis for Heterosexual HIV Transmission in Botswana," *New England Journal of Medicine* 367, no. 5 (2012): 423–434.
93. Jonathan S. Jay and Lawrence O. Gostin, "Ethical Challenges of Preexposure Prophylaxis for HIV," *Journal of the American Medical Association* 308, no. 9 (2012): 867–868.
94. Kachit Choopanya et al., "Antiretroviral Prophylaxis for HIV Infection in Injecting Drug Users in Bangkok, Thailand (the Bangkok Tenofovir Study): A Randomized, Double-Blind, Placebo-Controlled Phase 3 Trial," *The Lancet* 381, no. 9883 (2013): 2083–2090; Donald G. McNeil Jr., "Study Shows Pill Prevents H.I.V. among Drug Addicts," *New York Times,* June 13, 2013, http://www.nytimes.com/2013/06/13/health/pill-prevents-hiv-among-drug-addicts-in-a-study.html?pagewanted=all.
95. Catherine A. Hankins and Barbara O. de Zalduondo, "Combination Prevention: A Deeper Understanding of Effective HIV Prevention," supplement, *AIDS* 24, no. S4 (2010): S70–S80.
96. Supachai Rerks-Ngarm et al., "Vaccination with ALVAC and AIDSVAX to Prevent HIV-1 Infection in Thailand," *New England Journal of Medicine* 361, no. 23 (2009): 2209–2220.
97. Scott G. Hansen et al., "Immune Clearance of Highly Pathogenic SIV Infection," *Nature*, September 11, 2013, doi:10.1038/nature/12519; Donald G McNeil Jr., "New Hope for HIV Vaccine," *New York Times*, September 16, 2013, http://www.nytimes.com/2013/09/17/science/new-hope-for-hiv-vaccine.html.
98. Timothy J. Henrich et al., "Long-Term Reduction in Peripheral Blood HIV-1 Reservoirs following Reduced-Intensity Conditioning Allogeneic Stem Cell Transplantation in Two HIV-Positive Individuals" presentation, THAA0101 Oral Abstract, 19th International AIDS Conference, Washington, DC, July 22–27, 2012.
99. Donald G. McNeil Jr., "After Marrow Transplants, Two More Patients Appear HIV-Free without Drugs," *New York Times*, July 3, 2013, http://www.nytimes.com/2013/07/04/health/post-transplant-and-off-drugs-hiv-patients-are-apparently-virus-free.html.
100. Andrew Pollack and Donald G. McNeil Jr., "In Medical First, a Baby with HIV Is Deemed Cured," *New York Times,* March 4, 2013, A1.

101. "Microbicides," AIDS.gov, http://aids.gov/hiv-aids-basics/prevention/prevention-research/microbicides/ (accessed 9/30/13); Marianne W. Murethi et al., "Preservation HIV-1-Specific IFNy+ CD4+ T-Cell Responses in Breakthrough Infections after Exposure to Tenofovir Gel in the CAPRISA 004 Microbicide Trial," *Journal of Acquired Immune Deficiency Syndrome* 60, no. 2 (2012): 124–127.
102. Editorial, "Promises on AIDS Are Not Enough," *New York Times,* December 3, 2012, A24.
103. "Kaiser/UNAIDS Study Finds No Real Change in Donor Funding for HIV," Kaiser Family Foundation, http://kff/org/global-health-policy/press-release/kaiserunaids-study-finds-no-real-change-in-donor-funding-for-hiv/ (accessed 9/23/13).
104. UNAIDS, *Treatment 2015* (Geneva: UNAIDS, 2013).
105. UNAIDS, *Global Report: UNAIDS Report on the Global AIDS Epidemic* (Geneva: UNAIDS, 2013), 46.
106. Ibid., 47.
107. Ibid.
108. Citing research scientist Nelly Mugo in "Customizing HIV Prevention in a Global Pandemic," *VAX: The Bulletin on AIDS Vaccine Research*, August 29, 2012, http://www.vaxreport.org/Special-Features/Pages/default.aspx.
109. Michel Sidibé et al., "AIDS Is Not Over," *The Lancet* 380, no. 9859 (2012): 2058–2060 (advocating health system synergies in fighting AIDS).
110. Peter Piot, Thomas C. Quinn, "Response to the AIDS Pandemic: A Global Health Model," *New England Journal of Medicine* 368, no. 23 (2013): 2210–2218.

11. The International Migration of Health Workers

1. Paula O'Brien and Lawrence O. Gostin, *Health Worker Shortages and Global Justice* (New York: Milbank Memorial Fund, 2011). This chapter borrows from the content and analysis in that report.
2. Edward J. Mills et al., "Should Active Recruitment of Health Workers from Sub-Saharan Africa Be Viewed as a Crime?," *The Lancet* 371, no. 9613 (2008): 685–688; Solomon R. Benatar, "An Examination of Ethical Aspects of Migration and Recruitment of Health Care Professionals from Developing Countries," *Clinical Ethics* 2, no. 1 (2007): 2–7.
3. World Health Organization (WHO), *Human Resources in Health: Report by the Secretariat,* UN Doc. EB114/17 (April 29, 2004).
4. WHO, *Working Together for Health: The World Health Report 2006* (Geneva: WHO, 2006), 19–20.
5. Global Health Workforce Alliance, "About the Alliance," http://www.who.int/workforcealliance/about/en/ (accessed 9/30/13).
6. WHO, *Working Together for Health.*
7. James Dwyer, "What's Wrong with the Global Migration of Health Care Professionals? Individual Rights and International Justice," *Hastings Center Report* 37, no. 5 (2007): 36–43.
8. Kate Tulenko, "America's Health Worker Mismatch," *New York Times,* September 14, 2012, A23.

9. Mark W. Stanton, *Hospital Nurse Staffing and Quality of Care* (Rockville, MD: Agency for Healthcare Research and Quality, March 2004).
10. Dwyer, "What's Wrong with the Global Migration of Health Care Professionals?"
11. Jean-Christophe Dumont and Pascal Zurn, "Immigrant Health Workers in OECD Countries in the Broader Context of Highly Skilled Migration, Part III," in *International Migration Outlook* (Paris: Organization for Economic Cooperation and Development, 2007), 161–228.
12. Mona Mourshed et al., "Gulf Cooperation Council Health Care: Challenges and Opportunities," in Margareta Drzeniek Hanouz and Sherif El Diwany and Tark Yousef, *Arab World Competitiveness Report 2007* (Geneva: World Economic Forum, 2007), chap. 2.1, 55–64.
13. Julio Frenk et al., "Health Professionals for a New Century: Transforming Education to Strengthen Health Systems in an Interdependent World," *The Lancet* 376, no. 9756 (2010): 1923–1958.
14. World Health Assembly (WHA), Resolution WHA64.6, "Health Workforce Strengthening," May 24, 2011.
15. International Council of Nurses and Florence Nightingale International Foundation, *The Global Nursing Shortage: Priority Areas for Intervention* (Geneva: International Council of Nurses, 2006).
16. World Bank Human Development Department et al., *The Nurse Labor and Education Markets in the English-Speaking CARICOM: Issues and Options for Reform* (Washington, DC: World Bank, June 2009).
17. Patricia Pittman et al., *U.S.-Based International Nurse Recruitment: Structure and Practices of a Burgeoning Industry* (Washington, DC: AcademyHealth, November 2007); Linda H. Aiken, "U.S. Nurse Labor Market Dynamics Are Key to Global Nurse Sufficiency," *Health Services Research* 42, no. 3, part II (2007): 1299–1320.
18. Pittman et al., *U.S.-Based International Nurse Recruitment.*
19. UN Human Rights Committee, General Comment No. 27, "Freedom of Movement," UN Doc. CCPR/C/21/Rev.1/Add.9, November 2, 1999.
20. United Nations General Assembly (UNGA), Resolution 217A (III), "Universal Declaration of Human Rights," December 10, 1948, art. 13; UNGA, "International Covenant on Civil and Political Rights" (1966) entry enforced January 3, 1976, art. 12; UNGA, Resolution 45/158, "International Convention on the Protection of the Rights of All Migrant Workers and Members of Their Families," entry enforced July 1, 2003, art. 8.
21. UNGA, "International Convention on the Protection of the Rights of All Migrant Workers and Members of Their Families"; International Labour Organization, Forced Labour Convention, C029 (June 28, 1930); International Labour Organization, Freedom of Association and Protection of the Right to Organise Convention, C87 (July 9, 1948); International Labour Organization, Right to Organise and Collective Bargaining Convention, C098 (July 1, 1949); International Labour Organization, Equal Remuneration Convention, C100 (June 29, 1951); International Labour Organization, Discrimination (Employment and Occupation) Convention, C111 (June 25, 1958).

22. National Health Service Employers, *Code of Practice for International Recruitment* (April 24, 2012).
23. Memorandum of Understanding between the Government of the United Kingdom of Great Britain and Northern Ireland and the Government of the Republic of South Africa on the Reciprocal Educational Exchange of Healthcare Concepts and Personnel (October 2003).
24. The process began in 2004, with the Health Assembly urging member states to develop strategies and directing the Director-General to develop a code of practice (WHA Doc. 57.19). See Allyn L. Taylor and Ibadat S. Dhillon, "The WHO Global Code of Practice on the International Recruitment of Health Personnel: The Evolution of Global Health Diplomacy," *Global Health Governance* 5 (Fall 2011).
25. Margaret Chan, "Agreements at World Health Assembly: A Gift to Public Health," closing remarks at the Sixty-Third World Health Assembly, Geneva, May 21, 2010.
26. WHO, WHA Doc. A66/25 "The Health Workforce: Advances in responding to Shortages and Migration, and in Preparing for Emerging Needs," (April 12, 2013); Amani Siyam et al., "Monitoring the Implementation of the WHO Global Code of Practice on the International Recruitment of Health Personnel," *Bulletin of the World Health Organization* 91, no. 11 (2013): 816–823.
27. Allyn L. Taylor et al., "Stemming the Brain Drain: A WHO Global Code of Practice on International Recruitment of Health Personnel," *New England Journal of Medicine* 365, no. 25 (2011): 2348–2351.

12. Pandemic Influenza

1. Endang R. Sedyaningsih et al., "Towards Mutual Trust, Transparency and Equity in Virus Sharing Mechanism: The Avian Influenza Case of Indonesia," *Annals Academy of Medicine* 37, no. 6 (2008): 482–487.
2. David P. Fidler, "Negotiating Equitable Access to Influenza Vaccines: Global Health Diplomacy and the Controversies Surrounding Avian Influenza H5N1 and Pandemic Influenza H1N1," *PLoS Medicine* 7, no. 5 (2010): doi: 10.1371/journal.pmed.1000247.
3. Laurie Garrett and David P. Fidler, "Sharing H5N1 Viruses to Stop a Global Influenza Pandemic," *PLoS Medicine* 4, no. 11 (2007): e330, http://dx.doi.org/10.1371/journal.pmed.0040330.
4. World Health Organization (WHO), "Pandemic Influenza Preparedness Framework for the Sharing of Influenza Viruses and Access to Vaccines and Other Benefits," adopted in WHO, WHO Doc. A64/8, *Report by the Open-Ended Working Group of Member States on Pandemic Influenza Preparedness: Sharing of Influenza Viruses and Access to Vaccines and Other Benefits,* May 5, 2011.
5. WHA, WHA Doc. A64/10, "Implementation of the International Health Regulations (2005): Report of the Review Committee on the Functioning of the International Health Regulations (2005) in Relation to Pandemic (H1N1) 2009," May 5, 2011.

6. Patrick Adams, "The Influenza Enigma," *Bulletin of the World Health Organization* 90, no. 4 (2012): 250–251.
7. Cristoph Steffen et al., "Improving Influenza Surveillance in Sub-Saharan Africa," *Bulletin of the World Health Organization* 90, no. 4 (2012): 301–305.
8. Other formulations of essential prerequisites include the development of a pathogenic (disease-causing) flu strain in humans, readily transmissible from one person to another, and against which most of the world's population lacks protective immunity (effective antibodies).
9. Richard E. Neustadt and Harvey Fineberg, *The Epidemic That Never Was: Policy-Making and the Swine Flu Affair* (New York: Vintage Books, 1983).
10. Lawrence O. Gostin, "Public Health Strategies for Pandemic Influenza: Ethics and the Law," *Journal of the American Medical Association* 295, no. 14 (2006): 1700–1704.
11. "H5N1 Avian Influenza: Timeline of Major Events," WHO, December 13, 2011, http://www.who.int/influenza/human_animal_interface/avian_influenza/H5N1_avian_influenza_update.pd.
12. Margaret Chan, "Pandemics: Working Together for an Equitable Response," transcript, Pacific Health Summit, June 13, 2007, http://www.who.int/dg/speeches/2007/20070613_seattle/en/.
13. WHO, *WHO Strategic Action Plan for Pandemic Influenza* (Geneva: WHO, 2007).
14. Joachim Otte et al., "Impacts of Avian Influenza Virus on Animal Production in Developing Countries," *CAB Reviews: Perspectives in Agriculture, Veterinary Science, Nutrition and Natural Resources* 3, no. 080 (2008), http://www.fao.org/docs/eims/upload//251044/aj201e00.pdf.
15. "Cumulative Number of Confirmed Human Cases for Avian Influenza A (H5N1) Reported to WHO, 2003–2013," WHO, http://www.who.int/influenza/human_animal_interface/H5N1_cumulative_table_archives/en/ (accessed 11/17/13).
16. Margaret Chan, "Swine Influenza: Statement by WHO Director-General, Dr. Margaret Chan," April 25, 2009, http://www.who.int/csr/don/2009_04_25/en/.
17. David P. Fidler, "The Swine Flu Outbreak and International Law," *ASIL Insights* 13, no. 5 (2009), http://www.asil.org/insights090427.cfm.
18. Lawrence O. Gostin, "Influenza A (H1N1) and Pandemic Preparedness under the Rule of International Law," *Journal of the American Medical Association* 301, no. 22 (2009): 2376–2378.
19. "Updated CDC Estimates of 2009 H1N1 Influenza Cases, Hospitalizations and Deaths in the United States, April 2009 to April 2010," Centers for Disease Control and Prevention (CDC), May 14, 2010, http://www.cdc.gov/h1n1flu/estimates_2009_h1n1.htm.
20. Fatimah S. Dawood, "Estimated Global Mortality Associated with the First Twelve Months of 2009 Pandemic Influenza A H1N1 Virus Circulation: A Modeling Study," *The Lancet* 12, no. 9 (2012): 687–695.
21. "First Global Estimates of 2009 H1N1 Pandemic Mortality Released by CDC-Led Collaboration," CDC, June 25, 2012, http://www.cdc.gov/flu/spotlights/pandemic-global-estimates.htm.

22. WHO, "Implementation of the International Health Regulations (2005)."
23. Ron A. M. Fouchier et al., "Avian Influenza A Virus (H7N7) Associated with Human Conjunctivitis and a Fatal Case of Acute Respiratory Distress Syndrome," *Proceedings of the National Academy of Sciences of the United States of America* 101, no. 5 (2004): 1356–1361.
24. Laurie Garrett, "The Big One? Is China Covering Up Another Flu Pandemic—or Getting It Right This Time?," *Foreign Policy,* April 24, 2013, http://www.foreignpolicy.com/articles/2013/04/23/the_big_one.
25. Timothy M. Uyeki and Nancy J. Cox, "Global Concerns *Regarding Novel Influenza A (H7N9) Virus Infections," New England Journal of Medicine* 368, no. 20 (2013): 1862–1864.
26. "Number of Confirmed Human Cases of Avian Influenza A(H7N9) Reported to WHO, Report 10–data in WHO/HQ as of October 25, 2013, 14:45 GMT +1," WHO, http://www.who.int/influenza/human_animal_interface/influenza_h7n9/Data_Reports/en/index.html (accessed 11/17/13).
27. "Bird Flu Viruses Could Re-emerge in Upcoming Flu Season," Food and Agricultural Organization of the United Nations (FAO), September 16, 2013, http://www.fao.org/news/story/en/item/196736/icode/.
28. "FAO Launches Emergency Projects to Fight H7N9 Avian Flu," FAO, Regional Office for Asia and the Pacific, September 18, 2013, http://www.fao.org/asiapacific/rap/home/news/detail/en/?news_uid=197054.
29. Marcel Salathé et al., "Influenza A (H7N9) and the Importance of Digital Epidemiology," *New England Journal of Medicine* 369, no. 5 (2013): 401–404.
30. Nahoko Shindo, "Spreading the Word about Seasonal Influenza," *Bulletin of the World Health Organization* 90, no. 9 (2012): 252–253.
31. Pernille Jorgensen et al., "Unequal Access to Vaccines in the WHO European Region during the A(H1N1) Influenza Pandemic in 2009," *Vaccine* 21, no. 38 (2013): 4060–4062.
32. Jane Parry, "Clipping the Wings of Avian Influenza," *Bulletin of the World Health Organization* 90, no. 9 (2012): 638–639; Hongjie Yu et al., "Effect of Closure of Live Poultry Markets on Poultry-to-Person Transmission of Avian Influenza A H7N9 Virus: An Ecological Study," *The Lancet* (2013), doi: 10.1016/S0140-6736(13)61904-2.
33. "United States Seeks to Eliminate India's Restrictions on Various U.S. Agricultural Exports," Office of the United States Trade Representative, May 11, 2012, http://www.ustr.gov/about-us/press-office/press-releases/2012/United-States-Seeks-to-Eliminate-India-Restrictions.
34. WHO, *Pandemic Influenza Preparedness and Response: A WHO Guidance Document* (Geneva: WHO, 2009).
35. WHO, *Pandemic Influenza Risk Management: WHO Interim Guidance* (Geneva: WHO, 2013).
36. WHO, *Implementation of the International Health Regulations (2005),* 19.
37. WHO, *Pandemic Influenza Risk Management,* 3, 7.
38. WHO, *Global Pandemic Influenza Action Plan to Increase Vaccine Supply* (Geneva: WHO, 2006).
39. WHO, *Report of the Second WHO Consultation on the Global Action Plan for Influenza Vaccines (GAP)* (Geneva: WHO, 2012).

40. David P. Fidler, "Negotiating Equitable Access to Influenza Vaccines: Global Health Diplomacy and the Controversies Surrounding Avian Influenza H5N1 and Pandemic Influenza H1N1," *PLoS Medicine* 7, no. 5 (2004): doi: 10.1371/journal.pmed.1000247.
41. David P. Fidler and Lawrence O. Gostin, "The WHO Pandemic Influenza Preparedness Framework: A Milestone in Global Health Governance for Health," *Journal of the American Medical Association* 306, no. 2 (2011): 200–201; Nicole Jefferies, "Levelling the Playing Field? Sharing of Influenza Viruses and Access to Vaccines and Other Benefits," *Journal of Law and Medicine* 20, no. 1 (2012): 59–73.
42. WHO, *Pandemic Influenza Preparedness Framework: Distribution of Partnership Contribution among Companies* (Geneva: WHO, 2013).
43. WHO, *Pandemic Influenza Preparedness: Sharing of Influenza Viruses and Access to Vaccines and Other Benefits, Report of the Meeting of the Pandemic Influenza Preparedness Framework Advisory Group,* WHO Doc. A66/17 Add. 1 (May 14, 2013).
44. David P. Fidler and Lawrence O. Gostin, *Biosecurity in the Global Age: Biological Weapons, Public Health, and the Rule of Law* (Palo Alto: Stanford University Press, 2008).
45. Carl Zimmer, "Flu That Leapt from Birds to Seals Is Studied for Human Threat," *New York Times,* July 31, 2012, D3.
46. Terrence M. Tumpey et al., "Characterization of the Reconstructed 1918 Spanish Influenza Pandemic Virus," *Science* 310, no. 5745 (2005): 77–80.
47. Philip Hunter, "H5N1 Infects the Biosecurity Debate," *EMBO Reports* 13, no. 7 (2012): 604–607.
48. "Press Statement on the NSABB Review of H5N1 Research," National Institutes of Health, December 20, 2011, http://www.nih.gov/news/health/dec2011/od-20.htm.
49. John D. Kraemer and Lawrence O. Gostin, "The Limits of Government Regulation of Science," *Science* 335, no. 6072 (2012): 1047–1049.
50. David Malakoff, "Flu Controversy Spurs Research Moratorium," *Science* 335, no. 6067 (2012): 387–389; Denise Grady, "Bird Flu Scientists Agree to Delay Virus Research," *New York Times,* January 21, 2012, A3.
51. Bridget M. Kuehn, "International Debate Erupts over Research on Potentially Dangerous Bird Flu Strains," *Journal of the American Medical Association* 307, no. 10 (2012): 1009–1012.
52. WHO, *Report on Technical Consultation on H5N1 Research Issues,* Geneva: WHO, 2012).
53. David Brown, "Biosecurity Advisory Board Reverses Decision on 'Engineered Bird Flu' Papers," *Washington Post,* March 30, 2012, http://articles.washingtonpost.com/2012-03-30/national/35450272_1_national-science-advisory-board-ron-fouchier-h5n1.
54. Sander Herfst et al., "Airborne Transmission of Influenza A/H5N1 Virus between Ferrets," *Science* 336, no. 6088 (2012): 1534–1541; Masaki Imai et al., "Experimental Adaptation of an Influenza H5 HA Confers Respiratory Droplet Transmission to a Reassortant H5 HA/H1N1 Virus in Ferrets," *Nature* 486, no. 7403 (2012): 420–428.

55. Council Regulation 428/2009, Setting Up a Community Regime for the Control of Exports, Transfer, Brokering and Transit of Dual-Use Items, 2009 O.J. (L.134/1).
56. Robert Roos, "Dutch Export Rules Could Block Publication of Fouchier H5N1 Study," *Center for Infection Disease Research and Policy (CIDRAP), University of Minnesota*, March 12, 2012, http://www.cidrap.umn.edu/news-perspective/2012/03/dutch-export-rules-could-block-publication-fouchier-h5n1-study.
57. Robert Roos, "Dutch Court Affirms Limit on Publishing H5N1 Study," *Center for Infection Disease Research and Policy (CIDRAP), University of Minnesota*, September 26, 2013, http://www.cidrap.umn.edu/news-perspective/2013/09/dutch-court-affirms-limit-publishing-h5n1-findings.
58. Kraemer and Gostin, "The Limits of Government Regulation of Science."
59. Science and Technology Policy Office, *U.S. Government Policy for Oversight of Life Sciences Dual Use Research of Concern* (Washington, DC: The White House, March 29, 2012).
60. Science and Technology Policy Office, *United States Governmental Policy for Institutional Oversight of Life Sciences Dual Use Research of Concern* (Washington, DC: The White House, 2013).
61. U.S. Department of Health and Human Services (HHS), *Framework for Guiding Funding Decisions about Research Proposals with the Potential for Generating Highly Pathogenic Avian Influenza H5N1 Viruses That Are Transmissible among Mammals by Respiratory Droplets* (Washington, DC: HHS, February 21, 2013).

13. The "Silent" Pandemic of Noncommunicable Diseases

1. Rafael Lozano et al., "Global and Regional Mortality from 235 Causes of Death for Twenty Age Groups in 1990 and 2010: A Systematic Analysis for the Global Burden of Disease Study 2010," *The Lancet* 380, no. 9859: 2095–2128.
2. Christopher K. Hwang et al., "Rural Diabetes Prevalence Quintuples over Twenty-Five Years in Low- and Middle-Income Countries: A Systematic Review and Meta-analysis," *Diabetes Research and Clinical Practice* 96, no. 3 (2012): 271–285.
3. World Health Organization (WHO), *Global Status Report on Noncommunicable Diseases 2010* (Geneva: WHO, 2011).
4. Ibid., 11.
5. N. R. Kleinfield, "Modern Ways Open India's Doors to Diabetes," *New York Times,* September 13, 2006, A1.
6. Robyn Norton et al., "Unintentional Injuries," in Dean T. Jamison et al., eds., *Disease Control Priorities in Developing Countries,* 2nd ed. (Washington, DC: World Bank, 2006), 737–754.
7. David E. Bloom et al., *The Global Economic Burden of Noncommunicable Diseases* (Geneva: World Economic Forum, 2011), 27, 29.
8. Catherine de Martel et al., "Global Burden of Cancers Attributable to Infections in 2008: A Review and Synthetic Analysis," *Lancet Oncology* 13, no. 6 (2012): 607–615.

9. Anne E. Becker and Arthur Kleinman, "Mental Health and the Global Agenda," *New England Journal of Medicine* 369, no. 1 (2013): 66–73.
10. "New York Soda Cap Wouldn't Beat Obesity," editorial, *USA Today,* http://usatoday30.usatoday.com/news/opinion/editorials/story/2012-06-03/soda-16-ounces-Bloomberg/55366704/1 (accessed 10/4/13).
11. Ashley N. Gearhardt et al., "Preliminary Validation of the Yale Food Addiction Scale," *Appetite* 52, no. 2 (2009): 430–436.
12. Lawrence O. Gostin and Kieran G. Gostin, "A Broader Liberty: J. S. Mill, Paternalism, and the Public's Health," *Public Health* 123, no. 3 (2009): 214–222.
13. Roger S. Magnusson, "What's Law Got to Do with It, Part 2: Legal Strategies for Healthier Nutrition and Obesity Prevention," *Australia and New Zealand Health Policy* 5, no. 11 (2008): 1–17; Rob Stein, "New York City Starts to Monitor Diabetics," *Washington Post,* January 11, 2006, A03.
14. "Final Design of Consistent Nutritional Labeling System Given Green Light," UK Department of Health, June 19, 2013, https://www.gov.uk/government/news/final-design-of-consistent-nutritional-labelling-system-given-green-light.
15. "Finland Salt Action Summary," World Action on Salt and Health (WASH), http://www.worldactiononsalt.com/worldaction/europe/53774.html (accessed 10/4/13).
16. Erkki Vartiainen et al., "Thirty-five-Year Trends in Cardiovascular Risk Factors in Finland," *International Journal of Epidemiology* 39, no. 2 (2010): 504–518; Heikki Karppanen and Eero Mervalla, "Sodium Intake and Hypertension," *Progress in Cardiovascular Diseases* 49, no. 2 (2006): 59–75.
17. Institute of Medicine (IOM), *Food Marketing to Children and Youth: Threat or Opportunity?* (Washington, DC: National Academies Press, 2006), 169.
18. Corinna Hawkes, "Regulating Food Marketing to Young People Worldwide: Trends and Policy Drivers," *American Journal of Public Health* 97, no. 11 (2007): 1962–1973.
19. Children's Advertising Review Unit, *Self-Regulatory Program for Children's Advertising,* 9th ed. (New York: Better Business Bureaus, 2009).
20. Tirtha Dhar and Kathy Baylis, "Fast-Food Consumption and the Ban on Advertising Targeting Children: The Quebec Experience," *Journal of Marketing Research* 48, no. 5 (2011): 799–813.
21. Belinda Morley et al., "Public Opinion on Food-Related Obesity Prevention Policy Initiatives," *Health Promotion Journal of Australia* 23, no. 2 (2012): 86–91; Jennifer L. Harris et al, *Food Marketing to Children and Adolescents: What do Parents Think?* (New Haven, CT: Yale Rudd Center for Food Policy & Obesity, 2012), http://www.yaleruddcenter.org/resources/upload/docs/what/reports/Rudd_Report_Parents_Survey_Food_Marketing_2012.pdf.
22. IOM, *Food Marketing to Children and Youth: Threat or Opportunity?*; WHO Regional Office for Europe, *Marketing of Foods High in Fat, Salt and Sugar to Children: Update 2012–2013* (Copenhagen: WHO Regional

Office for Europe, 2013), 24; Simone Pettigrew et al., "The Effects of Television and Internet Food Advertising on Parents and Children," *Public Health Nutrition* (2013), doi: 10.1017/S1368980013001067 (accessed 10/30/13).

23. M. F. Jacobson and K. D. Brownell, "Small Taxes on Soft Drinks and Snack Foods to Promote Health," *American Journal of Public Health* 90, no. 6 (2000): 854–857; "Frequently Asked Questions about the WHO Global Strategy on Diet, Physical Activity and Health," WHO, http://www.who.int/dietphysicalactivity/faq/en/ (accessed 10/4/13).
24. Gary Sacks, "Denmark Scraps Fat Tax in Another Big Food Victory," *The Conversation*, 17 November, 2012, http://theconversation.com/denmark-scraps-fat-tax-in-another-big-food-victory-10689.
25. Kenneth E. Warner and David Mendez, "Tobacco Control Policy in Developed Countries: Yesterday, Today, and Tomorrow," *Nicotine and Tobacco Research* 12, no. 9 (2010): 876–887.
26. IOM, *Dietary Reference Intakes for Energy, Carbohydrate, Fiber, Fat, Fatty Acids, Cholesterol, Protein, and Amino Acids* (Washington, DC: National Academies Press, 2005). See also William H. Dietz and Kelley S. Scanlon, "Eliminating the Use of Partially Hydrogenated Oil in Food Production," *Journal of the American Medical Association* 308, no. 3 (2012):143–144.
27. "Notice of Adoption of an Amendment (§81.08) to Article 81 of the New York City Health Code," Department of Health and Mental Hygeine, http://www.nyc.gov/html/doh/downloads/pdf/public/notice-adoption-hc-art81-08.pdf (accessed 10/4/13).
28. Sonia Y. Angell et al., "Cholesterol Control beyond the Clinic: New York City's Trans Fat Restriction," *Annals of Internal Medicine* 151, no. 2 (2009):129–134; Sonia Y. Angell et al., "Change in Trans Fatty Acid Content of Fast-Food Purchases Associated with New York City's Restaurant Regulation: A Pre–Post Study," *Annals of Internal Medicine* 157, no. 2 (2012): 81–86.
29. Lawrence O. Gostin, "Bloomberg's Health Legacy: Urban Innovator or Meddling Nanny?," *Hastings Center Report* 43, no. 5 (2013): 19–25.
30. *In re N.Y. Statewide Coal. Hispanic Chambers of Com. v. N.Y.C. Dep't of Health & Mental Hygiene,* 970 N.Y.S.2d 200 (N.Y. App. Div. 2013).
31. Ronald Labonté et al., "Framing International Trade and Chronic Disease," *Global Health* 7, no. 1 (2011): 21.
32. WHO, *Globalization, Diets, and Noncommunicable Diseases* (Geneva: WHO, 2002).
33. Barry M. Popkin, "The Nutrition Transition and Obesity in the Developing World," *Journal of Nutrition* 131, no. 3 (2001): 871S–973S.
34. Andrew T. Kenyon, "Internet Content Regulation and the World Health Organization Framework Convention on Tobacco Control," *Scripted* 6, no. 2 (2009): 341–353; Luk Joosens et al., "The Impact of Eliminating the Global Illicit Cigarette Trade on Health and Revenue," *Addiction* 105, no. 9 (2010): 1640–1649.

35. Donald W. Zeigler, "The Alcohol Industry and Trade Agreements: A Preliminary Assessment," *Addiction* 104, no. S1 (2009): 13–26.
36. See, for example, Elaine D Kolish and Magdalena Hernandez, *The Children's Food and Beverage Advertising Initiative: A Report on Compliance and Progress During 2011* (Arlington, VA: Council of Better Business Bureaus, 2012), 13.
37. M Mar Romero-Fernández et al., "Compliance with Self-Regulation of Television Food and Beverage Advertising Aimed at Children in Spain," *Public Health Nutrition* 13, no. 7 (2009): 1013–1021.
38. Peter G Miller et al., "Vested Interests in Addiction Research and Policy. Alcohol Industry Use of Social Aspect Public Relations Organizations against Preventative Health Measures," *Addiction* 106, no. 9 (2011): 1560–1567.
39. Rob Moodie et al., "Profits and Pandemics: Prevention of Harmful Effects of Tobacco, Alcohol, and Ultra-processed Food and Drink Industries," *The Lancet* 382, no. 9867 (2013): 670–679.
40. Norbert Hirschhorn, "Corporate Social Responsibility and the Tobacco Industry: Hope or Hype?," *Tobacco Control* 13, no. 4 (2004): 447–453; Jill Stark, "Smokers Hazy on Use of Child Labor," *The Sydney Morning Herald*, September 29, 2013, http://www.smh.com.au/national/smokers-hazy-on-use-of-child-labour-20130928-2ulat.html.
41. Susan Kleiman, Shu Wen Ng, and Barry Popkin. "Drinking to Our Health: Can Beverage Companies Cut Calories While Maintaining Profits?," *Obesity Reviews* 13, no. 3 (2012): 258–274.
42. Michele Simon, "PepsiCo and Public Health: Is the Nation's Largest Food Company a Model of Corporate Responsibility or Master of Public Relations?" *CUNY Law Review* 15, no. 1(2012): 101–118; Mike Daube, "Alcohol and Tobacco," *Australia and New Zealand Journal of Public Health* 36, no. 2 (2012): 108–110;" "Performance with Purpose," Pepsico, http://pepsico.com/Purpose/Performance-with-Purpose (accessed 10/3/13).
43. William H. Wiist, "The Corporate Playbook, Health and Democracy: The Snack Food and Beverage Industry's Tactics in Context" in *Sick Societies: Responding to the Global Challenges of Chronic Disease*, edited by David Stuckler and Karen Siegel (Oxford: Oxford University Press, 2011), 204.
44. B. Samb et al., "Prevention and Management of Chronic Disease: A Litmus Test for Health-Systems Strengthening in Low-Income and Middle-Income Countries," *The Lancet* 376, no. 9754 (2010): 1785–1797.
45. Bryan P. Thomas and Lawrence O. Gostin, "Tackling the Global NCD Crisis: Innovations in Law and Governance," *Journal of Law, Medicine and Ethics* 41, no. 1 (2013): 16–27.
46. WHA, Resolution WHA53.14, "Global Strategy for the Prevention and Control of Noncommunicable Diseases," March 22, 2000; WHA, Resolution WHA57.17, "Global Strategy on Diet, Physical Activity and Health," May 2004; WHA, Resolution WHA63, "Global Strategy to Reduce the Harmful Use of Alcohol," May 21, 2010.

47. WHO, *2008–2013 Action Plan for the Global Strategy for the Prevention and Control of Noncommunicable Diseases* (Geneva: WHO, 2008).
48. WHA, Resolution WHA66.10, "Global Action Plan for the Prevention and Control of Noncommunicable Diseases 2013–2020," May 27, 2013.
49. WHO, *Set of Recommendations on the Marketing of Foods and Non-alcoholic Beverages to Children* (Geneva: WHO, 2010).
50. WHO, *A Framework for Implementing the Set of Recommendations on the Marketing of Foods and Non-Alcoholic Beverages to Children* (Geneva: World Health Organization, 2012).
51. "NCDnet—Global Noncommunicable Disease Network," WHO, http://www.who.int/ncdnet/en/ (accessed 10/4/13).
52. "Global Alliance for the Prevention of Obesity and Related Chronic Disease," World Heart Federation, http://www.world-heart-federation.org/what-we-do/advocacy/partnerships/global-alliance-for-the-prevention-of-obesity-and-related-chronic-disease/ (accessed 10/4/1313).
53. Sam Parker, "The UN High-Level Meeting on Non-Communicable Diseases: Raising Awareness but Little Else," *Harvard College Global Health Review*, October 19, 2011, http://www.hcs.harvard.edu/hghr/online/un-high-level-ncd/.
54. Allyn L. Taylor et al., "A WHO/UNICEF Global Code of Practice on the Marketing of Unhealthy Food and Beverages to Children," *Global Health Governance*, June 22, 2012, http://blogs.shu.edu/ghg/2012/06/22/a-who unicef-global-code-of-practice-on-the-marketing-of-unhealthy-food-and-beverages-to-children/.
55. The United Nations has held three high-level summits on AIDS: the UN General Assembly 26th Special Session (UNGASS) on HIV adopted the Declaration of Commitment on HIV/AIDS in 2001, http://www.un.org/ga/aids/background.htm; the UN held a second summit in 2006 (http://www.un.org/ga/aidsmeeting2006); and it held its most recent AIDS summit in June 2011, http://www.un.org/en/ga/aidsmeeting2011/.
56. "Two Days in New York: Reflections on the UN NCD Summit," Editorial, *Lancet Oncology* 12, no. 11 (2011): 981.
57. United Nations General Assembly, *Political Declaration of the High-Level Meeting of the General Assembly on the Prevention and Control of Non-communicable Diseases*, UN Doc. A/66/L.1, January 24, 2012.
58. WHO, "Global Action Plan for the Prevention and Control of Noncommunicable Diseases 2013–2020," 7.
59. Olivier De Schutter, *Report Submitted by the Special Rapporteur on the Right to Food*, United Nations General Assembly, Human Rights Council, December 26, 2011.
60. S. S. Lim et al., "Prevention of Cardiovascular Disease in High-Risk Individuals in Low-Income and Middle-Income Countries: Health Effects and Costs," *The Lancet* 370, no. 9604 (2007): 2054–2062.
61. Kumanan Rasanathan and Rüediger Krech, "Action on Social Determinants of Health Is Essential to Tackle Noncommunicable Diseases," *Bulletin of the World Health Organization* 89, no. 10 (2011): 775–776.

62. Robert Beaglehole et al., "Priority Actions for the Noncommunicable Disease Crisis," *The Lancet* 377, no. 9775 (2011): 1438–1447; "We Can End Poverty: 2015 Millennium Development Goals," United Nations, http://www.un.org/en/mdg/summit2010/ (accessed 10/4/13).
63. Hans V. Hogerzeil et al., "Promotion of Access to Essential Medicines for Noncommunicable Diseases: Practical Implications of the UN Political Declaration," *The Lancet* 381, no. 9867 (2013): 680–689.
64. Thomas J. Bollyky, "Access to Drugs for Treatment of Noncommunicable Diseases," *PLoS Medicine* 10, no. 7 (2013), doi:10.1371/journal.pmed.1001485 (accessed 9/30/13).
65. Shannon L. Marrero et al., "Noncommunicable Diseases: A Global Health Crisis in a New World Order," *Journal of the American Medical Association* 307, no. 19 (2012): 2037–2038.
66. Lawrence O. Gostin, "A Framework Convention on Global Health: Health for All, Justice for All," *Journal of the American Medical Association* 307, no. 19 (2012): 2087–2092.
67. Kathleen Strong et al., "Preventing Chronic Diseases: How Many Lives Can We Save?" *The Lancet* 366, no. 9496 (2005): 1578–1582.

14. Imagining Global Health with Justice

1. Lawrence O. Gostin, *Public Health Law: Power, Duty, Restraint* (Berkeley: University of California Press, 2008).
2. Isaac S. Kohane et al., "A Glimpse of the Next 100 Years in Medicine," *New England Journal of Medicine* 367, no. 26 (2012): 2538–2539.
3. World Health Organization (WHO), *The World Health Report 2010—Health Systems Financing: The Path to Universal Coverage* (Geneva: WHO, 2010).
4. Rodrigo Moreno-Serra and Peter C. Smith, "Does Progress towards Universal Health Coverage Improve Population Health?," *The Lancet* 380, no. 9845 (2012): 917–923.
5. Gina Lagomarsino et al., "Moving towards Universal Health Coverage: Health Insurance Reforms in Nine Developing Countries in Africa and Asia," *The Lancet* 380, no. 9845 (2012): 933–943.
6. Orielle Solar and Alec Irwin, *A Conceptual Framework for Action on the Social Determinants of Health: Social Determinants of Health Discussion Paper 2* (Geneva: WHO, 2010), 9.
7. Steven H. Woolf and Paula Braverman, "Where Health Disparities Begin: The Role of Social and Economic Determinants—and Why Current Policies May Make Matters Worse," *Health Affairs* 30, no. 10 (2011): 1852–1859.
8. John P. Bunker et al., "Improving Health: Measuring Effects of Medical Care," *Milbank Quarterly* 72, no. 2 (1993): 225–258.
9. Institute of Medicine, *U.S. Health in International Perspective: Shorter Lives, Poorer Health* (Washington, DC: National Academies Press, 2013).
10. "Social Status and Health Misery Index: Low Social Status Is Bad for Your Health," *Economist,* April 14, 2012, http://www.economist.com/node/21552539.

11. S. Jay Olshansky et al., "Differences in Life Expectancy Due to Race and Educational Differences Are Widening, and Many May Not Catch Up," *Health Affairs* 31, no. 8 (2012): 1803–1813, doi:10.1377/hlthaff.2011.0746.
12. WHO, *Closing the Gap in a Generation: Final Report of the Commission on Social Determinants of Health* (Geneva: WHO, 2008).
13. World Conference on Social Determinants of Health, Rio Political Declaration on Social Determinants of Health, Rio de Janeiro, Brazil, October 21, 2011, http://www.who.int/sdhconference/declaration/en/.
14. Moreno-Serra and Smith, "Does Progress towards Universal Health Coverage Improve Population Health?"
15. Organization for Economic Cooperation and Development (OECD), *Health at a Glance 2011: OECD Indicators* (OECD Publishing, 2011), 25; Institute of Medicine, *U.S. Health in International Perspective.*
16. Norman Daniels et al., "Why Justice Is Good for Our Health," *Daedalus* 128, no. 4 (1999): 215–251.
17. Till Bärnighausen et al., "Going Horizontal—Shifts in Funding of Global Health Interventions," *New England Journal of Medicine* 364, no. 23 (2011): 2181–2183.
18. Bernard Harris, "Public Health, Nutrition, and the Decline of Mortality: The McKeown Thesis Revisited," *Social History of Medicine* 17, no. 3 (2004): 379–407.
19. Simon Szretzer, "Rethinking McKeown: The Relationship between Public Health and Social Change," *American Journal of Public Health* 92, no. 5 (2002): 722–725.
20. WHO, *Global Health Risks: Mortality and Burden of Disease Attributable to Selected Major Risks* (Geneva: WHO, 2009).
21. Verra Mikkilä et al., "Consistent Dietary Patterns Identified from Childhood to Adulthood: The Cardiovascular Risk in Young Finns Study," *British Journal of Nutrition* 93, no. 6 (2005): 923–931.
22. Deborah Sontag, "Rebuilding in Haiti Lags after Billions in Post-Quake Aid," *New York Times,* December 23, 2012, http://www.nytimes.2012/12/24/world/americas/in-aiding-quake-battered-haiti-lofty-hopes-and-hard-truths.html.
23. "UNdata," accessed October 7, 2013, http://data.un.org.
24. UNICEF, *Narrowing the Gaps to Meet the Goals* (New York: UNICEF, 2010).
25. Andrew G. Berg and Jonathan D. Ostry, *Inequality and Unsustainable Growth: Two Sides of the Same Coin?* (Washington, DC: International Monetary Fund, 2011).
26. Norman Daniels, *Just Health: Meeting Health Needs Fairly* (New York: Cambridge University Press, 2008).
27. Gerard F. Anderson and Bianca K. Frogner, "Health Spending in OECD Countries: Obtaining Value per Dollar," *Health Affairs* 27, no. 6 (2008): 1718–1727.
28. Institute of Medicine (IOM), *For the Public's Health: Investing in a Healthier Future* (Washington, DC: National Academies Press, 2012).

29. IOM, "For the Public's Health: Investing in a Healthier Future," http://www.iom.edu/Reports/2012/For-the-Publics-Health-Investing-in-a-Healthier-Future.aspx (accessed 10/1/13).
30. IOM, *For the Public's Health*, 26–27.
31. Ilona Kickbusch and Kevin Buckett, eds., *Implementing Health in All Policies: Adelaide 2010* (Adelaide: Department of Health, 2010); "The Helsinki Statement on Health in All Policies," adopted at the Eighth Global Conference on Health Promotion, Helsinki, Finland, June 10–14, 2013, http://www.healthpromotion2013.org/images/8GCHP_Helsinki_Statement.pdf; Health in All Policies Framework for Country Action, draft for the Eighth Global Conference on Health Promotion, June 4, 2013, http://www.healthpromotion2013.org/images/HiAP_Framework_Conference_Draft_10_June.pdf.
32. Ian Forde, Kumanan Rasanathan and Rüediger Krech, *Public Health Agencies and Cash Transfer Programs: Making the Case for Greater Involvement; Social Determinants of Health Discussion Paper 4* (Geneva: WHO, 2011), 11–12.
33. Committee on Economic, Social and Cultural Rights, General Comment No. 14, "The Right to the Highest Attainable Standard of Health," UN Doc. E/C.12/2000/4, August 11, 2000, para. 45.
34. Michael Marmot et al., *Fair Society, Health Lives: The Marmot Review* (London: Marmot Review, 2010), 10.
35. UNAIDS, *"Three Ones" Key Principles: Coordination of National Responses to HIV/AIDS,* April 25, 2004, http://data.unaids.org/UNA-docs/Three-Ones_KeyPrinciples_en.pdf.
36. United Nations Population Fund (UNFPA), "Accelerating Progress in Maternal and Newborn Health: 'H4' Agencies Present Their Plan," September 29, 2009, http://www.unfpa.org/public/site/global/lang/en/pid/3918.
37. Christine Gorman, "Who Are the Health Eight (or H8)?," *Global Health Report*, April 29, 2008, http://globalhealthreport.blogspot.com/2008/04/who-are-health-eight-or-h8.html.
38. Mark Dybul et al., "Reshaping Global Health," *Policy Review* no. 173, June 1, 2012, http://www.hoover.org/publications/policy-review/article/118116.
39. Theodore M. Brown et al., "The World Health Organization and the Transition from 'International' to 'Global' Public Health," *American Journal of Public Health* 96, no. 1 (2006): 62–72.
40. UN Secretary General, "Implementation of the Declaration of Commitment on HIV/AIDS and the Political Declaration on HIV/AIDS," June 10, 2013, http://www.un.org/sg/statements/index.asp?nid=6888.
41. Michel Sidibé and Kent Buse, "A Framework Convention on Global Health: A Catalyst for Justice," *Bulletin of the World Health Organization* 90, no. 12 (2012): 870–870A.
42. WHO, *WHO Reforms for a Healthy Future: Report by the Director-General,* WHO Doc. EBSS/2/2 (October 15, 2011).
43. Andrew Sunil Rajkumar and Vinaya Swaroop, "Public Spending and Outcomes: Does Governance Matter?," *Journal of Development Economics* 86, no. 1 (2008): 96–111.

44. Devi Sridhar and Lawrence O. Gostin, "Reforming the World Health Organization," *Journal of the American Medical Association* 305, no. 15 (2011): 1585–1586.
45. Giorgio Cometto et al., "A Global Fund for the Health MDGs?," *The Lancet* 373, no 9674 (2009): 1500–1502. Others seek an even broader mandate, such as a Global Fund for Social Protection. See "Key Trade Union Priorities for the Post-2015 Development Agenda," Overseas Development Institute, January 2, 2013, http://post2015.org/2013/01/02/key-trade-union-priorities-for-the-post-2015-development-agenda/. See also Tim K. Mackey and Bryan A. Lang, "A United Nations Global Health Panel for Global Health Governance," *Social Science and Medicine* 76, no. 1 (2013): 12–15 (proposing a UN global health panel chaired by the WHO to coordinate public-private stakeholders).
46. Philip Stevens, *Diseases of Poverty and the 10/90 Gap* (London: International Policy Network, 2004).
47. *Novartis v. Union of India,* Civil Appeal Nos. 2706–2716 of 2013 (April 1, 2013), available at http://www.scribd.com/doc/133343411/Novartis-patent-Judgement.
48. WHA, Resolution WHA63.28, "Establishment of a Consultative Expert Working Group on Research and Development: Financing and Coordination," May 21, 2010. Consultative Expert Working Group on Research and Development: Financing and Coordination, *Research and Development to Meet Health Needs in Developing Countries: Strengthening Global Financing and Coordination* (Geneva: WHO, 2012), chap. 4.
49. James Love, "Balancing Options for Health Research and Development," *Bulletin of the World Health Organization* 90, no. 11 (2012): 796–796A.
50. Rebecca Hersher, "Pharma Backs Latest Attempt at a Global Health R&D Treaty," *Nature Medicine* 18, no. 6 (2012): 838.
51. WHA, Resolution WHA65.22, "Follow Up of the Report of the Consultative Expert Working Group on Research and Development: Financing and Coordination," May 26, 2012.
52. Aidan Hollis and Thomas Pogge, *The Health Impact Fund: Making New Medicines Accessible for All* (Incentives for Global Health, 2008), http://machif.com/wp-content/uploads/2012/11/hif_book.pdf (accessed 10/7/13).
53. Dybul et al., "Reshaping Global Health."
54. Ibid.
55. WHO, *History of the Framework Convention on Tobacco Control* (Geneva: WHO, 2009), 18.
56. American Public Health Association, "A Call for a Framework Convention on Alcohol Control," Policy no. 200615, November 8, 2006, http://www.apha.org/advocacy/policy/policysearch/default.htm?id=1339.
57. Allyn L. Taylor and Ibadat S. Dhillon, "An International Legal Strategy for Alcohol Control: Not a Framework Convention—at Least Not Yet," *Addiction* 108, no. 3 (2013): 450–455.
58. Lawrence O. Gostin, "Meeting Basic Survival Needs of the World's Least Healthy People: Toward a Framework Convention on Global Health," *Georgetown Law Journal* 96, no. 2 (2008): 331–392.

59. "About JALI and a Framework Convention on Global Health," Joint Action and Learning Initiative on National and Global Responsibilities for Health (JALI), http://www.jalihealth.org/about/index.html (accessed 10/7/13).
60. Lawrence O. Gostin et al., "The Joint Action and Learning Initiative: Towards a Global Agreement on National and Global Responsibilities for Health," *PLoS Medicine* 8, no. 5 (2011), doi:0.1371/journal.pmed.1001031; Lawrence O. Gostin et al., "Toward a Framework Convention on Global Health," *Bulletin of the World Health Organization* 91, no. 10 (2013): 790–793.
61. UN Secretary General, "Implementation of the Declaration of Commitment on HIV/AIDS and the Political Declaration on HIV/AIDS—Uniting for Universal Access: Towards Zero New HIV Infections, Zero Discrimination and Zero AIDS-Related Deaths," UN Doc. A/65/797, March 28, 2011.
62. Sidibé and Buse, "A Framework Convention on Global Health."
63. WHO, *WHO Reforms for a Healthy Future: Report by the Director-General,* WHO Doc. EBSS/2/2 (October 15, 2011).
64. Lawrence O. Gostin, "A Framework Convention on Global Health: Health for All, Justice for All," *Journal of the American Medical Association* 307, no. 19 (2012): 2087–2092.

Glossary of Abbreviations, Key Terms, and Actors in Global Health

Glossary of Acronyms and Abbreviations

AB	WTO Appellate Body
Abuja Declaration	Abuja Declaration on HIV/AIDS, Tuberculosis and Other Related Infectious Diseases
ACT UP	AIDS Coalition to Unleash Power
ACTA	Anti-Counterfeiting Trade Agreement
AIDS	acquired immune deficiency syndrome
AMC	advanced market commitment
ART	antiretroviral therapy
BIT	bilateral investment treaty
BSE	bovine spongiform encephalopathy ("mad cow disease")
CBD	UN Convention on Biological Diversity
CEDAW	UN Convention on the Elimination of All Forms of Discrimination against Women
CERD	UN International Convention on the Elimination of All Forms of Racial Discrimination
CESCR	UN Committee on Economic, Social and Cultural Rights
CIL	customary international law
CRC	UN Convention on the Rights of the Child
CRPD	UN Convention on the Rights of Persons with Disabilities
DALY	disability-adjusted life year
Doha Declaration	Doha Declaration on the TRIPS Agreement and Public Health
DSB	WTO Dispute Settlement Body
ECOSOC	UN Economic and Social Council
EIDs	emerging infectious diseases

FDA	U.S. Food and Drug Administration
FAO	UN Food and Agriculture Organization
FCGH	Framework Convention on Global Health
FCTC	WHO Framework Convention on Tobacco Control
FSPTCA	U.S. Family Smoking Prevention and Tobacco Control Act
FTA	free trade agreement
GATS	WTO General Agreement on Trade in Services
GATT	WTO General Agreement on Tariffs and Trade
Global Fund	Global Fund to Fight AIDS, Tuberculosis, and Malaria
GGH	global governance for health
GHG	global health governance
GHI	U.S. Global Health Initiative
GHL	global health law
GNI	gross national income
GOARN	WHO Global Outbreak Alert and Response Network
GPG	global public good
H1N1	a novel strain of influenza A virus often referred to as swine flu
H4+	Health 4+ (the WHO, UNAIDS, UNFPA, UNICEF, UN Women, and the World Bank)
H5N1	a novel strain of influenza A virus commonly known as avian flu
H7N9	an emerging strain of the avian influenza A H7 virus that typically circulates among birds
H8	Health 8 (the WHO, UNAIDS, UNFPA, UNICEF, Global Fund, GAVI Alliance, Gates Foundation, and the World Bank)
HCW	health care worker
HiAP	health in all policies
HIV	human immunodeficiency virus
HNP	World Bank Strategy for Health, Nutrition, and Population Results
ICCPR	International Covenant on Civil and Political Rights
ICD	WHO International Classification of Diseases
ICESCR	International Covenant on Economic, Social and Cultural Rights
ICJ	International Court of Justice
ICRC	International Committee of the Red Cross

IDU	injection drug user
IFFIm	International Finance Facility for Immunization
IGO	intergovernmental organization
IHL	international humanitarian law
IHP+	International Health Partnership
IHR	WHO International Health Regulations
IMF	International Monetary Fund
IP	intellectual property
JALI	Joint Action and Learning Initiative on National and Global Responsibilities for Health
LDC	least developed country
LGBT	lesbian, gay, bisexual, and transgender
LMICs	low- and middle-income countries
MDGs	UN Millennium Development Goals
MDR	multidrug-resistant
MFN	most favored nation (WTO principle)
MERS	Middle East Respiratory Syndrome
MEDICRIME Convention	Convention on the Counterfeiting of Medical Products and Similar Crimes Involving Threats to Public Health
MPP	Medicines Patent Pool
MSM	men who have sex with men
NCD	noncommunicable disease
NGO	nongovernmental organization
NTD	neglected tropical disease
ODA	official development assistance
OECD	Organization for Economic Cooperation and Development
OHCHR	Office of the UN High Commissioner for Human Rights
PAHO	Pan American Health Organization
PIP Framework	WHO Pandemic Influenza Preparedness Framework
PEPFAR	U.S. President's Emergency Plan for AIDS Relief
PHC	primary health care
PHEIC	public health emergency of international concern
PrEP	HIV pre-exposure prophylaxis
SARS	severe acute respiratory syndrome

SPS Agreement	WTO Agreement on the Application of Sanitary and Phytosanitary Measures
STD	sexually transmitted disease
TAC	Treatment Action Campaign (South Africa)
TASO	The AIDS Support Organization (Uganda)
TB	tuberculosis
TBT Agreement	WTO Agreement on Technical Barriers to Trade
TRIPS Agreement	WTO Agreement on Trade-Related Aspects of Intellectual Property Rights
UDHR	Universal Declaration of Human Rights
UN	United Nations
UNAIDS	Joint United Nations Program on HIV/AIDS
UNCTAD	United Nations Conference on Trade and Development
UNDP	United Nations Development Program
UNFCCC	United Nations Framework Convention on Climate Change
UNFPA	United Nations Population Fund
UNICEF	United Nations Children's Fund
UN Women	United Nations Entity for Gender Equality and the Empowerment of Women
vCJD	variant Creutzfeldt-Jakob disease
WFP	World Food Program
WHA	World Health Assembly
WHO	World Health Organization
WIPO	World Intellectual Property Organization
WTO	World Trade Organization
XDR	extensively drug-resistant

Glossary of Terms in Global Health

Accra Agenda for Action The Accra Agenda for Action (2008) is a follow-up agreement that is designed to strengthen the implementation of the Paris Declaration on Aid Effectiveness (2005). It calls for: (1) enhancing country ownership of development policies and processes, (2) creating more inclusive partnerships for development, and (3) improving accountability for results.

advanced market commitment An advanced market commitment (AMC) combats the problem of underinvestment in essential drugs and vaccines by guaranteeing that a certain level of funding will be available to purchase these products, thus ensuring a market and catalyzing research and development.

Alma-Ata Declaration on Primary Health Care The Alma-Ata Declaration on Primary Health Care (1978) (Alma-Ata Declaration) established principles for comprehensive primary health systems, with the promise of "health for all."

antiretroviral therapy Antiretroviral therapy (ART) is a drug regimen (or regimens) used in treating HIV/AIDS and preventing its spread.

Codex Alimentarius Commission The FAO and the WHO created the Codex Alimentarius Commission in 1963 to develop harmonized, international food standards and guidelines in the form of the Codex Alimentarius. The main purposes of codex are to protect consumer health, ensure fair trade practices, and coordinate global food safety standards. Codex guidance is not mandatory, but its adoption by states could reduce the threat of WTO legal challenges.

Committee on Economic, Social and Cultural Rights Created by the UN Economic and Social Council (ECOSOC), the Committee on Economic, Social and Cultural Rights (CESCR) makes recommendations to states regarding the ICESCR. The CESCR also issues general comments to further clarify the ICESCR, including General Comment 14 on the right to health.

customary international law Customary international law (CIL) refers to legal norms that have been established by general and consistent state practice.

Doha Declaration on the TRIPS Agreement and Public Health Promulgated by the WTO Ministerial Conference in 2001, the Doha Declaration reaffirmed the use of TRIPS flexibilities and stated that "the Agreement can and should be interpreted and implemented in a manner supportive of WTO members' right to protect public health and, in particular, to promote access to medicines for all."

Framework Convention on Global Health The Framework Convention on Global Health (FCGH) offers a new post-MDG vision for health grounded in the right to health and reducing global and domestic inequities. Originally proposed by Lawrence Gostin, a global coalition of civil society organizations and academics—the Joint Action and Learning Initiative on National and Global Responsibilities for Health (JALI)—has formed an international campaign to advocate for the convention.

G8 Formerly the G7, the G8 is an informal forum comprising the heads of state of eight industrialized nations, who meet regularly to discuss key economic and political issues. Current members include Canada, France, Germany, Italy, Japan, Russia, the United Kingdom, and the United States.

G20 Formally established in 1999, the Group of 20 is a forum for cooperation on economic and financial issues, bringing together finance ministers and central bank governors from nineteen countries—Argentina, Australia, Brazil, Canada, China, France, Germany, India, Indonesia, Italy, Japan, the Republic of Korea, Mexico, Russia, Saudi Arabia, South Africa, Turkey, the United Kingdom, and the United States—plus the European Union.

Gates Foundation The world's most influential and wealthiest private foundation, the Bill & Melinda Gates Foundation has distributed more than $15 billion in grants to global health causes and, as of 2013, has $38.3 billion in assets.

GAVI Alliance Launched in 2000, the mission of the GAVI Alliance (originally known as the Global Alliance for Vaccines and Immunizations) is to increase access to life-saving vaccines for the millions of children in developing countries who remain unvaccinated each year.

General Comment 14 Issued by the CESCR, General Comment 14 offers the most definitive interpretation of the right to health. It describes states' core obligations under this right, including the provision of health goods, services, and facilities that are accessible, acceptable, and of good quality. The general comment also makes reference to the underlying social and economic determinants of health, including access to adequate food, clothing, housing, and necessary social services.

Global Code of Practice on the International Recruitment of Health Personnel Adopted by the 63rd World Health Assembly in May 2010, the code sets out principles and practices for the ethical international recruitment of health personnel. It also provides guidance for improving the legal and institutional framework for recruitment, including bilateral and multilateral agreements, and promotes international cooperation.

Global Fund to Fight AIDS, Tuberculosis and Malaria The Global Fund was created in 2002 to dramatically increase resources to fight AIDS, TB, and malaria, and to direct those resources to regions of greatest need.

global governance for health Global governance for health comprises the collection of rules, norms, institutions, and processes that shape the health of the world's population. Governance strategies aim to organize divergent stakeholders and to manage social, economic, and political affairs to improve global health and narrow health inequalities. GGH is a broad concept that applies to diverse sectors that affect the public's health.

global health governance Global health governance refers to the use of formal and informal institutions, rules, and processes by states, intergovernmental organizations, and nonstate actors to address cross-border challenges to health through collective action. In standard usage, GHG is mainly limited to the health sector, such as the activities of the WHO and UNAIDS.

global health law Global health law is the study and practice of international law that influences the norms, processes, and institutions required for the world's population to attain the highest possible standard of physical and mental health. It includes formal sources of law, such as binding international treaties, as well as informal or "soft" instruments, for example, codes of practice negotiated between states. The field seeks innovative ways to stimulate research and development, mobilize resources, set priorities, coordinate activities, monitor progress, create incentives, and ensure accountability among a proliferation of global health actors. The value of social justice infuses the field, which strives for health equality for the world's most disadvantaged people.

Global Health Watch Considered an alternative to the World Health Report, the flagship annual WHO publication, Global Health Watch, is a civil society publication analyzing and offering recommendations on global health from the perspective of social justice, incorporating the voices of marginalized people. First published in 2005, a fourth edition is scheduled for release in late 2014. The People's Health Movement and four other organizations coordinate its publication.

global North "Global North" is used to describe a group of developed countries, predominantly located in North America and Europe, with high human development according to the United Nations Human Development Index. Most, but not all, of these countries are located in the Northern Hemisphere; Australia, for example, is a highly developed state located in the Southern Hemisphere.

Global Outbreak Alert and Response Network The WHO Global Outbreak Alert and Response Network (GOARN) is a group of institutions and networks that work together to rapidly identify, confirm, and respond to disease outbreaks of international importance.

global public goods Global public goods are those that are available to everyone but require collective action because no single state or private actor can provide the good in sufficient quantity. Traditionally they include, for example, clean air, uncontaminated water, and control of infectious diseases.

global South "Global South" is used to describe developing and emerging countries but also includes some countries with rapid industrial development/restructuring. Most, but not all, of the global South is located in South and Central America, Asia, and Africa, with many countries in these regions having lower human development according to the United Nations Human Development Index. Mexico, situated in North America, provides an example of a state usually included in the global South.

Health 4+ UNFPA, UNICEF, WHO, the World Bank, UNAIDS, and UN Women have formed a partnership known as the Health 4+ (H4+) to provide support to countries with the highest rates of maternal, newborn, and child mortality, in order to accelerate progress in achieving the health-related MDGs.

Health 8 The Health 8 (H8) is an informal group of eight health-related organizations (the WHO, UNICEF, UNFPA, UNAIDS, the Global Fund, the GAVI Alliance, the Gates Foundation, and the World Bank) created in 2007 to stimulate global urgency in reaching the health-related MDGs, and to increase harmonization among the activities of member organizations.

"health in all policies" "Health in all policies" (HiAP) is an approach under which governments commit to routine assessment of the health impact of policy initiatives outside the health sector, with a view to promoting optimal health outcomes. Sometimes referred to as the all-of-government approach, HiAP can apply at a national, state, province, or municipal government level.

Influenza A (H1N1) A novel strain of pandemic influenza A, H1N1 is known colloquially (but incorrectly) as swine flu because it is closely related to a viral strain found in pigs. Variant strains of H1N1 flu have been circulating for many years, but this novel subtype was first identified in April 2009 in the United States. It is highly transmissible from person to person, and in

June 2009 the WHO declared it pandemic. Although the pandemic ended in August 2010, H1N1 is still circulating as a regular seasonal influenza virus.

Influenza A (H5N1) The influenza A (H5N1) virus (also referred to as HPAI H5N1) causes a highly infectious, severe respiratory disease among birds. Human infections are relatively rare, and the key risk factor for contracting H5N1 is close contact with infected live or dead birds. Although H5N1 does not spread easily from person to person, it can cause serious illness in humans. A significant avian outbreak of the virus occurred in Asia in 2003, and although human cases of H5N1 peaked in 2006, the virus remains endemic in some countries, including Egypt, Indonesia, and Vietnam.

Influenza A (H7N9) Novel influenza A (H7N9) is an avian influenza A virus that emerged among humans in China in March 2013. Although H7N9 can cause severe respiratory illness and death, there is no evidence of sustained person-to-person spread of the virus. Human infection appears to occur through exposure to infected birds or contaminated environments, such as live-bird markets. Although the number of new cases has stabilized, the virus remains a concern because it is highly pathogenic in humans, but not in birds, and there is a risk that it will mutate and become more easily transmissible among people.

International Covenant on Civil and Political Rights The International Covenant on Civil and Political Rights (ICCPR) is a "twin covenant" with the ICESCR, and requires states "to respect and to ensure" civil and political rights, including the freedoms of expression, opinion, religion, conscience, assembly, and movement; freedom from slavery, torture, and arbitrary detention; and rights to privacy, equal protection, asylum from persecution, and free elections.

International Covenant on Economic, Social and Cultural Rights The International Covenant on Economic, Social and Cultural Rights (ICESCR), a "twin covenant" with the ICCPR, enunciates the definitive formulation of the right to health: "the right of everyone to the enjoyment of the highest attainable standard of physical and mental health." It also captures the key determinants of health: the right to "an adequate standard of living . . . including adequate food, clothing and housing, and to the continuous improvement of living conditions," as well as freedom from hunger. The ICESCR guarantees additional "economic, social and cultural rights" such as labor rights, social insurance, child protection, education, shared scientific benefits, and participation in cultural life.

International Bill of Human Rights An informal name given to the UDHR, ICCPR, ICESCR, and their Optional Protocols.

International Finance Facility for Immunization The International Finance Facility for Immunization (IFFIm) is a bond-selling scheme first presented by the then United Kingdom Chancellor of the Exchequer, Gordon Brown, at the 2003 G8 Summit. By selling "vaccine bonds" on the capital markets, the IFFIm accelerates the availability of funds for the GAVI Alliance to provide health and immunization programs in lower-income countries.

International Health Regulations Adopted by the World Health Assembly in 2005, the revised International Health Regulations (IHR) are the primary international rules governing global health security. Given the emergence of new infectious diseases, the IHR has become one of the most important global health treaties of the twenty-first century, with the WHO at the center of the governance regime.

International Monetary Fund The International Monetary Fund (IMF) is a specialized agency of the UN with 188 member countries, and the stated purpose of "working to foster global monetary cooperation, secure financial stability, facilitate international trade, promote high employment and sustainable economic growth, and reduce poverty around the world."

Joint Action and Learning Initiative on National and Global Responsibilities for Health The Joint Action and Learning Initiative on National and Global Responsibilities for Health (JALI) is a global coalition of civil society and academics that has formed an international campaign to advocate for a Framework Convention on Global Health (FCGH).

Kyoto Protocol Negotiated in 1997, and entering into force in 2005, the Kyoto Protocol to the UN Framework Convention on Climate Change created "binding targets and timetables" for emissions reductions. Expiring at the end of 2012, the protocol had only limited success in achieving its objectives.

Middle East Respiratory Syndrome Middle East Respiratory Syndrome (MERS, or MERS-CoV) is an emerging strain of coronavirus, with the first cases occurring in Saudi Arabia in 2012. The WHO has since identified infections in other Middle Eastern countries and in Europe. The likely reservoir for MERS appears to be camels or bats, although there is limited information available on the routes of transmission. Approximately half of known people who have contracted MERS have died, but the risk of sustained person-to-person transmission appears to be low. Health authorities remain concerned about the pandemic potential of MERS and the possibility that it will spread more widely around the world.

Millennium Development Goals The Millennium Development Goals (MDGs), which followed the Millennium Declaration (adopted by the UN General Assembly in 2000), are the world's most broadly supported and comprehensive development targets. The MDGs set numerical benchmarks that aim to reduce extreme poverty and hunger, and to address ill health, gender inequality, lack of education, lack of access to clean water and sanitation, and environmental degradation by 2015.

noncommunicable diseases Noncommunicable diseases (NCDs) (also known as chronic diseases) are diseases that are mostly nontransmissible and noncontagious, such as cancer, cardiovascular disease, diabetes, and respiratory disease. A significant minority of NCDs, however, are spread through communicable infections, such as the human papilloma virus, which causes cervical cancer. Together, NCDs account for 63 percent of global mortality annually.

Nomenclature Regulations A 1967 treaty, one of three negotiated under the auspices of the WHO, that established and revised international nomenclatures of diseases, causes of death, and public health practices, as well as standardized diagnostic procedures.

official development assistance Official development assistance (ODA) is government aid given to developing countries for the purpose of contributing to their development and welfare. ODA can be given as grants or loans, but for loans to qualify as ODA they must include a grant element of at least 25 percent.

Pandemic Influenza Preparedness Framework The Pandemic Influenza Preparedness (PIP) Framework for the Sharing of Influenza Viruses and Access to Vaccines and Other Benefits, adopted by the World Health Assembly in 2011, is a nonbinding agreement that brings together member states, the WHO, industry actors, and other stakeholders to secure global surveillance and sharing of benefits in regard to H5N1 and other influenza viruses with human pandemic potential.

Paris Declaration on Aid Effectiveness The Paris Declaration on Aid Effectiveness (2005) sets out the Paris Principles, covering five areas: (1) country ownership, meaning that countries establish their own strategies; (2) alignment, with development partners supporting country strategies and using local systems; (3) harmonization, that is, ensuring that development partners coordinate with each other and simplify their procedures; (4) results, with an emphasis on achieving measurable health improvements; and (5) mutual accountability, with countries and development partners being accountable to one another.

post-2015 sustainable development agenda The post-2015 sustainable development agenda will encompass a set of goals, benchmarks, and indicators to replace the MDGs when they expire in 2015. UN member states are set to finalize this agenda and establish the Sustainable Development Goals in September 2015, building on recommendations and lessons from global consultations that formally began in 2012 to determine the agenda's priorities. The post-2015 agenda is expected to combine the MDGs' focus on extreme poverty with a reinforced emphasis on sustainable development.

social determinants of health The social (or socioeconomic) determinants of health are the social and economic conditions in which people are born, grow, live, work, and age, and which have a fundamental impact upon the population's health. They include access to, and quality of, education, employment, and housing, as well as social and economic status, ethnicity, and gender.

TRIPS Agreement The WTO Agreement on Trade-Related Aspects of Intellectual Property Rights (TRIPS Agreement) establishes minimum levels of intellectual property (IP) protection that each government must afford to rights holders. TRIPS creates global rules that ensure greater uniformity between national IP policies, accompanied by an international dispute settlement system. The central mission of TRIPS is to protect and enforce IP rights for "the promotion of technological innovation and . . . the transfer and dissemination of technology, to the mutual advantage of producers and users of technological knowledge and in a manner conducive to social and economic welfare."

TRIPS flexibilities Contained in the TRIPS Agreement and recognized in the Doha Declaration, TRIPS flexibilities can be exercised for the protection of the public's health, including, but not limited to: the right of WTO members to grant compulsory licenses (e.g., for the production of generic medicines) and to determine the grounds on which such licenses can be granted; determine what constitutes a national emergency or conditions of extreme urgency; and establish their own regime for the exhaustion of intellectual property rights (which enables countries to engage in parallel importation).

TRIPS-plus TRIPS-plus agreements are bilateral or multilateral free trade agreements containing IP protections greater than those set out in the TRIPS Agreement.

UNAIDS The Joint United Nations Program on HIV/AIDS (UNAIDS) was created in 1996 to coordinate the work of six agencies on HIV/AIDS: the WHO, UNICEF, UNDP, UNFPA, UNESCO, and the World Bank. The World Food Program, the UN Office on Drugs and Crime, UN Women, and the International Labor Organization have since joined as cosponsors.

UNITAID Formed by Brazil, Chile, France, Norway, and the United Kingdom in 2006, UNITAID is based in Geneva and hosted by the WHO. The organization uses an innovative funding mechanism—a mix of airline levies and traditional grants from governments and foundations—to provide greater access to medicines and diagnostics for AIDS, tuberculosis, and malaria. In 2010 UNITAID founded the Medicines Patent Pool in a bid to lower ARV prices in the developing world.

World Health Organization The World Health Organization (WHO), with its constitution signed in 1946 and effective in 1948, is a specialized UN agency with an expansive health mandate, and with 194 member states as of 2013.

World Bank Formed in 1944, the World Bank Group consists of five organizations (three of which provide health-related funding), and has the mission of ending extreme poverty and promoting prosperity in low-income countries.

World Trade Organization The World Trade Organization (WTO) was established on January 1, 1995, at the conclusion of the Uruguay Round of multinational trade negotiations. It provides a forum for governments to negotiate trade agreements, as well as a mechanism for the implementation of these agreements and the resolution of any disputes arising under them.

Glossary of Actors in Global Health

Intergovernmental Organizations

IGO	*Mission*	*Major Health Initiatives*
United Nations (UN)	Ensure international peace and security, promote respect for, and observance of, human rights, protect the environment, fight disease, and reduce poverty	*Millennium Development Goals:* • Eradicate extreme poverty and hunger • Achieve universal primary education • Promote gender equality • Reduce child mortality • Improve maternal health • Combat HIV/AIDS and other diseases • Ensure environmental sustainability • Create global partnerships for development • *Post-2015 Sustainable Development Agenda (to be finalized in 2015):* • Universal health coverage? • Healthy lifestyles and NCDs? • Right to health?
World Trade Organization (WTO)	Ensure that global trade flows smoothly and predictably	• Agreement on Trade-Related Aspects of Intellectual Property Rights (TRIPS Agreement) • Doha Declaration on the TRIPS Agreement and Public Health • Doha Development Agenda

UN Specialized Agencies

Food and Agriculture Organization (FAO)	Improve nutrition, agricultural productivity, and the lives of rural populations	• Codex Alimentarius Commission develops safety standards and codes of practice under the Joint FAO/WHO Food Program
International Labor Organization (ILO)	Promote social justice and monitor compliance with human and labor rights treaties	• Program on Safety and Health at Work and the Environment (SafeWork) • Program on HIV/AIDS and the World of Work

IGO	*Mission*	*Major Health Initiatives*
Joint UN Program on HIV/AIDS (UNAIDS)	Coordinate a global response to HIV/AIDS	• Declaration of Commitment on HIV/AIDS • International Partnership against AIDS in Africa • World AIDS Campaign • Getting to Zero: Zero New HIV Infections, Zero Discrimination, Zero AIDS-Related Deaths
UN Entity for Gender Equality and the Empowerment of Women (UN Women)	Reduce poverty, violence, HIV/AIDS, and gender inequality	• Trust Fund to Eliminate Violence against Women
UN Development Program (UNDP)	Reduce poverty, preserve the environment, and strengthen democratic governance	• UN Capital Development Fund
UN High Commissioner for Human Rights (UNHCHR)	Promote and protect all human rights	• Promote the right to development • Mainstream human rights into humanitarian and development work
UN High Commissioner on Refugees (UNHCR)	Provide legal protection and emergency relief for refugees	• Research on mental and physical health of refugees; policies on HIV/AIDS
UN Human Rights Council	Address human rights violations and make recommendations on them	• Special rapporteurs monitor and recommend policies to advance the rights to health, water, food, and adequate housing, and to combat violence against women
UN International Children's Emergency Fund (UNICEF)	Secure the socioeconomic and health needs of women and children	• Baby-Friendly Hospital Initiative • International Code of Marketing of Breast-Milk Substitutes
World Bank Group	Provide loans, grants, and advice to low- and middle-income countries	• International Bank for Reconstruction and Development • International Development Association

(continued)

IGO	*Mission*	*Major Health Initiatives*
World Health Organization (WHO)	Attain the highest possible standard of health for all people	• Framework Convention on Tobacco Control • International Health Regulations • Global Code of Practice on the International Recruitment of Health Personnel • Global Strategy for the Prevention and Control of Noncommunicable Diseases • Comprehensive Mental Health Action Plan 2013–2020
World Organization for Animal Health	Promote animal welfare and prevent the transmission of disease between animals and humans	• Global Early Warning System for Animal Diseases Transmissible to Humans

Nongovernmental Organizations

This list is representative of NGOs that work in global health. Because there are hundreds of such organizations, it is not possible to include a comprehensive overview of them all.

NGO	*Mission*	*Primary Areas of Health Focus*
CARE (Cooperative for Assistance and Relief Everywhere)	Tackle the underlying determinants of poverty, with a special focus on women, to create permanent social change	Maternal health, gender-based violence
Doctors Without Borders/Médecins Sans Frontières (MSF)	Provide medical care to communities affected by natural disasters, conflict, epidemics, and poverty	Infectious diseases, disaster response, access to essential medicines
Family Health International (FHI)	Prevent HIV/AIDS and increase access to reproductive health care in developing countries	Reproductive health, HIV/AIDS
Health Opportunities for People Everywhere (Project HOPE)	Deliver health education, policy research, humanitarian relief, and socioeconomic development assistance	Infectious diseases (including HIV/AIDS), women's and children's health, humanitarian assistance

NGO	*Mission*	*Primary Areas of Health Focus*
International Committee of the Red Cross (ICRC)	Provide assistance and protection for prisoners of war and civilians affected by war	State compliance with the Geneva Conventions
Oxfam	Build a future free of the injustices of poverty	Public health, emergency response, health for all, agriculture and food prices
Partners In Health	Provide a preferential option for the poor in health care, based on solidarity and the right to health	HIV/AIDS, TB, cholera, women's and children's health, food, water, primary health care (including community health workers)
PATH (Program for Appropriate Technology in Health)	Advance health care in developing countries	Health training and education, contraceptives, injection devices, diagnostic tools
Physicians for Human Rights	Mobilize health professionals to advance health, dignity, and justice, and to promote the right to health	Women's health during conflict
Population Council	Coordinate international public health and biomedical research; strengthen local health care	Reproductive health, HIV/AIDS
Save the Children	Advance the health, education, and well-being of children to achieve immediate and lasting change in their lives	Child survival, hunger and nutrition, HIV/AIDS

(continued)

Partnerships

This list is representative of partnerships operating in global health, as it is not possible to include a comprehensive listing of all partnerships whose work affects global health.

Partnership	*Mission*	*Focus*
GAVI Alliance	Save children's lives and protect health by increasing access to immunization in lower-income countries	Vaccines
Global Fund to Fight AIDS, Tuberculosis, and Malaria	Dedicated to attracting and disbursing resources to prevent and treat HIV/AIDS, tuberculosis, and malaria	HIV/AIDS, TB, malaria
Global Health Security Initiative (GHSI)	Strengthen global preparedness for pandemic influenza and biological, chemical, and radio-nuclear terrorism	Influenza, health security
Global Health Workforce Alliance	Advocate and catalyze global and country actions to resolve the human resources for health crises; support health for all by increasing global access to a skilled, motivated, and supported health workforce, operating within a robust health system	Health workforce
Global Polio Eradication Initiative	Eradicate polio worldwide	Polio
Health Metrics Network	Strengthen health information systems and increase the availability of information for decisions to improve health outcomes	Health information systems
International Drug Purchase Facility (UNITAID)	Increase access to drugs and diagnostics for HIV/AIDS, malaria, and tuberculosis in high-disease-burden countries	HIV/AIDS, TB, Malaria
International Finance Facility for Immunization (IFFIm)	Accelerate the availability of funds for health and immunization programs through the GAVI Alliance in the poorest countries	Immunizations
Partnership for Maternal, Newborn, and Child Health	Ensure that all women, infants, and children not only remain healthy, but thrive	Maternal, newborn, and child health

Partnership	*Mission*	*Focus*
Roll Back Malaria	Reduce malaria morbidity and mortality by reaching universal coverage and strengthening health systems	Malaria
Stop TB Partnership	Serve every person who is vulnerable to TB and ensure that high-quality treatment is available to all who need it	Tuberculosis

Foundations

Foundation	*Mission*	*Focus*
Bill & Melinda Gates Foundation	Guided by the belief that all lives have equal value; works to help people who are most in need to lead healthy, productive lives, supporting this mission by "harnessing advances in science and technology to reduce health inequities and save lives in poor countries"	Vaccines, HIV/AIDS, TB, malaria
Clinton Health Access Initiative	Improve the management and organization of in-country health systems and global commodity markets while addressing key health systems barriers	HIV/AIDS, malaria, immunizations
Ford Foundation	Supports visionary leaders and organizations on the front lines of social change worldwide	Human rights, HIV/AIDS, sexual and reproductive health
Rockefeller Foundation	Promotes the well-being of humanity throughout the world	Health systems, disease surveillance, climate change, food security

Acknowledgments

This book was five years in the making—a period of time where my thinking and experience evolved and deepened thanks to many friends and colleagues. I originally proposed this book to Harvard University Press with a coauthor who is well known in global health law. David P. Fidler, at the University of Indiana, is an incomparable scholar whom I have admired and learned from throughout the years. Sadly, Professor Fidler had to withdraw from this book project, but his role in conceptualizing it was foundational.

The O'Neill Institute at Georgetown Law

I want to acknowledge the leaders and fellows of the O'Neill Institute for National and Global Health Law at Georgetown University, and especially Linda and Timothy O'Neill, whose remarkable generosity and ongoing intellectual guidance have enabled our institute to flourish. Bill Treanor (Georgetown Law's dean) and Oscar Cabrera (the institute's director) never failed to support this ambitious book project. I also thank Howard Federoff (dean, Georgetown University Medical Center) and Bette Jacobs and Martin Iguchi (respectively, former and current dean, Georgetown School of Nursing and Health Studies) for being such inspirational colleagues. President Jack DeGioia has been a staunch supporter of global health with justice, inviting me to join in a historic meeting with Ban Ki-moon and twenty-five university presidents to discuss the post-2015 sustainable development agenda in March 2013. His new global health advisor, John Monahan, was the first executive director of the O'Neill Institute.

The O'Neill Institute fellows with whom I have worked intensely are among the most intelligent, insightful, and hard-working colleagues I have ever had the privilege of learning from. They researched, wrote, edited, and conceptualized the book from the onset and throughout. They are the ones who provided the intellectual firepower that fueled the ideas and the prose in this book: Eric A. Friedman (human rights and international institutions), Kelli K. Garcia (interconnecting legal regimes), Anna Garsia (novel influenzas), Emily A. Mok (world trade), Emily Parento (international migration of health workers), and Bryan Thomas (tobacco and global health justice). They deserve all the credit and all of the gratitude I can muster.

My faculty colleagues, whom I greatly admire, have been deeply influential and supportive: Mark Dybul (former head of PEPFAR, now executive director of the Global Fund), Benn McGrady (director, O'Neill Institute Initiative on Trade, Investment and Health), Allyn Taylor (a world-class global health law scholar), Jeff Crowley (former director of the Office of National AIDS Policy), Nan Hunter (associate dean for Graduate Programs), and John Kraemer (a dynamic young global health scholar).

Talented fellows, staff, and students at Georgetown Law conducted research, thoughtfully read chapter drafts, and assisted with manuscript preparation, notably Ali Jones, Lisa Eckstein, Just Haffeld, Tyrone Manzy, Ayana Detweiler, Corey Kestenberg, Dina Jerebitski, Thandiwe Lyle, Kelsy Bennet, Jessica Band. A special thanks to Daniel Hougendobler, Alexandra Phelan, and Belinda Reeve.

JALI/Framework Convention on Global Health

If there were a single movement that shaped my thinking, it would be JALI (the Joint Action and Learning Initiative on National and Global Responsibilities for Health). JALI is part of an international campaign for a Framework Convention on Global Health—the founding vision of the O'Neill Institute. The leader of JALI and its unswerving and deeply passionate advocate is Eric Friedman. Robert Marten of the Rockefeller Foundation has offered generous support and intellectual guidance.

This global movement has brought me many friends around the world. To name just a few: Adila Hassim (SECTION27, South Africa), Anand Grover (Lawyers Collective, India, and UN Special Rapporteur on the Right to Health), Armando De Negri (World Social Forum on Health and Social Security, Brazil), Juan Garay (European Union), Attiya Waris (University of Nairobi/Tax Justice Network), Devi Sridhar (Oxford University, United Kingdom), Gorik Ooms (Hélène De Beir Foundation, Belgium), Harald Siem (Norwegian Directorate of Health), John-Arne Røttingen (Norwegian Knowledge Centre for the Health Services), Mark Heywood (SECTION27, South Africa), Mayowa Joel (Communication for Development Centre, Nigeria), Mulumba Moses (Center for Human Rights and Development, Uganda), Paolo Buss (Paulo Buss, Oswaldo Cruz Foundation [FIOCRUZ], Brazil), Shiba Phurailatpam (Asia Pacific Network of People Living with HIV/AIDS), Thomas Gebauer (Medico International, Germany), Mark Rosenberg (Task Force for Global Health, United States), and Tim Evans (BRAC University, Bangladesh).

International Organizations and Colleagues

I have the privilege of serving as the director of the World Health Organization Collaborating Center on Public Health Law and Human Rights. In that role, I have worked closely with insightful colleagues such as Ian Smith (Director-General's Office), Gian Luca Burci (general counsel), Helena Nygren-Krug (human rights), Rüediger Krech (ethics and trade), Heidi Jimenez (PAHO general counsel), and Javier Vasquez (PAHO human rights). I have also had enduring and fulfilling relationships with UNAIDS, ranging from its director, Michel Sidibé, to his senior adviser, Kent Buse, and its human rights officer, Susan Timberlake. I have also worked closely with David Patterson at the International Development Law Organization (IDLO) on a major report on public health law cosponsored by the WHO and the IDLO (with Roger Magnusson and Helena Nygren-Krug). Kevin Klock of the GAVI Alliance offered comments on Chapter 5, while colleagues at the Nossal Institute, Melbourne University—Rob Moody, Helen Robinson, and Katherine Taylor—reviewed Chapter 4. Kathryn Taylor warrants a special thank-you for helping design several figures in Chapter 4. My collaboration with Judy Wasserheit, Tom Quinn, Keith Martin, and many other colleagues on the Board of the Consortium of Universities for Global Health has been rewarding.

I have learned this field from the best and the brightest, notably Laurie Garrett (Council of Foreign Relations), David Heymann (Chatham House, London), James Hodge Jr. (Arizona State University), Peter Jacobson (University of Michigan), Ilona Kickbusch (Graduate Institute, Geneva), Roger Magnusson (University of Sydney), Wang Chenguang (Tsinghua University, Beijing), Benjamin Mason Meier (University of North Carolina), Art Reingold (University of California at Berkeley), Lindsay Wiley (American University), Jennifer Ruger (University of Pennsylvania), I. Glenn Cohen (Harvard University), Thomas Pogge (Yale University), and Julio Frenk, among many others.

I also want to express my deep gratitude to my editor at Harvard University Press. Elizabeth Knoll has nurtured this project intellectually throughout a five-year process. She is a remarkable editor.

As any author knows, writing a book of this magnitude takes a personal toll. My family has been wonderful, loving, and supportive. This book is for my wife, Jean; sons, Bryn and Kieran; and their loving partners, Jen and Isley.

Index